Luis Buñuel

WISCONSIN FILM STUDIES

Patrick McGilligan
Series Editor

Luis Buñuel

The Red Years, 1929–1939

Román Gubern
and
Paul Hammond

The University of Wisconsin Press

Publication of this volume has been made possible, in part, through support from the **Program for Cultural Cooperation** between Spain's Ministry of Culture and United States Universities, and from the **Anonymous Fund** of the College of Letters and Science at the University of Wisconsin–Madison.

The University of Wisconsin Press
1930 Monroe Street, 3rd Floor
Madison, Wisconsin 53711-2059
uwpress.wisc.edu

3 Henrietta Street
London WC2E 8LU, England
eurospanbookstore.com

Printed in the United States of America

Library of Congress Cataloging-in-Publication Data
Gubern, Román.
[Años rojos de Luis Buñuel. English]
Luis Buñuel: the red years, 1929–1939 / Román Gubern and Paul Hammond.
p. cm. — (Wisconsin film studies)
Originally published in Spain as Los años rojos de Luis Buñuel.
Includes bibliographical references and index.
ISBN 978-0-299-28474-9 (pbk.: alk. paper)
ISBN 978-0-299-28473-2 (e-book)
1. Buñuel, Luis, 1900–1983—Criticism and interpretation.
2. Buñuel, Luis, 1900–1983—Political and social views.
3. Motion picture producers and directors—Spain—Biography.
I. Hammond, Paul, 1947 July 19– II. Title. III. Series: Wisconsin film studies.
PN1998.3.B86G8313 2012
791.4302′33092—dc22
[B]
2011011630

Contents

Illustrations

Abbreviations

AAER	Association des Artistes et Écrivains Révolutionnaires (Association of Revolutionary Artists and Writers)
ACI	Alliance du Cinéma Indépendant (Alliance of Independent Cinema)
ADLAN	Agrupació Amics de l'Art Nou (Friends of the New Art Group)
AEAR	Association des Écrivains et Artistes Révolutionnaires / Asociación de Escritores y Artistas Revolucionarios (Association of Revolutionary Writers and Artists)
AEHC	Asociación Española de Historiadores del Cine (Spanish Association of Film Historians)
AGA	Archivo General de la Administración del Estado (General Archive of the [Spanish] State Administration)
AIEDC	Association Internationale des Écrivains pour la Défense de la Culture (International Association of Writers for the Defense of Culture)
BILR	Bureau International de Littérature Révolutionnaire (International Bureau of Revolutionary Literature)
BOC	Bloc Obrer i Camperol (Workers' and Peasants' Front)
CEA	Cinematografía Española y Americana S.A. (Spanish and American Cinema, Ltd.)
CGALI	Centralnyj Gosudarstvennyj Archiv Literatury i Iskusstva ([Russian] Central Archive of Literature and Art)
CGT	Conféderation Générale du Travail (General Confederation of Labor)
CIFESA	Compañía Industrial Film Español S.A. (Spanish Industrial Film Company, Ltd.)
CNT	Confederación Nacional del Trabajo (National Confederation of Labor)
Comintern	Communist International / Third International

CP	Communist Party
CPGB	Communist Party of Great Britain
CPSU	Communist Party of the Soviet Union
CPUSA	Communist Party of the United States of America
ECESA	Estudios Cinema Español S.A. (Spanish Film Studios, Ltd.)
ERPI	Electrical Research Products, Inc.
FAI	Federación Anarquista Ibérica (Iberian Anarchist Federation)
FIARI	Fédération International de l'Art Révolutionnaire Indépendant (International Federation of Independent Revolutionary Art)
FUE	Federación Universitaria Escolar (University Students Federation)
GECI	Grupo de Escritores Cinematográficos Independientes (Independent Film Writers Group)
Gestapo	Geheime Staats Polizei (German political police)
GPU	Gosudarstvennoe Politicheskoe Upravlenne (Soviet political police between 1922 and 1934)
JSU	Juventudes Socialistas Unificadas (Unified Socialist Youth)
KPD	Kommunistische Partei Deutschlands (German Communist Party)
LRS	*La Révolution surréaliste* (1924–29)
LSASDLR	*Le Surréalisme au service de la Révolution* (1930–33)
MGM	Metro-Goldwyn-Mayer
MNCARS	Museo Nacional Centro de Arte Reina Sofia, Madrid
MoMA	Museum of Modern Art, New York
MPPDAA	Motion Picture Producers and Distributors Association of America
NEP	Novaya Ekonomicheskaya Politika (New Economic Policy)
NKVD	Narodnyi Komissaryat Vnutrennikh Del (Soviet political police between 1934 and 1946)
OIAA	Office of Inter-American Affairs
OVRA	Organizzazione di Vigilanza e Repressione dell' Antifascismo (Organization for the Vigilance and Repression of Anti-Fascism)
PCE	Partido Comunista de España (Spanish Communist Party)
PCF	Parti Communiste Français (French Communist Party)
PFI	Progressive Film Institute
PNV	Partido Nacionalista Vasco (Basque Nationalist Party)
POI	Partido Obrero Internacional (International Workers Party)
POUM	Partido Obrero de Unificación Marxista (Workers Party of Marxist Unification)
PSOE	Partido Socialista Obrero Español (Spanish Socialist Workers Party)

PSUC	Partit Socialista Unificat de Catalunya (Unified Socialist Party of Catalonia)
RAPP	Rossiyskaya Assotsiatsiya Proletarskikh Pisatele (Russian Association of Proletarian Writers)
RCA	Radio Corporation of America
RGASPI	Rossiiskii Gosudarstvennyi Arkhiv Sotsialnoi i Politicheskoi Issledovanii (Russian State Archive of Social and Political History)
SFIC	Section Française de l'Internationale Communiste (French Section of the Communist International)
SIDE	Servicio de Información Diplomático y Especial (Diplomatic and Special Information Service)
SIM	Servicio de Investigación Militar (Military Investigation Service)
SOI	Secours Ouvrier International / Socorro Obrero Internacional (Workers International Relief)
UEAP	Unión de Escritores y Artistas Proletarios (Union of Proletarian Writers and Artists)
UFEH	Unión Federal de Estudiantes Hispanos (Federal Union of Spanish Students)
UGT	Unión General de Trabajadores (General Union of Workers)
UHP	Unión Hermanos Proletarios (Proletarian Brothers United)
UIER	Union International des Écrivains Révolutionnaires (International Union of Revolutionary Writers)
UN	United Nations
USSR	Union of Soviet Socialist Republics

Luis Buñuel

Introduction

The political earthquake of the First World War, one of whose seismic shocks was the Russian Revolution of October 1917, gave rise, following the peace of Versailles, to new currents of thought that would help to profoundly alter the intellectual map of Europe's developed societies. At the time it went all but unnoticed that a few days before signing the solemn treaty that expunged "the war to end all wars" (as it was called in an excess of irresponsibility), there would appear, in *Il Popolo d'Italia*, the Fascist manifesto signed by Benito Mussolini. The changes in the decade that followed were many and far from identical in each European country. In a Madrid that was still a "one-horse town in La Mancha," in the enlightened islet of the Residencia de Estudiantes, a group of young writers, intellectuals, and artists practiced, in their games and skirmishes, a boisterous subversion against the rancid clerical conservatism of Alphonsine society. Particularly outstanding among them were the Aragonese Luis Buñuel, the Catalan Salvador Dalí, and the Andalusian Federico García Lorca. They were to become the progenitors of a future culture as yet barely discernible on the horizon.

Outside Spain the changes were more profound. In January 1924 Vladimir Ilyich Lenin died in Nizhny Novgorod, and a troika consisting of Stalin, Kamenev, and Zinoviev replaced him in the Soviet leadership. On 6 April of that same year Mussolini achieved his first parliamentary majority in Italy, thus consolidating the political power of the Fascist Party. And in October, on the bloodless battlefield of ideas, André Breton launched his epoch-making *Manifeste du surréalisme*, which enthroned "psychic automatism" as a weapon in the service of "absolute non-conformism" (as the manifesto's last paragraph had it). These were three very different events, but their fundamental dialectical contradictions would finally become enmeshed in the following decade.

Before the advent of that decade, however, Buñuel, by now installed in Paris, produced and directed *Un chien andalou* (1929), based on a most unconventional script about the sexual tribulations of a young man, written in collaboration with Dalí, who had just put distance between himself and his former intimate, Lorca. Thus it was that two *révolté* members of that far-off Residencia de Estudiantes took the international floor as the founders of Surrealist cinema.

The release of *Un chien andalou* coincided with the Wall Street crash. The next ten years would be turbulent ones, with the masses of the crisis-bound capitalist democracies tempted by Fascism (which triumphed in Germany, Hungary, Japan, Portugal, and Spain, as it had triumphed before in Italy) and Leftist revolutionary illusions induced, until 1935, by the Stalinized Soviet Union, prior to giving way to the interclassist, anti-Fascist pacts of the Popular Fronts. Such polarization, which created its own magnetic fields in the artistic and intellectual world, helped dismast the impetuous, multifarious avant-garde impulse that—as "dehumanized" art (Ortega y Gasset *dixit*)—had occupied a central place in the European cultural life of the previous decade. Surrealism was perhaps the movement that most exemplarily registered such tensions and shocks—leading to successive schisms—which were promptly reflected in the programmatic texts drafted by André Breton, especially his *Second Manifeste du surrealisme* (1929–30) and *Position politique du surréalisme* (1935).

This political polarization promptly surfaced in Spain and met with a model instance in the ideological bifurcation of the trajectories of Buñuel and Dalí, who had previously collaborated on two films, *Un chien andalou* and the politically more radical *L'Âge d'or* (1930). While Dalí's undeniable artistic talents, managed by his wife Gala, were orientated toward economic profitability in the centers of capitalist power (in particular America), and while he flirted with Hitlerism, despite the admonitions of Breton, before kowtowing in 1940 to the Franco regime, Buñuel joined the Communist movement, considered directing in the USSR, and cultivated, in turn, the documentary of political denunciation and the production of popular cinema, before serving during the Civil War in the Spanish Republican Embassy in Paris. These two divergent political destinies had their counterpoint in the tragic fate of Lorca, "poet of the people" during the Frente Popular, who was shot by the Fascists in Viznar on 19 August 1936, thus definitively dynamiting the jubilant trio of the Residencia de Estudiantes.

The fact that this fraught decade would draw to a close with the Spanish tragedy—anteroom of the Second World War—gave a particularly meaningful dimension to these contrary itineraries, which partly acquired—notwithstanding the exceptional singularity of the protagonists—the status of political paradigms, paradigms that ought never to eclipse the rich and complex human characteristics of these individuals.

Despite Spain's relatively peripheral identity in the 1930s in terms of the major cultural currents that coursed through the Western world, the fratricidal war between Fascism and Popular Frontism, with the dramatic exile that succeeded it, lent the Spanish tragedy a historic exemplariness that goes on being a point of reference when it comes to understanding the avatars of the twentieth century.

This book, which focuses on the complex development of Luis Buñuel's biography in the least productive and most obscure years of his cinematic career, includes many hitherto unknown documents, obtained from archives in various countries, about that highly conflictive era and seeks to encourage reflection on a decade that was not only decisive for the political and cultural map of Spain, but also for the career and destiny of the man who would become, without a shadow of a doubt, its most famous filmmaker.

1

The Militant Surrealist

The appearance of *Un chien andalou* on the Paris intellectual scene was a bombshell for many, not least for the Surrealist Group around André Breton. The film was screened at an invitation-only session at the Studio des Ursulines art house on 6 June 1929, and its showing was tantamount to the epiphany of Surrealist cinema, hitherto dreamed of but never realized, and to the catapulting to fame of its makers, two provincial Spanish unknowns, Luis Buñuel and Salvador Dalí. With its public release at Montmartre's Studio 28 on 1 October a fresh chapter in the history of the Surrealist movement began, since not only did the twenty-minute movie blaze a new trail in terms of its creative genesis and its visual imagery, but it also heralded a struggle for its ideological appropriation on the part of Breton's group in order to prevent it from being claimed by different intellectual rivals.

The a posteriori accounts of when Buñuel and Dalí met this or that Surrealist, and the group as a whole, are vague and contradictory and impossible to verify today. The fact that *Un chien andalou* had been programmed to accompany the première of Man Ray's *Les Mystères du château du dé* at the Studio des Ursulines guaranteed, given the American artist's *Tout-Paris* connections, an elite audience. If not before, it can be said that on 6 June Buñuel—and he alone, for Dalí was in Figueres—would (or could) have met the Surrealists Breton, Louis Aragon, Max Ernst, Tristan Tzara, Joan Miró, Hans Arp, and Robert Desnos; artists like Fernand Léger, Constantin Brancusi, Jacques Lipchitz, and Le Corbusier; film director René Clair and the cinephile Viscount Charles de Noailles, who'd commissioned Man Ray's short and would have an immediate impact as a patron on the lives of the two Spaniards.[1] We also know that through the good offices of Miró, Dalí, in Paris for two months, partly for the shooting of *Un chien andalou* (which began on 2 April) but mainly to further his career as a painter, had met the Belgian art dealer Camille Goemans and signed a contract on 15 May that would provide him with a stipend enabling him to prepare his first one-man show six months later.

Goemans had introduced Dalí to René Magritte, then living near Paris, and whose work—as Agustín Sánchez Vidal has demonstrated—was already known to Dalí and to Buñuel, as revealed by several shots in *Un chien andalou* that are more or less facsimiles of Magritte's images.[2] (For example, there is a moment in which the male protagonist, Pierre Batcheff, stares fixedly at the palm of his hand—ants will later pour out of a stigmata-like hole in it—an image that replicates the Belgian Surrealist's 1928 painting *The Mysterious Suspicion*.) It seems that Dalí also visited Robert Desnos and crossed paths with Paul Éluard and his current girlfriend Alice Apfel (known as "La Pomme," a translation of her German surname), but not the absent Gala Éluard—that momentous meeting would come about later. On this occasion the French poet appears not to have registered Salvador's name, since in a letter from Paris to Gala in Switzerland, written sometime during the first half of July, he referred rather vaguely to Goemans going on holiday "with some Spaniards who have made an admirable film to Cadaqués, in Spain."[3]

Un chien andalou's frenetic Freudian satire on Jazz Age heterosexuality slotted perfectly into the local zeitgeist. Many a vanguard intellectual identified with the movie's take on the tragicomic vicissitudes of libidinal gratification and wanted to meet the perpetrator(s). Writing from Paris to Dalí in Figueres on 24 June 1929, Buñuel spoke exultantly of having encountered "*all* the Surrealists . . . , especially Queneau, Prévert, Max Morise, Naville, all 'splendid' and just as we'd imagined," before mentioning the loan of the film to Antonin Artaud and Roger Vitrac for a further restricted screening. Later in the same letter the debut director alludes to his great sympathy for Breton—without divulging if the two have already met—but laments that "he now finds himself surrounded by foul little Surrealist types like Thirion, Mégret and their friends."[4] Although he's aware that the arrangement with Artaud and Vitrac will have to be hushed up so as not to alienate Breton, for whom they are *personae non gratae*, Buñuel's outsider knowledge of the realpolitik of Surrealism is, we can say with hindsight, rather sketchy. Or, to be more precise, he lacks inside information on tensions within the group that are soon to come to the boil: aside from André Thirion and Frédéric Mégret, all the names he admiringly cites in his missive will become ex-Surrealists within a few months. This is by way of saying that the movement, ever prone to divisiveness given its compulsive search for perfect "peerage," was on the cusp of a more violent than usual reconfiguration of the ranks. And if the two Spaniards wanted to take their place within it they would have to rethink the issue of who was "foul" and who was not.

The August 1929 stay chez Salvador proved to be epochal. Summering in Cadaqués were René and Georgette Magritte, Goemans and Yvonne Bernard, Éluard and his wife Gala. The last to arrive was Buñuel, anxious to begin discussing a follow-up film with Dalí. The artist's mind was elsewhere, however: he'd fallen for Gala, thus endangering the harmony between the two scriptwriters, and he was hard at work on a series of extraordinarily inventive paintings for his upcoming Paris début. It was at this time that Buñuel and Dalí must have been briefed on the internecine warfare and the shifting alliances within Surrealism—in part by Goemans and Magritte, who'd demonstrated their solidarity with Breton during this parlous period, but especially by Éluard, who, a front-runner himself, was familiar with the thinking of his fellow pacemakers Aragon and Breton.

The latter, on holiday on the Île de Sein, off the Brittany coast, with his (soon to be ex-) lover Suzanne Muzard, plus Georges Sadoul, Pierre Unik, and Jeanette and Yves Tanguy, spent part of his summer drafting the "Second Manifeste du surréalisme," an audacious, illumined, melodramatic, occasionally pompous, position paper weaving together Hegelianism, psychoanalysis, dialectical materialism, hermeticism, and poetics into an irreducible whole. In part a purging of former adepts who'd opted for apolitical literary careerism or who'd joined forces in opposition to Breton's custodianship—the main target being the dissident faction around Georges Bataille and the magazine *Documents*—the manifesto also called for the further Bolshevization of Surrealism. Henceforth, the Surrealists would function as a fellow-traveling lobby in, but more often out of, step with the agitprop policies of the French Communist Party (PCF), the perceived enablers, along with the party's minder, the Communist International (Comintern), of the proletarian revolution, a revolution much yearned for by the *gauchiste* intelligentsia of Paris.[5] The "Second Manifeste" appeared in the twelfth and last issue of the magazine *La Révolution surréaliste* (*LRS*, 1924–29), soon to be followed by a new journal, *Le Surréalisme au service de la Révolution* (*LSASDLR*, 1930–33). The change of titles speaks reams.

What we must retain of all this, then, is that Buñuel (and Dalí) joined the movement at a moment of intense ideological crisis, during a reframing of Surrealism's revolutionary aspirations and its tactics; that the Surrealism of which they became part was anxious for politico-cultural instrumentality and would trade its critical, Left Oppositional stance vis-à-vis the PCF, dating from 1927, for a more orthodox position; and that in rallying to the general line in 1929–30 the Surrealists voiced no criticism of the totalitarian character the

USSR was assuming with the consolidation of Stalinism. That criticism would become tentatively public in 1933 and achieve critical mass as the stated Surrealist position after the last in a long line of thwarted rapprochements with the PCF, the International Congress of Writers for the Defense of Culture, held in Paris in June 1935.[6]

The perception of those who knew Buñuel in Paris after the devastating impact of his first film would be colored by his on-screen bearing in its unforgettable opening sequence: beefy and brutish as a slaughterhouse worker, given to cold-blooded, unthinkably perverse violence, seemingly on a whim. A dab hand with a cutthroat at dead of night. Along with his newly proven gifts as an incendiary image maker—and as an incendiary image in his own right—it was the perceived, omnipresent threat of this saturnine man losing his rag that created an aura around his person. In a collective much given to *action directe*, to propaganda by deed, such belligerence was an essential asset, and there are few witnesses who do not insist on Buñuel's potential for visiting retribution upon the enemy, a potential he was wont to underline, in the absence of the physical kind, by a penchant for verbal violence. And since Buñuel had forced his entry along with Dalí as a sort of double act, many of the portraits penned by their new comrades evoke the striking dissimilarity of their physiques. Georges Sadoul, the future film historian who assumes a certain importance in this book, described the first appearance of the two at the Surrealist café (which must have taken place at the only time both the Spaniards were in Paris, between 27 October and 18 November, probably closer to the former). Sadoul recalled that Breton "had convoked [the] creators [of the film] to our usual venue in order to admit them officially into our ranks. They came to the terrace of the [Café] Radio, one summer's evening. Dali had the large eyes, grace and timidity of a gazelle. To us, Buñuel, big and athletic, his black eyes protruding a little, seemed exactly like he always is in *Un chien andalou*, meticulously honing the razor that will slice the open eye in two."[7] Elsa Triolet, Louis Aragon's companion, likened Buñuel to gentle giant Mayakovsky, the literal and metaphorical colossus of Soviet avant-garde poetry and playwriting, while Aragon himself would speak of "this gentle, one-time boxer (who never dared use his fists from fear of killing his opponent)."[8] Breton, meanwhile, perhaps thinking of Man Ray's 1929 photo portrait of Buñuel wearing the same "prole" collarless shirt as in the prologue to *Un chien andalou*, emphasized the Spaniard's intimidating eyeballing: "When he spoke to me, he always gave me the impression of a ladder trying to lean up against me."[9]

As recounted by Buñuel, his first creative tryst with the cream of the Paris art world, including some of the Surrealists—at *Un chien andalou*'s première on 6 June 1929—aspires to the condition of myth: "Very nervous, as you might imagine, I remained behind the screen with a gramophone and during the showing alternated between Argentinean tangos and *Tristan and Isolde*. I'd put some stones in my pockets to throw at the audience in the event of failure. . . . I was expecting the worst. My stones were unnecessary. At the end of the film, behind the screen, I heard prolonged applause and I discreetly got rid of my projectiles on the floor."[10] And myth it must be, for it seems unlikely that the sensation-hungry sophisticates in the invited audience, habituated since the Dada days to aesthetic outrage, would be hostile to such cinematic brio, and that the director would lapidate the likes of Breton, Ernst, Léger, Brancusi, and Le Corbusier (to name but them). The anecdote works at the level of wishful thinking, though, as a magical overcoming, a dramatization of Buñuel's will to power, in a potential preemptive strike demonstrating that the Spaniard, being tougher than the tough guys, more scandalous than the scandalmongers, was worthy of belonging to their number. In any case, forty years later Aragon would tell Max Aub that the stones-in-the-pocket yarn was a fib: "He dreamed it up. He didn't have stones in his pockets nor was he behind the screen. He just waited anxiously to hear what we [the Surrealists] thought."[11]

Once *Un chien andalou* had been claimed by the Surrealists as their own, and its two creators formally inducted into the movement—which we date to late October 1929—it fell to them, almost as a rite of initiation and a test of their mettle, to wrest the film (and Dalí's paintings) from the ideological grasp of other, proscribed cultural entities.

In the 24 June letter cited above, a euphoric Buñuel speaks of the enthusiastic attention of a clutch of cutting-edge magazines—*Variétés*, *Cahiers d'Art*, and *Bifur*—toward *Un chien andalou* and their wish to feature it in their forthcoming issues. He cites one other magazine, *Du cinéma*, which, on being taken over by the publisher Gallimard, was about to become *La Revue du cinéma*. Two of its mainstays, Jean-George Auriol and Jacques-Bernard Brunius—the latter had gotten Buñuel to review films for *Cahiers d'Art* in 1927 and would himself pen a glowing critique of *Un chien andalou* in the July 1929 issue of the same magazine—had convinced the Spaniard to permit *La Revue du cinéma* to publish the scenario of *Un chien andalou* in its 15 November number. However, Surrealist intransigence was such that the new recruit was called upon by Breton, Aragon, and Éluard—the group's hard core—to rescind this agreement since the scenario was required as an exclusive for the final, 15 December 1929 number of *LRS*, where it would sit alongside the "Second Manifeste du surréalisme" and contributions by other newcomers such as René Char—another big fellow, being a rugby player—Dalí, Goemans, Magritte, and Tzara. And if Buñuel is to be believed—his account in *Mon dernier soupir* is, as so often, confused[12]—he did his rescinding in high style, descending on the publishers, hammer in hand, to smash the set type. It was too late, however: the number had already gone to press, and he had to settle for dispatching a strongly worded letter of protest, dated 19 November, to the editors of the chief Paris newspapers.[13] In any event Gallimard was an odd target to choose, for the publishers had placed an ad in the June 1929 Surrealist number of *Variétés* featuring the Surrealist writers it had been consistently publishing since 1921: a roster including Aragon, Breton, René Crevel, Éluard, and Benjamin Péret.[14] But Buñuel's vengeful foray may well have happened, for Gallimard ceased publishing the Surrealists around that time—although this may have had to do with dwindling sales or their commitment to the PCF, rather than to Buñuel's offensive—and it would be 1934 before their books reappeared with the Nouvelle Revue Française logo.[15]

Aside from the *Revue du cinéma* about-face, the reappropriation of a film that had been made as an approximation to Surrealism—a "surrealistic" movie that became truly Surrealist—was aimed, in the ongoing struggle among Left-modernist groupuscules seeking to occupy the moral high ground, at spiting the opposition, the *Documents* dissidents, especially Georges Bataille. In his September 1929 essay on the eye for the ongoing *Documents* dictionary, the author of *Histoire de l'œil* (1928) had written insightfully of the eroticized horror of the prologue of *Un chien andalou*. What's more, his text appeared opposite Dalí's 1927 painting *Honey Is Sweeter Than Blood*.[16] In this essay Bataille preempted the Surrealists, who were not to publish Dalí until *LRS* 12, by some three months. We get chapter and verse on this mini-crisis of legitimation in a letter dated 10 December 1929 from the Viscount de Noailles to Buñuel. Even at this late date, following the public screening of *Un chien andalou* at Studio 28 from 1 October onward, and after Dalí's sellout show at Goemans' gallery from 20 November to 5 December 1929 (with Breton writing the laudatory catalogue preface), the Surrealists, realizing just how close Dalí's—and to a lesser degree, Buñuel's—interests were to Bataille's, were intent on undermining the "excremental philosopher's" proprietorial claims. This fear of losing the two Spaniards to the dissidents demonstrates just how fulsome their contribution, present and future, was deemed to be by Breton and his followers.

Referring in passing to the Gallimard fracas, Noailles reveals that Éluard has written to ask him not to let Bataille reproduce a couple of Dalí paintings in a future *Documents*, paintings the Viscount had bought from Goemans; that Bataille had requested Noailles's authorization to do so with Dalí's blessing; and that Noailles has told Éluard that he feels duty bound to let Bataille publish the images, unless Dalí himself vetoes the arrangement.[17] Dalí did so: Bataille's ideas were exactly the opposite of his own, he tendentiously told Noailles in a

Published in the twelfth and final number of *La Révolution surréaliste,* this photomontaged frieze of portraits of the members of the Surrealist Group surrounds the image of a naked woman painted by Magritte. Starting at top left and continuing clockwise, we see Alexandre, Aragon, Breton, Buñuel, Caupenne, Éluard, Fourrier, Magritte, Valentin, Thirion, Tanguy, Sadoul, Nougé, Goemans, Ernst, and Dalí. (*La Révolution surréaliste,* no. 12 [15 December 1929]: 73)

letter. When Bataille came to publish his psychoanalytical reading of Dalí's painting *The Lugubrious Game* in the December 1929 number of *Documents*, he had to settle for a diagrammatic representation of it.[18] Buñuel's 14 December reply to Noailles is discretion itself: "Your reply to Éluard seems perfectly just to me and we'll come back to it."[19]

A day later the twelfth and final issue of *LRS* appeared, with Buñuel making three appearances therein. First, as one of the sixteen group members, each represented by a front-on photomaton portrait with closed eyes, who do not see "the . . . . . . hidden in the forest" (the dots standing for the self-effacing naked woman painted by Magritte around which the Surrealists are ranged). Then, as an answerer to one of the many inquiries, or *enquêtes*, which dot the history of Surrealism, this one on "love." And last, as the cowriter and introducer of the literary scenario of *Un chien andalou*. The director's preamble to the latter is legendary, but given what we've said above perhaps we may now nuance it a little. It reads:

> The publication of this scenario in *"La Révolution Surréaliste" is the only one I authorize.* It expresses, without reservations of any kind, my total adherence to Surrealist thought and activity. *Un chien andalou* wouldn't exist if Surrealism didn't exist.
>
> *A hit film*, that's what most of the people who've seen it think. What can I do, though, against the devotees of all kinds of novelty, even if this novelty flies in the face of their deepest convictions, against a venal or insincere press, against that imbecile crowd that has found beauty in what is basically nothing but a desperate, passionate appeal to murder.[20]

Stirring stuff, bespeaking urgency and anguish. But who was to murder whom, and why? Wasn't this mere rhetoric? An aping of Breton's infamous remark in the "Second Manifeste," in the same issue of *LRS*, about the simplest Surrealist act, the random shooting down of passersby in the street? (We shouldn't forget that the André Gide character from *Les Caves du Vatican*, Lafcadio Wluiki, advocate of unmotivated homicide, had been an exemplary figure for the Paris Dadaists.) A two-gun outrage, Breton's remark is partly predicted in *Un chien andalou* itself by actor Pierre Batcheff's trigger-happiness and was not to be elaborated upon until the long footnote the polemicist devoted to it in the revised version of the manifesto, when published in book form in June 1930: "As for that act I claim is the simplest—it is obvious that my intention is not to recommend it above all others just because it is simple."[21] (Elsewhere in the same footnote Breton declares, "Yes, I am anxious to know if an individual has a natural gift for violence before asking myself if, in that same individual, violence *portrays* or *does not portray* him"—a statement that applies to Buñuel in one way or another.) We've already argued that given the intellectual caliber and celebrity status of the invited audience, Buñuel's account of the first-ever showing of *Un chien andalou* was pure fantasy. Yet is there not something faux-naïf, or even ersatz, about his attack in *LRS* on the only viable audience for his twenty-minute first film—which played as a support, along with a Méliès, a Harold Lloyd, and a Michel Gorel documentary to an early Hollywood noir, *The Cop* (Donald Crisp, 1929)—to wit, the cinephiles who would knowingly buy a ticket to experience such a deliberate affront in a 337-seat art house in chic Montmartre? (But then an anti-cinephile cinephilia was always part of the Surrealist attitude.) And the venal press? Well, critics of the stature of Alexandre Arnoux, Brunius, Louis Chavance, André Delons, Desnos, and Philippe Soupault wrote perceptibly about the film. Indeed, it seems as if Buñuel's defiant stance was a response, knowing or otherwise, to his critical mentor Brunius's skeptical observation, in his July 1929 review in *Cahiers d'Art*: "For those who know something of the ways of art cinemas and avant-garde spectators, people who love being violated, it is easy to predict quite a bit of success for Buñuel among the snobs. May he take advantage of it without being led astray."[22]

Extending back to 1919, and the pre-Surrealist magazine *Littérature*, surveys like the one on love were a litmus test of private conviction and moral consensus. The themes chosen were dramatically existential—suicide, sexuality, humor, love—and called for candor and sincerity: die, screw, laugh, kiss . . . and tell. Truth telling as a gelling agent; the hypocritical bourgeois—and us. Here, and coming as the final statement of the last issue of *LRS*, the fifty-three responses to the questions are grouped in such a way as to pass from an outright hostility toward love or the Surrealist view of it (implicit in the questions) to a positive stance vis-à-vis the matter from non-Surrealists—these first two categories embracing thirty-seven replies—before arriving at the enthused Surrealists themselves: seventeen of them, but with a few changes in personnel from the sixteen in the photomaton frieze. The photomontage stands in an oblique relation to the inquiry proper; it's more a resonant supplement to it than its illustration. This enigmatic rapport is rendered even odder by the overall image itself: the solemn serial layout of the photos and the rebus-like oil in which a figurative representation of a naked, self-effacing woman stands in for the word "woman" and completes the autograph message. "I don't see the . . . . . . hidden in the forest." As Georges Sebbag has pointed out, a chance nocturnal meeting with a naked woman in a wood was a particular fantasy of Breton's, as he mentioned in *Nadja* (1928).[23] It isn't known who had the idea for the pose and the page layout, although Breton kept the original graphic and owned the

Magritte oil painting. It is possible that the latter suggested the image of the Surrealists "blinded by love," because in his paintings and photos in 1927–28 there are already figures, including the artist himself, with their eyes closed.[24] As it was, De Chirico's *The Child's Brain* (1914), with its heavy-lidded patriarch, had long been a fetish picture for Breton.

In terms of this visual argument, the photomontage of the self-blinded male egos is paired with the opening page of *LRS* 12, where Breton's "Second Manifeste" is preceded by the life-size red lip-prints of seven female companions of the Surrealists: Suzanne Muzard, Elsa Triolet, Gala Éluard, Alice Apfel, Jeanette Tanguy, Marie-Berthe Ernst, and Yvonne Bernard. Introduced in Paris in June 1928, the pioneering photomaton machine, located in the Jardin des Plantes, was soon co-opted as an avant-garde accessory and was already in use by the Surrealists before the hieratic intervention under discussion. This is borne out by Breton's personal collection of vintage photomaton strips, where the exuberant clowning of the Prévert Brothers, Marcel Duhamel, and Queneau contrasts with the stiff sobriety of the sixteen dreamers. The iconic status that the "I don't see" page has acquired through frequent republication means that it is an uncanny experience to view the alternative takes. Buñuel in particular seems to have "ratcheted" his head along a vertical axis during each freeze frame, as if exaggeratedly nodding his acquiescence.[25] He is in the top row, to Breton's left, in the alphabetically ordered sequencing. As chance would have it, coming third in the list in a top row of five, Breton occupies the pivotal position of the entire composition, immediately above and in line with the naked woman; it is as if *he* is the unseeing "je."[26]

It has been claimed that aside from differences of an aesthetic or political order, differences that culminated in the exclusions—and inclusions—announced in the "Second Manifeste," there was another fault line that led to the sundering of the group: Breton's divorce from his first wife, Simone Kahn, so as to satisfy the demands of Suzanne Muzard, his lover since the end of 1927. That is, many of the proscribed Surrealists had taken Simone's side.[27] We may say, then, that the questionnaire on love is overdetermined; that in consonance with the problematic "love life" of Breton—but not his alone!—the inquiry is charged with a desperate idealism. (Breton even had Suzanne answer on his behalf.) And that its manifest meaning—the overcoming of amorous alienation—is accompanied by a latent one: the promoting of male bonding around the issue of heterosexual desire. Whence the repetitive, equally rapturous replies of many of the seventeen Surrealists, and whence the absence of a potentially disruptive voice like Dalí's—after all, he was in the process of relieving a comrade of his wife; a fact that lends poignancy to Éluard's replies.

In the interests of legibility we have broken up the text of the questions and interlarded these with Buñuel's replies:

Q: What sort of hope do you place in love?

A: *If I love, every hope. If I do not love, none.*

Q: How do you envisage the transition from the *idea of love* to the *fact of loving?*

A: *For me only the fact of loving exists.*

Q: Would you sacrifice your freedom, willingly or otherwise, to love? Have you done so?

A: *I would willingly sacrifice my freedom to love. I've already done so.*

Q: Would you agree to sacrifice a cause you hitherto thought you had to defend if, in your opinion, it was necessary to do so in order not to be unworthy of love?

A: *I would sacrifice a cause out of love, but that would depend on the particular instance.*

Q: Would you agree to not becoming the person you might have become if this was the price for you to fully partake of the certainty of love?

A: *Yes.*

Q: How would you judge a man who would go so far as to betray his convictions in order to please the woman he loves? Can such a pledge be asked for, be obtained?

A: *I would judge him in a very positive light. But despite this I would ask that man not to betray his convictions. I would even go as far as to demand it of him.*

Q: Would you acknowledge the right to deprive yourself for a time of the presence of the being you love, knowing the degree to which absence is exalting for love, yet perceiving the mediocrity of a calculation of this sort?

A: *I would not want to separate myself from the being I love. At any price.*

Q: Do you believe in the victory of admirable love over sordid life, or of sordid life over admirable love?

A: *I don't know.*[28]

The agenda is Breton's; the questions are his and denote his current obsessions. That said, the exalted, "courtly love" feel they possess neatly complements the scabrous parting shot in the preceding number of *LRS*, another inquiry dominated by his person, the "Research on Sexuality."[29] Taken together, the two investigations flesh out the Surrealist notion of *amour-érotisme*, a notion already articulated in the slightly earlier defense of Charlie Chaplin's morals, "Hands Off Love," in response to press attacks at the time of his divorce from Lita Grey.[30] It is to this libertarian conception of carnal love that Buñuel cleaves.

Let us imagine, then, this question-and-answer sequence on love as a personal conversation between Breton and Buñuel. What comes over, in the first instance, is the orthodoxy of Buñuel's replies: one gets the impression he's saying what he thinks Breton wants to hear. But then he's not alone in this—many of the Surrealists respond in like manner, in part as an expression of their "blind struggle for the love of André," as Aragon would put it years later, speaking of the ultra-righteous attitude of neophyte group members.[31] Coming on the heels of this first impression is the feeling that this cannot be verbiage or ventriloquism alone, that the director must be telling at least *a* truth. As it is, the very terseness and pragmatism of his replies add to their note of conviction. Here is a man of action, and in a realm—"mad love," as it would be called—that seems to be belied by the little we know of his intimate biography. What, for instance, are we to make of Buñuel's claim to having already sacrificed his freedom for the sake of love? Who is the woman being alluded to here? Can it be Jeanne Rucar, his fiancée since 1926? And is this sacrifice so positive and "up-beat" as the triumphalist tone of much of the inquiry would have us believe? Or can we read it as a fatalistic response, as a depressed admission of entrapment? For all their seeming straightforwardness, such replies are deeply ambiguous, as are the questions set by Breton to which they respond. Perhaps the most convincing exchange is Buñuel's last, when he admits to not knowing which of the forces will win in the struggle between "admirable love" and "sordid life."

For one reason or another, neither the questions nor the answers seem to truly "fit" our man; the suit feels one size too big (or too small). On the other hand, both questions and answers *do* sit well on a figure who is about to play an important part in Buñuel's life; to wit, "The Honorable Monsieur X," the fictional character who will be played by Gaston Modot in the director's second film. If we put Monsieur X/Modot in Buñuel's place, so to speak, and have him answer Breton's questionnaire, things start to fall into place. (Not wholly, of course, because the character is as much an alter ego of Dalí as of Buñuel.) In that sense, the "Inquiry into Love" of December 1929 forms part of the source material generated by the movement—the "Research on Sexuality" and "Hands Off Love" being other elements—that finds its way into the *ur*-expression of cinematic Surrealism, *L'Âge d'or*, to which we now turn.

2

The Production of *L'Âge d'or*

In his capacity as an unofficial agent for *Un chien andalou*, Christian Zervos, the editor of *Cahiers d'Art*, would introduce the debutant director to the fabulously wealthy Viscount Charles and Marie-Laure de Noailles after the exclusive Studio des Ursulines session on 6 June 1929. Renowned for their patronage of the arts and for their avant-garde tastes, the cinephile couple had produced (and appeared in) the Man Ray vanity movie that *Un chien andalou* accompanied. Having been bitten by the dog, they began renting a print from Pierre Braunberger—who'd signed a world-rights exhibition contract with Buñuel on 12 June—for a set of screenings for the "right people" in the twenty-five-seat rococo projection room of their mansion on the Place des États-Unis. On 5 July, for example, their guests included filmmakers Carl Dreyer and Jean Lods, film critics Léon Moussinac and Jean Tedesco, the poet Léon-Paul Fargue, and Surrealists René Crevel and Michel Leiris.[1] So thrilled were the Noailles that they would soon commission Buñuel to do a remake of the same length, some twenty minutes. *La Bête andalouse*, as the new film was called during production, so as to underline its continuity with its predecessor, would cover the same narrative ground: the tragicomic courting of a libidinous but inhibited couple. We do not know if Buñuel, arriving in Cadaqués in mid-August, in part to brainstorm script ideas for their second film, was able to announce to Dalí that they might already have backers, illustrious ones at that. It seems unlikely, as Buñuel had left Paris for San Sebastián—where he vacationed with his family before crossing the peninsula to Catalonia—at around the date *Un chien andalou* was being viewed by Dreyer and the others, which would have left insufficient time for the necessary confidence between both parties to be built up. We do know

Charles and Marie-Laure de Noailles and their daughter, ca. 1930. (© Boris Lipnitski / Roger-Viollet)

that the Gala-besotted painter proved incapable of working on this hypothetical outline, and that in his frustration Buñuel almost strangled Salvador's paramour.

Restored to Paris and now a member of the Surrealist Group and maker of the new season's hottest film property—*Un chien andalou* having opened to great notices at Studio 28 on 1 October 1929—Buñuel began discussing his follow-up in earnest with the Noailles. By 18 November 1929 he had a sufficiently concrete proposal—whether contrived with Dalí or without him, we cannot tell—to convince the aristocrats to offer "the amount of money that will be necessary, which amount we [the producers] will determine with you [the director] when you have done your shooting script, but which will probably be around three hundred and fifty thousand francs."[2] The new project was envisaged to take just four months—as had *Un chien andalou*—with the shooting script (*découpage*) occupying a month and a half, and Buñuel being paid 9,000 francs in advance for this. For the filming of the as yet untitled movie, the director was to receive 12,000 francs a month. The producers were discretion itself: wintering in their "Dice Castle" in Hyères (near Toulon) for four months from 5 December, they would be notable by their absence, thus leaving Buñuel a completely free hand. The only thing the Noailles stipulated was that once the film was made, they might have an exclusive on privately showcasing the film for a month before arranging its rental to a distributor or selling prints of it abroad. Seventy-five percent of the monies from any future deal were to go to the Viscount until his investment was paid off; once this occurred, Buñuel would receive all the profits.[3]

Ten days after the agreement with the Noailles, Buñuel was once more in Cadaqués, where he spent a week or so discussing the film with Dalí. Flushed with the success of his sell-out exhibition at the Goemans Gallery—from which the Viscount had bought the notorious *Lugubrious Game*—Salvador was nevertheless in bad graces with his father, who had thrown him out of the family home in Figueres on account of a blasphemous canvas shown in Paris, *Sometimes I Spit with Pleasure on the Portrait of My Mother*, also known as *The Sacred Heart.* Since no documents survive, it is impossible to know how much the two scriptwriters achieved—thus leaving room, as with the gestation of *Un chien andalou*, for much mythmaking. Notwithstanding their separate admission, many years later, that their collaboration lacked the complicity of the January 1929 sessions that had produced the outline for their first opus, the letter Buñuel wrote to Noailles on 29 November communicated a certain serenity about the way things had gone: "I can already predict that the scenario will, I trust, be more interesting than *Chien andalou*'s. I feel very optimistic and above all I'm managing, at last!, to work with the greatest composure. I'll leave here only when the scenario is absolutely finished."[4] (But was that absent complicity a feature of the August–September sessions or the November–December ones? The accounts tend to conflate the two.) Buñuel went on to say that his intention, when he got to his mother's home in Zaragoza around 6 December, was to start work on the *découpage*. This would suggest that the Cadaqués sessions had been nothing short of fruitful, although it is interesting that he makes no mention of Dalí in these private letters, arrogating all invention to himself. This, of course, may simply be evidence of the fact that, for him, composing the shooting script was tantamount to inventing the film, as he had argued in his *La Gaceta Literaria* essay of October 1928, "'Découpage' or Cinegraphic Segmentation." Buñuel wrote, "The filmmaker—it is better to reserve this word for the creator of the film alone—is less so at the moment of directing than at the supreme moment of segmentation."[5] On the other hand, given the kudos Dalí had for the Noailles, who were now buying his pictures and were about to forward him the money to buy his fisherman's cottage in Port Lligat, why didn't Buñuel mention his input? Are we witnessing here the beginning of the end of a brief golden age of coruscating collaboration? And the end of the beginning of fifty years of conflicting authorial claims and disclaimers?

By the end of his Christmas stay in Zaragoza, Buñuel had all but finished the first version of the *découpage*, telling the Noailles so in a 27 December letter posted a couple of days before he returned to Paris, a letter in which he mentioned his plan of going to Cadaqués on 8 January 1930 to see Dalí and to discuss some further modifications to the scenario the two of them had come up with. On 10 January he would, as foreseen, travel to Hyères to show his patrons the first version of the complete *découpage.* In Paris Buñuel was surprised to bump into Dalí, who'd left Catalonia after being "irrevocably" banished by his notary father and more or less disinherited by him, a droll circumstance given the fortune the painter was about to make. The co-scenarists got down to making their script changes and to going through the *découpage.* It would be their final meeting until sometime in June when, with *L'Âge d'or* reaching completion in Paris, Dalí and Gala arrived at the French capital after their sojourn in Carry-le-Rouet, Torremolinos, and Madrid. In the meantime, Buñuel made his way to Hyères, arriving there on 10 January. On 16 January he gave Noailles a receipt for 100,000 francs, a third of the budget agreed upon seven weeks before, "to make a film." To get to that point he'd prepared a second *découpage,* which presumably integrated the revisions upon which he and Dalí had agreed.

If we are going into some detail about the development of the scenario—the informal storyline of the movie—and its next refinement, the *découpage*—the formal itemization used to frame and film each shot—it is because we think it is worth adding our voices to other writers (Petr Král, Agustín Sánchez Vidal, Jean-Michel Bouhours and Nathalie Schoeller, Ian Gibson) who have argued that despite the self-serving, mendacious statements made decades later by both protagonists, the writing of their second film was substantially, although not wholly, a joint affair; that Buñuel, a scriptwriter whose later career demonstrates how much he relied upon a collaborator when it came to writing his movies, planned three trips to Cadaqués to see the local *Wunderkind*; that the minimizing of Dalí's role has been a subterfuge on the part of all those who, with an ideological axe to grind and in the face of the invisibility of *L'Âge d'or* (until its first general release in 1980), have claimed that the Catalan contributed only one or two gags to it (the sight gag being the structural unit of this and their first film); and that by the time he cloistered himself with Gala in the Hôtel du Château in Carry-le-Rouet, near Marseilles, between 10 January and 8 March 1930, there to continue painting some of Surrealism's greatest pictures, to formulating some of its finest theory—his paranoia-critical method in embryo—and to mailing some exuberant script ideas to Buñuel in Paris in a series of letters (with storyboard-like drawings), Dalí had contributed much to *L'Âge d'or*'s basic script and was familiar with, and in agreement with, the film's first *découpage,* at least. Having said that, we must be careful not to veer too far the other way: to argue that Dalí's contribution was major is not to diminish Buñuel's—setting aside his *découpage* skills, skills of which Dalí was evidently incapable—he was already, and would remain, a brilliant gag writer.

The souvenir booklet printed for the new film's public release on 28 November, again at Studio 28, that hotbed of "devotees of all kinds of novelty," would open with the scenario, preceded by a short note by Dalí: "My general idea when writing the scenario of *L'Âge d'or* with Buñuel has been to present the straight and pure line of 'conduct' of a human being who pursues love in the face of ignoble humanitarian and patriotic ideals and other miserable mechanisms of reality."[6] The scenario that follows is a schematic résumé of some four hundred words written by Dalí specifically for the brochure in October or November 1930, following a viewing of the final version of the film—it is a literary text and not a founding, "authentic" argument. Dalí's manuscript, penned in badly spelled French in his miniaturist hand, was corrected and even rewritten by others, probably Éluard or Aragon. This was common practice among the Surrealists when faced with the chaotic manuscripts of the Catalan painter. Dalí would include this scenario as an appendix in the first British edition of *The Secret Life*, a book heavily revised by Gala. In 1948, the date of this new edition, the opportunist artist took care, however, to remove a sentence, the same one a panicky Charles de Noailles had asked the Surrealists to suppress in November 1930, but which they did not, namely, "The Count de Blangis is obviously Jesus Christ."[7]

In his correspondence with his indulgent producers, Buñuel returns time and again to this fetish object, his *découpage*—written in Spanish, with a French translation for the Noailles and, presumably, his technical crew and actors—tangible proof of his seriousness of purpose and his professionalism (or of his superiority over "mere" ideas man Dalí). Between the second *découpage* of 16 January and the start of filming on 3 March 1930 the director announced a series of changes, with more gags being added. The last of these additions dates from 7 March, with filming then under way. As before, Buñuel tells the Noailles that it is he who has found the new gags; Dalí is not mentioned as a possible source. In point of fact, the missives Dalí sent from Carry—and to which Buñuel must surely have replied, although no such letters have survived—are full of ideas. (A potential unknown is, of course, the number of telephone conversations they may have had.) Some of these ideas were integrated: the man with the slashed, bleeding face; the violin being kicked along the street; Modot's unbuttoned fly, for instance. Others were transformed by the director: the horrific ripping off of the female lead's fingernail by her crazed lover's teeth is transmuted into the implied biting off of the male lead's fingers by his enthused female counterpart. Still others were unusable: the complicated "paranoia-critical" metamorphosis

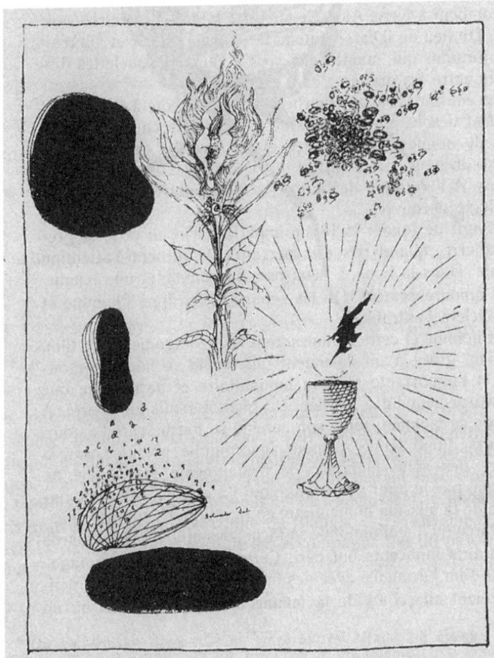

Drawing by Dalí of a blasphemous anal, oral, and genital flower, published in the 1930 booklet issued for the opening of *L'Âge d'or* at Studio 28. (© Salvador Dalí, Fundació Gala-Salvador Dali / VEGAP, Barcelona, 2010)

(using a tilted camera and superimposition) of the female lead's trembling lips into quivering labia, so as to realize Buñuel's "much dreamed-of cunt image in cinema."[8] Dalí would slip this image into the Studio 28 program in the shape of a drawing of an anal, oral, and genital flower, along with swarming ants and a shit-besmirched host and ciborium.

The independence with which Buñuel was able to work and the fertility of his own imagination, of Dalí's, and that of the friends (the Surrealist Group, for instance) and professional colleagues to whom he must have talked meant that the gestation of *L'Âge d'or* was a dynamic one. Such dynamism expressed itself in the film's ever-growing length. The original commission had been for a twenty-minute short. By February 1930 the Andalusian beast was forty-five minutes long and running at twice the planned budget. In an 8 February letter to the Viscount, the director proposed eliminating the location shooting in Cap de Creus (northeast Catalonia) and hence the need to build the set for the bandits sequence. "The film would begin, therefore, with the documentary on Rome you are familiar with, in which there would be the unveiling of a monument, with the placing, there, of the entrance of the main characters."[9] This would have shortened the film to two thousand feet, something like its original length, and reduced the budget to 500,000 francs. We would guess that the "new" beginning of the narrative was in fact its *original* point of departure and that the two earlier segments, the scorpion prologue and the bandits/Majorcans episode, were added later. That the basic script encompassed the Rome events, from the laying of the foundation stone to Modot defenestrating a series of incongruous objects, thus making the film something of a hysterical parody of a typical Lubitsch "high society" subject.

Noailles graciously okayed the longer version, a decision about which Buñuel was understandably delighted. And this was a decision that did not stay his hand, for during the March to May shooting further gags were improvised, taking the movie to just over an hour. By cutting corners the director was able to keep the final cost of the film to a figure (715,500 francs) very close to the budget agreed upon in February: 714,000 francs.

There is a further reason why *L'Âge d'or* expanded in terms of length as well as cost, a reason that has nothing to do with the ebullient independence of director and producer and everything to do with the constraints of the historical moment: namely, the arrival of talkies. Buñuel's second film had been mooted as a sound remake of his first, the silent *Un chien andalou* having been screened with a "live" accompaniment of gramophone records. As it is, the director's first two films exactly span the start date and end date of the battle being waged by foreign industrial capital for a controlling interest in the changeover from silent to sound cinema in France; the French themselves were incapable of making that change, more for reasons of financial investment than of technological backwardness. Between March 1929—as Buñuel was shooting *Un chien andalou*—and July 1930—when he left for Spain after completing *L'Âge d'or*—Tobis-Klangfilm, a Dutch-German company, challenged the American corporations ERPI (Western Electric) and RCA (General Electric) for control of the French film business as it submitted to the imperative of retooling for sound. In fact, the issue of sound, in one or another of its manifestations—foreign-language versions, dubbing, subtitling, and so forth—courses right through Buñuel's stuttering career in 1930s subaltern cinema, as we shall see.

As announced in the credits, *L'Âge d'or* was released as a *film sonore et parlant*: a sound and talking picture. In thrall to the inevitable imposition of sound cinema, French cineastes had been debating the relative virtues of *films sonorisés* and *films parlants* since 1928. The overall feeling was that with the *film sonorisé*, which was restricted to "speechless" sound effects and music, montage, the organizing principle of silent cinema, might survive as the key element. All-talking films—a garrulous filmed theater—would hasten its demise. The hybrid *film sonore et parlant* was a way of hedging one's bets at a time of tremendous uncertainty. In terms of sound, the *L'Âge d'or* we know bears the marks of each of the phases through which it passed: it's a larval work, a bit of a freak even. Years later, Claude Heymann, one the two young assistant directors (Jacques Brunius being the other) hired for their experience with sound, would reminisce about his duties. He describes going with Brunius to Buñuel's new rented apartment on Rue du Laos—the son of the concierge there would play the lad gunned down by his gamekeeper father—where "we got down to creating the technical *découpage*, in a single column, as was done at the time, because the film was envisaged to be silent. Only later did it become a sound film, then a sound and talking picture. In our *découpage* all the dialogues were envisaged as intertitles."[10] Theirs was not the definitive *découpage*, then; nor was it the first version.

For further detail we may avail ourselves of the incredible luxury of the Noailles/Buñuel correspondence, an inexhaustible mine of information. And what we read there seems to contradict Heymann's recall, forty-eight years after the events. In Buñuel's 29 November 1929 report to the Viscount on the second Cadaqués sojourn with Dalí, he puts in writing his intention to make "the talking picture" they'd discussed, although Noailles had remained silent about the sound option in his formal production proposal of 21 November.[11] By 8 February 1930 the director was speaking of a *film sonore et parlant*; the sonorization, sound-studio rental, and orchestra (for the occasional music and to act on-screen) adding 150,000 francs to a silent version budgeted at 564,000 francs. The 38 percent increase did not perturb the Noailles.

Film producers were not the only ones subject to the tensions of the time, however: exhibitors unwilling to assume the high cost of installing the new sound equipment in their cinemas were obliged to go on showing silent films. Buñuel's next letter reflects this. In it, he suggests making *two* versions of *La Bête andalouse*: one *sonore et parlant*, the other silent (*muet*). But it's not just a straight fight between these two categories; even within the sound camp there is uncertainty as to whether *sonore et parlant* will prevail over *muet et sonore* in the future evolution of the cinema. (This is basically the conflict between *films sonorisés* and *films parlants* alluded to above.) *Muet et sonore* involved a silent film that would still rely on intertitles, postsonorized with music and sound effects; *sonore et parlant* meant a film with short bursts of lip-synchronized dialogue recorded in the act in a studio built for the purpose, *plus* the music and sound effects of *muet et sonore*. Since a *film sonore et parlant* could not be shown silent—due to the boredom for audiences of seeing lip-synced actors talking without hearing them, and to the different shooting and projection speeds for talking and silent movies—a possible solution, "the one used by all the producers," says Buñuel, would be to hire a second "silent" cameraman to shoot the same scenes alongside the "sound" cameraman, each operator working at his own frames-per-second ratio and according to different compositional constraints.[12] When asked to choose, the forward-looking Noailles again elected the simple path: forget the silent version, they said. As it was, the aristocratic couple was soon to turn their Paris home cinema into the first in the country to be equipped for showing sound movies.

One way to define *L'Âge d'or* would be as a *film muet sonore parlant*, since it's a sort of missing link in the evolution from silents to talkies. It may be that Claude Heymann's memory wasn't so faulty after all, then: Buñuel's second movie combines the intertitles, sound effects, music, and silence typical of a *film muet et sonore* with the "talking heads" and voiceover dialogue specific to *sonore et parlant* cinema. A slave to the liminal nature of the technological moment, this combinatory quality, the Surrealist limits of which the director exploited to the fullest, is an element that adds to the movie's provocative heterogeneity. But it isn't the only such element, for last-minute alterations to the *découpage* would also affect the look of *L'Âge d'or*.

Buñuel was to keep astonishingly close to his final *découpage*—"in a slightly maniacal way, even," Heymann would recall.[13] Generally speaking, the transitions between shots and between sequences were smoother in the *découpage* than in the finished film; *raccord* (match cut) is an ever-recurrent word in the former. Changes were made, however, in response to unforeseen external factors. Originally, the scorpion prologue planned expressly for the movie in Cap de Creus was to pass, via a *raccord*, to a shot of the bandit sentinel in the same landscape, suggesting that bandits and scorpions are equivalents. Due to rain, and to shooting *Menjant garotes*—a five-minute Lumière-style home movie made by Buñuel and cameraman Duverger of Dalí's father and his spouse in their holiday home in Cadaqués, intended to appease the will-shaking patriarch and to facilitate filming in and around the town—the scorpions (supplied by the locals) could not be filmed, and so off-the-peg footage was bought in Paris in mid-April to replace it. The archaic, abraded look of *Le Scorpion languedocien*, a popular science documentary for schoolchildren based on the writings of Jean-Henri Fabre, a central figure in Buñuel's philosophical pantheon, and made by the Éclair Company in 1912 as part of their "Scientia" series, got this state-of-the-art feature off to a false start.

Inclement weather would dog the location shooting in Catalonia and Paris, disrupting Buñuel's tight schedule, and to make up for lost time the director fell back more than once on the use of stock shots. This tactic was already foreseen as part of his arsenal, as evidenced by the banal *Actualités Pathé* and *Éclair-Journal* footage used ironically—thanks to the play between image and intertitle—in the "founding of the city of imperial Rome" sequence; the film's original starting

Frame still of Salvador Dalí Sr. and his spouse from the five-minute vanity movie filmed by Buñuel in Cadaqués in 1930 and known by the informal Catalan title *Menjant garotes* (*Eating Sea Urchins*). (Doña Emilia Pomés, Cadaqués / Filmoteca de Catalunya, Barcelona)

point, as noted above. That is, whether *L'Âge d'or* commenced with the entomological clip or with the anti-city symphony material, it would begin bathetically, scandalously. In turning, out of necessity, to a greater amount of stock footage than planned, the appearance of the movie became increasingly fragmentary, with disjunctive collage taking over from seamless montage.

Narrative displacements across time and space—diachronic echoes based upon recurring details—form an ancillary structure embedded in the manifest storyline, often subliminally (at least on first viewing) and always in the name of humor. An example would be the four archbishops whose avatars are the four Marists on the footbridge whose avatars are the four Sadean profligates. There were more of these shifting signifiers in the *découpage*. The fourth of the Majorcan archbishops was to be a midget with a ludicrous handlebar moustache—the Catholic clergy is obliged to go clean-shaven, is it not?—whose comic physique would recur in the governor (played by the ceramist Josep Llorens Artigas) before resurfacing once more in a hirsute, dwarfish musician hired for the Roman garden concert. The first and last of these were dropped during filming. During the cod travelogue of Rome, a woman was to be briefly seen bawling her eyes out on a café terrace. In the (unshot) sequence of the urban chaos for which Modot, the bungling but unrepentant diplomat, has been responsible, a sobbing mother clutches the little dress of her dead daughter. The many innocent young victims, represented by an ever-growing pile of children's shoes—a fierce Stroheimian touch—would have echoed the little *girl* shot by her gamekeeper father. And doubling this brace of lachrymose women was to have been the bawling orchestra conductor crunching across the gravel to rob Lys from Modot, and the sobbing, cuckolded Modot stumbling toward his pseudo-cathartic ritual of defenestration. Omitting images like these, which might have bound the narrative more tightly, rendering it more homogeneous, increased the discontinuous feel of the story.

That Buñuel was intent upon creating a subversive work—albeit disguised as bona fide "standardized" cinema, just as Magritte's painting style masqueraded as academic realism—is clear from his perverse use of sound. At this point we should perhaps speak of Buñuel and Dalí, for the latter made various suggestions in his Carry-le-Rouet letters to do with the soundtrack. Just as they had employed the intertitle to tell lies (so to speak) in *Un chien andalou*, now they used the new Tobis-Klang technology against itself. With novice audiences struggling to make sense of the phonemes rattling eerily out of the new loudspeakers, it was indeed a provocation to offer nonsensical snatches of dialogue. For instance, Lys, monotonously reading her lines from an idiot card beside the camera, states that with the musicians they've hired for a garden party "we have enough, because just six close to the microphone make more noise than sixty placed a mile and a half away"—a dig at the ongoing sound revolution. The few who saw the film in the twilight days of 1930 must have found it hard at times to believe their ears.

Still other changes to the *découpage* were due to prudence, to pulling back from an awesome blasphemy: sitting on the toilet dreaming of Modot, Lys might have been garbed in white like the Virgin. More extreme was the elaborate joke at the end of the film, drawn from Sade's *Dialogue between a Priest and a Dying Man* and *The 120 Days of Sodom*—not many 1930 filmgoers would have got the reference to the latter, for the Marquis's magnum opus would only be published in a reliable version between 1931 and 1935. (Charles de Noailles, a collector of the manuscripts of Sade, who was an ancestor of Marie-Laure's, owned the scroll from which Maurice Heine prepared this edition.) Identified by intertitles, Sade's four vaginophobic, murderous libertines—the Duke de Blangis, Président Curval, Financier Durcet, and the Bishop de K—were to be costumed as Jesus, Confucius, Mohammed, and Luther, respectively, and it would be the latter who dispatched the bloodstained maiden. Yet if discretion be the better part of valor, Buñuel's idea to drop this multiple profanity—one still capable of causing a moral panic, as witnessed in Germany with the furor in 2006 over a staging of Mozart's *Idomeneo*—led to a less tendentious, more sublime visual gag: it is Christ who does for the maiden, off-screen, losing his beard in the process. That same Sade scholar, Maurice Heine, an ultra-Leftist sympathizer of the Surrealists, would criticize the director for not going through with his original plan in the pages of *LSASDLR*, an incident to which we return in a later chapter. Suffice it to say that this criticism continued to haunt Buñuel, although Dalton Trumbo, who must have gotten it from the Spaniard, slipped the image of the four defiled deities into his film version of *Johnny Got His Gun* (1971), on whose screenplay Buñuel worked in the 1960s.

As the first version of his *découpage* neared completion, Buñuel began penciling in his ideal crew, starting with his assistant director, cameraman, and *régisseur* (production manager). In his 29 December 1929 letter to the Noailles, Buñuel proposed Jacques Brunius as his assistant director. Of import was the fact that the twenty-three-year-old movie critic had recently made sound tests for Tobis-Klang of singer Yvette Guilbert and had assisted Henri Chomette, René Clair's brother, on one of Tobis's first *sonore et parlant* features, *Le Requin* (1929). For his cameraman, Buñuel turned to Albert Duverger, who'd shot *Un chien andalou*, as well as two movies on which Buñuel had himself assisted: *Mauprat* (Jean Epstein, 1926) and *La Sirène des Tropiques* (Henri Étiévant, 1927). Duverger, whose career extended from 1919 to 1933, is something of an unsung hero: his functionalist, deep-focus cinematography bears comparison with that of Elgin Lessley (who worked for Keaton and Langdon) or Georges Guérin (who filmed Feuillade's serials) as a cameraman who was capable of giving fleeting form to the "concrete irrationality" (as Dalí might have said) of the phenomenal world. Of Buñuel's potential *régisseur*, Maurice Morlot, we know very little, except that he assisted Jean Epstein on *La Glace à trois faces* (1927) and played some part in *La Chute de la maison Usher* (1928), on which, of course, Buñuel worked.

Ten days later, things were a little clearer. As well as informing the Viscount of his chosen team, Buñuel proudly underlines his own guile in reducing their fees, or in getting their services for nothing: an interesting insight into the director's obsessive budgeting, not to mention the workings of the class war. It's here that we realize how much he's relying on the Films Braunberger-Richebé infrastructure. The twenty-five-year-old Braunberger, who'd produced *En rade* (Alberto Cavalcanti, 1927), *Voyage au Congo* (Marc Allégret and André Gide, 1927) and *Tire au flanc* (Jean Renoir, 1928) and set up a distribution company in 1928 to promote a new generation of independent filmmakers—*Un chien andalou* was in his catalogue, along with films by Man Ray, Georges Lacombe, Germaine

Dulac, Eugène Deslaw, Jean Lods, and Boris Kaufman—had, in response to the solicitations of sound, gone into partnership with Marseilles cinema-owner Roger Richebé and bought Billancourt Studios, created by producer/director Henri Diamant-Berger in 1923, where some fifteen adaptations of stage plays and novels would be filmed (some in multiple versions) before the partnership foundered at the beginning of 1933. Needing the resources of an independent outfit to countenance his oddball ideas, Buñuel's stop-go career was often to intersect with Braunberger's—future "godfather" of the *Nouvelle Vague*—during this same period. Of assistance to the director on *L'Âge d'or* were Marc Allégret (casting), Georges Van Parys (occasional music), Michel Feldman (studio manager), and budget supervisor Roger Woog (or "Vogue" as the filmmaker calls him). And it was from the Braunberger-Richebé stable that his second assistant director came: Claude Heymann. Only twenty-two, Heymann had already assisted Renoir on three silents, co-scripting one of them (*Tire au flanc*), and had recently directed a short and co-directed a feature for Braunberger (*La Vie heureuse* and *Deux balles au cœur*, respectively). More to the point, he'd been assistant director to Robert Florey on the rickety but big-earning Braunberger-Richebé production *La Route est belle* (1929), shot in a silent and a *sonore et parlant* version at Elstree Studios in London.

Another collaborator announced in Buñuel's 8 February 1930 letter to Noailles is set designer Pierre Schildknecht—a.k.a. Schild—a Russian émigré whom the director had met when assisting on the Josephine Baker vehicle *La Sirène des Tropiques*, and who'd done the décors for *Un chien andalou*. In the same missive the director also mentioned Max Ernst.[14] As the leader of the bewildered bandits, Buñuel's aperitif-imbibing crony at the Surrealist café cuts a suitably ogreish figure in this, his initiation into cinema. Twelve months later he'd repeat the role in a three-minute comic advertising film commissioned by Meubles Barbès: *Au petit jour à Mexico*, directed by his brother-in-law Jean Aurenche (another of Buñuel's bandits). And a year after that he'd be the elusive subject of New York gallery-owner Julien Levy's *Portrait de Max Ernst: Film illogique* (1932), a minor addition to the Surrealist movie canon.

Since, like its predecessor, Buñuel's new film was built around the vicissitudinal romancing of a man and a maid, the question of the male and female leads was of paramount importance. Moreover, patrons and co-scenarist alike expressed their impatience to see photos of the main protagonists: their look and their acting ability would be crucial to the success of the film. Aged forty-two, the tried and tested Gaston Modot had appeared in some thirty films since 1919, including René Clair's first sound opus *Sous les toits de Paris* (1930). Buñuel, who must have seen Modot as an acrobat in the pre-1914 *Onésime* farces he loved

An image from *La Femme 100 têtes* (1929) and a frame still from *L'Âge d'or*. Years later, Max Ernst would claim that Buñuel's second film had been partly inspired by his collage novels. (© Max Ernst, VEGAP, Barcelona, 2010 / Collection: Paul Hammond, Barcelona)

as a boy—Modot also wrote gags for these—had met him on *Carmen* (Jacques Feyder, 1926), in which the Spaniard had a bit part. Modot had also been one of the founders of the Ciné-Club de France in 1926 (along with Cavalcanti, Clair, Gance, Marcel L'Herbier, and Moussinac). Although he was working for half his usual fee, the big money was on the actor—he was paid 5,000 francs a week to Buñuel's 3,000—and he proved to be worth every centime as, parodying his own screen persona as a hard case, he tragicomically laid about and lusted his way to abjection. This didn't stop the director complaining about his surfeit of technique.

The casting of the female *vedette* was to prove more difficult. Buñuel's first choice was the twenty-five-year-old Suzanne Christy, who'd acted in a dozen silent movies, eight of them nondescript titles made in Belgium, from whence she came, albeit with three Julien Duvivier French features to her name. Although Christy was destined not to be chosen, she is immortalized in a photo by cinematographer Duverger, who doubled as the taker of production stills, captioned "Are you cold?" and reproduced under the director's name in *LSASDLR*.[15] In it she is clutched by a plump, crosier-bearing bishop whose gloved hand cups her breast. The cleric is Marval, *régisseur* on Buñuel's first two films, who played one of the tugged, recumbent *curés* in *Un chien andalou* as well as the defenestrated bishop in *L'Âge d'or*. (We don't know if Marval and Maurice Morlot, both of whom were portly gentlemen, are one and the same, but it seems likely.)

On 13 February 1930 Buñuel shot screen tests of several potential female leads, including Kissa Kouprine (who'd appeared in *La Perle*) and Marie-Berthe Ernst, Max's painter wife and the sister of future scriptwriter Jean Aurenche. Marie-Berthe—the imprint of whose lips had appeared in *LRS*—was the most photogenic but turned out to be too nervous to carry the part. She would be an extra in the film, though, as a Cap de Creus crowd member and an invitee at the orchestral soirée. A Carry-le-Rouet letter from Dalí hints that the female lead ought to be a Louise Brooks look-alike. Brooks had recently made an impact in G. W. Pabst's *Diary of a Lost Girl* (1929). It was another, minor, Pabst actress, however, who'd become the *vedette*: Lya Lys, née Natalia Lyech in Berlin in 1907 (or 1908; sources differ). Lys had recently arrived from Germany after appearing in a talkie, *Moral um Mitternacht* (Marc Sorkin, 1930; produced by Pabst's Hom-AG für Filmfabrikation). With shooting under way, Buñuel would go into a rage at her ineptitude, reducing the actress to tears when precious film was wasted (as he saw it) reshooting her scenes. Heymann was of the opinion that she understood nothing in the movie, which was "wholly intentional on the part of Buñuel."[16] As it was, Lys would perform some of the strangest acts in cinema history, her emotive performance as a big-toe-sucker standing as a synecdoche for the entire film (and as a Surrealist in-joke about archrival Georges Bataille, perhaps). On the basis of her performance in *L'Âge d'or*, she'd be invited by MGM to Hollywood at the same time as Buñuel. There Lys would settle, doing the rounds of the big studios for the next ten years as a "Middle-European" character actress in a dozen or more minor features.

Of the other performers hired via the casting agencies—veterans of Films Albatros and La Société des Cinéromans in the main—Germaine Noizet and Bonaventura Ibáñez (the Marquess and Marquis de X) had recently appeared in another Louis Brooks vehicle filmed in Paris and San Sebastián, *Prix de beauté*. (Accustomed as we are to their mien in *L'Âge d'or*, it is uncanny to see them "adrift" in a two-shot in Augusto Genina's movie.) Ibáñez would ask for double pay to have flies glued to his face, and Noizet for a bonus of 100 francs to be slapped by Modot. (Lys would also make a fuss about having to kiss the bearded orchestra conductor, Duchange, "a fossilized old fool," in the director's opinion.)[17] Lionel Salem (the Count de Blangis/Christ) had played "The Turk," as Buñuel dubbed him, in one other movie: Julien Duvivier's *L'Agonie de Jérusalem* (1926). Many of the cast were friends and acquaintances who worked for nothing. Playing the bandits were members of the Spanish artists' colony in Paris, including future Falangist Francisco Cossio, who'd limped into shot in the park sequence in *Un chien andalou*. Manuel Ángeles Ortiz, the *mondain* painter about whose lady-killing qualities director and producer would joke in their correspondence, portrayed the infanticidal gamekeeper. Llorens Artigas, who acted the diminutive, mustachioed governor (to his six-foot-two wife, Mme François Victor Hugo, a doctor) had contributed to *Un chien andalou*, albeit invisibly: standing behind Simone Mareuil, he'd tugged the skin on her back to hitch up her naked breasts so that Pierre Batcheff might palpate them.[18] Surrealist painter Georges Malkine's girlfriend, Caridad de Laberdesque, would double as the scorched kitchen maid and the victim of the Sadean libertines; along with Paul Éluard, she'd also provide the voiceover in the garden: "What joy to have murdered our children!"[19]

Other friends were former Surrealists like Jacques Prévert, who is glimpsed as a passerby in the street, and his brother Pierre—who, with Marcel Duhamel, had codirected *Souvenirs de Paris*, a 1928 André Breton/Louis Aragon–inspired documentary shot by Man Ray and J. A. Boiffard. Possession of a white tie and tails or a cocktail dress sufficed to gain a part in the Roman soirée scene: whence the presence of English Surrealist Roland Penrose, a friend of Ernst's, and Brunius's sister Simone Cottance, part of the cinephile circle around *La Revue du cinéma*. Other concertgoers were Buñuel's former fellow students at Epstein's Académie de Cinéma, White Russians who were extras for Films

Albatros. The woman wearing "Anitta" nylons who descends from a Rolls with her ostensory is Ghislaine Auboin, the future wife of film director Claude Autant-Lara and a friend of the Préverts. Buñuel himself would appear for an instant as one of the four Marists on the footbridge (along with Brunius, Jean-Paul Dreyfus, and the unknown actor who plays the little Marist fiddler). When it came to the location shooting in Cap de Creus, apart from Modot, Lys, Ernst, and other bandit figures (Cossio, Aurenche, Juan Esplandiu, and Pedro Flores), plus Marie-Berthe Ernst, Llorens Artigas, B. Aliange, and Gilbert (the two policemen), the extras in the crowd scene were either friends from Barcelona like Buñuel's cousin Juan Ramón Masoliver (editor of the avant-garde literary magazine *Hèlix*, which had published two of the director's poems in May 1929), or local people from Cadaqués, Llané, and Tudela. This was why in order to have access to the locals Buñuel needed to placate Dalí's irate father, a figure much respected in the area who could have made his life difficult.

Since this was his début feature, and his first project using outside finance—*Un chien andalou* having been paid for by his mother—Buñuel was determined to keep to his carefully planned shooting schedule. Beating Billancourt studio manager Michel Feldman down from 3,500 to 2,000 francs a day for the biggest stage in the complex, the director had his designers Schild and assistant Serge Pimenoff begin supervising the building of the sets on 27 February. Between 3 and 5 March Duverger shot the scenes of the bandits' hovel, Selliny Castle, and the defenestration of the flaming fir tree, plough, giraffe, and bishop. The love scene in the garden and the orchestral evening were filmed between 6 and 14 March. After a weekend off, shooting of the Roman reception began on 17 March and terminated on 21 March. Nor was the filming without complications: for example, the doors to the salon had to be widened to accommodate the carousing workers' horse-drawn cart. Following another free weekend, the final studio sequences were completed between 24 and 26 March. These included the Normandy cow on the bed (which had to be specially reinforced). Five days later the sound shooting began at Tobis-Klangfilm in the former Éclair-Menchen studios at Épinay-sur-Seine, where fragments of the Billancourt sets had been installed for the tight talking head shots and the scene of Modot's investiture as a representative of the Ministry of the Interior. On one of the two Tobis days (31 March–1 April), the shoot went out into the street for some "live" dialogue—Modot's sarcastic, sing-song recitation of his upper-crust credentials to the cops—footage whose poor sound quality Buñuel blamed on the Tobis engineer, and he considered reshooting. (It seems unlikely he did, for even after digital restoration the spoken word in the film leaves something to be desired.) Other dialogue—Artigas's hilarious garbled speech as the governor during the laying of Rome's foundation stone, for instance—was postsynchronized along with the sound effects. The Spanish copy of the film has subtitles, according to which Artigas begins by saying, "Ladies and Gentlemen, shared out equally and worked in peace, our land is not destroyed but produces more. . . . In the land, we have many components that can be refined. We have the raw material, then. I mean, the clay that contains everything." Seconds later, he deposits an excremental pat of cement atop the stone.

On 4 April Buñuel, Brunius, Heymann, Duverger, Jeanne Rucar—who was a production assistant on the film, as she had been on *Un chien andalou* and would be on *Las Hurdes*—and the actors mentioned above traveled from Paris to Cadaqués. There, the exteriors of the exhausted bandits, the quartet of archbishops on the rocks, the landing of the faithful, and the ceremony to found Rome would be shot in the "grandiose geological delirium" (Dalí *dixit*) of Cap de Creus between 5 and 9 April.

It was there that the director was vexed by delays due to inclement weather and to the making of *Menjant garotes*, but he would keep on schedule by dropping the scorpion sequence. Back in Paris the downpours continued, and after a couple of frustrating days trying to shoot at a villa in Montmorency—where the arrival of the Roman guests (with ostensory), the gag of the stroller in the park with a stone on his head, and the gunning down of the gamekeeper's son were to be filmed—Buñuel laid off his crew until the weather improved. On 22 April he traveled to Boulogne-Billancourt to the editing rooms of G. M. Film, where he began a rough cut of his movie. (In his use of Billancourt Studios and G. M. Film, Buñuel was repeating his experiences on *Un chien andalou*.) Between 19 and 24 May the Montmorency exteriors were filmed, at times in the rain, although the "Stroheimian" kiddy catastrophe could not be filmed. It was dropped and replaced by footage from Henry King's 1923 MGM melodrama, *The White Sister*. By 27 May Buñuel had completed the silent rough cut, and on 29 May he presented it to Charles and Marie-Laure de Noailles at their first meeting in four months. In *Mon dernier soupir* the director tells us, "the Noailles . . .—they always said it with a slight British intonation—found the film 'exquisite, delightful.'"[20] Between 2 and 13 June Buñuel collaborated with Frank Clifford, Dr. Peter Paul Brauer, and Herr Kracht of Tobis-Klangfilm on the optical sonorization of what was no longer *La Bête andalouse* but *L'Âge d'or*. On 16 June the printing of copies from the master negative began at G. M. Film. By 30 June 1930 a pristine print of this *film muet sonore parlant* was ready to be shown to its first audience, the Surrealist Group.

It had taken Buñuel seven months to bring his (and others') image of Surrealism to the screen. Henceforth, *L'Âge d'or* would stand as the quintessential filmic statement of the movement's revolutionary aims and attitudes. This statement was made in several different ways. To begin with it imitated mainstream industrial cinema in order to undermine it, in the name of scandal and iconoclasm, by *densifying* both its form and content, thus confusing and disorienting the viewer. Claude Heymann would put it beautifully: "Making such a destructive film could assume its true value only to the degree in which it was exactly structured within the framework of a 'bourgeois' film."[21] As a sound remake of *Un chien andalou*, the new film would reuse many of the tactics of its predecessor: a "beside-the-point" prologue and epilogue; shots and shot sequences with an overdetermined, irrational content; narrative incongruities and non sequiturs; embedded narrative continuities that only repeated viewings bring to light; contradictory continuity cuts within a sequence; the use of mendacious or paradoxical intertitles leading to spatiotemporal "matching mismatches" or mystificatory ellipses; the in-joke as a generator of imagery; and so forth. What is new in *L'Âge d'or* are the colliding aesthetics and textures that come with the interpolation of found footage; the statelier cutting, at half the speed used in *Un chien*; the less arty camerawork (no slow motion, no soft-focus shots); and especially, in line with psychoanalysis, the planted parapraxes, the bungled actions, the visualized symptoms—a manifest latent content, so to speak. Added to this is the heterogeneity that comes from the soundtrack: an odd, already technically outmoded mixture of sound effects, talking heads, voiceovers, and silence punctuated by music.

Secondly, *L'Âge d'or* is rife with images one did not customarily see in Western cinema (except in films by Erich von Stroheim or Tod Browning). Blasphemous images, for instance, whose only peer might be the Soviet cinema of the time. Images of cruelty. Images of eroticism. For the film set out to represent a new kind of hero, a Surrealist hero whose inhibited will to love, which had its echo in the comic sublimations of Keaton, Langdon, and Chaplin, was charged with a histrionic fury that was not theirs, and that rendered any happy resolution illusory. What could be more disconsolate, in a film replete with gags about onanism, than that last image of Modot casting handfuls of white feathers into the void, seemingly for all eternity?

Thirdly, the film gave the viewer an insight into the private researches of the Surrealist movement in the shape of the kind of symbolically functioning objects that, under the aegis of Dalí, the Surrealists were to make. The paradigm here is the advertising poster we see of a woman's be-ringed hand reaching for a "Léda" powder puff. Modot fantasizes Lys's ring finger twitching onanistically: a quivering switch of hair has replaced the beauty aid and adds to the genital illusion. (His fantasy is generated by wordplay, since *la houppe* means both "powder puff" and "curls.")

While other Surrealists had made "amateur" films—Man Ray being the prime example—*L'Âge d'or* was the first (and last) "professional" movie to depict the program of Surrealism from within and to set out to project it beyond the avant-garde ghetto and into the wider world of mass culture. In this it would fail, of course, due to its almost instant prohibition. Unlike, say, *L'Étoile de mer* (Man Ray, 1928), Buñuel's masterpiece was the kind of film about which one could write a manifesto. And the Surrealists did, as we shall see.

3

A Fecund Scandal

Intent on showing *L'Âge d'or* privately to their aristocratic and intellectual friends for a month, as stipulated in their November 1929 contract with Buñuel, the Noailles had installed sound equipment in their home cinema in May–June 1930. The first group of spectators to see the sound print there were the Surrealists on 30 June. Although Charles and Marie-Laure de Noailles were on increasingly amicable terms with the latter—the Viscount being a neophyte collector of their artworks and manuscripts, as well as a defrayer of the costs of Éditions Surréalistes and of the group's new magazine, *LSASDLR*—they were not present on the last day of June, having diplomatically vacated their mansion for the evening.

Just how much the Surrealists, ever disposed to collective action, may have contributed to the brainstorming that went into *L'Âge d'or* must remain an open question, but it is clear that Breton and company were the primary audience for the film and that the director was anxious, as he'd been with *Un chien andalou*, for the Surrealists to give it their approval as a filmic expression of their (and his) worldview. We're not certain who was at the screening, aside from Buñuel, Dalí—who'd been in Paris for a month, following his creative self-exile in Carry-le-Rouet, Torremolinos, and Madrid—and Tzara, but there's every reason to suppose that the Surrealists were there en bloc—apart from Éluard, Crevel, and Péret, that is, who were in provincial France, Switzerland, and Brazil, respectively. It appears that a few Spanish friends, School of Paris painters like Joaquín Peinado, were also present.

That first screening on the Place des États-Unis was a fiasco, though, because the projector motor broke down, as Buñuel told the Viscount in a scribbled note left in situ for the latter's return. While waiting for the show to go on, those present had made inroads into the bar, imbibing, as the filmmaker laconically noted, "orangeade and liqueurs."[1] Forty years later, he'd give more detail on the evening: "They all arrived and Tzara began speaking very badly of the aristocrats and they emptied at least fifty bottles of alcohol and liqueur down the sink. The Viscount had the good taste not to say a word to me about it."[2] As a result of the technical hitch, and as a matter of some urgency, since Buñuel was due to leave for Spain on the following day, those present attempted to see the film later that evening at the Cinéma du Panthéon, the movie house that Pierre Braunberger had acquired in 1929, and that, reconditioned for sound, opened on 21 May 1930. This screening appears to have taken place, for a few days later Éluard was to complain in a letter to Gala that "everybody's seen it, except me."[3]

We left Buñuel's Surrealist trajectory hanging with his various contributions to the twelfth and last issue of *LRS*, published on 15 December 1929. Five weeks later the director, restored to Paris after his working holiday in Hyères, was writing to his patron to tell him that Breton was most happy that *La Bête andalouse* was going to be made. This is understandable since, whatever else may have been in play, the Surrealist linchpin, reeling from the counterattack against his person by some of those vilified in the "Second Manifeste," was in need of a major intervention such as this—the first professional sound film made under Surrealist auspices, after all—to serve as both a morale booster for the embattled movement and a demonstration to others of its ideological clout. Into the same envelope as his 24 January letter to Noailles, Buñuel put that anti-Breton tract, "Un cadavre," signed by a dozen former adepts, among them Bataille, Boiffard—who, with Eli Lotar, had done the famous photomontage of Breton wearing a crown of thorns by detourning his photomaton portrait from the "I don't see the . . . . . . hidden in the forest" image—Desnos, Morise, Prévert (Jacques), and Queneau. Some of these names are the ones Buñuel eagerly cited as being "splendid" Surrealists in his letter to Dalí of 24 June 1929. The director apologized for the physical state of the tract, published on 15 January: "The paper itself is extremely shabby and worn. What's more, it doesn't deserve to be clean."[4] Notwithstanding his devotion to Breton, Buñuel would nevertheless employ Jacques Prévert as an extra in *L'Âge d'or*, admittedly fleetingly and from the back, in a gesture that demonstrated his independence of mind—or his ambivalence when it came to total commitment.

For all his imposing physique and verbal violence, Buñuel did not take part in the 14 February raid on the sacrilegiously named "Maldoror" nightclub: by then he was busy screen-testing for the female lead of his film, and anyway a foreigner like him could not afford to fall foul of the *flics*. This sortie led to the Surrealists half-demolishing the place, to René Char getting stabbed in the leg, and to Caridad de Laberdesque, who would act in *L'Âge d'or*, distinguishing herself in defense of the self-proclaimed "guests of the Count de Lautréamont."[5] Buñuel would soon be on the receiving end, however, of some sectarian infighting that was embarrassing to his person. With the filming of *La Bête andalouse* entering its third week, he had heard via an assistant, probably Brunius, that Antonin Artaud and Raymond Aron—the founders, with Roger Vitrac, of the Théâtre Alfred Jarry in 1926—were putting it about that the director had written an insulting letter to his producer, boasting he was going to keep the entire budget for himself. "If it's Artaud who's spread the rumor," Buñuel tells the Viscount, "I'm not at all surprised because he's a bit cracked."[6] Although Buñuel had loaned *Un chien andalou* in June 1929 to Artaud (and Vitrac) for a private screening, the volatile poet-actor had more than once expressed his chagrin that his own relatively unrewarding collaboration with director Germaine Dulac, *La Coquille et le clergyman* (1928), had not been sufficiently acknowledged as a cinematic forerunner—which it was—of the Spaniard's first opus. Given his own fractious personal history with Breton and his friends, Artaud would not have been well disposed to any project that smacked of "official" Surrealism, as was the case with *L'Âge d'or*. Noailles's reaction was a sane one: tickled pink to be a focus of attention, he simply laughed the gossip off. That Buñuel was so sensitive to such tittle-tattle suggests that while he was happy to dish it out, he was less happy to take it.

That same month, March 1930, with Buñuel in the middle of shooting his film, his name appeared appended to two Surrealist tracts. The first of these, known as the "Second Prière d'insérer du 'Second Manifeste du surréalisme'" (Second Insert for the "Second Manifesto of Surrealism"), was a prospectus intended to accompany the revised version, issued in book form by Éditions Kra in June, of that polemical text, first published in the last issue of *LRS*. Since then, Breton had reworked his essay in order to hit back at the writers of "Un cadavre." While the 1924 *Manifeste* had focused, as the prospectus writers Éluard and Thirion observed, on the richness of unconscious mentation and on automatism as a means of tapping it, Surrealist attention had since been attracted (without jettisoning psychoanalysis) by "the extraordinary critical and theoretical monument erected by Marx-Engels on the ruins of Hegelianism and preserved by the world proletariat from the ravages of time."[7] Those listed at the end of the tract—Alexandre, Aragon, Buñuel, Char, Crevel, Dalí, Éluard, Ernst, Malkine, Péret, Sadoul, Tanguy, Thirion, Unik, and Valentin—gave their unconditional support to the contents of the *Second Manifeste* as a statement "of what is dead and what is more than ever alive in Surrealism," and to the figure of Breton as the guarantor of present and future prescience. The second tract to which Buñuel put his signature, also from March 1930, was a further prospectus, this time for the group's new organ, *LSASDLR*, which would reprint the declaration in its opening issue, appearing on 7 July 1930.[8] These ephemeral flyers were not without their importance: the roster of names, both old and new, provided tangible evidence of the overcoming of an epistemological conflict and of the reorientation of the movement, now heavily Bolshevized.

If the sudden revelation of *Un chien andalou* had led to a crisis of legitimation among the warring clans of Modernism, a crisis as to which publication of the scenario was the "official" one (see chapter 1), in the case of *L'Âge d'or* the Surrealists, taking no chances, were able to claim a scoop, in that three production stills from it appeared in the signature of halftones in the first issue of *LSASDLR*—and this while the film was still a thing of rumor, albeit one to which susceptible individuals like Artaud might react malevolently. Accompanied by the anticlerical photo of Suzanne Christy and Marval mentioned above, the three stills, duplicates of those Buñuel had been dispatching to Noailles and Dalí during filming, homed in voyeuristically on the eccentric gratification of Lya Lys (not exactly "money shots," but almost). The linking detail is the eroticized digit: aside from the iconic toe-sucking image, we see Lya biting Modot's fingers and swooning on the sofa after a relief massage. The captions are all mismatches, misquotations, encouraging us to read these freeze-frames (of a sort) differently from how we might view them in movement in the film. In July 1930, of course, the stills would have functioned as enigmatic prepublicity images for a movie few would have a chance to see until five months later. The captions are like comic-strip "think" balloons. While indulging her oral sadism, for example, Lya conjectures that "I've blasphemed, perhaps"—dialogue that was not included in the movie. And her post-orgasmic bliss is captioned "Sometimes on Sunday," which is in reality an intertitle from the deadpan documentary on the city of Rome. This disjunctive interplay between image and caption (or title), a familiar weapon in the Surrealist arsenal, gives the stills a poetic tension, makes them stranger than they already are.

Like that of his comrades, Buñuel's invisible signature is to be found on page one of this inaugural issue of *LSASDLR*, at the end of the famous collective telegram to Moscow. With the Depression making inroads into the global capitalist economy, thus increasing the danger of war—and of war against the USSR, as the Comintern saw it—the Muscovite International Bureau of Revolutionary Literature (BILR) had asked Breton what the Surrealists would do in the event of such aggression on the part of French imperialism. Written by Breton and

Aragon, the reply stated that the Surrealists would follow the directives of the Third International, as if they were members of the PCF—which, Thirion and Sadoul aside, they were not (or no longer, or not yet)—and in their capacity as revolutionary intellectuals: "We are at your disposition," the staccato reply reads. "In the current situation of non-armed conflict we believe it useless to wait in order to put at the service of the revolution the means which are particularly ours."[9]

By the time this declaration appeared, Buñuel was ensconced in his mother's house in Zaragoza at the start of his annual summer break with the family in Spain. The news from the Place des États-Unis is that the Noailles, as they'd done for *Un chien andalou*, have been showcasing *L'Âge d'or* to the intellectual and aristocratic habitués of their salon. Such has been its word-of-mouth success that the Viscount is to ask Yves Allégret to arrange a private matinee showing for *le Tout-Paris* at the Cinéma du Panthéon in mid-October.[10] While the producer professed delight at the film's reception, another contemporary account (in the journal of Julien Green, who was present at the 9 July screening along with playwright Édouard Bourdet, novelist and photographer Carl Van Vechten, and sculptor Jacques Lipchitz) divulges that certain conservative viewers, influential ones at that, had been infuriated by it. With the polarization and exacerbation of class sensibilities due to *la crise*, could Charles de Noailles really have been so blithe as not to see the writing on the wall?

Buñuel's own missives bespeak exhaustion, inertia. On 16 July he writes to the Noailles to say he's in no hurry to join the family in San Sebastián "because here I can relax better, despite the heat. I don't budge from my armchair during the whole day."[11] It was in his mother's house that a week later he received Andrés Ruiz Castillo, the representative in Zaragoza of the Cine-Club Español (a subsidiary of the film society Buñuel had founded with Ernesto Giménez Caballero in Madrid in 1928), the inaugural session of which, on 27 April 1930, had shown *Un chien andalou*. The motive for the visit was to interview him for *El Heraldo de Aragón*, Zaragoza's most important daily paper.[12] Finding his subject perusing Freud—probably *The Interpretation of Dreams*, in tune with Breton's work-in-progress, *Les Vases communicants*—the awestruck journalist, who bizarrely likens Buñuel's demeanor to Trotsky's, is perplexed by his belligerent rejection of the art film, pabulum of the film society movement, in the name of a militant cinema that would serve "as a medium for revolutionizing customs," says Buñuel, "for contributing to that grandiose work of social transformation. To me, the technical aspect of cinema is of no interest—only the human side preoccupies me. And this can be called Superrealism; Surrealism as they say in France. We aim to scandalize, with all its consequences."[13] With regard to his scandalous new film "in six parts," the director opines that these consequences may include the veto of the board of film censors in Paris. As it is, unlike its predecessor—aimed at a select minority—*L'Âge d'or* "is dedicated to the general public."

Buñuel left Zaragoza for San Sebastián on or around 6 August. A week later there was an important exchange of letters between director and producer. Noailles tells Buñuel that he's received a request from Jean Mauclaire, seeking an exclusive on showing *L'Âge d'or* to the public at Studio 28. In exchange, this well-heeled son of a member of the Académie de Médecine, the proponent in 1927 (with Jean Mitry) of the mounting of a cinémathèque, and the producer of avant-garde shorts by D'Arche and Hugnet, Lucie Derain, and Eugène Deslaw—in whose documentary *Montparnasse* (1929) Buñuel made a fleeting appearance—has undertaken not only to sonorize his 337-seat Montmartre cinema but also to wangle their movie past the censors, as he'd done for *Un chien andalou*. The Viscount's first reaction is to dismiss Mauclaire's offer. More attractive is the notion of approaching a brand-new movie theater owned by the Paris evening paper *L'Intransigeant*, Les Miracles, which is being equipped for sound and is due to open in October 1930 with *Hallelujah* (King Vidor, 1929) and *The Blue Angel* (Joseph von Sternberg, 1930). Buñuel would concur with his patron's anti-Mauclaire stance in the form of a categorical "Anything bar the avant-garde." And were Les Miracles to be a nonstarter, was there not always Braunberger's Cinéma du Panthéon to consider?[14] In fact, neither of these movie houses was any larger than Studio 28; they were more centrally located, that's all. Moreover, Buñuel has just been to see Braunberger in the seaside town where the latter has his holiday home, Saint-Jean-de-Luz, some twenty-five miles from San Sebastián in the direction of Biarritz, and the Frenchman has promised his cinema for the mid-October private screening Noailles is planning.

Another piece of news in Buñuel's 15 August letter, which he lets drop in a studiedly offhand way, will have resounding repercussions in the months ahead: "I don't know if I'd told you that this summer I was going to go to Russia with Aragon and Ella [Elsa Triolet]. But that I'd had to give up on it." And the reason? He was feeling under the weather, and the idea of such a long trip daunted him.

The five weeks of holiday left to Buñuel among the throngs of "Majorcans" holidaying in the Basque resort would do nothing to lift his spirits: aside from lolling on the sand and going to bullfights with Braunberger, the director remained cooped up indoors at his mother's rented house, staring into space for hours on end. In a snapshot with Jeanne Rucar on the Playa de la Concha, probably taken, given their tans, in September, the beefy director looks disgruntled and resigned. Even the possibility of collaborating on an article with

René Crevel could not motivate the neurasthenic Spaniard. A photo taken by Alfred Flechtheim of the tubercular Crevel in his Swiss sanatorium, posing next to photos of Buñuel and Dalí, had appeared in the German art magazine *Der Querschnitt* in February 1930.[15] Since then, through his close relationship with Marie-Laure de Noailles, Crevel had kept up with Buñuel's activities. Was the proposed collaboration to have been, perhaps, on the article Crevel would publish in *LSASDLR* (no. 2, October 1930)? "Bobards et fariboles" (Stuff and Nonsense) is a vitriolic attack on a servile press in thrall to politicians, clergy, police, and racist ideologues.

Buñuel was back in the French capital on 21 September. In the interim the Viscount's overtures to the cinema owners of central Paris had come to naught, and grudgingly a deal with Mauclaire had been struck. During the fourth week of September Mauclaire would prepare a fanciful synopsis of *L'Âge d'or*, the aim being to get the censors to grant it a visa on the basis of a résumé alone; that is, without actually viewing it. (This had been the Studio 28 owner's strategy with *Un chien andalou*, and it had worked.) Buñuel considered this document "a comic masterpiece," which it is: "This film, which begins with an extended and searching documentary on the life and manners of the scorpion, plus several fine sequences of the great outdoors and of rugged rocks, passes directly to the misadventures of one of those excitable types unhinged by modern life." And so on in the same vein before concluding, "The film redeems its difficult and unfathomable subject through a consistent and well-rendered sense of humor, which gives this obviously fanciful work an imprimatur of smiling philosophy."[16]

Instituted in France in 1909—not in fear of Eros but to prevent footage of a guillotining from being shown—film censorship was enforced after 1919 by a board appointed by the Ministry of State Education and Fine Arts. On 18 February 1928 the Center-Right government of Raymond Poincaré passed a decree designed to bring the provinces into line with Paris; to prevent films being censored *a second time* by local zealots. Article 6 of this decree outlined, with tremendous imprecision, the motives for banning a film: "The Board takes into consideration the entirety of national interests in play, especially the desirability of preserving morals and national traditions, as well, if foreign films are involved, as the ease of access of French films in the diverse countries of origin." In short, as barrister Robert Kiefé remarked during the anticensorship campaign waged by *La Revue du cinéma* between December 1930 and April 1931, the confusing of issues such as public order and foreign quotas had but one result: "The censors will ban films whenever it pleases them."[17]

It goes without saying that the censors' moral yardstick was ultraconservative and politically loaded. Formally, the power of the thirty-two board members devolved fifty-fifty to government functionaries and to laymen from inside and outside the film industry. In practice only two censors examined material, one from the Ministry of State Education and Fine Arts, the other from the Ministry of the Interior. Mauclaire had the ear, it seems, of Eugène Lautier, under-secretary of state at the Fine Arts Ministry, the equivalent of a minister of culture today. Of particular interest to the secretive work of the censors were "Bolshevik" films: only under private film society conditions could such movies be seen uncut. The late 1920s had witnessed an explosion of these politicized clubs, which liaised with specialized cinemas like Studio 28 to put on their member-only sessions. Often worker oriented, the clubs were subject to much surveillance, with one of them, Les Amis de Spartacus—set up by PCF stalwarts Vaillant-Couturier, Moussinac, Lods, Francis Jourdain, and Georges Marrane in March 1928—being forced to disband the following October by the Paris prefect of police, Jean Chiappe. This rabid anti-Communist protector of the Far Right was the frequent butt of Surrealist sarcasm in the pages of *LRS* and *LSASDLR*. Chiappe was something of a cinephile: in 1926 Gance even screen-tested him for the role of Napoleon, and his knowledge of Soviet cinema was second to none. He was known to manipulate Paul Ginisty, the liberal president since March 1928 of the Board of Film Censors, the man whose rubber-stamped signature was essential for getting one's movie shown.

With or without Lautier's intervention, Mauclaire's subterfuge worked: his tongue-in-cheek summary was accepted at face value without the lackadaisical censors even screening the film, from which they only requested the excision of one phrase from the long, rolling intertitle (intertitles were customarily presented in the form of a separate numbered list) that introduces the Sade/Christ segment: "who have but one God, their lust." (This is a misquote, in fact; the exact wording is "who have but one law, their depravity, *roués* without God.") It being taken as read that this cut would be made—it wasn't—*L'Âge d'or* was granted Visa number 39.872 on 1 October "for [its] public performance." Although there were a thousand other reasons for fearing a close inspection, the very fact that the minister of the interior himself was depicted in a ridiculous light in the film—inept at choosing his staff (i.e., Modot), he ends up a victim of suicide, absurdly plastered to the ceiling—would surely have endangered the film's future were the censors not to have stuck to Mauclaire's written précis.

Aside from the censorship issue, Buñuel's febrile first week back in Paris had been given over to negotiations with talent scout L. Laudy Lawrence apropos of a six-month stint at MGM's studios in Hollywood, due to begin in November, to work on foreign-language versions of its product, as detailed in the next chapter. Worth bearing in mind, in the light of Buñuel's later assertions about the moral choice he faced between going to the Soviet Union or to California, are the dates. Since he'd resolved not to go to Moscow—telling the Viscount so in his letter of 15 August—some six weeks before the Hollywood offer came up, his a posteriori account of asking the Surrealists to help resolve his dilemma of choosing careerism or political correctness would appear to be pure mise-en-scène.[18] The subtext of the story is revealing, however: whether he went west or east, he would avoid facing the consequences of his actions in person. He was certain to miss the public release of his new film.

Buñuel would also miss the private preview organized for the resumption of the "season" by his patrons on 22 October, and this on account of the week of 18–25 October he spent in Zaragoza bidding farewell to his mother—and in all probability seeking a handout—prior to crossing the Atlantic. The Panthéon screening—or screenings, because there is evidence that there were *two* shows, on 22 and 23 October—bears witness to the scope of the influence of the Noailles, to Buñuel's kudos as a cutting-edge creator, and to the osmosis between vanguard intellectuals and aristocrats at the end of the Jazz Age. Different factions, not all of them well disposed to each other, were present on that Wednesday morning in the 328-seat auditorium: Breton, Éluard, Ernst, Dalí, Heine, Man Ray, Tanguy, Thirion, and Tzara found themselves a few rows from the authors of "Un cadavre": Bataille, Boiffard, Desnos, and Leiris. Dreyer, Lods, and Painlevé were the filmmakers present. The artists included Brancusi, Braque, Duchamp, Giacometti, Miró, Léger, and Picasso. Composers Auric, Milhaud, Cole Porter, and Virgil Thomson were there, plus architects Le Corbusier, Lurçat, Mallet-Stevens, and Sert. Among the writers were Cendrars, Cocteau, Gide, Malraux, Gertrude Stein, and Valéry. These names speak for themselves, but it is more difficult to gauge the nobles present, French and English both, among whom were Lady Diana Abdy, the Duke de Gramont, Princess Léon Radziwill, Philippe de Rothschild, and members of the De Castellane, De Chimay, and De Polignac families. It was now that the rumored disaffection of some of the aristocratic spectators became a reality, the Noailles being snubbed by their peers as they waited in the foyer to receive the accolades for their new production. Yet not only were the couple rebuffed by the high-born that day; dragged along by Breton and Éluard to the reception in the Place des États-Unis after the show, André Thirion, inspired, perhaps, by Modot's behavior in the movie, would also act outrageously: "My intolerance at the time was so total that the role played by rich, titled people in the making of a revolutionary work disturbed me. . . . On mounting the great staircase, on the steps of which stood lackeys dressed *à la française*, my anger exploded. I went to the buffet and created a scandal there, breaking glasses, throwing bottles at the mirrors and major-domos, overturning everything I could, shouting insults. Charles de Noailles remained impassive. Marie-Laure was a young, dark-haired woman at the time, extremely slim, with an attractive décolleté. She had the elegance to say nothing."[19]

When allusions to the Panthéon "provocation" began appearing in the papers, suggesting that the Establishment was closing ranks, Jean Cocteau leapt to the defense of the Noailles—who were also *his* patrons on *La Vie d'un poète* (later *Le Sang d'un poète*, 1930)—praising them for their "big-heartedness" in the 9 November edition of *Le Figaro*.[20] Yet not all were brickbats: the Noailles received a pair of letters in praise of their new venture, one from the novelist and future Fascist Pierre Drieu la Rochelle, the other from Radical-Socialist deputy Gaston Bergery; the Viscount forwarded the letters to Buñuel in Hollywood. Both offer thought-provoking analogies to the film. Drieu states, "I have not had such a strong impression of liquidation since reading Eliot's *The Waste Land*." Meanwhile, Bergery asked if the scene in which Modot defenestrates the giraffe, burning fir tree, plough, and bishop had reminded the Noailles of the end of *Storm over Asia* (Vsevolod Pudovkin, 1928), "at the moment the storm sends the tins of food and the generals bowling head over heels in the dust?"[21]

Since its opening on 10 February 1928, Studio 28 had presented a new program every six to eight weeks. (Some programs were longer: *Un chien andalou*, for instance, had played there between 1 October and 23 December 1929, some twelve weeks, and was reprogrammed for fifteen days during the movie house's second anniversary in February 1930.) The program prior to the opening of *L'Âge d'or* ran from 7 July to 21 August 1930 and was of a format by now canonic in avant-garde cinemas and film societies: *Les Halles* (a documentary by Boris Kaufman and Galitzine, 1929); *Changements de rues* ("film de montage" by Paul Gilson, 1930); *À la conquête du Pôle* (Georges Méliès, 1912); *Prétexte: Divertissement visuel* ("film abstrait" by Alfred Sandy, 1928), and *The Love of Jeanne Ney* (G. W. Pabst, 1927). This would be Studio 28's last all-silent offering, since Mauclaire was now to install sound equipment in the Cocteau-designed auditorium, a costly commitment—and one for which the money came in part from his mother, who pawned her jewels to help her son—as part of the exclusive he had on premiering *L'Âge d'or*. Costly and complicated: nineteen days after the scheduled delivery of the machines on 6 November, an exasperated producer was writing to tell his director that he was still unable to confirm the date of the opening of their film, announced (at least to the Surrealist Group) for 12 November. In fact, *L'Âge d'or* would be unleashed on a suspecting public on Friday, 28 November. Due to a symptomatic ear infection that had kept him housebound for days, a by now reticent Noailles stayed away. Dalí was present, though, and he maliciously reported to the Viscount that the first night had been a disaster because of the malfunctioning of the sound system, but that they ought to look on the bright side: people had been unable to fully understand the film, which meant there was no scandal.[22]

Having taken the measure of *L'Âge d'or*, the Surrealist Group, sensing that the public release of the film would become the stuff of scandal, and hence of media coverage—and not just by Right-wing papers but the Communist press, too—elected to make a major statement in support of it. This involved the editing and publication, in an edition of one thousand, of a forty-eight-page "revue-program" to be sold at Studio 28, along with an exhibition of artworks and production stills in the cinema foyer and a display of Surrealist books and magazines for sale.

To begin with, the art exhibition: Arp, Miró, Man Ray, and Tanguy were represented by three artworks each; Ernst and Dalí, four. Interestingly, a list of these, probably annotated by Mauclaire, in the collection of the Fundació Dalí in Figueres, reveals that Dalí's paintings were by far the most expensive. One of them—*L'Hostie en bague*, a picture historians have been loath to identify—was selling for four times the price of many of the other works on show. Judging by the photos taken of the despoiled foyer after the Fascist raid of 3 December, there was at least one other artwork on display: a Man Ray "chessboard-style" photomontage of the Surrealist Group, their individual portraits arranged in alphabetical order by surname. The suitably gold cover of the booklet sports the name of the film in zigzag letters drawn by the American artist and photographer. The revue-program contains the Dalí scenario discussed in the last chapter; a list of intertitles and a montage of the dialogue; the long declaration "L'Âge d'or"; a list of the musical pieces heard in the film; a catalog of the artworks on display and an announcement of forthcoming Éditions Surréalistes publications; a list of Dada and Surrealist books from 1919 onward still in print and on sale at the Librairie José Corti; and fifteen pages of production stills. These texts are interspersed with graphic works by the artists who were showing in the foyer and a frame still from *Un chien andalou* of a nonchalant Buñuel honing his razor. Aside from the Dalí drawing of the oral, anal, and genital flower and an Ernst drawing of a praying mantis, the graphic works bear no relation to the film.

"L'Âge d'or," the collective declaration written by Breton, Crevel, Éluard, Aragon, and Thirion and signed by them and eight other group members (but not, since it's a homage to him, by Buñuel), is a didactic "introduction-cum-manifesto," as it was described in a later Corti catalogue, to the film. Assembled in haste, probably between the Panthéon screening on 22 October and 17 November, when proof copies were ready—and in Aragon's case, with even greater urgency, since he left Paris for Moscow (and the Second International

Conference of Proletarian and Revolutionary Writers in Kharkov) at the end of October—this dense, often inscrutable, Freudo-Marxist disquisition, aimed, it seems, at convincing the pro-Communist intelligentsia of Surrealism's scope and seriousness of purpose, has little of the pungent brio of the movie it celebrates—and that it apocalyptically describes as "this bird of prey so utterly unexpected today in the darkening sky, in the darkening western sky."

The general tenor of "L'Âge d'or"—and of *L'Âge d'or*, since the text functions as a hermeneutic gloss on the film—is that in order to upset the baleful, conservative balance of Eros and Thanatos, sublimated as "amorous egoism" and "passivity," respectively, the subject—Buñuel has to be included here, along with his alter ego Modot—must privilege one drive over the other. The frenzied violence of amorous egoism (later to be called "mad love") is best suited to performing this work of destabilization and to undermining the system of myths (the Golden Age is one) which, colonizing all mental activity, conscious and unconscious, subtend capitalist society. New myths, revolutionary moral allegories, are required. (Crevel recommends the erecting of statues of a blind couple devouring one another as a corrective, perhaps, to the myths of motherhood and old age.) Contemporary capitalist society is disintegrating; only the clergy and the police shore it up. *L'Âge d'or*'s anticlericalism and call to revolt is an "indispensable moral complement to the stock market scare." Moreover, Buñuel's new film joins the picky Surrealist pantheon of Clair and Picabia's *Entr'acte*, Mack Sennett, W. S. Van Dyke's *White Shadows of the South Seas*, early Chaplin, and *Battleship Potemkin*. Not only that: along with *Un chien andalou* it outstrips all these.

Dalí professed himself delighted with the revue-program in a 24 November letter to Noailles. The latter was less so. On 20 November, after examining a proof copy, he'd asked Mauclaire to remove a phrase from Dalí's scenario: "The Count de Blangis is obviously Jesus Christ." What's more, the Viscount inquired about the availability of production stills from the penultimate sequence that might show the three Sadean libertines *without* the "personage in white." Shortly after the fiasco of *L'Âge d'or*'s opening night the Noailles decamped to distant Hyères. Once Noailles had a finished copy of the revue-program in his hands he was mortified to find that the blasphemous analogy had not been removed. Dalí felt obliged to explain, which he did in a letter of 4 December, the morning after the Fascist sacking of Studio 28. Time had been of the essence; the scenario merely reflected what was visible on the screen. And anyway, the Catalan was honor bound not to betray Buñuel, who'd invented the Blangis/Christ gag in the first place, as Dalí knew from his stay in Carry-le-Rouet, thus suggesting that there *were* Buñuel letters (or phone calls) discussing the screenplay.

Dalí's own excision of the problematic phrase in his inclusion of the *L'Âge d'or* scenario in the first British edition of *The Secret Life* in 1948 is, we would suggest, an acting out, in the psychoanalytical sense, of this anxious episode.

In keeping with Studio 28's way of doing things, *L'Âge d'or*, the headlining feature, opened there on 28 November 1930 along with four supporting shorts. The first of these was Daniel Abric and Michel Gorel's *Paris-Bestiaux* (1930), on the abattoirs of La Villette. Perhaps inspired by Eli Lotar's already renowned photos in *Documents* no. 6 of November 1929, this implacable documentary, now lost, appears to be the blueprint for Georges Franju's harrowing *Le Sang des bêtes* (1949). Jean Mitry would place Gorel, a film critic whose real surname was Goreleff, among the 1929 "new wave" of documentarists along with Marcel Carné, Pierre Chenal, Deslaw, Jean Dréville, Georges Lacombe, Lods, and Vigo. After an unnamed comedy film, the third short on the bill was *Au village*, "film de montage" by Leonid Moguy, purportedly about the Five-Year Plan in operation on a collective farm in the USSR. In 1929 Moguy (Moguilevski) had moved from Moscow, where he'd run a laboratory producing scientific films, to Paris, becoming a renowned editor there before moving into direction with a series of uplifting social melodramas: *Baccara* (1935), *Le Mioche* (1936) and *Prison sans barreaux* (1938). The final offering before the intermission was a sound cartoon, probably a Walt Disney "Silly Symphony" or a Max Fleischer "Talkartoon." Taken together, the relatively strong fare of these movies would, in their respective grimness, utopianism, and humor, have "prepared" the audience for the last film on the bill. Up to a point.

No sooner had it opened than *L'Âge d'or* received a glowing review from Jean-Paul Dreyfus in *La Revue du cinéma*, the magazine Buñuel had railed against one year before for usurping the scenario of *Un chien andalou*. Not yet the PCF militant on film and theater matters that he would become during the Front Populaire, Dreyfus, who had a bit part in the movie, was nothing if not partisan: "If *L'Âge d'or* hasn't released unconscious feelings in you, if in your eyes and ears it hasn't possessed enough hidden or whole-hearted strength to reveal to you something of the real meaning of things, the release, the humor that goes as far as intolerable discomfort, I don't recognize you as one of my kind." The reading, by some critics, of Buñuel's second film as a technical regression in terms of his first, particularly in the patchy, stop/go use of sound à la *Sous les toits de Paris* (René Clair, 1930), another Tobis-Klang effort, cannot prejudice the film's "spiritual perfection." Dreyfus observes that truly blasphemous gestures like *L'Âge d'or* cannot be private affairs; their whole rationale is to reverberate in the public domain: "On these occasions it's a genuine piece of luck to cause reactions of confusion, embarrassment, aggressive anger even, in the adversary."[23] Fighting talk. Prophetic words.

There were five days of trouble-free screenings before events took the traumatic turn Charles de Noailles most feared. On Wednesday, 3 December, fifty Fascist troublemakers interrupted the show, hurling ink at the screen, letting off smoke bombs and stink bombs, and roughing up spectators before slashing and shredding the artworks, photos, and books on display in the Studio 28 foyer. In his letter of the morning after to the Viscount, Dalí, following newspaper reports, wrongly identified the perpetrators as Camelots du roi, the young Action Française volunteers whose forte was the sabotaging of Leftist cultural or political events. (Curiously, in his 26 July 1930 interview with Ruiz Castillo, Buñuel claimed that the Camelots had descended upon Studio 28 the year before with the aim of disrupting the showing of *Un chien andalou*, but they had been "disarmed, disqualified," and silenced by the harrowing violence of the opening sequence.)[24] In point of fact, the Fascist cohort pertained to Pierre Taittinger's Jeunesses Patriotes, a 1924 offshoot of the Ligue des Patriotes, founded by Paul Déroulède in 1892 as a response to the Boulanger crisis, and the Ligue Antisémite, founded by Maurice de Guérin in 1897 in reply to the Dreyfus Affair. With the formation of Charles Maurras's L'Action Française in 1899, the pre-1914 set of sinister far-Right "isms" was in place: anti-republicanism, anti-parliamentarianism, anti-Semitism, royalism, patriotism, militarism, and ultra-Catholicism, plus a shot of Maurice Barrès–style National Socialism. The Fascist leagues proliferated in France after 1918, drawing inspiration from Mussolini's *squadrista* and becoming ever more paramilitary, as in the case of Colonel de la Rocque's Croix de Feu, founded in 1927. Yet not only did the leagues recruit, as did La Rocque, many malcontent ex-servicemen—the universities, too, were a prime source of reactionary brawn.

On that fateful Wednesday it was at the appearance on screen of the ostensory that the ruckus began. Perhaps the impious juxtaposition of Ghislaine Auboin's shapely leg and the monstrance sufficed to trigger the violence, but if the Rightists had been looking for anti-Fascist allusions against which to retaliate, they were not wanting. For instance, the blind man Modot boots is a war veteran, an officer perhaps; the note taped to the Vicar of Christ's window is a gag about the 1929 Lateran Treaties between Mussolini and the papacy; being Majorcan is a synecdoche for the reactionary realpolitik between Italy and Spain; the bust Modot drops in his final frenzy looks very much like Il Duce; and so on. (Let's not forget that until Hitler came to power in 1933, Mussolini was the optimum signifier of Fascism.)

Eleven arrests were made, including one Ernest Sade, eighteen, in all likelihood a student. Five of the eleven detainees were aged between eighteen and twenty-two; the others were in their thirties. Taken to the eighteenth *arrondissement*'s Grandes Carrières police station in Rue Achille Martinet, a few streets away from Studio 28 in Rue Tholozé—and not far from *LSASDLR*'s editorial address at Breton's apartment in Rue Fontaine—the miscreants were released without charge shortly afterward. The projection continued with paper covering the stains on the screen. Later, some sixty anti-Fascist spectators signed a letter of protest, which was handed in to the police. Among them were composer Georges Auric and his wife Nora (great friends of the Noailles), photographer Gisèle Freund, filmmaker Daniel Abric (co-director of *Paris-Bestiaux*), Jules Monnerot (a Martiniquan student at the Sorbonne who would help launch the black Surrealist magazine *Légitime défense* in 1932), and Ferdinand Alquié (a Montpellier teacher and cinephile whose name crops up later in this book). For the rest of *L'Âge d'or*'s brief shelf life, from 4 and 10 December, it would be shown without incident under the watchful eye of a dozen gendarmes and a group of Communist workers, organized by Thirion and armed with clubs, who frisked all male spectators before allowing them entry.

The following day, 4 December, news of the assault appeared in the Paris papers, providing the parting shots in press campaigns from the Right—spearheaded by *Le Figaro* and *L'Ami du Peuple*, both of them owned by François Coty, the perfume magnate and backer of L'Action Française and the Croix de Feu—and the Left: *L'Humanité* (Communist) and *Le Populaire* (Socialist). The argument of the Right-wing journalists boiled down to *L'Âge d'or* being the work of cinematically incompetent Judeo-Bolshevik devil-worshipping Masonic foreigners. The Left countered with an attack on Chiappe and Coty for being at the beck and call of Fascism and the bourgeoisie. Somewhere in the middle came the censors, criticized by the Right for their lack of vigilance and by the Left for existing at all. While the most vociferous conservative critic, Gaston Le Provost de Launay, municipal councilor for the Champs-Élysées area, declined to identify Charles de Noailles in his 8 December letter of complaint to Chiappe, "out of respect for the name he bears," and while *Le Figaro* and *L'Ami du Peuple* tended not to name him, the more virulent yellow press attacked with headlines like "An important anti-Jewish demonstration. Down with the Jews! 'Noailles to Moscow!'" (*Libre parole*, 1 January 1931). Meanwhile, in the 3 January 1931 edition of *Aux Écoutes*, Marie-Laure was dubbed "the Viscountess née Bischoffheim"—her father was a Jewish banker; the insult was both anti-Semitic and anti-German.

Taken together with Mauclaire's deposition to the police, the "Exposition of the facts" and the press coverage quoted in the Surrealist tract "L'Affaire de 'L'Âge d'or'" of January 1931, to which we return below, plus the cuttings kept by Buñuel in a scrapbook (now in the collection of Filmoteca Española in Madrid), provide us with ample detail on the events of the first two weeks of December 1930.[25] On 4 December Mauclaire lodged a complaint with police inspector Gerardin of Grandes Carrières, holding the Fascist miscreants responsible for 30,000 francs worth of damage to his cinema. On 5 December Le Provost de Launay put a question to the Municipal Council about the scandal. In the meantime, M. Benoît of the Prefecture of Police conferred with Paul Ginisty at the Ministry of State Education and Fine Arts. That evening Mauclaire was instructed by the police to cut the scenes of the bishops on the rocky islet, which he did. The Right-wing press, however, put it about that the film had not been submitted to the censors at all and that the demonstrators had been "arbitrarily" arrested when going to Grandes Carrières to protest against the "immorality of this Bolshevist spectacle." *L'Ami du Peuple* asked Ginisty to comment: the film had passed the censors, he claimed, although personally he hadn't seen it. On 7 December the Coty papers called, in the absence of effective censorship, for vigilante action by Rightist militants against any nominally subversive piece of mass entertainment. In *Le Figaro*, Richard Pierre Bodin, the possibly embittered producer of a failed Sessue Hayakawa vehicle, *J'ai tué* (Roger Lion, 1924), addressed an open letter to Ginisty calling for tighter controls. Meanwhile, Le Provost de Launay attended the afternoon performance and purchased Surrealist books and magazines in the Studio 28 foyer, before addressing, on 8 December, an outraged missive to Chiappe demanding that the prefect crack down on "a spectacle conceived by neurotics and a hotbed of revolutionary propaganda." Hours later, the police requested Mauclaire first to edit out the "Christ" sequence and second, since Your Lord wasn't actually named on screen, to suppress the troublesome Blangis = Christ phrase in the revue-program. In *L'Humanité* Léon Moussinac signed a positive critique of the movie: albeit too formally difficult for the proletariat, in its attack on bourgeois institutions, cautious though this was, *L'Âge d'or* nevertheless served the proletarian revolution. On 9 December Mauclaire was requested to present the film before a censors' appeal board two days later, the Prefecture of Police having been advised that Aristide Briand, minister of foreign affairs, had received a complaint from Mussolini's ambassador that Artigas and Mme Hugo were on-screen caricatures of the Italian monarchs, Victor Emmanuel III and Queen Elena. That evening two agents from Chiappe's General Intelligence Department were in Studio 28, and it was partly on the basis of their detailed, but at times inaccurate, report that the decision was taken on 10 December to prohibit *L'Âge d'or*. Also weighing in the balance was Le Provost de Launay's letter to the prefect of police, promptly leaked to *Le Figaro* and published in an article signed by Gaëtan Sanvoisin, "Pour la fin d'un scandale." Elsewhere in his 10 December column, the latter compares the film's "series of blasphemies [and] degrading visions" to the Satanic narrative of *Là-Bas*. (Years later, in 1976, Buñuel would write a scenario with Jean-Claude Carrière based upon Huysmans's 1891 novel.) Further remarks by noted bibliomaniac Sanvoisin demonstrate that, like Le Provost de Launay, he'd spent money at the Studio 28 bookstall. The first issue of *LSASDLR* he'd purchased there is castigated for its generalized Leninist propaganda, with the threatening letter addressed to a cadet at the Saint-Cyr military academy called Keller by Surrealists Jean Caupenne and Georges Sadoul singled out for especial opprobrium. Sadoul's flight from the penal consequences of this scandal—his trip to the USSR with Aragon and Triolet—would have dramatic consequences for both Surrealism and Buñuel.

On 11 December the copy of *L'Âge d'or* delivered by Mauclaire was screened before the Censorship Appeal Board, consisting of Paul Léon, director of fine arts, M. Pilat of Foreign Affairs, and the censors who'd granted it a visa on 1 October. It was now that the face-saving mendacity began on either side. Mauclaire, handing over the projection print and the safety copy—a third print remained in the hands of the Librairie Espagnole in Rue Gay-Lussac, where Jeanne Rucar and Juan Vicens were fighting in Buñuel's corner—to inspector Gerardin of Grandes Carrières, signed a declaration recognizing that "a film technician" had omitted to make the cut to the rolling intertitle requested on 1 October. Short of reshooting the censored version of this intertitle, to black out the repressed sentence on each frame would have been extremely difficult. As mitigating evidence, Mauclaire added that the other offending phrase in the revue-program had been excised, which may not have been true. The tactical obfuscations of the appeal board are more reprehensible: to *L'Ami du Peuple*, as reported on 12 December, the minister of state education and fine arts stated that after a second viewing—a lie; the film had never been examined—it had noted that requested cuts—in the plural; a lie—had not been made, and that scenes that would not have been accepted had been added after the granting of a visa: a whopping lie. The net result of the board's bending of the truth was that it had recommended to Ginisty that the visa be withdrawn: *L'Âge d'or* seemed doomed. In the next day's *Figaro* it was rumored that Chiappe was to prosecute Mauclaire for infringing the censorship decree of 18 February 1928: if found guilty he could be fined 5,000 francs and have his cinema temporarily closed. The Coty press ratified its reactionary sympathies by printing a communiqué in the 12 December number of *L'Ami du Peuple* from the Ligue des Patriotes congratulating the activists arrested nine days before for their action and extending its thanks to Le Provost de Launay and to the prefect for repressing a spectacle that ridiculed religion, the patria, and the French family. At the other end of the political spectrum, *L'Humanité* of 12 December called for the workers to impose their own censorship "by preventing cinema showings of nationalist rubbish and newsreels—weapons in the moral preparation for imperialist war." The symmetrical call by both Right and Left extremes for direct action by its militants against offending media representations demonstrates just how much of an ideological battleground the diffusion of a reactionary or revolutionary cinema had become by 1930.

It was from many thousands of miles away that Buñuel experienced the traumatic prohibition of his second film. Yet the remove was not just physical; events unfolded in slow motion—and out of sync—on account of the time it took information to cross the Atlantic from Paris and Hyères to Culver City, the home of MGM, and back again. Added to this was a certain sluggishness (due to shock and disbelief, perhaps, but also to reticence and discretion) in the channels of communication between Mauclaire, Rucar/Vicens, and the Viscount de Noailles. On 12 December the first U.S. press report on the scandal appeared in the *New York Herald*. Did Buñuel see it on 12 December, or some time later? Probably the latter, since on 13 December, two days after the rescinding of Visa no. 39.872, Buñuel sent a cablegram—a telegram dispatched by underwater cable—to Breton expressing his delight at receiving the Studio 28 revue-program and yet saying nothing of the Paris debacle.[26] (The revue-program would have traveled by sea and rail; prior to airmail services between Europe and the United States commencing in 1939, a letter took between twelve and sixteen days to get from France to the West Coast.) Hours later on the same day Buñuel heard by cable from Noailles that their film was in all probability a lost cause: "Learn from papers that Age d'Or banned Paris stop Fear serious problems Believe it necessary to request return all copies rue Gaylussac stop Ask you this as personal service stop Prefer not to be named stop."[27] The director did not yet know, nor did his producer, that Mauclaire's two prints had been seized by the police on 12 December, and Buñuel replied by cable on 14 December, ordering the recovery of the prints (by Rucar/Vicens, it is understood) and assuming all responsibility. That same day Jeanne Rucar wrote to the Viscount, informing him of the seizure and of Mauclaire's intention to use his elastic (and enigmatic) political influence with the new government to get the ban overturned. The influenceable figure here was Radical-Socialist deputy Adrien Berthod, ephemeral under-secretary of state at the Fine Arts Ministry in the short-lived (six-week) cabinet of Théodore Steeg. On hearing from Rucar that the Studio 28 man was to fight on against the ban—recall that Mauclaire had installed sound equipment on the basis of his exclusive rights on Buñuel's new movie; he was also planning to open Studio 29 in Passy and Studio 30 in Montparnasse—the Viscount penned a letter, which may never have been sent, asking Buñuel to instruct the cinema owner to keep silent about the Noailles name. Aside from the furor over *L'Âge d'or*, the

Viscount's other 1930 production, Cocteau's *La Vie d'un poète,* had also been denied a visa: "We must be forgotten," was the anguished aristocrat's wish.[28]

By this time Buñuel's own ears may have been burning, for if he hadn't already seen the *New York Herald* piece, a new article by Alex Small appeared in the 15 December edition of the *Chicago Tribune.* Press reports of the sacrilege and subversion of *L'Âge d'or* were getting closer to home: in short order, Buñuel was able to read of the moral panic in the local *Los Angeles Examiner.* A little later, on 27 December, Janet Flanner (Genêt) would publish her own think piece in the *New Yorker.* Buñuel must have had mixed feelings about this media attention. On the one hand it signified a prestige of sorts, put his name on the map as a director of international renown; but on the other it represented a certain risk. Hadn't Eisenstein, in Hollywood at Paramount Studio's request, recently been sent death threats by a local Fascist group led by Major Frank Pease, whose scaremongering activities led to the Fish Committee—a forerunner of the McCarthy hearings of the 1950s—meeting in October 1930 to investigate Communist activities in California?[29] By early December the "Jewish Bolshevik" director was headed south of the border (and en route for further disappointment with *¡Qué viva México!*), but not before having his picture taken with the Spaniard, a belligerent critic of his Russian confrère on more than one occasion.

On 16 December Juan Vicens—an adolescent friend of Buñuel's in Zaragoza and now manager of the Librairie Espagnole, the Paris branch of León Sánchez Cuesta's Madrid bookshop—informed the Viscount by letter that the Rue Gay-Lussac print of *L'Âge d'or* had been rented to the flamboyant English heiress Nancy Cunard, Louis Aragon's former lover, for a single private showing in London at the Gaumont Theatre on 2 January 1931. (When she came to see the film, Nancy must have been amused by the appearance of a Cunard Lines poster in the street where Modot hallucinates about the Léda powder puff.) "Messieurs Breton, Dalí, etc. are very happy," wrote Vicens, "that the film is getting shown like this in England, and among this crowd."[30] Noailles, too, expressed his delight at the London outing; it was the possible resurrection of the film in France that dismayed him. The Viscount expressed this in a 22 December cable to Buñuel: Mauclaire's appeal against the ban must be subverted. Since the contract between the parties stipulated that were showings of *L'Âge d'or* to be interrupted for any reason the contract would be null and void, Noailles asked the director to refuse all future requests from the Studio 28 owner for a new contract. Buñuel cabled his agreement on 27 December.

The day before, Buñuel had penned an effusive and rather ingenuous (or faux-naïf) letter to the Noailles from MGM Studios: "I was far from expecting all this fuss, which is beyond belief. If what people tell me is true, many of the incidents that have occurred could easily feature as gags in the film. . . . Such is the outcome of a film that, over and above its violence, I took to be tender, and which would leave the public in a rather dreamy state instead of plunging it into a nightmare. . . . All these things have only made me feel that much closer to you both and ready to do anything to spare you further distress."[31] Buñuel goes on to say that he's cabled Vicens not to renew the contract with Mauclaire and not to rent the bookshop print to Nancy Cunard, but the message arrived too late to prevent this. Then he lets slip the rumor that MGM may terminate his own contract as a result of the Paris scandal. Finally, he asks Charles to thank Marie-Laure for a package containing press cuttings, another copy of the revue-program, and Jean Cocteau's new book, *Opium: Journal d'une désintoxication*, with its fulsome dedication to the director. A butt for the Surrealists, due in part to being an unrepentant aesthete and *pasticheur*, Cocteau had imitated some of the trick effects in *Un chien andalou* in his first film, *La Vie d'un poète*. *Opium* contained a eulogy to *L'Âge d'or*, but the poet divulges that he hadn't really understood the Spaniard's subversive quoting of—or wallowing in—mainstream industrial cinema: "The first anti-visual masterpiece. One slight reproach: in Buñuel strength is always accompanied by its conventional attributes. . . . For a Dreyer, Buñuel's technique must seem mediocre, as if in 1912 a painter had demanded that Picasso copy the newspaper page in trompe l'œil instead of gluing the newspaper page [to his canvas]."[32]

The Surrealist Group's hopes that *L'Âge d'or* might function as a public demonstration of its revolutionary credentials had been more than met with the banning of the film. The time had come to drive the message home, to retaliate. In early January 1931 a new tract was published, which made excellent use of the possibilities of juxtaposition to implement an ultra-ironic commentary on events. Composed by Éluard and Aragon, "L'Affaire de 'L'Âge d'or'" has four sides of text, which follow the double-column format of *LSASDLR*. Inserted between them is a loose leaf with captioned photographs on either side, the layout of which was Breton's work. The text includes an "Exposition of the facts," "Program extracts," and a "Questionnaire" in the main column, with "Press extracts" running alongside. Since we have elaborated on the facts above, and since the program extracts are drawn from the Studio 28 booklet (upon which we have also expatiated), we next focus on the press coverage, the questionnaire, and the photos.[33] It is worth remarking, though, that the fateful phrase, "The Count de Blangis is obviously Jesus Christ," is defiantly used as the opening quote to the program extracts section.

Taking the photos first: eight images, four to a side, provide the visual argument. On one page, a couple of stills from *L'Âge d'or*, the bishops squatting

The devastation to Studio 28 caused by a Fascist gang on 3 December 1930: staved-in canvases by Tanguy and Dalí, and a shredded photomontage by Man Ray. (Filmoteca Español, Madrid)

their Cap de Creus outcrop, "restore" the two images excised from the film on 5 December by order of Paul Ginisty. The live bishops are captioned with a quote from the young Marx: "The criticism of heaven is transformed into the criticism of earth, the criticism of religion into the criticism of law, and the criticism of theology into the criticism of politics." The putrefact bishops are paired with a *bon mot* by the French Romantic poet Maurice de Guérin, "There is no sweeter spectacle than the death throes of a priest." The sarcasm here is aimed at the *other* Maurice de Guérin, founder of the Ligue Antisémite. Below, a production still of the imagery that had so infuriated Mussolini's ambassador in Paris: the diminutive governor (Artigas) side by side with his towering wife (Mme Hugo). And below that, a press photo of Victor Emmanuel III and Queen Elena. The caption of the first alludes to the ambassador's complaint to the minister of foreign affairs; the second reads: "Their Italian Majesties, who have revolutionary workers killed—such as they are in sad reality." On the other side of the page are two photos of the aftermath of the 3 December Fascist raid. Among the debris we see two battered Tanguy pictures, Dalí's *Invisible*

Sleeping Woman, Horse, Lion, etc., now staved in, and Man Ray's photomontage, very much the worse for wear. The accompanying caption quotes Le Provost de Launay's 8 December protest letter to Chiappe: "We who have decided to react against the by now systematic poisoning of French society and its young people are ever more numerous." A detail of the ink-spattered Studio 28 screen is captioned "Christian illiteracy." Beneath it, in echo of the opening pair of images of the bishops, are the before and after states of *Invisible Sleeping Woman, Horse, Lion, etc.*—one of several versions Dalí produced during 1930, this one belonged to Éluard—with the following caption: "This painting, after the passage of young French bourgeois respectful of art and property."

The press extracts are ideologically grouped, beginning with plaudits from liberal newspapers like *Le Quotidien* and *L'Œuvre*, and ending with the tirades of the center- and far-Right press: *Le Figaro, L'Ami du Peuple, Echo de Paris, Journal des Débats, Le Petit Oranais, L'Œil de Paris.* Occupying the hallowed middle ground are citations from *L'Humanité* by contributors like Robert Caby, Jean-Claude, and Léon Moussinac. Ostensibly, the PCF paper's film and radio critic was no friend of the Surrealists, ever since a polemical exchange in January 1928, when the group's stance was Left-Oppositional and pro-Trotsky, but three years later things were different.[34] The pride of place granted to the *L'Humanité* extracts denotes just how much Breton and his companions were hoping to curry favor with the Stalinists. Hadn't the repression of *L'Âge d'or* proved that the Surrealists were at the cutting edge of revolutionary culture, much more so than rival fellow-traveling factions like Henri Barbusse's *Monde* collective? And that Surrealism was a homegrown movement that could produce attention-grabbing work on a par, in terms of mass-media agitprop, with the best of Soviet cinema?

Forming a climax to the tract, and signed by sixteen Surrealists (but not, once again, by Buñuel), the questionnaire is further proof of the group's harmony with the general line of the PCF and thus with that of the Third International. Resolutely anticlerical, anti-Fascist, and redolent with class-war rhetoric, the loaded questions suggest, for example, that the police ban legitimates the kind of retaliation recommended by *L'Humanité* on 12 December against religious imagery in the shape of "Catholic propaganda films, pilgrimages to Lourdes and Lisieux, centers of obscurantism like *Bonne Presse*, the Committee of the Index, churches, etc., the perverting of youth in church clubs, and military preparations, radio sermons, shops selling crucifixes, Virgins, crowns of thorns." Elsewhere, the banning of *L'Âge d'or* is compared to the state's hue and cry against movies from the USSR and to the recent suppression in Germany of *All Quiet on the Western Front* (Lewis Milestone, 1930) by "Hitler's police." The questionnaire, and the tract as a whole, end on a pro-Soviet note: "Since this intervention [by the police against the film] is made under the pretext of protecting children, adolescents, the family, fatherland and religion, may it be momentarily assumed that the goal of this obvious fascization is to destroy everything that tends to oppose the coming war? And especially the war against the USSR?"

The final sentence demonstrates—as does the telegram dispatched to the BILR in Moscow in late June 1930—the Surrealists' adherence to the Comintern's "Third Period" line, which determined the mental horizon of most Western Communists and their sympathizers between 1928 and 1934. The anti-religious campaign being waged in the USSR as part of the dekulakization program within the Five-Year Plan underpinned part of the Third Period strategy—also known as the "class against class" line—but its main thrust was the proscription of any united front with the Social Democrats, or "Social-Fascists" as the Stalinists dubbed them. The sophistry could reach absurd heights: for instance, as Arthur Koestler tells us, the Comintern would applaud Hitler's seizure of power in 1933 because it rid the proletariat of Socialist influence and therefore hastened Germany's chances of revolution.[35] The Third Period tactic has long been read as Stalin's attempt to forestall revolution in the West, since aggravating the disintegration of the Depression-hit capitalisms through a common-front strategy might have unleashed an attack on a Soviet Union that was still pushing through its crash industrialization and land-collectivization program, the Five-Year Plan. In the case of the Surrealists, the violent rhetoric of the Third Period line requited their own extremism, but in terms of the instrumental scope of the PCF this Comintern diktat was a disaster.

L'Âge d'or did indeed briefly function as an agglutinating agent for a movement that was ever-prone to fissiparity—and that had experienced, also in December 1930, the first rumblings of another crucial "Affair": the one involving Louis Aragon. In addition to providing an opportunity for the now-suspect Aragon to mend bridges, Buñuel's second movie, its suppression, and the publication of "L'Affaire de 'L'Âge d'or'" gave rise to the brief Surrealist allegiance of Francis Ponge, the future prose-poet of *Le Parti Pris des choses* (1942), and to exalted messages of support from such fellow travelers of the movement as *ultra-gauchiste* Sade scholar Maurice Heine and the psychoanalyst Jean Frois-Wittmann.[36]

In the meantime, the conflict of interests between Mauclaire and Noailles/Buñuel pursued its course. By the beginning of the new year the Viscount had brought in a solicitor, Maître P. Castaignet, to guarantee the respecting of the annulled contract. Despite pressure from both Castaignet and Vicens, Mauclaire pressed on with his salvage operation. At his behest, Adrien Berthod would indeed arrange a further "appeal" screening of *L'Âge d'or* on 15 January 1931 for high-ranking officials from the Ministries of Fine Arts (Ginisty and Léon, and a M. Verdier), the Interior (M. Migette), and Foreign Affairs (M. Chatagnon), plus M. Renard, "man of letters" (probably one of the laymen censors who never officiated) and André Benoist, head of the Criminal Investigation Department. The latter repeated the lie that after the granting of the visa the film had been illicitly modified, and he argued that although Berthod might envisage regranting the visa were these "clearly pornographic" sequences to be suppressed, the misdemeanor was a grave one and that, even bowdlerized, the movie would remain a threat to public order. Benoist's view held sway. *L'Âge d'or* was done for. Even if Berthod had won the day he would have been out of office a week later, when Steeg's government collapsed on 22 January, thus guaranteeing nothing.

Another issue of some urgency for the Viscount was the recovery of the negative, still in the safekeeping of G. M. Film in Boulogne-Billancourt, and this so as to preclude any further dissemination of *L'Âge d'or*. On 24 January the faithful and efficient Vicens delivered all the negative material to Place des États-Unis. Under lock and key in Rue Gay-Lussac was the print shown three weeks earlier in London. The Librairie Espagnole man had also undertaken to rescue the two remaining prints, once the police released them. As a result of his baptism of fire as a producer of talking pictures—by Buñuel and Cocteau—Charles de Noailles's interest in the movies rapidly waned. It would also seem that the scandal of *L'Âge d'or* and his subsequent blackballing by Armand de la Rochefoucauld, Duke de Doudeauville, president of the exclusive Jockey-Club, caused something of a separation between the Viscount and his wife, with Marie-Laure continuing as "Paris' première hostess" and Charles as a tender of his roses in far-flung Hyères.[37] And yet credit is due to him for his punctiliousness in archiving not just the negative but also all the documentation to do with the film, thus guaranteeing us, thanks to the splendid editorial work in 1993 of Jean-Michel Bouhours and Nathalie Schoeller, access to an unusually complete overview of the production, realization, exhibition, and repression of a sui generis masterwork.[38]

At first glance, one cannot help but feel sympathy for Jean Mauclaire, who in his ongoing struggle to get the ban on *L'Âge d'or* lifted, was pitted against both the French state and the producer and director of a film whose only chance of exhibition had been provided by him. Bouhours and Schoeller hint, however, that the resentful cinephile may have been behind the anti-Noailles press campaign of early 1931. Whatever the truth of this, Mauclaire would try to cut his losses with "a season of the least bad talking and sound films made until now," as *Paris Nouvelles* put it on 3 February. These stopgap movies were *Captain Lash* (J. G. Blystone, 1929), *Der Hund von Baskerville* (Richard Oswald, 1929), and *Das Land ohne Frauen* (Carmine Gallone, 1929): hardly the stuff of history. Bankruptcy would follow, with Mauclaire taking a slow boat to China in 1932, where he'd work for the League of Nations until 1937.

It is Mauclaire's very presence, his dogged activism, that is striking in all this. Buñuel, on the other hand, appears as something of a spectator vis-à-vis a scandal he'd been instrumental in causing. In his dealings with his patron, the director's probity is beyond question. This doesn't prevent us from asking why he accepted the Viscount's essentially apolitical sybaritic view of things. Or why he didn't struggle more vigorously, alongside his fellow Surrealists, against the repression of his film by the French authorities. Buñuel's physical and temporal distance, the distance he'd knowingly put between himself and his incendiary magnum opus, does not wholly explain his relative quietism. Be that as it may, it is now time to backtrack a little and to give an account of his deceptive four months in Culver City, the home of MGM.

4

A Brief Stay in Hollywood

Opening at the Madeleine-Cinéma in Paris on 13 November 1928 was *White Shadows of the South Seas*, a romantic, anticolonialist MGM movie set on a Polynesian island, which would captivate Dalí—as he declared in an article in the Barcelona daily paper *La Publicitat*—Buñuel, and the Surrealists as a whole.[1] One of the technical features of the film was that it had been sonorized with music and sound effects—breaking waves, birdsong, and so on—by the Movietone process. This *film muet sonore* by W. S. Van Dyke launched the sound era in France, an era that had its emphatic confirmation in the release on 30 January 1929 of Alan Crosland's seminal *The Jazz Singer* at the Aubert-Palace.

The fact that the linguistic aspect of sound film did away with the iconic universality of silent cinema and led to a crisis in the film industry has been abundantly described and studied. In the face of this challenge, one of the first solutions adopted by the big American and German companies was the production of talkies in various languages aimed at diverse linguistic markets and made by professionals contracted in different countries.

Buñuel was one such. However, the way in which he was contracted in Paris by L. Laudy Lawrence, MGM's representative in the French capital, for a stay of six months in Hollywood was due more to his personal contacts than to his professional career. It was Marie-Laure de Noailles, a friend of Lawrence's, who set the ball rolling, presumably at the suggestion, or at least with the acquiescence, of Buñuel, since it seems unlikely that she would have taken such an initiative without speaking to the filmmaker first. Lawrence had seen *L'Âge d'or* during a showing organized by the Noailles at the end of September 1930 and hadn't liked the film. Since neither its private screening at the Cine Panthéon on 22 October nor its public release on 28 November 1930 at Studio 28 had as yet taken place, the scandal attaching to it could not have acted as either a stimulus or a brake in terms of Lawrence's decision. The American talent scout's mistrust of the Spanish director is demonstrated by the fact that he asked for the endorsement of people who'd seen *L'Âge d'or.* As Buñuel explained years later to Max Aub: "I told the Viscount; he smiled and brought me the testimony of forty of France's most illustrious names."[2] The agreement was arrived at, therefore, with a certain amount of cynicism on both sides. For the producer it was of interest to attract young and rather inexpert Hispano-French talent to California and to keep it in reserve while the future of talking films was decided; whereas Buñuel had nothing to lose, being protected from the effects of the Great Depression in the Western world's idyllic Shangri-La. Lya Lys, the female lead in *L'Âge d'or*, would also be signed up by Lawrence in Paris and would prove to be far more active than her director in French versions like *Soyons gais* (Arthur Robison, 1930), *Buster se marie* (Claude Autant-Lara, 1931) and *La Veuve joyeuse* (Ernst Lubitsch and Marcel Achard, 1934), even going so far as to take part in a few English-language movies.

It was stipulated that Buñuel, like other compatriots contracted by MGM, would receive $250 a week during his professional stay of six months in Hollywood, during which time he would learn about studio working methods. On 18 October the cineaste traveled to Spain, where he stayed for a week, taking leave of his mother prior to embarking for New York. At that time the trip to Los Angeles by European filmmakers consisted of the following stages: Paris (Gare Saint-Lazare)–Le Havre, Le Havre–New York in five days of sea travel, and New York–Pasadena (Los Angeles station) by train, in a journey lasting three days and four nights. Thus, on 28 October 1930 Buñuel left Le Havre on board the S.S. *Leviathan*, in the company of the comedy writer and cartoonist Tono (Antonio de Lara) and his wife Leonor. Tono was traveling with a better contract than Buñuel's, since it was for five years, renewable every six months, to work in MGM's Spanish section. His engagement was due to the recommendation of writer and diplomat Edgar Neville, third secretary of the Spanish Embassy in Washington, who during a holiday spent in Hollywood had made friends with Charles Chaplin, Douglas Fairbanks, and Mary Pickford, thus giving him his start in films. Given that established Spanish theater types like Serafín and Joaquín Álvarez Quintero, Jacinto Benavente, and Carlos Arniches didn't want to travel to Hollywood, Neville convinced Irving Thalberg, vice-president of MGM, to sign up younger and more available names.[3] The first recruits were José López Rubio and Eduardo Ugarte, who sailed from Le Havre on 19 August 1930 on the *Île de France*, with contracts for two months, extendable to two years, at a salary of $250 a week. For his part, in Hollywood in 1930–31 Neville wrote or supervised the dialogues of *La mujer X*, *El presidio*, and *En cada puerto un amor*.

Making the crossing on the *Leviathan*, then, were two Spanish friends, albeit with different professional destinies: Tono, as a member of the second batch of writers destined for MGM's Spanish Department, while Buñuel was assigned to the French Department "to see what a 'real' studio was like, and to work in turn in various departments."[4] For all that, once installed in Hollywood Buñuel would claim to the Spanish press to be of a superior professional rank, as demonstrated by his letter of 25 February 1931 to the Madrid daily paper *ABC* rectifying an item published on 10 December, according to which he was going to work as an assistant to a Spanish director. In his missive Buñuel pointed out that he was contracted as a director and had no part in the Spanish section.[5] The late date of this letter, when it was already clear that he would not do any directing for MGM, reveals that Buñuel's public image in his own country mattered to him a lot.

After spending five days at the Algonquin Hotel in New York, attended by an Argentinean MGM employee, Buñuel, Tono, and Leonor boarded the train to California on 9 November or thereabouts. Tono recalled that during the trip Buñuel said to him: "Just imagine if when we get to Hollywood we find Charlot [Chaplin] waiting for us at the station!"[6] On the platform when they arrived, however, were Neville, López Rubio, and Ugarte, but no representative of the French Department for which Buñuel was destined, underlining the atypical nature of his situation. In fact, Maurice Lauzin, head of the French team, had never heard of Buñuel when his superiors announced his signing, which also corroborates just how anomalous the contracts arranged by Lawrence in Paris were, to the point that none have survived in the archives.

On arriving in Los Angeles, Buñuel, Tono, and Leonor went to have lunch at Neville's, who had a Japanese butler in imitation of his friend Chaplin. And that same night Buñuel broke bread with the British comedian and with Neville, for while Chaplin didn't speak Spanish he was a fervent Hispanophile, and his mansion would become a habitual meeting place for the Iberian colony, to the point that F. Scott Fitzgerald baptized it "the Spanish house." The emotional link was so long-lasting that in *Limelight* (1952) Chaplin called the composer, played by his son Sydney, Neville.

Buñuel settled into an apartment in Beverly Hills with Ugarte, and with the money his mother had given him he bought a Ford, a rifle, and a Leica. A couple of days after his arrival he had an interview with an executive who in his memoirs he calls Lewine, but who was none other than Albert Lewin, the future

The welcoming committee for Buñuel on his arrival in California in November 1930, consisting of (*from left*) José López Rubio, Edgar Neville, and Eduardo Ugarte. (Collection: José María Torrijos, Madrid)

director of a film canonized by the Surrealists, *Pandora and the Flying Dutchman* (1951). The French-speaking Lewin had already been assigned as the co-scriptwriter and producer of Jacques Feyder's first American film, *The Kiss* (1929), starring Greta Garbo, MGM's last silent production.

Producer Frank Davis was appointed to take care of Buñuel, and as the latter knew no English he was assigned a Spanish (not French) interpreter called Thomas Kilpatrick, who'd been a gold prospector in Mexico and would excel as the scriptwriter of *Dr. Cyclops* (1940), Ernest B. Schoedsack's 1940 fantasy film classic. Davis examined Buñuel's contract, which he found "odd," and asked him where he'd like to begin. The cineaste elected to observe an actual session of filming and chose *Inspiration*, a Clarence Brown movie in production in October and November 1930. Provided with due authorization,

Buñuel discreetly entered Stage 22, where the star, Garbo, was surrounded by her makeup artists. She spotted him, however, and gave orders for the intruder to be ejected. In his memoirs Buñuel adds, "From that day forth I decided to stay quietly at home and not go back to the studio, except on Saturdays to pick up my check."[7] The legend of Buñuel's total inactivity at MGM is not completely accurate, because in December 1930, at the instigation of José López Rubio, he played a bartender in Arthur Gregor's *La fruta amarga*.[8] This was the Spanish version of *Min and Bill*, directed by George Hill, the star of which, Marie Dressler, was to win an Oscar for her acting in the movie. Meanwhile, the American magazine *Cine Mundial* would draw attention to Buñuel's fleeting appearance.[9]

On 2 December—a day before the Fascist attack on Studio 28—Buñuel penned a long letter to the Viscount de Noailles, giving details of his unproductive stay in Hollywood.[10] He explained that he turned up at the studio at midday to have lunch and that at three in the afternoon he left for home. He added that he'd examined the detailed list of subjects deemed by MGM to be taboo in their films and that all the ones that interested him appeared right on that list. He summed up the situation, writing: "All the directors are directly and continually controlled by the supervisors, who set out to impose a respect for morality, public taste, political ideas, noble feelings and every kind of routine and human conventionalism. They are marvelously organized against any new ideas, except if these are to do with pure technique. I shan't speak to you of the material organization. It is even greater than I imagined. But I'm learning to despise this perfection and this marvelous organization placed at the service of the worst imbecility." And in a revealing aside he communicated to Noailles that "for my part and to justify my salary I've asked to direct dialogues in Spanish or to adapt foreign works," an offer that once again corroborates his association with MGM's Spanish rather than French Department. Such an arrangement would enable him to work on things that did not threaten his moral reputation vis-à-vis the Surrealists in Paris.

Buñuel and Ugarte parodied the rigid standardization of Hollywood production by drawing up a synoptic chart with four or five moveable columns indicating the different milieus, eras, characters, and so forth, and which allowed the storyline and the dénouement of films to be predicted. On one occasion Ugarte used the chart after Buñuel had returned from the première of Sternberg's *Dishonored* (1931) with its producer, Hector Turnbull, and dumbfounded the latter by deducing correctly that at the end of the film the heroine, Marlene Dietrich, was shot.[11]

Frank Davis became friends with the Spanish filmmaker, and they would meet again in 1938, when Davis was an active member of the American

An MGM poster for "the unforgettable movie" *El presidio* (Ward Wing, 1930). (Collection: Juan Bernardo Heinink, Getxo, Euskadi)

Communist Party and tried to help the then politically exiled Buñuel by involving him in a film project to do with the Spanish Civil War. As well as *La fruta amarga*, Davis supervised four other MGM Spanish-language productions in 1930–31: *Olimpia* (1930) by Chester M. Franklin (a version of *His Glorious Night*, Lionel Barrymore, 1929), *El presidio* (1930) by Ward Wing (a version of *The Big House*, George Hill, 1930), *En cada puerto un amor* (1931) by Marcel Silver (a version of *Way for a Sailor*, Sam Wood, 1930) and *La mujer X* (1931) by Carlos F. Borcosque (a version of *Madame X*, Lionel Barrymore, 1929).

In December 1930 MGM had more than sixty foreign actors, scriptwriters, and directors under contract at an estimated cost of $40,000 a week to film versions in Spanish, French, and German, plus the odd title in Italian. Productions in Spanish far outstripped all others, due to the size of the market for them. Such an ample geographical spread led to a diversity of dialect that turned—with the "war of accents"—into an obstacle to the overall acceptance of Hispanic films. Dramatist Gregorio Martínez Sierra's inclusion in MGM in January 1931 was as a final arbiter in disputes about dialect. The problem became chronic, despite the fact that on 18 January 1930 the Motion Picture Producers and Distributors Association of America (MPPDAA) had established the norm that "Any film whose action does not unfold in a country where given idioms or accents predominate will be made in the language that is used in the Spanish theater, and when individuals represent characters who in real life would use the accents and idioms of a given country, the typical idioms, accents and pronunciation of that country will be used." Then again, this output in Spanish was thought to be second-rate by the Hollywood studios: Benito Perojo—who traveled to California on an MGM contract, but who directed only one film for Fox, *Mamá*, in 1931—would recall: "To them, we were offal; they said that what sold was a Spanish sound. They weren't worried about the plot, direction or sets."[12]

The Catalan Salvador de Alberich, who'd saved Arthur Marcus Loew, vice-president of Loew's Inc., MGM's parent company, from drowning in the Pacific, had been rewarded by being made unofficial head of the studio's Spanish section, for which he'd been working in a lesser capacity for five years.[13] However, the section's output would be limited to only thirteen titles, starting with *Estrellados* (Edward Sedgwick, 1930), starring Buster Keaton (a version of *Free and Easy*, also by Sedgwick, of which there was also a French version), and ending in March 1931 with *El proceso de Mary Dugan* (Marcel De Sano, 1931), a version of *The Trial of Mary Dugan* (Bayard Veiller, 1931), which had French and German versions, too.

That said, Buñuel's ambiguous status in the company grabs attention, since although he was contracted by the French section (as was another compatriot of his, the Basque actress Conchita Montenegro), he only participated as a bit player in one Spanish-speaking production and was then required to supervise some dialogues in Spanish by the actress Lily Damita—an assignment he declined—but didn't take part in any Francophone productions. And neither was he required to collaborate on films that had Spanish as well as French versions, a potentially ideal task for him on account of his bilingualism.

The only testimony that seems to exist in Hollywood's Francophone colony of Buñuel's time in California is that of Claude Autant-Lara, a cineaste who also had a couple of avant-garde films to his credit. Fluent in English, the Frenchman was also signed up by MGM in Paris on a two-year contract, renewable every six months. Arriving in Hollywood, Autant-Lara had been dismayed to find that the document he'd signed for Lawrence granted him a salary of $400 a month, less than a stagehand's. After several months of idleness he was entrusted with directing the Francophone versions of two Keaton movies directed by Edward Sedgwick, copying the original versions shot by shot thanks to a moviola installed beside the set: *Buster se marie* (a version of *Parlor, Bedroom and Bath*, 1931) and *Le Plombier amoureux* (a version of *The Passionate Plumber*, 1931). In his memoirs Autant-Lara would explain that to MGM's French Department Buñuel was "the invisible man. As if he'd vanished into thin air," until the Frenchman bumped into him one Saturday while en route to pick up his pay.[14] Autant-Lara colorfully evokes his conversation with Buñuel during that encounter, recollecting the latter's eulogy to the magnificent rifles that could be bought in the United States, as well as his lack of interest in working in Hollywood and his contempt for the technique of American cinema, a jaundiced appraisal at odds with his earlier theories—shared by Dalí—about the superiority of "anti-artistic" films. Interviewed by Luis Gómez Mesa in 1929, Buñuel had stated that cinema was first and foremost an industry: "It stems from standardization, from the division of labor. The best cinema is the one deriving from a more perfected industry," which gave American cinema the edge over European.[15] Interviewed shortly afterward by Dalí for *L'Amic de les Arts*, he'd stressed: "When a genuine cinema industry exists in Europe, a genuine cinema will automatically emerge."[16] In his crepuscular memoirs the Spaniard would give the lie to his disdain for Hollywood by claiming that he left in 1931 with "marvelous memories of it."[17]

The finest account of Buñuel's perception of his American experience was published in August 1931 by Ernesto Giménez Caballero, just after the director's return to Paris: "[Buñuel] admires American cinema. And he admires the American system. And he admires American life. But the *comfort* suffocated him, crushed him and sent him running. It sent him running to see that when it came to making a film everyone was a cog in the machine who knew nothing of the movement of the other cogs. The objective rationalization of American life made him mad, evasive, tetchy."[18]

Albeit more nuanced, such an evaluation would emerge once again in an unpublished text Max Aub wrote years later about this experience. Buñuel, Aub said, "learns to *make* cinema in Hollywood. To put it together and take it apart. I'm speaking, naturally, of the profession. His cinema is very 'Spanish' at heart, but while his ideas are German or Italian, while his favorite poet is Péret, his *school*, his way of arranging things—not only his œuvre, but his life—is North American."[19]

There are no references to Buñuel in the relevant chapter of the memoirs of the most prestigious French-speaking director in Hollywood, Jacques Feyder, who directed 6 features there.[20] According to Dominique Lebrun, Hollywood's Francophone output was limited to 32 titles, made between 1929 and 1935, a much smaller figure than the Spanish-speaking one, which Heinink and

Dickson round out at 153 films, not counting those made in American studios in Europe.[21]

The testimonies we have also point to Buñuel's insertion in the Spanish and not the French colony, which gathered in Russian-American actress Alla Nazimova's mansion, known pompously as "The Garden of Alla."[22] The British filmmaker Ivor Montagu, who frequented Chaplin's house, would evoke the visit to the comedian's residence of Edgar Neville (whom he calls Count B., since Neville was also the Count de Berlanga del Duero), in the company of Ugarte and Buñuel, who played with the children of the actor and Lita Grey—whose divorce case had given rise to the Surrealist tract "Hands Off Love!" in September 1927—and chatted in Spanish with Sergei Eisenstein, who was trying at the time to sell his projects to Paramount. Montagu adds that two days later Neville dropped them off again at Chaplin's house and left, creating an awkward problem in terms of language, since it didn't occur to anyone to use French, in which Buñuel and Montagu were fluent.[23] Buñuel was friendly enough with Chaplin to propose organizing an orgy in his house, an old and always unsuccessful aspiration of the Spanish cineaste's, to which the comedian responded enthusiastically, but just as in so many Buñuel films, at the last moment desire remained unsatisfied because the invited girls, all wanting to sleep with Chaplin, began to argue among themselves and ended up leaving in a huff. It was almost a premonitory scene from *Le Charme discret de la bourgeoisie.*

Those pleasant social gatherings next to Chaplin's pool doubtless took place before 5 December, the date on which Eisenstein and his team crossed the Mexican frontier at the end of his controversial stay in California. Between that date and 24 December Buñuel received news from Paris about the *L'Âge d'or* scandal. Such news must have arrived by 13 December, as already indicated, with the telegram from Charles de Noailles. It's also possible, of course, that the cineaste could have found out via the *New York Herald* on 12 December or even via a telegram from Juan Vicens or Jeanne Rucar prior to that. Given that news of the Fascist assault on Studio 28 had broken in the press on 4 December, it's hard to believe that his friends from the Librairie Espagnole would not have warned him. What is important here is that once Buñuel sent a cablegram to the Viscount on 14 December, assuming responsibility for his film, he continued, despite the delay in communication between Hollywood and Paris, to be well informed about events and to intervene actively in them. But as far as we know he didn't divulge this information; he didn't make a single declaration to the American press in defense of his film. Neither does it seem that he explained the conflict to his French or Spanish or even American colleagues at the studio. Autant-Lara and López Rubio, for example, do not mention the scandal in their subsequent accounts of their Hollywood sojourns. Having heard rumors that his contract might be cancelled due to the negative publicity appearing in the newspapers—as he told Noailles in his 26 December letter—Buñuel kept his head down and his mouth shut. Such prudence does not mean, however, that he was not distressed and that this pain would not reappear in the form of violence.

Actor Roberto Rey explained that "on account of the language the Spanish colony lived completely independently of other actors."[24] And a decade later López Rubio would recall that the Spanish film people "made up a kind of big family. Our first Christmas Eve was full of nostalgia and memories of our fatherland."[25] López Rubio's reference to the celebration of Christmas Eve 1930, held in the house of Tono and Leonor, was overly decorous or exceedingly forgetful. Present at the soirée were Buñuel, Neville and his wife, Chaplin and the actress Georgia Hale, López Rubio, Ugarte, the actors José Crespo and Julio Peña, Benito Perojo, Gregorio Martínez Sierra and his companion Catalina Bárcena, Rafael Rivelles and his wife María Fernanda Ladrón de Guevara, and Valentín Parera. During the party Buñuel, Ugarte, and Peña laid waste to the Christmas tree as an angry riposte to Rivelles's misjudged recitation of Eduardo Marquina's patriotic paean to the sixteenth-century Tercios (Spanish regiments) of Flanders. The destruction of the Christmas tree was a rebellious initiative reminiscent of a scene at the end of the recently banned *L'Âge d'or*, when the main protagonist throws a flaming fir tree out of a window. Was this also an attempt to vindicate the subversive impulse of Surrealism vis-à-vis the conformist, commercialized citadel of Hollywood?

Buñuel's unilateral break with MGM came about, he claimed, when Kilpatrick conveyed Thalberg's assignment to him that he supervise a dialogue in Spanish by French actress Lily Damita. To Kilpatrick Buñuel replied, "Firstly, I was hired as a Frenchman and not as a Spaniard. And secondly, tell Mr. Thalberg I'm not about to listen to whores."[26] Buñuel added in his memoirs that the next day he handed in his notice and prepared to leave, a causality that remains doubtful, since his return to Europe coincided with the abandonment on the part of MGM in March 1931 (albeit decided in February) of all its Spanish-speaking productions and the ensuing cancellation of the contracts of the professionals working on them.

Buñuel's refusal to listen to Lily Damita's Spanish is worth examining. Lily Damita (Liliana Marie Madeleine Carré) had made her debut in French cinema in 1921 under the (slightly subversive) Spanish pseudonym Damita del Rojo, before acquiring her definitive one in 1923. According to the vox populi of the day, she was King Alfonso XIII's lover, which in Spain earned her the nickname

Buñuel with Georgia Hale, the female lead in *The Gold Rush* (Charles Chaplin, 1925), in Beverly Hills at the end of 1930. (Centro Buñuel Calanda, Spain / Courtesy Javier Espada and Herederos de Luis Buñuel)

Lily Dinamita.[27] Settling in Hollywood in 1928 under contract to Samuel Goldwyn, she participated a year later in the silent movie *The Bridge of San Luis Rey*, a version of the Thornton Wilder novel set in the Spanish viceroyalty of Peru. Although Lily Damita wasn't Spanish she had a Latin appearance and was given the role of Camila Perichole. When Thalberg subsequently decided to sonorize this silent film with dialogue, the need arose to check the diction of the polyglot actress, and this was probably the origin of the incident with Buñuel, who was unlikely to feel any sympathy for her. Later on, Tono was assigned to do a similar test with the actress for a Spanish version that never got made.[28] In February 1931 the monthly magazine *Cinelandia* announced that "Lily Damita has been contracted by Metro-Goldwyn-Mayer Studios to make films in French, which of the five languages she speaks is the only one she doesn't murder. Her first movie will be called *¡Divertámonos!*, something which doesn't displease Lily."[29] That French-speaking production would be entitled

Soyons gais, directed by the German filmmaker Arthur Robison (a version of the American *Let Us Be Gay*, by Robert Z. Leonard), and appearing alongside the actress were none other than Lya Lys and Adolphe Menjou, a fetish actor in the cinephile mythology of Dalí and Buñuel, to whom the latter had devoted his eulogistic article "Variations on Menjou's Moustache" in the June 1928 issue of *La Gaceta Literaria*.[30]

It was in mid-February 1931 that MGM decided to suspend its Hispanic output. Finalized in March, *El proceso de Mary Dugan* became the colophon of the Spanish-speaking cycle. MGM bought back the contracts of the Spanish film people at half price, although actors José Crespo and Juan de Landa refused to sell theirs and went on collecting their weekly pay for five months, until their contracts expired. In June 1931 *Cine Mundial* remarked on the exodus of MGM's Spanish professionals (including in its list Buñuel, in spite of his French contractual affiliation), writing, "From Metro have gone writers Edgar Neville, Eduardo Ugarte and José López Rubio; artistes María Tubau, María Fernanda Ladrón de Guevara, María Luz Callejo, Rafael Rivelles and Luis Peña; directors Benito Perojo and Luis Buñuel, set designer Fernando Mignoni, and one or two more I may have forgotten. Most of the redundancies didn't get to fulfill their respective contracts, bought by the company, which paid as little as possible and never more than fifty percent."[31] And listing the inactivity of some of the Spaniards under contract, the magazine added: "The same thing happened to avant-gardist Luis Buñuel (so as not to remain idle, the latter offered to be an actor in *La fruta amarga*)."

Ginette Vicendeau summed up the failure of the operation when arguing that "the multi-version revealed itself to be at once too standardized to correspond to the cultural diversity of its intended public, and not sufficiently so as to be profitable."[32] This diagnosis turned out to be valid for the different linguistic teams, and in August 1931 the French weekly *Ciné-Journal* wrote: "The French artistes under contract in Hollywood to film French versions of talking pictures have returned. The orange has been squeezed."[33]

This cancellation explains why Buñuel didn't fulfill the six months of his contract, thus turning Greta Garbo's high-handed act and his own derogatory remarks about Lily Damita into episodes that were irrelevant to his continuity in the company. Buñuel renounced his contract two months before it expired, as proved by Frank Davis's standard letter of farewell to the cineaste, dated 27 February 1931, which invokes the suspension of Spanish-speaking productions as the cause, demonstrating that Buñuel was no longer attached to the French Department. At the same time as Davis salutes the filmmaker with a breezy "hasta la vista," he refers to "the fact that you anticipated our situation by

CULVER CITY, CALIFORNIA February 27, 1931

Mr. Luis Buñuel,
Metro Goldwyn Mayer Studio,
Culver City, California

Dear Mr. Buñuel:

It is only the fact that it has become the policy of this company to suspend the production of pictures in the Spanish language that forces me with deep regret to say, "Hasta la vista." Yours has been one of the most pleasant associations this department has experienced and the fact that you anticipated our situation by voluntarily relieving us of our contractual obligation to you has shown us aside from your many talents, that you are thd kind of person that we want with us when we go into production again.

Please let us know how you fare on the many voyages you are planning and if there is ever a time when we can help you in any way I hope you will not hesitate to communicate with us.

Very sincerely yours,

Frank Davis

SUPERVISOR OF SPANISH PRODUCTION

NO AGREEMENT OR ORDER WILL BE BINDING ON THIS CORPORATION UNLESS IN WRITING AND SIGNED BY AN OFFICER

MGM's "scratch-my-back" letter of farewell, signed by producer Frank Davis, which Buñuel received at the end of February 1931. (Archivo Buñuel, Filmoteca Española, Madrid)

voluntarily relieving us of our contractual obligations," as did all the Spanish professionals, with the exception of Crespo and De Landa.

In a letter of the same date as Davis's, Buñuel wrote from Beverly Hills to the Viscount de Noailles to announce his departure on 16 March for Oceania and Asia (Hawaii, Japan, China, Manila, Singapore), arriving in Marseilles in May via the Suez Canal.[34] The attraction exerted by exotic worlds was very strong in those years of scant tourist activity—years in which a still highly limited commercial aviation was beginning to emerge—and all the more so for the exalted Surrealist imagination. This trip, moreover, sounded like an echo of the one Gala, Paul Éluard, and Max Ernst made in 1924 as a *ménage à trois*. But when Buñuel recalled a horoscope Breton had cast for him (of one page, not two hundred, as the filmmaker jestingly claimed), predicting that he would die at sea on the other side of the world, he abandoned the project and traveled to New York instead, where he remained for ten days before embarking for Le Havre on 24 March on the *Lafayette*, on which a few French actors were also returning to their country. In the mid-Atlantic Buñuel had a chance to carry out one of his last public acts of Surrealist subversion when acting disrespectfully in public during the playing of the American and French anthems. At the time he didn't know that another, more profound political adventure was awaiting him almost as soon as he set foot in Europe, with the proclamation of the Second Republic in Spain.

It would also be politics—the proximity of defeat in the Spanish Civil War—that would drive Buñuel to the United States once more in September 1938, there to meet up again with his friend Frank Davis. Davis had gone on working as an independent producer for MGM on titles such as *Forsaking All Others* (W. S. Van Dyke, 1934), *Petticoat Fever* (George Fitzmaurice, 1936), *The Devil Is a Sissy* (W. S. Van Dyke, 1937), and *Lord Jeff* (Sam Wood, 1938). When Buñuel reached Hollywood at the end of 1938 he immediately got in touch with his old supervisor, as described in the final chapter of this book.

Tom Kilpatrick would also reappear in the second North American phase of Buñuel's career, since after an abortive plan with the Spaniard to coproduce films in Argentina in 1939, in May 1943 he would become head of production for the Office of Inter-American Affairs in New York, on whose program of propaganda documentaries for Latin America Buñuel had been working for more than two years.[35]

The interpretation Buñuel was to make of his frustrating reencounter with Hollywood in 1938 would hark back to his refusal to cooperate with its industry in 1930, a refusal that, as he saw it, placed him among a group of filmmakers who were notorious for their rebelliousness. He would perceive this as his Achilles heel, to the extent that when he composed his "Auto-Biography" in July 1939 in the hope of getting taken on at the Museum of Modern Art in New York or the American Film Center in Los Angeles, he omitted all reference to the unproductive four months he'd spent in Hollywood at the service of MGM.

5

The Coming of the Spanish Second Republic

Having crossed the Atlantic with the unruly Buñuel on board, the *Lafayette* docked on 1 April 1931 in Le Havre, where he had filmed the final sequence of *Un chien andalou* two years before. This destination may have seemed a symbolic link hinting at the continuity of his career in a Surrealist vein, but the reality was to be very different.

The director would give various accounts of his subsequent travels, the most precise being the one to Max Aub: "In New York I spent all the money I had. I got to Paris on a Wednesday and that Friday—Good Friday—I was beating my drum in Calanda. I took a taxi as far as Hendaye, and from Hendaye to Calanda, a second. On the Sunday I went to Zaragoza and on the Monday or the Tuesday I awoke to the *Himno de Riego*. Boy, that was really something! Never have I seen so much enthusiasm or so many people in the street. There I was, in the café, with [Rafael] Sánchez Ventura and [José] Gaos, who was a professor at the University. My father would've been delighted."[1]

The municipal elections of 12 April 1931 that gave rise two days later to the Second Republic expressed a repudiation by the masses of a monarchy that had backed the dictatorship of General Primo de Rivera and of an omnipresent ecclesiastical power that had supported the ancien régime, representative of a sociopolitical system by now obsolete on the European scene. María Teresa León would sum up such freedom in a beautiful metaphor: "We were sporting a new set of clothes. Clothes without sleeves, which constricted us."[2] It has to be remembered that the republic's coming was supported by neither the anarchists nor the Communists. The anarchists declared that a bourgeois Republic was not their affair, but they didn't attack it.[3] Meanwhile, amid the euphoria on 14 April, Communist militants cruised the streets of Madrid in a lorry shouting, in line with the slogans of the Comintern, "Long live the soviets!" "Long live the workers' and peasants' government!" and "Down with the bourgeois Republic!"[4] In his memoirs José Bullejos, general secretary of the then minuscule Spanish Communist Party (PCE), would admit that the Communist votes cast in Madrid amounted to some two hundred.[5]

What was Buñuel's attitude to these political events? When Max Aub asked him if he'd voted in the April 1931 elections, his response was, "No, I didn't. I couldn't have cared less. What's more, I was never a Republican." From a reading of different statements Buñuel's juvenile sympathy for anarchism becomes clear, which isn't surprising given the huge presence in his native Zaragoza of the Iberian Anarchist Federation (FAI).[6] Buñuel corroborated this when he stated, "At the time, those who, like me, were interested in the sociopolitical aspect of the period, couldn't help but have a rapport with anarchism."[7] He declared that when attending the tertulia in Madrid's Café de Platerías, frequented by the Ultraists in the early 1920s, "I began to be an anarchist, and I would like to point out that I continued with the same ideas until 1930."[8] His libertarian ideology led him to celebrate the political assassinations by the anarchists of José Canalejas (November 1912), Eduardo Dato (March 1921), and Cardinal Juan Soldevila Romero, Archbishop of Zaragoza (June 1923), and as late as 15 April 1931 he co-presided over an anarcho-syndicalist meeting in the bullring in Zaragoza with art historian Rafael Sánchez Ventura.[9] (Four months prior to this, Sánchez Ventura had participated, with the teacher and artist from Huesca, Ramón Acín, in the abortive pro-Republican uprising in Jaca, and it was the proclamation of the Republic that enabled them to emerge from hiding.) In his memoirs, however, Buñuel recalls that the general rejoicing that greeted the Republic "subsided extremely quickly and gave way to unease, then to anguish."[10] In any case, following the euphoric Republican celebration in Madrid, Buñuel returned at the end of the month to Paris.

The opinion of his ex-collaborator Salvador Dalí of those same political events was much more drastic and denunciatory. In his autobiography he described, in apocalyptic tones, the proliferation of political parties and schisms, which portended that "something phenomenal was going to happen in Spain, something like a universal deluge in which, instead of a simple downpour of water, there would rain archbishops, grand pianos and rotten donkeys," in an allusion to the Surrealist iconography of his two film collaborations with Buñuel.[11] But the fact of the matter is that at that time Dalí also had ultra-Leftist opinions, albeit more personal and heterodox ones, as demonstrated by the lecture he gave on 18 September 1931 in Barcelona, at the request of the Workers' and Peasants' Front (BOC), a group of anti-Stalinist Communists, and in which his exalting of the social revolution included the defense of masturbation, exhibitionism, and assassination.[12]

Less than a month after the inception of the Second Republic, popular anticlerical violence flared up with the conflagration, on 10 May 1931, of the Jesuits' church on Calle de La Flor in Madrid. In the days that followed, the burning of religious establishments extended throughout Madrid (eleven fires) and spread to Málaga (forty-one), the Valencia region (twenty-one), and Alicante (thirteen). As a result the government declared martial law in Madrid on 12 May, an ordinance that was soon extended to seven provinces in the south and east, as well as to Logroño.[13] The torching of religious establishments in Spain was applauded euphorically by the Surrealists, who put out an inflammatory tract entitled "Au feu!" signed by twelve of the group, to which were added ten signatures "on the part of foreign comrades."[14] In light of this enthusiastic plea, it is more than likely that the Aragonese Buñuel was one of the drafters of the text: "With the great materialist clarity of burned-down churches opposing all the bonfires once erected by the clergy of Spain, the masses will contrive to find enough gold in the coffers of those churches to arm themselves, to struggle and to transform the bourgeois Revolution into a proletarian Revolution. For the restoration of the Our Lady of the Pilar in Zaragoza, for example, the public subscription of 25 million pesetas has already been half met: let this money be reclaimed for revolutionary ends and may the Basilica of the Pilar, where for centuries a virgin has served to exploit millions of people, be razed to the ground!"[15]

Although the names of Buñuel and Dalí did not appear among those signing the tract, they were doubtless included among the ten foreign comrades, whose names were concealed to avoid police harassment. Dalí's case is of particular interest, since after his return to Francoist Spain in June 1940, fleeing the German advance into France, and his cordial encounter with Falangist leaders and intellectuals (Eugenio Montes, Dionisio Ridruejo, Rafael Sánchez Mazas), he distanced himself from the revolutionary past of his younger days, thereby removing any impediment to his integration in the new regime. His denunciation of the blasphemy and anticlericalism of *L'Âge d'or* in his book *The Secret Life of Salvador Dali* was but one of his expedient gestures of exculpation. Yet once again it has to be remembered that immediately following the tumultuous screening of *L'Âge d'or* at Studio 28, Dalí wrote in December 1930 to its producer, the Viscount de Noailles, defending the anti-religious content of the film.[16] And shortly after the church and convent burnings in Spain in June 1931, he exhibited, at the Galerie Pierre Colle in Paris, *The Profanation of the Host*, a 1929 canvas depicting a Great Masturbator look-alike who spits on a luminescent wafer hovering above a chalice. In his self-justifying memoirs of 1942 Dalí would call this expression of anti-Catholic militancy "a painting of Catholic essence."[17]

Shuttling between France and Spain, Buñuel still maintained enough of a rapport with Dalí in 1931 to write on 19 October to the Viscount about the project with the painter to be created in Hyères, where the Noailles had their sumptuous mansion.[18] Buñuel spent most of that winter in Spain, however, and his future wife Jeanne Rucar recalled that "he got very excited about politics and the ideas that were everywhere in pre–Civil War Spain."[19] We know that on 22 November 1931 he organized a private screening of *L'Âge d'or* in the Palacio de la Prensa in Madrid, of which he recalled that, on leaving, Lorca—perhaps in retaliation for the purported slight of *Un chien andalou*, which he took to be an allusion to his person—said to him, "Luis, I didn't like your film one bit."[20] Buñuel would admit to Noailles that his movie was greeted with coolness.[21] Ernesto Giménez Caballero glossed the negative reaction in this way:

> How Buñuel's face must have looked when, after a tremendous hour-long screening, the only thing produced in the cinema was a perfect silence of the most refined sort.
>
> The classic silence of the Spanish elite: the silence of the smart set who are not to be fooled in a land of fools. . . .
>
> I understand that nobody is going to struggle for *L'Âge d'or* here because nobody struggles for the Age of Gold in life: for neither God nor Devil.
>
> What I don't understand—how monstrous it begins to seem—is this horrible coldness, this being above it all. This boorish aristocracy of ours, which considers that emotion and sincerity are only useful for invoking before the people and then charging it expenses in the form of a republic.
>
> *L'Âge d'or* is a "film" that is moving and sincere, and poetic and great. I state this with all my might. And I would have burst into applause had they not taken me for a friend of the director, for a Surrealist or something of the kind.[22]

On 5 December 1931 Buñuel wrote from Zaragoza to Noailles, informing him that he would stay in Spain until the end of year, in part to work on a script for Braunberger.[23] Seven weeks later he wrote once more to the Viscount, this time from Paris: "Here I am, back again, after that long stay in Spain. Things are really exciting right now and if I hadn't made a brave decision I'd have remained there for a long while yet."[24] From this statement we can deduce that it was now that Buñuel became active in the "exciting" political scene in Spain—not as an anarchist, however, but as a Communist.

Given the way things were developing, it is as well to give some information about the situation of the PCE during this period. The party had begun as a scission of the pro-Bolshevik wing of the Young Socialists in the Spanish Socialist Workers Party (PSOE), but it remained dormant during the dictatorship of General Primo de Rivera and was a minority movement prior to 1936. It was chaperoned by the more numerous and influential PCF, in the shape of the Spanish-speaking Jacques Duclos, a central committee member after 1926, politburo secretary after 1931, and by 1935 a member of the executive committee of the Third International. Following the suppression of the German Communist Party (KPD) by the Nazis in 1933, the PCF became the most influential Western Communist Party, and during the Civil War it would monitor the situation in Spain, in accordance with the Comintern.

In 1931 the PCE was a minority party with a thousand or so militants.[25] One of its main centers of proselytism in Madrid was the Ateneo, a traditional forum for intellectual and ideological debate, of which Buñuel had been a member since October 1924. According to Julio Caro Baroja, among the PCE's founders was the Aragonese *Ateneísta* Mariano García Cortés, who formed part of his uncle Ricardo Baroja's circle in the Ateneo—which he joined in November 1930—a circle also frequented by other Marxists like the Cárdenases, Pinillos, and even the general secretary of the party, José Bullejos.[26] In June 1931 a meeting was held in the Ateneo that gave birth a few days later to the Spanish American Union of Revolutionary Proletarian Writers, as a section of the International Union of Revolutionary Writers (UIER) founded in the Soviet Union. Two of its leaders—the novelist Joaquín Arderius and the painter and essayist Ricardo Baroja—would immediately join the PCE. In his memoirs Bullejos evoked the militancy emerging in the Madrid Ateneo: "Various Left-leaning *Ateneístas*—Captain Francisco Galán, the brother of Fermín Galán, Wenceslao Roces, Jiménez Siles, Joaquín Arderius, Ricardo Baroja and Castillo García Negrete—served the party, first as sympathizers, then as members. César Falcón, with his group the Anti-Imperialist League, came within the orbit of Communism, and months later, in 1933, joined the party."[27]

During this period a sympathy for Marxism extended to different intellectual circles, although this did not lead automatically to joining the PCE. For example, Lorca—who was never an active party member, despite the pressurizing of Alberti—proclaimed in September 1931 that "all current Communist and Socialist social movements proceed from one great book: Karl Marx's *Das Kapital.*"[28]

Militating on behalf of popular theater in La Barraca, Lorca stated in October 1933 that "in the theater we have to admit the public in espadrilles."[29]

So it was that after 1932—and doubtless at the instigation of its French comrades, who had more experience in the matter—the PCE began admitting intellectuals, who were subject to a more flexible discipline than that granted to the workers. On 14 November 1931, with the economic support of the PCF, it began publishing the paper *Mundo Obrero*, which disseminated the party line and broadcast its slogans, which were not always very realistic.[30] For instance, after the heavily supported workers' demonstrations of May Day 1931 in Seville, the PCE leadership was summoned to Moscow and given orders to speed up the revolutionary process, since as far as the Comintern was concerned, Republican Spain was in a situation similar to that of Russia in 1917, a conviction the national leaders did not share.[31] On 17 March 1932 the PCE's Fourth National Congress got under way in Seville with the attendance of 257 delegates, representing 12,000 members.[32]

Constituted a year after the Comintern set up the Association of Revolutionary Writers and Artists (AEAR) in Paris in March 1932, in which Buñuel was active, the Spanish branch of the association never exceeded two hundred members,[33] although in June 1933 Rafael Alberti and María Teresa León managed to launch their eye-catching review, *Octubre*. In Valencia, with the legalizing of the Spanish section of the AEAR, a group of Communist intellectuals formed the Union of Proletarian Writers and Artists (UEAP), since the civil governor, Luís Doporto, refused to countenance the term *Revolucionarios*, which was replaced by *Proletarios*, a designation already in decline in party terminology. In January 1935 it began publishing the magazine *Nueva Cultura*.

In the years prior to the Civil War the PCE demonstrated its force of attraction in the intellectual world. One of its founders had been the Basque writer Eduardo Ugarte, Buñuel's friend and colleague in Hollywood in 1930 as well as in Filmófono five years later. The Córdoban poet and journalist Juan Rejano also militated in the PCE from the mid-1920s onward and was the secretary of Editorial Cenit, a publishing house dependent on the party. The writer and politician from Alicante, Ángel Gaos, was active in the PCE after 1930. The Valencian poet Juan Lacomba was connected with the party in Galicia in 1931, the same year the poet José Herrera Petere joined, as did the Valencian painter and poster artist Josep Renau and the graphic artist Helios Gómez. Much admired by Buñuel, the poet Pedro Garfias became a PCE member around this time. César Muñoz Arconada joined in 1932, the same year in which, invited by the UIER, Alberti and León went to the USSR in December on an initiatory trip, extending their stay there for two months before returning to Spain and setting up *Octubre*. April 1933 saw the creation of the Spanish Friends of the Soviet Union, an organization launched by Ugarte, writers María Lejárraga and Ramón J. Sender (in his evolution from anarcho-syndicalism to filo-Communism), lawyer Luís Jiménez de Asúa, politicians Victoria Kent and Juan Negrín, and caricaturist Luís Bagaría, along with other comrades. Three months later there were already seven thousand fellow-traveling Friends.[34] As a "para-Communist constellation" of intellectuals during the Second Republic, Joan Estruch cites the writers Ramón del Valle-Inclán, Ramón J. Sender, Joaquín Arderius, César Muñoz Arconada, José Díaz Fernández, José Antonio Balbontín and José Bergamín, lawyer and professor Wenceslao Roces, artists Ricardo Baroja and Luís Bagaría, journalists Julián Zugazagoitia and Amaro del Rosal, politicians Juan Negrín, Margarita Nelken, Luis Jiménez de Asúa, and Julio Álvarez del Vayo.[35] The names could be added of many contemporary artists and intellectuals who militated in the Communist movement, some as prestigious or notorious as the poets Luis Cernuda, Juan José Domenchina, and Emilio Prados, writers Arturo Serrano Plaja and Álvaro Custodio, sculptor Alberto Sánchez, architect Luis Lacasa, filmmakers Antonio Del Amo and Fernando G. Mantilla, and film critic Juan Piqueras. Luís Buñuel was no exception, as we shall see. In the PCE's extended plenary session of July 1934, its new general secretary, José Díaz, claimed that in all Spain the party had some 25,000 militants.[36]

6

A Stormy Year

When Buñuel declined to travel with Louis Aragon and Elsa Triolet to the Soviet Union in August 1930, his decision had two consequences. First, he left the door open for MGM's future summons to Hollywood, with its ensuing deception in terms of his ambitions as an "anti-artistic" movie director. And second, he missed out on an ideological equivocation that would change the trajectory of that with which he was most in sympathy, Surrealism, and in so doing change his own trajectory. This ideological equivocation marked the start of the "Aragon Affair," which would lead to another major rift in the Surrealist Group, the second in two and a half years. It was the seesawing exaltation and melancholia of this crisis-ridden period that subtended Buñuel's own stay in the movement.

Moreover, Buñuel's option of going east or west neatly encapsulated the wanderlust of many Western European intellectuals of the time, and their fascination with pharaonic displays of either Socialist creativity (a blast furnace in Magnitogorsk) or capitalist invention (a film studio in Culver City). Perhaps it is overly simple to label this as revolutionary or reactionary tourism: suffice it to say that the perception from Paris, London, Berlin, or Madrid was that something ultramodern and magnificent was stirring in these two isolationist subcontinents.

By the time Buñuel was U.S.-bound at the end of October 1930, Aragon, Triolet, and Georges Sadoul were in Moscow, staying in Mayakovsky's apartment, courtesy of Elsa's sister Lili Brik, the late poet's ex-lover and a film actress (in *Shackled by Film*, Nikandr Turkin, 1918) and director (of *Jews on the Land*, a 1926 documentary, and, with Vitali Jemtchoujny, *The Glass Eye*, a mélange of documentary and fiction made for Mezhrabpom in 1929). Although Aragon had recently applied to rejoin the PCF, the trip was not overtly political but rather to visit Lili and do some sightseeing in the One Country of Socialism. Nevertheless, shortly after their arrival the two Surrealists had been invited, probably through the machinations of Triolet, to travel to Kharkov as "consultative" French delegates at the Second International Conference of Proletarian and Revolutionary Writers, "one of the first great cultural events of the Stalinist era," as Jean-Pierre Morel defined it.[1] The first such congress had taken place three years earlier in Moscow, when the BILR was founded. It was to the BILR that the Surrealists had directed their pro-Soviet telegram in July 1930, thus providing Aragon and Sadoul with credentials. According to Stephen Koch, the threesome journeyed from Moscow to Kharkov in the company of Aleksandr Fadaev—a dubious companion when one considers that as prime mover of the Russian Association of Proletarian Writers (RAPP) Fadaev had orchestrated the literary baiting of Mayakovsky that contributed to his suicide.[2] Held between 6 and 15 November 1930, this Comintern junket in the Ukraine was attended by 134 Communist Party (CP) and fellow-traveling writers from fourteen countries. In commending the general line on "proletarian" art—in the shape of the *rabcor* "worker-correspondent" movement—and praising the rigor of the GPU—the Soviet political police—Aragon established his credentials as a pliable servant of the Cause, albeit an as yet contentious one: his attack on the pacifist "confusionism" of absent party favorite Henri Barbusse, leader of the *Monde* collective and a major obstacle to the Surrealists' attempt to convince the PCF, and the Comintern, of their peerless worth as revolutionary artists and writers, outraged many of the faithful. But not all: such major figures in the RAPP and the BILR as the Polish Communist Bruno Jasienski, author of the apocalyptic novel *Je brûle Paris* (1929), had been waging an anti-*Monde* campaign for some time. Aragon's opportunistic bending of the knee was such that he was co-opted onto the controlling body of the newly formed UIER and onto the editorial board of its periodical *Littérature de la Révolution mondiale* (but then so was Barbusse). The price for such empowerment was that, seemingly from the first, Aragon and Sadoul were, under pressure from Jasienski, required to denounce the "counterrevolutionary" ideas of Breton, Freud, and Trotsky in a letter sent to the Secretariat of the UIER and the leaders of the PCF.[3]

Taken, at the end of the congress, on a tour of a vast dam-building project on the Dnieper—a showpiece of Stalin's crash industrialization program—Aragon, who had doubtless never visited a French dam in his life, would enthusiastically pen the first of many pro-Soviet propaganda poems. Before leaving the USSR on 10 December he'd compose another, "Front rouge," which would become a *cause célèbre.* "Running with the wolves" in Kharkov, as Morel puts it, the French poet added his grain of sand to the international "chekaization" of Leftist culture.[4]

It fell to Sadoul, arriving in Paris in advance of Aragon and Triolet, to explain their about-face to the Surrealists on the same day the prefect of police impounded copies of *L'Âge d'or.* Soon afterward the two waverers were urged by an aghast group to produce "Aux intellectuels révolutionnaires," a tract intended to outflank any future leaking of their Kharkov statement. The text rehabilitated Breton and Freud—though not Trotsky—and ratified Surrealist synergy with the aims of the Third International. In passing, Aragon and Sadoul applauded Breton and Thirion's recent initiative, the Association of Revolutionary Artists and Writers (AAER), a pro-PCF intellectuals' trade union, an initiative discountenanced, however, by the party's agitprop department.[5]

Before long Aragon was back in the thick of things, cowriting the January 1931 broadside, "L'Affaire de 'L'Âge d'or.'" As already indicated, Buñuel, still in Hollywood, didn't sign this retort to institutional "fascization." When, after witnessing the birth of the Second Republic in Spain, he finally returned to Paris on 27 April 1931, conscious that he'd sat out the two big scandals of the day—one of them his own doing—he was readier for the fray. In the meantime Aragon, Sadoul, and two other Surrealists—Pierre Unik and Maxime Alexandre—had been admitted to the PCF. For Aragon and Unik it was their second time: together with Breton and Éluard they'd been accepted as candidate-members in 1927, only to depart months later, disillusioned by the *arrière-garde* obtuseness of the party satraps. (Sadoul had been a candidate-member prior to becoming a Surrealist in 1926.)

Writing on 30 April to the Noailles about a future get-together—their first since 27 October 1930, the day before Buñuel left for Hollywood—the director reassured his still-jittery backers that, as an update from friends had led him to believe, the *L'Âge d'or* scandal appeared to have blown over. "Now I'm looking for work," he affirmed, "and I have hopes of getting into Paramount in the Spanish section. I've volunteered for anything apart from directing."[6] In May 1930 Paramount had begun refilming their American movies in as many as five different languages in their recently acquired studios at Joinville-le-Pont, near Paris. This was factory filmmaking at its most exploitative, two weeks being the common turnaround time. An application Buñuel made to join mainstay directors Florián Rey, Adelqui Millar, and Manuel Romero on the Spanish roster was turned down, thus putting a different cast on his words to the Noailles.[7]

Were the anecdote to be true, it would have been around this time—late April to early May 1931—that Buñuel, just back from Spain, was asked to go on the Dakar-Djibouti Ethnographic and Linguistic Mission as a documentarist. Since his name appears nowhere in the literature, the likeliest possibility is that the out-of-work filmmaker did the asking via the Viscount, one of the sponsors of this trans-African fact- and artifact-collecting expedition organized by the Paris University's Institut d'Ethnologie and the Musée Nationale d'Histoire Naturelle (in the shape of its annex, the Musée d'Ethnographie du Trocadéro).[8] Buñuel also knew one of the mission's organizers, Georges-Henri Rivière, subdirector of the Trocadéro museum. Rivière, coeditor of the recently defunct *Documents*, had helped engineer his meeting with Noailles in June 1929, shortly after the première of *Un chien andalou*. By this late date—the eleven-man team left Paris for Dakar on 10 May 1931—the cameraman's position had gone to Éric Lutten, the mission's technology adviser. Although Lutten would shoot footage of Dogon funerary rites, the taking of still photographs took precedence: the expedition returned with some six thousand of these, but very little movie film. In *Mon dernier soupir* Buñuel claimed that he'd turned down the invitation to participate—the twenty-month mission was a nonsmoking affair!—and had suggested to Michel Leiris that he make the trip in his place.[9] This is surely a mystification: we cannot thank Buñuel for furthering the writing of *L'Afrique fantôme* (1934) because Leiris had been recruited by expedition leader Marcel Griaule in January 1931, while our man was still in Hollywood. Dakar-Djibouti remains the stuff of legend: as stated in the voiceover of *Sur les traces du renard pâle*, Luc de Heusch's 1983 film on Griaule and the Dogons, it was Henri Storck who'd been invited to go as the expedition's filmmaker, although poor health obliged him to decline. Buñuel's fabulation is significant: it suggests that by May 1931 he was already mulling over the possibility of setting fiction filmmaking aside and setting off down the documentary road. His next cultural intervention, moreover, would at least hint at Spain as a potential subject for such a film.

On the same day that the ethnographic mission left Paris for Dakar, the Spanish masses, disenchanted by the Republican-Socialist government's vacillation in introducing radical reforms, particularly the promised separation of church and state, reverted to a century-old tradition and began torching ecclesiastical property. As indicated in the last chapter, the Surrealists greeted this arson with a ferociously anticlerical tract, "Au feu!" But not just anticlerical: penned by Thirion, beefed up by Aragon, and printed on flame-red paper, the text was very "Third Period" in tone. That is, it followed the Comintern line in arguing that the Republic, as a fomenter of democratic "illusions," was the true enemy of the proletariat. "If the first concern of the bourgeois Republic," the squib stated, "has been to declare that the Catholic faith remains the State religion, its second task is to use force to curtail those who have resolved to pull down all consecrated buildings. . . . The quaking bourgeoisie will maintain the clergy on its land because the partition of ecclesiastical property can only be the signal for a secular partition. . . . They will not be able to separate Church and State. Only the terrorism of the masses can effect this separation."[10]

We have already argued that Buñuel's (and Dalí's) name must have appeared among the ten "foreign comrades" who signed the tract in invisible ink. Elsewhere in "Au feu!" we can see that the Spanish iconoclasts were putting into effect the program of retaliation against religious propaganda recommended by *L'Humanité* and promoted by the Surrealists in "L'Affaire de 'L'Âge d'or.'" Not only were ecclesiastical buildings razed, but a number of establishments pertaining to the Catholic press were also burned to the ground.

The "magnificent bouquets of sparks appearing over the Pyrenees" did not, of course, catch the Surrealists unaware. On 4 May 1931, a week after Buñuel's return to Paris, and at the behest of Breton, the group had elected a three-man committee consisting of Dalí, Éluard, and Thirion to present a set of concrete proposals for rescuing the group from its despondency by intensifying its activity as a collective. The report this committee presented on 12 May, two days after the pyromania began in Spain, identified two axes, the fight against religion and the resumption of experimentation into objective perception.

Aside from the report's intrinsic interest, the fact that Buñuel's name appears therein justifies a closer look. The first section, written by Thirion, proposed an agitprop campaign built upon the atheistic writings of the eighteenth-century French materialists D'Holbach, La Mettrie, Sylvain Maréchal, and Sade, as well as Feuerbach, Marx and Engels, Lenin. This campaign was to be waged in the pages of a new monthly bulletin: "The title is to be decided upon at the meeting on Thursday the 14th [of May]. Print run: 5,000. We request Ernst, Tanguy, Dalí, Trouille and Malkine to each submit collages, drawings and caricatures that might serve as illustrations."[11] The chief editor of this "Bulletin of the worldwide struggle against religion, now and henceforth" would be Aragon, the editorial secretary Tzara, with a press committee consisting of Breton and Albert Valentin. The four-page newsletter was never to appear under Surrealist auspices, however. Number 3 of *LSASDLR* (December 1931) did, though, carry an advertisement for the PCF's magazine *La Lutte: Bulletin mensuel de la Libre-Pensée Antiréligieuse et Prolétarienne*, edited by R. Levasseur, which suggests that the Surrealist project ran parallel to the party's own and was absorbed by it. We don't know if Buñuel subscribed to *La Lutte*, but Breton certainly did: a photograph exists of his subscription card, dated 10 October 1931, Aragon being the collector of the annual fee.[12] During his first year in the PCF Aragon would work on the editorial staff of *La Lutte*—he'd get Giacometti to do illustrations for it—and in

1932 he'd publish a little book of poems for children in the party's "Bibliothèque antiréligieuse" series called *Aux enfants rouges: Éclairez votre réligion.*[13] Sadoul was another activist and would liaise from Paris with the Liga Atea (Atheist League) in Madrid via PCE members Juan Vicens and María Luisa González ("Comrade Justine").

The second half of the report, probably written by Éluard, argues for the need to complement the group's public politicking with a private experimentation that was irremediably at odds with the anti-Freudian worldview of the puritanical PCF. Watched over by a series of four-man subcommittees, this activity was meant to reinvigorate past areas of Surrealist exploration, such as the researches into sexuality (Dalí, Tanguy, Crevel, Purnal), dream interpretation (Thirion, Unik, Tzara, Char), games (Breton, Char, Tzara, Dalí), and the study of simulation, as in the simulations of psychotic utterance contained in Breton and Éluard's recent *L'Immaculée Conception* (Ernst and Thirion would serve on this panel together with the authors of the book).[14] The other subcommittees devoted themselves to an examination of humanitarian and anti-humanitarian feelings (Aragon, Dalí, Crevel, Valentin) and to the two categories that involved Buñuel: diurnal fantasies and objective perception. As to the first of these, the report reads: "transcription of diurnal fantasies; it is obvious that these fantasies must not be consciously provoked, but appear in the same way dreams do; just as for dreams, these fantasies will have to be commented upon and critiqued. Gestures, atmosphere, circumstances, and any rapport with oneiric life are to be noted." Buñuel was to work with Tanguy, Breton, and Aragon on this. As to the second, the report says: "examination of objective perception; each person is to note down at the same time each day what especially strikes him in sensory terms, and the immediate associations of ideas these perceptions entail. Assembly of documents and critique." Buñuel's colleagues here were Unik, Valentin, and Éluard.

In mid-May Buñuel and his patrons met face-to-face for the first time in seven months. Although the outcry over their two recent productions had cooled the ardor of the Noailles for moviemaking, Buñuel heard enough to know that the Viscount's goodwill would not be withdrawn. Before long the two men set about renting copies of *L'Âge d'or* to film societies in Berlin, Buenos Aires, Madrid, and Amsterdam. Or better still, selling: Charles didn't need the money, but Luis most certainly did. In his letter to Noailles of 29 June 1931 Buñuel announced that he'd be staying in Paris all summer, a rare occurrence given that he usually vacationed in Zaragoza and San Sebastián.[15] Perhaps his labors on booking his banned movie, or in furnishing his new apartment at 39, rue Pascal, or simply looking for work kept him in the French capital.

Be that as it may, there is a gap of more than two months in our knowledge of his movements.

Most of the Surrealists were out of town, taking the country air, but by early September they were back, organizing "La Vérité sur les Colonies," their riposte to the May–June Colonial Exhibition. Funded by the Anti-Imperialist League, an adjunct of the Comintern, this counter-exhibition, which began on 20 September 1931, was hung by Thirion, Sadoul, Éluard, Tanguy, Aragon, and Elsa in the Soviet Pavilion built by the Vesnin brothers for the 1925 Exposition des Arts Décoratifs. Just as Buñuel's unstated signature is, we believe, to be found at the end of "Au feu!" so it may be appended as that of a "foreign comrade" to the tract "Ne visitez pas l'Exposition Coloniale" of May. And by the same token it may be added to the "Premier bilan de l'Exposition Coloniale" of 3 July, which alludes to "the purifying acts of the Proletariat in burning the monasteries of Spain."[16]

The political activity of the Surrealists is a subject that almost never comes up in the Buñuel/Noailles correspondence, so when writing to the Viscount on 17 September the director makes no mention of the anticolonialist exhibition. He does, though, emphasize his penury: for want of money he's been unable to hire a viewing theater to show *L'Âge d'or* to a potential Dutch customer, probably a representative of the Filmliga, the Leftist film society run in Amsterdam by Joris Ivens. He will, however, get to show the film to this Dutchman because Victoria Ocampo, who wants it for her Buenos Aires film society, is willing to pay for a rescreening. "I remain idle," Buñuel tells Noailles, "forever seeking something that for the moment I do not find, according to my desires."[17] In the meantime he'd been pounding the pavements and working on a book. Was the latter another attempt to anthologize his 1920s poetry?

After the summer recess the Surrealists began meeting again. André Thirion has left us a description of the tensions in the collective generated by the discussions of autumn 1931: "Two groups took shape during the debates, that of the Communists around Aragon and Thirion, and that of the poets around Éluard. In the voting, a majority, of which Breton was the fulcrum, and of which I was always part, prevented a swing towards excessive politicization or towards an exclusively aesthetic attitude. Giacometti and Unik often took the side of Aragon, with whom I sometimes parted company. Crevel, Tanguy and Buñuel never disagreed with Breton."[18] On 6 October an important session took place in Tzara's Adolf Loos-designed house in Montmartre, and the "directeur de conscience" was there. Breton's manuscript of *Les Vases communicants* was the ostensible subject of discussion, but the talk soon turned to the dispiriting fact that in more than a year the first two issues of *LSASDLR* (published in July and October 1930, respectively) had sold only 350 copies apiece. The question was begged: who were the Surrealists writing for? Things took a surprising turn when, donning his Communist cap, Breton stated that he for one was capable of vulgarizing his writing in order to reach a wider audience: "as I don't want to provide any fodder for aristocrats and bourgeois I intend to write for the masses." The subject arose of Surrealism's autonomy: "Even if it means abandoning Surrealism," Breton railed, "the public will have to be renewed at all costs." The meeting ended with Aragon proposing that a future session be devoted to "dialectical materialism in all its forms, however distant." Breton, Sadoul, Aragon, Thirion, Éluard, Tzara, Léo Malet, and Giacometti put their hand to this measure; Buñuel too.[19]

Buñuel's next missive to the Viscount two weeks later has him expressing his thanks for the advance paid for the "show in Hyères." This is the divertissement he's been asked to mount at a Noailles garden party to be held six months hence. Our man is still in the French capital, delaying a trip to Madrid to show *L'Âge d'or*, waiting for Dalí to get back from Port Lligat. Salvador, who is occupied with the paintings for his first show in the United States, as well as with "Rêverie," a text that will reverberate in both their careers, is to collaborate on the Hyères spectacle. "I've found," says Buñuel, "a workable, but very individual, idea for us to do together." As long, that is, as the two of them didn't get into their "number."[20]

That proved to be impossible, for Dalí did not return to Paris, and after waiting a week or so Buñuel took off for Madrid, arriving there with his film on 29 October. Given the recent unrest in Spain, the police had forbidden any public showing of *L'Âge d'or*, and the director was obliged to content himself with a private screening to an invited audience of some three hundred people in Ricardo Urgoiti's Cine Palacio de la Prensa at midday on 22 November. Among those present were Lorca and Ugarte, who had recently begun planning "La Barraca," the student theater group whose ambition, in line with the Pedagogical Missions but independently of them, was to take classic plays to the villages of deepest Spain. Although Lorca expressed his dislike of the film, it appears that Buñuel did some of the spadework for La Barraca.[21] His verdict on the Palacio de la Prensa session was typically laconic: "Most people . . . thought the film was bad," he told Charles de Noailles, "but as always there were a few fans. Soon they're going to show it in Barcelona, where the reception will doubtless be just as unfavorable."[22] During the month spent in the capital he also discussed with Tota Cuevas de Vera and Carmen Muñoz—countesses both—the possibility of bringing Breton to Madrid to lecture to the Courses and Conferences Society at the Residencia de Estudiantes, but this lecture never took place.[23]

Nine days after the screening in Madrid of *L'Âge d'or*, the director left for a week in Zaragoza and then a further eight days in Toledo, where, aside from taking Crevel—a new knight in the parodic "Order of Toledo" invented by Buñuel and his friends as a caricature of aristocratic rituals—to view Goya and El Greco, he intended to work on a scenario for Pierre Braunberger. Was he already cogitating *Wuthering Heights*? We don't know, but it is at least worth floating the hypothesis that Crevel had spoken to him of the novel; in 1930 the French writer had published a study of the Brontës: *Les Sœurs Brontë, filles du vent*. It may be that Buñuel came up with nothing, for in his Zaragoza letter of 5 December to the Viscount he complains of "an unspeakable idleness" that has prevented him from sending his contribution to issue 3 of *LSASDLR*: perhaps the as-yet unpenned text "Une girafe," on which the Hyères intervention would be based, or his contributions to the researches into diurnal fantasies and objective perception. "They [the Surrealists] must be mad with me," he adds.[24] Although he told the Viscount that after a further three weeks in Zaragoza, he'd be back for the new year, Buñuel stayed a month longer than anticipated in Spain, until 25 January 1932. This, we have argued, is the moment of his conversion to Communism.

When Buñuel received word of his Surrealist comrades, in the shape of numbers 3 and 4 of *LSASDLR*, published simultaneously in December 1931, he must have had mixed feelings. While Aragon praised *L'Âge d'or* as an expression of Surrealism's subversive authenticity in the opening essay in number 3, a few pages further on Maurice Heine took the director to task for what he saw as intellectual cowardice. We don't know if the addressee of "An Open Letter to Luis Buñuel," written by the great Sade scholar immediately after a visit to Studio 28 in December 1930, saw the screed before its belated publication a year later. Heine's argument was that while *L'Âge d'or* was to be venerated for being the first film ever to depict an episode from Sade's writing, the stepping back on the part of the cineaste from extending his blasphemous gag about the Duke de Blangis being Jesus Christ to having his three libertine companions be Mohammed, Moses, and Confucius—thus combining *Dialogue between a Priest and a Dying Man* and *The 120 Days of Sodom*—was to be regretted: "Why don't you give Jesus rivals of equal stature? Why don't you simultaneously level the charge of a quadruple blasphemy against the world's four great religions? For you to attack only one of them—is this not to play implicitly into the hands of the other three?"[25] Demonstrative of the fact that there is always someone more extremist than oneself, Heine's critique is comradely, if rather Jesuitical, in tone. Blinded by his admiration for Sade—whose two books, cited above, he had published in 1926 and 1931, respectively—he seems not to have registered the sight gag of the de-bearded Son of God, Buñuel's solution, perhaps, to the uncinematic (and pedantic) repeating of the same joke four times over. Heine's criticism, published by the Surrealists against one of their own, thus converting what was essentially a private affair into a public one, still pained the director decades later. "Maurice Heine penned an article against me," Buñuel told Jean-Claude Carrière, "stating that the Divine Marquis would have been extremely peeved. He'd actually attacked all religions, without restricting himself, like me, to Christianity alone. I replied that my intention was not to respect the ideas of a dead author, but to make a film."[26] That said, Dalton Trumbo, who must have got the idea from the Spanish filmmaker, slipped the image of the four religious figures filing past in his film *Johnny Got His Gun* (1971), on whose screenplay Buñuel worked in the 1960s.

Appearing elsewhere in number 3 of *LSASDLR* was Dalí's important taxonomic text "Objets surrealistes," while number 4 contained his delirious erotic fantasy, "Rêverie," reworked by Éluard and Breton from the Catalan's chaotic original. Dalí's reproduced artworks and objects, plus the ads for his books—*La Femme visible* (1930) and *L'Amour et la mémoire* (1931)—are evidence of his fecund hyperactivity in different media. Not so Buñuel: his other appearance in these two December 1931 issues—albeit in neither instance as a direct contributor—occurs in number 4, as a visual element in Max Ernst's 1931 collage, "Au Rendez-vous des Amis," a sequel to the artist's 1922 painting of the same name now in the MoMA (Ernst's collage is also known as *Loplop Introduces Members of the Surrealist Group*). Here, a scruffy, sullen Buñuel, clipped from a photo taken by Dalí in Cadaqués when they were working together in November 1929 on the scenario of *La Bête andalouse*, stands with an escapologist towering over him to his right and a display of knives to his left. Scorpions are also present elsewhere in this Dada-style montage of the male Surrealists, since the only woman depicted is Gala, the lover of three of the group—Dalí, Éluard, and Ernst—who repeats her equally solitary role in Ernst's 1922 picture.

If the advertisements appearing in numbers 3 and 4 of *LSASDLR* are anything to go by, the high point of Surrealism's commitment to the PCF was reached by December 1931. While the first two issues (July and October 1930) carry ads for the publishers and vendors of books by members of the group and for various galleries specializing in modern and primitive art, the third and fourth issues forego the latter and propose a host of Marxist-Leninist magazines instead—*Les Cahiers du Bolchévisme*, *La Lutte*, *L'Étudiant Pauvre*, *La Défense: Organe du Secours Rouge Internationale*, *Les Cahiers de Contre-enseignement Prolétarien*, and so on—and the writings of Hegel, Marx and Engels, Lenin and Stalin. By the time numbers 5 and 6 appeared simultaneously on 15 May 1933 the publishers, booksellers, and galleries were back, the agitprop literature gone.

Max Ernst (1891–1976), *Loplop Introduces Members of the Surrealist Group*, 1931. New York, Museum of Modern Art (MoMA). Cut-and-pasted gelatin silver prints, cut-and-pasted printed paper, pencil, and pencil frottage on paper, 19 ¾ x 13 ¼″ (50.1 x 33.6 cm). Purchase. Acc. no.: 267.1935. © 2010. (Digital image, The Museum of Modern Art, New York / Scala, Florence. © Max Ernst, VEGAP, Barcelona, 2010)

In extending his Zaragoza stay by a month Buñuel missed a crunch meeting of the Surrealists—forever on the cusp of another schism around the issue of just how much ideological ground to give to the Communists—on 6 January 1932. After deploring the PCF's philistine hostility toward recent issues of *LSASDLR*—the "pornographic" content of Dalí's "Rêverie" had outraged the party bureaucracy—Breton lamented the increasingly divided group's vulnerability to such attacks. His uneasiness was augmented by the announcement in the previous day's *L'Humanité* of the constitution of the AEAR (the French section of the UIER), the party's remodeling of his and Thirion's AAER scheme of a year before. Rumors that only the "Communist-Surrealists" would be admitted were alarming. What, Breton asked, would the position of Aragon, Sadoul, Unik, and Alexandre be if the PCF showed the other Surrealists the door?

Despite the obstructive politicking of party powerbrokers Jean Fréville and Léon Moussinac—respectively, literary editor and art/film critic of *L'Humanité*—the "Surrealist-Communists" (that is, the ones more resistant to forgoing the movement's irreducibility in the name of political expediency) pressed their claims to belong to the AEAR, but before the organization could even get off the ground another bombshell exploded. On 16 January Aragon was belatedly charged with "demoralization of the army and of the nation," as a consequence of his histrionic paean to Stalinism, "Front rouge"—a title that alludes to the KPD slogan, *Rot Front* (Red Front), pronounced with the clenched fist held high. Originally appearing in the July 1931 issue of *Littérature de la Révolution mondiale*, this poem "in the manner of Mayakovsky on an off day," as José Pierre put it, opened Aragon's new collection, *Persécuté Persécuteur*, published on 25 September 1931. If found guilty, Aragon faced a prison sentence of up to five years. Within days the group had issued a tract, "L'Affaire Aragon." The text spoke of "the magnificent words" of "Front rouge," denounced the judicial fallacy of interpreting a lyrical poem literally, and invoked the imminent "proletarian Revolution under the leadership of the Communist Party (SFIC) [French Section of the Communist International], a Revolution in the likeness of the admirable Russian Revolution that is now building Socialism in one sixth of the globe."[27] In a display of group solidarity the signatures of Alexandre, Sadoul, and Unik accompanied those of the non-PCF Surrealists. The names of Buñuel and Dalí are absent, probably due, once again, to their vulnerable status as aliens.

Buñuel was back in Paris by 25 January 1932 or so. On Friday, 29 January, two crucial events were to take place. The first was triggered by Dalí's brilliant onanistic, sodomite, and pedophile fantasy, "Rêverie." As a consequence of it, party members Aragon, Unik, Sadoul, and Alexandre had been summoned to

PCF headquarters to receive a dressing-down for their implicit approval of a text that sought "to complicate the exceedingly simple and healthy relations between men and women." Although he isn't named in some accounts of what occurred on that Friday, Buñuel accompanied them. Relating this episode to Max Aub almost forty years later, Buñuel explained, "I never belonged to the [Communist] Party. When I went with the others to *L'Huma*[*nité*] for them to be reprimanded, Aragon said, 'Comrade Buñuel's here, he's come with us.' 'Let him in,' said Legros. But I wasn't a member of the Party."[28] However, this internal dressing-down, to which "comrade Buñuel" was admitted, was related differently by one of those present, Pierre Unik, who on 30 January 1932, only one day after the event, wrote the following to Maurice Thorez, general secretary of the PCF since July 1930:

> I joined the Party last winter on my return from military service. . . . And then yesterday, 29 January, I was summoned, along with various Party comrades (Alexandre-Aragon-Sadoul and Buñuel from the Spanish CP), by a comrade from Agit-Prop in order to have to hear him say that Surrealism was a movement of bourgeois degeneration, . . . that one couldn't be at once a member of the CP and collaborate on the magazine [*LSASDLR*]. . . . What will the rank-and-file comrades say the day I have to announce to them, "Comrades, I no longer have the right to militate amongst you . . . because I'm a degenerate bourgeois." I reckon, comrade, that the mates from the rank and file will think it's a bit of a joke at first, but maybe afterwards they'll think it's a bad joke because the mates don't like to be fucked about, because the mates don't give much of a fuck whether I'm a Surrealist, dentist or somnambulist.[29]

In chronological terms, Unik's letter to Thorez is the earliest contemporary document we have that formally states that Buñuel was a member of the PCE. In the cited meeting it was not, as Buñuel said, Legros—the pseudonym of Maurice Tréand—who admonished the Communist-Surrealists, but Claude Servet, a Russian-Swiss militant whose real name was David Retchisky.[30] A former graduate of the Comintern's Lenin School and a member of the PCF's agitprop committee since February 1930, Servet presented an already prepared document condemning Dalí's text, and Surrealism in general, for the five waverers to sign. They refused to do so, and Aragon (a pornographer himself, given his 1928 novel *Le Con d'Irène*) fired off a telegram of protest to the UIER in Moscow, and the harassment ceased, at least for the time being.[31]

A couple of comments are called for here. First, why was Buñuel, a member of the PCE, convoked along with the Surrealists who were PCFers? We believe the answer is that, like any other member of a foreign Communist Party on

French soil, he was subject to the discipline of the *French* party.[32] He was not some masochistic dilettante along for the ride that day, but a militant under party control. Buñuel's mobility between France and Spain would permit him to utilize, ambiguously and to his own advantage, the contrary argument of national discipline in order to avoid tasks he deemed unpalatable or dangerous. In this, we may observe a kind of rerun of his Hollywood stay: his tactic of claiming, when it suited his purpose, to be on the French or the Spanish team. Moreover, we may infer that Buñuel—assuming he didn't lie to his French comrades—joined the PCE during his three months' stay in Spain in winter 1931–32, all of which puts a different gloss on his statement in his 27 January 1932 letter to Noailles: "Here I am, back from that long stay in Spain. These are really exciting times and if I hadn't taken a brave decision I'd have remained there for even longer."[33] Was new party member Buñuel politically active in Madrid, Zaragoza, and elsewhere? Was he in touch with the Aragon faction—the Communist-Surrealists—from afar? Did he return from Spain especially for the meeting with Servet?

That Friday, 29 January, was indeed a highly charged day, since as well as the encounter with Servet, a hundred-strong exploratory session of the AEAR took place in the evening, at which, along with Giacometti, Ernst, and Tanguy, Buñuel represented the Surrealists. The four were there to test the waters. "They received an extremely warm welcome," Éluard wrote to Gala, "but we haven't done with all the difficulties Aragon has created for us."[34] Written two days before the AEAR meeting, Buñuel's 27 January letter to Noailles as usual makes no mention of the Leftist infighting that was preoccupying its writer and his comrades; instead he keeps the chat to things cinematic. (It could be the letter of a dutiful son writing home to his father.) While *L'Âge d'or* is booked for a one-off showing in Marseilles on 15 February, and Brussels three months later, the rest of the news is bad. Buñuel's immediate career prospects look grim: the Braunberger project—the scenario he referred to in his 5 December 1931 missive to the Viscount—is on hold because Braunberger is broke, can't finish his updated version of *Fantômas* (directed by Paul Fejos, assisted by Yves Allégret and Claude Heymann), and has decided to shut down Billancourt Studios for several months. The Pathé-Nathan outfit—another potential employer, one assumes—is similarly straitened. Paramount-Joinville's Spanish duplicate versions have been put on ice. But all is not black for Buñuel: "I'm going to try and get taken on as a director in Russia, something that shouldn't be too difficult, according to what certain people in the know tell me."[35] No names are mentioned, but an educated guess would posit those of Paul Vaillant-Couturier and Louis Aragon, with the former in the pole position of power and the latter as go-between.

A founder (and at times political pariah) of the PCF, as well as chief editor of *L'Humanité* between April 1926 and September 1929, and again from July 1935 until his sudden death at the age of forty-five in October 1937, Vaillant-Couturier still awaits his biographer. In February 1932 this intellectual aider and abettor—of whom Buñuel would say: "I loved him with all my heart, a wonderful man"—returned to Paris after an eleven-month stay at Thorez's instigation in the USSR, where he'd written an enthusiastic account of the Five-Year Plan, published in three slim volumes as *Les Bâtisseurs de la vie nouvelle.*[36] While in Moscow Vaillant-Couturier also wrote a film script called *La Commune de Paris* for the Mezhrabpom studio. Slated to be directed by Erwin Piscator, this project came to nothing, but it did further the French Communist's contacts with the nascent Soviet sound cinema, just then entering a phase of ideological restructuring and needful of foreign artists to write and direct foreign-language versions of its feature films.[37] Since we return in a later chapter to the activities of Mezhrabpom and to Buñuel's ongoing interest in working for it—prior to his contract with Filmófono in May 1935—we merely remark that as expressed in his letter of 27 January 1932, his professional hopes were not to come to any fruition for some seventeen months.

Vaillant-Couturier returned to Paris with the mission of furthering the PCF's (and the Comintern's) cultural ambitions by shaping the policy of the AEAR. (The French Friends of the Soviet Union organization was another propaganda exercise mounted by him at this time.) Vaillant-Couturier's restoration to the French capital in February is synchronous with the formal launching of the AEAR and with the unfolding of the "Front rouge" controversy. Indeed, the two are intimately related, and he is in there somewhere, moving the pieces. In order to capture something of the complexity of these overdetermined politico-cultural episodes, and of the personal ambitions expressed therein of, say, Aragon and Breton, but also Buñuel, we essay a crosscutting account of them. In a later chapter we attempt a more general overview of this material.

Since the publication of "L'Affaire Aragon" in the third week of January 1932, the tensions within the Surrealist Group had mounted, with both sides—the Surrealist-Communists and the Communist-Surrealists—becoming increasingly polarized. On 29 January there had been the meeting with Servet and then the exploratory session of the embryonic AEAR. During February letters of support for "L'Affaire Aragon" came pouring in: by early March three hundred European intellectuals had endorsed the tract. Breton duly cited them at the beginning of his new thirty-page polemic, "Misère de la poésie: 'L'Affaire Aragon' devant l'opinion publique," published on 9 March. Buñuel's name is there; so is Dalí's, plus those of the other Surrealists who didn't sign the earlier tract: Ernst, Giacometti, Malet, Man Ray, Clovis Trouille, and Tzara. Spanish signatures that catch the eye are those of Altolaguirre, Arniches, Gaos, Garfias, Lacasa, Moreno Villa, Piqueras, Sánchez Ventura, Vicens, and Viñes. Among the French: Boiffard, Brunius, Dreyfus, Heine, Prévert, Vigo. And Benjamin's and Brecht's amid the German. A day or two before publication, Georges Sadoul had sent Breton a virulent letter of rupture, full of quotes from Lenin and references to the class struggle, repudiating the Surrealist leader's change of position with regard to "Front rouge" and its author. While Aragon had displayed an admirable lack of restraint in attacking the "pro-Fascist" French bourgeoisie and in toeing the Comintern line, "Front rouge" itself was, Breton now argued in "Misère de la poésie," a mere *poème de circonstance* and thus regressive from the poetic point of view. And if poetically regressive, it was, ipso facto, politically regressive too. Breton then attacked Moussinac and Fréville by brandishing, in the war of citations typical of Communist culture, Lenin against their vulgar Marxism, and by scorning the retrograde concept of proletarian art as promulgated by the PCF. In so doing he ran the risk of burning his and his co-religionists' bridges vis-à-vis the AEAR.

On 10 March, one day after the publication of Breton's tract, and even though he had, with reservations, endorsed its contents, Aragon issued the following statement in *L'Humanité*: "Our comrade Aragon informs us that he has absolutely nothing to do with the publication of a brochure entitled 'Misère de la poésie: "L'Affaire Aragon" devant l'opinion publique,' signed by André Breton. He wishes to make it clear that he disapproves of the content of this brochure in its entirety and the stir it may cause as to his name, every Communist being obliged to condemn the attacks this brochure contains as being incompatible with the class struggle, and thus objectively counter-revolutionary."[38] So be it: after a distressing twenty-four months of constant inconstancy, a friendship going back fifteen years had ended for all time. Aragon was done with Surrealism—although the movement would go on obsessing him. With Sadoul already a defector, it was only a matter of time before the other Communist-Surrealists would have to show their cards. Commenting on Aragon's about-face in a 14 March letter to Gala, Éluard bitterly remarked: "So the scoundrel shows his true character at last. Sadoul is following him. I don't know whether Buñuel will, but I fear so."[39]

On 17 March, one week after Aragon's statement, some 200 adherents were present at the AEAR's constitutive assembly. Approximately 80 were writers, 120 were artists. Buñuel was one of them. Although the PCF fraction numbered only 36, all the executive posts in this gathering of (mainly) fellow travelers went to the party's cultural commissars: Vaillant-Couturier, Moussinac, Fréville, Paul Nizan, and Aragon. Five days later the AEAR manifesto was published in

L'Humanité. After ritual condemnation of the Fascist and "Social-Fascist" bourgeoisie, the manifesto called for the propagation of a Marxist-Leninist art and literature that would pave the way for the dictatorship of the proletariat.[40] Notwithstanding the ongoing discord in its ranks, and with Aragon putting obstacles in its way from within the PCF, the Surrealist Group persisted in its ambition to play a part in the association.

Also on 17 March, Buñuel wrote to Charles de Noailles apologizing for not having been in touch because of "the eternal Surrealist complications" and went on to say that "for extremely complex reasons there has been a new split, which this time includes Aragon, Sadoul, Unik, Alexandre, Giacometti and me. The break has come about as a result of Breton's publication: 'Misère de la poésie.'"[41] Here, Buñuel situates himself among the Communist-Surrealists. (Giacometti wasn't a party member and would return to the Surrealist fold in mid-May.) Things were not so black and white, for all that: dining chez Buñuel on 13 March with Tota Cuevas and Manuel Ángeles Ortiz, the filicidal gamekeeper in *L'Âge d'or*, Crevel must have spoken of the anti-Aragon, pro-Breton tract he'd coauthored with Char and Thirion. Signed by the three authors, plus Dalí, Éluard, Ernst, Péret, Tanguy, and Tzara—the definitive Surrealist-Communists—"Paillasse! (Fin de 'L'Affaire Aragon')" was finally published sometime between 15 and 22 March.[42] Juxtaposed in it was the document disavowing Breton, Freud, and Trotsky that Aragon and Sadoul had signed in Moscow on 1 December 1930—leaked here not, as was feared at the time, by the PCF but by the Surrealists themselves!—and "Aux intellectuels révolutionnaires," the tract the two vacillators had published in Paris that same month renouncing the renunciation. It was now that a distraught Aragon sent a telegram to Buñuel, asking for his moral support: not only had the Surrealists publicly embarrassed him, but Elsa had left, and the party was debating his exclusion. (The next day Elsa was back, and Aragon would do nothing but rise in the party.) Buñuel still recalled the encounter with emotion fifty years later: "As evidence of that day, I've kept a copy of *Persecuté Persécuteur* in which Aragon wrote a dedication saying it is good, at certain times, to have friends to come and shake your hand 'when you feel there is not much time left.'"[43] In an understatement typical of their correspondence, Buñuel summed up the atmosphere for Charles de Noailles: "All these goings-on are very sad and you can imagine the terrible times we've all lived through."

All was not doom and gloom, however: there were always the movies. Aside from a "superb" Eddie Cantor musical comedy, *Palmy Days* (A. Edward Sutherland, 1931), Buñuel had recently seen "the best French film of these last few years," Jean Renoir's *La Chienne*, produced by Braunberger. Although

Buñuel had been trying to get it screened, *L'Âge d'or* seemed condemned, thanks to the censor, never to pay its way. "Apart from that, I'm often busy 'dubbing' at Paramount," he reports.

As in other missives where something momentous is involved, Buñuel casually reveals that he's received a long, violent communication from Dalí, which, he tendentiously remarks, proves that his erstwhile collaborator "now represents the Surrealist far-Right." Buñuel gives no more detail, but even if this document had not survived, we could intuit something of its vitriolic tone from an Éluard letter to the Catalan artist: much affected by Dalí's remarks, Buñuel is considering disowning *L'Âge d'or*. Éluard has been shown the letter by Unik—whom Éluard is trying to "save" from the grips of Aragon—and has replied that "if Buñuel disowns *L'Âge d'or*, I will consider that it is he who has really destroyed my 'Lion, Horse, Sleeping Woman' [*sic*]," the Dalí painting owned by the poet and lacerated by the Fascists during the Studio 28 riot of 3 December 1930.[44] Fortunately, Dalí's letter—which we date to between 10 and 16 March 1932—has survived in two forms: as a rough draft in the collection of the Fundació Gala-Salvador Dalí in Figueres, and as a transcription by Perpetua Barjau (Max Aub's wife) of a copy of the original (with a couple of annotations by Buñuel), in the Fundación Max Aub in Segorbe, this second version being the more elaborate.

It is easy to imagine how appalled Buñuel must have been by Dalí's reply to a now lost letter of his own, apparently written to defend his siding with Aragon, his disavowal of Surrealism, his acceptance of Communist Party discipline, his approbation of the tenets of Marxism-Leninism, his defense of recent Soviet films and of proletarian art, and his agreement with the AEAR project. In short, his belief in "the morrows that sing," which, as Vaillant-Couturier propagandized, Communism was preparing. Dalí was doubtless still seething about the PCF's reproof of "Rêverie" and in his letter (which is the second document of the time that speaks of Buñuel's CP membership) he wrote: "I see you completely abandon the ideas (Surrealist ones) that we'd hitherto shared and all this owing to the discipline of the party. . . . It's surprising that the mere fact of becoming a member of the Communist Party nullifies all trace of intelligence even in individuals like Aragon and you." Dalí pulled no punches when it came to the obscurantism of the Stalinists and their repressive attitude toward Surrealism, psychoanalysis, and much of modern science: "Today, everything is violently censured by the Stalinists, who are preparing the most *chaste*, backward society history has ever known: playing draughts, physical culture and so-called wholesome, natural love (!)." His letter was tantamount to a character assassination:

> Since your new Communist stance I feel you as far away as Federico [García Lorca] with his book *Romancero gitano* (!) All this represents a spiritual weakness that is frightening and makes me think that you have never felt Surrealism *the way I do*. Surrealism will succeed in reinforcing itself with the future split since such wretched political dilettantism was preventing it from developing, and we'll be able, from now on, to denounce the crap irrespective of the fact it's proletarian. Actually, it's been some time since Aragon existed as a Surrealist. You, *theoretically*, have brought nothing to Surrealism, despite the fact that *I was expecting a lot*. Surrealism is the only moral consolation there is: you have no idea of how I reproach you for your attitude. Down with the reactionary, bourgeois optimism of the Five-Year Plan! Long Live Surrealism![45]

Of interest is what Dalí says of cinema:

> As for the [Soviet] films—you seek to diminish the gravity of this matter with a phrase that is unthinkable in you: "You don't forgive their artistic errors." Artistic errors! It isn't a question of artistic errors (and there are some). The films, the proletarian literature shit, etc., etc., these are films and works with a *message*, with an aim that's exclusively to do with propaganda, they are the *exact* expression of the spiritual and moral state to which people *aspire*, these are works with a *message* not only permitted . . . by the government, but made by that selfsame government and in these films and in this literature there are nothing but *abominations*, a state of mind of pure assimilated moral crap, filthy mysticism, *concealed* sanctity, etc., etc. All this made Aragon weep when watching Dovzhenko's ignoble film *Earth*—and not due to its artfulness, but to its *spiritual content*.

Since Buñuel, his chances of directing in France or Hollywood seemingly blocked, had already announced his intention of going to the USSR to make films, should the occasion arise, Dalí's scathing allusion to Dovzhenko's grandiloquent hymn to the *kolkhoz* must have been doubly wounding. As it was, Dalí had already written to Breton on 5 March 1932 that "in Barcelona, Soviet films arouse the enthusiasm of the most bourgeois kind of audience," probably in reference to Nikolai Ekk's *The Road to Life* (1931), which had just been shown with great success in a Cineclub Mirador session at the Cine Fantasio.[46] It may even be that Dalí had taken it upon himself to lead a campaign among the Surrealists against contemporary Soviet cinema—a campaign that would have dramatic consequences, as we shall see.

Buñuel was not, as Éluard feared, to disown *L'Âge d'or* but to do something much more catastrophic: to expurgate it. Writing to Noailles on 23 March, the director confessed to feeling distanced from the spirit in which he'd made his second film—namely, the spirit of Surrealism—and needful of pastures new. (On that same day Éluard wrote to Gala: "Let Dalí rest assured as to Buñuel, Unik, Alexandre, Sadoul, Giacometti. There is no question of anyone amongst us remaining in contact with them."[47] The poet also sent her his vicious new anti-Aragon tract, "Certificat.") Buñuel went on to outline an idea proposed by Braunberger to reduce *L'Âge d'or* to a twenty-minute short—its length when first commissioned in November 1929, but which represented a third of its final running time—and to give it a different title. Since Braunberger had agreed to pay all expenses in exchange for the rights, the project would cost the Viscount nothing. Once topped and tailed, the "new" movie—renamed *Dans les eaux glacées du calcul égoïste* (*In the Icy Waters of Egoistical Calculation*, a phrase taken from *The Communist Manifesto*)—stood a chance of getting past the censors, of becoming commercially viable as a short.[48] (Just how viable, though, could a short film be in money terms?) As chance would have it, the Viscount opened Buñuel's letter of intent in the presence of Breton and Éluard, just then in Hyères: "We spoke of you with much regret," he tactfully remarked. In his reply of 25 March, Noailles, relieved, no doubt, to disburden himself of his cinematic cross, agreed to this "most elegant solution," his only request being that the sequences of the ostensory, the ever-troublesome "personage in white," and the hirsute cross be dropped.[49]

This director's cut would be postponed, however, due to the urgency of finalizing the "surprise" for the garden party to be held by the Noailles on 20 April. Buñuel's presentation would follow a concert by Georges Auric, Darius Milhaud, Francis Poulenc, Igor Markevich, and Henri Sauguet; Christian Bérard was to fancy dress the guests, Cocteau to design the programs. Given Crevel and Dalí's withdrawal from the project for political reasons, the original short-list of collaborators on Buñuel's offering was now reduced to two: Giacometti and himself. Notwithstanding his claims in October 1931 to having a viable scheme, the director was still seeking advice from the Viscount at the eleventh hour as to what form his intervention should take. This might have been the moment when, seeking inspiration, a panicky Buñuel came up with—or went back to—a piece of poetic prose of his own confection, "Une girafe," as the blueprint for an object to be mounted in the grounds of the Hyères mansion. As published, the text is a set of instructions for fabricating said object:

> This giraffe, life-sized, is a simple board cut out in the shape of a giraffe. . . . Each of its spots, which from ten or twelve feet away looks perfectly ordinary, is actually formed either by a cover that each viewer can easily open by making it

> turn on a small hinge placed invisibly on one side, or by an object, or by a hole revealing the light of day—the giraffe is only a few inches thick—or by a concavity containing the various objects detailed in the following list.
>
> It should be noted that this giraffe doesn't make complete sense until its full potential is realized, that is to say, until each of its spots performs the function for which it was intended. If this realization is extremely costly, it is not, for all that, any less possible.
>
> EVERYTHING IS ABSOLUTELY REALIZABLE.

The main body of the text then goes on to describe the micro or macro contents of each spot in hallucinatory detail: "To conceal whatever objects are behind the animal, it must be placed in front of a black wall thirty-five feet high and a hundred and thirty feet long. The surface of the wall must be intact. In front of this wall, a garden of asphodels needs to be kept up, one with the same measurements as those of the wall."[50] This was the maximum program for what would now be called an installation.

Synchronous with Surrealist interest in the object—as expounded in articles by Dalí, Giacometti, and Breton in *LSASDLR* number 3 of December 1931—"Une girafe" could be the text Buñuel confessed in that same month to not having yet written for the magazine. If this were true, then at least the first draft must have been composed between December 1931 and late January 1932 in Spain, or between late January and mid-April in Paris and Hyères, with perhaps further elaboration between the latter date and its publication in the last number of *LSASDLR* in May 1933. However, Buñuel's a posteriori account of the genesis of "Une girafe"—that it was produced, at Breton's instigation, in an hour-long fit of automatic writing—must be taken with a grain of salt.[51] This account not only reduces the complexity of automatism but seeks to legitimate the director's Surrealist orthodoxy as a practitioner of "Surrealist magic art," despite the fact that said orthodoxy had entered into crisis between December 1931 and April 1932. Whatever the truth of it, "Une girafe" is surely a contrivance, an ad hoc collage of individual short pieces: some old, originating in Buñuel's unpublished poems of the 1920s; others new. At least one section seems to be an outtake from the script of *L'Âge d'or*. Any, or all, of these segments may have been automatic in origin, but they had, as is habitual in such writing, undergone much secondary elaboration. In the absence of the original manuscript, who can say? Neither do we know whether Unik, who corrected Buñuel's French, had more than a secretarial role. What is certain is that by 10 April 1932, when Buñuel and Giacometti traveled to Hyères to actually make and install their giraffe, they had at least some ideas from which to work.

There is a snapshot of the two of them in the garden of the Noailles, standing before a rudimentary wooden cutout of a giraffe some twelve feet tall. The picture must have been taken on or around 20 April. Hands in his pockets, Buñuel has a relaxed, devil-may-care mien. Giacometti, on the other hand, looks furtive, ill at ease; he seems to be holding up his pants, as if he thought he might be caught with them down. Can this crude, cutout creature, with its clear echoes of the defenestrated giraffe in *L'Âge d'or*, really have taken ten days to construct? The markings, remember, were hinged doors behind which were written descriptions of twenty ghastly and blasphemous bits of business: recipes for a series of kinetic assemblages. Yet one looks in vain for hinge or handle on this lay figure. On the day, did Buñuel function as a fairground barker and simply read out the list of contents? As it was, the Noailles were apparently deceived: "It'd been announced to the guests that there was a surprise," Buñuel tells us. "Before dining they were requested, with the help of a wooden stepladder, to go and read the inside of the spots. They obeyed and seemed to enjoy it. After coffee I returned with Giacometti to the garden. The giraffe was gone. It had completely vanished, without any explanation. Had it been thought too scandalous, after the scandal of *L'Âge d'or*? I don't know what became of the giraffe. Charles and Marie-Laure never made any allusion to it in my presence. And I didn't dare ask the reason for this sudden banishment."[52] His rationalization of this disappearing act, that the giraffe was too transgressive for his patrons, doesn't stand up to scrutiny. How could such acculturated, avant-garde aristos have been fazed? Didn't they know their man? The embarrassment was surely of some other kind.

While the Hyères cutout is far from being scandalous, the text as published *is*. Akin to the numbered shots in a film *découpage*, each of the twenty niches frames an ever more sadistic staging, describes an interactive object or event "with a symbolic function" (to use a Dalinian term of the time). An example of one such delirious object would be the nineteenth spot: "A model less than three feet square representing the Sahara Desert beneath an overwhelming light. Covering the sand, a hundred thousand miniature Marists made of wax, their white aprons standing out against their cassocks. In the heat, the Marists melt little by little. (Several million Marists must be kept in reserve.)" Yet among the disorienting details there are some that are more limpidly autobiographical, akin to those opening long shots in a movie that establish time and place. In spot 1, for instance, is an album of photos of "very miserable, tiny and deserted squares. They are those of old Castilian towns." In spot 6, a washerwoman (Buñuel's mother) scrubbing clothes in a river. In spot 11, seen through a hole punched in a pig's bladder, "a very poor cottage [in Masada del Vicario, four

Buñuel, Giacometti, and their giraffe cutout in the garden at the "Chateau de Dé," the home of the Noailles in Hyères, in April 1932. (Centro Buñuel Calanda, Spain / Courtesy Javier Espada and Herederos de Luis Buñuel)

miles from Calanda], whitewashed, in the midst of a desert landscape. . . . At this moment an old plowman will perhaps come out of the house, barefoot." To emphasize these specifically Spanish allusions is to create an artificial order in the mixed bag that is this Surrealist text, but we do so because Buñuel's deadpan evocations of a premodern, feudal land of dusty rural backwaters, landless peasants, Catholic icons, and putrefaction are to resound in his next film, *Las Hurdes*.

That Unik was called upon to lend Buñuel a hand is of some relevance to the future, to his participation in the writing and filming of *Terre sans pain*.

Sadoul, it will be recalled, had quit Surrealism on 7 March 1932; Aragon three days later. Of the Communist-Surrealists, that left Unik, Alexandre, and Buñuel still out on a limb. On 5 April Unik and Alexandre published "Autour d'un poème," their take on recent events. For them, Breton's ultimately idealist assessment of "Front rouge" was erroneous; yet Aragon, too trusting in the anorexic ideology of proletarian art, was wrong to denounce him as a counter-revolutionary.[53] In a context in which the battle lines were clearly drawn, their even-handed assessment can have pleased no one. Unik and Alexandre now inhabited a no-man's land between Surrealism and Communism. Buñuel continued to drag his feet.

Leaving Hyères on 21 April, Buñuel traveled east to Monte Carlo with another Noailles houseguest, composer Roger Désormière, who was to conduct a series of Ballets Russes performances there. The Spaniard's fantasies of spending a libidinous weekend in the principality misfired and by Sunday 24 April he was back in Paris. Three days later there was a private screening of "the famous Surrealist film by Luis Buñuel" under the aegis of a film society called Les Spectateurs de l'Avant-Garde, at La Bellevilloise, a cinema run by a workers' cooperative in the twentieth arrondissement. Supporting *L'Âge d'or* was a program "chosen by the filmmaker," the contents of which are unknown to us. This screening, which would be repeated on 30 April, was organized by Jacques Brunius and Jean-Paul Dreyfus—collaborators, both, on *L'Âge d'or*—who'd taken over the three-year-old film society in January 1932, remodeling it along the lines of the defunct Amis de Spartacus and upping the class war rhetoric of the house magazine, *Spectateurs*. "A couple of screenings of the film have been given in the most complete silence," Buñuel dolefully remarked to Noailles two weeks after the event. "At the end, a bit of applause, with the public shuffling out very depressed. No protests."[54] Three among the audience had not been so lukewarm, however: documentarists Jean Vigo, Boris Kaufman, and Henri Storck were enthused by *L'Âge d'or* at the second Spectateurs session and during a month's stay in Paris would regularly meet Buñuel in the Closerie de Lilas.[55] In a first flush of enthusiasm, the politico-cultural orientation of the month-old AEAR—or more precisely, of its "photo-cinema section"—must have been a major topic of conversation between them.

Aside from Buñuel and Vigo, both of them activists in the photo-cinema section, the latter included Moussinac (its chief ideologue), his brother-in-law Jean Lods, Jean Painlevé, Man Ray (briefly), J-A Boiffard, Henri Cartier(-Bresson), Maurice Henry, Jean Lévy, Yves Allégret, and Eli Lotar. Dreyfus and Brunius were also members, which suggests that the April screenings of *L'Âge d'or* squared with the AEAR project. Sympathizers included Joris Ivens, Storck, and Kaufman (brother of Dziga Vertov and Mikhail Kaufman). We lack detail on the activities of the section during this early period, but it would seem that it followed the directives of the UIER's "cinema bureau" in Moscow. In the short term this involved the showing, in a film society context, of the work of the Russian directors Dalí excoriated in his mid-March letter to Buñuel. In the longer term it included the producing of workerist documentaries and newsreels focusing on the class struggle. Although there is evidence that a series of *Actualités prolétariennes* was in production by mid-1933, a more ambitious film-making program would only take off in November 1935 with the founding of the Alliance du Cinéma Indépendant, and then in August 1936 with its metamorphosis, the Ciné-Liberté cooperative.[56]

The two private screenings of *L'Âge d'or* at La Bellevilloise were low-key affairs, announced only in a dozen Parisian bookshops. One of these was the Librairie Oliviero in the sixth arrondissement, run by Yolande Oliviero, "a slightly lame but very beautiful bookseller," as Buñuel describes her in *Mon dernier soupir*. There, he evokes the evenings spent playing Surrealist games with Oliviero, Pierre Unik, and Unik's seventeen-year-old girlfriend Agnès Capri, plus "a photographer called Denise."[57] The latter was Denise Bellon, and both she and Oliviero were recent recruits to Surrealism during the convulsions following Aragon's 10 March 1932 communiqué in *L'Humanité*. The two women would contribute to the experimental research into irrational knowledge published in the last *LSASDLR*, the same number in which "Une girafe" appeared. Bellon, the cofounder in 1934 of one of the first photo press agencies in Paris, was to photograph the famous mannequins displayed at the 1938 Exposition Internationale du Surréalisme. Oliviero was on the literary panel of the AEAR (as was Unik and, briefly, Breton) and acted in the agitprop stage performances mounted by the Groupe Octobre. In 1936 she had a bit part in the film Renoir supervised for the PCF, *La Vie est à nous*. Also an AEAR stalwart, future chanteuse and nightclub owner Capri was a friend of the Préverts; Buñuel would use her as an actress in *La Voie lactée* (1969) and *Le Fantôme de la liberté* (1974). These soirées, which are partly dateable to February 1933, demonstrate the relatively fluid nature of personal relationships in and around Surrealism: the reluctance to break once and for all with one's erstwhile comrades; the wish to keep one's options open.

There were, however, moments of plain speaking, of the emphatic taking of a position. One such is Buñuel's letter of demission. Although for Breton there can have been little mystery about Buñuel's political alignment since mid-March 1932, it was only a month and a half later that the cineaste formalized his break in writing. Why? Ambivalence? Procrastination? Cowardice? Whatever the reason, on 6 May 1932 the director finally did type and post a six-hundred-word missive to the Surrealist leader. In terms of chronology, this document is the third we possess that states Buñuel was a CP member, and the second to declare that he was a member of the PCE. More importantly, it is the first in which the subject himself declares this. Here is the letter in full:

102

Paris 6 Mai 1932

Mon cher Breton : Je ne crois pas que malgré mon retard,ne soit encore temps de,par cette lettre,prendre position vis a vis du groupe surréaliste et faire face aux dernières évenènents qui ont marqué une étape aussi particulièrement grave dans l'avenir même du surréalisme.

Quand il y a quelques années j'ai voulu joindre mon activité a la votre,je voyais -a part d'autres qualités d'ordre purement poétique- le grand reconfort moral,autentiquement subversif representé par le surréalisme,se dressant impitoyablement contre la pourriture intelectuelle de la bourgeoisie dont moi même je sortais et contre laquelle depuis longtemps je m'étais revolté. Le seul fait d'avoir uni mon prope devenir ideologique a celui du surréalisme a pû me conduire quelque temps après a donner mon adhesion au P.C.E. et je vois là,tant subjective qu'objectivement,une preuve de la valeur revolutionnaire du surréalisme,ma position actuelle étant la consequence obligée de notre collaboration de ces dernières années. Il y a seulement quelques mois je ne croyais pas a la possibilité qu'une contradiction apparemment violente allait se lever entre ces deux disciplines,surréaliste et communiste. Or,les derniers événements on demontré qu'aujourd'hui ces deux activités semblent être incompatibles,et d'une part et de l'autre. Vous comprendrez,que sans ma recente adhesion au P.C. -avec tout ce que cela represente dans le terrain ideologique et pratique-le problème ne se poserait même pas et que je continuerais a travailler avec vous,mais dans l'état de choses actuelle ne saurait être question pour un communiste de douter un instant entre le choix de son parti et de n'importe quelle autre activité ou discipline. Je ne me crois pas très doué politiquement et je pretends que mes possibilités seraient plus avantageusement employées dans le surréalisme mais il me manque la conviction que je servirait mieux la revolution parmi vous que militant dans le parti auquel,tout de même,j'ai des moyens pour aider.

Le fait de ma separation de votre activité n'implique pas l'abandon total de TOUTES vos conceptions mais seulement de celles qu'AUJOURD'HUI s'oppossent a l'acceptation du surréalisme par le P.C. et que,je veux bien le croire,sont d'ordre purement formel et passager. Par exemple,poétiquement,il n'est pas question que je puisse avoir d'autres conceptions que les votres tout en pensant qu'il est impossible aujourd'hui

de maintenir une conception "fermée" de la poésie au dessus de 103
la lutte de classes. C'est dans ce mot "fermée" que j'appuie une possible discrepance avec vous. La valeur subversive même de la poésie hors de ce contenu de classe ne pourra être que subjetive sans que cette consideration m'empeche de penser que, du point de vue emotive et de l'amour le poème "Union Libre" ne soit pour moi tout ce qu'il y a de plus admirable. Je ne suis pas appelé a resoudre ce difficile problème et en attendant je me contents d'admettre, a coté de la poésie telle que vous l'entendez ou plutôt telle que je l'entends d'après le surréalisme, une forme d'expression moins pure qui puisse servir pour la propagande et qui arrive a toucher directement aux masses. C'est dans ce sens que j'ai toujours aimé le poème "Front Rouge", ou tout au moins son intention.

Avant de finir cette lettre, que j'ai reduite juste pour dire l'essenciel, je veux vous exprimer également mon desaccord total et profond avec les tracts et brochure qui ont suivi "Misère de la Poésie", et tout specialement avec "Paillasse". Comme j'ai toujours crû, je continue a croire a votre sincerité de revolutionnaire mais cela n'empeche que, si je tiens compte des "circomstances" qui ont precedé l'accusation dans l'Huma de votre brochure par Aragon, et du sens "stricte et litteral" de la dite accusation, je puisse le moins du monde me joirdre a rien venant du groupe surréaliste, et qui tenterait de ruiner l'activité revolutionnaire d'Aragon dont l'affaire est loin d'être fini.

Très amicalement votre

Bunuel

Buñuel's letter to Breton of 6 May 1932, in which he announced his abandonment of Surrealism after he joined the Spanish Communist Party. (Bibliothèque nationale de France, Paris)

My dear Breton: I don't believe my lateness means there is still not time, through this letter, to take a position vis-à-vis the Surrealist Group and to confront the recent events that have marked a particularly serious stage in the very future of Surrealism.

When a few years ago I sought to unite my activity to yours, I saw—apart from other qualities of a purely poetic kind—the great, authentically subversive moral consolation represented by Surrealism pitilessly rising up against the intellectual putrescence of the bourgeoisie from which I myself came and against which I had long since rebelled. The sole fact of having united my ideological development to that of Surrealism has contrived to lead me some time later to give my adherence to the PCE and I see in this, both subjectively and objectively, a proof of the revolutionary value of Surrealism, my current position being the unavoidable consequence of our collaboration during these last few years. Only a few months ago I did not envisage the possibility that a seemingly violent contradiction was going to arise between these two disciplines, Surrealist and Communist. As it is, recent events have demonstrated that these two activities appear to be incompatible today, from one side as well as from the other. You will understand that without my recent adherence to the CP—with all that this represents in the ideological and practical realm—the problem would not even crop up and that I would continue working with you, but in the current state of things there can be no question of a Communist doubting for a moment about the choice between his party and any other activity or discipline. I don't consider myself very gifted politically and I maintain that my possibilities would be more advantageously employed in Surrealism but I lack the conviction that I would serve the revolution better among you than by militating in the party to which, nevertheless, I have [obliterated] the means to help.

The fact of my separation from your activity does not imply the total abandonment of ALL your conceptions but only of those that TODAY stand in the way of the acceptance of Surrealism by the CP and that, I would really like to believe, are of a formal and momentary kind. For example, poetically, there is no question that I could have other conceptions than your own while thinking that it is impossible today to maintain a "closed" conception of poetry that is above the class struggle. It is on the word "closed" that I base a possible discrepancy. The actual subversive value of poetry outside this class content cannot but be subjective, without this consideration preventing me from thinking that from the emotive point of view and that of love the poem "L'Union libre" represents for me all that is most admirable. I am not called upon to resolve this difficult problem and in the meantime I am content to admit, alongside poetry such as you understand it or rather such as I understand it according to Surrealism, a less pure form of expression which might serve as propaganda and which manages to directly touch the masses. It is in that sense that I've always liked the poem "Front rouge," or at least its intention.

Before ending this letter, which I've kept short so as to say just what is essential, I also want to express to you my complete and profound disagreement with the tracts and brochure that have come after "Misère de la poésie," and particularly with "Paillasse." I continue, as I always have, to believe in your sincerity as a revolutionary but this doesn't mean, if I take into account the "circumstances" that preceded the indictment in L'Huma[nité] of your brochure by Aragon, and the "strict and literal" meaning of said indictment, that I can by any means join in with anything proceeding from the Surrealist Group, and which would attempt to destroy the revolutionary activity of Aragon, whose affair is *far* from being over.

With my very best wishes,

Bunuel.[58]

Buñuel's reframing of the moral-poetic imperative is patent here: morally, Communism takes precedence over Surrealism; poetically, objective propaganda has the edge over subjective hermeticism. "Front rouge" is of more service to the Revolution than Breton's lyrical love poem "L'Union libre." As a militant, Buñuel is prepared to submit his moral and aesthetic activities to party control. Although there are several allusions to the fact of becoming a party member in the letter, they are too vague to really help us to date this precisely. That said, the fact that the cineaste joined the PCE would suggest that this occurred on Spanish soil—otherwise he'd have entered the PCF—thus endorsing our suggestion that this step was taken between 26 October 1931 and 25 January 1932, during Buñuel's extended stay in Madrid, Zaragoza, and Toledo, and at a time when many friends or intellectual companions of his generation had taken or were taking the same step.

That Buñuel was an activist in the PCE, at least in the short term, is borne out by an anecdote that he relates in his memoirs. There we read: "During a meeting of foreign labor held in Montreuil-sous-Bois, in the suburbs of Paris, I was brought face to face with Casanellas, one of the supposed murderers of Prime Minister Dato. Having taken refuge in Russia and become a colonel in the Red army, he was in France clandestinely. As the meeting was dragging on and on and I was getting a bit bored, I got up to go. One of the participants then said to me: 'If you go and Casanellas gets arrested, it's you who'll have denounced him.' I sat down again."[59] This secret meeting can be dated to between April 1932 and the end of October 1933, when the former anarchist and now Communist Ramón Casanellas Lluch—the assassin, with syndicalists Pedro Matheu and Luis Nicolau, of Spanish prime minister Eduardo Dato in March 1921—arrived secretly from Moscow as an emissary of the Comintern and member of the politburo of the PCE in Paris, from where he was bound for Barcelona with the mission to "embark on an active struggle against the National Confederation of Labor [CNT]."[60] Casanellas would die in a motorcycle accident on 27 October 1933. Although Buñuel recounts the incident as if it were an almost irrelevant fact, it is obvious that in a clandestine political meeting with a Red Army colonel on a subversive mission, not just anybody would have been admitted.

As a footnote to the episode of the letter to Breton, in later life the director would come to regard "L'Union libre" as his "finest literary souvenir of Surrealism."[61] Likewise, the seventy-seven-year-old Aragon would opine that it was "a poem that is perhaps the finest, the greatest, of this century," while his own "Front rouge" had become "that poem I detest."[62] Back then, however, Buñuel, like Sadoul, like Unik, would walk in the shadow of "Le Paysan de Tout-Paris"—as the Surrealists later dubbed him—for most of the 1930s. On 6 June, one month after the letter to Breton, we find Buñuel interceding between the Stalinist poet and the Viscount, trying to sell the latter the manuscript of *Persecuté Persécuteur*—which included "Front rouge."[63] The sale was of some urgency: Aragon and Triolet were to leave the next day on their second trip to the Soviet Union—a visit that would secure the poet (and his spouse) star billing in the cultural apparat of the party—and desperately needed money. Their stay would last ten months, during which time Aragon was to strengthen the links between the UIER and the AEAR, and like other *engagé* writers and filmmakers, to compose his canticle to the new industrial complex at Magnitogorsk, a poem cycle called *Hourra l'Oural*. While in Moscow the couple would attempt to repay Buñuel by touting for work for him there as a director.

Buñuel's status as a Communist was not unknown in Spanish intellectual circles. In a later portrait, Ernesto Giménez Caballero described him thus: "Surrealist, revolutionary and anti-everything. Buñuel: Paris, Russia, Mexico."[64] Carlos Fernández Cuenca, when studying Republican cinema during the Spanish Civil War, wrote: "The two great hopes for the Communist party as regards cinema were Juan Piqueras and Luis Buñuel," information confirmed by the Communist filmmaker Antonio del Amo, who worked under him during the *contienda*.[65] For his part, Buñuel's friend Carlos Saura declared: "I see him much more as an anarchist than as a Communist, although he was in the Party—he said he wasn't, but it's known he was."[66] And Santiago Carrillo recalled that in the Paris of the 1960s, "we always treated each other as comrades."[67] The most conclusive testimony comes, however, from the Communist poet Rafael Alberti, who complained to Max Aub: "I don't understand how it's possible for Luis to repeatedly deny having been in the party. How come, if he was in it until 1940?"[68]

We have observed how one bone of contention between Buñuel and Dalí was their respective vision of cinema; that their personal credos differed as to the value of the Communist propaganda produced by the Stalinized Soviet film industry; that Buñuel felt compelled to state in March 1932: "I find myself very far from the spirit of *L'Âge d'or* and I dream of new things that are a far cry from my last film."[69]

Unlike Buñuel, who'd produced no theoretical writing since becoming a Surrealist—"You, *theoretically*, have brought nothing to Surrealism, despite the fact that *I was expecting a lot*," being Dalí's reproach—the Catalan was a preeminent theorist who, on the cinematic plane, would make his position clear in a new book, a book that demonstrated his fidelity, in practical filmmaking terms, to the frenetic line traced out in *Un chien andalou* and *L'Âge d'or*, and his infidelity, in aesthetic terms, to many of the positions he, in concert with Buñuel, had held in their pre-Surrealist days (1927–29). That book, published in July 1932, was *Babaouo*.[70]

7

Time-Serving at Paramount-Joinville

When it came to the rather unproductive phase that followed the repression of his second film and his separation from the Surrealist Group, Buñuel wrote in the July 1939 autobiography he drafted in the United States: "To earn a living I began to collaborate anonymously in my profession, entering as a writer in Paramount Studios in Paris, adapting pictures from English to Spanish."[1] In fact, following his return from Hollywood and his subsequent trip to Spain, where he witnessed the proclamation of the Second Republic, Buñuel told Charles de Noailles that he was seeking gainful employment and was contemplating the possibility of entering the Spanish section of Paramount, although he didn't want to work there as a director.[2] The banning of *L'Âge d'or*, along with the uncertainty involved in the shift from silent to sound cinema and the professional frustration he had just suffered at MGM, had put Buñuel in a difficult position, but in order to preserve his prestige he was not prepared to become a director of Paramount's insipid, standardized talkies. Anonymous, subaltern work in the company's Spanish section was more palatable to him.

Paramount's plan to produce sound films in different languages in France was a complex affair. In May 1929 Jesse L. Lasky, studio vice-president, traveled to France in the company of Walter Wanger, his production manager, and announced his project for multilingual production to the press. In December of that year *Cinémagazine* informed its readers: "One of Hollywood's most important producers, Robert T. Kane, has announced the creation of a Franco-American group with a capital of 250 million francs for the production of talkies filmed entirely in French; the first movie should be finished by 15 April [1930]. The Studios des Réservoirs in Joinville have been rented on a long-term basis and carpenters and bricklayers are there getting ready for the equipping of the studios with Western Electric machines. The production contemplated is for twenty-four films a year, maybe more."[3]

Kane would become, in effect, the architect of a project that far outstripped this initial idea. His participation as an officer in World War I had won him the Belgian Croix de Guerre, but he spoke neither French nor any other European language. In the States he had worked as an independent producer for Paramount and First National. In 1928 he'd begun running the small New York company Sound Studios Inc., which, equipped with RCA's Photophone system, sonorized such famous silent films as *King of Kings* (Cecil B. DeMille, 1927).

In January 1930, with the backing of film distributor Adolphe Osso, managing director of the Société Française des Films Paramount founded in Paris in 1920, Kane began renting Gaumont's former Studios des Réservoirs in Joinville-le-Pont, some six miles southeast of Paris. After the renovating and modernizing of its five stages and then an adjacent studio in Saint-Maurice, the complex, which officially opened in April, had seven stages and its own laboratories. While this modernization work was underway, Kane began his multilingual production in March 1930 in the old Gaumont studios in Buttes Chaumont with an adaptation of the comedy *Un trou dans le mur* by Yves Mirande and Gustave Quinson, directed by René Barbéris. To take advantage of the same sets, within a month were added a Spanish version, *Un hombre de suerte*, directed by Benito Perojo (with dialogues by Pedro Muñoz Seca), and a Swedish one, *När rosorna sla ut*, by Edvin Adolphson.

At the closing dinner of the annual Paramount congress held in Paris in March 1930, Osso announced the agreement signed with Kane to distribute the French-speaking movies that his company, Société Cinéstudio Continental, was going to produce in France. The fusion between Kane and Paramount would not be legally formalized until July 1930, an event reprised by *La Cinématographie Française*: "The Société Cinéstudio Continental has assumed the new name of Studios Paramount and has increased its capital from 6M to 10M francs."[4] In the new managerial structure Kane became the managing director of the company, presided over by J. C. Graham, with Osso as vice-president. Kane was seconded in turn by two trusted assistants, Richard Blumenthal and Jacob Karol.

In frantic shift work, Paramount's round-the-clock production spooled out, as the company's own publicity had it, in fourteen different languages: French,

Swedish, Spanish, Italian, German, Portuguese, Czech, Danish, Hungarian, Rumanian, Yugoslavian, Polish, Norwegian, and Russian.[5] According to Donald Crafton, in relation to the initial figures announced, the first year's spectacular increase in output was because the costs of this venture were much lower than if the films had been produced in Hollywood.[6] The accelerated rate of production and the criteria of standardization that gave rise to such a reduced outlay led to a series of anodyne, impersonal films, and it is perfectly understandable that Buñuel would wish not to figure as the director of any of them. It is also worth pointing out that Kane, aware of the phenomenon, decided to recruit a few directors with cultural credentials in an attempt to artistically "gentrify" his output. He signed up Alberto Cavalcanti, whose Impressionist film *Rien que les heures* had been praised by Buñuel, and the Brazilian director made five titles for the company.[7] Although the first of these, *Toute sa vie* (the 1930 French version of Dorothy Arzner's *Sarah and Son*, the Portuguese version of which was also filmed by Cavalcanti), was deserving of polite praise from Juan Piqueras, the fact is that this phase of Cavalcanti's career has been forgotten.[8] Kane also signed up another prestigious director with avant-garde connections, the Estonian Dimitri Kirsanoff, but his *Les Nuits de Port Said* remained unfinished, the ruins of it being used by the Austrian Leo Mittler—who'd directed the "proletarian" movie *Jenseits der Strasse* (1929) for the Communist concern Prometheus Film GmbH in Berlin—to flesh out the film of the same name released by the studio in French, German, and Spanish versions. Kirsanoff, the sensitive avant-garde director of *Ménilmontant* (1926) and *Brumes d'automne* (1929), who was, according to Georges Sadoul, a precursor of French poetic realism and Italian neorealism, would never rediscover his creative impetus.[9] In the meantime Mittler ventured to direct the Spanish-speaking *La incorregible* (1931) for the studio.

The picturesque figure of Ricardo Baroja was one who tried his luck as an actor there—he played in *La incorregible*—and he has bequeathed us a sarcastic account of the time he misspent in Joinville:

> A gigantic doorman in full uniform was the man in charge of asking for the personal details of all those who sought to enter there. Never were the precautions taken in the most carefully guarded fortress greater.
>
> The doorman's office was a cavernous room with benches along the walls. Seated on them were lots of men, lots of women. Young men and young women. All elegantly dressed, all with the eccentric appearance of circus people or comedians. Rouged cheeks, painted lips, red-varnished nails. . . . The studios form a conglomeration of hangars, hastily knocked together in brick. Some painted grey; others, bottle-green. . . . The disorganization of the big

> American company is there for all to see, apparently. Here, everyone, without being useful for much, is useful for everything. He who was hired as a set painter is assigned to literary (!) correction of the translations made from English into the other languages. If he's an electrical technician working on sound recording he occupies the post of head gardener. The dancer becomes a make-up artist, the hairdresser a film director, the electrician has to accompany the foreign actresses around Paris. You'd say the most irrational people of Europe and America have gathered on the banks of the Marne to gobble up the dollars contributed by gullible American shareholders.[10]

Buñuel offered his services as an employee in Paramount's Spanish section, doubtless because his anonymity would be better protected there than in the French section, and so as not to sully his good name with his ever-sensitive Surrealist colleagues. One of these, Albert Valentin, would be expelled at the end of 1931, in point of fact, for having worked as René Clair's assistant on *À nous la liberté*, a film denounced by Éluard and Crevel as being "seriously counterrevolutionary."[11]

Launched by Benito Perojo in April 1930, the helm of Paramount's Spanish production was almost immediately taken by the Chilean actor and director Adelqui Millar, who had begun his film career in Holland in 1916 and pursued it in England in 1922.[12] From May 1930 onward Millar would make six films at Paramount, becoming the driving force of the Spanish-speaking section and its most prolific director, as well as making an incursion into Francophone production. According to Piqueras, the running of the section was confided to Mittler in February 1931.[13] Paramount's Spanish production totaled seventeen features, plus two shorts that brought it to a close in December 1932: *La casa es seria*, by the Frenchman Jaquelux (Lucien Tonlet, whose Spanish credentials resided in the fact that he'd just directed, with the help of Germaine Dulac, a film called *Le Picador*), and *Buenos días* by Florián Rey.

Leo Mittler's leadership of the Spanish section, if indeed he really exercised it, was very brief. In June 1931 the weekly magazine *Popular Film* announced that the Canary Islands writer Claudio de la Torre had been hired to create the Spanish literary department in Joinville and to choose the films that were to be shot there in that language.[14] Five years older than his friend Buñuel, de la Torre had been educated at Brighton College and the Crystal Palace School of Engineering in London, which vouched for his linguistic competence as far as the American company was concerned. In 1924 he'd been awarded the National Literature Prize in Spain and had made a name for himself as a successful playwright. His friendship with Buñuel was a close one, as expressed in his article

"El tranvía al ralenti (Caminos para Luis Buñuel)," in which the writer attempted to replicate, in literary form, the slow-motion effect of film in the tram ride taking him to the studios in Épinay where Jean Epstein was shooting *La Chute de la maison Usher*—with the Aragonese filmmaker as his assistant—a film that repeatedly used slow-motion photography for dramatic effect.[15]

De la Torre's connection with Paramount Studios would last until 1934, and he would fulfill a variety of tasks. He was the writer and adapter of dialogues in Spanish for *¿Cuándo te suicidas?*, which the Argentinean Manuel Romero filmed in August 1931, and for *El cliente seductor*, shot that same summer by Richard Blumenthal to promote Maurice Chevalier's movie *The Smiling Lieutenant*, directed in Hollywood by Ernst Lubitsch, in the Spanish-speaking market. When Paramount abandoned their multilingual versions of American films and decided to adapt original scripts alone, de la Torre directed a film in French, *Pour vivre heureux* (1932), described by Harry Waldman as a "little-seen, mildly cynical" comedy.[16]

Buñuel was able to start working at Paramount thanks to de la Torre, but their collaboration was somewhat overshadowed by the campaign Piqueras was mounting against Spanish-speaking versions. On 29 June 1930 he had published an article in the Madrid newspaper *El Sol* entitled "Paris-Cinema: The Translation of Yankee Films Presents a Danger for European Cinema." In a letter he wrote from Paris to Nicolás Planells on 20 November 1930, when Buñuel was living in Hollywood, Piqueras explained that he'd been involved in a polemic "in a French paper with a local journalist who defended Paramount (from whom I didn't want to accept 5,000 francs a month for an unlimited period)."[17] This attempted bribe would be mentioned in June of the following year in an interview with Benique Sellés, in which Piqueras explained that "Paramount wanted to deprive me of my independence with a few thousand francs a month."[18] At the time Buñuel was on the point of joining Paramount, where he would once again rub shoulders with another frustrated MGM colleague: Claude Autant-Lara.

Claudio de la Torre's arrival in Joinville in summer 1931 occurred at the traumatic moment multilingual production was suffering an unexpected interruption. During the second half of the year the specialized French press repeatedly published reassuring communiqués from Paramount denying that its multilingual production was about to be canceled. In December 1931 and January 1932 the trade journal *La Cinématographie Française* published various reports about the poor economic results of American Spanish-speaking productions, specifying that their exploitation in Spain recovered 60 percent of their cost, the remaining revenue being obtained in the depressed markets of Latin America.[19]

The Spanish film press also anxiously followed the development of the situation in Joinville. In February 1932 a note in *Popular Film* informed readers that M. Bacos, the treasurer of Paramount Studios in Joinville, had returned after conferring with the company heads in New York about the new program for the films to be made that year in French and Spanish.[20] In December 1932, the month in which Spanish-speaking production was definitively canceled in France, the American magazine in Spanish, *Cinelandia*, published a message of optimism, announcing Paramount's unexpected decision to resume the large-scale "synchronization" of films in Spanish. Sixteen films were to be synchronized—that is, dubbed—eight made in French at Paramount-Joinville and a further eight shot in English in Hollywood.[21] By then it was clear that dubbing—which Mussolini had imposed as a patriotic obligation in Italy in October 1930 and which was more or less perfected as a technique—was going to become, along with subtitling, a simple and cheap alternative to multilingual versions.

The Paramount-Joinville move to dubbing, an episode Ilya Ehrenburg satirized in his *Fábrica de sueños* (*Dream Factory*, 1931), also posed certain union problems.[22] In July 1930 the Artistes Union of France forbade its members to take part in the dubbing of foreign films, which was considered a "plundering of the personality of the actor." This union conflict did not spill over into the Spanish dubbing section where Buñuel was working at the considerable salary of 300 francs a day.[23] On 17 March 1932, right in the middle of the ongoing political crisis of the Surrealist Group, the proletarianized filmmaker wrote to the Viscount de Noailles, "I'm often busy with 'dubbing' work at Paramount." Given that Buñuel declared on one occasion that he worked for two years at this task,[24] it must be inferred that it occupied him until 1934, the year of his marriage to Jeanne Rucar and of de la Torre's dismissal by Paramount. His occupation there was intermittent, however, for in the summer of 1932 he spent time in Sallent de Gallego (Huesca), Jaca, Zaragoza, and San Sebastián, and in the spring of 1933 he shot his documentary about Las Hurdes in Spain, although after finishing it he rejoined Paramount in June. At the beginning of 1934 Buñuel began to collaborate on dubbing work for Warner Bros. in Madrid. By July 1935, when yet another plan for reorganizing a debilitated Paramount was approved by its top brass, the studio's European adventure already belonged to the past.

To begin with, Buñuel worked at Joinville under the orders of the Slovakian-German Rudolf Sieber, the husband of Marlene Dietrich. In 1923 this obscure figure had been the assistant of Joe May, a highly successful director of adventure serials, on *Tragödie der Liebe*. In a casting session for it Sieber chose the young, almost unknown actress, a Max Reinhardt alumna, for a small role.

He soon became the lover and artistic mentor of Dietrich, whom he married in May 1923, and in December of the following year they had their only child, Maria. Following the success of *The Blue Angel*, directed by Josef von Sternberg (a Viennese Jew like Joe May), the actress—by now Sternberg's lover—traveled to Hollywood in April 1930 at Paramount's request, while Sieber remained in Berlin, working as an assistant producer for its German subsidiary. Different versions exist about their separation. Some claim that Sieber, who had met a new companion, refused to go to Hollywood in order just to become "Mr. Dietrich." Others assert that Paramount moved Sieber from Berlin and found a post for him in Paris in order to be done with the idle gossip and off-color jokes in his professional milieu, since the love affair between his wife and Sternberg was well known. And a still further version alleges that after visiting his wife in Hollywood in summer 1931, Sieber was incorporated into the Joinville studios in August because Sternberg himself negotiated his new position with executives of the company. The real reason may have contained ingredients from all three versions.

During this period Buñuel managed to seriously study English and on 15 September 1932 was promoted to head of dubbing, for on 14 November of that same year he wrote to Noailles, "I've been two months at Paramount as head of Spanish dubbing and I usually work from six in the afternoon to two in the morning."[25] Employed under him on the afternoon/night shift was the musician Gustavo Durán, an interesting and complex figure if ever there was one, since after his Communist militancy in the Spanish Civil War he would work for the American State Department and the United Nations. In his travailing Buñuel fell back on the voices of friends of his who were living in Paris, such as the Granada painter Manuel Ángeles Ortiz—who'd acted in *L'Âge d'or*—who has left an eloquent account of his experience:

> I remember the dubbing of a film in which the owner of a factory had a son and it was the first child that was born there. All Buñuel did was say to me, "Go easy with your Andalusian accent, the film is in Castilian [i.e., formal Spanish]." And I replied, "A worker can be from anywhere." But he insisted, "No, Manolo, no, in Castilian." That was very difficult for me. We rehearsed the scenes a few times and I always came in at the wrong time, because I was nervous about the accent and I wasn't able to synchronize voice with image. Until one day Luis said to me, "Look, I'll be at your side and the minute I give you a signal by pressing my knee against yours, you do your stuff." But as I was so nervous, when he gave me the sign I started stammering horribly and that was the end of my dubbing work. It was a pity because they paid you well and I had a lot of fun.[26]

Also in Buñuel's employ, it seems, was the actor José Nieto, who recalled in an interview that he spent two years doing dubbing work in Paris, being paid 350 francs a day.[27] Buñuel's professional meticulousness didn't really fit in with an ambience that was both Taylorist and Stakhanovite, in which "such-and-such an Italian actor dubbed this or that Spanish or Rumanian, the main thing being that he had a foreign accent."[28] It is worthy of note, however, that Buñuel, who in his 1939 autobiography kept mum about his unproductive stay at MGM, admitted to his activity during this phase at Paramount, a phase that, if hardly glorious in artistic terms, provided evidence of his dedication and professional discipline when it came to seeking a job in his American exile.

8

The Mutations of *L'Âge d'or* and Other Projects

On 22 September 1930, a month before the private première of *L'Âge d'or* at the Cinéma du Panthéon, Charles de Noailles wrote a breezy letter to Dalí that began with his thanks for the photos of the fisherman's cottage in Port Lligat that Salvador and Gala had bought with the monthly stipend paid to the painter by the Viscount after the collapse of the Goemans Gallery. Including Marie-Laure in his effusion, Noailles went on to tell Dalí, "We are passionately interested in all your projects, films, poems, etc."[1]

Film projects. In the physical (and emotional) distance that was increasingly separating Dalí from his erstwhile collaborator, Luis Buñuel, Dalí's exuberant creativity had continued, and would continue, to throw out ideas for movies. All of these were to remain unmade, during the 1930s, at least. One such was *Cinq minutes à propos du surréalisme*, an undated scenario for a didactic five-minute documentary about the movement that has been plausibly ascribed to sometime between the première of *Un chien andalou* (June 1929) and the filming of *L'Âge d'or* (March 1930).[2] We suggest a start date of autumn 1929, for in her autobiography Janine Bouissounouse, a member of the *Revue du cinéma* collective, states that Dalí consulted her about making a Surrealist animated film—*Cinq minutes* was planned to have such sequences—and that she put him in touch with Frans Masereel, author of *L'Idée* (1927). Masereel, who wanted to do an animated version of his libertarian graphic novel, was about to begin work with Berthold Bartosch, who would animate *L'Idée* between 1929 and 1932. The placing of this anecdote in Bouissounouse's chronological account implies a date of October or November for Dalí's inquiry, which would tie in with the formal induction of Buñuel and himself into the Surrealist Group in Paris.[3] The crisply typed manuscript in impeccable French suggests that Dalí, ever cavalier with words, had been helped by Gala or Éluard or Breton to compose it. Divided into three columns representing, respectively, a voiceover or synchronized dialogue, an image track, and a soundtrack of music or noises, *Cinq minutes* is, like *L'Âge d'or*, an example of the ephemeral *muet sonore parlant* hybrid, "a sort of missing link in the evolution from silents to talkies." And as in that film, the relation of sound to image is now consonant (and comforting), now dissonant (and disorientating). To give a sense of the compass of the scenario, which set out to introduce a few basic ideas about Surrealism—the creative role of play; collective research into the object; the primacy of the ideas of Freud and, by implication, Emil Kraepelin—a single synchronic reading across the columns will suffice. At one point the voiceover says: "The Surrealists have in fact been the first, dark lantern in hand, to wander through the forbidden, deep, dark and unknown domains of human thought," while on the screen the group would be seen descending the steps of the Métro. On the steps "are a few moving automata, a half-naked woman. Before entering, all of [the Surrealists] will open their umbrellas." At the same time on the soundtrack one would hear the wind getting increasing louder.[4] The dénouement of the documentary would have Breton lecturing to camera.

Although Dalí relied on the collaboration of the Surrealist Group in this "official" portrait of its current credo, the project was his baby: he wrote the text and was to undertake the frame-by-frame animation of various diagrammatic drawings, including a "paranoiac" metamorphosis of the contents of his *Sleeping Woman, Horse, Lion, etc.*, the Éluard-owned painting that would become a prime target during the Fascist disturbance in Studio 28 months later. (Who might have directed the other sequences remains an open question. It is unlikely Buñuel was slated; he was too busy creating his second film.) And the wider purpose of *Cinq minutes*? Our hunch is that it was meant as a supporting short for *L'Âge d'or*, its simplified description of Surrealism being aimed at a popular audience at a time when it was still believed that Buñuel's new movie would be launched in a major cinema on one of the boulevards of Paris.

The artist's next foray into film was also for a didactic documentary, this time on the family, which would draw on psychoanalysis but be imbricated with historical materialism and subtended by Dalí's own recent history: the row with his father during the first quarter of 1930 over the *Sometimes I Spit with Pleasure on the Portrait of My Mother* picture—a row Buñuel would attempt to smooth over by portraying a peaceable Dalí Senior on film in *Menjant garotes*. *Contre la famille* has been dated by Dawn Ades to early 1932.[5] Agustín Sánchez Vidal, however, suggests that "one can date its genesis to the very beginning of the decade," and places the text between *Cinq minutes* and the third project in the "cine" section of Dalí's written *Obra completa*, *La Chèvre sanitaire*, from the second half of 1930 or early 1931.[6] Aside from a single reference to "the film," Dalí's outline gives no hint as to its visual transposition to the screen. Indeed, *Contre la famille* reads more like a loosely structured collation of ideas drawn from his most recent reading (Freud, Otto Rank, Engels), ideas used to buttress a scathing critique of a neurotic social institution founded on generational conflict. In the absence of a scenario, we might still admire the scope of this embryonic project. Who but a fanatical *révolté* like Dalí would even imagine putting intrauterine dreams, polymorphous perversity, and the castration complex on celluloid, and, moreover, of making the link between psychoanalysis and Marxism while doing so? (The closest any filmmaker had come to this didactic approach was G. W. Pabst in *Secrets of a Soul* [1926], with the collaboration of psychoanalysts Karl Abraham and Hanns Sachs. The technophobic Freud refused to collaborate on any film about psychoanalysis; indeed, it's thought that he never once went to the cinema in his life.) Despite Dalí's positive allusions to Engels and to Marx, he appears to be skeptical about sex under constituted Communism: "Social deviance, condition of the woman as an object to be used, [under capitalism, it is understood] set against the Communist idea of the female comrade, in which erotic relations are in fact ruled out."[7] Here we have the origin of some of the remarks in his devastating March 1932 missive to Buñuel. In fact Dalí seems to have gone back to *Contre la famille* in February of that year, announcing this in a letter to the Catalan poet and journalist J. V. Foix.[8] Furthermore, the project prefigures, ironically to be sure, the PCF's call, made by Vaillant-Couturier in 1935, the year in which the Surrealists broke definitively with the party, to *save* the French family.

Far more complex is Dalí's next cinematographic intervention, *La Chèvre sanitaire*. On 15 December 1930—four days after the Prefecture of Police impounded copies of *L'Âge d'or* and Sadoul was called upon to explain his and Aragon's Kharkov betrayal to the group—Éditions Surréalistes published Dalí's first book, *La Femme visible*, a compilation of three essays, "L'Âne pourri," "La Chèvre sanitaire," "L'Amour," and a poem, "Le Grand Masturbateur." (The *prière d'insérer*, or loose-leaf blurb, was by Breton and Éluard, further evidence of the esteem in which they held the Catalan.) The film treatment that takes its name from the second essay has been dated to the second half of 1930 or early 1931. Attack Buñuel as he might for making no contribution to Surrealism in terms of theory, at times Dalí's own theoretical writing is murky in the extreme.

Witness "La Chèvre sanitaire," a study of the crisis in contemporary poetic thought and its remedy—an exaltation of the gratuitous—which is not discussed here since it has only a limited bearing on the eponymous film narrative. Or rather several narratives, plus programmatic statements about the image/sound nexus, for *La Chèvre sanitaire* is a somewhat protean manuscript now in the Fundació Gala-Salvador Dalí in Figueres, with unrelated notes and drawings. For the standard version of this manuscript, we would direct the reader to volume three of *La obra completa*, to Sánchez Vidal's notes therein, and to another recent essay of his.[9] Here, we tentatively suggest another order to this heterodox amalgam of images. Doing so enables us to come up with three discrete treatments.

First, there are a number of reiterations of the phrase "L'âge d'or," along with passages that seem to be gags Dalí invented for the film, in which case we'd have to revise the opening date of the manuscript to the first half of 1930. Did he communicate these gags to Buñuel? Yes, at least in part, in the case of an enigmatically smiling woman at the first-floor window of an Art Nouveau house with, on the ground floor, a sliding coffin that enters the front door unaided: one of Dalí's letters from Carry-le-Rouet quotes the last image. Perhaps, in the case of a character's "hypnagogic" vision of a multitude of crucified women: think of the last shot in *L'Âge d'or* of the female scalps on the cross.

Second, another "family" film built around the animation, so to speak, of the iconic contents of a scabrous Leonardesque drawing by Dalí, *The Butterfly Hunt*, of 1929. This narrative is intertwined with a triple tale of forbidden love (brother and sister), reciprocal love (Romeo and Juliet), and love for love's sake (Don Juan), with the same actor playing all three male roles. In the recurring image of the butterfly hunt, it is the first of these—a seemingly autobiographical fabulation expressing the artist's incestuous desires for his sister Ana María—that has pride of place. Romeo and Juliet or Don Juan do not reappear, at least on the face of it. Emptying the butterfly net of its unseen catch on the part of the now largely clothed family unit is an excuse for the sort of histrionic acting out typical of *Un chien andalou* and *L'Âge d'or*: bitten lips, rolling eyes, terrified glances, animal-like cries. Less caustic than *Contre la famille*, this segment appears to be about the not unproductive hold neuroses have on personality; about the bliss of sublimation.

Last, there is the "sound film" *La Chèvre sanitaire*, per se: "The spirit of the film has to be orientated towards the principles [of the essay] and must, therefore, be directed towards the idea of the gratuitous." Opening with a reading of the poem "Le Grand Masturbateur," accompanied by the fast cutting of images that now replicate the description on the soundtrack, now contradict it, Dalí seemed to be after an "alienation effect" that would not enlighten the audience, à la Brecht, but (to use one of his favorite expressions) "cretinize" it instead. This segment of the manuscript is strong in shot sequences and in programmatic statements—often to do with image/sound incongruities—and both are encapsulated in the (unstated) notion of converting the heterogeneous miniaturist events conflated in the stage-like space of Dalí's paintings into live action before a movie camera, using the conventional editing of "anti-artistic" cinema. For example: a man is seen from the rear playing a piano, the sad music of which swells to a crescendo on the soundtrack. The man, whose physique resembles Breton's, sports a feminine chignon and many rings on his fingers. His music evokes the exterior of an Art Nouveau-style house—suggested by a dissolve and slow focus pulling—with windows that reflect images of white horses and fire. On the soundtrack is the noise of breaking surf. A cut and a pan downward reveal that the feet of both man and piano are submerged in seawater. The iconography of Dalí's "William Tell" cycle of paintings (1930–31) is well to the fore here.

In July 1931 Dalí announced a new Surrealist film project to the Catalan art critic Sebastià Gasch: *Le Troisième Faust*, based on a treatment by Breton and Aragon. Albert Valentin was to direct, Dalí to do the animated drawings, George Antheil the music.[10] Another source has Aragon trying unsuccessfully to interest Breton in 1930 in the writing of an opera libretto, *Le Troisième Faust*, to be filmed by René Clair.[11] The two versions are not necessarily contradictory: Valentin, like Dalí and Buñuel a new recruit in 1929, was poised to become Clair's assistant on *À nous la liberté*, for which he'd be ejected from the group in December 1931. Twenty years later, in 1952, a respected director and scriptwriter by now, Valentin would offer to create the entry on Surrealism for *L'Encyclopédie filmée*, a Paris-based project for short movies that never got beyond the letter A (Jean Grémillon did the entry on "Alchemy"). Was this a distant echo of Dalí's *Cinq minutes* project? And might Valentin have been slated to direct the non-animation sequences of the latter? Like *Cinq minutes*, *Le Troisième Faust*—at least as outlined in the Gasch letter, a contemporary document, after all—suggests that in 1929–31 the Surrealist Group was hoping to express itself to a wider audience through the medium of film; that the cinematic apparatus functioned as a jelling agent for their collective identity; and that Dalí was a central figure in all this. By 1932, however, his ideas about film were changing, as his third book in two years—*L'Amour et la mémoire* being the second—made clear. One of the most cogent Surrealist statements on (and of) cinema, this book was *Babaouo, scénario inédit: Précédé d'un Abrégé d'une histoire critique du cinéma et suivi de Guillaume Tell, ballet portugais*, published by Éditions des Cahiers Libres on 12 July 1932. That is, sixteen weeks after Buñuel had announced the *Dans les eaux glacées du calcul égoïste* project and ten weeks after he'd penned his letter of resignation to Breton.

The change in ideas is less evident at the scenario level, for *Babaouo* ploughs the same furrow as *Un chien andalou* and *L'Âge d'or*, and if it differs from them it is in being more formally conventional, more linear, more "Hollywood," so to speak. Babaouo—from the Catalan *babau*, and the Spanish *bobo* or *babieca*, meaning "simpleton"—is the name of the protagonist of this multigeneric opus: now melodrama, now comedy, horror film, noir, musical, but always preposterous, forever luxuriating in ambiguous kitsch. The movie is set in the near future (1934) in a European country in the throes of civil war. France is a candidate, although the story soon shifts to Portugal, where Communist soldiers are in control. (In 1932 António de Oliveira Salazar was in fact elaborating his proto-Fascist *Estado Novo*, a bulwark, precisely, against Communism.) A chip off the Batcheff/Modot block, Babaouo is oblivious to political events and is only intent upon answering the plea of his lover, Mathilde Ibañez, that he rescue her from her solitude in a Portuguese chateau. The first part of the film describes Babaouo's peregrinations, full of disturbing tragicomic events, especially those in a deserted Lusitanian town under martial law, perhaps; his arrival at the enigmatic chateau; and his subsequent blinding in a motor accident that Mathilde does not survive. In the second part, or epilogue—which may have been a later addition—our hero, his sight restored years later by surgery, has become a Sunday painter intent upon depicting the folkloric aspects of the Brittany countryside and its picturesque inhabitants, including a weird family of fisherfolk based on Lidia of Cadaqués and her two sons. When, out of the blue, Babaouo is shot dead, a deadpan footnote—a final intertitle?—declares: "It's a Surrealist film."

The scenario is rife with images from Dalí's paintings: blindfolded cyclists with a stone or a loaf on their heads, soft watches, an extruded spoon, eggs on a plate without the plate, a felled cypress lying on an eighteen-foot-long bed. Or from his own filmography: the "extremely well-known little cape of white cloth," first seen on Batcheff's back in *Un chien andalou*; the toiling orchestra conductor from *L'Âge d'or*.

Many formal ideas are reworked from *La Chèvre sanitaire*, suggesting that the latter was less a rounded entity, more a disparate work-in-progress. The provocative use of dead time, when, for instance, the audience would have its patience tried by watching Babaouo wait five whole minutes for the subway. Or the systematic use of elements in "sterile discord" with the action or decor, as when a grand piano comes crashing down a hotel stairwell, in an incident ignored by the people in the lobby. Or an illustration of the following note: "a blind man may arrive at the same notion of reality as a paranoiac," when, following the car crash, the blinded Babaouo gropes various objects among the debris, believing they might form the still-living body of Mathilde.[12]

Technically, *Babaouo* is a talkie, albeit largely reliant on sound effects (sometimes deafening) and on music, represented by the tango *Renacimiento*—a recording by the Orquesta Típica Argentina Bachicha, released by the Odeon record company in 1931—which acts as a leitmotif, along with Wagner's *Tannhäuser* overture, which, comically, never gets going.[13] There is little dialogue, and some of it is deliberately irrelevant, as when Babaouo and an acquaintance discuss the plans for converting a Figueres farmhouse, problems with a bookbinder, and so forth. Although far from being a shooting script, *Babaouo* does make technical reference at times to close ups, dissolves, and medium shots, but mostly to a recurring traveling shot that keeps behind Babaouo's shoulder as he penetrates the tunnel-like deep space of such locations as the Paris Métro or the rose-strewn streets of the Portuguese ghost town. At one point the movie goes from black and white to color and back to black and white again.

In among all the parody are some barbs aimed at Dovzhenko, whose "ignoble" *Earth* Dalí had reviled in his terrible March 1932 letter to Buñuel. In the mock documentary on Brittany that opens the epilogue, there is a series of shots of apple orchards, with piles of apples and snot-nosed children: a sarcastic allusion to the beginning of *Earth*.

The final part of *Babaouo* (the book), *Guillaume Tell, ballet portugais*, is subtitled "extract from the previous film" but is manifestly a stage production, a clear homage to the plays and novels of Raymond Roussel. Although certain signifiers, both visual and aural, are carried over from *Babaouo* (the scenario), it is hard to see where in the film the ballet might be inserted. Among the arcane rituals depicted is one in which a female harpist slices a baguette by banging it against the strings of her instrument—a genuflection to Harpo Marx and his brothers, the overarching influence on Dalí's would-be movie.

Although published in July 1932, *Babaouo*—or at least a version of it—may be dated to June 1931 at the latest, for in *The Secret Life* Dalí claims that on the very day that he completed *The Persistence of Memory*, the "soft watches" picture first shown at the Pierre Colle Gallery in Paris that same month, he had "received from a moving-picture studio a rejection of a short scenario that I had laboriously prepared, and that was the profoundest possible summary of all my ideas."[14] Several commentators have suggested that this scenario was *Babaouo*, which seems almost certain.[15] Unfortunately, we don't know which film company this was, although we can say that Buñuel was not, so to speak, part of the "package." We know this because the director himself says so in a letter to Pierre Unik of

16 August 1932: "I've read Babahouo [*sic*]. There is the odd thing in it, above all some very amusing moments. But nothing new and impossible to make due to Le Chien and to L'Âge. The theoretical part more amusing still. Man Ray, whom I've seen in Saint-Jean, told me Dalí is very hopeful a director will make the film."[16] The suggestion here is that Buñuel considers *Babaouo* to be "more of the same," and that he, for one, is intent on following another path.

Two days later Buñuel wrote to Charles de Noailles to say that Salvador and Gala had invited him to Port Lligat—where Crevel was already in situ and Breton and Valentine Hugo were due to arrive—adding, euphemistically, that he had neither the time nor the money to make the trip. Were the Surrealists hoping to tempt Buñuel back into the fold? The slim possibility that Dalí might still have been trying to seduce the filmmaker, to win him round to directing the scenario, is belied by the circumspect, even defiant, dedication inscribed in the director's copy of *Babaouo*: "To Luis Buñuel, in the hope of agreeing as much as 'possible,' yours, Salvador Dalí."[17] Buñuel was right; Dalí indeed had his sights set elsewhere, namely on the dream factories of California. As hinted above, *Babaouo* was, all things considered, even more Hollywood in essence than, say, *L'Âge d'or*, itself "a very American film," in Dalí's words. In line with such thinking, the author also sent his book to Edgar Neville, who'd returned to Madrid from Hollywood as a result of the advent of the Second Republic and of MGM's shift from foreign-language versions to dubbing, with a dedication that read: "Dear Neville, you'd be doing me a phenomenal favor if you sent me some private addresses in America, big wheels in the cinema, so I can send them my scenario."[18]

Although when writing to Unik, Buñuel confessed to finding the theoretical preface even more amusing than the scenario proper, in his letter to Noailles he claimed that the former was "rather bizarre."[19] The changes in the artist's ideas on film are indeed most evident in this preface, the *Abrégé d'une histoire critique du cinéma* (Abstract of a Critical History of the Cinema). At times these ideas add up to a 180-degree shift, especially in terms of the "cinergy" Dalí and Buñuel had developed in a series of call-and-response essays—ideological *billets doux*, almost—published between 1927 and 1929 in *Cahiers d'Art* (Paris), *La Gaceta Literaria* (Madrid), *L'Amic de les Arts* (Sitges), and *La Gaseta de les Arts* (Barcelona). Whereas Dalí had once argued for the superiority of cinema over theater, now he privileged theater over cinema, argued for the virtue of filmed theater. While he had once praised the superiority of brand-new, machine-made, standardized objects over outmoded, handcrafted, ornamental ones, now he reversed that set of values; thus, hypermodern Esprit Nouveau gave way to recently outmoded Art Nouveau. Such values were, as before, also applied to cinema. Although

Dalí had once concurred with Buñuel's views on segmentation, *découpage*, photogenia (founded on the insert shot), and rhythmic editing, now he judged "cinematic cinema" to be the enemy, the quick-fire visual rhetoric of 1920s silent film undermining the expression of "concrete irrationality."

Dalí, the eternal masquerader (to paraphrase Ramón Gomez de la Serna), liked nothing more than to fly in the face of received wisdom (even that of his closest allies), and his writing of film history—still a young discipline in 1932—was perverse in the extreme. Primitive cinema, particularly Méliès, represented the medium's experimental, metaphysical phase. Then came a gray period when technique was perfected—the cursed progenitor of all this being D. W. Griffith, whom Buñuel had vaunted in his essay "Del plano fotogénico" (April 1927)—after which there emerged the Golden Age of "the first materialist films of the Italian School" from 1910 to 1920: "I am speaking here," Dalí continued, "of the grandiose epoch of hysterical cinema . . . , of that cinema so marvelously, so properly close to theater, which not only has the immense merit of offering us real, concrete documents of psychic disturbances of all kinds . . . but also the merit of having attained complete possession over its essential technical means. From this moment on cinema rapidly enters its decadent phase."[20]

This lauding of "diva cinema" had its parallel in the artist's recent cult of Art Nouveau architecture and his imminent mystique of *pompier* painter Meissonier. (Moreover, it's a displacement of Surrealist interest in the "old-fashioned" movies of Louis Feuillade.) In the *Abrégé*, Dalí singled out a film called *Il fuoco* for special praise. Directed in 1915 for Itala Film, Turin, by Piero Fosco, the pseudonym of Giovanni Pastrone, *Il fuoco* starred Pina Menichelli and Febo Mari (not Gustavo Serena, as Dalí claims). The scenario was the work of Mari and Pastrone; the photography and special effects were by Segundo de Chomón, another of Aragón's great filmmakers. The film historian Juan Gabriel Tharrats has described *Il fuoco* (*The Fire*) as "the story of a mad love, impassioned and impossible, that catches like a spark, flares into a sudden blaze and ends in ashes."[21] Dalí was particularly sensitive to the fact that the predatory lovemaking between, here, a highborn poetess and a modest painter took place in a Boecklin-esque setting, "in an unending night of cypresses and marble stairs." In evoking *Il fuoco* Dalí was perhaps reconfiguring a powerful preteen erotic experience, for he may not have seen the movie since April 1916, when it was released in Catalonia. At the fantasy level, of course, the relationship between Mari and Menichelli bore an uncanny resemblance to his and Gala's.

What Dalí prized in obsolete *drames mondaines* like *Il fuoco* was the depiction of "the most impure aspirations and fantasies." Irrational, too, since one definition of "concrete irrationality" would be the objective imaging of delusional states of mind, of hysterical symbolization, of the return of the repressed as symptom. (Contemporary scholarship bears him out: diva cinema is now read as a radical, proto-feminist representation of female hysteria.)[22] Moreover, the reproduction of concrete irrationality was expedited by the formal conservatism of diva films, with their long takes, static camera, deep-focus photography, unhurried cutting between medium shots and close-ups. And their restrained acting style, due in part to the sheer length of the take: mugging for a whole minute before a static camera would have been both ludicrous and exhausting.

But not everything is anachronism in the *Abrégé*: there is much that is consistent with Dalí's earlier thinking about cinema. Such as his view that the *locus classicus* of concrete irrationality is silent Hollywood comedy, particularly the work of Mack Sennett and Harry Langdon. And now sound comedy, too, for with the arrival of talkies the Marx Brothers had risen to stardom, and the artist was an unconditional fan, situating their second film, *Animal Crackers* (Victor Heerman, 1930), based on their 1926 stage play of the same name, "at the summit of comedy film's development."[23] After a viewing of the Marxes' third opus, *Monkey Business* (Norman Z. McLeod, 1931), Buñuel begged to differ, finding the film "excessively comic."[24] Of most interest to Dalí was the aphasic, erotomaniacal Harpo, with his "face of persuasive and triumphal madness, at the end of the film as well as during the all too brief moment when he interminably plucks the harp."[25] This is quintessential Dalí, sarcastically raising *ennui* and schmaltz to a subversive aesthetic category. By 1934 he'd be claiming that the "latest mode of intellectual excitation" in cinema involved "a monotonous and persuasive abjection of sorts; preferably films of 'tenors, exhibitionists, salivary of tongue and with dazzling teeth,' Jean Kiepura-style."[26] Kiepura was a Polish opera singer who achieved fame in the early 1930s in a series of operettas filmed in Berlin in German, English, and French versions. *Das Leid einer Nacht* and *Tell Me Tonight* (1932), for instance, were directed by Anatole Litvak; *La Chanson d'une nuit* by Henri-Georges Clouzot. Dalí's mischievous preface ended on a white lie: "In 1929 Buñuel and I wrote the scenario of *Le Chien andalou* [*sic*], in 1930, the scenario of *L'Âge d'or*. These are the first two Surrealist films. Apart from revolutionary Communist films, which are justified by their value as propaganda, what one can expect of Surrealism and what might be expected of a certain 'comedy' cinema are all that merit being considered."[27] Knowing what we know of his true feelings about films like *Earth* and *The Road to Life*, Dalí was surely speaking tactically, and perhaps at the behest of the group, in order to appease the PCF and to further Surrealist entry into the AEAR (which would occur in November 1932). Was he also tending an olive branch to Buñuel, smoothing over their quarrel about Dovzhenko and Ekk?

By the time he received *Babaouo* in August, Buñuel had long since begun reshaping *L'Âge d'or* into *Dans les eaux glacées du calcul égoïste.* Moreover, he'd written a screenplay of Emily Brontë's *Wuthering Heights* with Pierre Unik. As the 1930s developed, Unik (along with Sadoul) would, in the absence of the estranged Dalí, evolve into a frequent collaborator of Buñuel's. Son of a Polish-born tailor (a freethinking Jew who was far from being the "rabbi" Buñuel mentioned in his memoirs), the atheistic Unik had joined the Surrealists in 1925 at the age of sixteen, becoming an assiduous contributor to the debates and the publications of the group. Called on two years later by Michel Marty to choose between the PCF and Surrealism, he'd opted for the latter. On completing his military service in September 1930 Unik considered working as René Clair's assistant. (Was this on the *Troisième Faust* project?) Proletarianized in Rheims in winter 1930–31, he was to rejoin the PCF. In September 1931 Éditions Surréalistes published his *Théâtre des nuits blanches*, a slim volume of poetry dedicated to Breton and Éluard. During this period of self-questioning as to the nature of his commitment, Unik began an autobiographical novel, *Le Héros du vide*, describing his gradual shift from the "infantile malady" of Surrealism to a "real" Communist position.[28] In April 1932, in the circumstances described in an earlier chapter, this "marvelous young man . . . , ardent and brilliant" quit Breton's group.[29]

The first vague reference we have to Buñuel writing a screenplay that may or may not have been based on Emily Brontë's novel emerges in his 5 December 1931 letter to Charles de Noailles: the following day he was to go to Toledo for a week, where he intended to work on "a script for Braunberger. He absolutely insists I do something."[30] His traveling companion would be René Crevel, author of a recent study of the Brontë sisters. Buñuel's dreams of transposing *Wuthering Heights* to the screen, however, went back to his early days in Paris: Santiago Ontañon remembered him proposing to film the book, read in French translation—Frédéric Delebecque's, published in 1925 by La Nouvelle Librairie nationale, which pertained to Action Française (!)—prior to *Un chien andalou.*[31]

The first concrete reference to the *Wuthering Heights* screenplay is a *pneumatique* from Buñuel to Unik of 19 June 1932: "Read the novel at your leisure without making a summary of it: there's no need to as I'm disposed to make this film. Just mark the passages that interest you most in pencil. Monday evening, I'll expect you here at 7 pm to dine. Sadoul will come too. Bring the book and we'll talk about it."[32] The idea jelled, for on or around 6 July Buñuel traveled with Unik and the Sadouls, Georges and Nora, to Cernay-la-Ville, a village some twenty-five miles to the southwest of Paris, where the three men set to work. A tale of the complexities of mad love prized by the Surrealists, the one testimony

Working on *Wuthering Heights* in Cernay-la-Ville, July 1932. *From left to right*: Buñuel, Nora Sadoul, Pierre Unik. Snapshot by Georges Sadoul. (Private collection. Courtesy Librairie Emmanuel Hutin, Paris)

to have come down to us as to why *Wuthering Heights* interested Buñuel is Ontañón's, who wrote in his memoirs that "the hatred of the protagonist for the family of the girl he doesn't get to love strongly attracted him. That hatred in the novel seemed marvelous to him. And that's pure Surrealism."[33] We may speculate, then, about the degree to which Buñuel and company were seeking to affirm a certain continuity with the ideas of the movement they had recently left ("Brontë" is, after all, an anagram of "Breton"). In the case of Buñuel, great passions—especially pathological ones—have been a decisive raw material in his filmography.

Whatever the truth of the matter—and it may be that the impoverished collaborators were primarily looking for a viable film project to bring in some ready cash—the scheme moved swiftly ahead, although Sadoul dropped out after the Cernay sessions. By 21 July Buñuel was writing to "Pedro el Único" from Sallent de Gallego, a village in the Aragonese Pyrenees seven miles or so from the French border, insisting that he make the trip from Paris to continue laboring on "the script I've already finished and enlarged with dialogues."[34] Unik did so and reported to Sadoul on 11 August that he and Buñuel had worked well in Spain "for throne and altar"—meaning, we imagine, for the temporal and spiritual power of the movie business as incarnated in Pierre Braunberger.[35] On 16 August, Buñuel wrote from San Sebastian to tell Unik that their potential producer had dropped by on 13 August to pick up the completed scenario and that on 15 August the director had traveled the twenty-five miles to Saint-Jean-de-Luz, where Braunberger summered every year, to discuss the script: "He thinks it's very good and is intent on making it. He'll start seeing about everything on returning to Paris. I fear that even if all goes well it'll be two months before the film gets under way. It's necessary to talk to the moneymen, etc., to prove to them it's a commercial film." Buñuel proceeded to give some precious details of this 1932 version of *Wuthering Heights*: the script had an epilogue, but Braunberger suggested dropping this and ending with "the scene of the cemetery," while heightening the tension by adding material "between the love scene and the death of Lisbeth" (Lisbeth being the substitute name for the novel's Catherine Earnshaw).[36] More information is forthcoming from an 18 August letter to the Viscount: this "beautiful love film" would not have original music, which was a disappointment to Buñuel since he'd have liked to collaborate with Igor Markevich and Nikolai Nabokov, the two Russian-born composers he'd met through the Noailles.[37]

A month later the project still had the green light. Restored to Paris, Buñuel went on working on the script—probably with Unik—telling the Viscount so in a 24 September letter: "Things are moving along very nicely and the idea is to begin directing in two months. I have a lot of interest in this work. . . . I think I've preserved the overall spirit of the book in the script."[38] It's here that we would beg to differ with Jean-Michel Bouhours and Nathalie Schoeller, editors of the Buñuel/Noailles correspondence that has been so vital to this part of our study. They state that the book to which the director alludes is Maurice Legendre's *Las Jurdes* (1927), which will provide the inspiration for his next realized film, *Las Hurdes*, while also hinting that the latter project was already well under way; that the "scenario" for the future documentary was already written. However, as shown in the next chapter, such a document, including the voiceover commentary, would not exist until March 1934. A comparison between Buñuel's letter to Unik of 16 August and this one to Noailles—witness the repeated phrase about beginning the filming in two months' time—indicates that the reference is to the adaptation of Emily Brontë's novel. The end of September 1932 would appear to be the start date for the Las Hurdes project, perhaps as a consequence of Buñuel's perception, notwithstanding his optimistic letter to the Viscount, of the dwindling possibilities of directing *Wuthering Heights*, for, sadly, this version was doomed, due precisely to the intrusion of the "moneymen, etc." cited above.

Since its creation in June 1930, the main backer of Établissements Braunberger-Richebé had been Braunberger's cousin, Marcel Monteux, whose father had made a fortune by inventing right and left footwear (until then shoes were undifferentiated). Alas, unlike his progenitor, Montreux was no accumulator of money, but a squanderer, and by the end of 1932 his credit with the banking fraternity was running out. A year later he would take the production company down with him. As to the screenplay, the manuscript of which has not survived, Braunberger doesn't mention it once in his 1987 memoirs.

Or does he? We would contend that the eighty-two-year-old producer confuses *Wuthering Heights* with another nineteenth-century novel much favored by the Surrealists, M. G. Lewis's *The Monk*. Thus, when he has Buñuel adapting Lewis in 1938—at the height of the Civil War—he really means Brontë in 1932. If this hunch is correct, then Braunberger unwittingly describes the fate of the scenario: namely, that it disappeared during the Gestapo ransacking of his Paris office in 1940, prior to his deportation as a Jew to the Drancy concentration camp. This would explain why, when Buñuel finally came to make *Wuthering Heights* in 1954—as *Abismos de pasión*—he did so with a new script, cowritten with Julio Alejandro and Dino Mauri.[39] It is worth noting that this new version retained the dénouement in the cemetery, as suggested by Braunberger in August 1932. Another loss is a *second* version of the script, on which Jean Grémillon purportedly collaborated when in Madrid to direct *¡Centinela alerta!* for Filmófono. If the Spanish Civil War hadn't intervened, might this version have become another "Producción Filmófono"?

To be sure, there were enough echoes of Lys and Modot in the figures of Cathy and Heathcliff to suggest that Buñuel's enthusiasm for the project belied his stated ambition to do something completely at odds with *L'Âge d'or*, but what was perhaps more prescient, now, in terms of the immediate future—in terms of *Las Hurdes*, that is—was the novel's backwoods setting, its Social Darwinism, and the dispassionate account, delivered by a participant-witness, of events redolent with a fateful grimness. Was there a sort of "bleed" at the imaginary level between the waning *Wuthering Heights* scheme and the waxing Las Hurdes one?

The month of September 1932 was indeed a busy one for Buñuel: not only did he finalize the *Wuthering Heights* script and set the *Las Hurdes* project in motion by making an exploratory trip to the area with Unik, Lotar, Rafael Sánchez Ventura, María Teresa León, Rafael Alberti, and Gustavo Durán, but he was also appointed head of the Spanish dubbing department at Paramount, which involved working a daily eight-hour shift in its Joinville-le-Pont studios. On top of that, on 23 September the censors would refuse to grant a visa to his "new" film, *Dans les eaux glacées du calcul égoïste*.

The reader will recall that Buñuel, mortified by the vicious letter he'd received from Dalí in mid-March and unsettled by the violent polarization of the

Surrealist Group, had resolved to recut *L'Âge d'or,* to render it down into a twenty-minute short. By thus paring his magnum opus, a labor that we may assume commenced at the end of March and lasted intermittently until 21 September, when it was re-presented to the French Board of Film Censors, not only was the director getting back at Surrealism by potentially depriving it of the jewel in its cinematic crown, but he was simultaneously settling a personal score with the film's co-scriptwriter. But the aggressiveness of his gesture also rebounded upon himself: couldn't this desperate act only ever be a Pyrrhic victory? A humiliating self-castration, even?

When approving the original scheme, Noailles had specifically asked for the sequences of the ostensory, the "personage in white," and the hirsute cross to be eliminated. At the eleventh hour Buñuel also excised the kicking of the blind man, "due to no longer being in agreement with its spirit."[40] In the absence of "*L'Âge d'or bis,*" which, soon after his run-in with officialdom, the cineaste probably destroyed—or left to its own fate—it is impossible to know what its content was. We would guess, though, that the final result centered on the mis-mating of Modot and Lys; that it opened with the travelogue of "Imperial Rome"—thus doing away with the scorpion prologue and the bandits sequence—and closed on the shot of Modot casting white feathers into the abyss. Other material from this segment would have had to be excised to get *Eaux glacées* down to twenty minutes, of course. Moreover, the new title resonated ambiguously with the mad love depicted on the screen, put a moralizing frame around it; a frame more in accord with the puritanical views of the PCF. Such a short would have been palatable to its target audience, the kind of politicized public that attended, say, La Bellevilloise, where *L'Âge d'or* had been shown on 27 and 30 April, since it depicted the aristocracy, police, and clergy in a manner consonant with the agitprop films of Soviet cinema. Having said that, given the suppression of the movie, can't the *Eaux glacées* scheme be read as a somber example of the price to be paid for seeking, as Buñuel said in his letter of resignation to Breton, "a less pure form of expression which might serve as propaganda"?[41]

Breton would certainly suggest that the director dismembered his film after receiving a party mandate to prepare a simplified, "worker-friendly" version, thus flying in the face of Buñuel's claim that the scheme had been proposed by Braunberger. In a sense, Buñuel was rectifying his film in response to an observation made by Moussinac in *L'Humanité* on 7 December 1930, when the critic argued that *L'Âge d'or* was too formally difficult for the proletariat, even though it did contribute to the proletariat's revolutionary mission. Still smarting, four years later, over the vandalizing of a prime expression of Surrealism, Breton wrote, "I feel tremendous sadness to think that Buñuel has subsequently gone back to this title; that, at the request of a few bogus revolutionaries bent on subjecting everything to their immediate propaganda aims, he has consented to an expurgated version of *L'Âge d'or* being shown in the workers' cinemas."[42] Breton was whistling in the dark, for all that: could he name anyone who'd actually seen this version? The Surrealist leader would return to this charge when on 17 May 1938 he presented a showing of *Un chien andalou* at the Palacio de Bellas Artes in Mexico City. There, he denounced the director's submission "to the orders of a party" and, after lamenting that he had authorized the circulation of an expurgated version of *L'Âge d'or*, added: "Buñuel, on the poetic plane, has abdicated."[43]

In 1942 Dalí would state that "when Buñuel abandoned Surrealism, he expurgated *L'Âge d'or* of its frenzied passages and made a number of other alterations without asking me my opinion."[44] In the recently published manuscript version of *The Secret Life*, from which this quotation comes, the Catalan was more specific, and wrote in his peculiar French (which we translate literally here): "Later, when Buñuel became a Communist, he cut/expurgated *L'Âge d'or* of those ultra-frenetically erotic passages, adapting it to Marxist ideology, going so far as to change its title for another he takes from a phrase by Marx! If the film had a value it was that of Anarchy."[45] In 1942 Dalí rounded off his allusion by stating, "This altered version I have not seen." Of course not! Because besides Buñuel and the French censors, plus, in all probability, its putative producer, Braunberger—and, completely by chance, Edmond T. Gréville, the French B-movie director whose œuvre is now sometimes compared to Mexican-period Buñuel—nobody was ever to view *Dans les eaux glacées du calcul égoïste*. While editing his fourth feature, a bread-and-butter opus called *Plaisirs de Paris* (1932), at Braunberger-Richebé's Billancourt Studios, the twenty-six-year-old Gréville came across "a pile of old cans containing outtakes. In one of them, a roll of film bore the label: *Les Eaux glacées du calcul egoïste*. It was handwritten by Buñuel, who must have worked in this same room on the editing of *L'Âge d'or*. I put the roll on the moviola straightaway. It was a compilation of certain scenes the Mexican director had rejected from *Un chien andalou* and from his last film. It constituted a sort of digest of Surrealist cinema. The discovery of a previously unseen movie by the man I consider to be one of the greatest filmmakers alive plunged me into a transport of delight."[46]

It's clear from this anecdote, recorded thirty years after the event, that Gréville remained ignorant of *Eaux glacées* as an autonomous project, and that he thought he'd stumbled across the outtakes from the cutting of *L'Âge d'or* in April 1930. Had they been the outtakes, why would Buñuel have spliced them together? No, although delighted with his good fortune, Gréville was simply unaware of what he had before him. The allusion to *Un chien andalou* is intriguing, for all that, albeit unlikely: why would the Spaniard have included such material? After all, he was trying to diminish the heterogeneity of *L'Âge d'or*, not to add to it, as this description would suggest. What Gréville's account does communicate, though, is an air of abandonment—witness the old film cans—as if he'd encountered a jettisoned print of *Dans les eaux glacées du calcul égoïste*, consigned to the wind and the waves by its disgruntled maker.

For Buñuel was indeed bitter and despairing at the censors' decision. Firing off a letter on 24 September to the Noailles, he would observe, "So there you see a bit of revenge on the part of this *dame* [*Dame Anastasie*, colloquial French for the institution of censorship] because the film had nothing worth censoring in it. . . . Am I to assume that for having directed *L'Âge d'or* I must make no more films? . . . If I had any influence I would mount a big campaign against this totally Fascist arbitrariness. As I can't, nobody will learn of this new form of 'castor-oil purge.'"[47]

The film that Buñuel had momentarily despaired of and had attempted to "de-surrealize" would remain a touchstone for the movement during the 1930s, as demonstrated by Breton's melancholic ruminations of 1936 in *Minotaure* on the expurgated version.[48] In point of fact, during the planning of *Minotaure* in 1933, when the project was still in the hands of Georges Bataille and André Masson, before Breton and others wrested control of it from them, the original title of the magazine had been *L'Âge d'or*, in homage to the movie. The banishment of the latter to the "Enfer des films" by the French state served to keep its power to scandalize intact. For instance, during the ephemeral rapprochement between Breton, Bataille, and their respective followers in the ultra-Left group Contre-Attaque (October 1935–March 1936), it was proposed to show *L'Âge d'or*—probably assistant director Brunius's copy; he was a Contre-Attaque member—"with a view to causing a widespread incitement to revolt," in the name of an anguished anti-Fascism, anti-Stalinism, anti-French imperialism.[49]

In their manifesto-style defense of Buñuel's second film in 1930, the Surrealists had called for the invention of new myths to undermine the old myths of capitalism. *L'Âge d'or* turned into one such myth. A final anecdote suffices to corroborate this. In December 1934 Buñuel received a polite request from Breton to borrow a print of the film, this being the sine qua non of an invitation from the Tenerife Surrealists of *La Gaceta de Arte* to the Surrealist leader to mount an international exhibition in Santa Cruz and to lecture there; a series of public screenings of the banned movie would, it was thought, defray the costs of the trip.[50] These screenings were not to take place, either before the departure from the Canary Islands of Breton's party—Jacqueline Lamba and Benjamin Péret accompanied him—on 27 May 1935 or in May or June, "hot" months of social protest against the Lerroux-Gil Robles government. The local Catholic bourgeoisie, with the pro-Fascist archbishop Fray Albino Menéndez-Reigada in the van, mounted a strident press campaign that resulted in any showing of the film, which had been left in the islands, being repeatedly deferred by the civil governor. Only with the advent of the Frente Popular in February 1936 was *L'Âge d'or* screened: almost a year to the day after the Paris Surrealists had left, it could be seen in Santa Cruz.[51] In late June the film traveled to Las Palmas de Gran Canaria and into the safekeeping of a German friend of the *Gaceta* group.

In July the military uprising led by General Franco, army commander of the archipelago, occurred and the generous German, whose name has not come down to us, fearing reprisals, buried the reels in waste ground near his home. After World War II he disappeared from view, and a house was built on the land. Some forty years later Domingo Pérez Minik, one of the original *Gaceta* hosts, offered his personal interpretation: "It is quite possible that it's still lying there, turned to sand, mixed with cement, beneath bricks, converted into dust or into a dangerous scorpion. . . . Also following the natural course of *L'Âge d'or*, it is very likely that the latter might have been turned into a strange rock, already fossilized, as one more stone on the island."[52] Coming full circle from the mica-schist of Cap de Creus to the basalt of Gran Canaria, this is poetic justice indeed, a fabulous transubstantiation of the imaginary into the real.

Turning the clock back once more: Buñuel's original announcement of the remodeling of his first feature-length film arrived a week after the formal founding of the AEAR on 17 March 1932. With the suppression, six months later, of *Dans les eaux glacées du calcul égoïste* we may pose the question: was this emasculated film, then, the first fruit—the first bitter fruit—of the pro-Communist program of the association's photo and cine section?

During those same six months, the AEAR had evolved, in line with ideological changes in the USSR. Although the UIER in Moscow subsisted until December 1935, the dissolving of the RAPP in April 1932 heralded a new pluralism, with the hard-line ideology of "proletarian realism"—founded on the "worker-correspondent" movement, or *rabcors*—gradually giving way to a more amorphous "Socialist Realism," officially and definitively adopted in August 1934. In France, no effort was now spared to attract fellow-traveling intellectuals to the Communist cause. The AEAR, with Vaillant-Couturier as its president after September 1932, was to be the bridgehead of this common cultural front. Barbusse was rehabilitated, Gide courted, the Surrealists inducted. In November 1932 Breton, Char, Crevel, Éluard, Ernst, Giacometti, Man Ray, Péret, and Tzara were finally admitted into the association, due in part to

Aragon defending their admission in the face of Soviet opposition, but also to Surrealist indulgence vis-à-vis Stalinism.[53]

L'Humanité had just launched a proletarian literature competition, and Breton, a new member of the AEAR's five-person literary bureau, albeit a skeptic as to the plausibility of such literature, was invited to sit on the competition jury as a replacement for Unik, who was suffering from appendicitis. Breton would later characterize the Surrealist position as "more or less . . . that of the Left Opposition (Trotskyist)."[54] Angered by *L'Humanité*'s misrepresentation of his statement about the results of said competition, he would resign from the bureau on 28 February 1933. A month before, Vaillant-Couturier had asked the Surrealist leader to edit the association's new bimonthly review. Unable to reach agreement about a platform, the project came to naught, and the review, entitled *Commune*, now with Aragon at the helm, would only appear in July. *Commune* was to play an important role as a major cultural vector of the Comintern until September 1939, the month World War II broke out. Between February and May 1933 the names of the Surrealists appeared once again alongside those of Aragon, Sadoul, and Unik on three AEAR tracts. One of these, "Protestez!," condemning Nazi terror, the Reichstag fire, and the imprisoning of Leftist writers in Germany, was also signed by Buñuel.[55] In the face of Communist reservations about the Freudo-Marxism of Breton's new book, *Les Vases communicants*, published on 26 November 1932, his impatience reached the boiling point, and on 11 March he confided to Éluard: "I believe more and more in the need for a resounding break with these *cocos* ["Commies" or "Reds" of the AEAR] and for resuming Surrealist activity of the most intransigent kind."[56] That definitive rupture would occur in July.

The seven months between November 1932 and July 1933 mark, then, a brief rapprochement between the Surrealists and those who had quit the movement at the time of the Aragon Affair, particularly Buñuel and Unik. This explains the appearance in *LSASDLR* of two Unik poems in number 5 and of Buñuel's "Une girafe" in number 6, published simultaneously on 15 May. That same period saw an influx of new members of the Surrealist Group: Roger Caillois, Arthur Harfaux, Maurice Henry, Georges Hugnet, Marcel Jean, Gilbert Lély, Jules Monnerot, César Moro, Guy Rosey; and several women, including Denise Bellon, Claude Cahun, Suzanne Malherbe, and Yolande Oliviero. It was with Bellon and Oliviero that Buñuel and Unik forged a special relationship, as revealed in a 23 February 1933 letter from the director: "Dear Pierre: Shall we meet on Sunday [the 26th] at 7.00 pm in the Café Cluny? We can dine together and at 9.30 go to my place, where I've 'convoked' Yolande and Denise. Do your best to keep this evening free. We have lots to talk about."[57]

Even though Buñuel found the long political meetings of the AEAR not to his liking, his presence in the organization seems to have been a relatively high-profile one. In an article published in *La Revue des vivants* in September 1932 entitled "Littérature révolutionnaire en France," the Communist intellectual Paul Nizan provided a survey of the AEAR's current activities. Aside from professional writers, journalists, and philosophers, "the Association also groups together painters, architects like Lurçat, filmmakers like Buñuel."[58] A great admirer of the Spaniard, Nizan and his close friend Jean-Paul Sartre had recently composed a scenario à la Buñuel entitled *Tu seras curé*, shot by Nizan's brother-in-law Jean-Paul Alphen and acted by Paul and Henriette Nizan, Simone de Beauvoir, Sartre, and "the young wife of Emmanuel Berl" (namely, Suzanne Muzard, Breton's former lover and the inspiration for his "L'Union libre").[59] Neither scenario nor film has survived, alas.

Proof that Buñuel's commitment to the AEAR was explicit and sought after is provided by the fact that his name appeared alongside those of fifty others in the list of select anti-Fascists and anti-imperialists in a twenty-four-page pamphlet published by the association in June 1933: *Ceux qui ont choisi: Contre le fascisme en Allemagne; Contre l'impérialisme français.*[60] In his preface, Vaillant-Couturier observed that after a year of existence the AEAR had some 550 adherents in its different sections: literature, the plastic arts, architecture, music, theater, film, and photography. With Hitler in power since January 1933, the extent to which AEAR/UIER sectarianism was giving way to a common-frontist rhetoric was revealed in the pamphlet by the repeated invocation of a proletarian art and literature marching arm in arm with bourgeois centre-Left culture under a revolutionary guise. This embrace of the broad spectrum of fellow-traveling intellectuals on the part of the PCF's cultural machinery—a tactic that displeased the Surrealists, who found their names alongside those of old enemies like Rolland and Barbusse—found expression in Vaillant-Couturier's extravagant praise for André Gide, a recent sympathizer. Indeed, the "headlining" testimony in the pamphlet was Gide's opening address as president of an anti-Nazi, anti-imperialist rally held by the AEAR in the Salle du Grand Orient on 21 March. An address that included a certain criticism of state repression in the Soviet Union—a price the party was willing to pay to demonstrate its pluralism and to win the famous author over to its side. Buñuel was in Paris at the time and surely must have been among the two thousand people who attended—probably alongside Unik and Lotar, with whom he was about to embark on his Las Hurdes documentary.

Buñuel's importance as a committed cineaste was such that Moussinac would mention him in a lecture delivered at La Bellevilloise in 1933. This took place sometime before April, because by then Moussinac was in Moscow to take over from Aragon as a delegate of the UIER. Since *L'Humanité*'s film and theater critic was one of the main ideologues of the AEAR and a leading light in its cine section, it is worth pausing over this lecture, "État du cinéma international," for it perfectly describes the Communist viewpoint.[61] The international cinema of which Moussinac speaks is neither American nor Russian, which he sees as being in direct opposition to one another, but European (French and German). European cinema exists in a traumatized state, due to the hegemonic ambitions of the American film business. One consequence of the economic recession and the arrival of talkies, both of which originated in the United States, has been the demise of the French avant-garde (from which Moussinac came), with experimentation giving way to routine and stereotyping. The patronage that was able to produce *L'Âge d'or* is now a thing of the past. Innovators like the French "Impressionists," who were once promoted by small, independent, production companies, long since defunct, have been reduced to wage slavery. It is only a matter of time before the relative independence of Vidor, Stroheim, Pabst, and Clair is completely undermined.

Meanwhile, American standardized entertainment is regressive, both formally and ideologically. The average consumer of a Hollywood war, detective, or musical film leaves the picture palace a bit more brutalized than the week before. Technical advances only reveal the decadence of bourgeois culture. Money rules. But the whole Depression-hit system is crumbling, hence its recourse to pacifist, nationalist, and religious propaganda that uses pornography—"American sex-appeal"—to drive the message home. "It is a fact," stated Moussinac, "that the bourgeoisie reaps a reward from the psychological misery of the masses. It has, therefore, an *interest* in increasing this misery. Propagandistic claptrap and the unbridling of instinct—this is what facilitates the launching of the requisite butchery, heralds the era of 'sacrifices.'"[62] A venal press, but more especially government censorship, guarantees the prevalence of crypto-Fascist, reformist propaganda, keeps any idea of revolutionary change at bay. Moussinac cites the French state's harassment of Russian movies by Yutkevich and Vertov and protests the recutting by Abel Gance's own distribution company of works by Eisenstein, Ermler, and Trauberg. *The Road to Life* has been one of the few Russian films not to suffer censorship (apart from the *Internationale* being wiped from the soundtrack). In response to the limited penetration of Socialist cinema from the USSR, the French film industry exalts individualism, the division of labor, a return to the land, naturism, and sport, while the Comité Catholique du Cinéma has gone into production and extended its press and film society activities. Albeit rarely, a few nonconformist movies do get shown, be they

American: *I Am a Fugitive from a Chain Gang* (Mervyn Le Roy, 1932), *The Crowd* (King Vidor, 1928), *Lonesome* (Paul Fejos, 1928), and *City Lights* (Charles Chaplin, 1931); or "international": *Niemansland* (Victor Trivas, 1931), *Kameradschaft* (G. W. Pabst, 1931), *Kuhle Wampe* (Slatan Dudow and Bertold Brecht, 1932), *À propos de Nice* (Jean Vigo and Boris Kaufman, 1929–30), *À nous la liberté* (René Clair, 1931), and *L'Âge d'or*. Moussinac also alludes approvingly to the work of Ivens, Lods, and Prévert.

In capitalist countries, Moussinac continued, science outstrips the economic context, which acts as a brake upon it. Any technological innovation will, like sound cinema, be held back until the big companies decide on the opportune moment to launch it. The patents for recent inventions like television are in the hands of trusts that cannot implement them for fear of destabilizing the already fragile market. In the USSR, science lags behind the economic conditions. Soviet Socialist society, which could make radical use of inventions like color or 3-D cinema, lacks access to them, and although sound film is less developed there than other sectors of industry, rapid modernization is rectifying this. Only the USSR can develop experimental sound film, "because the interests of the Revolution would derive an advantage from it." To end, Moussinac returns to the technology of television, which is at odds with the reactionary profiteering, both pecuniary and symbolic, of capitalist society: the revolutionary needs of Socialist society alone can release the potential of the new medium.

It is not our purpose to criticize this 1933 lecture, which provides a good example of the extent to which the unquestioning vaunting of Socialism in One Country was an essential part of the culture of the PCF (and the PCE). In passing, we might recall how far Dalí was from sharing Moussinac's view of screen operettas. Buñuel, on the other hand, must have sympathized with much of the Communist critic's argument: he'd been in Hollywood and observed its nefarious workings; what's more, he'd twice fallen foul of the French censors. With the film industries of the United States and France closed to him, it was to the USSR that he now looked for gainful employment. (Spain, its industry weighed down by the difficult lift-off of sound cinema, was not, as yet, a viable alternative.) As mentioned in an earlier chapter, the cineaste's first allusion to directing in the Soviet Union is synchronous with Aragon's public denial of Breton, the formal launching of the AEAR, and the return of Vaillant-Couturier from Moscow. It would, however, be seventeen months before this project assumed concrete form, in the shape of a screen version of André Gide's 1914 absurdist novel, *Les Caves du Vatican*, to be filmed in the USSR.

In June 1932, if not earlier, as his "clandestine Eckermann," Maria Van Rysselberghe (also known as "La Petite Dame," the Little Lady), revealed in her notebooks, the illustrious novelist had been tempted by the idea of "making a film of *Les Caves* that would be used by the Russians as a satire on the bourgeoisie, on religion." Van Rysselberghe mentioned this in the same breath as another scheme that much excited Gide: a fact-finding trip to the Caucasus, Georgia, Turkistan, and southern Siberia with Lucien Vogel, fellow-traveling publisher of the picture magazine *Vu* and also the father of Vaillant-Couturier's wife, Marie-Claude, and of Nadine, the future wife of film director Marc Allégret, Gide's "nephew."[63] By 9 January 1933 Gide, Vogel, and Marc Allégret were discussing the "material conditions" of the Siberian journey and those of an accompanying "cinematic mission," the nature of which remains something of a mystery, although it is apposite to recall that Gide had already accompanied Allégret in 1927 on the expedition that generated the documentary *Voyage au Congo*, distributed by Braunberger. La Petite Dame's diary entry for 16 May 1933 tells us that on leaving the Soviet Embassy that day, Gide had been buttonholed by Louis Aragon, back the month before from his ten-month stay in the USSR. "He told me," Gide informed her, "that if I wanted, they were fully prepared in Russia to edit a film adapted from *Les Caves du Vatican*, but there you are, they want to make some changes, in order to make the attack more violent, more effective, they'd want the crooks to be real priests. . . . I don't see how I could agree to that at all," the Protestant writer continued, before upbraiding Aragon and the Communists for playing dirty with the Catholics, for refusing to fight them "with weapons that are fair."[64] Aragon backed off, but on 23 May he would announce that the screenplay of this agitprop version was already well under way (which may have been a lie). What he didn't say was that Buñuel, his diary blank after finishing the shooting of *Las Hurdes* on 22 May, was to be included in the package as co-scriptwriter and director. Some spadework was indeed done on a treatment, as Buñuel described years later: "Gide received me and said he felt flattered that the Soviet government had chosen his book, but that personally he knew nothing about cinema. For three days—but only an hour or two a day—we chatted about the adaptation, until one fine morning Vaillant-Couturier announced to me, 'That's it, they're not making the film.'"[65] The veto had come from Gide himself, who, fearful of his own capacity for compromise—"I am for all the world that chameleon which, placed on a piece of tartan, explodes because it doesn't know which color to adopt!"[66]—did not give in to the blandishments of the AEAR president, even though the latter attempted to sugar the pill by having the book serialized in *L'Humanité* in June 1933. "Au revoir, André Gide," would be Buñuel's terse comment on the affair.[67] After three years of fitful courtship by the PCF and the Comintern, Gide would eventually become a thorn in the side of Stalinism with the publication of his skeptical travel log, *Retour de l'U.R.S.S.* (1936) and *Retouches à mon Retour de l'U.R.S.S.* (1937).

But which Soviet film company might have produced *Les Caves du Vatican*, with Buñuel as its director? In an interview with Max Aub, Buñuel refers to Mezhrabpomfilm. This seems reasonable, since Vaillant-Couturier had worked as a scriptwriter for the studio on *La Commune de Paris*, the unmade Piscator movie to which we've already alluded. But also because Mezhrabpomfilm's prime mover, Willi Münzenberg, the Communist propaganda chief who'd fled his native Germany after Hitler's arrival in power, had reached Paris by March 1933, from where he would spearhead the Comintern's anti-Fascist campaign. In addition, his right-hand man, Otto Katz (aka André Simone), had labored at the Moscow studio as an executive between the end of 1930 and spring 1933. Buñuel would have been in good company: between 1924 and 1936 Mezhrabpom—the Russian acronym of Workers International Relief (SOI), the Communist aid organization—would produce films by Yakov Protazanov, Lev Kuleshov, Pudovkin, Boris Barnet, Ekk, Piscator, Hans Richter, and Ivens. To direct *Les Caves du Vatican* at Mezhrabpom would indeed have been a prestigious undertaking. Yet once the scheme collapsed, and although Buñuel continued to nourish the fantasy of working in the Soviet Union, he remained consistently vague about the concrete nature of the project. Writing to Unik from Madrid on 10 January 1934, while in the grip of a long and excruciating bout of sciatica, he would say: "I don't know if, given the bad state of health I'm in, they will accept me in the USSR. It goes without saying that this project pleases me enormously and that if I can I will go and work over there."[68] Maybe this lack of detail was due to his being dependent on news of the distant maneuvering on his behalf of powerfully placed figures like Aragon.

By the summer of 1934 Aragon and Triolet were in the USSR once more, in part to attend the First Soviet Writers Congress during the last two weeks of August, a much-publicized event at which Socialist Realism would be promulgated as the official aesthetic of Stalinism. (Alberti and León, clones of the French couple, were the Spanish AEAR representatives at the congress.) After recuperating from a gallbladder operation in a deluxe Comintern sanatorium, Aragon journeyed in October with Triolet to Odessa, in response to a request to turn his new, as yet unpublished, Socialist Realist novel *Les Cloches de Bâle* into a screenplay. Both the novelist and his producers, Ukrainfilm, would ultimately find the five hundred pages of intrigue too intractable, but not before AEAR stalwart Jean Lods had arrived in town to direct it.[69] There, Lods shot a documentary instead, *Histoire d'une ville, Odessa*, based on an Isaac Babel idea.[70] Aragon went back to Moscow in late November, and after witnessing Stalin shedding crocodile tears over the corpse of Sergei Kirov, whose murder would launch the "Great Terror," he returned to Odessa a fortnight later. From there he wrote on 20 December 1934 to Buñuel in Madrid, inviting him to come to the Ukrainfilm studios.

Aragon's letter is worth quoting at length because it is the only document we have that sets out the parameters of a potential Buñuel collaboration:

> I recall that two years ago, at the very moment you were to go to America, you told me that if you received an assignment elsewhere you'd drop America. Well, at the time I wasn't able to arrange things. Now it's different. I'm on the spot at the minute, and am working myself for a studio [Ukrainfilm] where they're dead keen for you to come and work. Only they can't do anything, of course, without knowing if you would leave the job you're doing, which must be interesting; in the event that this might interest you, you can let me know through Pierre [Unik], because I travel a lot and my current address would be useless to you. The studio is, it's true, extremely rudimentary in terms of means: but it might improve. Moreover, I don't think this is an issue for you. As a scenario, you could write one yourself or take a ready-made one, at any rate that would be something to discuss here, once you'd arrived. Right now, an ultra-modern Spanish operetta, of the Olé, olé! kind, the Caramba! kind, in short the Carmen kind, would certainly meet with a favorable reception; but this isn't obligatory, Père Ubu. Maybe things could be arranged so that you film a scenario of mine (a love story set in 1904), or no matter what by someone else.
>
> Personally, I strongly urge you to accept, as long as it doesn't force you to give up a job you don't want to leave, of course. I'm sure all your friends in Madrid would be delighted with the film you could make here, and if they advise you to come, let yourself be led. You'd only have to pay your travel expenses, which isn't that much money. Following that, you'd have everything: a room, living expenses, etc. You could come alone or with Jeanne [Rucar], as it suits you. As you will pass through Paris, note that I return there at the beginning of February [1935]. Which means that I could explain everything far better to you than by letter. I think that the most agreeable thing for you would be to come in March. But for that I'd need a positive reply so I could do some bargaining here before my departure.
>
> Drop me a line, in any case. Since you will understand that if you don't want to come now I also have to know: it would be very inconvenient to remain without a reply.[71]

This concrete proposal on the part of Aragon put Buñuel to the test. Under such modest conditions as these, would his cherished dream become reality? Well, no, and it would indeed have been surprising were Buñuel, who'd been contracted in July 1934 at an abundant salary to head the Warner Bros. dubbing department in Madrid, to have left such a well-paying job in order to journey at his own expense to an under-equipped studio on the Black Sea to direct folkloric potboilers. Moreover, Aragon was unaware that Luis and Jeanne now had a son. The "love story set in 1904" is a reference to *Les Cloches de Bâle*, a novel the director may just have read, since it was published in Paris late in 1934, with its author still in the USSR. (Incidentally, one of the main characters, Catherine Simonidzé, is named after Catherine Earnshaw of *Wuthering Heights*.) Buñuel might have been able to doctor the shelved script, to help salvage the project: "The truth is," Aragon would write, "I was as incapable of writing a film script, even drawn from a novel of mine, as a basset hound is of running across a tightrope."[72] The admiring Madrid friends to whom Aragon alludes in the letter must surely have been Alberti, Arconada, Garfias, Lacasa, León, Roces, and Ugarte, among others. The opinion that "true" cinema only existed in the Soviet Union was common coin among Spanish Communist intellectuals.

The enabler in Paris of this December 1934–January 1935 exchange of letters between Aragon and Buñuel was Pierre Unik, who'd recently joined the editorial board of *Commune*, and it was Unik who wrote to the director on 10 February 1935, asking if he still intended to go to the Soviet Union, which suggests that Buñuel was dragging his feet when it came to responding quickly, as Aragon had asked.[73] In any event, Buñuel's Russian campaign was finally nullified by the signing of his Filmófono contract in May. Yet perhaps the thing did not end there, for Aragon's Odessa proposal has a certain resonance with the populist *zarzuelas* and melodramas the Spaniard would produce in Madrid in 1935–36.

In the three years that he clung to the Soviet fantasy, Buñuel seems not to have thought twice about working in the conditions imposed by the new boss of the Soviet film industry, Boris Shumiatsky. During his eight-year tenure, which ended in 1938 when, accused of "sabotage," he was dispatched to the gulag, this party cadre with no experience of cinema was given carte blanche to Stalinize the movies. That is, to Taylorize the studio system, to purge a denigrated modernist avant-garde, and to impose the Socialist Realist method: uplifting stories with positive heroes, and no fancy montage. From 1930 onward the crash industrialization program was extended to the incipient sound cinema, with, at the level of image, mass entertainment and ideological legibility as the immediate goal, the aim being to arrive at a politically correct consumer product to vie with Hollywood. (It's here that we see how idealist, how out of touch, Moussinac's 1933 Bellevilloise lecture was.) Given the shortage of able scriptwriters, the apparat favored the adaptation of Russian and foreign literary works. This is the context of the *Caves du Vatican* and *Cloches de Bâle* proposals, and although these came to nothing, they suggest that after the problematic reception (or lack of it) of his first three films, Buñuel had mentally opted for the more viable, conventional path of transposing fiction to the screen. (He'd taken the first step with Unik, and to a lesser extent with Sadoul, in July–August 1932, of course, in scripting *Wuthering Heights.*) It could be that the CPSU (Communist Party of the Soviet Union) denunciation of the formalist "aberration" of the 1920s—its nadir reached with Eisenstein's public humiliation in 1935—segued with Buñuel's abiding distaste for "artistic" cinema. What are we to make, though, of his potential willingness to work under bureaucratic and relatively philistine party control?

Not all Left intellectuals of the period were in awe of Soviet cinema—Soviet cinema under the pall of Stalinism, that is. Witness Dalí, and his 5 March 1932 letter to Breton claiming that in Barcelona the "most bourgeois sort of audience" was queuing up to see Ekk's *The Road to Life*, a first fruit of Shumiatsky's reconfiguration of the cinema industry in the USSR. This issue of the "politically *incorrect*" audience for Soviet films had already exercised the Surrealists: in January 1928 Breton and others had addressed an extremely violent letter to Moussinac criticizing his presentation of Pudovkin's *Mother* (1926) before "a public of bourgeois profligates."[74] Dalí's complaint was subtly different, however: he was suggesting that by 1932 the content of Soviet cinema had become sufficiently reactionary as to be perfectly palatable to conservative Western audiences.

Produced by Mezhrabpom, *The Road to Life*, the first Soviet sound film to circulate outside the USSR, triumphantly illustrated the virtues of the pedagogical theories of Anton Seminovich Makarenko, for it depicted the re-education of asocial, delinquent youngsters—the *bezprizorni*, children who'd been orphaned in the civil war of 1919–21—through the shared task of constructing a railway line, and was enthusiastically applauded by the entire filo-Communist Western intelligentsia. Artur London, for example, would confess, "Who had not wept as he watched the superb film, *The Roads of Life* [*sic*]? That was why my comrades and I could never suspect the Moscow trials."[75] Dalí was to write to Breton once more on 4 October, mocking Communist bureaucrats and *The Road to Life*, whose repeat showing in Barcelona had been mounted by the Young Catholics Organization, an event that ratified his earlier dismissal. The artist cannot have known that some 150 miles away from Port Lligat, in Carcassonne, a pro-Surrealist cinephile was soon to address a letter to Breton complaining, quite independently, of the abject content of Ekk's film. And that the publication on 15 May 1933 of this letter in *LSASDLR* number 5 would lead to a final break with the AEAR, thus putting the already fraught relationship with the PCF under tremendous strain.

On 28 January 1933 *L'Âge d'or* was projected for the first time in Montpellier in a private session organized by Les Amis du cinéma, a film society run by teachers at the local university. The screening was introduced by one of their number, Ferdinand Alquié, signatory of the collective letter in favor of the film following the tumultuous aggression suffered during its opening (and closing) run in Paris. One week later, Les Amis du cinéma presented *The Road to Life*, thus prompting Alquié's indignant missive to Breton, dated Carcassonne, 7 March.[76] The letter began with a critique of Aragon's recent career in the service of "the wind of systematic cretinization that blows from the USSR" and went on to denounce Ekk's film, pointing out that his "indignation exploded during the screening of *The Road to Life*, at the sight of some young twerps for whom work is the only goal, the only means of living, who pride themselves on a train guard's uniform, who only enter the brothel—where at least there are songs and forsaken bodies—to abuse the women, and to frenziedly rip up the paper heart on which shine out the words—those words which, when all is said and done, I would willingly adopt as a program—'Here we drink, sing and kiss the girls.'"[77]

At the sight of this critique, Vaillant-Couturier, seconded by Marcel Willard, Paul Servèze, and Pierre Unik, sent Breton a letter on 10 June in the name of the AEAR, in which they reproached him for publishing the text, alleging that it contributed to the anti-Soviet campaign and demanding his "immediate repudiation" of Alquié's remarks. In the face of Breton's silence, Vaillant-Couturier summoned him before an AEAR Commission of Control, which the Surrealist declined to attend. On 4 July Breton received another letter, which notified him of his expulsion, ratified by a general assembly, from the association. As a result, the other Surrealist members—Char, Crevel, Éluard, Ernst, Giacometti, Man Ray, Péret, and Tzara—immediately resigned, in a decision that must have delighted Dalí, for whom the AEAR, whose affairs he'd remained resolutely aloof from, was a "bunch of mediocre bureaucrats."[78]

Although on the surface it was the implied endorsement of Alquié's views by the Surrealist Group that angered the party ideologues, there were other provocations in the last two issues of *LSASDLR* that contributed to this dramatic rift. Dalí's irreverent painting, *Hallucination: Six Images of Lenin on a Piano*, for one. But more importantly, a sarcastic reference to Gide's speech at the AEAR's anti-Fascist rally in the Salle du Grand Orient on 21 March, plus a typically ribald verse by Péret at the novelist's expense: "Monsieur Comrade Gide / sings *The Young Guard* among his mates / and tells himself the time's come to exhibit his belly like a Communist / red flag."[79] Given the fact that Unik, who had two poems in number 5, was on the literary panel seeking to win over Gide, and given the fact that Buñuel, who had a prose text in number 6 and was at that moment collaborating—or on the point of doing so—with Gide on the screen treatment of *Les Caves du Vatican*, the irreverence of the Surrealists must have been embarrassing to their former colleagues. Unik's signature at the bottom of the AEAR letter of condemnation would signify his final taking of a distance with the movement, and his commitment to the Communist cause. As for Buñuel, the evidence suggests that much the same applied to him during the 1930s, although he, like Unik, retained a certain interest in the doings of the people, especially Breton, who had recently meant so much to him.

With the appearance of the first issue of *Minotaure* on 1 June 1933, it became clear that the Surrealists were no longer at the service of the revolution, at least the one the Stalinists of the PCF proposed. The inclusion, even, of five Surrealist names in the list of *Ceux qui ont choisi: Contre le fascisme en Allemagne; Contre l'impérialisme français* was out of sync with developments on the ground. Henceforth, the group would ally itself with, and make the front running in, the anti-Stalinist opposition, from the group around Boris Souvarine and the Socialist Left to, finally, the Trotskyists.

Dalí was to become a *Minotaure* mainstay, with many of his finest essays and pictures appearing in its pages and a design of his gracing the cover of number 8 in 1936. Perhaps his omnipresence forms the subtext of Buñuel's tendentious claim—he, the receiver of aristocratic patronage!—that it was the "deluxe snobbery" and the "fashionable bourgeois" look of the new magazine that caused him to stop going to meetings of the group.[80] The chronology is awry here: by the time *Minotaure* started appearing, Buñuel had been out of Surrealism for the best part of a year. Even the disgrace of Dalí's interest in Hitler in February 1934, at the time of the momentous Fascist riots in Paris, could not invalidate his centrality to the movement. Until May 1939, that is, when Breton finally broke with him in "Des tendances les plus récentes de la peinture surréaliste," an article appearing in the final issue (number 12–13) of *Minotaure.*

Once the Surrealists and the AEAR had parted company in July 1933, Buñuel would continue siding with the culture of Stalinism until leaving Europe for the United States in September 1938. A couple of public statements of this—discreet ones, of course—are his would-be contributions to two fellow-traveling literary reviews dating from 1935: *El Tiempo Presente* (whose editors were César Arconada, Emilio Delgado, and Arturo Serrano Plaja) and *Tensor* (edited by Ramón J. Sender). Published in Madrid, both magazines were pro-Aragon and pro-AEAR, anti-Breton and anti-Surrealism. Bearing in mind Bunuel's ongoing epistemological break with the latter at the time of planning, shooting, and editing his third film, the "AEAR" documentary *Las Hurdes*, will help us understand the complexity of this new path taken by the avant-garde.

9

From *Las Hurdes* to *Terre sans pain*

Las Hurdes (or Jurdes), a wild and mountainous region in the province of Cáceres at the northern tip of Extremadura, abutting on to Portugal and with some fifty centers of population, has traditionally occupied a special place in the Spanish popular imagination as a source of both attraction—because of its mythic potential—and repulsion, due to its atavistic misery. In 1614 Lope de Vega published the comedy *Las Batuecas del duque de Alba*, presenting the region, which he knew only by hearsay, as a legendary place covered in snow. The original population of that remote and rather inaccessible area derived from Jews fleeing Christian persecution and, later on, from bandits on the run from the law or from Protestants who, fleeing the severity of the Catholic authorities, took refuge there. Some of its place-names bespeak the passage of foreign communities, such as the Camino Morisco, or Moorish Trail, a reminder of the Muslims who crossed and occasionally took refuge in the area and who also gave a name to places like La Alberca. In 1834, with Isabel II's arrival on the throne, Las Hurdes was freed of its feudal ties yet remained an isolated, miserable enclave. Moreover, the arrival of the new century—a century of electricity and techno-scientific revolution—demonstrated that its centripetal attraction had not diminished, since instead of trying their luck in foreign climes, many Hurdanos who emigrated to America to work on the building of the Panama Canal returned to their depressed place of origin after fulfilling their contracts.

The study and scientific description of Las Hurdes took a huge leap forward in 1910 when Maurice Legendre, secretary of the Casa de Velázquez in Madrid (an annex of the Institut Français), began making an annual tour of the region, except during World War I and in the summer of 1926, when he wrote his lengthy PhD thesis, *Las Jurdes: Étude de géographie humaine*, published in Bordeaux in 1927. The following year the Frenchman gave a lecture at the Residencia de Estudiantes called "Some Data on the Historical Conditions of Las Hurdes," of which Buñuel may have learned. In the highly detailed descriptions by Legendre (a Catholic fundamentalist like Jean-Henri Fabre, who also influenced Buñuel a great deal) there is something of the vision of the entomologist, a vision also cultivated by the future cineaste when he was a student of natural science in Madrid and one that would persist in many of his films. Legendre's gaze is that of an enlightened ethnographer, one typical of a Regenerationist, as Jordana Mendelson has put it.[1] Legendre took more than two thousand photos of the inhabitants, landscapes, and dwellings of that isolated and depressed area, forty-nine of which he reproduced in his book.

Following a description of the features of the physical geography of the region, Legendre devotes the greater, and most interesting, part of his book to its inhabitants and their systems of subsistence. The positivist logic of his description appears to be guided by an ineluctable determinism or fatalism. Accordingly, Legendre writes on the opening page of his study: "Nature has denied Las Jurdes all that may attract man and permit him to subsist; it has surrounded the region with barriers that are difficult to cross. . . . Ringed on all sides by dense barriers, it must have seemed a refuge to the persecuted, the defeated and the outlawed, before revealing itself to them, all too late in the day, as a desert."[2]

This idea persists throughout the book, in such observations as this: "One would say that the land has made a prisoner of man. . . . Man has walked into a trap; he is caught" (3). Legendre remarks that Malthus's theory is unfailingly fulfilled in the region (161), and referring to the adaptation to their environment of the fugitives who took shelter in Las Hurdes, he detects a sort of inverted Darwinism, since the Hurdano "evolves, except that he can only evolve by degenerating" (487). The French scholar notes that "through misery, their humanity was distorted" (lviii), according to a sinister syllogism, for "poverty breeds sickness, which breeds poverty. Poverty favors alcoholism, which makes poverty worse. Poverty favors demoralization, which makes poverty worse. Poverty causes outbursts of wastefulness, which make poverty worse" (339–40). Legendre also observes that until two years earlier—that is, until 1925—there were neither doctors nor civil guards in the area, the social redemption of which he sees as being problematic because, referring to the schooling of the children, "it is difficult to improve education without improving everything else" (380). One jarring aspect of that moral misery lay in the fact that it was situated at little more than an hour from the cultured university town of Salamanca.

Buñuel never concealed the fact that the source of inspiration for his 1933 Hurdano documentary was to be found in Legendre's remarkable work, as well as in four illustrated reports in the Madrid magazine *Estampa* in August–September 1929. Just as in Legendre's book, he subtitled the film "an essay in human geography," while the subsequent title of *Terre sans pain* also derives from Legendre's observation that "far from being fundamental to their nutrition, bread for them is a product of luxury" (162). We need do no more than look at the photos published in Legendre's book—the woman with goiter, the typical female costumes of La Alberca, the slate roofs of the houses, the mountains, and so on—to verify the debt owed by the iconography of Buñuel's documentary to its source. But this debt does not end there. Legendre mentions a medical report referring to the population of Aldehuela "with its generalized dwarfism, and characters worthy of Velázquez" (318), which has its visual echo in a scene from the film. And Legendre's observation that "death besets and haunts [the Hurdanos] on all sides" (490) provides the key to the film's last sequence, with the old woman tolling a bell and announcing that "there is nothing that keeps us more alert than thinking at all times of death."

Accounts as ancient as that of the Baron de Bourgoing's (in *Nouveau Voyage en Espagne* of 1798) exist of travelers visiting Las Hurdes. With the twentieth century under way, Blanco Belmonte and photographer Venancio Gombau toured the region in 1909 and published *Por la España desconocida: La Alberca, Las Hurdes, Las Batuecas y Peña de Francia*, a reportage that excited the interest of Unamuno and led him to visit the region with Legendre in the summer of 1913, a journey that resulted in four articles in *El Imparcial*. In April 1922, during Holy Week, a government-sponsored committee consisting of Doctor Gregorio Marañón, the surgeon José Goyanes, anthropology professor Luis Hoyos Sainz, and provincial health inspector Doctor Bardají visited Las Hurdes in order to write a report for the Ministry of the Interior, informing it of the sanitary conditions of the region and proposing measures to resolve its problems. As a consequence of this episode Alfonso XIII visited Las Hurdes in the spring of 1922, accompanied by the minister of the interior, the head of the royal palace, Doctors Marañón and Varela, photographers José Campúa and Alfonso, and cameraman Armando Pou, who shot news film of the visit.

The group set off on its travels on 20 June, and the king toured the region on horseback until 24 June, when he left it by car. The expedition received wide media coverage, with the reports in the weekly magazine *Blanco y Negro* of 2 July and in *La Esfera* of 8 July, using photos by Campúa, being particularly memorable.

As a result of the royal visit, the building of a road from La Alberca to Las Batuecas and Las Mestas was undertaken. In March 1930 Alfonso XIII would repeat the journey. These widely publicized initiatives have been linked to the difficult moments the Crown was going through on both occasions: the first tour, because of the colonial army's humiliation at the Battle of Annual in Morocco, which had besmirched the king's name and led to a change of government the month before; while the second visit followed the collapse of the Primo de Rivera dictatorship, backed by the monarch, on 30 January 1930. With his gestures of interest in the disinherited of Las Hurdes the king attempted to improve his public image. The advent of the Second Republic in April 1931 saw the Royal Board of Trustees of Las Hurdes give way to the National Board of Trustees of Las Hurdes, with Gregorio Marañón occupying the presidency.

Before getting round to the genesis of Buñuel's documentary, it is worth examining the extent to which *Las Hurdes* was inscribed within the tradition of ethnographic documentary—a genre that was already consolidated by 1933—particularly of the "sensationalist" sort.

The fourth session of the Cineclub Español, held in the Palacio de la Prensa in Madrid on 19 March 1929 and programmed by Buñuel from Paris, featured *Moana* (1923–25), the documentary shot by Robert Flaherty in Samoa. Of it, Robert Desnos had written in *Le Soir*: "Due to the appeal it made to our most precious imaginative faculties, to our heartfelt feelings and sensuality, *Moana* . . . is one of the most beautiful dreams we may ever have experienced."[3] Although Flaherty is usually considered to be the father of ethnographic cinema with his *Nanook of the North* (1922), travel films to exotic climes were invented by the Lumière Brothers and their peripatetic cameramen, although the dramatization of travel documentaries probably got under way with Gaumont's *Scott's Antarctic Expedition* (Herbert G. Ponting, 1911–12), a visual logbook with a tragic ending that filled Colette with enthusiasm.[4]

Many ethnographic documentaries of the time took an overtly sensationalist tack. A good example is *In the Land of the Head-Hunters* (1914) by American ethnographer Edward S. Curtis, about the life of the Kwakiutl Indians of Northwest Canada, which enjoyed wide distribution in Spain thanks to the efforts of the Selecciones Julio César company. Released in Europe in 1931 were a number of ethnographic documentaries with great impact, such as *Au pays du scalp*, made by the Marquis de Wavrin of his expedition to Amazonia to visit the Jivaro Indians, who practiced headshrinking. Opening in November 1931 in Paris, when Buñuel was once again living there, was *Chez les buveurs de sang*, filmed during the Gourgand-Rychner expedition to Africa (1930–31), which showed Masai tribesmen drinking the blood of animals. In the same year *Untamed Africa*, a documentary about the Wynant D. Hubbard and Earl Frank expedition, was released in France, while in Spain Filmófono distributed *Africa Speaks* (1930), about the Paul L. Hoefler expedition.

Although we have referred to ethnographic films of a sensationalist kind, it is worth noting that from time to time a militant magazine as rigorous as *Nuestro Cinema* published photos from such documentaries on its cover and in its pages. Indeed, its first number, in June 1932, opened with a cover photo from *¡Hasta la vista Africa!*, a practice adhered to in subsequent issues. By this time the French expedition film had a string of its own classics, the first being *La Croisière noire* (1926), a report by Léon Poirier of the crossing of Africa by a Citroën team. This was followed by *Voyage au Congo* (1927) by Marc Allégret, who was accompanied by André Gide, at times presented as the filmmaker's uncle or godfather, when in reality their relationship was a sentimental one. In January 1930 Buñuel got to know Marc Allégret personally in the studios of Billancourt, and it may be that the latter described the details of the filming of *Voyage au Congo* to him.

Along with these generic antecedents, which are more or less remote from *Las Hurdes*, there are some that are much more specific. For the second session of the Cineclub Español on 26 January 1929 Buñuel programmed the French documentary *La Zone* (1928), the first film by Georges Lacombe, who had been René Clair's assistant on *Entr'acte*; the film bore the expressive subtitle *Au pays des chiffoniers (Étude des coins ignorés de Paris)*. In part this was an exploration of the slums surrounding Paris's orbital road in the area of Clignancourt and showed *chiffoniers* (ragpickers) raking around in the rubbish. Influenced by the Soviet documentary school, *La Zone* depicted the reverse side of the lively and frivolous Paris of the tourist postcard. Lacombe's film, which interested Buñuel, may be seen as a possible precursor of *Las Hurdes*.

Opening in January 1926 at the Ciné Madeleine in Paris, where Buñuel might have seen it, was the startling American documentary *Grass* (1925), by Ernest B. Schoedsack and Merian C. Cooper, which showed a tribe of Kurdish herdsmen in the west of Iran making an arduous annual migration in search of fresh pasture for their livestock. It is fitting to speak of this much-bruited release in relation to *Las Hurdes*, which not only shows the fraught exodus of a group of Hurdanos but contains a sequence of a mountain goat plunging down a cliff that is very similar to one Schoedsack and Cooper included in *Grass*.

Lastly, during a break from filming *Komsomol* in the USSR, Joris Ivens visited Paris and met Buñuel there in April 1932. Perhaps the Dutchman spoke to him of a movie he'd seen in Tiflis on his first trip to Russia in spring 1930. Of *Salt for Svanetia* (1930), directed and photographed by Mikhail Kalatozov, Ivens said: "Although it was a documentary, it had an intensity and a violence that the

European Surrealists would have adored had they been able to see it."[5] Jay Leyda went much further and confessed that *Terre sans pain* and *Salt for Svanetia* "are always linked in my mind—they are both sur-realist in the literal sense of the term, both with a harsh pity for the tragedies of their subjects that is far more moving than any appeal for sympathy."[6] Much influenced by Eisensteinian formalism, Kalatozov's film (which is not strictly speaking a documentary) is based on the account of a visit to Svanetia, in the Caucasus Mountains, by Sergei Tretyakov and describes the impoverished life of an isolated village dominated by religious superstition but above all by its distressing lack of salt. Like *Terre sans pain*, the film begins by showing a map of the region and describes the struggle for survival of its people and animals. Thus, a goat licks the sweat of a sleeping man, because in sweat there is salt. The urine of a peasant who pees in a field attracts a herd of cows for the same reason, as the blood-smeared corpse of a stillborn child draws a salt-seeking dog. This collective and violently anti-clerical tragedy, which also shows men emigrating to find work, might rightfully be called *Terre sans sel*. In the end intrepid Communists dynamite the mountains and end the isolation of the population. The American critic Harry Alan Potamkin described *Salt for Svanetia* as the "summit of the ethnographic film I saw in Moscow last year," deeming it to be "a drama that calls forth high emotional response and commands immediate action."[7]

As theoretically interesting as these antecedents of *Las Hurdes* are, there is a further source that is rigorously concrete and historical in relation to the genesis of Buñuel's project, one involving Yves Allégret, Marc Allégret's brother. As her dowry, Yves's wife, Renée Naville—sister of Pierre Naville, ex-Surrealist and future partisan of Trotsky—received the Cinéma du Panthéon in Paris, and in order to put it to good use she went into partnership with producer Pierre Braunberger, the two of them having a big commercial hit with the release of Ernst Lubitsch's *The Love Parade* (1929).[8] Yves Allégret, by sympathy a Trotskyist—in May 1933 he refused to sign a text eulogizing Stalin—associated with the agitprop theater group *Octobre*, had made *Prix et profits / La Pomme de terre* in 1931, a Marxist documentary about the exploitation of the peasantry produced by Célestin Freinet's Coopérative de l'Enseignement Laïc, on which the Prévert brothers, who were also members of *Octobre*, collaborated. A reading of Legendre's book deeply impressed Allégret, and he decided to film a documentary in Las Hurdes, as he already had professional experience as an assistant to Alberto Cavalcanti, Jean Renoir (on *La Chienne*, 1931), Paul Fejos, and his brother Marc.

In the spring of 1932 Allégret traveled to Spain with Renée and cameraman Eli Lotar (Eliazar Lotar Teodoresco), son of the Rumanian poet Tudor Arghezi, armed with a camera supplied by Braunberger. Lotar, a future squire in the

Date and location uncertain. Possibly a meeting of the Order of Toledo in the Venta de Aires inn on the outskirts of the city, ca. 1932–34. *From left to right*: Eli Lotar, Pierre Unik, Manuel Ángeles Ortiz, Buñuel, Pepín Bello, María Teresa León, Rafael Alberti, Unknown. (Private collection. Courtesy Librairie Emmanuel Hutin, Paris)

Order of Toledo, was known for his photographs of the slaughterhouses of La Villette in the "Abattoirs" reportage—which in its cruelty presaged *Las Hurdes*—featured in the sixth number of *Documents* in November 1929. Lotar had filmmaking experience as a cameraman on the documentaries of Jean Painlevé (*Caprelles et pantopodes*, 1930, for instance), Joris Ivens on *Nous bâtissons* (1930) and *Zuiderzee* (1930)—whose life-and-death struggle of men against the sea bore some resemblance to *Las Hurdes*—and Jacques Brunius on *Un Voyage aux Cyclades* (1931). The Préverts wrote a script that Lotar was slated to direct, *Le Fils de famille (ou attention au fakir)*, the tale of a money-grubbing family that unwittingly sells its idiot son to the Devil and then tries to get him back.[9]

Allégret's project—which bore the *Groupe Octobre* hallmark—miscarried, however, when the threesome was detained by Spanish police in Carmona (Seville)—Andalusian anarchist uprisings were also one of Allégret's interests—and then freed (thanks to the diplomatic intercession of Radical politician Édouard Herriot). Deemed to be "dangerous Communists," they were expelled from the country. In Cádiz they took the first available boat and ended up in the Canary Islands, where they filmed the documentary *Ténérife*. It would be four years before they managed to edit it and add a soundtrack commentary by Jacques Prévert—despite which it was rejected by the distributor, Pathé.[10] It was Lotar or Allégret who spoke to Buñuel of their stillborn Las Hurdes scheme, which the Aragonese director inherited, so to speak, along with its cameraman, and even the camera Braunberger had supplied.

To sum up, it was Yves Allégret's failed plan, a reading of Legendre's book, and the four news reports *Estampa* published in August–September 1929, signed pseudonymously and with photos by Benítez-Casaux, which gave rise, along with Buñuel's previous visits to the area, to the definitive documentary. On 23 March 1932 Buñuel had written to Noailles that he felt distanced from

Frame and production stills from the documentaries *Ténérife* (Yves Allégret, 1932) and *Las Hurdes* (Luis Buñuel, 1933), both of them photographed by Eli Lotar. (*Ténérife*: Gaumont Pathé Archives, Saint Ouen; photo: Iconothèque of the Cinémathèque Française, Paris / *Las Hurdes*: Filmoteca Española, Madrid)

the spirit of *L'Âge d'or* and was thinking about new projects that were a far cry from it.[11] At the time the failure of Allégret's scheme had still not occurred, but the by now Communist Buñuel cleaved to a new sensibility that would render him receptive to the tale of the Hurdano misadventure.

As has been related on numerous occasions, the project supposedly got off the ground thanks to the lottery ticket with which the teacher, artist, and anarchist militant from Huesca, Ramón Acín, won the Christmas draw in December 1932. In Zaragoza's Café Ambos Mundos he had told his friend Buñuel in front of Rafael Sánchez Ventura that were he to win the prize he would pay for a film.[12] In the draw Acín won 100,000 pesetas, 20,000 of which he gave to Buñuel, to notable protests from his anarchist comrades, who wanted to share the money between them. This is the official version, since in 1951 Pierre Kast deduced from the witnesses he consulted—among them Lotar and Hernando Viñes—that it was Buñuel who loaned Acín the cash to buy the lottery ticket, saying "if you win you have to give me money to film a short in Las Hurdes."[13] However, when compiling his professional autobiography in the United States in 1939, Buñuel wrote laconically that the money came from Acín's savings, an elliptical way, perhaps, of summing up the incredible origin of the investment.

Buñuel used 4,000 pesetas of that money to buy an old Fiat, which he repaired himself when necessary.[14] In those days, notwithstanding their ideological differences, it was not unusual to come across collaborations between anarchists and Communists—two revolutionary groups, both of them enemies of the bourgeois Second Republic—all the more so if personal friendship intervened, as in this case. Some sources—such as J. F. Aranda and Conchita Mantecón—maintain that Buñuel's mother also contributed production money, which seems likely.[15] And the fact that Pierre Unik would have his travel expenses paid by Lucien Vogel, owner of the illustrated magazines *Vu* and *Lu*, to do an article meant a saving for the project.

Even before the financing for the film was in place, Buñuel visited Las Hurdes with a group of friends at the end of September 1932. Rafael Alberti and María Teresa León were later to evoke this trip to the region under the guidance of the filmmaker. They first recalled that accompanying the three of them were Unik, Lotar, and the musician Gustavo Durán (all Communists, bar Lotar), and that they spent the night in the Monastery of Santa María de Guadalupe in the province of Cáceres.[16] León, meanwhile, claimed that Buñuel said to them: "Do you see this marvelous valley? Well, hell starts from here on in."[17] The beauty of the place would prompt Buñuel to conceive of buying the monastery of Las Batuecas in June 1936, but the operation was thwarted by the outbreak of the Civil War.[18] Evoking the phase prior to the filming, Buñuel stated: "I visited the region ten days before with a notebook. I jotted down 'goats,' 'little girl ill with malaria,' 'anopheles mosquitoes,' 'there are no songs, no bread,' and later on I began filming according to these notes."[19] Invited in March 1940 to give a talk at Columbia University, he explained that after touring the area for three days, he put together a synopsis divided into different sections: "Hurdano foodstuffs, school, constructing fields for cultivation, burial, etc."[20]

Buñuel prepared the filming by getting the written approval of Marcelino Pascua, another member of the Order of Toledo, general director of health in the Republican government and future Paris ambassador during the Civil War, and of Ricardo Urueta, general director of fine arts, who backed his scheme for an "artistic" film about Salamanca and a "picturesque" documentary about Las Hurdes.[21] A very different movie was to result, however.

In his study of the documentary Carlos Rebolledo attributes a "zero degree of culture" to the Hurdanos.[22] This is inaccurate, and Buñuel would make a point of emphasizing the contrary, as he did in his lecture to the students of Columbia University:

> There are a number of strange ideas about Las Hurdes. The most persistent is the belief that the people are savages. Nothing could be further from the truth. If these people are unlike anyone, they are unlike savage tribes. Among savages life is not nearly so hard. Man has only to reach out his hand to gather the fruits of nature. There is no spiritual conflict between the savage and his circumstances. A primitive civilization has a primitive culture. But in Las Hurdes a primitive civilization goes with a modern culture. These people have the same moral and religious principles as we have. They speak our language. They have the same needs as we have. But in their case the means for satisfying those needs are hardly any better than those of the cave man.[23]

On the other hand, a bit further on he did admit to their lack of spiritual and instrumental culture: "Another point hard to believe is that here there is no folklore. The whole time we were there we never heard one song. The men are silent at their work, and have no songs to make their task a little lighter." Unamuno's testimony was at odds with Buñuel's when it came to music, for in Las Hurdes he claimed to having heard "the occasional human song ascending to the heavens from out of a ravine."[24] Buñuel also observed in his lecture: "The few utensils which are seen have been brought in from Castile or Extremadura by some who went off begging in those regions. In the district of Las Hurdes nothing is made. There is no skilled labor." And on the film's soundtrack commentary the diagnosis is that "the degeneration of this race is due principally to hunger, to the lack of hygiene, to misery and to incest." And with regard to nutrition, the observation that "bread was until very recently almost unknown in Las Hurdes" gave rise to the definitive title of the film in 1936: *Terre sans pain.*

Buñuel referred to the fracture in Las Hurdes between spiritual culture and material scarcity. In relation to the first, it has to be remembered that the Second Republic made a considerable, albeit insufficient, effort when it came to building schools and providing teachers. Buñuel completed the filming of *Las Hurdes* in the spring of 1933, just as the Spanish Parliament was discussing the closing of religious schools, approved in May. Marcelino Domingo, the Republican minister of education, would claim that 12,988 schools were created between 1931 and 1933, although this amount has been reduced by historians to between 10,000 and 11,000, figures that are nevertheless praiseworthy.[25] In the documentary a long shot is accompanied by the comment: "This village, La Aceitunilla, is situated in one of the poorest valleys. The white building is the school, recently built." Sadoul would add in 1936, doubtless from information afforded him by Buñuel, that the school was built "for the King's visit."[26] And as to the extreme debility of the region in terms of agriculture, it has to be remembered that in September 1932 Parliament approved a very limited program of agrarian reform that was dismantled in May 1934 by the conservative government.

On 26 March 1933 Buñuel had a work session with cameraman Lotar, who left Paris for Spain on 20 April, according to his personal notebook.[27] This information concurs with a letter to Lotar and Unik written by Sánchez Ventura from Las Batuecas, dated 16 April 1933, in which he gives them detailed instructions about leaving Paris on 20 April at the latest—if possible, on 19 April—for Madrid in order to meet him or Acín at the central station or the Hotel Dardé there. Sánchez Ventura adds that on 24 April "there's a splendid social gathering to film," namely the ceremony of decapitating cocks in La Alberca. The signing of the letter is revealing, for in it we read: "Communist greetings, Buñuel / Anarchist regards, Acín / Cheers! Sánchez Ventura."[28]

According to Buñuel's statement to the Columbia University students, his technical equipment consisted of two old cameras, one of them lent by Braunberger: a hand-cranked Éclair and an Eyemo, although this lacked the swiveling head to take the different lenses.[29] Mentioned in Lotar's notebook is a four-hundred-foot-capacity Debrie with 25, 35, and 50 mm lenses, to which Aranda adds a Kinamo camera.[30] In a talk Buñuel gave at the MoMA in April 1940 he recalled that they had only four thousand feet of film available, potentially forty minutes of projection, material that was also provided by Braunberger.[31] As there was no electricity in the region, reflecting screens of silver paper were used to illuminate the interiors by day, although for the night scenes (of promiscuous sleeping arrangements or the old woman who bids people to pray) torches were used. The photography was a faithful echo of the illustrations in Legendre's book, but it is also possible to encounter other connections: the open mouth of the sick girl, her throat and gums inflamed, has often been linked to Boiffard's photograph *Bouche*, published with a commentary by Bataille in *Documents* (second year, number 5, 1930), a magazine on which Lotar collaborated.

The team's home base was in the sanctuary of Las Batuecas, a sixteenth-century ecclesiastical building converted into an inn after the sale of church property in the nineteenth century, which had a dozen rooms with cold running water, a luxury at the time. This hostel-cum-abbey was run by a Carmelite brother turned layman who, according to Sadoul, was an "odd and truculent monk."[32] In the team, besides Lotar, there was Unik, Sánchez Ventura, and Acín, whose name Buñuel did not mention in the credits of the film. The one-month stay in the region led to the team's total isolation from the outside world, although Buñuel would call a halt to the filming in order to participate—perhaps *à distance*, by telephone—in the launch of the first manifesto of the Spanish AEAR in support of German writers who had fallen foul of the Nazis (said launch took place in Madrid on May Day). Unik spoke of their isolation in a letter sent to Sadoul from La Alberca on 30 April, with the greetings of Buñuel and Sánchez Ventura annotated in the margin—the absence of Acín's signature would suggest he had already left the project. Sketching three flags, Unik asked Sadoul for news of home, telling him he didn't know which banners were now flying on the buildings of Paris, whether the French, the Third Reich's, or that of the USSR.[33]

The filming only took place in Las Hurdes Altas, the more depressed area—the one also toured by Unamuno—which ideally suited Buñuel's political purpose. During the filming the team rose at four in the morning, journeyed for two hours by car, and then continued on foot, hefting their equipment, in order to arrive at the previously chosen location around midday. They worked until three in the afternoon before returning to their base in Las Batuecas to eat.

The production of the documentary in situ lasted from 23 April to 22 May 1933. On 24 May the team returned to Madrid, and on 22 June Buñuel got back to Paris to continue his dubbing work at Paramount. That same summer Buñuel and Unik began working on the commentary, as is shown by a *pneumatique* dated 22 July, in which Buñuel makes an appointment in a café near the *L'Humanité* office, adding, "Tonight we can go to my house and read Las Hurdes," that is, to presumably go through Legendre's text in order to establish the script of the edited material.[34] The editing of the documentary, however, was not done until the end of the year in Madrid, without a moviola and on a kitchen table, with the help of a magnifying glass.[35] The commentary written to accompany the images is dated March 1934. The first screening, with a live voice-over by Buñuel, took place in December under the Lerroux government, which did not authorize the film. Furthermore, in January and March 1935 Unik published a couple of reports on Las Hurdes, with photos by Lotar, in the magazine *Vu*, under the title "Ten hours from Paris: At the 'Sultan of Las Hurdes'; Terra incognita, a strange, primitive tribe."

Thanks to Buñuel's Columbia University lecture, and confirmed by the outtakes of the film preserved in the Cinémathèque de Toulouse, we know that the documentary was based on reenactments by the individuals seen on screen, following prior rehearsal by Buñuel. In short, this is a highly interventionist, refined mise-en-scène that distances the film from the spontaneity traditionally (and ingenuously) attributed to the documentary genre. In his lecture Buñuel explained: "All the footage you are going to see in the film had to be paid for. Our budget was a modest one, but luckily it squared with the few pretensions of this poor people. The village of Martilandrán, which is one of the most squalid, placed itself at our disposal in exchange for two goats that we killed and roasted and for twenty big loaves of bread that the people ate communally during a lunch supervised by the mayor, perhaps the hungriest of the lot."[36] Mercè Ibarz has referred to the feast as "the Martilandrán deal."[37]

This pact was truly important because the appreciative local official became a crucial intercessor (as both filter and negotiator) between Buñuel's team and the subjects of interest to it. We do not know the extent to which he became Buñuel's orthopedic gaze in Las Hurdes, but his collaboration—unattested to in the credits—was surely relevant. (Another, similarly invisible figure is "Vicente," servant to the doctor of the village of Nuñormoral, who worked for the team as a guide and thus go-between.) This system of mediations and of rigid mise-en-scènes explains the well-known disqualification of the film by anthropologist Pío Baroja. Lotar's statement confirmed this: "Everything is reconstructed, elaborated, interpreted. The Hurdano peasants *perform* their own roles the way actors do."[38] By working this way Buñuel did nothing, in fact, but prolong the "constructivist" tradition instaured by Flaherty with *Nanook of the North*, which established that in filmic representation reality and truth are not necessarily synonymous.

The list of controlled stagings is long. The goat hurtling from the crags was brought down by a shot, the smoke from which is just visible in the lower right-hand corner of the frame, and one of the outtakes preserved in Toulouse shows Buñuel firing at it with a pistol. Of course, Buñuel had to pay the animal's worth to the Hurdanos. Unik explained that they shot and killed a donkey after it was attacked by bees. The scene in the school when the boy writes "Respect thy neighbor's property" on the blackboard was organized according to Buñuel's instructions. The little girl who appears with an infected mouth did not die, as claimed in the voice-over. And the sequence of the dead baby and its famous river burial was total fiction. Herminia Alba Añe, who represents the mother in the scene, was not the mother of the supposedly dead child and was paid twenty *reales* (five pesetas) for her performance. The choice of individual was so happy that André Bazin would deem her to possess "all the beauty of a Spanish Pietà."[39] And her supposed child was not dead but sleeping. The theme of the river burial would reappear in two of Buñuel's Mexican feature films: *Subida al cielo* (1951) and *El río y la muerte* (1954).

Due to the freedom of their construction, Buñuel's first two films were in a way cine-poems, while *Las Hurdes* opts clearly for cine-prose, of a distinctly harsh kind in which, notwithstanding the predominance of exterior shots, the photography and editing construct a claustrophobic, concentration-camp-like terrain. In that respect the documentary constitutes a visual equivalent of the region's *huis clos* quality, described in a literary manner by Legendre. Javier Herrera Navarro has rightly pointed out that Buñuel inverted the 1930 itinerary of the king, who concluded it in the festive atmosphere of La Alberca ("a redemptive end-of-journey celebration," Herrera Navarro calls it), while Buñuel begins it in the fiesta in La Alberca, prior to the descent into the Hurdano hell.[40] While the classic itinerant structure of the travel documentary is retained, the joyous release comes first, thus accentuating the dourness of the subsequent expedition to the miserable Hurdes Altas.

The description of the setting of La Alberca is an exercise in cultural anthropology, which commences with its monuments and continues with its inhabitants. The all-seeing gaze of the camera before a facade, typical of an art documentary, shows us two skulls in their niches and the religious inscription over the door. The power of the church will become an overarching theme. From stones we pass to human beings, with an elaborate feminine hairdo and the rite of the recently married young men who, on horseback, pull off the heads of cocks suspended from a rope by their feet. Exorcizing the threat of castration, this bird decapitation—a scene cut or abbreviated in the French and English versions—is a sadistic provocation similar to that of the razored eye in *Un chien andalou*, but now in a documentary context. The Dionysian festival of blood and sex is brought to a close with the fruit of sexual union—the close-up of a baby baroquely festooned with Christian medallions, conjuring up, the commentary tells us, pagan amulets from Africa or Oceania. Thus begins Buñuel's discourse on the hegemony of religious power, which continues with the monk of Las Batuecas—the "Sultan" of Unik's *Vu* essays—who lives surrounded by a harem of women servants, continues with the precept to "Respect thy neighbor's property" taught to the impoverished children in school, and ends with the observation, before a splendid altar, that "the only thing of luxury we have found in Las Hurdes is the churches." The closure, with the nocturnal cry of the old woman who preaches that "there is nothing that keeps us more alert than thinking at all times of death. Say an *Ave Maria* for the repose of the soul of . . . ," is in keeping with Legendre's observations about the obsession of the Hurdanos with death, but its text proceeds literally from the news reports cited in the magazine *Estampa.* The old woman accompanies her sermon with the ringing of a bell, an instrument that also occupied a privileged place in the memory of Buñuel, who time and again recalled the bells of Calanda, "which toll all day long. Who's dying? Bells, bells for mass, for the rosary, the death knell."[41] This obsessive recollection finds a place in *Tristana* (1969).

Agustín Sánchez Vidal has drawn attention to the three levels on which the documentary unfolds: its realist aspect, its tragic structure, and its overtures to the unconscious (like the beheading of the cocks or the phallic tower of Las Batuecas).[42] But *Las Hurdes* is also rich in intertextual references within Buñuel's œuvre itself. For instance, the wretched outlaws of *L'Âge d'or*, led by Max Ernst, prefigure the Hurdanos the director filmed three years later. As Alberto Farassino has written: "Played by Parisian intellectuals, the ragged, debilitated bandits from the beginning of *L'Âge d'or* have the same tragic look as the emigrating Hurdanos who advance with difficulty."[43] But the references do not end there, for the characters in *Los olvidados* (1950) live in miserable, rundown suburbs that are like Las Hurdes with asphalt. And in their social marginality the Hurdanos have a family resemblance to the beggars of *Viridiana* (1961). Their existential precariousness reminds us of the harsh desert island loneliness of the figure of *Robinson Crusoe* (1952), or the protagonist of *Nazarín* (1958), in self-exile from his society, or to those of *Él* (1952) and *Simón del desierto* (1965), adrift in the solitude of their pathological inner world. Finally, the physical and endogamic isolation of the Hurdanos anticipates the enforced cloistering of the characters in *El ángel exterminador* (1962), which propels them implacably toward a degradation of the most sordid kind.

Another familiar iconographic motif in the documentary is the donkey killed by bee stings, which in fact dramatizes an episode that impressed Buñuel in his childhood, when as an eight-year-old he came across the body of a donkey in the countryside "surrounded by enormous buzzards that looked like priests."[44] This "rotting" donkey would appear for the first time in *Un chien andalou* (1929), with the bodies of two burros laid atop a pair of grand pianos. And in the close-up of the eye of the dead donkey surrounded by bees there is an apparent echo of the sliced eye in that film. In *Las Hurdes* there are shots of toads and snakes, demonstrating the interest the former natural sciences student had in the animal world, something exhibited repeatedly in his subsequent filmography. And this interest, now with didactic intent, reappears in the brief lecture on mosquitoes, using an illustration from an essay on entomology to distinguish the dangerous anopheles mosquito, which is the bearer of malaria, from the inoffensive culex mosquito. Buñuel admired the scientific documentaries of Jean Painlevé, which he wanted to screen in the Residencia de Estudiantes, and inserted a short documentary on scorpions as a prologue to *L'Âge d'or*.

The narrative logic of *Terre sans pain* flies in the face of any kind of hope, as Ado Kyrou first pointed out in 1953.[45] The voice-over informs us that spring—the season of love and gaiety—is the hardest period for the Hurdanos, since hunger causes them to gorge themselves on cherries, but as these are still green they produce dysentery. In short, every glimmer of hope seems to be contradicted by its outcome: the olive trees bear fruit, but this is devoured by insects; the bites of certain snakes are not fatal, but the victim puts medicinal plants on the wound that cause infections, and so on. And along with this logic of pessimism, there are the instances of irrationality that reveal the filmmaker's Surrealist origins: hence, after a few descriptive images of La Alberca, the film's eighth shot shows, as if it were the most natural thing in the world, a black ox coming out the door of a house in an eye-catching contextual displacement that evokes the cow lying on the bourgeois bed in *L'Âge d'or*. Another contextual dissonance appears in the print of an elegant, Louis XV-style lady on the wall of the poverty-stricken school in Aceitunilla, frequented by barefooted children. And a new outburst of strangeness emerges with the images of the dwarfs and cretins, about whom the commentary points out that "the realism of a Zurbarán or a Ribera comes a poor second in the face of a reality such as this."

The Surrealist sparks that fly at certain moments in Buñuel's documentary enable us to reopen the controversial question of its aesthetic affiliation. In keeping with his Surrealist militancy, Kyrou wrote: "This film does not differ in the least from *L'Âge d'or*, its realism is the same and so, therefore, is its Surrealism."[46] And with identical determinist tenacity, Freddy Buache stated, "There is no hint of a hiatus between *L'Âge d'or* and *Terre sans pain*."[47] When Kyrou and Buache wrote such pithy affirmations very little was known of Buñuel's withdrawal from Surrealist activity in 1932 and even less of his subsequent Communist militancy, which shed quite a lot of light when it came to contextualizing his documentary. More judicious, as to the Surrealist aspects of the film, is Patrick Bureau's assessment that "the real, due to its coefficient of the monstrous, the inconceivable, leads to a Surrealist reality."[48] What is forgotten in these assessments, however, is that in the early 1930s a "rehumanization" of art (in contrast to its earlier avant-garde "dehumanization") occurred in Spanish culture, and it is within the framework of this new collective social sensibility that Buñuel's film must be situated.

The often shrewd Ernesto Giménez Caballero described Buñuel as "Goyaesque, Quevedoesque and Solanaesque, introducer of the *tremendismo* [harsh realism] of Cela."[49] Setting aside Camilo José Cela, who is much later in chronological terms, the allusion to Buñuel's *tremendismo* is interesting, not least because the cineaste would confess to Max Aub: "As for me filming the worst, it was true. If not, why bother?"[50] At the time there already existed in the visual arts a tradition of *feísmo*, the vaunting of ugliness, in whose lineage were to be found Goya, Toulouse-Lautrec, James Ensor, Regoyos, Otto Dix, and George Grosz. In Spain this tradition's main exponent at the time was José Gutiérrez Solana, author of the book *La España negra* (1920) and painter of cruel and bitter canvases in which the macabre and the grotesque are magisterially brought together. Solana's *tremendismo* is the one that comes nearest to that of Buñuel's film, and it is no accident that his visual work was exhibited in the Spanish Pavilion at the 1937 International Exhibition of Art and Technology in Modern Life in Paris, since it represented to perfection, and more explicitly so than *Guernica*, the tragic Spain of the Civil War. As a young man, Buñuel had defended—along with Dalí—the "anti-artistic" ideal in cinema and had eulogized as "repugnantly magnificent" the sordid naturalism of Stroheim's *Greed* (1923).[51] His documentary remained faithful to these ideas by demonstrating that reality could be transformed into nightmare, with the collaboration of another *tremendista*, Eli Lotar, who had so incisively photographed the abattoirs of La Villette.

Buñuel not only filmed "the worst" of Las Hurdes, as he confessed to Aub; elsewhere he would add: "It's a tendentious film. In Las Hurdes Bajas there isn't the same huge amount of misery," and, "it's maybe the least gratuitous film I've made."[52] This was a utilitarian or, more precisely, an *engagé* movie expressive of the aspirations of a young generation of politicized, pro-Communist filmmakers. It is fitting, therefore, to examine the situation of the PCE at that moment.

When General Sanjurjo's attempted military coup took place on 10 August 1932, the PCE replied with the order to "defend the Republic," but this was immediately disavowed by the Comintern, for whom the only valid slogan was "Long live the soviets!" As a result, the PCE leaders were summoned to Moscow, admonished, and dismissed, with José Bullejos being replaced as general secretary by José Díaz. At the same time the party was henceforth to be monitored by an

Old Highland Woman, etching by José Gutiérrez Solana, ca. 1933–34. (Collection: Galería Leandro Navarro, Madrid)

Detail of the back cover of the first issue, dated June–July 1933, of the magazine *Octubre*, organ of the Spanish AEAR, with a text by its coeditor Rafael Alberti forming a caption to a still from *Las Hurdes*. (Collection: Román Gubern, Barcelona)

Italian-Argentinean named Vittorio Codovila, a hard-line Stalinist agent.[53] Accordingly, in the elections of November 1933 the PCE went on using the watchwords authorized by the Comintern: "Down with the bourgeois Republic!" "For a workers' and peasants' government!" and so on.

In the light of these facts, it can be seen that the social and political message of Buñuel's documentary virulently contradicted the image of rural Spain being disseminated at the time in the photographs and documentaries of the Pedagogical Missions (1931–36), an enlightened and Regenerationist didactic front with which Buñuel never collaborated. Not only did he not collaborate, but he pitted the revolutionary intentions of his documentary against the Missions by angrily denouncing the negligence of the monarchy and the bourgeois republic toward that miserable region. This political intention was immediately corroborated when in its first number, dated June–July 1933, the organ of the Spanish AEAR, the magazine *Octubre*, opened with an essay by Friedrich Engels and published photographs from Buñuel's film on its front and back cover. On the front was Herminia Alba Añe, the mother of the supposedly dead child, while the caption read: "Thus are the peasant women of Spain, who struggle and suffer for possession of the land." (This young, anachronistically blonde Hurdana would appear, transfigured, in a Surrealist scenario composed in Las Batuecas by Pierre Unik, *La Suédoise d'Aceitunilla*.)[54] Meanwhile, on the back cover the schoolchildren of that same village appeared seated at their desks accompanied by a text (by Alberti) stating: "The children of Extremadura go around barefoot. Who stole their shoes? The heat and the cold get to them. Who made off with their clothing?" The Valencia magazine *Nueva Cultura*, pertaining to the Union of Proletarian Writers and Artists (UEAP), published a photo of one of the dwarves who appear in the film.[55] The importance that Alberti and León, the prime movers of *Octubre*, gave to Buñuel's collaboration was so significant that when the poet evoked the creation of the magazine in his memoirs more than half a century later, the first name he cited in his list of collaborators was Buñuel's.[56]

Later on we will see how, when putting a soundtrack on the documentary in the middle of the Spanish Civil War, this revolutionary intention would metamorphose into one of anti-Fascist struggle, thanks to an explanatory title stuck on the end as a coda. It is interesting today to read a review published at the time in France by a militant PCF organ. In *Commune* (the AEAR's magazine) Pierre Robin wrote: "The very existence, in a country of Europe, of such an island of misfortune would suffice to indict a regime that has done nothing to do away with this state of affairs. . . . This is the image of a Spain committed to feudal reaction, which today attacks and murders the masses, ready to give up their lives."[57]

Earlier on we observed that Buñuel did not edit his documentary until the end of 1933. Between 6 and 8 September of that year Henri Storck discussed his *Borinage* project—about the consequences of a lengthy miners' strike in the Borinage area of Belgium—in Paris with cineastes from the AEAR like Lods, Buñuel, and Piqueras, to whose names Hans Schoots adds that of Vladimir Pozner.[58] On account of this, certain similarities between *Misère au Borinage*—co-directed by Storck and Ivens—and *Terre sans pain* have been pointed out, similarities like the prematurely aged faces, pauperized children, the contrast between the impoverished masses and the church, and so forth. And the poignant discourse about human misery in Buñuel's film was to be continued by Lotar in 1937 when filming the documentary *Les Maisons de la misère* with Storck.

On 29 March 1934 Buñuel and Unik finished drafting the text of the commentary in French that was meant to appear on the soundtrack of the documentary, although the film would not be sonorized until December 1936. Urged on by Acín, who wanted to recoup his investment, Buñuel decided to project his documentary in public.[59] In its silent version it was presented by the Madrid film society Cine-Studio Imagen, run by the San Sebastián critic Manuel Villegas López, with a screening at the Palacio de la Prensa (belonging to the Urgoiti chain) in December 1933. Completing the program was a silent German documentary, *Natur und Liebe* (Wolfram Junghans and Ulrich K. T. Schulz, 1927). The presentation program of *Las Hurdes* stated: "In showing this universally awaited film, IMAGEN is secure in the knowledge of offering its public the biggest cinematic event of the day." Buñuel contributed his improvised commentary, as the text cowritten with Unik did not exist as yet. We have various accounts of that screening, which was coolly received, commencing with the recollections of Buñuel himself.[60] In his autobiography he recounts that "the film was silent and I did the commentary on it myself at the microphone." The most interesting descriptions would be provided by two of those present, Carlos Serrano de Osma and Florentino Hernández Girbal.

Serrano de Osma, the future Falangist director, recalled the projecting "of a silent rough cut in the Palacio de la Prensa in Madrid, with an improvised commentary on the elementary loudspeaker system the movie theater had at the time, and on coming out from the screening the government police requested all of us who were there to show our identity papers: Villegas López, Buñuel himself, Gonzalo Menéndez Pidal, Rafael Gil and Antonio del Amo."[61] Hernández Girbal remembered that "not having a commentary, it was Buñuel himself who volunteered to do it. I witnessed this. He went up to the projection booth, took the microphone and started talking as he watched the film through the little window, what was happening, what each thing was, what had been proposed, etc. He gave a sort of lecture, illustrated by the film."[62] Pierre Kast claimed that Jean Grémillon was present at the screening and that he controlled the excerpts from Brahms on the record player while Buñuel was delivering his commentary, an affirmation that might be endorsed by the French director's move to Spain to film *La Dolorosa* (1934) at Estudios C.E.A. in Madrid.[63]

Although all the accounts agree that the film met with next to no enthusiasm, the Communist writer César M. Arconada saw fit to praise it in the pages of *Nuestro Cinema*:

> There is nothing in the film—although it might lend itself to it—of a morbid relapse into the terrible. Buñuel has interred, partly voluntarily and partly conventionally, his fame as a child-eating ogre and his complicated ways of doing things in order to place himself before nature with precision, restraint and realism. Nature always takes the most extreme fantasies by surprise and, whether we like it or not, with her we must have the same sobriety and extol or recount her with realism, as we see her and not as we dream her.
>
> In this, Buñuel demonstrates that he is a great director. The director who accepts with dignity the lesson dictated by the scenario he has before him, a distinguished lesson, because he must be among the distinguished. And the

> lesson owed Buñuel by Las Hurdes, with its untamed nature, its inhospitality and misery, was one of simplicity, of dissemination.
>
> To the extent that Buñuel has pulled it off, to the extent that Buñuel has managed to descend from the complicated intellectualism of his earlier films—magnificent ones, by the way, the definition of which we shall not attempt right now—to the misery and the primitive, brutal existence of a number of human beings, it appears to us that Buñuel is a great artist. . . .
>
> With *Las Hurdes*, which is a reportage about misery and injustice, Buñuel embarks on a new phase.[64]

Arconada's critique is politically significant, inasmuch as it celebrates Buñuel's resurgence in a "new phase," following his earlier stage as a "child-eating ogre," a stage marked by a "complicated intellectualism," that is, Surrealism. At that time the Communist movement had definitively discredited all avant-garde movements and, in August 1934, around the time Arconada was writing his text, instituted the new aesthetic dogma of Socialist Realism.

When *Las Hurdes* was screened in December 1933 the conservative forces that had won the elections in November were already in power, and the Lerroux government did not authorize its showing; in addition, it also instructed all Spanish embassies to protest its screening abroad. Urged on by Acín, Buñuel decided to show the film to Doctor Gregorio Marañón, president of the National Board of Trustees of Las Hurdes, in the hope that he might intercede. The filmmaker has related the episode in various places. To his Mexican interlocutors he said: "We saw it together at a private screening in a cinema on Gran Vía. At the end Marañón dumbfounded me. He said, 'You've been to La Alberca and all you could think of was to film a horrible and cruel event in which they pull the heads off live cocks. La Alberca has the most beautiful dances in the world and its peasants dress in magnificent seventeenth-century costumes. And I'll tell you something, Buñuel, in Las Hurdes I've seen carts fully laden with wheat pass by.' I said to him, 'Carts full of wheat in Las Hurdes? Why, I've been in seventeen villages where bread is unknown, even. You talk like a member of the Lerroux government. Adios.' And the ban on the film continued."[65]

Not long after the screening of *Las Hurdes* in Madrid, Buñuel, now definitively installed in Madrid, wrote to Unik on 10 January 1934, setting out the reasons that, as he saw it, had led to the refusal to authorize the movie: "More than likely you don't know that the 'Hurdes' film has been banned everywhere, in Spain and abroad, and I've learned that the ban comes from the Spanish Embassy in Paris. It seems that [Lucien] Vogel has tried to blackmail the embassy with your article and to wheedle money out of them not to publish it. The embassy has been put on its guard and at its request the Minister of the Interior from here has banned the film. I have this information from absolutely reliable sources."[66] The information passed on to Unik by Buñuel doesn't square all that well with the correspondence maintained during 1934 between Rafael Sánchez Ventura and Juan Vicens, in which they inform the filmmaker of the existence of potential buyers of the documentary in France. This would require an economic investment to put the final touches to its editing and to run off new copies, something that neither Buñuel nor Acín nor Sánchez Ventura was in a position to finance, as is explained in their letters. The interest of Sánchez Ventura and Vicens in the matter tends to underline the political affiliation of the film, in which producer-exhibitor Pierre Braunberger and exhibitor Saul Colin had also shown an interest (in January and April 1934, respectively), not to mention the invitations of Hernando Viñes and Tristan Tzara to mount private screenings of it in Paris.[67]

According to Bunuel, he showed his documentary in the town of Saint-Denis, near Paris, on the initiative of its Communist mayor Jacques Doriot, to an audience of Spanish immigrant workers, among whom were four or five Hurdanos.[68] It is likely that on this occasion, too, Buñuel did a live commentary on the film. The sociopolitical context suggests that this was a session of agitprop, in line with the directives of the AEAR. Given that Doriot resigned as mayor on 9 April 1934, it may be presumed that this screening took place in the first quarter of that year.[69] Notwithstanding its lack of government authorization, *Las Hurdes* had an outing in Zaragoza in June 1934 and the odd private screening in Paris, as confirmed by a report in *ABC* in March 1934 cited by Mercè Ibarz.[70]

When at its Seventh Congress, held in Moscow from 25 July to 17 August 1935, the Comintern adopted the policy of the interclass, anti-Fascist alliances of the Popular Fronts as a substitute for the revolutionary goals of the "class against class" line, the subversive radicalism of *Las Hurdes* remained out of step with the new Communist political orthodoxy, although this did not affect the ban on it, obviously. And its stigma would extend to the Franco regime. When on 26 May 1937 the civil governor of La Coruña issued an order for the pursuit and capture of Buñuel, describing him as a "morphine addict and alcoholic," he did not fail to point out that "he was the writer and director of a film about Las Hurdes that was to the genuine discredit of Spain."[71]

After the victory of the Frente Popular in February 1936, *Las Hurdes* was authorized and shown once again at Cine-Studio Imagen in April in a silent version. Antonio del Amo praised it in *Cinegramas* as "the universally most perfect, sincere and realistic type of Spanish documentary."[72] And in the General Archive of the Spanish Civil War there is a letter from Pedro Garrigós of Cine-Studio Imagen, dated 15 April 1936, inviting minister of state education Marcelino Domingo to a showing of *Las Hurdes*, as well as the minister's reply, stating that he was very interested in seeing the film and would attend one or other of its screenings.[73]

As stated above, in March 1934 Buñuel and Pierre Unik (with whom he would also collaborate in Paris on film propaganda during the Civil War) wrote the soundtrack commentary in French, doubtless in the hope of releasing the documentary—still banned in Spain—in France. The commentary, the typescript of which is in Filmoteca Española, Madrid, is written in the present tense and the first person plural to express the point of view and the voice of the expeditionary team that descends into the Hurdano inferno, discovers its horror, and invites the audience to share in its discovery. As the preserved text has many crossings-out, corrections, and handwritten additions, at least two observations of interest can be made after reading it.

The first is that the original written commentary is much more verbose and detailed that the one finally adopted and had to be cut down, in part due to the limited duration of the film of 259 shots and twenty-nine minutes, twenty seconds. Thus, for example, the original commentary enlarges at length on the psychoanalytical meaning of the decapitation of the cocks in La Alberca. And epithets that are strange to the spirit of the film appear. For instance, when showing a little girl sick with malaria leaning languidly against a balcony, the text adds: "Moreover, this balcony, in all its poverty, has a certain poetry." At the end the text indicates, "We abandoned this land after a month-and-a-half's stay among the Hurdanos." We know this to be false, since the group spent only a month there, but in the final sound version the duration of their stay was increased to two months.

On the other hand, the original 1934 commentary is much more radical than the definitive one and so reflects the original intention of the film as an AEAR shock item to denounce the shiftlessness of the bourgeois governments—including the Republican ones—that had kept the region in such a miserable state. The outbreak of the Civil War led, however, to a reformulation of the political intention of the documentary, for while in 1933 the film criticized the centuries-old abandonment of Las Hurdes, which the Republic did nothing to rectify, in 1936 it had to be reused ideologically in order to defend a regime being attacked by Fascism and by the interests of the big landowners who were guilty of that state of affairs.

Although Buñuel always claimed that the sonorization of the documentary undertaken in Paris in December 1936 in French and English—for its international distribution—was financed by the Spanish Embassy, headed by Luis Araquistáin, the official documentation suggests otherwise.[74] It indicates that the film was presented to the French Board of Film Censors by producer Pierre Braunberger of the Société du Cinéma du Panthéon and Charles Goldblatt, head of La Propagande par le Film, a company belonging to the PCF.[75] (In this way it appeared before the public as a production without links with the Spanish government.) The print mentioned none of these names, only that of the distribution company, Panthéon. Of Braunberger we have spoken at length, but not of Goldblatt. A friend of Jean Vigo's, Goldblatt had written, to Maurice Jaubert's score, the lyrics of the songs in *Zéro de conduite* (1933) and *L'Atalante* (1934). As a scriptwriter, perhaps he came across Buñuel at Paramount-Joinville when the two of them worked there. As an actor under the pseudonym of Charles Dorat, he had an important role in Julien Duvivier's *La Belle Équipe* (1936), an emblematic film of the Front Populaire period. Years later Dorat/Goldblatt would be the co-scriptwriter with Buñuel, Luis Alcoriza, and Louis Sapin of *La Fièvre monte a El Pao* (1959).

During this postproduction process some important changes occurred, however. In the first place *Las Hurdes* was a geographically meaningless title as far as any foreign general public was concerned, due to which the film came to be called, in 1936, *Terre sans pain*—a much more dramatic and functional title for a piece of political propaganda aimed at the international market. Victor Fuentes has pointed to the title's proximity to that of a book much read in the revolutionary circles of Spain at the time, Kropotkin's *The Conquest of Bread*.[76] To this we would add the resonance that *Terre sans pain* produced, in French Communist culture at least, with the pro-Soviet book by Vaillant-Couturier, *Terre du pain, champs de blé et champs de pétrole*.

In order to give meaning to the new anti-Fascist political message, a written text was added to the end of the film that read:

> The misery this film has just shown us is not a misery without remedy. In other areas of Spain, highlanders, peasants and workers had already managed to improve their living conditions by mutually helping one another and asserting their claims before the public authorities. This trend, which guided the people toward a better life, had determined the last elections and given rise to a Popular Front government.
>
> The rising of the generals, aided by Hitler and Mussolini, was aimed at reestablishing the privileges of the big landowners. But the workers and peasants of Spain will defeat Franco and his accomplices.
>
> With the help of anti-Fascists the world over, peace, work and happiness will take the place of civil war and make the centers of misery this film has showed you disappear forever.

So it was that Buñuel's film passed from its first state as a denunciation of a centuries-old political abandonment that went unremedied by the Republic (the revolutionary choice) to a denunciation of warlike Fascist aggression supported by the big landowners. It was a didactic text that Sánchez Vidal has appositely associated with the one Buñuel would later use to begin *Los olvidados*.[77] It is worth recalling here that the filmmaker did not include his documentary in the film screenings he programmed for the Spanish Pavilion at the 1937 International Exhibition in Paris, doubtless because, despite its didactic coda, it offered an overly barbaric and primitive image of his country and inevitably suggested, in an implicit way, a criticism of the public authorities who had permitted that situation to persist.

The actor Abel Jacquin read the text of the commentary in French, with Buñuel accompanying his voice with the background music of Brahms's romantic Fourth Symphony, thus creating a Surrealist-tinged audiovisual collage with the horrifying images. Buñuel was to reveal in more than one place that this melody was sounding in his head as he edited the film and that he noted how well it fitted the images.[78]

Terre sans pain was released in Paris on 19 December 1936 at the Cinéma du Panthéon. It was shown as a support to the Soviet feature *Love and Hate* (1935), by Albert Gendelstein. In response to a number of protests, especially in the press of Haute-Savoie, angered by the appearance at the beginning of the documentary of a map that showed this French region as being one of the most backward in Europe, the censors proceeded to cut the shot.

Immediately following its release, many reviews of *Terre sans pain* were published in the French papers, reviews that have been compiled and analyzed by Javier Herrera Navarro.[79] Highlighted here are some of the more significant ones. Georges Sadoul, for example, became a faithful mouthpiece of the political intentions of Buñuel, who had shown him the film before its sonorization and its release, still with its old title, when writing, "*Las Hurdes* is a love song to the living Spain, a cry of hate against the Francos who wish to turn the peninsula into an immense Hurdes-like land."[80] The political readings of the documentary from both Left and Right were very varied. In *Le Travailleur du Centre Ouest* (12 November 1937), from Limoges, one could read, "After seeing this film we can understand why the Spanish Republicans struggle in such a ferocious manner for the Republic and their independence." Meanwhile, the anonymous critic of *Choisir* (10 January 1937) opined: "The French commentary accompanying it makes an effort to be objective, but, taking the origin of the production into account, one clearly sees a second Communist intent denoted by the unkind allusions to Catholic religion." More devious was the conservative reasoning of

Front Latin (March 1937): "When authority, religion and property fail in their duty, misery and revolution is their Siamese twin. And it is a humiliating task to defend these essential forces of civilization, although they might not have managed to fulfill their mission. Such is the inner drama of the Spanish tragedy of today." Most of the French reviews, though, set aside any ideological interpretation and underlined the objectivity, realism, testimonial value, or cruelty of *Terre sans pain*. For instance, L. W. (probably Lucien Wahl) wrote in the influential magazine *Pour Vous* (24 December 1936): "The images it offers us are of a brazen eloquence, with no artificial effect having been sought at any time. The text, read in voiceover, refers to facts: it doesn't comment, it has no need to comment." And Jean Kress, in *Avant-Garde* (2 January 1937), insisted on the same idea: "The commentary that accompanies the film simply points to the facts and its sobriety accentuates the Dantesque vision."

Terre sans pain was also shown at a number of screenings organized by the French Communist cooperative Ciné-Liberté and by town councils ruled by the PCF.[81] It also had the odd outing in one or another European country. It was distributed in Belgium by Flora Films of Brussels in April 1937 and presented as *Land without Bread* at the Film Society in Manchester in November 1937. The English documentary filmmaker Basil Wright called it an "extraordinary film" and, after a brief description of its content, added, "Such are the facts that Buñuel's camera quite unemotionally presents. They are presented without sympathy and without rage. He was there with a camera: he saw these things; he photographed them. That is all." However, he had some misgivings about the English commentary and the music by Brahms.[82]

Someone who also must have seen the documentary was Elsa Triolet, Louis Aragon's companion, for in *Dix jours en Espagne* (1937) she wrote—doubtless in reference to *Terre sans pain*—about "poverty in the cinema," which had enabled her to see its "deformed, crippled, hunchbacked" people in places "where baking bread is unknown."[83]

In mid-November 1939 Iris Barry, founder and director of the MoMA Film Library in New York, who had met Buñuel on a trip to California and had immediately hit it off with him to the point of putting him up in her New York apartment, took measures to obtain, via the intercession of *The March of Time* newsreel in Paris, the negative of the documentary deposited in the Éclair Tirage laboratory. After receiving it, Barry showed the film to progressively minded filmmakers like Joris Ivens, Joseph Losey, and Robert Flaherty. According to her, it impressed Flaherty so much that in a moment of the screening he cried out and covered his eyes with his hand; his documentary *The Land* (1942), about the tragic erosion of American soil, would be clearly indebted to Buñuel's film.

Terre sans pain, then, turned into the filmmaker's calling card vis-à-vis the cinephile community of North America. When showing the film to her students, Barry introduced it by saying that the truth is usually disconcerting and went on to call the film "alarming." After the screening a discussion took place between Buñuel and the spectators, in which Iris Barry and Jay Leyda also intervened, to which we've already referred. The MoMA Film Library catalogues the film in its archives under the generic label "Travels and Anthropology."[84] And the brief résumé that appears in the MoMA catalogue states: "it anticipated the social documentary movement in Western Europe; but it is so unusual a work that it resists inclusion in any mainstream."[85]

Following the Paris release of *Terre sans pain*, Paramount considered taking over international distribution of the film, perhaps due to Buñuel's administrative efforts with his former employers in Joinville. But the threat of reprisals from the Franco authorities dissuaded it from such a venture, notwithstanding the fact that during the Civil War years the company did not receive a single import permit from Francoist Spain.[86]

After World War II the commercial exploitation of *Terre sans pain* would generate certain tensions between Buñuel and Braunberger, who had collaborated on the production, sonorization, and showing of the film in Paris. According to the producer's account: "The two of us had equal rights on *Las Hurdes* and *Un chien andalou*. In 1945 Buñuel received an important offer (to which he had a perfect right) and proposed 'splitting things down the middle' with me. He left me *Las Hurdes* and kept *Un chien andalou*. I accepted, thinking that *Las Hurdes* was rights-free. However, I later found out that during the [Second World] war he'd made some sales of the film, in particular in the United States, where he'd resold the rights for the entire territory. Hence the differences between us."[87] In the book from which this quote comes, Braunberger reproduced, as a proof of the dispute, a letter from Buñuel dated from Mexico City, 29 September 1964, in which the director claimed 1,500 francs from the producer for exploitation of the documentary.[88]

10

Dubbing at Warner Bros.

By mid-1934 Luis Buñuel's cinematic status in Spain was that of a living, if somewhat outlandish, legend. Though adored by a small minority of cinephiles, because of his lack of activity as a filmmaker the niche he occupied was becoming clogged with dust. Perhaps due to Dalí's intervention, *Un chien andalou* and *L'Âge d'or* had been shown at the Cine Lido in Barcelona on 13 January 1933. The screening was to be accompanied by a public debate between Guillermo Díaz-Plaja and Lluis Montanyà, but this never took place.[1] On 18 May 1934 *L'Âge d'or* had a further outing at Barcelona's Cine Fantasio, along with a recent Fox production, a melodrama much prized by the Surrealists, *Berkeley Square* (Frank Lloyd, 1933). This Sesión Mirador annoyed Dalí, who wrote indignantly to poet J. V. Foix protesting the omission of his name in the advertising for the show in *La Publicitat* of 11, 15, and 16 May—only Buñuel's authorship was mentioned—and asking Foix for a rectification that never came.[2] On 7 June *L'Âge d'or* was again projected privately in Barcelona (at Sinera Estudis Espanyol) for members of the Friends of the New Art Group (ADLAN), the main platform of the Catalan avant-garde since its founding in 1932. In the attendant publicity it was announced that the film would not be subject to "the mutilations of the public screening,"[3] which leads us to infer that the civil governor of Barcelona, responsible for local censorship, had made some cuts in earlier sessions, although we do not know which segments were eliminated. The echo of these screenings was, in any event, extremely modest.

Buñuel's professional inactivity in France, along with an ever more chronic sciatica that the cold and damp climate of Paris did nothing to improve, impelled him to settle definitively in Madrid during the spring. Years later, in a résumé of his return to the city, he would declare, "I returned [to Spain] around 1934 because I had sciatica and wanted to get over it. Warner Brothers made me an offer to supervise their films in Spain. They paid me magnificently for doing almost nothing. (Warner had thirty films a year for dubbing into Spanish.) I merely chose the speaking voices, got the dialogues corrected, and then checked that the synchronization and sound were OK. I was working on that when the October revolution began in Asturias."[4] And in his 1939 professional autobiography he added, "I have a pleasant memory of my association with that company and of its chief in Spain, Mr. Huet."[5]

Unlike Fox and Paramount, Warner Bros. Spanish-language productions were very thin on the ground, with only six titles, five of them directed by William McGann. The cycle opened with *El hombre malo*, a Spanish version of Clarence Badger's *The Bad Man*, filmed alongside the original in its Burbank studios in May 1930—a French version was also shot—and closed with *El cantante de Nápoles* by Howard Bretherton, filmed in August 1934, by which time Buñuel was the head of Warner's dubbing program in Madrid.[6]

Warner Bros.–First National Films, a Spanish corporation, had been set up as a distribution company in November 1932, with its head office in Barcelona and a branch in Madrid. In its first year of activity it imported twenty-two films, which were shown in subtitled versions as was habitual in Spain ever since the Madrid distributor Exclusivas Diana had introduced the practice. Warner's first big hit in the Spanish market was a subtitled *I Am a Fugitive from a Chain Gang* (Mervyn Le Roy, 1932), based on an autobiography by Robert E. Burns, two-time escapee from a brutal prison in Georgia. A model example of the social cinema Warner was turning out during those years, it won Oscar nominations for its main protagonist (Paul Muni) and for its soundtrack. *I Am a Fugitive* opened in Madrid on 27 March 1933 and was shown in Barcelona at a Sesiones Mirador film society screening that same month.[7] When José Castellón Díaz asked Buñuel about the movies he took to be exemplary, he duly cited it.[8] And after seeing the film in Paris, Juan Piqueras, usually so hard on American cinema, pointed out that it was "one of those films that very occasionally appear in Yankee filmmaking in frank opposition to the political and social line of its cinema," since it showed the penitentiary system of a country "in whose prisons thousands and thousands of workers suffer the rigors of a regime that does not hesitate to commit the worst abuses so as to guarantee its dominion over, and repression of, the working classes by the dominant bourgeois classes."[9]

At the end of 1933 René Huet, the French managing director of Warner Bros. in Spain, adopted a policy of dubbing some of its material, a commercial strategy MGM had already embarked upon that same year in its Barcelona studios, following the final cancellation of its Spanish-speaking versions. The first assignment Buñuel received was on 8 January 1934 to dub *Captured* (Roy del Ruth, 1933).

On 23 June 1934, on a lightning visit to Paris, Buñuel married Jeanne Rucar; on 11 July she joined her husband in Madrid and spent three months in Spain, also sharing the director's summer break in Zaragoza, Calanda, and San Sebastián. Thanks to the experience he had acquired at Paramount, Buñuel had consolidated his position as dubbing director of part of Warner Bros.' imported product, earning 4,000 pesetas a week, a princely sum for the period.[10] The technical infrastructure for performing this task was very limited in Spain at that time. In 1934, however, Estudios CEA (Cinematografía Española y Americana), which had opened the year before in Madrid, abandoned their initial function as a producer and turned to filming and dubbing work, with Jerónimo Mihura named as director of the dubbing department. Mihura has related how "because there was no other place that was suitably equipped, Buñuel came in with some Warner films he wanted dubbing one day, and we had to invent the dubbing process. Buñuel rapidly explained how it was done and then we did it, with my brother [Miguel] adjusting the dialogue and me directing the dubbing."[11] We know that the brilliant comedy writer Miguel Mihura also prepared dialogues for such dubbing sessions, and it is worth recalling that he rewrote the absurd exchanges of the Marx Brothers in *A Night at the Opera* (Sam Wood, 1935)—released in Madrid in June 1936—and that they tallied perfectly with the madcap humor of the comedians.

Of such tasks we also have the testimony of another technician who was working at Estudios CEA, the editor Eduardo García Maroto, who recalled that "Warner Bros commissioned CEA to dub its films and appointed Luis Buñuel as the supervisor of these. He was extremely meticulous and on more than one occasion made me retouch some shots so as to try and improve them, since at the time the adjustment was made in the editing, by 'bodging' phrases and words when they were a bit out of sync, although if the actor made them too short or too long you had to go and do them again."[12] Following the huge commercial success of *I Am a Fugitive*, Warner Bros. of Spain imported a batch of musicals by Ruby Keeler, Joan Blondell, Al Jolson, and Ginger Rogers, which were often shown subtitled due to the difficulty of translating the songs. Among the jewels Warner released in the 1933–34 season was Tay Garnett's *One Way Passage* (1932), the story of an impossible love affair between Kay Francis and William Powell during a transatlantic crossing, which became a fetish film for many Surrealists, with Breton in the van.

On 16 August 1934 Buñuel wrote to Georges Sadoul from Madrid, summing up his personal situation: "My life right now is extremely dull and rather soul-destroying on account of the work I have to do. Fortunately, I don't bother too much about it and at times I get whole days off. What's more, my boss is in Barcelona. I'm in Madrid for reasons of health, ever since five months ago I started suffering from sciatica, which prevents me from doing anything. At times I've the feeling of being a 'huge invalid' and that I've 'been in the wars.' I fear the winter will keep me in bed and put me completely out of action."[13] In his letter Sadoul had suggested to Buñuel that they meet in Barcelona, but in his reply, on Residencia de Estudiantes notepaper, the director told Sadoul he never traveled to Barcelona but offered to meet him in Madrid. Such an encounter did take place, as Sadoul recalled: "On the last afternoon of our stay in Madrid I was present with Luis in the University Stadium at a meeting of the Communist Party (the last one authorized by the Lerroux government). Everybody was talking about big things happening in the days to come."[14] This must have been the event held on 16 September in Madrid's Estadio Universitario, at which the Socialist and Communist Youth attempted to establish the bases of a joint militancy.[15] Faced with Hitler's expansionist threat, the French Communist Party, with the approval of the Comintern, had already come to an agreement in July with the Socialists to establish an interclass alliance that would lead to the formation of an anti-Fascist Front Populaire. In Spain a similar political strategy involving an alliance of Leftist forces was beginning to emerge.

This episode tends to corroborate the fact that Buñuel was still militating in the PCE at the time, although his political activity was low-key. In a letter to Unik sent during the *bienio negro*—the two-year period under the conservative government—he wrote: "We are always on a war footing and this for fear that people might speak of the infamous repression of the movement. Hitler has done a lot less than our [Alejandro] Lerroux and Gil [Robles]. I've sent a letter to Hernando [Viñes] for him to forward to you, a letter from a Radical-Socialist deputy to Lerroux, which in my opinion is a valuable document when it comes to furthering the international campaign against the repression. I have to say that with my illness and my being confined to bed I'm a bit out of touch with politics at the moment."[16] Buñuel told Aub that by the time he started his new job a pile of twenty-one films needed dubbing, and he asked the musician Gustavo Durán—who'd already worked with him at Paramount—to help him do this. Buñuel met with a certain opposition, he claimed, because Durán was a notorious Communist, but he managed to get the company to take on the musician.[17]

We know that in May 1935 Buñuel began working for the Filmófono production company, but until September he synchronized this new task with his work for Warner Bros. Warner's Madrid offices were run by Antonio Balonga, who was replaced at the beginning of 1935 by Isidoro Martínez Ferry, recorded more as the progenitor of the filmmaker of the same name, nominal co-director of the remarkable Marco Ferreri movie, *El pisito* (1958), and director of other less memorable ones such as *Escala en Hi Fi* (1962).[18]

The final months of 1934 were important ones as far as Buñuel's private life was concerned. On 9 November his son Juan Luis was born in Paris, and both mother and son traveled to Madrid on 1 March 1935 in order to settle definitively in Spain in a large apartment Buñuel had at the intersection of Calle Menéndez Pelayo and Calle Doctor Castelo.[19] That same year, moreover, his relationship with Lorca, which had known periods of estrangement, was totally reestablished, and on 29 December he attended the opening night of *Yerma*, at the Teatro Español in the capital.[20] Lorca's tragedy was obviously foreign to Buñuel's creative imagination, but in 1934 the artistic intransigence of his youth, which had led him and Dalí to repudiate *Romancero gitano*, had evaporated. In his memoirs, however, Buñuel recalled that he was present at the performance with his mother and his sister Conchita while suffering a strong attack of sciatica and that the play irritated him so much he left the theater. He summed up this experience by writing, "My passage through Surrealism had distanced me—for quite a while—from this supposed 'avant-garde.'"[21] Dalí was earning a lot of money by now with the commercialization of his Surrealist formula abroad, while Buñuel had taken refuge in a modest, if profitable, artisanal anonymity, one that could not be compared to the social recognition that greeted the work of Lorca and Dalí. Of the three old friends, Buñuel appeared to be the least favored, professionally speaking, a lack of status of which he must have been aware, although we know little of his feelings about this, except for his perception of the "soul-destroying" nature of his life—according to his epistolary confession to Sadoul—albeit one with lots of free time and handsome economic compensation.

Although his name had all but disappeared from the annals of cinema, on 20 December 1934 the Barcelona weekly magazine, *Popular Film*, published a curious article by Luis M. Serrano, comparing Buñuel's œuvre to Picasso's.[22] In his article Serrano wrote: "Here are two artists who have triumphed in those different branches of art outside Spain, in Paris, and their works, a product of their intelligence, have come down to us—for obvious reasons—when their names were often on foreign lips, when they scaled the final rung of glory. And despite this, of the first [Picasso] we have only seen a brief exhibition, and of the second only one of his films, in a semi-private film society session." Serrano went on to compare their two styles: "In the picture by the painter from Málaga we see two figures—a man and a woman—intertwined, embracing, but with nothing morbid about them, without outwardly expressing their feelings. In a scene from *Un chien andalou*, by the filmmaker from Valencia [*sic*], we observe similar figures, scathing ones, outwardly expressing their feelings. Picasso paints the soul, Buñuel portrays the body. But both of them move—by separate paths—toward a common idea: to objectivize art." The Valencian origin attributed to Buñuel in this text is indicative of just how little his personality was known at the time in Spain, even on the part of some of his admirers, as the writer obviously was. Although confused, this article must surely have been comforting for the Aragonese director.

In the second half of 1934 Warner Bros. began distributing in the Spanish market the recent work of such directors as William Dieterle, Archie Mayo, Michael Curtiz, Busby Berkeley, Lloyd Bacon, and Frank Borzage.[23] In its special number of summer 1936, which would be the magazine's last before the Civil War saw it off, *Arte y Cinematografía* published an eye-catching Warner Bros. ad that announced, with much ballyhoo, thirty-two titles for its new season, twelve of which were dubbed into Spanish; that is, just under a third of the films it imported.

During the Civil War René Huet fell victim to a series of accusations in which professional jealousies and political sensibilities played an important part. Three Barcelona cinema owners taking refuge in Francoist San Sebastián—Modesto Castañé (owner of the Astoria, Avenida, and Victoria cinemas), Fernando Pascual (of the Metropol and Principal Palace), and Lorenzo Fargas (of the Publi-Cinema and Maryland)—accused Huet and other local impresarios of having traveled to Paris with leaders of the CNT to negotiate the importing of films into the Republican zone. A few impresarios displayed their political loyalties by passing to the Francoist zone, but René Huet fled to France and managed to reach safety.[24]

11

Commerce, Art, and Politics

Prior to the outbreak of the Spanish Civil War, Luis Buñuel worked closely with the engineer and impresario Ricardo Urgoiti Somovilla in his cinematic activities, activities that culminated in the production of four feature-length movies for Urgoiti's company, Filmófono. The son of Nicolás María de Urgoiti, prime mover of the paper manufacturing, publishing, and newspaper industries in Spain at the start of the twentieth century, Ricardo extended these multimedia activities to the audiovisual sector, first to radio—with his Unión Radio station in Madrid and the publication of specialized magazines like *Ondas*—and next to cinema, covering the areas of exhibition, sonorization, the film society movement, dubbing, and production. Given his frenetic activity, Ricardo Urgoiti deserves the title of Media Baron of the Generation of '27 and of the Republic. There is nothing surprising, then, about the fact that the General Archive of the Spanish Civil War in Salamanca preserves his Francoist police record, which has him down as a freemason, invoking, as proof of this, his inscription on page 110 of the 1934–35 *Anuario Rotario*, or Rotary Yearbook.[1]

Chronologically speaking, the first cinema-related phase of the Urgoiti business empire was devoted to exhibition. In March 1920 Urgoiti's uncle, Ricardo Urgoiti Achúcarro, became president of the cinema circuit known as Gran Empresa Sagarra, named after its founder, Carlos Viñas Sagarra. In 1923 Antonio Armenta was appointed manager of the company after rising from being the projectionist, ticket seller, and head of personnel at the Cine Príncipe Alfonso.[2] After returning in 1924 from studying electronics in the United States, Ricardo Urgoiti Somovilla was named managing director. Armenta, who lived his moment of glory with the opening in 1929 of the Cine Palacio de la Prensa, the circuit's flagship and an emblem of Republican rationalist architecture, would leave his post in 1931, at the beginning of the sound period, and was to die at the beginning of 1934.[3]

A floridly rhetorical notice published in the trade magazine *Arte y Cinematografía* in 1933 gave a measure of the company's ambitions: "Madrid festoons itself with a wealth of movie houses. Due to the drive and boldness of its managing director, Señor Urgoiti, and to its general manager, Don Roberto Martín, Gran Empresa Sagarra opens the doors of its three cinemas, the Ópera, Monumental and [Palacio de la] Prensa, into which they have put all their love of enrichment; they open their doors, we repeat, sure of the satisfaction of the public, which is the whole of Madrid." The correspondent went on to praise other movie houses in the capital: the Palacio de la Música, Cine Avenida, Coliseum, Astoria, Callao, Cine Madrid, Cine Génova (formerly the Príncipe Alfonso), Cine Delicias, Cine Actualidades, and Cine Bellas Artes.[4] According to J. F. Aranda, prior to the Spanish Civil War Filmófono also acquired control of some four hundred theaters in Latin America, forty of which actually belonged to it.[5] On 18 October 1934 Ricardo Urgoiti Achúcarro died, but his nephew went on promoting the company, which in 1935 grew with the incorporation of the cinemas Palacio de la Música, Goya, Argüelles, and Dos de Mayo.[6]

Born in 1900, Ricardo Urgoiti Somovilla began studying radiotelephony in 1923 at the General Electric head office in Schenectady, New York, before returning to Spain in August 1924.[7] In June 1925 he launched his Madrid station Unión Radio (EAJ-7), which on 14 April 1931 broadcast Niceto Alcalá Zamora's speech proclaiming the Second Republic, and whose film section was in the hands, from 1932 to 1935, of Manuel Villegas López, the first exhibitor of *Las Hurdes*. In May 1927 Urgoiti introduced the Filmófono system for sonorizing films, based on two synchronized turntables, each with an independent potentiometer for controlling the volume, thus enabling the user to do sound dissolves and add background sound effects or music. This system was employed for the first time in public to sonorize, with gramophone records chosen by the musician Felipe Briones, the projection of Erich von Stroheim's *Greed* (1923) in the seventh session of the Cineclub Español, held on 26 May 1929 in the Cine Goya. Buñuel, who deeply admired the film, had wanted to kick off the sessions of the Cineclub Español with it in December 1928. The Filmófono sound system was the first in a line of rudimentary and ephemeral Spanish systems for sonorizing films via gramophone records (like the Melodión and Parlophone), the first Spanish-patented photographic sound system being the Laffon-Selgas, constructed as a prototype in 1934. A few collaborators from that inaugural session of Filmófono's acoustic apparatus, such as the musician Fernando Remacha and Buñuel (as the founder of its film society), would become collaborators in its later business activities.[8]

Setting aside a few faltering precursors, it may be said that sound film arrived in Spain on 19 September 1929 when the Cine Coliseum in Barcelona launched the Paramount movie *Innocents of Paris* (Richard Wallace, 1928), with Maurice Chevalier, although the American engineer who was monitoring the projection booth only permitted the parts with singing to be heard, in order to avoid the protests of the public at the dialogues in English. Mindful of the reality of the new sound cinema, Ricardo Urgoiti had meanwhile envisaged putting a sound system in the Real Cinema, pertaining to Gran Empresa Sagarra. Supplied after much delay by the Radio Corporation of America (RCA), the new system was, after numerous installation problems, publicly inaugurated on 12 October 1929 with the screening of *Lady of the Pavements* (D. W. Griffith, 1929), distributed by United Artists and premièred in January of that same year in Los Angeles, but the acoustics left a lot to be desired.

Urgoiti was also a pioneer in the production of Spanish sound films, since at the end of 1929 he organized, in the British International Pictures Studios in Elstree, and with the collaboration of the distributor Saturnino Ulargui, the shooting of the interiors of *La canción del día*, which, directed by the Englishman G. B. Samuelson, was completed with the filming of exteriors in Madrid. The cinema press of the day announced its filming as the "first all-talking, completely synchronized Spanish production,"[9] and it is worthy of note that the first "hundred-percent" French sound movie, André Hugon's *Les Trois Masques*, was also filmed in 1929 in an English studio by Pathé. The screenplay of *La canción del día* was by Pedro Muñoz Seca and Pedro Pérez Fernández, the music by Jacinto Guerrero, and the models, set, and costume designs by the painter Gustavo de Maeztu. It was released on 19 April 1930 in the Real Cinema in Madrid, equipped with acoustic equipment by Urgoiti. Urgoiti also ceded the ground floor of the Cine Palacio de la Prensa and, according to Manuel Rotellar, intervened in the production of the review-style entertainment movie *Yo quiero que me lleven a Hollywood* (1931), which Edgar Neville filmed intermittently at the request of producer Rosario Pi, who had proposed he shoot screen tests of aspiring young actresses.[10] Sonorized with the Seletone system in the Studios Baroncelli in Paris, it had songs and a discourse by popular raconteur Federico García Sanchiz.[11]

The technology of sound film was to a large extent a byproduct of different electronics laboratories intent upon resolving the problems of radiophony. Samuel Warner, for example, became interested in sound film after buying a Los Angeles radio station.[12] The introduction of this technology in cinema precipitated an economic battle between America's two most important financial groups: the Morgan group (telephonic interests) and the Rockefeller group (radiophonic interests), which would end up winning the contest in a field that constituted a crossroads between the entertainment and communications worlds.[13] A similar capillarity also occurred in Spain between the radiophonic and sound film businesses. Inaugurated on 24 November 1924, EAJ-1, Radio Barcelona, Spain's first broadcasting station, was set up by the engineer José María Guillén García, who in May 1932 would also equip the city's Estudios Orphea, the first to shoot sound film using technical equipment imported from France. Urgoiti also came out of radiophonics, and he made reference to this during the fifteenth session of the Cineclub Español, held on 29 November 1930 in the Palacio de la Prensa, when his amplified voice stood in for his visual presence as he presented Walter Ruttmann's sound documentary, *Deutsche Rundfunk* (1928), which the publicity for the screening announced as "a radio-cinematic avant-garde movie."

On 28 August 1931 a document was signed in the presence of a notary founding Filmófono, a limited company launched with the financial support of Banco Urquijo and Unión Radio, which together contributed 1.5 million pesetas. The objectives of the company were listed as film production and distribution, the sale of sound equipment for movie theaters, film synchronization and dubbing, and the recording of discs with original compositions for films. Ricardo Urgoiti became the company's managing director and went on to give financial aid to magazines like *Cinema Sparta*, with its headquarters in the Palacio de la Prensa, and Piqueras's Marxist magazine *Nuestro Cinema*.

The figure of Valencian film critic Juan Piqueras deserves particular attention. Settling in Paris in May 1930, he immediately joined the PCF.[14] He went on to found *Nuestro Cinema* (published in Paris and Madrid from June 1932 to August 1935), coedited by the Communist Antonio del Amo from Spain, and to collaborate on, among other publications, *La Gaceta Literaria*, *El Sol*, and *Popular Film*, as well as *Mundo Obrero*, the PCE newspaper. In 1934 or 1935 Piqueras spent several weeks in Moscow, and his militant activities extended from the promoting of Soviet cinema in Spanish film circuits to the writing of proclamations and manifestos in favor of "proletarian" cinema.[15] In terms of his film society work, it may seem surprising today that his Cine Studio Nuestro Cinema would open in Madrid in December 1934 with a screening of Leni Riefenstahl's *The Blue Light* (1932), presented to much praise by comrade del Amo. At the time the collaboration of Hungarian Communist Béla Balázs on the script and direction of the film must have seemed enough of an ideological guarantee. Piqueras would become a key figure in the Filmófono distribution operation through his work in selecting the films in Paris that the company would disseminate in Spain.

The magazine *Arte y Cinematografía* celebrated the birth of the new distribution company by declaring, "Here is a new firm in the field of Spanish cinema, whose birth coincides with the appearance of the first sound films in Spain, and which, faithful to its origins, has finally crystallized into one big film rental and distribution house, with a firm footing in our Spanish arena."[16] Around the same time Ernesto Giménez Caballero composed a colorful pen portrait of the dynamic orchestrator of the project when writing: "Ricardo Urgoiti—the American *Ricardito* of our Iberian cinema—is the only significant example of Americanism in Iberia. He exhales a landscape of machines, business deals and sportiness. . . . He makes films. . . . And his circuits struggle in the poverty of our movie houses as racing cars would struggle on a track for scooters. . . . For me, Ricardo Urgoiti has been a sort of try-out of the extent to which Spain has been able to Yankee-ize itself. Very little."[17]

From Paris Piqueras selected the films Filmófono distributed in Spain, a selection that was vetted in Madrid by a committee consisting of Buñuel, César M. Arconada, Germán Gómez de la Mata (who had been a correspondent for the weekly magazine *La Pantalla* in Paris), the Basque architect and filmmaker Nemesio Sobrevila, and Manuel Villegas López, although its members changed over the course of time. Given that the Hollywood majors had branches in Spain, Piqueras's selection concentrated on European (mainly French) films and, as was only to be expected, on his beloved Soviet cinema. Piqueras's widow, Ketty González, recalled that "of a morning he saw perhaps two or three films with a view to buying them for Filmófono."[18] As Piqueras was also working in Paris as a correspondent for the Valencia magazine *Semana Gráfica*, whose proprietors owned Cifesa (the other Spanish major), when Filmófono rejected his suggestions he could, with its permission, offer them to that company through another Valencian, Daniel Falcó.[19] In the first consignment of imports publicized by the distributor were *Sous les toits de Paris* (1930), *Le Million* (1931), and *À nous la liberté* (1932), all by René Clair, *Westfront 1918* (1930) and *Kameradschaft* (1931), both by G. W. Pabst, and the Soviet film *Blue Express* (Ilya Trauberg, 1929).

In order to promote a programming that was so demanding from the cultural point of view, Urgoiti created, with Buñuel directing things in the shadows, Estudio Proa-Filmófono, a Madrid film society intended to pre-release their more difficult titles (whence its allusion to the "avant-garde prow"), although some of the films presented therein never reached the point of being commercially released for the general public. Its illuminating advertising slogan read "Artistically progressive films. Cultural, social and documentary titles." For this reason it is

Poster by Enrique Herreros to promote Estudio Proa-Filmófono, the Urgoiti company's Madrid film society, which programmed commercially risky movies from Paris that were selected by Juan Piqueras. (Fundación Enrique Herreros, Madrid)

essential to examine first the cutting-edge activity of the Cineclub Proa-Filmófono, which both Buñuel and Urgoiti contemplated as being a prolongation of the Cineclub Español, launched by the former in Madrid in December 1928, and whose sessions were interrupted just after the birth of the Second Republic, with the enthused screening of *Battleship Potemkin* (1925) on 9 May 1931.

On 20 December 1932 Estudio Proa-Filmófono commenced its screenings at the Palacio de la Prensa, with the projection of Pabst's *Kameradschaft*. Urgoiti considered that this session inaugurated the fourth season of the Cineclub Español, of which it was taken to be the continuation after several months of inactivity, and so he invited Ernesto Giménez Caballero, its cofounder along with Buñuel, who performed the function of a link between the two forums or stages. However, Giménez Caballero publicly declined the invitation and bitterly criticized Urgoiti in the pages of *La Gaceta Literaria* for his own exclusion from the new initiative, associating it in part with the new Republican political climate.[20] The author of this reproach was beginning to see himself as a victim of the Republican regime, in an acrimonious slalom that was to turn him into a genuine "literary Crusoe," as he would define his solitude shortly afterward.

The first Estudio Proa-Filmófono session was a social and artistic success, with the presence of the authorities and the diplomatic corps, judging by reports in the press.[21] Despite this, Piqueras's ideological intransigence would be shown in his disqualification of Pabst's film in a review published in *Nuestro Cinema*, in which he wrote: "And the miners of *Kameradschaft* coming from Germany to rescue the French are driven by humanitarian feeling, not by class feeling, as it should have been."[22]

The preeminence accorded by Piqueras to Soviet cinema was made evident in the first Estudio Proa-Filmófono catalog, which was almost exclusively devoted to Russian films, of which it was planned to screen fourteen titles, subsequently reduced to twelve.[23] In 1929 Julio César S.A. had entered into negotiations with the Moscow producer Mezhrabpomfilm via the Paris company Albatros, formed by Russian exiles, in order to import into Spain a batch of Soviet movies, beginning with Pudovkin's *Storm over Asia* (1928), which was the first film shown publicly in Spain at Barcelona's Cineclub Mirador on 28 November 1929.[24] Fear of the Spanish censors meant that the remaining titles were less politically committed, however; they included *Revolt in Kazan* (Yuri Tarich, 1927) and *The Yellow Ticket* (Fyodor Otsep, 1928). At that time Spanish censorship emerged, in fact, as a major impediment to the operation, but with the advent of the Second Republic the situation changed, and Filmófono rapidly became the main importer of Soviet cinema into Spain.

Estudio Proa-Filmófono's standard of programming was truly spectacular. In 1932 it showed *Old and New*—with a special dispensation from the censors[25]—*Das Lied vom Leben* (Alexis Granowsky, 1930); *Turksib* (Victor Turin, 1929); *À nous la liberté*; *Melody of the World* (Walter Ruttmann, 1929); *Berlin-Alexanderplatz* (Phil Jutzi, 1931), *Romance sentimentale* and *October* by Eisenstein; *Earth* (Aleksandr Dovzhenko, 1930); *The Crowd* (King Vidor, 1928); *Die Koffer des Herrn O.F.* (Alexis Granowsky, 1931); *Le Sang d'un poète* (Jean Cocteau, 1930), and *The Wind* (Victor Sjöström 1928). Meanwhile, in 1933 the Estudio screened *Die Dreigroschenoper* (G. W. Pabst, 1931); *The Road to Life* (Nikolai Ekk, 1931); *Rain* (Joris Ivens, 1929); *Une idylle à la plage* (Henri Storck, 1931); *La Chienne* (Jean Renoir, 1931); *Vampyr* (Carl Dreyer, 1931); *Entr'acte* (René Clair, 1924), and *Kühle Wampe* (1932), the German Communist indictment by Slatan Dudow, the negative reception of which in Madrid and in Barcelona's Studio Cinaes prompted Piqueras to publish an impassioned defense of this example of proletarian cinema in *Octubre*.[26]

Some of the movies imported by Filmófono for its film society, including *Blue Express* and *Old and New*, were also screened in the Sesiones Studio Cinaes in Barcelona's Lido Cine. Most of the film societies that flourished in the 1930s in Spain were, however, associated with noncommercial workerist or cultural groups. An article published in *Popular Film* in July 1933 stated that in Madrid alone there were Proa-Filmófono, Cinestudio FUE (pertaining to the Federación Universitaria Escolar, a cinephile entity founded by Carlos Velo, which held its sessions in the Palacio de la Prensa), Cinestudio 33, and the Cineclub Proletario de los Empleados de Banca y Bolsa, which produced *El despertar bancario*, a film about the history of the Banking Trade Union.[27] The Cineclub Popular would have to be added to that list before the end of the year, while on 11 November 1933 the influential GECI (Grupo de Escritores Cinematográficos Independientes) was launched, which published a series of books on the cinema. By July 1934 the list had expanded spectacularly, with new entities like the Cineclub de la Juventud Roja, Cine-Studio Lyceum Club Femenino, Centro Cultural Deportivo Obrero "Avanti," Cineclub "La Lucha," Cineclub "Trabajadores de la Distribución y Producción de Material Cinematográfico," Cineclub de Trabajadores de Comercio, Cineclub del Socorro Obrero Español, Cineclub Frente Universitario, Cineclub del Socorro Obrero en el Cinema, and Cineclub de la Biblioteca Circulante de Chamartín de la Rosa, run by Julio González Vázquez, a ubiquitous *cineclubista* who featured in the activities of various "proletarian film societies."[28] In October 1933 in the pages of his magazine *Nuestro Cinema*, Piqueras called for the creation of a federation of Proletarian Film Societies.[29]

Filmófono, then, was the major importer of Soviet cinema to Spain, although the censorship of the *bienio negro*—the two-year period in office of the center- and far-Right extending from November 1933 to January 1936—slowed it down. In August 1935 Piqueras denounced the Republican government for forbidding the showing of *Patriots* (Boris Barnet, 1933), about an episode in a Russian village in World War I; *The House of the Dead* (Vasili Fyodorov, 1932), a biography of Dostoyevsky; *Golden Mountains* (Sergei Yutkevich, 1931), the story of a strike in Baku in 1914; *Lieutenant Kizhe* (Aleksandr Feinzimmer, 1934), a farce set in the time of Peter I; and *The Earth Thirsts* (Yuli Raizman, 1930), about land collectivization in the eastern Soviet Union.[30]

Piqueras was a dogged propagandist for Soviet cinema, and when announcing the projection in the Cineclub Español in November 1930 of the Ukrainian film *Taras Shevchenko* (Pyotr Chardynin, 1925), which he'd signed up in Paris, he wrote in *Popular Film*: "The Spanish censors have put the brakes on the technical and ideological innovations of Soviet cinema. And this, obviously, is an injustice. Not so much with regard to the political order of the latter, but with regard to the artistic—the cinematic. Seeing as Russian cinema—made by the masses, for the masses—would reach the people, the Spanish masses, in its entirety. The Russian masses, the life of the peasants, the workers' contingent—full of fervor, enthusiasm, faith in the future—would be received by the Spanish masses, by the peasant and by the worker with that same fervor and that same enthusiasm."[31] In *Nuestro Cinema* Piqueras published articles on Soviet cinema by the likes of Eisenstein, Anatole Lunacharsky (the USSR's former commissar of education and enlightenment), Moussinac, Karl Radek, I. Anissimov, Agustín Aragón Leyva, and Ramón J. Sender, among others. To these articles must be added those that Piqueras himself wrote and published.

Piqueras's enthusiastic Communist militancy led him to sometimes make declarations of a surprising ingenuousness, as when he praised Soviet censorship for being of "a severe and incorruptible rigor," to the point that "of the 110 films shot during the last seven months, the Censors have authorized only eight."[32] When formulating his project for an exemplary Spanish cinema, Piqueras wrote: "I would immediately make documentary cinema in the knowledge that it would be at the same time revolutionary cinema. Through this cinema the Basque miners would know how and why their Andalusian comrades struggle and vice versa. This cinema could also teach the proletariat on the move towards the class struggle many things that were concealed from it, many facts that would strengthen its demands."[33]

Piqueras identified this revolutionary cinema with the Soviet one, established as an exemplary model for Spain, without taking their different politico-industrial structures into account, although his subtler comrade César M. Arconada warned against this simplification.[34] Piqueras not only supported the Soviet cinema in doctrinal terms but, prior to his collaboration with Filmófono, imported into Spain and supervised the titling of the silent *Women of Ryazan* (Olga Preobrazhenskaya, 1927), screened at the Cineclub Español on 20 January 1930, and in 1936 he did the subtitling of *Chapayev* (Sergei and Georgi Vasiliev, 1934), a personal favorite of Stalin's.

On arriving at this point we might ask ourselves if Piqueras's organic function in Paris, and perhaps that of his comrades Buñuel and Arconada at the service of the Filmófono distribution machine in Madrid, formed part of the propaganda project organized by German Communist Willi Münzenberg, in consequence of the assignment Lenin gave him in 1921 to create a network of international solidarity with the USSR in artistic and intellectual circles. Through a German intermediary—Aufbau, Industrie & Handels A.G.—Münzenberg acquired the distribution rights for German films in the USSR. With the profits from this, in December 1925 he set up the distribution company Prometheus Film GmbH in Berlin, with shares amounting to 10,000 marks, divided in equal parts between the German Communist Party (KPD) and Mezhrabpomfilm, a Soviet SOI entity created in August 1924, whose appointed task was furthering good relations abroad.[35] Mezhrabpomfilm's mission was twofold: disseminating Soviet cinema beyond its own borders and winning over foreign filmmakers to its projects. Prometheus made its debut in April 1926 by importing into Germany *Battleship Potemkin*, whose running time was some four minutes shorter, due to censorship.[36] In that same year the first German-Soviet co-production was filmed in Germany. *Superfluous People*, based on Chekhov and with German actors (Werner Krauss, Heinrich George, Fritz Rasp), was directed by the veteran Aleksandr Razumni and distributed by Prometheus. It met with little success. Prometheus broadened its activities to include production, quickly becoming the mainstay of German proletarian cinema (also called *Arme-Leute-Filme*: the cinema of the poor), although it was also obliged to make commercial movies, the "quota quickies" needed to be able to import Soviet films.

In 1927 Münzenberg created a subsidiary production company in Berlin, Welt-Film-Gesellschaft, specializing in noncommercial and agitational films that were shot by ad hoc worker-cameramen. Seeking after the sort of universality inscribed in its own name, Welt-Film devoted itself to the distribution of Soviet films on 16 mm for the film society market in Europe and the United States. We may speculate as to just how much these companies inspired the militant Piqueras when, with the complicity of Buñuel and Arconada in Madrid, he turned Filmófono into the biggest Spanish importer of Soviet movies, with such emblematic titles in the Communist imaginary as *October* and *Old and New*. The suspicion that they did increases when it becomes clear that, as J. F. Aranda pointed out, the showing of Soviet films was not profitable. Were this to be true, we would have to see in Urgoiti—who also financed Piqueras's magazine *Nuestro Cinema*—a complaisant "fellow traveler" of the cause Piqueras defended.

In his memoirs Buñuel evoked the shock of seeing *Battleship Potemkin* in Paris, where the film was presented by the Cine-Club de France on 13 November 1926 and re-screened on 12 April 1928 by Les Amis de Spartacus.[37] A piece of information that serves to remind us that Prometheus and Spartacus were the names adopted by Communist organizations the world over in the cultural field: Joris Ivens's *Spanish Earth* (1937), for example, was distributed in the United States by Prometheus Pictures. And to be done with Münzenberg for the time being, we must mention that his right-hand man on things cinematic was Otto Katz, head of the German section of Mezhrabpomfilm, future promoter of the Anti-Nazi League in Hollywood, as well as the occasional lover, it is said, of Marlene Dietrich.

Making its appearance during the 1931–32 season was the first batch of Filmófono's Soviet films. As well as the titles already cited, these included *The Murderer Dimitri Karamazov* (1931), made in Germany by Russian director Fyodor Otsep. Otsep had absconded from the USSR by taking advantage of the 1929 Mezhrabpomfilm/Prometheus co-production of *The Living Corpse* in Berlin. He wasn't the only Soviet film professional to desert his country: actors Valeri Inkizhinov, Anna Sten, and Vera Malinovskaya used joint ventures with Prometheus to flit the USSR. Of *The Murderer Dimitri Karamazov* Jorge Luis Borges wrote that it was an "extremely powerful" film, and that "its presentation of a genuine, candid happiness following a murder is one of its high spots."[38]

Also featuring prominently in the Filmófono list were comedies, a genre that thrived during the Depression. As well as those by René Clair, the comedies included the Franco-German co-production that inaugurated the sound career of Julien Duvivier, *Here's Berlin* (1932); *Peter Voss Who Stole Millions* (E. A. Dupont, 1932); *The Lovers of Midnight* (Augusto Genina, 1931); and *Madame Pompadour* (Willi Wolff, 1930). Evidence of the company's rapid prosperity is provided by the fact that in Barcelona Filmófono's first films were distributed by another firm, Febrer y Blay, which represented it in Catalonia, Aragón, and the Balearic Islands. In spring 1932, however, Filmófono dispensed with the firm's mediation and opened its own branch in the city.[39]

Walt Disney's *Silly Symphonies* proved to be an important trump card in this good fortune. Disney hadn't found a representative or distributor in Spain until by chance Urgoiti met a Disney representative in Paris.[40] The Disney shorts, which were dubbed in the Estudios Ballesteros, went on to form the American quota of Filmófono's programming. In Spain Mickey Mouse was baptized "Ratoncito Pérez" (a name that was used simultaneously with the original), while the series became the "Sinfonías Grotescas." Their success was so great that they were shown at the end of the session, after the feature films.[41] These hits could not have been produced without efficient teamwork. Enrique Herreros was the head of publicity, and among the poster artists he signed up for the company was Josep Renau. Fernando Remacha directed the dubbing operation, and in order to reduce costs he equipped a suitable annex at Unión Radio headquarters in October 1933.

In June 1933 *Popular Film* announced that Filmófono had acquired the entire production of Pathé-Natan, thus corroborating the weight of French cinema in its lists.[42] When asked a few months later which genre predominated in the new season, Urgoiti answered "Comedy. Given that the times are not exactly happy ones, I've tried to make sure spectators have fun watching our films."[43] In order to promote the René Clair comedy *Quatorze Juillet* (1933), Urgoiti invited its main protagonist, Pola Illery, to the launch in Madrid and Barcelona, which didn't prevent Piqueras from writing on this Filmófono film in *Nuestro Cinema*, "The fact of avoiding a subject that might reveal to the masses the decomposition of capitalism and today's bourgeoisie—presenting, moreover, these elements with completely false directions—leads to a social statement of a bourgeois tendency, and therefore a well-finished and resolutely political film, due precisely to its apolitical nature."[44]

Featuring in the list for the 1934 season was a batch of films by Julien Duvivier: *David Golder* (1931), *Poil de carotte* (1932), *Les Cinq Gentlemen maudits* (1932), *Le Petit Roi* (1933), and *Le Paquebot "Tenacity"* (1934); in addition were *L'Homme à l'Hispano* (Jean Epstein, 1933), *Le Lac aux dames* (Marc Allégret, 1933), and *Cette nuit-là* (G. W. Pabst, 1934), reputable directors, all, albeit entering their decline. Taken as a whole, this was a less ambitious list, artistically speaking, than in earlier years, a list penalized, what's more, by the stringency of the Right-wing government's censorship of Soviet cinema.

In 1934 Filmófono's distribution arm lost money, which disturbed the Banco Urquijo representatives on the company's board of directors. On the eve of the Civil War it continued importing French titles, some of which are not without interest: *Le Dernier Milliardaire* (René Clair, 1934), *Maria Chapdelaine* (Julien Duvivier, 1934), *Mauvaise Graine* (Billy Wilder, 1933), and *Sans famille* (Marc Allégret, 1934). As a novelty it also began importing the occasional Mexican title, such as *Chucho el roto* (Gabriel Soria, 1934), starring Fernando Soler, a future actor in Buñuel's filmography.

In 1935 Filmófono had offices in Madrid, Barcelona, Valencia, Seville, Bilbao, La Coruña, Oviedo, Las Palmas, and Palma de Mallorca. By this time Urgoiti was thinking about entering the film production business—as the distribution companies Exclusivas Diana and Cifesa had already done—as can be deduced from a text he published as a foretaste, along with those of other impresarios, in the 1935 *Anuario Cinematográfico Español*:

> Today, the cinema exercises a decisive influence over the masses, and it has created problems that the public authorities must confront, both inside and outside the country. The cinema is a formidable tool for the propaganda of ideas and customs, which far outstrips anything hitherto imaginable, and so, properly used, it has provided countries like the United States of America and Russia that have made use of it with the most terrible and effective weapon of spiritual invasion.
>
> Spain can and must make its own film propaganda—about its monuments and examples of natural beauty, about the lofty spirituality of our race, about its new political regime, its organization, ideals and quintessential individuals. Finally, all this calls, in each case, for prudent consideration of the circumstances as being apt and opportune to be disseminated before the eyes of millions of spectators who, the world over, go daily to the cinema.[45]

12

Filmófono

In the autobiography he compiled in 1939, Luis Buñuel wrote:

> If I left Warner Bros. it was only because I began to produce pictures in Spain for my country and for South America. For this purpose I entered into partnership with a young Spanish financier, Mr. Urgoiti, who owned the best chain of theaters in Madrid. I was the anonymous producer of several films made by Filmófono, which was the name of the company. Although it had started, there did not yet exist in Spain the specialized work of the Hollywood studios, and I had to develop directors, writers, etc. The pictures were an economic success, the principal ones being, *Don Quintín, el amargao, La hija de Juan Simón, ¿Quién me quiere a mí?, Centinela, alerta.* They are nevertheless mediocre if compared from an artistic standpoint to similar American ones; although intellectually and morally they are no worse than those which the Hollywood studios produce.
>
> Our experiment was going marvelously, when the work was suddenly stopped by the Spanish civil war on July 18, 1936.[1]

The following year, on 10 April 1940, during his encounter with the students of Columbia University, Iris Barry asked him, "How about your commercial films?" Buñuel replied in somewhat erratic English that he'd produced several, "the most awful ones," although he admitted that they had met with a lot of success.[2] Buñuel was always reluctant to speak of this phase of his career, and his cousin Juan Ramón Masoliver told Max Aub that the commercial movies he made then "embarrassed him quite a bit."[3] Also in 1940, in a letter to Ricardo Urgoiti from New York dated 1 April, he referred, not without irony, to the

"Filmófono school" as a school "as cheap and lacking in artistic and moral sense as Buñuel-Remacha's." At the same time, however, he declared himself ready to make films "much viler than the famous daughter of Juan Simón."[4]

In May 1935 the Spanish film press announced that Filmófono was "getting ready to set up a production company, so covering all aspects of the cinema." On 20 May, in fact, shooting began on its first production, *Don Quintín, el amargao*, but Urgoiti's decision to go into production was a *fuite en avant*—a mad rush—cogitated a few months earlier due to the poor economic results of his distribution arm and the pressure forthcoming from the Banco Urquijo. Such a priority seems to be corroborated by the interview Buñuel gave to José Castellón Díaz, published in the February 1935 issue of *Nuestro Cinema*, in which the director alluded to the legitimacy of producing a commercial cinema "that may be seen by millions of eyes."[5] This appeared to provide confirmation of the title Moussinac had given to an article, also published in *Nuestro Cinema*: "Death of the avant-garde."[6]

In his memoirs Buñuel claimed that he contributed 150,000 pesetas, borrowed from his mother, to the Filmófono production plan,[7] but the contractual relationship with Urgoiti was rather more complex, as Josetxo Cerdán and Luis Fernández Colorado's recent biography of the impresario has revealed. As these authors showed, the contract between the two men stipulated a fixed weekly salary for the cineaste for a minimum period of twelve months, renewable in accordance with the success obtained by the first production. Other clauses included the possibility of intervening financially in future productions in exchange for a percentage of their eventual takings at the box office; the chance to return behind the camera as the director of a personal project, depending on the profitability of the first five films; and full executive powers, with the obligation to report to Urgoiti on a daily basis. The authors add that as managers of his production company Urgoiti had previously discountenanced Nemesio Sobrevila, given his megalomania and inclination toward extravagance, and Juan Piqueras, due to his lack of practical experience in professional terms and his residence in Paris.[8] Of special interest is the option Buñuel reserved for himself of directing a "personal project," if the first five films made money. Would he have made his Filmófono debut, perhaps, with his version of *Wuthering Heights*, a project replete with melodramatic ingredients?

Cifesa, the Valencian distributor that went into film production in 1934, would become, with Filmófono, the nearest thing to the studio system that the wretched Spanish Republican cinema had, the first inspired more by the German model, which the Cifesa head, Vicente Casanova, knew from his travels, and the second by that of Hollywood, which Buñuel had experienced firsthand.

With his businesslike organization, stable personnel, production norms, and division of labor, Buñuel did no more than confirm the ideas about "anti-artistic cinema" he'd expressed in 1929. Interviewed at the time by Luis Gómez Mesa for *Popular Film*, he declared that "[the cinema] is an industry. It stems from standardization, from the division of labor. The best cinema is the one that derives from a more perfected industry. I'm of the opinion that film ought to be anonymous, like the cathedral."[9] And shortly afterward he reiterated to his friend Salvador Dalí: "When a true cinema industry exists in Europe, true cinema will automatically appear."[10] This was the premise of the industrial cinema he was now trying to make at Filmófono.

Buñuel's right-hand man at Filmófono was the Navarrese composer Fernando Remacha. Remacha had studied music in Rome and on his return to Spain been a violinist in the string section of the Madrid Symphony Orchestra. He also worked for Unión Radio, where he introduced the sound syncing of records, which was a signal on the score for the gramophone to lower its pickup at the desired moment. Using the Filmófono system he sonorized silent films like *Red Hair* (Clarence Badger, 1928) and *Sunrise* (F. W. Murnau, 1927), screened in the cinemas owned by Gran Empresa Sagarra. Next he became head of dubbing for Filmófono distribution, with dubbing directors like Felipe Briones and Santiago Reyes working under him. And when the Civil War broke out, with the resulting exodus of professionals, he became head of the company. Following the Republican defeat he was to suffer imprisonment and ostracism.

The stable team Buñuel organized at Filmófono worked well together and as a result was able to keep costs down. Another fundamental member of the team was the Basque Eduardo Ugarte, grandson of a Carlist general and son of a writer, lawyer, and minister in three Conservative cabinets between 1900 and 1913. Ugarte had been a leading light in the Socialist Students Group, which would adhere to the Third International. In 1919 he traveled to Russia to enlist in the Red Army, but the German police detained him and sent him back to Spain, where he became one of the founders of the PCE. He was, like Urgoiti, a knight in the mythical Order of Toledo and, with Lorca, co-director of La Barraca, the theater group that in November 1931 had joined the Federal Union of Spanish Students (UFEH), of which Ugarte was secretary. In 1928 he had married Pilar Arniches, daughter of playwright Carlos Arniches, while her sister Rosario did likewise with José Bergamín, thus making Ugarte and Bergamín brothers-in-law. This family connection meant that Filmófono would adapt two Arniches plays, *Don Quintín, el amargao* and *¡Centinela, alerta!*, while Urgoiti, in his Argentinean exile, was to produce *La canción que tú cantabas* (1939), also deriving from Arniches and directed by Miguel Mileo. Ugarte would be co-scriptwriter on all the Filmófono productions and occasional director of *¡Centinela, alerta!* in the absence of its official *metteur en scène*, Jean Grémillon.

The company cameraman was the Aragonese José María Beltrán, son of a professional photographer, who had experimented with microphotography in 1921 before moving in 1924 to Madrid, making his debut in professional cinema there the following year. Having become the most competent Spanish cameraman, he collaborated with Nemesio Sobrevila on *El sexto sentido* (1929) and shortly before starting work for Filmófono photographed *La Dolorosa* (1934) for Grémillon. Like Buñuel and Ugarte, he would go into exile as a result of the Spanish Civil War. Handling the company advertising was the Madrid writer and designer Enrique Herreros, creator of its posters and slogans and, during the Civil War, one of the founders on the Francoist side, along with Tono and Miguel Mihura, of the weekly humorous magazine *La Ametralladora* (1937–39).

Filmófono assembled its own roster of stars, beginning with the hugely popular flamenco singer Angelillo, who was nicknamed "the nightingale of Andalusia" and even "the Fleta of Andalusian lyric art"—Miguel Fleta (1897–1938) being an internationally acclaimed Spanish opera singer of the day. Angelillo appeared in *La hija de Juan Simón* and *¡Centinela, alerta!* Later, taking advantage of his Argentinean exile, Urgoiti would give him the lead role in Buenos Aires of *La canción que tú cantabas* and *Mi cielo de Andalucía* (1942), in which he shone with six songs. Ana María Custodio was the female lead in *Don Quintín, el amargao* and *¡Centinela, alerta!* The comedian Luis de Heredia appeared in *Don Quintín, el amargao*, *¿Quién me quiere a mí?*, and *¡Centinela, alerta!*, and Buñuel would rehabilitate him in 1961 as one of the beggars in *Viridiana.* Other habitual cast members were Manuel Arbó and José María Linares Rivas. All those cited, minus Arbó and Heredia, chose exile after Franco's victory.

Buñuel organized the team and its production methods in a highly disciplined way, with a daily work schedule of eight hours, a detailed shooting script, and rehearsals prior to filming, with the right to a maximum of two takes. J. F. Aranda has written that Buñuel "put into practice his incredibly cheap methods (incomplete sets with only one possible camera angle, one or two takes at the most, etc.), and a rigorous timetable for the filming. . . . When he arrived at the studios everybody paid obeisance to the 'Señor Bishop,' and Buñuel went by leaning on his walking stick as he was suffering an attack of sciatica."[11] And Manuel Rotellar collected the testimony of Pilar Muñoz, actress in *La hija de Juan Simón*, who told him that Buñuel was "an authoritarian gentleman, very handsome, with green eyes, who had everybody, actors included, at his beck and call."[12]

This brings us to the much-debated question of what the cineaste's real intervention in Filmófono's films was. As a condition for his collaboration in the production company, Buñuel imposed the strictest anonymity, the same that had protected him during his stay at MGM in Hollywood, Paramount-Joinville in Paris, and Warner Bros. in Madrid. And indeed, it is in vain that one looks for his name in the numerous news items, advertising announcements, and press releases of the period to do with Filmófono's productions, apart from one exception, discussed below. His invisibility in the professional media reached the point that in the list of directors and technicians published in the *Anuario Cinematográfico Español* for 1935 his name does not appear, although Urgoiti's does, along with his photograph.

Buñuel alluded on several occasions to his different tasks in the company, allusions that are couched in vague language that does little to clarify the facts of the matter. When referring in his memoirs to *Don Quintín, el amargao*, he categorically stated that "at times I openly intervened in the directing."[13] The director of the film, Luis Marquina, corroborated this when, on the point of directing his next movie, *El bailarín y el trabajador* (1936), he declared to *Cinegramas*: "This is the first film I'm directing under my own responsibility. On *Don Quintín, el amargao* I had invaluable help and advice."[14] Elsewhere, Buñuel claimed that "I was only the executive producer: I supervised the script, the work in the studio, the sound recording . . . My function was to make sure the production kept within budget."[15] And to Max Aub he gave an even more modest version: "I did nothing more than see that they made the films as quickly as possible, spending as little as they could."[16] Another filmmaker, José Luis Sáenz de Heredia, who figured as the director of two of the company's productions, remarked in various places that the real director of his first film—*La hija de Juan Simón*—was Buñuel.[17] Moreover, Buñuel admitted to having directed certain scenes in *¡Centinela, alerta!*

Buñuel's being omnipresent head supervisor—from script to sound recording—has given rise to many different versions about his true responsibility in these films. The critic Florentino Hernández Girbal, for example, published an article in the Urgoiti-financed magazine *Cinema Sparta* attributing the direction of both *Don Quintín, el amargao* and *La hija de Juan Simón* to him.[18] Buñuel denied this in a letter to the magazine, dated 15 January 1936, in which he defined himself as "the firm's production manager, a merely technical and administrative position." He went on to invite the critic to visit the Estudios Ballesteros, where Sáenz de Heredia was currently preparing *¿Quién me quiere a mí?*, a film in which, due partly to Buñuel's back pain and partly to complications in the preparation of the following film *¡Centinela, alerta!*, he had little personal presence, as

Production still from *Don Quintín, el amargao* (Luis Marquina, 1935) showing a tumultuous scene in a café in which the irascible Quintín (*on the left*) threatens the customers with a pistol. (Archivo Buñuel, Filmoteca Española, Madrid)

would be noticeable in its unsatisfactory outcome. More than sixty years after this episode, when asked about whether Buñuel intervened in the directing, Hernández Girbal answered, "No, but he gave advice, he was supervisor at the same time."[19]

The slightly ambiguous conclusion of all this is that Buñuel imported into Filmófono the American figure of the producer, with powers as wide-ranging as they were authoritarian, as he had seen exercised during his stay at MGM by his friend Frank Davis. In any case, evoking this period of a Buñuel in full swing, Pepín Bello would recall, "he confessed to me it was perhaps the happiest time in his life."[20] Moreover, the financial rewards that went with it enabled him to buy an eight-cylinder Ford, as well as to financially help the PCE. In fact, Buñuel would confide to Max Aub: "I was making a lot of money with Filmófono and the government was going to embargo *Mundo Obrero* [the PCE's newspaper]. So I went along and embargoed it for a sum of money we pretended it owed me. Once embargoed by one person it couldn't be embargoed by another."[21]

An ample consensus exists about Buñuel's organizational and money-saving skills, virtues he'd already demonstrated during the production of *L'Âge d'or*. Urgoiti expressed his boundless admiration for such ability to various people. To Aranda he declared that "Luis was marvelous and incredibly cheap. He saved, *centimo* by *centimo*, every foot of raw stock, every minute. I'd given him a ridiculous budget. I sat in my office waiting for him to come and ask me for more. Three weeks later he came in with the finished film in one hand and part of the money I'd given him in the other. Here's the change, he said, keep it for the next one."[22] Bello recalled Urgoiti admitting to him: "Look, as the manager of a company, who's there to run things and to make money, the first time deadlines and budgets [were] exactly adhered to is with Luis Buñuel."[23] And in a letter of 5 July 1946 he praised the latter for having taught him how to get the "maximum out of the minimum."[24]

By mid-1935 Buñuel's position on the Spanish and European cultural scene was very far from what it had been in 1929–30. While his old friends Dalí and Lorca had augmented their international prestige with a plentiful body of work, Buñuel was travailing anonymously, hidden away in a production company that manufactured a plebeian cinema of *sainetes* (comic sketches), *españoladas*, and popular comedies. A number of objective factors existed to explain this situation. In the Republican-Socialist *bienio* of 1931–33, the technical difficulties presented by the new sound cinema hampered any use of the medium by the Left, while in the 1933–35 *bienio*, when the technique and infrastructures of sound cinema had been consolidated in Spain, political hegemony was in the hands of the Right, so that the objective conditions for making a progressively orientated cinema did not exist. This is verified in *Don Quintín, el amargao* by Felisa (Luisita Esteso), a young woman with ambitions to be an actress, who states in the film that "right now the cinema in Spain is in very bad shape." Doubtless Buñuel was thinking of all this when he replied to Castellón Díaz, in the interview in *Nuestro Cinema* mentioned above: "Within the current framework of our society I don't think the creation of a really popular cinema is possible. The existence of censorship, among other things, does its all to prevent it."

Although we examine each of the four films produced by Filmófono in 1935 and 1936 in some detail, it is worth saying something about the imaginary configuration structured by these films. First, all four movies present strong, schematic, and recurrent archetypes that rough in many of the themes and characters that reappear in the commercial films Buñuel made years later in Mexico. They are archetypes deriving from the national popular tradition, the stereotypes of which had been successful since the mid-nineteenth century, being linked to the thematic constellation known as the *españolada*. Let's not forget that in December 1934 Aragon had written to his Spanish comrade from Odessa suggesting he make a film in the USSR, proposing "an ultra-modern Spanish operetta, of the Olé, olé! type, the Caramba! type, in short the Carmen type, [which] would certainly meet with a favorable reception." And proof is given of the hold this idea had by Juan Piqueras, who wrote somewhat cryptically that "with a different ambience, *Le Chien andalou* [*sic*], by Buñuel and Dalí, might have been the first great authentic *españolada*."[25]

To sum up, the "sob story" model developed in the films presents innocent female victims placed in difficulty by their irregular (or seemingly irregular) status as mothers, grappling with domineering men with social power who act as sexual predators or exploiters. In the end the virtue of the humble is finally rewarded, but without the intervention of either clergymen or supernatural elements as was habitual in films by Filmófono's rival, Cifesa. An inventory of the characters is evidence of this: *La hija de Juan Simón* and *¡Centinela, alerta!* feature destitute mothers who laboriously cart their natural offspring around. In *Don Quintín, el amargao* we encounter an upright, pregnant wife repudiated by her husband, who is also responsible for the abandoning of his baby daughter. Meanwhile, *¿Quién me quiere a mí?* features the abduction of a little girl, snatched away from her mother by the latter's unscrupulous husband. Where the men are concerned, the jealous, irascible protagonist of *Don Quintín, el amargao* is the one who triggers events by throwing his honorable pregnant wife out of his house. In *La hija de Juan Simón* an unmarried mother is driven by economic necessity to work as a hostess in a cabaret (read brothel) run by an overbearing spiv and pursued by lecherous clients. In *¿Quién me quiere a mí?* a criminal husband decides to kidnap his daughter from his wife and to ask her for ransom money. And in *¡Centinela, alerta!* an unscrupulous playboy gets a young woman pregnant and then abandons her; later, when she is successful in economic terms, he tries to rob her. In every instance a positive male counterpoint exists, an honorable young man who finally saves the female victims—although the woman is shown as the weaker, more vulnerable element in the couple. With regard to this dramatis personae we must, however, carefully nuance the judgment of Jo Labanyi, when she states that these films portray "male sexual anxieties."[26]

While it is clear what the Filmófono production company meant in Ricardo Urgoiti's managerial structure in terms of compensating for its problems in the distribution sector, it is much less clear what it meant in the professional career of Buñuel, after the political manifesto of *Las Hurdes*, which he didn't even take the trouble to sonorize for the French market in Filmófono's readily available sound facilities. It is pertinent to have a look at the evolution of the Communist movement during those same years.

With Hitler already in power in Germany, the Fascist riots that took place in France in February 1934, in which twenty people died, alarmed the French Left and led to a defensive rapprochement between the Communist and Socialist parties that marked the beginning of the move toward the Popular Fronts. In May of that year Georgi Dimitrov, secretary of the Comintern, met Maurice Thorez in Moscow and approved the new alliance, which deferred the class struggle in the capitalist countries and gave priority to the defense of the USSR against the expansionist threat of the Nazis. In October Thorez formally proposed the new interclass, anti-Fascist alliance, and on 14 July 1935 the pact between the Communists and the Socialists for the *Rassemblement Populaire* was signed in Paris.

Although it occupied a peripheral place on the European map, Spain was not, for all that, absent from the new scene. In Paris the AEAR organized the first International Congress of Writers for the Defense of Culture from 21 to 25 June 1935, a united anti-Fascist initiative that witnessed André Breton's final clash with the Communists (a clash that led to his physical confrontation with Soviet delegate Ilya Ehrenburg) in his doomed attempt to have the Surrealist movement collaborate with the PCF. The congress was presided over by Gide and, bringing together 230 delegates from thirty-eight countries, marked the starting signal for the intellectual world to support the watchword of the Popular Front. The Spanish Socialist Julio Álvarez del Vayo intervened in the sessions, but the Spanish delegation also counted on Ramón del Valle Inclán, Bergamín, Alberti, María Teresa León, and Arturo Barea. An executive committee—the International Bureau—was created, consisting of twelve members, one of whom was Valle Inclán. And secretariats were created in different countries: directing the Spanish one were Ricardo Baeza and Bergamín, who proposed in Paris that the Second International Congress take place in Spain in 1937.

A month after this emblematic conclave the Seventh Congress of the Comintern, beginning in Moscow on 25 July, officially approved and promulgated the political line of interclass and anti-Fascist Popular Fronts, thus postponing the revolutionary aims of the national Communist parties in favor of the new doctrine of "collective security." As a result of the new context, the Mezhrabpom-film production company was dismantled, and the Communist paradigm of proletarian cinema was abandoned. Juan Piqueras had insistently defended the cause of proletarian cinema in the pages of *Nuestro Cinema*. By the time it started coming out again in January 1935 after a break of more than a year the magazine's slogans and language had changed, and as Carlos and David Pérez Merinero were to observe, it subsequently seemed "very moderate in its approach."[27] Significantly, the final number of *Nuestro Cinema* is dated August

1935, in consonance with the political change ordained that summer by the Comintern.

The new rallying cry also reached Spain. After the defeat of the insurrection of October 1934, the Comintern had asked the PCE to create a broad anti-Fascist front that would include Manuel Azaña's Izquierda Republicana. In March 1935 the National Committee of Prisoners' Aid was created, in which the Socialist and Communist parties and their youth sections participated. On 2 June the PCE, through its secretary José Díaz, proposed a "popular anti-Fascist rally," and on 2 November the slogan of the Frente Popular was formally coined.

It is precisely in May 1935 that Filmófono embarks upon its production program, which can no longer be perceived as being incompatible with radical political ideas by the Communist Buñuel. Not only that: Filmófono's managerial framework may have been seen as an operative infrastructure for consolidating a popular cinema (equivalent, in a way, to the populist cinema some filmmakers were making at the time in a more cultured France), while waiting for circumstances more favorable to explicit political action. More than thirty years after the events, Buñuel explained to Max Aub: "One morning, following a strong bout of sciatica during which I'd read a lot of plays by Arniches, I turned up at Ricardo Urgoiti's house and said to him, 'Right, here's 20,000 *duros* [100,000 pesetas] for us to make *Don Quintín, el amargao*.' 'Are you going to direct it?' 'Certainly not. We've got Marquina. We give him 2,000 pesetas.' It was a huge hit. We made pots of money."[28] This might have been the origin of Filmófono's film production, except that the figures Buñuel gave Aub are erroneous and even contradictory in terms of those he offered elsewhere.

It has to be remembered that during the Republican years (1931–39) Arniches's theater underwent a revival as a source of popular culture, due to its cordial vision of humble characters and milieus, its liberal traditionalism, its criticism of social hierarchies, and its witty punning. Of him Gonzalo Torrente Ballester wrote: "Of all the comedy writers of our time, none has known the glory Arniches has among ordinary folk, a glory that is above all their gratitude for having elevated them to the rank of protagonists."[29] He was eulogized by, among others, Bergamín (who saw him as "the Larra of the *género chico*"; that is, of the short, light, musical play), Ramón Pérez de Ayala, Gregorio Marañón, and Edgar Neville, who defended him in 1944 as a model, in contrast to the Falangist cinema of imperial nostalgia.[30] The symbiosis between *sainete* and cinema was important during the Second Republic: on the eve of the Civil War Julio Romano published an article called, eloquently enough, "The public for Madrid's *sainetes* has gone over to the cinema."[31]

With admirable assurance Arniches cultivated a genre in which a pre-absurdist quality has sometimes been detected. *Don Quintín el amargao o el que siembra vientos . . .*, which belongs to the cycle of his "bourgeois comedies," is a two-act play he wrote with Antonio Estremera, which, with music by Jacinto Guerrero, opened at Madrid's Teatro Apolo on 25 November 1924. The following year it was adapted for the screen by Manuel Noriega for Cartago Films. And its popularity was so great that the dialogues and the music from it were broadcast on 20 April 1929 by Unión Radio.

News of the project to film *Don Quintín el amargao* first appeared on 2 May 1935 in the magazine *Popular Film*, its direction being attributed to Benito Perojo.[32] This choice is not so odd, for Perojo—a liberal, secular filmmaker, unlike Florián Rey, a Cifesa man—was currently enjoying his period of greatest commercial success. On 14 September 1928 the young Buñuel, who was trying to break into the film world, had written to Pepín Bello that the production company Julio César was on the point of signing him up: "The company makes its films in France, Germany and England. Our brilliant Perojo is under contact there." Buñuel's professional recognition of Perojo—two filmmakers who'd met professionally in Paris and used the same French actors and technicians (Modot, Duverger, Schildknecht) on their shoots—came from way back, then. By the time the news emerged in *Popular Film*, Perojo had closed a deal with Cifesa.[33] It was with good reason that *Nuestro Cinema* could exclaim at the time, "How the producers argue over Perojo!"[34] According to José Cabeza San Deogracias, Perojo's films ran for fifty weeks in Madrid during the Civil War, proof that "no Spanish director was so loved by the public."[35]

With Perojo ruled out, Buñuel chose Luis Marquina, an industrial engineer who'd trained as a sound technician in the Tobis studios in Paris and Berlin, returning to Spain in 1933. He was the son of Catalan poet and playwright Eduardo Marquina, a friend of the Dalí family, and the person responsible for the painter being admitted into the Residencia de Estudiantes, meaning that Buñuel had met him during his stays in Cadaqués in Dalí's house. At the time Buñuel asked him to collaborate, Marquina was working as a sound engineer at Estudios CEA in Madrid, where *Don Quintín, el amargao* would be filmed. The decision to hire a specialist in sound was a prudent one, since Florián Rey had just come to grief in the making of *El novio de mamá* (1934) at Estudios Cinema Español S.A. (ECESA) thanks to its disastrous soundtrack, which had to be rerecorded during postproduction. Buñuel hired Marquina for a thousand pesetas as director.

On 7 May 1935 the contract to produce *Don Quintín, el amargao* was signed by Urgoiti and Buñuel. According to its terms, Buñuel was to contribute 75,000 pesetas, while Filmófono undertook to come up with the remaining money. Decisions would be taken in relation to the proportion of the capital contributed. The film would be distributed in Spain and Morocco by Filmófono, with the help of a 30 percent remuneration. Within the two weeks following each period of three months, starting in January 1936, Filmófono would present its statement of account to Buñuel and pay him his share, guaranteeing him a minimum of 50,000 pesetas. These data have been presented by Cerdán and Fernández Colorado in their biography of Urgoiti when indicating that the film cost 331,021 pesetas, a sum spread over different contributions: Urgoiti (125,000), Buñuel (85,000), Luis de la Peña (35,000), Aurora Gutiérrez, Urgoiti's wife (15,000), the composer Jacinto Guerrero (5,000), Arniches (2,500), Antonio Estremera (2,500), and Filmófono (61,021), an amount that was in fact a loan from Unión Radio.[36]

The filming of *Don Quintín, el amargao* began on 20 May at CEA, whose sound engineer (León Lucas de la Peña) and set designer (José María Torres) played a part in its production. Don Quintín was played by Alfonso Muñoz, who had been the leading man in Margarita Xirgu's company, while his abandoned daughter was played by the Sevillian Ana María Custodio, who had made her debut at the Teatro Calderón in Madrid in 1927 and formed part of the Lola Membrives and Irene López Heredia companies, before starting out in the cinema in 1931 in Hollywood, under contract to Fox for a couple of Spanish-language versions. Shooting ended on 21 July and editing was completed by the end of August.[37]

The only reliable account we have of that production was provided by its editor, Eduardo García Maroto, who wrote in his memoirs: "The script, written in collaboration with Eduardo Ugarte, was by Buñuel. As I looked after the editing of the film, I read it time and again and to me it seemed extremely well constructed and perfectly planned. The filming began, then; Luis Marquina was directing, Buñuel supervising and correcting, and I was doing the editing. Buñuel was exacting, something that pleased me because so was I in my work, and so nothing untoward happened. The film got released later on and its success gradually increased with the re-releases of it. Although Buñuel was not entirely convinced—which was natural given his preferences—to me it seemed the best thing that had come out in terms of Spanish folkloric films."[38] The absence of Buñuel's name in the many news reports published during the production of the movie is, as we've already said, striking. Perhaps his most eye-catching lack of visibility (so to speak) occurred on the occasion of the celebration of the end of the filming, to which the Madrid press was invited. The account in *Popular Film* went thus:

> Last week the most lucid delegation of Madrid's film critics visited the CEA Studios in the Ciudad Lineal in order to attend the filming of the final scenes of Filmófono's first production. The journalists, presided over by the learned editor of *La Libertad*, Don Antonio Pérez Camarero, member-elect of the Film Council, were courteously received and attended to by Señors [Rafael] Salgado and [Enrique Domínguez] Rodiño of the CEA, and by the Filmófono top brass, Señors Roberto Martín, Fernando Remacha and the excellent designer Enrique Herreros.
>
> The event was an intimate, cordial and pleasant one. After the filming, in which Ana María Custodio, Luisita Esteso, Consuelo Nieva, Porfiria Sánchez, Alfonso Muñoz, Luis de Heredia, Fernando de Granada, José Alfayate, Manuel Arbó and José Marco Davó took part, under the direction of Luis Marquina, a splendid lunch was served by the indispensable barman, Perico Chicote. The illustrious authors of *Don Quintín, el amargao*, Carlos Arniches and Antonio Estremera, were also present at the congenial gathering.[39]

Buñuel's name is conspicuous by its absence.

Don Quintín, el amargao gets under way with the resentful and jealous Don Quintín (Alfonso Muñoz) arriving at his house one day and surprising his wife (Porfiria Sánchez) talking to a man behind a curtain. Convinced she is having an affair, he throws her out of their home, despite the fact that she is pregnant. She gives birth to a girl in the Maternity Hospital and, penniless, wanders the streets with her daughter. To move him to pity, she decides to leave the baby in her husband's house, but by night Quintín in turn leaves the infant in the doorway of the house of a modest road worker, with a letter announcing a monthly payment to the family for it to maintain the child. Meanwhile, Quintín's personality is ever more disagreeable, and his mistress (Consuelo Nieva) leaves him after stealing money from the strongbox of the casino he owns. His daughter, Teresa (Ana María Custodio), is cared for by her adoptive parents, along with their own daughter Felisa (Luisita Esteso), although the father, a hardened drinker, frequently vents his bad temper on Teresa. On her deathbed Quintín's wife swears to her husband that the girl is his daughter, and so he decides to reclaim her, but on the very day he sends his assistant Angelito (Luis de Heredia) to the house of the adoptive parents, Teresa runs away with Paco (Fernando de Granada), a young mechanic who is to use his savings to buy a taxi, and who installs the girl in the house of his aunt while they prepare for their wedding. Chance has it that one day Teresa and Paco go into a café where Quintín is drinking with two of his employees, Angelito and Sefiní (José Alfayate). Quintín harasses the couple by throwing olives at them, but Paco faces up to and humiliates him, and so Quintín decides to take revenge on him. Quintín's unpleasant character even gives rise to a song (the only one retained from the play), which goes:

> Don Quintín
> no es un malandrín
> no es un maleducao
> no lo hace con mal fin . . .
> Don Quintín, el pobre, está amargao.
> [Don Quintín
> is not a ruffian
> not a boor
> he doesn't do it with evil intent . . .
> Don Quintín, the poor chap, is embittered.]

In the meantime Angelito has begun an affair with Felisa, Teresa's adoptive sister, a girl who aims to triumph in the entertainment world and become "the Spanish Garbo." One day when Paco and Teresa attend a function in which Felisa performs, the sisters meet again, and Angelito then follows Teresa to where she lives. In this way Quintín is able to track down the couple in order to revenge himself for his earlier humiliation. He confronts Teresa without knowing she is his daughter. She curses him, and Sefiní then explains that she is his daughter, saying, "He who sows hate reaps curses." Quintín goes storming off and upon reaching his house encounters Teresa and Paco, with whom he is reconciled. Next, Angelito and Felisa arrive with a barrel of olives, from which they extract Quintín's grandson, a beautiful baby the grandfather takes in his arms, at which point the infant urinates on him.

The leading character of *Don Quintín, el amargao* is a male figure related to the main protagonist of *Es mi hombre*, the "grotesque tragedy" by Arniches that Perojo brought to the screen in that same year, 1935. Don Quintín is denounced as a representative of *machista* despotism and egoism since, believing his wife has a lover, he throws her out of the house, while he himself is having an affair with another woman. The counterpoint to him is his daughter, personification of the humiliated, absent mother, who ends up triumphing over the bad father at the same time as, happily, she gets him back in what also entails for her an advancement in social terms. And appearing alongside them are the "comic characters" who act as the despot's henchmen, Angelito and Sefiní (a Gallicism for *C'est fini*), although the former also had the plot function of putting the father in contact with his lost daughter.

José María Torres's impressive urban décor for *Don Quintín, el amargao*, which reveals the influence of the populist Paris sets Lazare Meerson had designed earlier for René Clair. The lamppost in the foreground emphasizes the depth-of-field effect of the photography. (Archivo Buñuel, Filmoteca Española, Madrid)

The urban sets of a populist Madrid were a modest, but effective, echo of the Paris presented by René Clair in *Sous les toits de Paris* and *Quatorze Juillet*, although there were no film cranes at the time in Spain, so that the framing was necessarily static.[40] At the end, during the nocturnal scuffle in the street between Paco and Don Quintín, the camera shoots from a high angle with an illuminated lamppost in the foreground to lend depth to the composition. Beltrán's lighting was impeccable, and the scene at the beginning, when the main protagonist discovers the silhouettes of his wife and a friend behind a curtain and thinks they are tricking him, appeared to come from the German Expressionist film *Shadows* (Arthur Robison, 1923), which was shown in June 1930 at the Cineclub Español.

The handling of the match cuts and ellipses revealed an absolute professionalism. In the opening sequence we see high-angle shots of a Madrid street filled with street vendors' barrows. From this general view we cut to a medium long shot of Quintín buying fruit at one of the stands before entering the doorway of his building. The most spectacular ellipsis was produced after the shot showing the two babies (Teresa and Felisa) on a bed, transmuting them via a dissolve into two nubile grown-ups lying on the same bed. Certain ellipses bore the imprint of the narrative economy of American cinema, as when Don Quintín requested a cardsharp to step into his casino office, and in the next shot his employees carry the wrongdoer out unconscious. At times the ellipsis was transformed into a metaphor, like the one alluding to Teresa's future maternity: Paco's aunt is seen making clothes for the unborn child, while Teresa waters some plants in a flowerpot. The ellipsis immediately gives way to the same plants in flower, while Paco and Teresa rock the cradle with their baby in it. At times the associations were more distant. The scene in the café where Quintín threw olives at Paco and Teresa—which ridiculed the noble confrontations in so many westerns, according to Jean-André Fieschi[41]—shot in angle/reverse angle with depth of field, served for the olives of discord to turn into their opposite, since it is from a bountiful barrel of olives that Don Quintín's grandson is plucked in the final sequence.

The spirit of the recently outmoded proletarian cinema found its way into the distressing scenes of the ejected wife begging in the streets. She is shown in the queue of a soup kitchen, from which she does not get to profit because she lacks a bowl. Out of solidarity a worker who is eating a sandwich leaves a bit of it on the edge of the bench he is sitting on so that the poor woman can reach it.

To the script Buñuel added a few amusing allusions to cinema through Felisa, who, wanting to triumph as an actress, stares enthralled at a fan magazine containing photos of Greta Garbo in *Queen Christina* (1933) and then says, "Every girl has her dreams. But in this godforsaken place who's going to notice one's charming incognitos?" Teresa replies, "The only thing you're going to get is that your father will put an end to such charms with a thrashing the day he sees you in one of those poses." Felisa aspires to become the "Spanish Greta Garbo" and to win the Miss Spain beauty contest. In the same May 1935 issue of *Cine Español* announcing the start of the filming of *Don Quintín, el amargao*, there was a report on the same page of the making of *Reportaje de Miss España 1935* by Sabino A. Micón, to the greater glory of Alicia Navarro, who would go on to win the title of Miss Europe in London, a sign of the modernizing of leisure in Republican Spain. Later on, when Felisa meets Angelito, she tells him he isn't her type, her type being Gary Cooper. Full of irony, Buñuel's cinephile jokes culminate during a subsequent meeting of the two characters in this dialogue:

> ANGELITO: Are you still thinking of the Seventh Art?
>
> FELISA: No, because right now the cinema in Spain is in very bad shape and the Hollywood people don't call you that easily.

Teresa meets Paco when the young man makes a violent swerve to avoid running her over on the highway, a swerve that sends the car (from which he's jumped clear) hurtling down a ravine. Enrique Herreros had got hold of a 1932 Hudson for the shooting of this scene (in Buñuel's 1951 Mexican version of the film the scene would be reduced to a sudden braking). The scene has a savage feel to it, which makes one think of the atmosphere of *L'Âge d'or.* This isn't the only note of a Surrealist sort in the film, for in the final scenes Angelito gets around the streets of Madrid on a child's scooter.

When Buñuel arrived in Mexico in 1946 he found a dozen copies there of what he considered to be his best Filmófono production, and from these he re-edited a master copy, which he used to show to his Spanish friends in exile: Ugarte, Luis Alcoriza, Ignacio Mantecón, and José Moreno Villa.[42] His 1951 Mexican remake of the movie, *La hija del engaño*, which boasts a more elaborate mise-en-scène and cinematography (by José Ortiz Ramos), has a number of significant differences, although the appearance of the main character (Fernando Soler), also mustachioed, is similar to that of the Spanish protagonist. It is clear that the jealous and irascible Quintín prefigured Francisco, the paranoid protagonist of *Él*, made the year after *La hija del engaño*.

Don Quintín, el amargao opened on 3 October 1935 at the Cine Palacio de la Música, pertaining to Gran Empresa Sagarra, with the slogan "A Madrid *sainete* with the rhythm of an American film." Fox, which had sold a batch of films to the company, sent its Movietone newsreel cameras to capture the premiere, an event a few newspapers picked up on due to its novelty value. Three weeks later the film was used to launch the same circuit's Cine Salamanca. Its success was overwhelming, and in the first quarter of 1936 it made more than 300,000 pesetas at the box office, while in the first six months the takings in the Spanish market exceeded 900,000 pesetas.

In his highly favorable review in *El Sol* (a daily paper founded by Ricardo Urgoiti's father), José Pizarroso wrote: "A doughty zarzuela subject to rules and norms that are not in the least bit photogenic has been suppressed, or better yet, transformed into something visual. Time and again the dialogue has been supplanted, happily, by very beautiful and synthetically expressive shots."[43] Two weeks later the same newspaper printed a somewhat unusual article since it did not emanate from a regular film critic but from José Moreno Villa, another member of the Order of Toledo. In "Don Quintín and the World" the poet and painter argued that if before the Spanish archetype was Don Quijote, now it is Don Quintín, which is why "the presentation of Don Quintín on the screen is highly opportune, because I'm afraid that we as a nation are doing a Don Quintín in the concert of Europe." He went on to define such an archetype: "Don Quintín is a lonely, punctilious man. But due to this he lacks social power. He lives from the limited tyranny he can exercise over his wife and his cronies.

A homemade tyranny, vulnerable to the fact that a man in the street can bring it down at any time."[44] A distant view of the film came from the correspondent in Spain of the New York magazine *Variety*, who, signing himself Ziff, thought it was slow and that it could be cut by twenty or thirty minutes, but that it could be successful in the markets of Latin America. Of the actors, he thought that Luisita Esteso stole the film from Ana María Custodio—in which he was not mistaken—and that Alfonso Muñoz overacted.[45]

In the same 21 July 1935 number in which *El Sol* announced the end of the filming of *Don Quintín, el amargao*, another item on the same page informed the reader that Filmófono would next bring to the screen an adaptation of the comedy *La Papirusa*, by Leandro Navarro and Adolfo Torrado. A few days later the film press came out with the same bit of news.[46] One week later this information was rectified, with Filmófono announcing that prior to doing *La Papirusa* it would make *La hija de Juan Simón*, a play by the Basque cineaste, architect, and inventor Nemesio M. Sobrevila.[47] As it was, until June 1936 *La Papirusa* was repeatedly announced as being one of Filmófono's upcoming productions, although nothing ever came of it.

La hija de Juan Simón was a popular drama written by Sobrevila and the cleric José María Granada (José María Martín López) and was based in turn on their film script inspired by a popular song about the fate of the daughter of the gravedigger Juan Simón. The original song, a *milonga* composed by Manuel Escacena in 1926 and an immediate success as a recording by El Niño de Marchena, told of the misfortunes of a village woman abandoned and forced into prostitution in the city, whose body was buried by her father, the gravedigger Juan Simón. The song was so well known at the time among the Spanish public that newspapers like *ABC* (13 February 1934) satirized the Fascist party Falange Española by saying that its initials corresponded to "Funeraria Española" (Spanish Undertakers), due to which its founder, José Antonio Primo de Rivera, deserved to be called Juan Simón, the gravedigger of the popular song.[48] The stage play deriving from the song, dedicated to Manuel Machado, featured Carmen, the gravedigger's daughter, who, enamored of the singer Pepe Luis, is bearing his child. Imprisoned for a crime he did not commit, Pepe Luis is told on being released that Carmen has died, when in reality she is working in a brothel. When Pepe Luis goes to visit the brothel, Carmen commits suicide. The drama thus combined two archetypes typical of popular culture, the wrong culprit and the woman as abandoned victim who is finally immolated.

Sobrevila, coauthor of the play premiered at the Teatro La Latina in Madrid on 28 May 1930, had moved from architecture to experimental filmmaking as the producer, scriptwriter, director, and set designer of two unusual movies, *Al*

Cover of the 1930 edition of the stage play of *La hija de Juan Simón*, by José María Granada and Nemesio M. Sobrevila, with the inducement of a Julio Romero de Torres reproduction of his archetypal Andalusian woman wielding a phallic guitar. (Collection: Román Gubern, Barcelona)

Hollywood madrileño (1927) and *El sexto sentido* (1929). With Urgoiti, he had also compiled the report, *El cinema y el Estado*, published in July 1931, proposing measures to the new Republican government for fomenting Spanish cinema. In addition, he sat on the Filmófono distribution selection committee.[49]

One of the most important assets of the new production was the presence of the singer Angelillo (Ángel Sampedro Montero) in the leading role. Born in Madrid on 12 January 1908, he had been an apprentice jeweler and later worked in a stove-repair workshop. In 1924 he won an amateur singing competition and made his professional debut under contract to the influential impresario Juan Carcellé. In 1929 he formed a company with Estrellita Castro, another presence who would become popular on the screen, thanks mainly to her work with Benito Perojo. Angelillo's first film appearance was in the bullfighting movie *El sabor de la gloria* (Fernando Roldán, 1932), which made little impact, but he was the joint lead in his next outing, *El negro que tenía el alma blanca* (1934), in the role of the shoeshine boy Nonell, a highly successful version of the Alberto Insúa novel brought to the screen by Perojo. Angelillo's songs in *La hija de Juan Simón* were composed by Daniel Montorio, but the most famous of the ten he intoned therein, "Soy un pobre presidiario" (A Poor Convict Am I), was anterior to it and had been made popular by Angelillo himself. *La hija de Juan Simón* constituted, then, an interesting example of intermedia complicity, since the stage play adapted to the cinema proceeded from a script based on a popular song and incorporated in its film version musical material from outside that had already been a hit on the market.

La hija de Juan Simón was financed by Urgoiti (100,000 pesetas), Sobrevila (65,000), and Filmófono (379,473.88), by means of loans from Unión Radio and the Banco Urquijo. It was shot in Madrid's Estudios Roptence, inaugurated shortly before by Benito Perojo with his version of *Es mi hombre*, by Carlos Arniches. Sobrevila began directing on 9 September, using sets he designed. However, his slow, perfectionist direction irritated Buñuel so much that when the film went a week behind schedule he fired Sobrevila. According to Urgoiti's statement to Roger Mortimer, Buñuel directed the film for a few days at Urgoiti's and Ugarte's request, receiving extra pay for this.[50] To replace Sobrevila, Filmófono recruited José Luis Sáenz de Heredia, first cousin and co-religionist of José Antonio Primo de Rivera. Sáenz de Heredia had studied architecture and worked on film subtitling, making his debut as a director when standing in for Fernando Delgado, sacked by his producer from the filming of *Patricio miró a una estrella* (1934), an interesting comedy about the star system. On various occasions Sáenz de Heredia would describe how Remacha received him in the Roptence studio, saying, "Look, I'm going to speak frankly. Actually, we need a director, but more in name than in reality. The person who in actual fact is going to direct the film is Buñuel."[51] When Sáenz de Heredia replied that what he wanted was to learn, Remacha offered him 1,500 pesetas for his work and he accepted. Years later he would supply more detail to Antonio Castro:

> Buñuel had fired Sobrevila. What was needed was a director to put his name on the film, given that the real director was Buñuel, who'd agreed to work in Filmófono out of friendship for Ricardo Urgoiti but didn't want to sign the films, since it would put an end to his fame as an *enragé* avant-gardist. . . . [Sobrevila] must have taken his role seriously. He had ideas of his own about a film he'd written himself, and this led to problems with Buñuel. In short, they gave him the boot. They'd already been a week with the film at a standstill when I presented myself. The musician on the film, someone called Remacha, received me, and I put myself forward to direct the film. He arranged to meet me in the afternoon and said, "I prefer to tell you the truth: the person who's going to run the show is Señor Buñuel, you'll be there for the sake of appearances, to be in the studio and to do what Señor Buñuel tells you." I replied that it was fine by me, I was ready to be a good sergeant. . . . Every morning Buñuel explained to me what he wanted. Generally, he didn't go on set; we viewed the takes together and it was he who chose which ones, and in the editing room I didn't even set foot, he did it himself, directly.[52]

This last description of Buñuel's input squares with what Sáenz de Heredia would tell Roger Mortimer later on: "Each day before the filming I saw Buñuel and he told me exactly how he wanted each scene to be shot. I supervised the filming in the studio. At night Buñuel examined the takes and did all the editing. He also intervened on the script. Although he didn't interfere in the shooting, it was he who made the film."[53] The first scene Sáenz de Heredia tackled was Carmen Amaya's dance on a tabletop, which was filmed in a building behind the Palacio de la Música.

As to the personal relationship between the Falangist Sáenz de Heredia and the Communist Buñuel, the former would recall that "Buñuel and I became great friends, although our political opinions were diametrically opposed; I was a Falangist and he a Communist. Some mornings we met in Bakanik, an elegant café, the most rightwing in Madrid, to discuss politics. Buñuel liked it because he said it had the best scotch in town."[54] Among those who frequented Bakanik was José Antonio Primo de Rivera, who, as Emilio Sanz de Soto told us, greeted Buñuel when he saw him by saying, 'Bonjour, Monsieur le chien andalou,' with Buñuel correcting him: 'Monsieur *un* chien andalou.'"

La hija de Juan Simón gets going with a lugubrious general shot of a cemetery at night, as two gravediggers bury a woman. Juan Simón (Manuel Arbó) says, "She's been everybody's and now she's nobody's, not even her family's." After this prologue, we meet Juan Simón's daughter, Carmela (Pilar Muñoz), who is in a relationship with Ángel (Angelillo), notwithstanding the opposition of her mother, Angustias (Ena Sedeño), in contrast to the benevolent understanding of her father. Carmela is pregnant by her boyfriend, who tells her he's decided to go to the capital to triumph as a flamenco singer and earn a lot of money, although he assures her he'll return to the village for her. In Madrid, in a tavern in which Carmen Amaya dances, Ángel sings a song, a fight ensues, and the lights go out. When they come back on there's a man dead on the floor, and Ángel is accused of his murder and imprisoned. Simón reads in a newspaper of the fight over a woman and Ángel's subsequent imprisonment. Such an ill-fated piece of news causes a family row, and the father consoles his daughter, who decides to leave for the capital. Carmela gives birth to a son and is offered work as a waitress, but in reality she is hired as a hostess in a nightclub. Her son is handed over to her family, who are told that Carmela has died, but Angustias rejects the child. Later on, she repents of this and asks her husband to go in search of their grandson. Shortly before leaving prison Ángel receives a letter in which he is told that Carmela died during childbirth, and he bursts into tears. He gets over his sadness and begins to triumph as a singer, which enables him to send money to Carmela's parents to look after his child. Parallel to the triumph and spectacular social ascent of Ángel, who installs his son in his house, Carmela suffers the sordid life of a nightclub hostess, pursued by lecherous customers and subject to the despotism of her boss, Don Paco (Fernando Freyre Andrade). One day Ángel receives, through a client of the nightclub, news that Carmela is alive and goes in search of her, but she, ashamed and depressed, decides to kill herself in her dressing room by swallowing Veronal. Ángel arrives and manages to save her, so that in the following scene the two of them appear on horseback, riding happily through Ángel's country estate, while their son plays with a cat.

La hija de Juan Simón was an outrageous tearjerker replete with clichés, with an unmarried mother gone astray and a humble farmhand, wrongly imprisoned, who finds glory and saves the fallen woman. Apropos of this, Aranda observed: "This time Buñuel was unable to lend dignity to an unpardonable genre; what he did instead was to exaggerate it, to heap up its more odious conventions, taking these to a kind of delirium."[55] Manuel Rotellar, however, nuanced this assessment when writing, "With its occasionally crude dramatic structure modified, it draws to a close in a sugary-sweet submission to the box office, with its happy ending, when in the original stage play a rural tragedy was aired, without potential compromises."[56] Notwithstanding the complaisant, artificial ending, *La hija de Juan Simón* dramatized, albeit melodramatically, the very real phenomenon of the migration from country to city, accompanied by the dream of personal or professional success on the part of the depressed rural classes.

Despite this happy ending, *La hija de Juan Simón* was a somber movie, rich in chiaroscuro, with a blackness that at times owed something to the modeling of Gutiérrez Solana. The film opens mournfully with a burial by night, a fake scene but one that accentuated its melancholy aspect (and which anticipates the atmosphere of the dénouement of *Abismos de pasión* in 1953). Aranda saw in it a "reminder, perhaps ironic, of *La Chute de la maison Usher*," on which Buñuel had worked as an assistant to director Jean Epstein.[57] When the gravediggers lower the coffin into the grave, Juan Simón pronounces, "She's been everybody's and now she's nobody's, not even her family's." The premonitory phrase introduces the theme of the "fallen woman," concording with that of the wretched predestination of the grave digger's daughter. There have been those who have seen in this scene the beginning of a flashback, but Juan Simón's comment on the dead woman refutes this since his daughter is not involved, although it is interesting to observe that when Ángel thinks Carmela has died, in a scene that evokes his loved one in a song—"she died of sorrow / being good"—a brief superimposition is inserted of the opening scene in the cemetery, a subjective evocation of the protagonist that may induce a feeling of trickery about the function of that scene—dependent on the original song and stage play—in the narrative structure of the film.

The architecture of the film rests on two parallel, asymmetrical actions, which fulfill the dramatic law of fall-and-rise, since we are present at Ángel's ascent toward the star system as a famous singer after a setback has sent him to jail and the simultaneous social descent of an unmarried mother driven to working in a nightclub (the euphemistic equivalent of a brothel). Ángel's rise to stardom is described in a somewhat impressionistic way, with a sequence of shots of posters showing his image, newspaper headlines, and so on, and with the voice-over of his song dedicated to Carmela.

One of the most famous scenes in *La hija de Juan Simón* is that of Ángel in a prison cell, accused of having killed the flamenco tavern customer in a fight. This scene is remembered for the intentional (and comically misspelled) political inscriptions on its walls—the hammer and sickle, "Long liv freedum!" "Death to Lerrox" (*sic* for Lerroux, the *bienio negro* prime minister who'd put down the workers' insurrection in Asturias in October 1934)—and for the movie's most popular song, "Soy un pobre presidiario," which Ángel sings together with a chorus of prisoners and jailers. (The assertion that Buñuel appeared as one of these is, we believe, erroneous.) It was a song Angelillo himself had previously made popular, and its fame was so great that he sang it three times during the film: in jail; as a dance number in the nightclub, and at the end, against a black background, in dramatic contradiction to the happy ending of the reunited couple.

The discourse of *La hija de Juan Simón* with regard to gender roles is neither simplistic nor schematic. Carmela is harassed by her intolerant mother but protected by her father, suggesting an Electra complex that causes Angustias's rejection (family roles that invert those of the stage play, which hints at their intentional modification by Buñuel in the new screenplay). Carmela uninhibitedly sleeps with her boyfriend and becomes pregnant without any sense of guilt. Ángel migrates to Madrid to earn some money and come back for her afterward and, later on, like the character in *Don Quintín, el amargao*, sends money to the village to maintain his son. Carmela is certainly harassed sexually by the clients of the nightclub and by her boss, Don Paco. Presented as a Madrilenian spiv, Don Paco is ridiculed by the director, who has him come out with some truly Surrealist dialogue with a customer: "What's happening is that there's no principles, or reason, or morality—nowt. Schopenhauer said as much. Have you read," he consults a book, "*The Fourfold Origin of the Principle of Sufficient Reason*, eh?" And as a counterpoint to Carmela's submission, the brief appearance of the splendid and young Catalan gipsy dancer Carmen Amaya (in a scene Buñuel considered to be the finest of Filmófono's entire output) is used to have her say, "Nobody rules over my body and I do with it what I want," a phrase that will find a tardy echo in the figure of Conchita in *Cet obscur objet du désir* (1977). An evocation would have to be added of the fateful garden of *L'Âge d'or* in the final scene on Ángel's country estate, and it is not hard to imagine the singer fixing his attention, in echo of said film, on the foot of the statue of Venus glimpsed in the bower behind the happy couple. Notwithstanding its more conventional appearance, then, *La hija de Juan Simón* turns out to be an undoubtedly progressive representation of sexual roles, which does not censure a free, premarital erotic relationship (something infrequent in Spanish cinema of the time) and thus subscribes to the modernizing of customs of Republican reformism.

The uninhibited sexual relationship during Ángel's and Carmela's courtship is presented via an expressive metaphor after a fairground scene, which begins with a still photo of Ángel on a wooden horse in front of a window in which Carmela is framed. The photo comes to life before the photographer who takes it, and scenes of popular amusements succeed one another: the doughnut stand, the merry-go-round, the tombola, the Catherine wheel—a rapid mosaic that evokes Ernesto Giménez Caballero's short film, *Esencia de verbena* (1930). Following this sequence, we see an image of Ángel and Carmela seated on a bench: Ángel kisses her, and she moves toward the end of the bench, accidentally sending a cage with a canary in it falling to the ground. This erotic metaphor, typical of silent cinema, also evokes the metaphorical use of the caged bird in Stroheim's *Greed*.

The slogan accompanying *La hija de Juan Simón* on its release was "Like the music of Falla or the gipsy ballads of García Lorca: the transcending of art's popular roots," a description that linked the intention of the film—voluntarily or otherwise—to the neopopularism typical of the Generation of '27. It opened at the Cine Rialto in Madrid on 16 December 1935 and immediately went on to be shown in seven more cinemas in the capital: the Salamanca, Opera, Metropolitano, Monumental, Argüelles, Dos de Mayo, and the Toledo. The review in the daily *La Voz* ably described the look of the film when pointing out, "The director, Sáenz de Heredia, has filmed images of pathos, somber shadows, that convey an extremely intense feeling of emotion to the mind of the viewer."[58] The *Cine Español* reviewer opined, "It is essential to highlight the direction of *La hija de Juan Simón* as a decisive point in the creation of Spanish cinematic technique," words that become all the more meaningful if we consider that it was Buñuel himself who directed many scenes.[59]

In Barcelona *La hija de Juan Simón* opened at the Cine Urquinaona, with an end-of-screening performance by Carmen Amaya, along with a concert with music by Albéniz, Granados, and Falla.[60] Predictably, the Catalan critics took exception to the sob-storyline. Accordingly, Lope F. Martínez de Ribera wrote: "It's a shame the subject matter doesn't contain higher values for the director and actors. The film is well put together, the actors manage to conduct the mind of the spectator along the pathways of emotion, managing this without affectations that would abnormalize the general line of the film. We cannot ask more of them; but the subject matter lets them down. . . . It's a pity."[61] *La hija de Juan Simón* was a spectacular commercial success: the sale of the records of its songs alone covered its costs. (Such success also generated a parody in animated cartoon form.) In the first quarter of 1936 *La hija de Juan Simón* made some 600,000 pesetas and three months later it had already surpassed the million mark. When programming the Spanish Pavilion at the 1937 International Exhibition in Paris, Buñuel chose it as the only fiction film and as a counterpoint to the documentary testimonies of the drama of the Civil War. In 1956 Gonzalo Delgrás directed a feeble remake, with Angelillo's role taken by Antonio Molina and Pilar Muñoz's by María Cuadra.

While Buñuel struggled against his persistent sciatica and toiled anonymously in plebeian cinema in the Filmófono factory with a young Falangist director, his old friends Lorca and Dalí had reencountered each other at the height of their fame and had decided to resume their collaboration. On 19 January 1935 Dalí and Gala set sail from New York after the artist's first triumphant American trip. Notwithstanding his friction with Breton due to his political heterodoxy and his interest in Hitler, the Catalan had signed the Surrealist critique of the International Congress of Writers for the Defense of Culture, "Du temps que les surréalistes avaient raison" (published in August 1935). On various occasions during that same year Lorca manifested his distance from Surrealism. The discrepancies between Lorca and Dalí were not just aesthetic. In July 1935 Dalí published his essay "La Conquête de l'irrationel," redolent with Fascist ideology, while Lorca would soon declare: "The USSR is tremendous. Moscow is the opposite pole to New York. I would really like to get to know Russia personally, because the effort of the Russian people is fantastic. It's a work of virility, of nerve, an important reaction of the masses. Look at Soviet literature!"[62] Lorca joined the Friends of the USSR and collaborated on various PCE initiatives, but he resisted Alberti's pressure to join the party. And although a month after his paean to the USSR he declared to Jordi Jou that "in the face of social reality the poet must become enthused," and "he can certainly not remain unmoved," Lorca added to this his criticism of the attempt by the state to control art and literature in the USSR.[63]

As Sobrevila embarked on the filming of *La hija de Juan Simón*, the "poet of the people," who would soon support the Frente Popular with his signature, met Dalí in Barcelona the day after publishing his 27 September eulogy to the USSR. All the indications are that it was a very emotional meeting, with Dalí asking Lorca to collaborate with him on an opera he was preparing, the main characters of which were Sacher-Masoch and Ludwig II of Bavaria. These were two characters who could not leave the poet, tormented by his closet homosexuality, indifferent. Lorca gave his agreement to Dalí's scheme, as demonstrated by his letter of 4 October to Josep Palau i Fabre, in which he explained that he would write a work with Dalí and that they would do the sets together.[64] This would be the last encounter between the poet and the painter, but what interests us here is that as the two now-famous friends from the Residencia resumed their collaboration, Buñuel was all but invisible on the cultural scene.

Filmófono's next production was *¿Quién me quiere a mí?*, whose credits indicate that its story was by "[Enrique] Pelayo and [Carlos] Caballero," but which a contemporary news item in *El Sol* attributed to Enrique Herreros.[65] The screenplay itself was the work of Buñuel and Ugarte—who also appeared as a barrister in the final courtroom scene—although the credits give no scriptwriter's name. Sáenz de Heredia recalled that the script "was awful," but the film got under way because the preparations for *¡Centinela, alerta!*, based on a play by Arniches, were behind schedule.[66] It is also worth noting that the music was composed by the inevitable Remacha with the collaboration of Juan Tellería, writer of the Falangist hymn *Cara al sol*.

Although it was initially announced that Berta Román would, along with the young Mari-Tere, be the female lead in *¿Quién me quiere a mí?*, her name soon gave way to that of the Madrid actress Lina Yegros (Avelina Yegros Antón), a blue-eyed blonde, which gave her an American look. Yegros was popularly known as "the gentle weeper," due to having starred in a couple of highly successful tearjerkers, *Sor Angélica* (Francisco Gargallo, 1934) and *La bien pagada* (Eusebio Fernández Ardavin, 1935). In the credits of the film her name shared double billing with Mari-Tere's.

The worldwide popularity of American child star Shirley Temple, who had made her debut in the cinema in 1932 at the age of four, led to attempts to emulate her in different countries, Spain included. With the production of *¿Quién me quiere a mí?* underway, the America distributor Hispano Fox Film sponsored a competition called "Does a Spanish Shirley Temple exist?," the winner of which was announced in April as Mary Carmen López.[67] She had, however, been forestalled by Mari-Tere (Antoñita Barbosa), who was blonde and not yet five years old, like the original Shirley Temple; according to Sáenz de Heredia she had been discovered in a radio competition by Carlos del Pozo, who also worked on the film.[68] Santiago Aguilar took advantage of the contrast in age of the two leading actresses, publishing in *Cinegramas* an article called "Interview of the day: The big star and the little star; Lina Yegros and Mari-Tere."[69]

Although a news item published in *Popular Film* in November 1935 stated that Sáenz de Heredia was going to proceed with *Nada sé de ti* at Estudios Ballesteros, the fact is that Buñuel, doubtless encouraged by the excellent results of his earlier film, entrusted him with directing Filmófono's third production.[70] In addition, Sáenz de Heredia found his salary increased to 3,000 pesetas, and as he confided to Aranda, "I was authorized to direct it almost entirely, with Buñuel's superficial control."[71] *¿Quién me quiere a mí?*, the filming of which commenced on 27 January 1936, was shot at Estudios Ballesteros Tonafilm, where Sáenz de Heredia had begun his career with *Patricio miró a una estrella*, and it is probable that he acted as a mediator for the hiring of its installations on favorable terms.[72] Years later he would explain that although the script was very bad, "the film was well worked out and had everything it needed."[73] Its cost ascended to 300,806.46 pesetas, provided by Filmófono, apart from 10,000 pesetas from

Poster by Enrique Herreros for *¿Quién me quiere a mí?* (José Luis Sáenz de Heredia, 1936), featuring a Pacheco portrait of Mari-Tere, Spain's shortlived "Shirley Temple." (Fundación Enrique Herreros, Madrid)

Buñuel. Filming ended in March, when the Frente Popular had already won the elections and the government presided over by Manuel Azaña had taken power.

¿Quién me quiere a mí? begins with Marta Vélez (Lina Yegros), a diva of the opera, bringing her career to a close with a performance of Gounod's *Faust*. She has decided to abandon her profession and to take care of her newborn daughter Mari-Tere, but above all because she has been reconciled with her husband Eduardo (José María Linares Rivas) and wishes to consolidate her family and her home. The unscrupulous Eduardo, however, has proposed this reconciliation solely to get the money from his wife to pay his debts. When she doesn't agree to his demand for cash he organizes the kidnapping of their daughter, so as to get Marta to pay a ransom. A couple of beggars, in league with him, kidnap and hide the little one. When they proceed to transport the baby inside a suitcase, two crooks (Luis de Heredia and Fernando Freyre Andrade) steal it and then discover to their surprise that it contains a baby girl. Although they initially want to get rid of the infant, they end up taking her to their house. There, she will grow up in the care of a neighbor, the composer Alfredo Flores (José Baviera), who is on hard times due to his avant-garde music projects. An ellipsis shows Mari-Tere (Mari-Tere), aged four, playing the piano, tutored by Alfredo, who has become her adoptive father. It is in Alfredo's house where thanks to an anonymous letter Marta will reencounter her daughter. She hits it off with Alfredo and launches his opera, *The Black Doe*, to great success. Marta and Alfredo fall in love, and the latter urges her to get a divorce so that they can get married, but Marta fears the reprisals of her cruel husband. After the opening night of *The Black Doe* Marta and Alfredo go to dine in a restaurant. Using a ploy, Eduardo has Marta leave the table, and Alfredo, puzzled by her non-appearance, goes in search of her, only to find her grappling with her husband. Eduardo threatens Alfredo with a pistol and in the fight that ensues falls dead from a gunshot wound. In the trial for homicide Alfredo is absolved, and at the end the impresario, Don Román (Carlos del Pozo), toasts the success of Alfredo's next première, to be starred in by Marta, who will now be able to marry her composer-lover.

¿Quién me quiere a mí? was, in the words of Emilio Carlos García Fernández, "a comedy with certain dramatic overtones" that reiterated the classic theme of a woman caught between two men, a constant since *Don Quintín, el amargao*, in this instance between a perverse husband and a kind-hearted composer, who, moreover, acts as a surrogate father for the daughter kidnapped on the orders of his opponent.[74] The film again featured a woman, financially well-off on this occasion, who sacrifices her professional life in order to rebuild her marriage, but

who is tyrannized by a despotic, unscrupulous husband whose male counterpoint is a humble and good-natured composer. Not only is the wife the victim of a perverse husband—so is her daughter, who is kidnapped on his orders.

Inevitably, a certain kinship can be recognized between the plotting of *¿Quién me quiere a mí?* and the beginning of the French film *L'Affaire est dans le sac* (1932) by Pierre Prévert, with a script by his brother Jacques, the action of which has its origins in the project to kidnap the daughter of a millionaire, an attempt that leads to a series of unexpected situations. Given a rough ride by the critics of the time, this absurdist comedy must have been seen in Paris by Buñuel, a friend of the Préverts. It is also fitting to refer to the relationship between the beggars responsible for kidnapping the baby and the underworld, since scenes of a similar complicity were depicted by Fritz Lang in *M* (1931) and by G. W. Pabst in *Die Dreigroschenoper* (1931), a film distributed in Spain by Filmófono. The anxiety of Alfredo as he waits for Marta in the restaurant is expressed in a disturbing and "symptomatic" big close-up, with him consulting his watch by taking a table knife to push back his cuff. This rapid shot hints at mutilation, like the eye and hand in *Un chien andalou* or the hands in *L'Âge d'or*.

In *¿Quién me quiere a mí?* there are two allusions to divorce. Following the successful opening night of *The Black Doe*, the smitten composer urges Marta to file for divorce, but she fears the reaction of her husband; and in the final courtroom scene a witness states that the husband was an obstacle to Alfredo marrying Marta "because they weren't divorced." In January 1932 the divorce law had been approved, albeit with rather restrictive conditions, but there were few divorces: only 3,500 in 1932–33, according to legal sources. This law, however, provided an example of the modernization of customs in the Republican period. As an echo of this, the film comedy *Madrid se divorcia* (Alfonso Benavides and Adelqui Millar, 1934) was released in 1935 with the advertising slogan "Can a woman in love with her husband be unfaithful to him without being guilty?"—a libertine dilemma that reflected the moral changes during the permissive era of the Second Republic. As the new divorce law was being discussed in Parliament, the complications of the situation were summed up by a free-thinking bachelor who inserted an announcement in the press that read "Young millionaire devotes half of his fortune to paying for the divorce of married women who desire it and lack their own means, as well as providing a substantial sum for them to start living on their own."[75] Certifying the new situation, in the film press articles appeared with titles like "Our artistes also get divorced" (in reference to actresses María Ladrón de Guevara and Carmen Navascués) and "A year of divorces."[76] In *¿Quién me quiere a mí?* divorce was presented as a desirable solution to the affective dissatisfaction of the female protagonist, who did not dare take the step on account of her husband's threats, undoubtedly reflecting a social reality that helps explain the low number of divorces in that era. That the violent death of the husband appeared as a solution for the union of the amorous couple constituted a civilized and convincing line of argument in terms of divorce propaganda.

¿Quién me quiere a mí? was technically superior to *La hija de Juan Simón*, but its storyline, screenplay, and rhythm were markedly inferior. Sáenz de Heredia made the transitions between scenes with match cuts that would open with visual motifs analogous to those of the preceding shot (the husband's face, clocks, etc.). And although the comedy was claustrophobic, since it took place almost entirely in interiors, the camera was more fluid than in the earlier film. García Fernández described Sáenz de Heredia as "a young director who is more concerned with making a real go of each shot than with a conjunction between the directing of actors and the visual narration."[77] The absence of Buñuel's supervision is undoubtedly evident, although Mari-Tere shone in a charming dance scene in a bar, surrounded by small-time crooks.

¿Quién me quiere a mí? was launched to the advertising slogan "A Spanish film? Yes, but also a European one." And on the eve of its premiere a publicity item in *El Sol* reiterated the same idea when claiming that after films based on Madrilenian and Andalusian local color, "Filmófono has sought to touch on an international theme by shooting a thoroughly cinematic novel that can just as easily be set in Madrid as in Vienna."[78] The movie opened on 11 April 1936, Easter Saturday, at the Palacio de la Música in Madrid and the Cine Urquinaona in Barcelona, the Madrid premiere again being covered by Fox Movietone's newsreel cameras. Its reception was lukewarm, however, and Jo Labanyi has attributed its failure to the fact that the male lead was a down-on-his-luck composer of avant-garde operas, with whom the popular public was unable to identify, unlike with the popular flamenco singer Angelillo.[79]

Despite his sympathy for Urgoiti, the reviewer of the daily *El Sol* did not hide his reservations about the film when writing, "In order to get away from those zarzuela-type titles or from novels in installments, the authors of the story have created a script that is neither one thing nor the other in terms of the positive aspect these kinds of works can have."[80] More generous was Antonio Guzmán Merino in his review in *Cinegramas*, when pointing out that "One observes in this film a praiseworthy desire to flee from themes and situations that have become clichés in our cinema. . . . Nothing is superfluous and nothing is lacking in the logical development of the action, which flows along as spontaneously, continuously and naturally as life itself."[81] In general, the Barcelona critics were hard on *¿Quién me quiere a mí?* In *Popular Film* Lope F. Martínez de

Ribera criticized Sáenz de Heredia for "his lack of emotion, which is apparent in the more dramatic scenes in the film. . . . The photography feeble; the sound very irregular and the dialogue wretched."[82]

The collaboration between Filmófono and Mari-Tere did not end with this film, since Aranda divulged that during the preparation of *¡Centinela, alerta!* (1936) the Filmófono team shot a film called *Ojos cariñosos* in two weeks, the direction being something of a joint effort.[83] According to Emilio Sanz de Soto, this was a promotional short to consolidate the popularity of Mari-Tere, with a title very similar to *Bright Eyes*, the 1934 David Butler film featuring Shirley Temple, which had not yet been released in Spain.[84]

In May 1936 the film press announced that Filmófono would produce *¡Centinela, alerta!* and, following that, *La Papirusa* and *El último mono*, by Arniches.[85] Although in the credits of *¡Centinela, alerta!* it read "Story written for the cinema by Carlos Arniches," this ambiguous formula concealed the fact that the story was a free adaptation of *La alegría del batallón*, a one-act military zarzuela by Arniches and Félix Quintana that had opened at the Teatro Apolo in Madrid on 11 March 1909. In 1925 it had been adapted for the cinema by Maximiliano Thous under its original title. For *¡Centinela, alerta!* the zarzuela was turned into a screenplay by Arniches himself, with the collaboration of Ugarte, the action being transposed from the Carlist Wars to the present day.[86]

A few months before, in January, the press announced that Angelillo had signed a 117,000 peseta contract with Filmófono to act in two films, which meant a return to the model of *La hija de Juan Simón*, after the mediocre commercial success of *¿Quién me quiere a mí?*[87]

With Eusebio Fernández Ardavín, a friend of Urgoiti's since 1923, ruled out as director of the new production, the most notable thing about this project lay in the fact that the person chosen to direct it was French filmmaker Jean Grémillon, who had begun his career in the avant-garde and who enjoyed a certain amount of artistic prestige in his own country. This unusual professional signing calls for clarification. In France, 1934 was a year not just of political crisis—with the Fascist riots of February—but also of an incipient crisis in the cinema, with 126 national films being released in contrast to the 143 of the year before. For the French Confederation of Intellectual Workers Grémillon compiled a report called *A Plan for the Creation of a Corporate Organization* (a forerunner of what in the postwar period would become the Centre National du Cinéma). Juan Piqueras, who knew of Grémillon's Hispanophilia and his musical training, suggested that he film, for the Valencian outfit Producciones Cinematográficas Españolas-Falcó y Compañía—whose Paris correspondent was Piqueras—a version of the zarzuela *La Dolorosa*, by the great composer José Serrano. Aureliano

Cover of the Ediciones Bistagne novelization of *¡Centinela alerta!*, with a photomontage showing Angelillo, Mari-Tere, José María Linares Rivas, and Ana María Custodio. (Collection: Román Gubern, Barcelona)

Campa, co-producer of the film, was Serrano's son-in-law, which helped when it came to obtaining the adaptation rights. In Grémillon's hands *La Dolorosa* became a baroque melodrama with *surréalisant* touches.

Grémillon and Buñuel had met in 1929 in Billancourt Studios, where the Frenchman was filming *Gardiens de phare* on the stage next to *Un chien andalou*'s.[88] Buñuel recalled hiring him to direct with an exceptional salary of 15,000 pesetas and a generous shooting schedule of four weeks. In his memoirs he stated: "Grémillon, whom I'd known in Paris and who was a big fan of Spain, where he'd already shot a film, accepted, on condition that he didn't put his name to it, which I readily conceded, since neither did I. On the other hand, I had to direct various scenes in his place, or have them directed by my friend Ugarte, on the days Grémillon didn't feel like getting out of bed."[89] And in an interview he added that Grémillon "directed the film with admirable skepticism. One day he said, 'Luis, I'm not coming in tomorrow, I've got to go to the dentist's.' And I replied, 'Very good, but what do we do with this scene?' 'Whatever you like,' so I directed the scene. In making the film we were taking the rise out of ourselves."[90] The different versions by the historians who are specialists in that period do not concur. Aranda wrote that toward the end of the film Grémillon fell ill and Buñuel personally took care of finishing it, while Fernández Cuenca and Rotellar claimed that the relations between the two men became increasingly tense, due to Grémillon having to work to the commercial strictures Buñuel imposed on him, the reason why, for the third time in his career—after *Daïnah la métisse* and *Pour un sou d'amour* (both 1931)—he refused to sign the film.[91] In any case, *¡Centinela, alerta!* was released without the director's name as "Filmófono Production No. 4."

In his collaboration with Filmófono Grémillon hooked up again with three of his colleagues on *La Dolorosa*: cameraman José María Beltrán, actor José María Linares Rivas, and composer Montorio. According to Aranda, Buñuel obliged him to take the plane back to Paris on 14 July 1936, the day after the tit-for-tat killing of Monarchist politician José Calvo Sotelo by Left-leaning Assault Guards, which heralded the outbreak of the Civil War, and Buñuel finished the editing of it.[92] During World War II Grémillon undertook cinematic tasks for the Resistance and in 1946 prepared *La Massacre des innocents*, a trilogy that was to cover the period from the Spanish Civil War and the Munich Agreement to the end of World War II.[93]

The filming of *¡Centinela, alerta!* got under way on 20 April 1936 at Estudios Roptence in Madrid. Its cost would ascend to 400,866.47 pesetas, provided by Filmófono, plus other contributions by Luis de la Peña (50,000) and Buñuel (10,000). Serrano's original music was eliminated and replaced by a score by composer Daniel Montorio, who had begun his film career providing musical accompaniment for silent films in the modest cinemas of his home town, Huesca, and had written the score for *El sabor de la gloria*, in which Angelillo made his debut before the camera, and then *La Dolorosa*.

The action of *¡Centinela, alerta!* shows how *señorito* Arturo (José María Linares Rivas), the womanizing scion of a wealthy family, assaults Candelas (Ana María Custodio) after she has been bathing in a river, gets her pregnant, and leaves the village. With her baby daughter in her arms, Candelas goes in search of Arturo to Valdenogales, where he has gone to claim an inheritance. An infantry battalion on maneuvers has also settled in the area, and the soldiers Angelillo (Angelillo) and Tiburcio (Luis de Heredia) protect the young woman, going so far as to organize a concert to raise money to help her. Arturo, meanwhile, evades his responsibility toward Candelas and flees Madrid. Once demobilized, Angelillo forms a couple with Candelas, while Tiburcio works as a shoeshine boy next door to the tobacconist's run by the young woman. Arturo finds out where Candelas is and, in financial straits and planning an escape to Buenos Aires with a girlfriend, decides to steal the money she keeps in her shop. He goes to see her and feigns repentance, promising to legalize the situation of their daughter (played by Mari-Tere, demoted here to the status of an extra). Later on, he returns to her house and steals the key to the tobacconist's. Angelillo discovers them together and, enraged, rips up Candelas's photo and decides to leave Spain. Tiburcio, however, playing the detective, has found out about Arturo's scheming and arranges to meet Angelillo in the tobacconist's at night. There, Angelillo comes across Arturo just as he is about to rob the shop, and in the ensuing fisticuffs they knock over an oil lamp that sets fire to the premises, with Arturo perishing in the blaze. Angelillo is going to perform for the last time in Spain as a singer, but Tiburcio takes Candelas to the theater, and on the stage the couple are happily reunited.

The permissiveness of the Republican period had led to the novel appearance of barrack-room farces in the wake of Jean Renoir's brilliant *Tire au flanc* (1928). Not by chance was it a Frenchman, Raymond Chevalier, who, after being Florián Rey's cameraman on *Sierra de Ronda* (1933), got the genre under way in Barcelona with *El tren de las 8,45* (1933) by filming a Georges Courteline novel that had already been adapted in France by Georges Pallu in 1927. The Bilbao director Mariano Lapeyra continued the cycle with *Amor en maniobras* (1935). Released at the start of 1936, it was banned in the part of Spain under Francoist control, its ban being reaffirmed at the end of the Civil War.

As well as being an "army game" comedy, *¡Centinela, alerta!* set out to replicate the European film musical of the time. It featured seven songs by Angelillo, the most famous of which, with choruses and a lot of crowd input, was "Si yo fuera capitán" (If I Were Captain). In the song Angelillo sang to collect money for Candelas and her daughter he looked straight at the camera, a novel practice imported into Spanish film from the Hollywood musical. And in the posters announcing his final performance he is dubbed "Angelillo, the nightingale of Andalusia," thus blending fiction and the reality of his publicity slogan on the music scene. Notwithstanding this modernizing look, *¡Centinela, alerta!* remained faithful to Filmófono's melodramatic norms and was in particular an echo of *La hija de Juan Simón*, after the negative outcome of *¿Quién me quiere a mí?*, since it depicted an unmarried mother, the victim of a sexual predator, protected by a man of the lower classes who ends up triumphing in the musical world. *¡Centinela, alerta!*, however, had added comic value with the scene of the drilling of the company of raw recruits, Tiburcio being one of their number, adding up to a hilarious satire of the army on the eve of its mutiny.

In the middle of the Civil War and prior to the film's release, Fernando Remacha alluded in a letter to Ricardo Urgoiti of 27 February 1937 to "a risk of the film being banned due to its particular nature, which doesn't fit in with the political trajectory [the authorities] want to give to movie performances."[94] In effect, the military satire might have proved inconvenient at a time when the government was attempting to set up a disciplined, efficient Popular Army by placing the autonomous militias that had been active until then under centralized control. Rafael Abella has described the Madrid moviegoing public at that time as "mainly consisting of people in uniform, of the many who were garrisoned at the nearby front and who took advantage of any bit of leave to have themselves a good time."[95]

¡Centinela, alerta! opened on 12 April 1937 at the Teatro Lírico in Valencia, on 12 July at the Rialto in Madrid, and on 13 September at the Salón Cataluña in Barcelona. According to Ramón Sala it was screened "to the indifference and hostility of the critics, who considered it to be a vulgar barrack-room comedy that was being inappropriately distributed at the height of the *contienda*."[96] *El Sol* was of the opinion that "it is frankly brutalizing. It represents exactly the social and moral climate against which the Spanish people is struggling."[97] Moreover, as a major novelty, both *El Sol* and *Ahora* of 16 July made Luis Buñuel responsible for the outrage, in complicity with Grémillon, thus blowing the cover of anonymity the Spanish director had scrupulously guarded since his beginnings at Filmófono. Despite its discrediting, *¡Centinela, alerta!* was shown for forty-two weeks in a besieged Madrid, making it the most viewed film during this period, ahead of *A Night at the Opera* (Sam Wood, 1935) with the Marx Brothers, *Modern Times* (Charles Chaplin, 1936), and *Morena Clara* by Florián Rey, the

biggest-grossing movie in Republican cinema.[98] *La hija de Juan Simón* was shown in Madrid for nineteen weeks and *¿Quién me quiere a mí?* for eighteen. The empathy of encircled Madrid with the irreverence of Grémillon and Buñuel's barrack-room farce lends itself to succulent considerations about the relaxing, liberating function of satire.

Writing about the film many years later, the Francoist historian Fernández Cuenca argued: "While the thematic development of *¡Centinela, alerta!* is full of concessions to the gallery and the displays of the main character's repertoire of songs often appear to be introduced any old how, the visual harmony of the film is surprising, the tone of the basic scenes has quality and the direction of the actors reveals painstaking care, to the point that in his film career Angelillo may never have given the same sensation of being an actor as in this movie, of an undoubtedly minor category within the overall career of the great French cineaste [Grémillon], but highly superior to what is usually meant to be ultra-commercial cinema with touches of 'fakelore.'"[99]

Franco's victory in the Civil War decisively affected the fate of *¡Centinela, alerta!* A fiche in the National Film Department dated 14 February 1939 indicates that the movie was directed by Edgar Neville.[100] This surprising attribution for an unsigned film may have been the result of the disinformation of a bureaucrat, but it also suggests various hypotheses: perhaps Neville wanted to do his friends Buñuel and Urgoiti a favor, or Filmófono attempted to protect its anonymous film by attributing it to a director who militated in the Francoist ranks. In any event, this error is not repeated in the abundant documentation that *¡Centinela, alerta!* later generated. The fact is that in that same month the National Film Department censors re-examined the film and made various cuts, including the satirical scene of the drilling of the squad of dimwits, and this censored version was screened in Bilbao. But on 21 March 1939 Antonio Tovar, general manager of Radiodifusión, which was dependent on the Ministry of the Interior, sent a letter to Manuel Augusto García Viñolas, head of the National Film Department, in which he complained of the distribution of a film that "on account of its plot and the episodes in it presents a lamentable vision of a tourist Spain, with particular harm being done to the respect our Army ought to deserve at all times and above all right now. Moreover, I must make known to you that the disposition of said film is of a clearly Communist nature inasmuch as in it there is posed the hackneyed problem of the Andalusian *señorito* who abuses his servants and seduces a young girl." As a result of this letter, the minister of the interior ordered the banning of *¡Centinela, alerta!* on 23 March 1939. In spite of this, the voluminous censorship dossier on the film was reopened, and the case dragged on for several years, with appeals presented by Filmófono. The most remarkable document in the thick dossier is the complaint the army minister sent to Franco about the showing of this film, a complaint that the head of state's private secretary retransmitted on 2 February 1940 to the undersecretaryship of press and propaganda. In his answer of 5 February the technical secretary of the latter replied that the representative named by the army for the Superior Board of Film Censors authorized the film with a number of cuts. And he added: "This criterion was taken into account, given that the film was made prior to the Glorious National Movement, in a demo-liberal period that chose its subject matter in old stage plays like 'La alegría del batallón' and 'El cabo 1°,' of a coarse humor and caricature lacking in subtlety. So as not to prejudice the economic interests of a Spanish company, instead of a total banning of the film, it was authorized with major cuts. Furthermore, this film, now an old one in terms of Spanish markets, is of little interest to the public."[101] Notwithstanding this exculpatory report, the film was re-examined, and this time the report by the military spokesman of the Board of Film Censors, Señor Múzquiz, was less complaisant, since he wrote that "It must be banned because it contains various scenes in the first five reels of the film in which, albeit of a pronounced comic character, it may be considered that the prestige of the military uniform of the Army and the discipline of the latter, which is taken in some scenes as a comic pretext, suffers damage." It is interesting to observe that the definitive banning of the film was pronounced on 12 February 1940, while the military spokesman's report is from 16 February, which means that as a result of the high-ranking origin of the complaints the decision was taken beforehand. It comes as some surprise, however, to note that in 1942 and 1946 Filmófono was still presenting appeals for re-examination to the Board of Film Censors, proposing new cuts in the movie.

The fifth and sixth Filmófono productions were slated to be the long-announced *La Papirusa*, a comedy by Adolfo Torrado and Leandro Navarro that opened on 29 January 1935 at the Teatro Victoria in Madrid, and *El último mono o el chico de la tienda*, based on a *sainete* in three acts by Carlos Arniches about a young man employed in a shop, premiered by Aurora Redondo and Valeriano León's company at the Teatro del Centro in Madrid on 10 November 1926. Interestingly, in 1948 Buñuel went back to considering the making of both of these in Mexico, which corroborates the continuity of the "Filmófono spirit" in much of his Mexican output. In both instances the addressee of the proposal was Oscar Dancigers, the future producer of *Los olvidados*. On 5 September 1948 Buñuel wrote to his friend José Rubia Barcia, resident in Los Angeles: "In Spain in 1935 and 1936 I produced various Arniches films to amuse myself and to earn money. I didn't put my name to them. But today, fifteen years later, it turns out I'm going to direct 'in earnest,' and putting my name to, Carlos Arniches' *El último mono*."[102]

The outbreak of the Spanish Civil War put an end to all of Filmófono's projects. Ugarte went on to work in the press facility of the Fifth Regiment, a Communist military unit whose film service, on which Buñuel collaborated briefly, was run by Antonio del Amo. Aranda recapitulated that "for 1937 Buñuel had limned the outlines of fourteen films based on literary works by Galdós (two of whose books he would film later on), the novelist Pío Baroja (such as *La lucha por la vida*) and others of the Generation of '98, much loved by the Madrid para-Surrealists of the 1920s, as well as a Dostoyevsky."[103] Aranda's list is excessive and hardly in keeping with the line of production followed hitherto by the company. For all that, different testimonies about Filmófono buying the rights in 1935 to three novels by Pérez Galdós, an author Buñuel took a shine to during his inactive stay in Hollywood in 1930–31—namely, *Angel Guerra*, *Doña Perfecta*, and *Fortunata y Jacinta*—permit us to speculate as to whether one or other of their adaptations would have been one of the "personal works" Buñuel reserved for himself as a director in the contract signed with Urgoiti in May of that same year.[104]

Feeling threatened, Ricardo Urgoiti fled to Paris in February 1937. With great difficulty, Filmófono's negatives were placed out of harm's way in France in March, thanks to an invitation extended to Remacha by the Spanish Embassy in Paris, arranged by Buñuel, under the pretext of his performing in a concert in the French capital. As it was, Remacha's collaboration on the Spanish Pavilion in the 1937 International Exhibition would mean that he was purged in the *posguerra*—the immediate post–Civil War period. In July 1937 Urgoiti moved to Buenos Aires, just as the villainous *señorito* of *¡Centinela, alerta!* had aimed to do, and there he had further recourse to Arniches and Angelillo when producing *La canción que tú cantabas*. Following that, he was the producer and director of the nostalgic *Mi cielo de Andalucía*, on which such other exiles as composer Julián Bautista and actor Enrique A. Diosdado joined forces. In this country estate comedy the opposed pair personified by Fernando (Diosdado) and Rafael (Angelillo) represented the two faces of the lost, yearned-for fatherland: that of the hard-working engineer, in whom Urgoiti himself was projected, and the stereotype of the happy-go-lucky young man, witty, hedonistic, and irresponsible, a *gracioso* typical of so many *españoladas*, who finally became supportive of a shared cause. The film said more than its images appeared to do.

Meanwhile, in Spain Angelillo's name was proscribed, and he could only be referred to as "the nightingale of Andalusia," to the point that the owner of the Cine Avenida in Barcelona was fined 1,000 pesetas for naming the singer in publicity.[105] On the other hand, engineer León Lucas de la Peña, editor Eduardo García Maroto, and composer Daniel Montorio continued working in Francoist cinema, with the first two collaborating actively on its film propaganda program during the Civil War.

13

The Outbreak of the Spanish Civil War

Three weeks before the elections of 16 February 1936 that led to the triumph of the Frente Popular, a meeting was held in Madrid between the Socialist leader Francisco Largo Caballero and the Communist Jesús Hernández with a view to creating a revolutionary Marxist party. This was the clearest expression of the ideals of the Frente Popular. Yet when the electoral victory arrived, Manuel Azaña formed a government containing neither Socialists nor Communists, although both gave it their support in Parliament. Keeping to the announced plan, the Young Socialists and Young Communists joined forces on 1 April 1936 to form the Unified Socialist Youth, which would be led, following a consultative trip to Moscow, by Santiago Carrillo. When Azaña became president on 10 May, Santiago Casares Quiroga formed a new government in which the Socialists and Communists did not, once again, participate. Meanwhile, social unrest was growing, with a group of big landowners, financiers, and generals already conspiring to overthrow the Republic. Falange Española chose the path of direct action and on 8 May assassinated Captain of Engineers Carlos Faraudo, thus launching its campaign of *pistolerismo*. The following day the response arrived in the form of church burnings in Cuatro Caminos (Madrid). Tension mounted during the summer. On 11 July a Falangist squad assaulted the Valencia premises of Unión Radio (belonging to the Urgoiti chain) and broadcast a statement speaking of a coup d'état. The next day in Madrid its gunmen shot and killed Assault Guard Lieutenant José del Castillo, which produced the murder of the Monarchist deputy José Calvo Sotelo in retaliation.

The die was cast on 17 July, when the army rose in Morocco. That same Friday afternoon the government took control of Unión Radio, in order to use it as a mouthpiece for its official statements.

The military insurrection plunged Madrid into chaos, as witnesses of the time later recalled. The Socialist Julián Zugazagoitia wrote that "smashed to smithereens, public authority was in the street, a bit of this authority being at the behest of each anti-Fascist citizen, who wielded it in the way that best suited his temperament."[1] Santiago Carrillo concurred, in that "effective power was in the hands of the workers' parties and organizations, but each one wielded it as he saw fit and for his own side, which left a lot of room for uncontrollable types."[2] One of the victims of such anarchist *incontrolados* was Pepín Bello, Buñuel's companion and friend since the Residencia de Estudiantes days. According to José Moreno Villa, a group of revolutionaries made a search of his house, and the finding of a fake parchment of the parodic Order of Toledo, invented by Buñuel in 1923, got him into a jam because he was taken for a genuine aristocrat.[3] On 18 July 1936 Buñuel was lunching in the house of his friend Claudio de la Torre and his wife, Mercedes Ballesteros. A car suddenly arrived bearing an FAI patrol, one of whose members was a cousin of the maid who was waiting table. The maid took off her white cap in order to attend to the new arrivals, who asked her if there were holy images in the house. She answered no, and the patrol made off. It was a scene typical of those hours of disorder and confusion that would drive de la Torre to later take refuge in the Mexican Embassy in Madrid.

Given that years later Buñuel stated that in such circumstances he went to ask Santiago Carrillo for a gun, it is well to remember what the reaction of the authorities was with regard to handing out weapons to the people. On 18 July Casares Quiroga—who in addition to being head of government was minister of war—refused to distribute arms, against the opinion of his minister of the interior, General Sebastián Pozas, and declared, "Whoever supplies arms without my consent will be shot." At 9 p.m. on that same date of 18 July the Central Committee of the PCE and the Executive Commission of the PSOE issued statements mobilizing all their militants and offering themselves to the government. And on the night of 18–19 July, disobeying orders, Lieutenant Colonel of Artillery Rodrigo Gil issued five thousand rifles from the artillery depot, with which the JSU (Unified Socialist Youth) and UGT (General Union of Workers) armed themselves.

Following the collapse of Casares Quiroga's government—which despite many previous warnings had not believed in a military uprising—it was replaced on 19 July by a cabinet presided over by the Left Republican José Giral, which in its first meeting decided to hand out rifles to the worker organizations, although most of the rifles lacked bolts, which were in the rebel-held barracks, the Cuartel de la Montaña. Be that as it may, by 2 p.m. on 20 July the Fascist uprising in Madrid had been defeated. And with the armaments available the JSU quickly created the battalions Octubre, Largo Caballero, Joven Guardia, and Pasionaria.

In this confused setting, and prior to being sent to the embassy in Paris, Buñuel was involved in a certain amount of film activity. The cineaste's own references to this period are forever fragmentary and vague. During the Francoist dictatorship, and with understandable wariness, he declared to J. F. Aranda: "I didn't have any official post during the war. The direction of film services was in the hands of a Cuban [Manuel Colino], now living in his own country. Like everybody else I was mobilized, they gave me a boiler suit and a pistol and I remember I did 'guard duty' with current director Antonio Del Amo in the Plaza de la Independencia. There was some shooting and I confined myself to hiding behind a tree."[4] And in his autobiography he offered a few new details, explaining that he'd met Santiago Carrillo, JSU General Secretary, and went to ask him for a weapon, but there were none left. All the same, he managed to get a rifle. However, in the middle of an exchange of fire, and while sheltering behind a tree, he didn't know who to shoot at: "What was the use, then, of having a rifle? I returned it."[5]

When asked about this episode of requesting a weapon, Santiago Carrillo could not remember it, although added that this did not mean it was a lie on the filmmaker's part.[6] The most interesting thing about all this is that Carrillo was absent from Madrid until August 1936, when he arrived from Barcelona after a trip to Paris, where he had had to cancel various political meetings due to being overtaken there by the military uprising.[7] This means that if the cineaste's request to Carrillo in August for a weapon was true, we do not know what Buñuel did in the first few weeks of the Civil War.

To Max Aub and to Jean-Claude Carrière, Buñuel explained that he got ahold of both Socialist and Communist identity documents: a UGT union card and a *Mundo Obrero* pass.[8] According to Bello, after the outbreak of the fighting Buñuel told him, "Don't tell anyone, but I'm off tomorrow. I'm leaving the house and all its furniture. I've been to the Communist cell, I've made a gift to them of my car and tomorrow I'm off."[9] And to the question of whether the director was afraid, Bello answered, "Yes, incredibly, horrifically. The word 'afraid' is inadequate. He was terrified, panic-stricken," a perception corroborated by Aub, who said, "And as soon as he saw violence, a dreadful feeling of panic took hold of him and he left Madrid."[10] In his biography of Ramón J. Sender, Jesús Vived Mairal also says of Buñuel that, "panic-stricken, he played no part in those famous days."[11] It would be wrong to interpret these words pejoratively. Zugazagoitia, a privileged witness of these events, has put on record that in the summer of 1936 the members of the government "were breathless, and if the word is not too strong, I will add that they were scared."[12] Closer to Buñuel, his friend Santiago Ontañón would also write that "in war, one discovers, without admitting it, one's own fear."[13] The fear derived from two opposed fronts, the *incontrolados* on one's own side and the aggressors of the enemy camp. Like many other historians, Gabriel Jackson has argued that "the first three months of the war were the period of maximum terror in the Republican zone."[14] And as for enemy terror, it suffices to recall that the first aerial bombardment of Madrid took place on 7 August 1936.

On the other hand Buñuel has bequeathed us, if not precise data about his conduct in the Civil War, at least some very illuminating ideological reflections or conclusions. In his memoirs he said, "It was not long before the incredible joy and revolutionary enthusiasm of the early days gave way to a disagreeable feeling of division, disorganization and total insecurity, a feeling that lasted until around the month of November 1936."[15] And to Aub he explained: "The fact is that with the war in Spain everything we'd thought about, at least everything I'd thought about, became reality: the burning of convents, war, killings, and I was scared stiff, and not only that, I was against it. I'm a revolutionary, but revolution horrifies me. I'm an anarchist, but I'm totally against the anarchists."[16] This attitude was reflected in his categorical disqualification of the behavior of the latter during the Civil War, which even led him to confront, along with Remacha, an anarchist group that was attempting to make off with some bottles of wine from a restaurant, the son of whose owner had been seriously wounded in fighting the Fascists.[17] And Buñuel added: "Every night whole brigades of anarchists descended the Sierra de Guadarrama, where the fighting was taking place, to loot the wine cellars of different hotels. Very thin on the ground at first, but growing stronger week by week, organized and disciplined, the Communists seemed to me—and still seem to me—irreproachable. They put all their energy into conducting the war. It's a pity to have to say it, but it has to be said: the anarcho-syndicalists hated them even more than the Fascists, perhaps."[18] A little further on he denounces "the arbitrary acts" of the POUM (Workers Party of Marxist Unification), a Left-Oppositional, anti-Stalinist group.

It is all but unnecessary to underline the contrast between Buñuel's political position and that of Salvador Dalí. After the summer, when Jaume Miravitlles—who'd appeared in *Un chien andalou*—organized the Commissariat of Propaganda in Barcelona in October 1936, Dalí wrote to him from Paris suggesting he be appointed "General Commissioner of Public Imagination," with a possible headquarters in Gaudí's La Pedrera, a suggestion Miravitlles declined.[19] In his autobiography, written after sealing his complicity with the victors in the *contienda*, Dalí wrote narcissistically: "The Spanish Civil War changed none of my ideas. On the contrary it endowed their evolution with a decisive rigor. Horror and aversion for every kind of revolution assumed in me an almost pathological form. Nor did I want to be called a reactionary. This I was not: I did not "react"—which is an attribute of unthinking matter. For I simply continued to think, and I did not want to be called anything but Dalí."[20]

Coming back to Buñuel, in his few statements about his wartime activities we have seen how on two different occasions he mentioned that he'd been involved in a shootout that obliged him to take shelter behind a tree in the Plaza de la Independencia. This occurred while he was on guard duty with the cineaste Antonio del Amo—mention of which brings us to Buñuel's film activities in Spain prior to his trip to Paris.

Two sources of information exist about the poorly documented cinematic activities of the director during the first few weeks of the war: the declarations of Antonio del Amo, and Juan Vicens's archive in the Residencia de Estudiantes. In the latter there is a receipt signed by Luis Buñuel, dated 25 August 1936, which reads: "Received from Leo Fleischman the sum of £490 for the purchase of film material, for which I assume the responsibility of repaying at some future date." Leo Fleischman was an American engineer, a New Yorker, the brother-in-law of Juan Vicens, which is why this document is in his archive. Before the first American volunteers would embark at the end of the year in New York to fight on the Republican side, Fleischman, who was probably spending his summer holidays in Spain with the Vicenses, enlisted in the Fifth Regiment and died in combat in October 1936.[21]

On 20 July the PCE had organized the Fifth Regiment, consisting of Communist militiamen—harangued that day by Pasionaria—whose first headquarters were in the Salesian convent on Calle Francos Rodríguez in Madrid. In its ranks it introduced "political commissars" on the Soviet model—the painter Ramón Pontones was one of them—and by the end of July it had already sent a thousand combatants to the Sierra de Guadarrama front. Eduardo Ugarte would join the Fifth regiment's press service, in which he was chief editor of the newspaper *Milicia Popular*.

An economic relationship between Buñuel and Fleischman existed, then, within the confines of filmmaking activity at the start of the war, when Buñuel had already abandoned Filmófono. The fact that he was the recipient of a rather large sum to buy film material with would suggest that his function was that of an administrator, manager, or organizer. The comments by Communist

1

He recibido de Leo Fleischman la cantidad de cuatrocientas noventa libras esterlinas para compra de material cinematografico de las que me hago responsable para saldarlas en su día.

Madrid 25 Agosto 36

Son #490£,, Luis Buñuel

Receipt in Buñuel's handwriting, dated 25 August 1936, in which he acknowledges the loan of £490 by American International Brigades member Leo Fleischman for the purchase of film material. (Archivo de la Residencia de Estudiantes, Madrid)

filmmaker Antonio del Amo about his activities during that period point in the same direction. The earliest and most illuminating were made to Antonio Castro. "When the war started," del Amo told him, "I, who had always intended to become a director and had tried without success to become Perojo's assistant, asked a great friend of mine, Buñuel, what I had to do to make films, and Buñuel gave me a 16 mm camera, a hand-cranked Éclair, a good one, and made a present of film he'd got himself from Kodak. With the camera, the negative film and a few cameramen friends I went to the front with Mantilla; in actual fact I went as an assistant to Fernando G. Mantilla, who was Carlos Velo's collaborator."[22] Del Amo was twenty-five years old at the time and was known as a movie critic and film society activist, while the likewise Communist Mantilla, a philosophy and arts graduate in 1931, film critic for Unión Radio, and since 1935 co-director of various documentaries with the Galician biologist Carlos Velo, had greater professional experience. It is usually claimed that Mantilla's first Civil War documentary was *Julio 1936*, which was commented upon that September in the film press.[23] Produced by the improvised Cooperativa Obrera Cinematográfica, consisting of Communists and a few Socialists, its Communist orientation was evident, since it began with an address by José Díaz, general secretary of the PCE, and concluded with a speech by Pasionaria. It is likely that the workers cooperative film unit had some connection or other with the Fifth Regiment, given the Communist predilection for centralized, unified activity, and it is also plausible that Buñuel was not foreign to its pioneering wartime initiative. In February 1937 the Cooperativa Obrera Cinematográfica presented a project to the Ministry of Press and Propaganda for the reorganization of the film industry, a document in whose gestation Buñuel could have intervened before leaving for Paris.

Buñuel, then, provided the camera and virgin film that del Amo utilized in his early Civil War work. More than twenty years after his statement to Antonio Castro, and with Buñuel dead, del Amo came up with a more self-serving and colorful version of their professional relations during the war, affirming that he went to film with Buñuel at the front, under his direct orders, "and we launched ourselves into the adventure of filming all the confrontations that were taking place on all the battlefields."[24] More reliable researches indicate that del Amo was Mantilla's assistant on the documentaries *España 1936* (which must not be confused with the film of the same name made in Paris by Buñuel/Dreyfus), produced by the Alliance of Anti-Fascist Intellectuals for the Defense of Culture, and *Nueva era en el campo* (1937), a Film Popular production for the Ministry of Agriculture.[25] Del Amo was extremely active during the Civil War. He directed the Cinema Section of the Forty-Sixth "El Campesino" Division (led by Valentín González, who was nicknamed thus) of the Fifth Army Corps, following the death of its chief, the Italian cameraman Antonio Vistarini. For it he co-directed, with Rafael Gil, the remarkable *Soldados campesinos* (1938), using nonprofessional actors. Del Amo was condemned to death at the end of the war, a sentence commuted to thirty years' imprisonment, thanks to the negotiations of his ex-collaborator Gil, whose life he had previously saved in the opposite political camp. Mantilla, meanwhile, went into exile in Mexico.

The names of Buñuel and Antonio del Amo also appear alongside each other in the dossier held in the General Archive of the Spanish Civil War in relation to the tragic end of the Communist critic Juan Piqueras.[26] In July 1936 Piqueras, who was suffering from a stomach ulcer, traveled from Paris to the Spanish border in response to an invitation from his comrades in Asturias. Once on Spanish soil on 9 July 1936, however, he began to cough up blood and was obliged to take shelter in the inn of the railway station in Venta de Baños (in the province of Palencia) in order to recover. It was there that the military uprising overtook him. On 19 July he wrote a poignant letter to the Communist painter Hernando Viñes in Paris, informing him in detail of the incoming news he had been noting down since the day before. It is worth reproducing this dramatic document, conserved in Vicens's archive, which begins thus:

Juan Piqueras, the Valencian film critic, Communist activist, and close collaborator of Filmófono who was assassinated by the Fascists in July 1936. The portrait dates from 1930. (Institut Valencià de Cinematografia Ricardo Muñoz Suay, Valencia)

Dear Hernando,

I've been in Venta de Baños for ten days now. Just imagine that when making my way on Thursday the 9th to Asturias, twenty minutes or so before reaching Venta de Baños, I suffered a hemorrhage in the stomach. I had to put up at the Station Inn, where I'm confined to bed, being cared for by the local doctors. [Juan Antonio] Cabezas came from Oviedo and hasn't moved from my side. He and the comrades from here have looked after me. In a few days I shall go to Valladolid and get an X-ray done. If I have to be operated on again I'll go to Madrid. If not, to Oviedo. Don't say anything to my wife and if you let on to my friends tell them to be very careful not to say anything so that she doesn't find out. Given all that's happening I'm very upset about the useless state I'm in. Never have I felt the revolution so close and me here in bed. It's infuriating. Since I can't move, I've decided to send you a few notes about the information I'm getting. If you give it to the comrades at *L'Humanité*, warn them not to say that a sick comrade's involved, etc. Greetings and best wishes,

Piqueras

You can write me c/o the *Hotel de France. Valladolid.* I expect to be able to move in the next four days.

As I get to find out things I'll send them to you. Go and see [Paul] Nizan because I'm sure they must be of interest to him and to *L'Huma.*

On seeing Cabezas and the other comrades armed and ready to defend our February victory, and seeing myself in the state I'm in I was unable to repress an attack of nerves in the face of my uselessness. Cabezas tries to console me a bit. From the stairs we say goodbye with a *UHP* [Proletarian Brothers United] and our fists held high.

The train stops 1 ¼ hours late.

Greetings

Rot Front [Red Front]

Venta de Baños (Palencia)

Saturday 18 [July]: confused and very vague rumors have been arriving all day, last night's Madrid press says nothing. This morning's appears with huge blank spaces, imposed by the censors.

At 3 pm some comrades told me they'd heard on the radio that the Minister of the Interior had stated that in Tetuán and other cities of the protectorate [in Morocco] the forces of the Foreign Legion had risen to the cry of "Viva España!" which is the cry of degenerate patriots, the working population confronted them and two hours later they told me once again that in the streets of Tetuán the working masses were fighting the Legion.

At 6 pm they informed me that Largo Caballero has said on the Madrid radio, in the name of the UGT, that in all those places where military forces or Fascist elements show themselves, the workers will respond with the General Strike.

The CNT and UGT have ordered an all-union general strike in all those places where the state of war is declared.

Saturday, 20.00: around 8 pm Cabezas arrived from the Casa del Pueblo where he'd met the committee, which was interceding to defray the costs occasioned by my illness in Venta de Baños. Moments later, a comrade arrived requesting he go because an individual from Asturias had turned up asking for assistance. When asked if he knew Cabezas he said yes. When he went he was able to discover that the man was a common swindler.

Saturday, 21.00: an hour later Cabezas arrived with two more comrades. He told me they were going to look for arms and to detain all the suspicious people in the village. It appears that this order had been given by the Governor of the province. They'd been in a meeting in the Casa del Pueblo studying the ways in which they could prevent the forces in Palencia and Valladolid from uniting. In Valladolid there are three dangerous reactionary regiments and the one in Palencia is the one that already rebelled in Alcalá de Henares. They want to avoid at all costs that in the event that the forces in these provinces are mobilized, they can unite.

Saturday, 22.00: Cabezas has just arrived with some comrades. He tells me they've managed to mobilize a hundred men and that he has them ready in case it's necessary to go and help the men in Palencia.

A bit later he leaves and returns armed with a carbine. He comes with two or three more comrades. They've locked up the village Fascists and are going to Palencia. I'm very agitated due to not being able to move.

Cabezas tells me Pasionaria spoke on the Radio along with the Minister of the Interior telling the Communists and workers that they should get weapons and fight. There is no leadership save that of the civil authorities.

At 11 pm the government dismissed five generals. Franco. Mola. Queipo de Llano and two others.

At the same time it announced the dismissal of various members of the high command of the Civil Guard.

Palencia: at 3 am the Civil Governor of the province telephoned the Mayor of Venta de Baños to get him to send the workers' forces he can, the aim being that on arriving in the town they split up and try and take the strategic sites.

At 3.30 am the mayor, who has been visiting me every day (a good man with anarchistic ideas to whom I'm pointing out the mistaken tactic of the FAI people at this time of a Popular Front in Spain) and who finds himself, precisely, in the Station Inn, where the telephone and telegraph service is installed, has just come up to see me in order to reassure me and he tells me he'd discovered the existence of five wagons full of explosives in the Station. I think their discovery is due to the fact that Cabezas, accustomed to Asturian dynamite, began to ask right away if there were explosives. The mayor, pressed by our comrades, has asked permission of the Governor to requisition them. This he denied to begin with. But moments later he sent him a telegram saying, "Make use of them now and whenever."

Palencia 5 am. Cabezas has just telephoned the Station Inn telling them to tell me the government is in control of the situation there and that they will return straightaway.

Miners' train. They assure me the Government has asked for help to the workers' forces and that a miners' train is coming from Oviedo.

They tell me that instead of one, two will come and that before reaching Madrid they'll bring the Fascist forces in Valladolid to book.

Judging by what's happening here the people identifies with the government.

Seville. General Queipo de Llano seditiously declared a State of War in the Province. The workers replied to this provocation with a General Strike. It seems they took possession of the radio station from which they announced the province is theirs. On the other hand the Minister of the Interior says the Civil Guard and the Assault Guards are facing them and putting up a fight.

4 am, Sunday. Better impressions from Sevilla. The radio is again in the hands of the State.

Malaga 5 am: the Fascists were defeated and a huge popular demonstration took place, which cheered the government forces.

Burgos 5 am. The Commander-in-chief is in military prison.

Valladolid. In this province, where the right-wingers are very strong, it appears that General Mola (that famous assassin of the students of the Universidad de San Carlos in Madrid a few months before the Republic of 14 April [1931]) has taken the railway station with a task force and demands that travelers shout "Viva España!" and "Viva the Fascio!"

[Annotated in the margin] 5 generals replaced at 11 pm.

Sunday 5 am. It appears the seditious forces and soldiers are in the street with machine-guns. A Fascist captain has phoned Venta de Baños to say they're waiting for the miners' train to riddle it with bullets. Our comrades have taken all sorts of precautions.

Sunday 5 am. They've just told me a new Government has been formed:
Presidency: [Diego] Martínez Barrios
Ministry of the Interior: [Augusto] Barcia
War: General [Carlos] Masquelet
S[tate] Education: M[arcelino] Domingo
Treasury: [Enrique] Ramos
Navy: [José] Giral. etc. etc.

I'm waiting for the train to Paris to pass at any moment. That's why everything's so topsy-turvy.

The train ought to have passed here at 4.30. It's 5.15 and still it hasn't passed. This shows that in Valladolid or in Madrid there's something that's stopped it leaving or traveling normally.

The postmark on the envelope in which Piqueras sent this letter, by express mail, bears the date of 19 July. In the Francoist dossier that contains the documents confiscated from Piqueras there are various interesting items, among them a telegram from Buñuel and del Amo to Piqueras, sent from Madrid on 15 July, which reads "We await a decision to come tomorrow," which implies that Piqueras had informed his comrades in the capital of his misfortunes. A letter from del Amo to Piqueras the next day was more explicit, since it divulged that Piqueras's illness was taken as read, and informed him that a meeting of the PCE cell had taken place, before adding:

> The first thing I did was phone Buñuel, to say that he was the one who could help me out with his car, since I couldn't leave for Venta de Baños without money. Buñuel reassured me. He told me you'd written to Urgoiti about your getting better. Anyway, I sent you a telegram, which I suppose you'll have received, because Buñuel advised me that we oughtn't to go to Venta de Baños without you informing us of the need there was for it. Today I've waited for news from you, but have received nothing before reaching the end of this letter. I hope if you continue being poorly you'll let me know if it's essential I come to Venta de Baños. I don't have money for the trip, if not I would have come already, even though your state of improvement wouldn't have made it necessary.

In 1980 Antonio del Amo nuanced this information in a letter to Juan Manuel Llopis, Piqueras's biographer, when relating, "The thing I remember is that I said [to Buñuel], 'We've got to get to Venta de Baños somehow. We can go in your car.' And he said, 'They've requisitioned my car' (it was common at the time to requisition cars from all those who had them, be it for the political parties, trade unions and the militias themselves that were springing up at every moment like mushrooms). 'We might go by train, or in another car, one way or another,' I interrupted him. And he told me, with good reason, 'And by what route, if the Somosierra and Alto de los Leones and Navacerrada roads are blocked?'"[27] A certain confusion may be observed in the chronology, since while the correspondence with Piqueras took place before the military uprising, del Amo is referring years later to dates posterior to the insurrection, when Buñuel had already handed over his car to his Communist cell, as Bello explained. In any case, if Buñuel restrained his comrade's impulse to go and visit the sick man, it is very possible that this somewhat unsupportive attitude saved the two of them from being captured by the Fascists, as occurred to their friend.

In any case, figuring in the dossier of charges the Francoist military authorities initiated against Juan Piqueras were the following confiscated documents:

1. An anti-Fascist manifesto to be published in *Nuestro Cinema*, proposing the creation of a federation of proletarian film societies (a text that had appeared in the October 1933 issue of the magazine).
2. A letter from Piqueras to Buñuel dated 13 November 1935, in which he told Buñuel that a Paris company was interested in distributing *Un chien andalou*, *L'Âge d'or*, and *Las Hurdes* in Switzerland, Belgium, the Netherlands, Scandinavia, Denmark, and the United States, adding that he (Piqueras) was active in the AEAR and living with miners who've emigrated from Asturias (a phrase underlined in pencil by the Francoist authorities). It may seem strange that Piqueras would carry a six-month-old letter for Buñuel

that the latter had already received, but this was doubtless a copy to determine the eventual details of the scheme for the international distribution of the films listed therein.

3. A letter with a PCF letterhead, dated 23 June 1936, in which the party ceded to his magazine *Nuestro Cinema* the sales rights of the French propaganda film *La Vie est à nous* (1936), coordinated with the PCE, at the price of 4,500 francs per copy.
4. An authorization from the PCF cooperative Ciné-Liberté to Piqueras of 8 July 1936 for him to organize the exchange of film information for the newsreels of the Front Populaire.
5. The letter and telegram cited above from del Amo and Buñuel to Piqueras of 15 and 16 July 1936.

According to Llopis's researches, Juan Piqueras was executed by the Francoists during the night of 28–29 July.[28] Evoking these events decades later, Buñuel commented, "I believe they tied him to a chair and shot him in the station itself."[29] Georges Sadoul, whose project to write a history of the cinema was, according to some French sources, inspired in 1937 by Piqueras's example, honored his comrade with an article published in both *Commune* and *L'Humanité*.[30]

In contrast to the cruelty the rebels manifested toward the ailing Piqueras, Buñuel saved the life of Falangist filmmaker José Luis Sáenz de Heredia in an episode that was rather incredible. Like so many tales of the Civil War, the versions of those who participated in the affair—Sáenz de Heredia, Santiago Ontañón, and Luis Buñuel—do not always agree. Let us begin with the Falangist director's account. According to Sáenz de Heredia, after a few days of roaming Madrid, going from one hiding place to another, he turned up at Estudios Ballesteros, where he'd begun his career in 1934, and asked for asylum from the Workers' Committee, whose members he knew. They granted his request, and he installed himself in what had been his office, sleeping on a mattress on the floor, and succored by Santiago Ontañón's sisters—Sara Ontañón was a film editor—who supplied him with food. On 24 August, however, a group of militiamen detained him, imprisoning him in the *cheka*, or secret sectarian prison, in Calle Marqués de Riscal until he was freed. He then took refuge in the Cuban Embassy, where he managed to get a Cuban passport, before escaping to the Francoist side.[31]

Santiago Ontañón offered a complementary version that omits the sheltering of the cineaste in the Estudios Ballesteros: "One day I was astonished to meet [Sáenz de Heredia] in the street: 'What're you doing here?' I asked him, and he replied, 'As you can see, hopping like a rabbit from bush to bush.' Apparently, he'd been hiding in a house. His window looked out at street level and one morning while he was shaving he heard a kid shout, 'In my house we have the *señorito* Sáenz de Heredia!,' so he hightailed it from there in a state of panic. I took him to my building, where we had a doorman called Lorenzo, and he spent the day, the idiot, praying in the hallway and telling the fifteen mysteries of the rosary a few yards from the CNT, and I spoke to Buñuel who interceded for him when they'd already detained him."[32] In his autobiography Buñuel recalled that he found out about Sáenz de Heredia's detention through Ontañón, thus tallying with the version above. He then went to the Estudios Roptence, where the Falangist director had filmed *La hija de Juan Simón*, and talked to its Workers' Committee, whose members endorsed the prisoner's good conduct. And in the company of six or seven workers armed with rifles Buñuel went to the *cheka* to free him.[33] Many years later Sáenz de Heredia recounted to Antonio Castro that he only found out that Buñuel had got him out of the *cheka* when the latter told him so in an encounter in Cannes.[34] Given this, the version of the episode offered by Juan Antonio Porto does not seem plausible: namely that on taking leave of each other after being freed, Sáenz de Heredia said to Buñuel, "I hope I won't have to do the same for you."[35] The contrast between Buñuel's behavior toward Sáenz de Heredia and that of the rebels toward Piqueras could not be more marked. Another member of Filmófono, the also Falangist Enrique Herreros, went into hiding in the Peruvian Embassy for six months, but he was then detained and suffered imprisonment in Madrid, Valencia, and Barcelona.

María Zambrano recalled that around April 1936 meetings began in Madrid of a group of intellectuals and artists with a view to forming an association similar to the one created in France as an outcome of the International Congress of Writers for the Defense of Culture mounted by the AEAR in Paris in June 1935.[36] The outbreak of the Civil War speeded things up. As it was, before the founding manifesto of the Alliance of Anti-Fascist Intellectuals for the Defense of Culture was even able to appear, in Paris the Surrealist Group published a tract (on 20 July) denouncing the Fascist insurrection and calling for the arrest of the ultraconservative deputy José María Gil Robles, who had taken refuge in Biarritz.[37]

The founding manifesto of the (Spanish) Alliance of Anti-Fascist Intellectuals for the Defense of Culture appeared in July 1936 (without indicating the day), being seconded by sixty-one signatures, including several that would end up supporting the Francoist cause, like Ramón Gómez de la Serna. The signatories relating to filmmaking were Buñuel, del Amo, Ugarte, Santiago Ontañón, and the critic Miguel Pérez Ferrero. The Alliance's headquarters were in the mansion of the Marquis de Heredia Spínola in Madrid, and María Teresa León became its secretary. Edited first by Ricardo Baeza and then José Bergamín, its organ of expression was the magazine *El mono azul*, which appeared in August, while the alliance's Catalan section published *Meridià*. The organization of the Second International Congress of Writers for the Defense of Culture, held in July 1937 in Valencia, Barcelona, and Madrid, would be its biggest public coup.

By September the Alliance had already mounted a theater section—Guerrillas del Teatro, promoted by León—and was preparing its cinema section, in accordance with the directives of the Ministry of State Education and Fine Arts. Under the government presided over by Largo Caballero, this ministry was headed by the Communist Jesús Hernández—ex-alumnus of the Lenin School in Moscow, deputy for Córdoba in the Cortes (the Spanish Parliament), editor of *Mundo Obrero*, and a painter—his undersecretary being the jurist Wenceslao Roces, professor of Roman law and the translator of *Das Kapital* into Spanish. The office of director general of fine arts, meanwhile, went to Valencian painter and poster artist Josep Renau. The policy of this ministry had a strong ally in the platform of the Alliance of Anti-Fascist Intellectuals, to the point that many of its projects, connected directly or indirectly with wartime propaganda, would be carried out by its administrative organization.[38]

In its film production program the alliance privileged the theme of the defense of Madrid, a theme that was otherwise related to the intervention of the International Brigades in the protecting of the capital. Outstanding among its documentary filmmakers was Arturo Ruiz Castillo, a collaborator on La Barraca and the Pedagogical Missions, who made good use of his Eyemo 35 mm camera, with its single 50 mm lens and hundred-foot capacity (after the Civil War, however, he ended up serving Francoist cinema).

In the network of international aid to the Republic, France constituted a fundamental geographical, logistic, and political link. On 13 August 1936 the International Committee of Coordination and Information for Aid to Republican Spain was created in Paris. Serving on it were members from nineteen countries; Willi Münzenberg was one such member. The following month saw the creation of the Committee for the Defense of Spanish Culture, founded and headed by Aragon, who was succeeded by Tristan Tzara in January 1937. It organized tours in France of the Cobla de Barcelona music ensemble, Valencian dancers, and children's companies. Its Spanish representatives in the French capital would be Max Aub and then Bergamín and Juan Larrea.[39] Returning to the subject of film in relation to international aid, in his memoirs Alberti evoked his reception, as secretary of the alliance with Bergamín, of a truck from the International Writers Association of France, fitted with projection equipment for screening movie propaganda at the front.[40]

In the Spanish film industry a dramatic political polarization took place in July 1936 between the professionals of Cifesa and Filmófono. The head of the first, Vicente Casanova, supported the military uprising from Cifesa's branch in Seville, while his colleagues director Florián Rey and actress Imperio Argentina joined the ranks of Falange Española. Rey, moreover, denounced Ricardo Urgoiti to the Francoist authorities as a "Red" and requested the blocking of Filmófono's accounts abroad.[41] At Filmófono, Fernando Remacha was named president of the Workers' Control Committee, holding this position until June 1937. While the Filmófono professionals were dispersing, Buñuel collaborated assiduously with the Alliance of Anti-Fascist Intellectuals, as Alberti and del Amo, among others, recalled.[42] Among the people he frequented in its Madrid headquarters, Buñuel would mention Alberti, Bergamín, Corpus Barga, Altolaguirre, Chilean composer Acario Cotapos, and Claudio de la Torre.[43]

In the face of the lack of support on the part of the Western democracies for the aggressed Republic, José Giral sent a letter on 25 July 1936 to the Soviet ambassador in Paris—the USSR's geographically closest representative—asking for weapons and military equipment for resisting the military rebellion. Inside the country, furthermore, the Communists were displaying enormous energy and great initiative, as the creation of the Fifth Regiment demonstrated. The daily newspaper *El Sol* started to depend on the PCE, and almost 40 percent of the commentaries on cinema published therein were devoted to Soviet films, always in extremely positive terms.[44] It is no exaggeration to say that the creation of the Alliance of Anti-Fascist Intellectuals was to a large degree due to Communist insistence.

As a consequence of Giral's diplomatic initiative, the first-ever Soviet ambassador, Marcel Rosenberg, with experience at the League of Nations, arrived in Madrid on 28 August 1936. To reciprocate, on 21 September Giral sent, as ambassador to Moscow, the Socialist doctor Marcelino Pascua, who was general director of health when Buñuel appealed to him for a recommendation to facilitate the shooting of his Las Hurdes documentary. Pascua obtained his new diplomatic assignment thanks to the groundwork of his colleague Juan Negrín and left Barcelona on 25 September for Moscow. He and Buñuel would meet once again when Pascua was put in charge of the Spanish Embassy in Paris from April 1938 to February 1939.

The mediation of the PCF was essential in setting up Soviet aid to the Republic, and in August the Spanish Communists' "big brother" sent its Spanish-speaking members Jacques Duclos and André Marty to the Iberian Peninsula. In September Marty would organize and direct the recruiting of the International Brigades (whose center was in Rue Mathurin Moreau in Paris). To them the Comintern would add the Italian Palmiro Togliatti, who used the pseudonym Alfredo Ercole Ercoli. Manipulating the mass media with great effectiveness, the Communists created a potent revolutionary mythology, albeit not without its contradictions. Hence, the mythical Dolores Ibárruri, "Pasionaria," was defined by José María Quiroga during his intervention in the conference of the International Writers Association on 25 July 1938 as "the mother of all Spaniards. We all feel we're the children of Pasionaria."[45] As the historian Joan Estruch has pertinently observed, this was the Frente Popular's substitute Virgin Mary myth, a "secular Lady of Sorrows" of sorts.[46]

On 8 August 1936 the Léon Blum government closed the French frontier to military traffic, while 24 August witnessed the creation of the Non-Intervention Committee, which held its first meeting in London on 9 September. In this situation of abandonment on the part of the Western democracies the Republic had to rely on Soviet military supplies. On 30 August the head of the Soviet intelligence service in Western Europe, General Krivitsky, received the order to create spurious companies to buy arms in Germany and in various small European countries and then ship them to Spain on Scandinavian ships with false documentation, in which it would give the destination as Latin America or the Far East, an issue discussed in chapter 15.[47] In this situation of external helplessness, diplomatic activity constituted a fundamental priority for the Republican government. Spain's embassy in Paris had been headed by the factious Juan F. de Cárdenas, who in the first week of the war sabotaged the buying of arms for the Republican side. Cárdenas was replaced, however, after Fernando de los Ríos's urgent temporary spell in office, by Álvaro de Albornoz.

On 4 September 1936 Largo Caballero formed his first government, which assumed its duties the next day. It consisted of six Socialists, four Republicans, two Communists, one member of Esquerra Republicana de Catalunya, and one from the Partido Nacionalista Vasco. In this cabinet, in which Jesús Hernández occupied the post of minister of state education and fine arts (which included propaganda), Julio Álvarez del Vayo was appointed foreign minister (then known as the minister of state). A pro-Soviet Socialist, Álvarez del Vayo also possessed a singular cinephile streak. He'd been an early visitor to the USSR in 1922, 1924–26, and 1929, which had borne fruit in his books *La nueva Rusia* (1926), *Rusia a los doce años* (1929), and *La senda roja* (1934). On one of these trips he'd met Eisenstein, and when Giménez Caballero attended the Congress of Independent Cinema held in La Sarraz in September 1929 and met the Soviet director, the latter asked him to pass on his greetings to Álvarez del Vayo.[48] Neither side could know that they would meet each other again in December 1930 in Mexico, during the director's ill-fated travels in the country. Due to the breaking off of diplomatic relations between Mexico and the Soviet Union in January 1930, following the assassination of General Obregón, and to the political suspicions of the Mexican authorities, Eisenstein and his team were arrested two weeks after their arrival in the capital, which led to an intervention in their favor by Spanish Ambassador Álvarez del Vayo, and they were freed the following day. Furthermore, on 2 September 1931 he projected in his embassy, as a scoop, an hour's worth of scenes from *¡Qué viva México!* before a select audience including many high-ranking Mexican officials.[49] It is not surprising, therefore, that Álvarez del Vayo was chosen to give an introductory talk to the first-ever screening of a Soviet film in Madrid on 20 January 1930, when in its ninth session the Cineclub Español, founded by Buñuel, showed *Wings of a Serf* (Yuri Tarich, 1926) and *Women of Ryazan* (Olga Preobrazhenskaya, 1927).[50]

Married to the sister of the wife of Luis Araquistáin, Álvarez del Vayo favored any agreement between the Socialists and the Communists, due to which Stanley G. Payne had not the slightest doubt in labeling him a "crypto-Communist."[51] He was a member of the Friends of the Soviet Union association and a promoter of the fusion of the Communist and Socialist Youth organizations, so much so that in his memoirs Carrillo related that in 1934 he held meetings in Álvarez del Vayo's house with Vittorio Codovila, the Comintern agent, to formalize said fusion, which would give rise to the JSU.[52] And Azaña stated in his *Diaries* that when Negrín formed his government in May 1937 and dispensed with Álvarez del Vayo, the PCE and the UGT put pressure on him to allow the latter to continue in his post.[53]

Eugeni Xammar, press attaché at the Spanish Embassy in Paris in 1936, has given us some choice anecdotes about the incompetence of Ambassador Álvaro de Albornoz, who didn't even understand French, due to which the new government decided to replace him.[54] On 14 September the head of government convoked Luis Araquistáin and offered him the ambassadorship in Paris, so that when the Spanish press reported a fresh interview on 18 September between Largo Caballero and Araquistáin, accompanied by the president of the Anti-Fascist League of North America, the report described him as "the new ambassador to Paris." On 24 September Araquistáin arrived in Barcelona and from there caught the afternoon train that would take him to his destination.[55]

We do not know from whom the initiative came to appoint Buñuel as an attaché of that legation. Araquistáin, who had already been labor minister and ambassador to Berlin, was Largo Caballero's intellectual mentor and represented the more radical wing of the PSOE, in harmony with the new prime minister, so much so that the magazine *Claridad*, which Araquistáin published, was wont to polemicize with the more moderate *El Socialista*. When he was named ambassador to Paris, Araquistáin already knew Buñuel, since on the occasion of a public dispute in 1921 between the politician and the writer "El Caballero Audaz" (José María Carretero), the Ultraist group, including Buñuel, had offered a banquet in Araquistáin's honor at the Hotel Palace in Madrid.[56] And Araquistáin had amply demonstrated his interest in the cinema, not only in different writings, but as the instigator of the didactic documentary *¿Qué es España?* (ca. 1929), which has, happily, recently been found by the Filmoteca de Valencia.[57] It is more than likely, then, that it was Araquistáin who suggested Buñuel's name to Álvarez del Vayo.

Like no other Spaniard of the time, the director was acquainted with the Parisian intelligentsia, and it was legitimate to assume that he would be able to give an international orientation to the film propaganda program, of which the Republic was so much in need in order the combat the Non-Intervention blockade. All the same, for some of his friends his appointment turned out to be somewhat enigmatic. Thus, Alberti recalled that when he arrived in Madrid from Ibiza, "Buñuel—it was already August—was all set to leave. He was going—he never really explained what it was—on a mission, a mysterious mission."[58]

The accounts of the origin of the trip and its dates are also rather confused, and so we attempt here to clarify the chronology. In his memoirs Buñuel stated that "at the end of September [1936] they fixed up a meeting in Geneva for me with the Republic's Foreign Minister, Álvarez del Vayo, who wanted to see me. He would tell me what about in Geneva."[59] However, prior to this meeting and even to the formation of the Largo Caballero government on 4 September, Buñuel received the assignment to take a sum of money from the government to the Soviet agent Willi Münzenberg in Paris, as the cineaste recounted to Max Aub:

> Arias asked me in the Ministry of War in Madrid at the end of August 36: "I know you're going to Paris. Would you do me the favor of taking these £400 and handing them over to Münzenberg?"
>
> [Aub:] Were you not on a government mission, from the Ministry, then?
>
> [Buñuel:] No, alright, yes, partly. When [Arias] found out I was going he ordered me to call. Apparently he didn't have a reliable agent to give the money to, so I stepped in. And he gave me a secret code in order for us to be able to communicate.
>
> [Aub:] So that you left . . .
>
> [Buñuel:] On 4 September. And I returned five times during the war. To Barcelona, Madrid, Valencia.[60]

And a little further on Buñuel explains that "Ogier was the one who sent me to Paris. He said, 'Go. You'll be more useful to us there. We'll be there within two weeks.' Then Arias called me and gave me the £400 for Münzenberg. I delivered them, in front of him, to Otto Katz, for an unrecorded German who was going to go to Burgos, entering via Portugal."[61] This was, therefore, an intelligence mission, in which he carried out tasks entrusted to him by Ogier and Arias, the precise details of which—save for the parsimonious information Buñuel offered Aub—we do not know.

Let us begin by identifying Ogier and afterward Arias, of the War Ministry. "Do you remember Ogier?" Aub asked Buñuel. "Sure do. A good bloke," replied the director.[62] Supposedly a member of the legendary anarchist group the Bonnot Gang, French-born Ogier Preteceille had lived in Valencia since 1913, working there as a journalist on Blasco Ibáñez's newspaper *El Pueblo*, and as a prestigious translator—his 1926 Spanish version of Samuel Butler's *Erewhon* (1872) is still considered a classic. A collaborator on such Left-leaning Socialist magazines as Araquistáin's *Leviatán* and *Claridad*, as well as on Renau's Stalinist *Nueva Cultura*, Preteceille was jailed for his political activities during the insurrection in Asturias in October 1934. While under lock and key in the Model prison in Madrid, his companion in misfortune Luis Quintanilla drew a portrait of him. A high official of the UGT, as well as the union's press secretary, the polyglot Preteceille would soon follow on the heels of Buñuel and take his place in the embassy in Paris, where he worked as Araquistáin's private secretary.

Apropos of Arias, it has to be remembered that the first government of Largo Caballero, who also assumed the minister of war's portfolio, remodeled the military General Staff, and it was during that reorganization that Fernando Arias Parga was incorporated. A civilian who was also a reserve officer, Arias would look after the intelligence services, precursors of the Military Investigation Service (SIM), which was not organized until August 1937.[63] The episode related by Buñuel indicates that prior to September Arias was already working in the embryonic military intelligence service hurriedly set up by the Republic.

Buñuel left Madrid for Barcelona on 4 September. In the Catalan capital he changed trains, which led to his chance meeting with José Bergamín, Eugenio Imaz, and Ricardo Muñoz Suay, member of the national committee of the Spanish Federal Students Union (UFEH), who were traveling with a dozen students to Geneva to attend an International Congress of Students. During the leg to the French border on 8 or 9 September Bergamín and Muñoz Suay entered the restaurant car, in which was Buñuel, and the writer made the introductions.[64]

At the Spanish frontier, Buñuel, who had his travel papers in order and a letter from *Mundo Obrero*, found his journey obstructed by an impertinent anarchist unit, since it was they who controlled the political situation in Catalonia at the time. The cineaste overcame its resistance with a torrent of blasphemies and was able to continue his journey.[65]

The key to establishing the chronology of this journey is found in the appointment with Álvarez del Vayo in Geneva during his presence in the assembly of the League of Nations. On 18 September the opening session was held, and the Spanish press reported that that same night the Spanish minister had a meeting with the British delegate, presumably to talk about the Non-Intervention Committee, which had met in London the day before. On 21 September, following a banquet in his honor, Álvarez del Vayo addressed the press correspondents present in Geneva. On 25 September he gave a speech before the assembly, in which he defined the unpunished Italian and German intervention in Spain as "a juridical monstrosity," a recurrent argument in Álvarez del Vayo's interventions in this forum and one that would be included in the documentary produced by Buñuel, *Espagne 1936*. On the night of 1 October he returned to Madrid. It was, therefore, between these two dates that the interview took place between the filmmaker and the minister, an interview that lasted only twenty minutes.[66] In it, Álvarez del Vayo, who undoubtedly knew of the secret mission Buñuel had just successfully completed in Paris, told him of his assignment to the embassy, and Buñuel left immediately for the French capital, in order to place himself under the orders of Araquistáin, who'd just been named ambassador.

Preserved in the Prefecture of Police in Paris is form number 21241 of 28 October 1936, which Buñuel had to complete in order to get an identity card as a resident in France. In this document it states that Buñuel, a "writer" by profession, entered French territory on 20 September via the frontier at Bellegarde, namely the Franco-Swiss frontier. This means that, once they were on French territory on 8 or 9 September, the itineraries of Buñuel and Bergamín and his group bifurcated, with the latter continuing to Geneva and Buñuel going on to Paris to deliver the money with which Arias had entrusted him. Since in the police form it says that the cineaste was in possession of a Spanish passport issued—by the Spanish diplomatic services, obviously—on 19 September 1936, this means that after some ten days in Paris executing the instructions received in Madrid, Buñuel went to Geneva and met with Álvarez del Vayo on the afternoon or evening of 19 September or the morning of 20 September, the date on which the director left for Paris, as the police document shows.

We know that following Buñuel's departure, his spacious apartment on Calle Menéndez Pelayo in Madrid was occupied by the future Republican general, Vicente Rojo, a Catholic, who according to certain published accounts also gave shelter to refugee nuns and several Francoists. This cohort also included Alamán and Tuero, defenders of the besieged Alcázar of Toledo, it being remembered that on 9 September 1936 Rojo had requested Colonel Moscardó, the officer in command, to surrender.[67]

We imagine that the duties with which Álvarez del Vayo entrusted Buñuel in Paris were wide ranging and vague, such as taking care of information and propaganda, public relations, counter-information, and espionage. Also included, in a very specific way, was the issue of international film propaganda, since Buñuel recalled that figuring among his tasks was the cataloguing of Republican propaganda films made in Spain.[68] While Buñuel and Álvarez del Vayo were parleying in Geneva, in New York the film editor Helen Van Dongen, under the supervision of Joris Ivens, was on the point of beginning her first montage on the Spanish Civil War—entitled *Spain in Flames*—using the scant material on hand.

The Spanish film industry had been paralyzed by the outbreak of the war. In April 1938, in a highly critical article about Spanish moviemaking, Luis Gómez Mesa was still able to ask what directors like Benito Perojo, Florián Rey, Fernando Delgado, Luis Buñuel, Edgar Neville, and Luis Marquina were up to.[69] Gómez Mesa's ignorance is surprising, since by then Perojo and Rey were providing Francoist cinema with *españoladas* filmed in Berlin, Delgado and Neville were creating propaganda documentaries for the rebels, Buñuel was in Paris on a diplomatic mission, and Marquina had fled to Argentina. The political heads of Republican cinema produced numerous propaganda documentaries and tried, with difficulty, to get them shown abroad. Francisco Ayala, who served in the Republican embassy in Prague, was, however, to write in his memoirs: "We'd been able to ascertain the mistake our government was making by having—through payment, of course—French cinemas project newsreels of the atrocious bombardments suffered by our civil population, since instead of awakening the indignant reaction it was meant to, all it had achieved was to demoralize the viewing public even further, leading it to the conclusion that it would be preferable to support the diktats of the Germans provided it escaped such horrors."[70]

This was one of the problems Buñuel would try and resolve from his new post in the Spanish Embassy in Paris.

14

A Two-Year Mission in Paris

In the beginning, Buñuel's mission to the French capital was as makeshift as the Propaganda Section of the Spanish Ministry of State Education and Fine Arts that sent him there in September 1936. In an interview four months later he recalled the Republican authorities suggesting in August that he make a grandiose war film in the studios of Madrid along the lines of *Battleship Potemkin*, a project he took to be unrealistic.[1] Only with the reorganization of film production by Jesús Hernández, the Communist minister of state education in Largo Caballero's new government of national defense, formed on 4 September, was a more viable goal envisaged: the mounting of a national and international propaganda campaign based on the making and showing of documentaries and film reports about the Civil War.

As it was, the remark made in the ministry by Ogier Preteceille in early September about the cineaste being more useful to "us"—to the PSOE/PCE political machine—as an attaché at the embassy in Paris must have been music to Buñuel's ears, for it spirited him away from the terror, White and Red, rife in the country. Understandably, he had every intention of avoiding the tragic end of his friends Piqueras and Lorca. What's more, being an embassy official gave him the perfect excuse to refuse the summons of PCE fundamentalist Wenceslao Roces, Hernández's second in command, who requested him to return to Spain to film the fighting. "I'd been in Paris for a while," Buñuel would say, "when one day I received a telegram at the Embassy from Roces, who was under-secretary of state education, summoning me to Madrid to do some filming. I went down to see Araquistáin and showed him it. 'What do you want to do?' he asked. 'Stay here. Filming in the trenches is impossible. The front's no good for that. Now, if it's to make a film, better to do it in the studio, so you can see everything. But I don't think this is the case.' I stayed."[2]

This must have been late in the month, some time after 25 September, when Araquistáin arrived to take up his new post as ambassador. Buñuel wasn't the only one to express his reservations about filming at the front: a year later the Communist filmmaker Fernando G. Mantilla would argue: "The big battles occur along a front several miles long. The artillery and aviation duels are impossible to record. . . . Sniping from the trenches isn't very photogenic, you might say."[3] Any excuse would do to keep Buñuel away from the bombs and bullets: according to Max Aub, when Roces asked him to return to Spain Buñuel replied that he belonged to the PCF, that by implication he was in Paris on party business and under party control, and that in order to get him to return, he (Roces) would have to discuss it with the French politburo.[4]

Leaving Madrid on 4 September 1936, the day Largo Caballero formed his cabinet, Buñuel reached Paris on 8 September, or perhaps the following day. His wife Jeanne and son Juan Luis had been there since the end of June, and on his arrival the family moved into an apartment at 409 Square Albin Cachot belonging to Jeanne's sister, Georgette Rucar, who had taken over the Librairie Espagnole, that crucial redoubt of resistance during the *L'Âge d'or* scandal, when owner Juan Vicens returned to Madrid in 1932.[5] In the Civil War the bookshop would be used as a mail drop for Republican documents, and during the German Occupation a certain amount of material was moved for safekeeping to the house of Jeanne and Georgette's mother. What became of it afterward is unknown.[6] Buñuel's first act in Paris must have been to deliver the £400 sent by Arias to Münzenberg and Katz, thus proving himself to be a reliable intermediary between the embryonic intelligence service of the Spanish Republican state and the Comintern apparat. To simplify communication between them, Münzenberg gave the cineaste a secret code.

Although Álvaro de Albornoz was in his sixth week as ambassador when Buñuel arrived, his days were numbered. In fact, it was only with the replacing of this non-French-speaking Izquierda Republicana politician by that theorist of the Bolshevization of the PSOE, Luis Araquistáin, an appointment announced on 19 September, that Buñuel's nebulous assignment came into sharper focus. Armed with his new passport, granted by the embassy that same day, he made a lightning visit to Geneva to discuss the fine-tuning of his mission as coordinator of Republican film propaganda with Julio Álvarez del Vayo (Araquistáin's brother-in-law; their wives were Swiss-German sisters).[7] Said mission would exploit both the organizational skills the cineaste had acquired at Paramount in Paris and Warner Bros. and Filmófono in Madrid, and his excellent connections,

The pro-Soviet Socialist Julio Álvarez del Vayo, foreign minister in the Largo Caballero government, in a frame still from *Espagne 1936* (Jean-Paul Dreyfus and Luis Buñuel, 1937). (Filmoteca Española, Madrid)

filmic and extra-filmic, with the Communist and fellow-traveling intelligentsia of the French capital. His duties, however, were to extend beyond all things cinematic, to embrace diplomatic protocol and public relations, counter-information and espionage.

Buñuel would remain for two years, almost to the day, at the Spanish Embassy, his time there being spent under three different ambassadors, whose rotation denoted not only the political changes taking place within the Republican government in response to events in Spain but also the revising of the propaganda imperative in the light of the military successes of the insurgents, overtly aided by Nazi Germany and Fascist Italy; the non-interventionism of France, Great Britain, and the United States; and the more covert aid provided by the USSR in terms of matériel and military and intelligence personnel. Ramón Sala Noguer has judiciously summed up the two main aspects of Republican propaganda on celluloid (and in other media): "The first would insist on proving the Fascist nature of the insurgent movement and its alignment with the Axis powers. The second would attempt, instead, to gain the confidence of the European democracies by playing down the fear of a 'Sovietization' of the country, namely the collapse of Republican institutions overwhelmed by popular organizations, precisely what the propaganda of the nationalist zone was trying to demonstrate."[8]

On 4 November 1936, two days before the Largo Caballero government decamped from Madrid to Valencia, the improvised Propaganda Section of the Ministry of State Education and Fine Arts, formed under Jesús Hernández on 4 September, gave way to the newly created Ministry of Propaganda, entrusted to Carlos Esplá Rizo, novelist Vicente Blasco Ibáñez's one-time secretary and a member of Izquierda Republicana. The new ministry's purview included cinema, radio, the press, book publishing, and exhibitions under a single, unified plan, albeit restricted to civil society, since the Undercommisariat of Propaganda of the General Commisariat of War, which intervened among the armed forces, was to subsist under the control of the Ministry of War. While the action of the short-lived Propaganda Section was restricted to the management of the cinemas Capitol and Monumental in Madrid and their programming of uncensored Soviet films—with Socialist-Realist titles like *We from Kronstadt* (Efim Dzigan, 1936) and *Chapayev* (Sergei and Georgi Vasiliev, 1934) received with fervent empathy by the beleaguered citizens—the Ministry of Propaganda shifted the emphasis from exhibition to the production of militant documentaries. In its seven-month existence it would release four of these: *El 'Komsomol' en Valencia*, a reportage, to the strains of Wagner and *The Internationale*, on the protest demonstrations in the city following the sinking by the Franco forces of a Soviet ship bearing foodstuffs; *Discurso del Presidente de la República Don Manuel Azaña*, in which the oratory of the politician was supplemented by compilation footage of the progress of the war; *Todo el poder para el Gobierno*, on a PCE and UGT-backed demonstration in Valencia on 14 February 1937 calling for greater centralization of state power and a further purge of the Republic's military leaders; and lastly, and most famously, the compilation film on which Buñuel collaborated in Paris, *España 1936*. These four titles were made between November 1936 and February 1937. During the three further months before its demise, the Ministry of Propaganda shifted its attention away from filmmaking proper and toward the mounting of the Spanish Pavilion at the International Exhibition in Paris.

Buñuel considered that Araquistáin, whose period in office ran from 19 September 1936 to 27 May 1937—that is, during the life span of the Largo Caballero government—"was an excellent ambassador, as good as [his successors] Ossorio and Pascua were bad."[9] Eugeni Xammar, chief press officer at the Paris Embassy from the start of the Civil War, was of the opinion that with Araquistáin's arrival the "absurd situation" under Álvaro de Albornoz had given way to political pragmatism: "The Embassy began being frequented by slightly more serious people and the ambassador fondly imagined that from the embassy he could involve himself in politics, a natural response for someone who accepts an embassy. Those politics took several directions."[10] Xammar goes on to cite Araquistáin's secret negotiations with the Italian ambassador in London to end the war. Undertaken in early 1937 at the request of Largo Caballero and Azaña, these negotiations would, once Álvarez del Vayo had revealed them to the PCE and the Soviet secret service, contribute to the removal from power of the PSOE leader, as well as his intellectual mentor in Paris.

The Socialist Luis Araquistáin, who took up his post as head of the Spanish Embassy in Paris on 25 September 1936. (Fundación Pablo Iglesias, Madrid)

The terrible endophagy of the Barcelona "events" of May 1937, during which the militias of the FAI and the POUM were suppressed by the forces of the PCE, PSUC (United Socialist Party of Catalonia), and the Generalitat, and Largo Caballero was replaced as head of government by Juan Negrín, foregrounded the ever-increasing influence of the Communists in the political life of the Republic, both at home and abroad. Buñuel would maintain a manifestly pro-Soviet view of these events, a view emphatically at odds with that of Breton and the Surrealists.[11] In Paris, Araquistáin, victim of the CP's machinations, resigned on 27 May and was replaced by the former ambassador to Brussels, Ángel Ossorio y Gallardo, a moderate Catholic politician, legal expert, and writer, whose time in office may have been hit and miss in terms of internal organization and diplomatic finesse but was nevertheless marked by an unflagging activism. In April 1938, as a result of a government reshuffle in which Negrín relieved Prieto of his post as minister of defense, thus causing a definitive rift in the PSOE/PCE ranks, Ossorio was replaced by Marcelino Pascua. Brought from—or sent by—Moscow, where no further Republican ambassador replaced him, thus demonstrating Paris to be the diplomatic (and espionage) frontline as far as the Kremlin was concerned, Pascua was the antithesis of Ossorio, being a meticulous, even fanatical, organizer. Xammar spoke of him burning any ribbon used to type a secret telegram with, for instance.[12] Although to Pérez Turrent and de La Colina, Buñuel defined the polyglot Pascua as a close friend, he was ungracious about this "guest of the guests of the shield-bearers of the Order of Toledo" in an interview with Aub: "That Pascua . . . With his dog, his intractable ways. He shut himself away with some young boy or other, I now know, and there was no talking to him."[13]

In the administrative reshuffle after 17 May 1937, the Ministry of Propaganda in Valencia ceded to the State Department (the Ministry of State) and its new Undersecretariat of Propaganda, fronted by rationalist architect Manuel Sánchez Arcas, a PCE militant and one of the founders of the Alliance of Antifascist Intellectuals for the Defense of Culture. The Undersecretariat had its own Film Service, whose head was Manuel Villegas López, the well-known critic and author of the books *Espectador de sombras* (1935) and *Arte de masas* (1936); as a film society animator he'd screened *Las Hurdes* in Madrid in December 1933. Villegas López would eventually direct several documentaries—commencing with *Madrid* (1937)—an activity complemented by the interventions of his Undersecretariat colleagues Fernando G. Mantilla and Francisco Camacho, who was in charge of the international versions in French and English of *España al día*, the weekly newsreel of the Barcelona-based PCE/PSUC/UGT organization, Film

Popular.[14] Film Popular and the Film Service of the Undersecretariat of Propaganda were, in fact, to work hand in hand after May 1937. Between that date and the end of the Civil War on 1 April 1939 the Film Service produced some twenty documentaries, of lengths varying from ten to forty-five minutes, plus a dozen or more "trailers," each two or three minutes long, illustrating the government watchword of the moment and created by Villegas López, Mantilla, and Camacho.

In Paris Buñuel was to play only a limited role in this œuvre, originated in Valencia and Barcelona, although one Film Service compilation, *Espagne 1937* (1938), is partly attributable to him. Other significant documentaries made by the Undersecretariat were *Un año de guerra* (1937), mounted by Arturo Ruiz-Castillo, a member of the Alliance of Anti-Fascist Intellectuals for the Defense of Culture; *Campesinos de ayer y de hoy* (1938), directed by Carrasco de la Rubia, leader of the Grupo Cinemático; *Defendemos nuestra tierra* (1938), the work of Juan M. Plaza, film critic, contributor to Piqueras's *Nuestro Cinema*, and mainstay of the Film Services of the Army of the Center; and *La toma de Teruel* (1938), edited by the Basque filmmaker Mauro Azcona. The Undersecretariat's most ambitious project was undoubtedly the co-producing, with Productions Corniglion-Molinier and (in a lesser capacity) the ex-Surrealist Roland Tual, of André Malraux's feature-length *Sierra de Teruel/Espoir* (1939). While our listing of these government-funded movies is aimed at providing a context for Buñuel's two contributions to the ideological war effort, *Espagne 1936* and *Espagne 1937*, before getting to them we must backtrack a little.

During October 1936 the newly appointed coordinator of Republican film propaganda in Paris moved into his own office at 24, Rue de la Pépinière, in the same eighth arrondissement as the Spanish Embassy at 13, Avenue George V. Interviewed in February 1937 by Karl Obermann, a German exile and KPD member working for the Münzenberg press in Paris, Buñuel not only articulated his current ideas on film but also gave an implicit summary of his own recent experience as a cineaste. The tardy advent of a modern Spanish film industry in 1935—due in large part to the Filmófono operation—has been curtailed by the Fascist uprising, he remarked. The producers have fled—Ricardo Urgoiti, for example, reached Paris that same February—and the occupation of the studios by the workers has, given the senselessness of continuing to produce "bourgeois" fiction films based on the star system, resulted in their closure. The sociopolitical drama of events has spawned a more prescient genre, which takes as its subject the Spanish masses themselves, whether at the front or in the rear. "Right now, the news film [*film de reportage*] is the film of Republican Spain," Buñuel told Obermann. "We can do nothing better at present than to show reality through the film."[15] And the paradigm for this new genre? Buñuel's documentary on the Hurdano rural proletariat.

Buñuel's first propaganda project was, in point of fact, to put a soundtrack on *Las Hurdes*, a work that Georges Sadoul announced was under way in an article published in the Communist illustrated weekly magazine *Regards* on 29 October 1936. Retitled *Terre sans pain* in its Francophone version and *Land without Bread / Unpromised Land* in its Anglophone rendering, and with a new anti-Fascist coda that reframed the message of what, in 1933, had been an essentially *anti*-Republican opus, the sonorized documentary would serve as an opening shot in the pro-Republican campaign. This campaign set out to remind French, British, and North American public opinion of the baleful effects of their governments' policies of non-intervention; namely, the potential victory of the same forces of obscurantism that had doomed Las Hurdes to radical underdevelopment. Since we discuss the production and reception of *Terre sans pain* at length in chapter 9, we merely emphasize a few points here.

First, Buñuel must have spent part of October revising, with Pierre Unik, the first draft of the French commentary they had finalized on 29 March 1934 with a view to producing, at the request of Pierre Braunberger, a sound version of *Las Hurdes*. The last mention of Unik in these pages evoked his query, made on 10 February 1935, as to whether Buñuel still intended to go to the USSR to make movies. In recent times Unik had held a sub-editorial post on *L'Humanité*; contributed poems, reviews, and news items to the AEAR monthly magazine *Commune*; and in April 1936 been appointed editor of *Regards*, the association's "showcase for the 'man in the street,'" as Lucien Logette has described it.[16] The young ex-Surrealist had also been active in Communist film culture, collaborating on the collective docudrama *La Vie est à nous*, produced by the PCF for the general election of April–May 1936 that would instaure the Front Populaire. Directed by Jacques Becker, Jacques Brunius, Henri Cartier (-Bresson), Jean-Paul Dreyfus, Jean Renoir, and André Zwoboda, Unik had been co-scriptwriter—along with Brunius, Dreyfus, Maurice Lime, Marc Maurette, Renoir, Zwoboda, and Paul Vaillant-Couturier, whose idea the film was—and had also briefly appeared in it as PCF Central Committee member Marcel Cachin's (fictional) secretary. Screened for the first time before invited audiences at La Bellevilloise on 7 April and on 10–11 April at Braunberger's Cinéma du Panthéon, *La Vie est à nous* was refused a visa by the French Board of Film Censors, and, restricted to the echo chamber of the already converted, can have had only a limited impact on the election campaign.[17] Later, Unik would write the French commentaries for such pro-Republican documentaries as *Espagne 1936* (with, it is usually claimed, Buñuel), *Cœur d'Espagne / Heart of Spain* (Herbert

Kline and Géza Karpathi, 1937; commentary cowritten with Nina Martel-Dreyfus, Jean-Paul's wife) and *Victoire de la vie / Return to Life* (Henri Cartier (-Bresson) and Herbert Kline, 1938), as well as cowriting with Dreyfus *Le Temps des cerises* (Jean-Paul Dreyfus, 1937), a social melodrama about the plight of retired workers without a pension produced by the PCF for the local elections in October of that same year.[18]

Second, since the issue of Soviet cinema has run like a proverbial red thread through this study, it is worth repeating that *Terre sans pain*'s first public outing was as a support to Albert Gendelstein's *Love and Hate* at the Cinéma du Panthéon, where it would play from 19 December 1936 to 4 February 1937, when this Russian film gave way to *Two in the Dark* (Benjamin Stoloff, 1936). *Terre sans pain* was retained as its support, however, and would end up as the headlining opus on a double bill that showed until 13 March, making a run of twelve weeks in all. Before directing *Love and Hate*, Gendelstein had assisted Pudovkin on *The End of St. Petersburg* (1927) and Fyodor Otsep on *Land in Captivity* (1928). All of these Russian titles were Mezhrabpomfilm productions, but by the time of the French release of Gendelstein's Civil War drama—in which, to music by Dimitri Shostakovitch, White saboteurs are foiled by the doughty womenfolk of a group of miners—the studio, debilitated by the Stroheimian financial excesses of Erwin Piscator during the making of *Revolt of the Fishermen* (1934), and decimated by the political purges unleashed as the first big Stalinist show trials got under way in August 1936, was on the point of closing.[19]

By 23 August two Soviet cameramen, Roman Karmen and his assistant, Boris Makaseev, were in Spain, and between that date and July 1937 they would send over 55,000 feet of film to Moscow, where, supplemented by material shot by Spanish cinematographers, it was transformed by a team of thirteen Soyuz-kinochronica technicians and editors into a series of twenty newsreels, each (for the most part) between six and eleven minutes long, called *Events in Spain*.[20] It is worth noting that the eleven months Karmen and Makaseev spent in Spain were more or less congruent with the period of maximum Soviet military assistance to the Republic. Using as an interpreter the Polish-born photographer Chim (David Szymin, known as David Seymour), who was reporting on the Civil War for *Regards*, the two cinematographers began filming the fighting in Irún and San Sebastián with their handheld 35 mm Eyemo cameras. Once shot, the material was dispatched to Paris, where lavender copies of the negatives were made prior to continuing on their way to Moscow.[21] Raw film stock was also forwarded to the two shutter-happy cameramen from the French capital.

Accompanied at times by the writer and *Izvestia* journalist Ilya Ehrenburg, and at other times by Mikhail Koltsov, *Pravda*'s envoy to Spain (and a good

Soviet documentary moviemaker Roman Karmen filming in the trenches with his 35 mm Eyemo camera, in the company of bespectacled *Pravda* correspondent Mikhail Koltsov. (photographer unknown)

friend of the Aragon/Triolet couple), over the next eleven months the two Russians would film the Fascist bombing of Barcelona and Madrid, the formation of the International Brigades, frontline combat in Huesca, Oviedo, the Álcazar in Toledo and Jarama, and the siege of the Spanish capital, where they insisted on remaining even after the Republican government had moved to Valencia on 6 November. Not surprisingly, figures from, or close to, the PCE feature strongly in *Events in Spain*: Dolores Ibárruri (Pasionaria), José Díaz, Enrique Líster, André Marty, and Julio Álvarez del Vayo are much in evidence.

Yet Paris was not just a clearinghouse for Soviet footage en route to Moscow: that same footage was to find its way into other compilations confected in New York, London, Madrid, and Paris itself. Berlin, too, since the German newsreel *UFA Wochenschau* used, almost before the USSR itself, shots taken by the two Russians and illegally duplicated on their way to Moscow, shots framed within a wholly different ideological discourse.[22] In the case of the first three cities, this was because as well as passing through the hands of the commercial delegation at the Soviet Embassy in Paris, lavender copies of the Soyuzkinochronica material were also inspected at the Spanish Embassy's annex at 24, Rue de la Pépinière. "Officially," Buñuel states in *Mon dernier soupir*, "in my Rue de la Pépinière office I saw about regrouping all the Republican propaganda films shot in Spain."[23] The word "all" must be taken to include the Karmen/Makaseev material. Indeed, as the Russian film historian Natalia Nussinova tells us, there are editing sheets dated to the end of September 1936 in the Roman Karmen collection in the CGALI (the Central State Archive of Literature and Art in Moscow) that are annotated in French and that make reference to the striking of lavender copies.[24] Nor was it simply a question of collating this material: Buñuel acted as a filter for it. A censor of sorts, even, for it was through him that selected segments were rerouted to Spain, England, and North America.

Spain in Flames, a sixty-three-minute anti-Fascist compilation edited by Helene van Dongen, produced by Film Historians Inc. and released through Amkino, the Sovkino agency in New York, opened there on 28 January 1937. A paradigm of sorts—*Espagne 1936* would owe it much—this was a work of two halves, each with a different narrator: the first, "The Fight for Freedom," was filmed by Spanish cameramen; the second, "No Pasarán: They Shall Not Pass," was culled from the newsreels of Soyuzkinochronica. Van Dongen was Joris Ivens's companion and the editor of many of his films in the 1930s; Ivens, who like Van Dongen was in New York at the time, helped select the footage received from Paris for this documentary. Film Historians Inc., which would rapidly metamorphose into Contemporary Historians Inc., was a CPUSA (Communist Party of the United States of America) front organization founded in autumn 1936. Consisting of John Dos Passos, Lillian Hellman, Ernest Hemingway, Archibald MacLeish, Clifford Odets, Dorothy Parker, and Herman Shumlin, its stated mission was to raise funds to produce a major pro-Republican propaganda film to be made in Spain by Ivens. Supplementing the money collected by this organization was the much greater sum provided by a Münzenberg creation, the North American Committee for Spain.

By the time *Spain in Flames* was released—and immediately banned in several U.S. states—Ivens was in the Iberian Peninsula to direct *The Spanish Earth*, using funding from Contemporary Historians. But first he visited Paris to link up with cameraman John Ferno (or Fernhout), who'd arrived there from Amsterdam, and to parley with Münzenberg, who was coordinating aid to Spain on behalf of the Comintern, and Katz, the head of Agence Espagne, a key press agency set up by Münzenberg and Álvarez del Vayo.[25] Another port of call was 24, Rue de la Pépinière, where Ivens and Buñuel signed a contract apropos of the as yet unnamed movie on 14 January 1937. The contract stipulated that the negative footage was to be conveyed to Paris from Spain in the embassy's diplomatic bag, "in order to avoid the surveillance of customs officers," and to be developed by the Laboratoires Cinéma-Tirage L. Maurice in Gennevilliers, a laboratory located in a small town on the northern outskirts of Paris whose mayor between 1934 and 1939 was Jean Grandel, a Communist, and which was used by the PCF, as indicated in a 1939 documentary featuring Maurice Thorez, now in the Archives communales d'Ivry-sur-Seine. Once developed, the negatives "will be controlled by a person duly mandated by the Spanish Embassy," namely Buñuel. Following the indications given by him, "lavender copies will be made of certain parts, or all, of the developed negative."[26] The embassy was to facilitate payment for these lavender copies, which it would then forward C.O.D. to poet Archibald MacLeish at *Fortune Magazine* in New York. Founded in 1930 by Henry Luce of *Time Magazine* and edited by MacLeish, *Fortune* was America's foremost business journal—although artists like James Agee and Walker Evans contributed to it—and provided the perfect cover for Contemporary Historians Inc. It was thought that Ivens would shoot some thirty thousand feet of negative, which would cost 11,000 FF (French francs) to develop; the check for $500 that *Fortune* was asked to lodge with the embassy would pay for this developing.

Perhaps the most revealing aspect of this contract is the amount of control exercised by Buñuel, who, with Ivens's agreement, was to have power of decision over which segments of the negative material sent to him by his old AEAR comrade ought to be contretyped. In a sense, then, Buñuel would act as the first editor of *The Spanish Earth*, and in a lesser capacity as a production manager: it was he who provided Ivens and Ferno with their passes to fly from Toulouse to Valencia, seat of the Republican government, where they began shooting their film on 21 January 1937 (he'd do the same for Hemingway and Dos Passos, among others). On 21 February the two Dutchmen were back in Paris, where they showed their developed footage to a hundred invited guests, including Renoir, Unik, Dreyfus, Louis Daquin, and Vladimir Pozner.[27] It is hard to believe that Buñuel was not there too, although, as so often happens, he melts into thin air in the historical accounting. His own view of *The Spanish Earth*—first shown in public in the United States on 13 July 1937—was positive, in that it "demonstrated that our army did not consist of murderers"—meaning anarchists—"but of disciplined people, with political sense," to wit, Communists under Soviet control.[28] When Buñuel saw the completed movie, however, he was appalled that, calling on Dos Passos's record collection in New York, Ivens had mistakenly put Catalan *sardanas* on the soundtrack of a narrative that takes place in and around Madrid, an error that was corrected in the Spanish version.[29] Now lost,

Tierra española took time to reach its country of origin—distributed by Film Popular, it was first shown in Barcelona on 25 April 1938—so much so that a disgruntled Ivens wrote to Hemingway on 28 January of that same year to say that he suspected Buñuel of "keeping the print away from Madrid," or that there was "some kind of sabotage somewhere in the [Spanish] embassy—too many party people in the picture."[30] Ivens's meaning is hard to grasp. Is he saying that there were too many Communists in the embassy, and that *Tierra española* was being sabotaged for being too positive about the Socialists or the CNT? Or is he saying that since the Frente Popular tactic was to play down the PCE's role in the war, the on-screen presence of Líster, Díaz, Irraburi, Gustav Regler, and Vittorio Vidali (the sinister GPU agent and political commissar of the Fifth Regiment), figures whose identity would not go unremarked in Spain, made that role too explicit?

To return to the Soyuzkinochronica footage shot by Karmen and Makeseev—some of which would find its way into *Espagne 1936*—and reiterate the centrality of Paris as the clearinghouse for it, it is worth observing that Ivor Montagu, a member of the Communist Party of Great Britain (CPGB), whom Buñuel had known in Hollywood in 1930–31 in the company of Chaplin, Eisenstein, Neville, and Ugarte, used such footage in a propaganda piece put together by his London-based production and distribution company, the Progressive Film Institute (PFI), *Crime against Madrid* (1937). Shown at party-political and trade-union gatherings throughout the UK, this thirty-minute documentary was distributed on 35 mm by the PFI and on 16 mm by its sister organization, Kino Films. The same held true for the prints of two titles imported from across the English Channel, *La Vie est à nous* and *Land without Bread*.[31]

Buñuel's filtering of this early, and prime, Soviet material did not just take in London and New York, however—Madrid also came into the picture. Years later our man would express his remorse at an incident involving the Soviet commercial representative in Paris. Araquistáin had given the cineaste a letter from the Propaganda Section of the Ministry of State Education or the Ministry of Propaganda—he doesn't remember which; the first metamorphosed into the second in November 1936—in which the head of news information, Manuel Colino, complained that footage by Karmen and Makaseev hadn't reached the Spanish capital from Paris. Buñuel went to complain in turn to the Soviet Embassy, where he was treated uncivilly by an official, who asked him why he wasn't at the front. (By now the director may have had a bit of a complex about this; see the Roces incident cited earlier.) The official's superciliousness, Buñuel told Aub, "made me so angry that I made four copies of a letter I wrote and sent one each to Araquistáin, the French Party [the PCF], Álvarez del Vayo and Roces. A few months later they recalled him to Moscow and shot him."[32]

Ambiguity has long surrounded Buñuel's next venture, *Espagne 1936*: ambiguity as to this propaganda film's identity; ambiguity as to his part in it; ambiguity as to its status within his œuvre. First let us identify the object of study. In the *Catálogo general del cine de la Guerra Civil*, edited by Alfonso del Amo García and María Luisa Ibáñez Ferradas, and published in 1996, we read:

> [Entry] 297
> *España 1936*
> Title of the Italian version: *Espagna [sic] 1936*
> Title of the French version: *Espagne 1936*
> Other titles used: *Madrid 1936*, *España leal en armas*
> 1937 Spain
> Producer: Undersecretariat of Propaganda of the Government of the Republic
> Director: (Jean-Paul Le Chanois)
> Producer, choice of material and script: Luis Buñuel
> Commentary: Luis Buñuel, Pierre Unik
> Voiceover of the French version: Gaston Modot
> Editor: (Jean-Paul Le Chanois)
> Original language: Spanish, French
> Length: 35 minutes.[33]

Other sources add further information, and at times further confusion. In Francisco Aranda's much earlier biography of Buñuel, it says:

> 1937 *Espagne 1937* (*España leal en armas*)
> Production: Spain and France. Ciné-Liberté. Documentary. 4 reels (40 minutes).
> Film material supplied by Luis Buñuel.
> Photography: Roman Karmen, Manuel Villegas López and a Spanish cameraman.
> Editing: Newsreels and documents, by J. P. Dreyfus (Le Chanois).
> Supervision: Luis Buñuel.
> Commentary: Pierre Unik and Luis Buñuel.
> Voiceover: Gaston Modot.
> Music: Luis Buñuel (Beethoven's 7th and 8th Symphonies).[34]

Observe that there is already a discrepancy between the two entries as to the title—*España 1936* and *Espagne 1937*—a discrepancy that Yasha David's filmography in *¿Buñuel: La mirada del siglo!* tries to get around by having *Espagne 1937* as the French title and *España 1936* as the Spanish.[35] Moreover, in the main text of Aranda's pioneering study the film appears as *Espagne 1936*. And to further complicate matters, the *Catálogo general* lists two documentaries entitled *España 1936* (the second, produced by the Alliance of Anti-Fascist Intellectuals for the

Defense of Culture, and directed by Mantilla in 1937, is now lost); and "another" *España 1937*, with a French version: *Espagne 1937* (unidentified director/editor, 1937). There is also a potential contradiction in the *Catálogo general* as to the producer of *Espagne 1936*: the Undersecretariat of Propaganda of the Government of the Republic only came into being in May 1937, months after the French release of this co-production. The titles *Madrid 1936* and *España leal en armas* were evoked by Carlos Fernández Cuenca, according to his recall forty years later.[36] However, as Magí Crusells has pointed out, newspaper reviews of the film on its release in Madrid in June 1937 refer to it as *España 1936*.[37] In fact, it opened at the Cine Actualidades on 8 June and ran for a week, until 15 June, solely in the morning sessions from 8 a.m. to 2 p.m.; in the afternoon, commercial movies were shown. The Madrid public much preferred the Buñuel production *¡Centinela alerta!*, which played during the war for forty-two weeks.[38] Fernández Cuenca's assertion cannot be tested as all the Spanish copies of the film were consumed in the calamitous fire at the Cinematiraje Riera laboratories in Madrid in August 1945. We would propose jettisoning the titles *Madrid 1936* and *España leal en armas* as being confusing.

But we, too, must be careful not to add more confusion at this point by harping on the errors of the past. Let us say, in consonance with historians such as Wolf Martin Hamdorf and Inmaculada Sánchez Alarcón, that the root of the problem lies in the fact that *two* propaganda films, namely *Espagne 1936* and *Espagne 1937*, on both of which Buñuel collaborated to varying degrees, have been conflated as one.[39] The job at hand, then, is to disentangle them, a task made no easier by the fact that neither film has any credits. The filmographic descriptions above were, and are, a posteriori reconstructions, therefore educated guesses on the part of historians. Hence the anomalies.

In the absence of credits, much of the attention devoted to *Espagne 1936* has arisen from the perceived need to establish, and to measure, the part Buñuel played in it; to see if that part is extensive enough for the film to be included in his filmography as a valid authorial work—in short, to posit Buñuel as its director (of sorts). However, it is redundant to speak of a director for this, a compilation film consisting of Second Republic, Civil War, and other footage shot over a period of years by various, usually anonymous, hands. This is the problem faced by Aranda and Fernández Cuenca, two scholars marked by auteurism: they scan the film for images or juxtaposed shots that bear the mark of the all-pervasive magus, as if, had they not existed, Buñuel might have planned and actually filmed them. For Aranda, a man crossing the deserted Plaza del Callao in Madrid, bearing a diminutive child's coffin on his head; for Fernández Cuenca, superstitious peasants praying for rain and technocrat dam builders providing water. In an age in which access to prints was nowhere near as easy as it is today, such historians may be forgiven for citing "Buñuelian" sequences that are not even in the film.

Yet when, as here, a director is absent, who is the determining figure? Is it he who selected the images in the first place, a role traditionally ascribed to Buñuel? Or he who then put them together in a certain order, a role that has been accredited to Dreyfus? Historical reckoning demands there be a prime mover, a final arbiter, but in the case of these two men, neither the one nor the other was particularly anxious to claim that role—thirty or forty years after the event, that is.

Buñuel's various versions of events are equivocal. To Aranda, he said that after being sent to the Spanish Embassy in Paris, "I dealt with the (film) material shot in Spain and even gave orders for a compilation film, whose title I don't recall, to be made."[40] To Aub: "All I did was supervise the editing that Jean-Paul Dreyfus, who today calls himself Jean-Paul le Chanois, did using the material the Undersecretariat of Propaganda was sending us."[41] To Pérez Turrent and de la Colina: "Le Chanois edited a film with the material I received and supervised. Some books point to the film as being mine, but this isn't so."[42] To Aranda, on another occasion: "'So,' I asked Buñuel, 'you didn't intervene in the editing?' 'I'm not that frivolous!' he replied. 'I supervised the editing at the rough cut and positive print stages, and during the sonorization.'"[43] In *Mon dernier soupir* the director makes absolutely no mention of *Espagne 1936*.

Dreyfus/Le Chanois's own account hovers at the edge of amnesia but is revealing for all that. In a 1978 interview with Philippe Esnault, he said: "When the Franco insurrection occurred, the generals' coup d'état, let's say, I made *Espagne 36* in Paris, about the victory of the Frente Popular." And where did the documents come from? asks Esnault. "I got them from Spain and from French newsreel companies. It was a two-reel compilation film and got shown in the cinemas." Esnault then asks: "There's an *Espagne 36* film attributed to Buñuel. What's the relationship between them?" And the dialogue continues:

A: I don't know. At the time he was a cultural representative of the Republic in Madrid. It's possible he might have helped us.

Q: Buñuel wasn't in on it, then?

A: It's possible he might have financed the film. Ciné-Liberté, who'd produced it, relied on film enthusiasts. I was one of the few professionals, and at the same time a militant.

Q: Moreover, you were an excellent editor.

A: I was just a beginner at the time. One learns one's trade by practicing it.[44]

A solution to the dilemma of ultimate responsibility would be to see *Espagne 1936* as a structural echo, within that still nascent genre, the compilation film, of a recent predecessor: *Spain in Flames*, with Buñuel in the Ivens role as first filter of the available footage and Dreyfus as the Helene van Dongen figure, the one who actually mounted the celluloid. Moreover, Dreyfus/Le Chanois's recollections imply that the project was marked by a zero sense of intimate contact, of common purpose, between himself and the Spaniard, their remoteness being connoted by the Frenchman mistakenly placing Buñuel in Madrid during the editing process.

Fernández Cuenca's claim to having seen Buñuel's as the headlining name on the print of *España 1936*—or *Madrid 1936* or *España leal en armas*—that he viewed in the summer of 1937 can neither be proved nor disproved. Nor can his assertion that in foreign prints Dreyfus's name was the more prominent, since, as previously stated, there are no credits on the extant French (and Italian) version. There is, however, one contemporary voice that ascribes the film to Buñuel: that of Claude Aveline. As well as being the new film critic of *Commune*, the fellow-traveling Aveline—another old friend of Jean Vigo's—was a member of Ciné-Liberté and must have been aware of the part his comrade Dreyfus had played in the editing, but when he came, in 1937, to introduce a screening of *Espagne 1936*, it was the Spaniard's name alone that he cited: "While it wasn't shot by Buñuel, this film has at least been edited thanks to him. . . . I will make no comments on this film. I simply want to evoke, in a few words, an image that isn't in it, that couldn't be in it. . . . A short episode, one death among a hundred thousand." This episode was the murder of Juan Piqueras, a name that cast a long shadow: hadn't Piqueras been at the origin of a project to interchange newsreel footage with Ciné-Liberté just before the military uprising in Spain? A project that would bear fruit in the collaboration, however ambiguous, between Buñuel and Dreyfus, and the organizations behind them.

Sponsored by Paul Langevin, Jean-Richard Bloch, André Chamson, and Élie Faure of the Franco-Spanish Committee called "Against the Blockade of Spain / For the Security of France" and intended to raise funds for Republican hospitals, the 6 April screening of *Espagne 1936* took place at La Mutualité, in the Latin Quarter, and was co-introduced by Gaston Modot, general secretary of Ciné-Liberté. This was the second time the committee had shown the movie, the first being at the Studio Pallas Athénée on 8 March, when it was introduced by Faure.[45] Moreover, the committee's secretariat was at 26, Rue de la Pépinière, next door to Buñuel's office at number 24. Aveline's presentation was reprinted in July 1937 in number 8 of *Soutes: Revue de Culture Révolutionnaire Internationale*,[46] and in September he would make a further reference to Buñuel's editorial responsibility (so to speak) for *Espagne 1936* in his "Cinéma" column in number 49 of *Commune.* This allusion was refuted in the November issue (number 51) of the same magazine, presumably by the Spanish cineaste himself: "Apropos of this film, may we take the opportunity to rectify an error, which Aveline managed to repeat: the editing has certainly not been done by Buñuel, who has not collaborated on this compilation film."[47]

The filmmaker's disavowal was immediate, then, and in keeping with the sought-after anonymity that marked his professional trajectory through contemporary industrial cinema, from MGM in Hollywood in 1930–31 to Filmófono in Madrid in 1935–36. Notwithstanding his private wish, sustained between January 1932 and February 1935, to direct in the Soviet Union, in terms of his public profile Buñuel wanted both his salaried and his *engagé* activities to be kept under wraps; he prized the image of his freewheeling independence as a director subject to no constraints, political or commercial. Moreover, when Buñuel was called upon to narrate his career toward the end of his life, and he sought to depict himself as a moralist who'd never "really" contravened the ethical precepts of Surrealism, there was every reason *not* to include a film that, as a work of state propaganda (and pro-Stalinist, to boot), was entirely at odds with the subversive values promulgated by Breton & Co.

Whatever the reason (or reasons) for it, Buñuel's repudiation of his involvement in *Espagne 1936* lacked consistency, for when it suited his purpose, and depending on the ideological context, he was ready to let this anti-Fascist exercise be included in his filmography. A second contemporary witness, albeit one who was only to express himself on the matter a few years later, is worth quoting here. The Communist writer Álvaro Custodio was well positioned to have access to inside information: his wife, Isabel Richart Sotes, worked with Manuel Colino, one of the enablers of the *Espagne 1936* project. In a well-documented article on Buñuel published in the Mexico City magazine *La Semana Cinematográfica* in January 1949, an article on which the subject seemingly collaborated, and one intended, by establishing his "credentials," to gain him another chance in the Mexican film industry after the relative failure of *Gran casino* (1947), Custodio had no hesitation in attributing *Espagne 1936* to Buñuel: beneath a photo of the mustachioed, pipe-smoking director is the caption "Luis Buñuel, the great director to whom are owed *Le Chien andalou* [*sic*] and *L'Âge d'or*, the two greatest films of Surrealism, and the magnificent documentaries *Tierra sin pan* (*Las Hurdes*) and *España 1936*. His name has been cited alongside those of the best directors in the history of cinema."[48]

Dating the *Espagne 1936* project presents little difficulty. We suggest a start date of the beginning of November 1936 (at the earliest) and a certain end date of the third week of February 1937. The former is more tentative but would coincide with both the last datable bits of footage—the arrival of Moroccan troops in Oviedo in the first week of November—and the mutation of the Propaganda Section of the Ministry of State Education and Fine Arts into the Ministry of Propaganda on 4 November. Determining this start date is rendered more problematical by the fact that Buñuel was also working on the sonorization of *Las Hurdes* at this time; namely, between the end of October 1936 and its release as *Terre sans pain* on 19 December 1936. For the end date, we possess a document that fixes this: on 20 February Buñuel sent a telegram from Rue de la Pépinière to diplomat Francisco García Lorca—brother of the assassinated poet and knight founder in 1923 of the Order of Toledo—at the Spanish Embassy in Brussels, instructing him not to give a copy of *Espagne 1936* to anyone without his (Buñuel's) written permission.[49] The film was finished by 20 February, then.

It comes as no surprise to find that the Republican officials at the Spanish Embassy in Paris were being spied upon by the French state. In keeping with such surveillance, a copy of Buñuel's telegram was forwarded by the director general of the Sûreté Nationale to the prefect of police on 6 March 1937. A follow-up report, prepared in April for the French minister of the interior, provides further detail: "With a view to attracting worldwide attention in its favor, the Spanish Government has decided to embark on a campaign of film propaganda abroad. For this purpose, the Spanish ambassador in Paris has designated one of his attachés, M. Buñuel Don Luis, born 22 February 1900 (diplomatic passport of 22 December 1936), who, in October last, rented an office at 24, Rue de la Pépinière to this end. Only M. Buñuel is entitled to negotiate the renting of propaganda films, following the favorable opinion of the French censors. Only one of the films envisaged has hitherto been made. It is called *Espagne 36* and has already been screened in many cinemas in the capital."[50] What a pity this omniscient police spy did not enlarge on the list of planned films!

It is only by cross-referencing the data of the two filmographic fiches that we may get a more accurate idea of who produced *Espagne 1936*: namely, the new Ministry of Propaganda in Valencia and Ciné-Liberté in Paris. Ciné-Liberté was a second metamorphosis of the cinema section of the French AEAR, the first being the short-lived Alliance du Cinéma Indépendant (ACI). The ACI was founded in November 1935 as part of the Communist Maison de la Culture organization promoted by Louis Aragon, which devoted itself, on behalf of the proletariat, to the defense and propagation of bourgeois culture in the face of Fascist attacks upon it. The activities of the ACI seem to have been limited to private screenings of movies that had failed to pass the censors;

spectatorship was its goal, then. Ciné-Liberté marks a more militant phase of pro-Communist film production, and between its inception in late January 1936 and its demise three or so years later the cooperative was responsible for two major works—*La Vie est à nous*, produced for the PCF; and *La Marseillaise* (Jean Renoir, 1938), produced for the Société "La Marseillaise" and paid for in part by public subscription—plus a series of lesser ones, which it originated, at times using funding from the PCF, or made for other organizations, or then again adapted as French versions. Its original works include *Grèves d'occupation* (1936); *14 juillet 1789–14 juillet 1937* (1937); *Hommage à la Commune* (1937); *Magazine Populaire n° 1* (1937), and *Magazine Populaire n° 2* (1937), all of these made by the Ciné-Liberté collective, plus *À l'aide du peuple basque* (Jean-Paul Dreyfus, 1937). The original works it produced for the PCF are *Le Souvenir* (1937), *La Vie d'un homme* (1937), and *Fils du peuple* (1937), all directed by Dreyfus, plus *La Grande Espérance* (Ciné-Liberté collective, 1938). *Le Temps des cerises* (Jean-Paul Dreyfus, 1937) was produced for the PCF and the Société "La Marseillaise."

Espagne 1936 may be filed under the heading of the Ciné-Liberté production for other organizations—in this instance the Republican Ministry of Propaganda in Valencia—as may the following: *L'ABC de la liberté* (Jean-Paul Dreyfus, 1937) for the Société "La Marseillaise"; *Sur les routes d'acier* (Boris Peskine, 1938) for the Fédération des Cheminots and the CGT; *Les Bâtisseurs* (Jean Epstein, 1938) for the Fédération Nationale du Bâtiment and the CGT; and *Les Métallos* (Jacques Lemare, 1938) for the Union des Syndicats Métallurgiques de la Seine and the CGT. French adaptations of English-language films are *Victoire de la vie* (Henri Cartier[-Bresson] and Herbert Kline, 1938) and *Cœur d'Espagne* (Herbert Kline and Géza Karpathi, 1938), both produced by Frontier Films along with different American, Canadian, and French medical aid organizations; plus *Refuge* (Irving Lerner, 1939). Ciné-Liberté also distributed *Terre d'Espagne*, the French version of *The Spanish Earth*. Between May 1936 and March 1937 the Communist cooperative published a monthly magazine, *Ciné-Liberté*. Interestingly, no mention is made therein of *Espagne 1936*. In passing, Dreyfus's hyperactivity during 1937 would suggest that the attention he gave to *Espagne 1936* cannot have been of the lingering kind.

It is here that we must pause to consider the authorship of the commentary that accompanies the images of *Espagne 1936*. Within the deficient historiography of the division of labor on this movie, the commentary is ascribed now to Buñuel and Unik, now to Unik and Buñuel, presumably with a connotation of primary and secondary responsibility. It was Aranda who first put forward this attribution when he said: "Trying to remember in response to our questions, Buñuel recently recalled an episode in which he didn't take part: in 1938 his co-scriptwriter and coauthor of the commentaries of *Las Hurdes, Tierra sin pan* and of this new documentary, [*Espagne 1936*] took Jean-Paul [Dreyfus], who was attempting to monopolize the copyright of the work, to the trade-union courts in Paris. Sentence was passed in favor of Pierre Unik."[51]

This, we believe, is a false memory on Buñuel's part. A legal dispute did arise between Unik and Dreyfus about a script credit, and there was a court case, but this concerned *Le Temps des cerises*, and Unik lost. There is a major contradiction within the memory trace: is it possible that the commentary of a compilation film that didn't even have credits would be the cause of litigation? Aside from the remark made to Aranda during the 1960s, nowhere else in the literature does Buñuel mention his collaboration on the voice-over text of *Espagne 1936*—he may disavow several other roles having to do with this film, but that one never comes into the frame. In the light of this, we would suggest that the commentary be attributed to Unik alone, although Buñuel may have acted in an advisory capacity when it came to explicating the content of the source material. There are several reasons for this: (1) the first version of the movie was the French one, as proved by the three-month delay before the release of *España 1936*, namely the time it took to prepare a Spanish version; (2) Unik was deeply involved in the cinema at the time, especially with Dreyfus, and given his track record and political leanings, Unik must have been a member of Ciné-Liberté; (3) Unik's involvement in cinema was more or less restricted to writing descriptive commentaries; and (4) stylistically speaking, the *Espagne 1936* commentary bears his stamp.

Espagne 1936 opens with a title:

> A great film report / *Espagne 1936* / The documents that are to be placed before you have been shot on the various fronts in Spain by different cameramen, always under difficult conditions and often at the risk of their lives. Objectively, we have sought, turn and turn about, to present those whom public opinion calls "rebels," "Loyalists," "nationalists" and "Reds." In 1937 the cinema must devote itself to following world events, to reproducing them, to publicizing them, to revealing them to the men of all countries. This documentary on the war in Spain, this unique film report, has no goal other than serving the cause of history. / In 1931 the Spanish Monarchy collapses, to great popular enthusiasm. The Spanish Republic is born.

After repeated viewings of *Espagne 1936* and close scrutiny of the 1,500 diverse frame stills and 889 entries of the splendid *Catálogo general del cine de la Guerra Civil*, plus our own experience as film viewers, we are in a position to identify some of the source material. The bulk of it consists, naturally, of newsreels. We

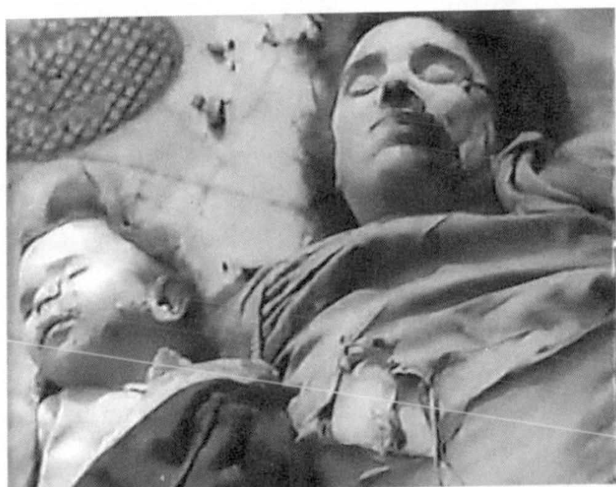

Image filmed by Karmen of a dead mother and her child, the victims of a Fascist air raid, which was used in *Espagne 1936*. (Filmoteca Española, Madrid)

The poignant image of rows of waiting coffins in *Espagne 1936*, from footage shot by Karmen. (Filmoteca Española, Madrid)

have already insisted on the multidirectional recycling—due to Buñuel, we believe—of the Spanish footage shot by Karmen and Makaseev, so it will come as no surprise that some of the most striking and iconic imagery in *Espagne 1936* is theirs: a shot of a working-class Madrid woman in a shawl on the verge of tears after a bombing raid; a "No pasarán" banner straddling a Madrid street; a close-up of Buenaventura Durruti, "Head of the Catalan column," as the quietistic voice-over euphemistically puts it; the nocturnal burning of the Mercado del Carmen, Madrid. Most dramatic of all are Karmen's eerie close-ups of the pallid, bloodied corpses of mothers and children killed during a bombardment, followed by a warehouse full of modest coffins; a climactic sequence that is all the more moving because of the accompanying silence on the soundtrack. Originating in *Events in Spain* numbers 10, 11, and 12, seen in the USSR in November 1936, many of these shots, as well as being included in *Espagne 1936*, would be recycled once more in a ten-minute Soviet compilation,

Madrid Aflame (1937), released in French, English, and Spanish versions; the latter (*Madrid en llamas*) was distributed by Laya Films.

Laya Films, the Barcelona-based production and distribution company created in November 1936 by the Commissariat of Propaganda of the Generalitat de Catalunya (the Catalan autonomous government), was a source of some of the images in *Espagne 1936*, images taken from its newsreels numbers 2 and 3 (January–February 1937): militiamen crossing snow-covered terraces in the Pyrenean foothills north of Huesca, for instance; or a zigzagging line of Republican trenches on the southern front. A Laya Films mainstay was Joan Castanyer, who'd been part of Buñuel's expatriate circle in Paris after 1925 and had appeared as an extra in *L'Âge d'or*. In 1935 Castanyer originated the idea for *Le Crime de M. Lange* with its director, Jean Renoir, before Jacques Prévert got down to writing the script; Castanyer was also assistant director and joint set designer on this pre–Front Populaire comedy. The head of the Commissariat of Propaganda was Dalí's boyhood friend, and himself a bit-part player in *Un chien andalou*, Jaume Miravitlles. In February 1937 Laya Films was to briefly collaborate with Film Popular to co-produce the important newsreel series *España al día*, issued in Spanish, Catalan, English, and French editions. (In May–June Film Popular would become sole producer of *España al día* until January 1939.) Carmen Meana, the wife of Cuban Communist Manuel Colino, whose name appears above, was a Film Popular employee.

The greater part of the footage used in *Espagne 1936* originates in the weekly French newsreels *Éclair Journal* and *Gaumont Actualités*, stripped, of course, of their original voice-overs. In September 1936 *Éclair Journal* produced a digest of its Civil War material called *La tragedia española* for distribution in Spanish-speaking areas. Since many an image from it resurfaces in *Espagne 1936*, it may be that Buñuel/Dreyfus looked no further than this. It seems more likely, however, that they scrutinized the common source for *La tragedia española*: the weekly installments of *Éclair Journal*, starting with number 8 (19 February 1936) and ending with number 45 (4 November 1936). We invoke some of the more vivid shots from these: seminarists crossing the border at Hendaye under the impassive gaze of the gendarmes; nationalist troops in a rain-soaked square in Vera de Bidasoa, near San Sebastian; the warship *Churucca* in the port of Tangiers (all from *Éclair Journal* number 31 of 29 July). Militiamen guarding boxes of art treasures in Barcelona (number 34 of 19 August). Before an enthusiastic crowd, General Queipo de Llano histrionically kissing the Spanish flag (number 35 of 26 August). Also in Sevilla, Joaquín Miranda, the head of Falange Española in Andalusia, leaving his office amid Fascist salutes; a column of Francoist militiamen on horseback, with rifles and straw sombreros, on the road from Sevilla to

A frame still from *Espagne 1936* showing seminarists fleeing from Spain across the border at Hendaye at the start of the Civil War. (Filmoteca Española, Madrid)

Córdoba (the two from *Éclair Journal* number 36 of 2 September; the episode is entitled "What Goya Didn't See"). And last, an animated image of pliers closing around the word "Madrid" (number 43 of 21 October). *Gaumont Actualités* images include the following shots: militiamen drilling unarmed recruits (installment of 7 August); fighting near Irún, with militiamen crossing a road and attacking a farmhouse (installment of 28 August); and Dolores Ibárruri pronouncing a message of solidarity with the French people in a fluty voice (installment of 11 September). Interestingly, *Gaumont Actualités* also used material shot by Roman Karmen in its 18 December 1936 segment, which consisted entirely of his footage of the bombardment of Madrid. Buñuel/Dreyfus used some of the same shots, like those of an enormous bomb crater in the Puerta del Sol and enemy planes flying over the city, but it is likely that their source was a more direct one: the commercial delegation at the Soviet Embassy in Paris. Judging by the fifty or so *Pathé Journal* frame stills from the Second Republic and Civil War period included in the *Catálogo general*, the makers of *Espagne 1936* did not use this, the third major French producer of newsreel footage, as a resource.

Espagne 1936 grew out of ideological (and practical) urgency: when necessary, Buñuel/Dreyfus were capable of appropriating the near at hand. There are several newsreel shots transposed from *La Vie est à nous* (of which Dreyfus was both co-director and co-scriptwriter): a swastika plus goosestepping Wehrmacht soldiers and a speechifying Hitler (in silence on the *Espagne 1936* soundtrack; to the sound of a barking dog on *La Vie est à nous*); a fasces and a speechifying Mussolini; a violently foreshortened cannon on a warship; an exploding farmhouse; the pouring of molten steel; and so forth.

To continue on the theme of newsreel footage, Aranda was obviously right to list Karmen as a cinematographer (by proxy) in his entry on *Espagne 1937* [*sic*], but we believe he was wrong—as have been all the historians who've followed him—to do so in the case of Manuel Villegas López. While Villegas López's *Madrid*, compiled toward the end of November 1937, uses some of the same material as *Espagne 1936*, there is no evidence that this head of the Film Services of the Undersecretariat of Propaganda after May 1937 was active as a filmmaker before that date.

But newsreel is not the only resource used in *Espagne 1936*. In the preamble to the outbreak of the Civil War there is a brief sequence of Masereel-style black-and-white drawings of the Asturias uprising of October 1934 by Communist artist Helios Gómez. There are fleeting images of still photographs by Robert Capa (taken in November–December 1936) and Chim. Capa (Endre Ernö Friedmann), a Hungarian, and Chim (to whom we've already alluded) were in Spain photographing for, respectively, *Vu* (published by Lucien Vogel, Vaillant-Couturier's father-in-law) and *Regards*. As the editor of *Regards*, Unik was in a privileged position to have instant access to the photojournalism arriving from both frontline and rear. There is an animated map, a common enough device in didactic documentaries. (In this instance the animator may have been Griffoul, Ciné-Liberté's in-house specialist; is the map in *Terre sans pain* his, too?) An animated diagram of the balance of power in the Republican government avoids the initials CNT, employing the word "syndicalists" instead. Perhaps most strikingly, there is fiction film, which is granted the same status *qua* verisimilitude as the "actuality" footage. Clips from Lewis Milestone's *All Quiet on the Western Front* (1930) served to depict the "muck and bullets" of contemporary (1936) trench warfare. At another point in *Espagne 1936* we see the victims of an execution, represented by fedora-wearing silhouettes subsiding before a brick wall illuminated by automobile headlights; we would hazard a guess that this footage comes from a Hollywood noir, perhaps a version of the Saint Valentine's Day Massacre: according to Carlos Clarens, the first such version was *Bad Company* (Tay Garnett, 1931),[52] which we've never seen; there is a very similar sequence in *Scarface* (Howard Hawks, 1932), but it doesn't quite "fit." And the images of fleeing citizens at night—from a Soviet movie, perhaps—are an echo of Buñuel's use of almost identical footage from *The White Sister* in *L'Âge d'or*. As a matter of fact, it is worth pointing to the long-distance continuities between Buñuel's second film and *Espagne 1936* in terms of the insouciant use of heterogeneous found footage: newsreels, documentaries, fiction films. All have the power to convince; all are equally "real" within filmic discourse.

Attention has been drawn by film historians to the striking opening shot in *Espagne 1936*, a shot that makes explicit reference to Eisenstein's *October* (1927),

The first shot in *Espagne 1936*, which describes a rhetorical figure symbolizing the fall of the Spanish monarchy, and also constitutes a quote of the opening sequence in Eisenstein's *October* (1927). (Filmoteca Española, Madrid)

thus yoking the film—for the discerning cinephile, at least—to the iconosphere of the Soviet avant-garde, by then expunged. What we see, in imitation of the destruction (and, later, reverse-motion restitution) of a statue of Tsar Alexander III in Saint Petersburg, is—and the identification is Aranda's—the equestrian statue of Felipe IV in Madrid's Plaza de Oriente turning head over heels in a similar synecdoche, one connoting the recent abdication of Alfonso XIII. Rather than rotating the camera to achieve this effect, we would posit the gyration of a still photograph before the lens. Like the rest of *Espagne 1936*, this shot was doubtless inducted from some other source. But which? One prime candidate would be the documentary begun in 1931 by Carlos Velo and Fernando G. Mantilla and finished by them for Cifesa in 1935: *El Escorial de Felipe II*, known today in a mutilated version, following some drastic re-editing, particularly of the anti-royalist commentary, on the part of the Francoists in 1939 (the handiwork was Ruiz Castillo's, in point of fact). Were this attribution to be correct, the shot would be by José María Beltrán.

Where the soundtrack is concerned, a comparison between *Espagne 1936* and *Terre sans pain* suggests that the commentary might have been delivered by the same voice, that of Abel Jacquin, a middle-of-the-bill French screen actor whose career began in 1930 with the arrival of sound, and who also co-directed a comedy, *Les Deux "Monsieur" de Madame*, in 1933. Such a strategy would have a certain logic, since Buñuel was working on the two projects at the same time. On the other hand, the voice may belong to Gaston Modot, as stated in all the literature that draws on the entry contained in Aranda's biography. This, too, would be logical, since Modot was a committed member of Ciné-Liberté, the co-producers of the film. Doubt must remain on this point. We can state definitively, however, that no Beethoven is to be heard in *Espagne 1936*, the identifiable music consisting of snatches of *The Internationale*, the *Himno de Riego* (a nineteenth-century song that became the Republican anthem), and the *sardana*, *Els Segadors*. It is worth remembering here that in Paris in February 1937 the PCF's Éditions Sociales Internationales published a three-record set, by La Cobla de Barcelona, which included the last two songs. Starting the film with Catalonia's national hymn, while the monarchy "falls" in that opening synecdoche, may have been an allusion to the 1640 Catalan uprising against Felipe IV; to Catalonia, rather than encircled Madrid, as the spearhead of resistance to the forces of reaction. The remaining music is of the anonymous "mood" variety. For example, a jaunty tune accompanies footage of the plucky Republic at work; or bugles and drums, when it's on a war footing. Mimetic sound effects are used to underline the images; but so is silence, at times more tellingly so. Appearing at the very end of *Espagne 1936* are the words "Contrôle, L. Maurice C.T.M., Gennevilliers, France." Patronized by the PCF, the Laboratoires Cinéma-Tirage L. Maurice would, as stipulated in the contract between Buñuel and Ivens vis-à-vis *The Spanish Earth*, be used for the developing of the negative material shot in Spain by Ferno.

In keeping with the general thrust of pro-Republican propaganda in the print and audiovisual media during the Civil War, *Espagne 1936* puts forward four theses: (1) The uprising is by officers who swore allegiance to the Republic; they are, therefore, traitors and their movement is unlawful. (2) Germany and Italy give military aid to the rebels, a fact denounced by Álvarez del Vayo at the Society of Nations in Geneva. (3) The Republic is a civilized and peace-loving regime, a democracy just like France, Great Britain, and the United States; hence anarchist and anticlerical excesses are hidden. (4) The war threatens peace in Europe; a title states that Madrid has become Spain's Verdun, and the last sentence of the commentary says: "When will this monstrous war, which endangers the peace of Europe, end?" In verbal terms, such ideas are expressed in a commentary that is both terse and stoical; one that, like Buñuel and Unik's work on *Terre sans pain*, employs an unruffled tone of neutrality.

We are now in a position to propose a new, more accurate fiche for *Espagne 1936*, with the proviso that such an entity is always open to revision and refinement, and that educated guesswork has played a part in some of the following:

Espagne 1936
Title of the Spanish version: *España 1936*

Title of the Italian version: *Spagna 1936* (made ca. 1945)
1936–37 France
35 mm, b & w
Date of release: French version, 8 March 1937 (Paris); Spanish version, 7 June 1937 (Madrid)
Producers: Ciné-Liberté in Paris and the Ministry of Propaganda of the Government of the Second Republic in Valencia
Logistical support from Valencia: Manuel Colino
Choice of material and supervision at the rough cut and positive print stages: Luis Buñuel
Filmed sequences: Roman Karmen and Boris Makaseev of Soyuzkinochronica, Moscow, between 23 August 1936 and February 1937; Laya Films, Barcelona, newsreels 2 and 3, January–February 1937; *Éclair Journal*, Paris, numbers 8–45, 19 February–4 November 1936; *Gaumont Actualités*, Paris, installments of August–September 1936; material from *La Vie est à nous* (Jacques Becker, Jacques Brunius, Henri Cartier, Jean-Paul Dreyfus, Jean Renoir, and André Zwoboda, 1936); from *All Quiet on the Western Front* (Lewis Milestone, 1930); from an unidentified Hollywood film noir; from *El Escorial de Felipe II* (Carlos Velo and Fernando G. Mantilla, 1931–35); drawings by Helios Gómez; photographs by Robert Capa and Chim; maps by Griffoul.
Commentary: Pierre Unik
Editing: Jean-Paul Dreyfus
Voiceover of the French version: Gaston Modot or Abel Jacquin
Music: *Els Segadors*, *The Internationale*, *Himno de Riego*, plus anonymous "mood" music
Supervision of the soundtrack: Luis Buñuel
Processing: Laboratoires Cinéma-Tirage L. Maurice, Gennevilliers
Original language: French, Spanish
Length: 35 minutes

Espagne 1936 was one of four films available for release by the Ministry of Propaganda between November 1936 and February 1937. On 27 February the first stone was laid in Paris of the Spanish Pavilion for the International Exhibition of Art and Technology in Modern Life.[53] Henceforth, and until it closed on 25 November, priority would be given by the government in Valencia and the Spanish Embassy in Paris to the propaganda opportunity provided by the exhibition.

The appointment in late September 1936 of Ambassador Araquistáin had marked a brusque change from the peacetime project—mooted in March 1935, in response to the French invitation, but never implemented—of promoting Spain as a simple destination for business and tourism, to one in which the pavilion was to serve as a vector, across a wide variety of media, for the ideological values of a beleaguered but defiant Republic. One of Araquistáin's first acts, with the collusion of Álvarez del Vayo, was to set the wheels in motion to replace the chief organizer of the Spanish contribution to the exhibition, Carlos Batlle (who'd been appointed the day before the military uprising), with the philosopher, PSOE activist, and rector of Madrid University, José Gaos. With Gaos's appointment, and that of architects Josep Lluis Sert and Luis Lacasa, a certain urgency would be applied to the planning and construction of the diaphanous Corbusian pavilion, sited, symbolically, in the shadow of the Third Reich colossus designed by Albert Speer and obliquely facing the USSR's "plinth-building" for a gigantic Socialist-Realist sculpture by Vera Mukhina. Despite all the urgency, the Spanish pavilion would not be inaugurated until 12 July 1937, seven weeks after the opening of the exhibition proper.

Wearing his cap as a film programmer, Buñuel was to play a part in this media offensive. But before getting to this episode, it is worth citing the pavilion personnel who were old friends or comrades of his. Much earlier in this book we came across Gaos in the company of Buñuel and Sánchez Ventura in Zaragoza at the founding of the Second Republic; that day the cineaste, who was on the point of joining the PCE, would make fun of Gaos's Socialist convictions. Communist graphic designer Mariano Rawicz recalled a visit from co-religionists Lacasa and Buñuel to his Madrid apartment on the eve of the insurrection in Asturias in October 1934.[54] The general secretary of the pavilion, the artist Hernando Viñes—whose wife Loulou was the daughter of PCF stalwart Francis Jourdain, a prime mover of the AEAR, and the goddaughter of art historian Élie Faure—was a knight of the Order of Toledo, and snapshots exist of Buñuel and the Viñes couple in a Toledo bell tower, taken on 10 May 1936. The Viñeses also served on the Franco-Spanish Committee. A founding member of said order, painter José María Ucelay, was Basque Country Commissioner—both Euskadi and Catalonia were represented in the pavilion as autonomous entities. Among the cultural attachés in the embassy was prose writer and editor José Bergamín, the "foul Jesuit" (according to Breton) who in 1938 would preface an abject anti-POUM pamphlet signed by Max Rieger, pseudonym of the *L'Humanité* journalist and NKVD (Soviet secret police) amanuensis Georges Soria.[55] Juan Larrea was another attaché. In 1937 the typescript of his unfinished tale, *Ilegible, hijo de flauta*, dating from 1927–28, was literally borne off on the wind in Vallecas, but after hearing Larrea describe it ten years later in Mexico, Buñuel would work intermittently with him on a screen version that was abandoned only in 1963.[56] Also present in the embassy—presumably to act as a liaison with the PCF and its media arm—were Georges and Jacqueline Sadoul. Urged on by the late Juan Piqueras and by Léon Moussinac, Georges Sadoul had recently embarked on his mammoth film history project; his wife Jacqueline (or Nora, as she was known) was Henri Cartier's sister; Cartier would become Henri Cartier-Bresson. Indeed, her husband was to write the commentary for her brother's last-gasp documentary, *Espagne vivra* (1939). Nora had been present in July 1932 when Buñuel, Unik, and Sadoul roughed out the *Wuthering Heights* scheme in Cernay-la-Ville. Proximity to Buñuel did not, however, guarantee access to inside information about his nebulous activities or his political penchants: thirty years later Max Aub, cultural and propaganda attaché at the embassy after December 1936, as well as assistant curator of the exhibition, would devote his final energies to ascertaining, not wholly with success, just what those activities and politics had been in the institution where they worked side by side.

The Spanish Pavilion was on three floors, the ground floor being occupied by a patio-cum-auditorium with a capacity of five hundred, where plays, folk dancing, and music events were to be staged. Films would be shown there, too. Picasso's *Guernica* and Calder's *Mercury Fountain* were also on permanent display in this semi-open-air space. The second floor, to which visitors acceded next, was divided into two sections, the first devoted to the regions of Spain, with images of the nation's landscapes, architecture, and customs presented in photomural form—the work of Josep Renau and his team—alongside traditional handicrafts. The second section was given over entirely to the visual arts, much of it of an anti-Fascist, Socialist-Realist orientation. On descending to the floor below, visitors passed Miró's *The Reaper*. The first level also had two sections, one dedicated to the Republic's social welfare and education programs, information about the Civil War, and statistics about industry and agriculture; the other section was devoted to the graphic arts: posters, illustrated books, magazines. Again, Renau's Lissitzky-style handiwork was much in evidence here. The grounds of the pavilion, meanwhile, were dotted with the eye-catching sculptures of Picasso, Alberto Sánchez, and Julio González.

On 15 June *L'Humanité* printed a roundup of the pavilion's future "live" performances:

> After the inauguration of the Spanish Pavilion, that is, around the end of this month and during the entire Exhibition as a whole, a series of dance and film shows, etc., will take place in the pavilion patio. The shows will unfold in the following order:

1) During peak times, record concerts of classical music and Spanish popular songs.
2) In principle, a private session will be organized every Wednesday evening to present documentary films and newsreels, which will be screened for the public on the other evenings of the week. These film shows will alternate with performances devoted to regional dance and music.

   Among the films that will be shown, and which will number some forty titles, are: *Reforme agraire, Guerre dans la campagne, Route de Don Quichotte, Symphonie basque, Espagne 36, Madrid, Escorial, Guadalquivir, Almadrabas, Tribunal des eaux, Juan Simon.*
3) Every two or three weeks the groups listed below will follow one another. These groups will appear twice a week and on each occasion will give four performances a day.

   These matinée and evening performances will follow one another every half-hour.

   The Castilian group, Basque group, Catalan group, Valencian group, Aragonese group, Asturian group, Andalusian group.
4) Towards the end of August or the beginning of September the university theater group "La Barraca" will give matinée and evening performances for two weeks.
5) Twice a month writers will read or recite literary texts or poems.[57]

In his rather glum report addressed to President Negrín on 21 July about the continuing delays in installing the final exhibits in the now inaugurated pavilion, Gaos commented that at least the film projections were going ahead: "Thanks to Buñuel, we have the cinema up and running for two or three weeks."[58] The recorded music recitals were also functioning, courtesy of the Cuban musicologist and journalist Alejo Carpentier (the future theorist of "the marvelous real" had been a signatory of the 1930 anti-Breton tract *Un cadavre*). Gaos's remarks imply that Buñuel took part in selecting the films listed in the *L'Humanité* article, although it is impossible to say whether or not the choice was exclusively his. According to the anonymous journalist, those eleven titles were but the first installment: some forty movies were planned to fill the twenty or so weekly slots planned until the International Exhibition ended in November. And this because, as revealed in a 21 June communiqué by Gaos, the pavilion screenings were to include two one-reelers—a reel runs for some ten minutes—one a news bulletin and the other a documentary, plus the occasional two- or three-reeler, which could be a fiction subject.[59] All of this adds up to forty titles, two to a program.

Buñuel's contribution was, moreover, probably a one-off, stopgap affair, for the baton was swiftly handed off to an official commission headed by Manuel Villegas López, assisted by Juan M. Plaza and the composer Rodolfo Halffter. One of the founders of the Alliance of Anti-Fascist Intellectuals for the Defense of Culture, Halffter was head of the music department of the Undersecretariat of Propaganda and had written scores for fiction films by Harry d'Abbadie d'Arrast and Edgar Neville, as well as for two documentaries by Velo and Mantilla: *Infinitos* (1935) and *Castillos de Castilla* (1936). During the Civil War his music was to accompany four further documentaries—three of them distributed by Film Popular—directed by Rafael Gil, Jean Lordier, and Mauricio A. Sollin. Among the exiled Halffter's many screen credits in Mexico are *Los olvidados* and *Nazarín*.

Of the eleven films programmed by 15 June, seven were documentaries of a historical, monumental, cultural, or work-related nature, the majority of them produced in the years immediately before the outbreak of the Civil War: *La ruta de Don Quijote* (Ramón Biadiu, 1934), *El Guadalquivir* (Heinrich Gaertner or Jesús Romo Raventós, 1935), *Reforma agraria* (unidentified director, 1935), *El Escorial de Felipe II* (Carlos Velo and Fernando G. Mantilla, 1935), *Almadrabas* (Velo and Mantilla, 1935), *Sinfonía vasca* (Adolf Troz, 1936), and *El Tribunal de las Aguas* (Ángel Villatoro, 1937). A further three were anti-Fascist documentaries on the origins and effects of the fighting in the Republican zone: *Guerra en el campo* (Arturo Ruiz Castillo, 1936), *Espagne 1936* (Luis Buñuel/Jean-Paul Dreyfus, 1937), and *Madrid* (Manuel Villegas López, 1937). The eleventh and last title was a fiction film: *La hija de Juan Simón* (José Luis Sáenz de Heredia and Nemesio M. Sobrevila, 1935).[60] Aside from these, we know of the certain projecting of three other titles: *Castillos de Castilla* (Carlos Velo and Fernando G. Mantilla, 1935), *Galicia Saudade* (Carlos Velo, 1936), and *Finisterre* (Fernando G. Mantilla, 1936). The last two films were entered for the more general "Exhibition Grand Prize of French Cinema," on whose jury sat Buñuel and Aub, with Velo's documentary receiving an award and Mantilla's a diploma of honor.[61]

This wasn't the only time Buñuel would serve with Aub on a jury. In his official appointment, signed on 17 December 1936 by Wenceslao Roces, undersecretary of the Ministry of State Education and Fine arts, Aub was mandated to form, along with Lacasa, Bergamín, and Louis Aragon (representing "French writers"), the Delegate Committee for the Expansion of Spanish Culture Abroad. As part of this effort it was proposed that Aub collaborate with Piscator on a production of Lope de Vega's *Fuenteovejuna* in Paris in May 1937. In a 10 April report to Araquistáin on the Piscator project, Aub mentioned contacting Dreyfus, in his capacity as organizer of the Union des Théâtres Indépendants de France, on budgetary matters, and alluded to the forming of a committee consisting of Buñuel, Bergamín, Lacasa, and himself to control the staging of *Fuenteovejuna*. The project would come to naught, however, following Roces's negative reaction to a screening in Valencia of Piscator's Mezhrabpom movie, *The Revolt of the Fishermen*.[62]

As far as the eleven listed films are concerned, the foregrounding of positive documentary images of peacetime Spain under the Second Republic, with the entwining of modernizing as well as archaic strands, and the playing down of the war, its political causes and consequences, especially the internecine strife among the Left, underlined the relatively muted ideological narrative visible on the walls of the pavilion. Although the film program privileged the "realist" genre of documentary, even a popular melodrama like *La hija de Juan Simón*, given its progressive depiction of contemporary gender relations, might resonate with, say, Renau's juxtaposed photos of "old" and "new" Spanish womanhood: the former a richly bedecked "Albercana" bride—her groom could be one of the horsemen we see at the start of *Terre sans pain*—and the latter a boiler-suited militiawoman.

It is likely that Buñuel's two contributions to the pavilion's screenings—*Espagne 1936* and the Filmófono movie—were programmed by him during those first few sessions in July and August 1937. Thanks to his efforts, and to those of Jean Grémillon and Ricardo Urgoiti, the master negatives of the four Filmófono productions—including *La hija de Juan Simón*—had arrived in March from Spain, where their complicated exit had been coordinated by Fernando Remacha. According to one source, it was the musician from Navarre, Buñuel's right-hand man in Filmófono, who presented *La hija de Juan Simón* in the pavilion.[63] *Espagne 1936* had, of course, been shown in Paris prior to the Exposition, first in the *huis clos* of Communist film culture, with screenings at the Studio Pallas Athénée on 8 March 1937 and La Mutualité on 6 April, but then also commercially: that is, from 9 to 15 April at the Cine Ce Soir, with *Nitchevo* (Jacques de Baroncelli, 1936); from 16 to 22 April at the Artistic, with *The House of the Dead* (Vasili Fyodorov, 1932; a Mezhrabpomfilm production written by Viktor Shklovsky); from 23 to 29 April at the Maine-Palace, with *Mr. Deeds Goes to Town* (Frank Capra, 1936); from 21 to 27 May at the Bellevilloise, with *Josette* (Christian-Jacque, 1936, starring Fernandel), and at Le Flandre, with *It's in the Air* (Charles Reisner, 1935, a Jack Benny comedy).[64] *Espagne 1936* also formed part of a PCF propaganda package, along with *La Vie est à nous* and *La Fête de l'Huma à Garches* (Jacques Lemare [attrib.], 1936), which could be hired from Films Populaires, the party's own agency, for screenings in locations off the beaten track. One of three vehicles, especially equipped with projection material by the PCF's Book and Press Diffusion Centre, undertook to deliver.[65]

One Buñuel film, a film to which he put his name, unlike the two that were shown at the International Exhibition, was conspicuous by its absence: *Terre sans pain*. Even with the ideological reframing provided by its anti-Fascist coda, the image it depicted of rural Spain under the Republic was too black, too corrosive, to segue with the "redemptive narrative" (as Jordana Mendelson has called it) of the Spanish Pavilion's "international discourse"—a discourse, that is, in harmony with the Comintern tactic of portraying Spain as a democracy under siege, struggling against Fascism, and not as a revolutionary state. A non-alarmist discourse aimed at currying favor with the Western powers, which on the face of it persisted in their policy of non-intervention.[66] *Terre sans pain* would be visible elsewhere during the International Exhibition, however. Advertised with the subtitle "Visions of Spain," it played between 6 and 11 October at the Ce Soir-Italiens with *Police mondaine* (Michel Bernheim and Christian Chamborant, 1937).

When it came to attracting public attention, the pavilion possessed one of the International Exhibition's biggest draws: Picasso's *Guernica*. Although he would claim to have disapproved of its grandiloquent propagandizing, Buñuel helped hang the huge canvas, along with other embassy officials. According to Larrea, the Spanish government, disappointed by the lack of manifest partisanship displayed by Picasso—whom Edgar Neville tried to win over to the Francoist cause—even considered removing the picture from the pavilion wall.[67] Invited by Renau, director general of fine arts, Picasso had been officially named as director of the Prado on 19 September 1936, the same day that Araquistáin's appointment as ambassador to Paris was announced and Buñuel received his brief from Álvarez del Vayo in Geneva. In December 1936 Renau arrived in the French capital to get the collaboration on the future pavilion of Picasso and other Paris-based Spanish artists such as Miró and Julio González. The second name on his list after Picasso's was Dalí's. The encounter between the latter, an anti-Stalinist of the first order, and Renau, a PCE hardliner, was, predictably, a disaster. The versions of what happened are disparate, and as entertaining as they are self-serving.

In his typically perverse narrative, Dalí offers to do a big mural "because at the time I wanted to test the Communists, and as I had a Republican passport there was no reason to refuse me doing a painting in the pavilion; but I knew it wouldn't work because there were all the party people and they knew my ideas and all; . . . and it didn't."[68] According to Renau's account:

> With a view to preparing [the] interviews [with the artists on his list], the Embassy put at my disposal a small office with a telephone and a secretary-cum-typist. Shortly after my second interview with Picasso, as I was dictating something to the secretary, Salvador Dalí burst unexpectedly into the office. Without so much as a by your leave he began to upbraid me at the top of his voice: saying that in the Government they knew nothing of what was happening in Paris; that Picasso was already finished and was a "tremendous" reactionary; that the only Communist Spanish painter in Paris was him; that we ought to let him take first place. The "visit" stunned me. At that time I was rather impulsive, and my self-control failed me. With one bound I was out of my chair and telling him I wasn't accustomed to having anyone shout at me: that if he had something to complain about he could do it right there and then—pointing to the telephone—to my Minister, the Head of the Government and even the President of the Republic himself. . . . I looked nervously for my address book (which was in my mac on a coat stand behind the table). When I turned round with the book in my hand, Dalí had disappeared. . . . The secretary told me he'd gone pale. Weeks later—I don't remember how many—he took part in a violent meeting organized in Paris by the POUM and the FAI against the Government of the Spanish Republic.[69]

Renau's final claim is nonsense, although it certainly reveals his own political paranoia. Given that Dalí is usually depicted as a craven, cynical fence-sitter when it comes to the Civil War, it is worth recalling that the exhibition proposal was his second attempt to put himself at the service of the Republic; the first being his wish to work for the Generalitat's Commissariat of Propaganda as "General Commissar of Public Imagination." To be sure, the seriousness and selflessness of these two offers must remain open to question.

Although Picasso painted *Guernica* for free as his gift to the Republic, Aub convinced him to accept a symbolic sum from the government to cover his expenses. We know this from an embassy document dated 31 May 1937 referring to "sums handed over by the cashier's office of the special acquisitions service for propaganda."[70] These sums extend from 3 October 1936 to 28 May 1937, the day Picasso received his check for 150,000 FF, and add up to a total of 4,300,851.10 FF. Of the sixty-four payments made, nine are to Buñuel and come to 464,000 FF. The first entry, dated 20 October, is annotated by hand: "Intelligence service, Paris," and the second, from 26 October: "Ditto . . . Spain," which may be a reference to *Espagne 1936*, meaning that the project was under way by then (70,000 FF were involved). Are these payments the secret funds for which, according to his own testimony, Buñuel did not need to account?[71] Or at least the ones dating to Araquistáin's time in office? With regard to the Ossorio and Pascua periods, while figures are cited for their mandates in a classic study of the Spanish Embassy and espionage, the sums are given over to agencies rather than agents; Buñuel isn't mentioned, in any event.[72]

It is worth drawing attention to some other names on the Embassy payroll. One is that of Arthur Koestler, the Hungarian-born polymath and future anti-Communist, at that time a committed KPD member, who on 12 October received 3,000 FF as "travel expenses." Said trip was probably to London, for Koestler's activities as a journalist and spy for the so-called Münzenberg Trust were triangulated between the British capital, Paris, and Spain. It is possible that the recipient of the £400 delivered by Buñuel in September for "an unidentified German who was going to go to Burgos, entering via Portugal" was for the Hungarian, whose first language was German.[73] Koestler's name appears once on the embassy's balance sheet, nothing like the nineteen times someone called Jean Laurent is listed. We have been unable to trace this man—Jean Laurent may have been a pseudonym—but what is important is that the first reference to him on 13 October is annotated "Agence Espagne," and that of the total propaganda budget, 2,425,000 FF—some 60 percent—was passed via Laurent to this agency.

Agence Espagne was set up by Münzenberg and Álvarez del Vayo; although appearances may have suggested otherwise, its de facto boss was Otto Katz. In December 1936 del Vayo would officially designate Ricardo Marín, a Communist who'd hitherto worked in the Soviet Embassy in Madrid, to serve as the agency's director. In his Christmas Day letter to Araquistáin confirming Marín in the post, the minister of foreign affairs insisted that the ambassador was to have the last word on controlling the agency. Del Vayo also referred in passing to getting Juan Vicens to assist in the operation. A few days later he wrote again, "Having thought it over, neither our friend Marín, whom I've sent you, nor Vicens, and probably none of those who'd like to make their mark in Paris right now is the man to *direct* the propaganda campaign. The leadership must always come from you."[74] Luis Araquistáin, that key figure in the Paris propaganda world, was eventually to fall foul of the realpolitik of the Third International, but at the beginning of his tenure his posture was assiduously pro-Soviet. In his personal archive there is a letter from Münzenberg dated 30 October 1936, which we quote in full since it gives an insight into the collusion of the propaganda machinery of the Comintern, the Spanish Embassy, and Agence Espagne:

Willi Münzenberg in Paris, ca. 1936. (Random House Archive and Library, Rushden, UK)

Dear Friend,

I've talked with my friends again and we've come to the conclusion that the book on the atrocities of the Whites must be published as soon as possible, especially after yesterday's terrible catastrophe in the Madrid school and after the Burgos people [Franco et al.] have proclaimed, in a huge announcement (2–3 pages in the *Times*, which is quite something), the publication of a book about our supposed atrocities. As a result, in order to get things moving we've convinced one of our best writers, comrade Koestler, who is familiar with both fronts, and have commissioned him to write the book immediately.

I earnestly request you to help him and to give him all the material and images, in accordance with the promise you gave me, especially the images the Spanish delegation of journalists brought back, and were it to be possible, today, so that our friend can start work tomorrow morning.

Furthermore, I would ask you to speak to comrade del Vayo by telephone so that finally all the material he and Rubio have on this affair is either brought immediately to Paris by special courier or, better still, is fetched by a special courier sent by you. In this way we would be sure the material is actually and rapidly obtained. We ought to include the material about the first big bombing of Madrid, especially of the schools, photos of wounded kids with descriptions of their lives, etc., since this material should have a chapter to itself in the book.

As it was you yourself, dear friend, who underlined the great importance of such a book during our conversation, I am convinced that you will help in this matter with all speed. We will make the preparations to guarantee rapid publication of the book in England, America and France, and also in the German language.

Comradely greetings,
Your W[illi].[75]

Koestler's book, complete with atrocity photos of mangled bodies following the bombardment of a children's home in Getafe, was to be published in January 1937 in German as *Menschenopfer Unerhört: Ein Swarzbüch uber Spanien*, and in French as *L'Espagne ensanglantée*, by Éditions Carrefour, a Paris press that, prior to being colonized by Münzenberg in spring 1933, had published two of Ernst's collage novels, *La Femme 100 têtes* (1929) and *Une semaine de bonté* (1930).[76] The Karmen/Makaseev footage included in *Espagne 1936* would obviously ratify, and resonate with, those Getafe atrocity photos.

As Koestler tells us, Katz, who was the anonymous author of several sensationalist anti-Nazi "Brown Books," including *The Nazi Conspiracy in Spain*, by the Editor of *The Brown Book of the Hitler Terror*, was "the unofficial chief of the Spanish Government's propaganda campaign in Western Europe, and had large funds (partly of Spanish, partly of Comintern origin) at his disposal.[77] These funds played a considerable part in securing the sympathy of influential French journalists, and of entire newspapers for the Loyalist cause. In fact, Otto was the grey eminence of the propaganda war, and was treated as such by everybody in the Spanish Embassy, including Álvarez del Vayo himself."[78] Thierry Wolton has provided a little more detail on this "slush fund" aimed at the media: "It was under the cover of Agence Espagne, created for the occasion, that Katz distributed his manna. His means were considerable, but we don't know the exact sum in the bank account opened at Morgan & Cie, 14, Place Vendôme. As a guide, we would draw attention to the fact that the Spanish government—the agency's main financial backer—was to lodge a complaint against Katz in 1939 (in the United States), accusing him of having diverted part of the money to the Comintern's account. The total amount embezzled was 2.5 million francs, that is, around 7 million of today's francs [i.e., in 1993], a tidy sum for fronting the influence-peddling operation over a period of three years (1936–39)."[79]

Beginning on 4 January 1937, a branch of the agency at 13, Rue de l'Ancienne Comédie, in the sixth arrondissement, published a daily newsletter in French under the rubric "Agence Espagne: Informations télégraphiques et téléphoniques de dernière heure."[80] In effect, an updated edition of this mimeographed one-page bulletin appeared every two hours. Its official director was Jean Fouquet, compiler of the monthly "Par le temps qui court" column in *Commune* between July 1936 and the magazine's demise in September 1939 (with his articles often appearing alongside Unik's). One of the agency's correspondents was Jeanette Vermeersch, Maurice Thorez's companion.

As well as the print media, Katz also dabbled in film production. On the basis of the success of *The Defense of Madrid* (1936), filmed for the PFI by Ivor Montagu and Norman McLaren on 16 mm color stock (later transferred to black and white), the institute would be given funds by Katz, Negrín, and the Spanish Embassy—for which, read "Buñuel"?—to make three twenty-minute films in Spain, including *Spanish ABC* and *Behind the Spanish Lines* (Thorold Dickinson and Sidney Cole, 1938).[81] Katz, that "smooth and slick operator" (in Koestler's words), was to meet a sorry end. After spying on Münzenberg for the Soviet secret service and deserting his boss when the latter broke with the Comintern in 1938, he was executed in December 1952 along with ten other defendants, many of them former members of the International Brigades, following the Slansky show trial in Prague.

Frontage of the Spanish Tourist Office on the Boulevard de la Madeleine in Paris with its window display of atrocity photos being scrutinized by a large crowd, ca. 1937–38. (Courtesy of the Tamiment Library, New York University)

Another important entity in the divulgation of pro-Republican propaganda was the Spanish Tourist Office, situated in the eighth arrondissement at 12b, Boulevard de La Madeleine, at its intersection with Rue Vignon. Run by the National Tourist Board, the office had been opened by the Primo de Rivera government in 1928 to publicize the 1929 expositions in Barcelona and Sevilla. During the Second Republic it continued to function as a vitrine for promoting the country as a tourist destination. With the outbreak of the Civil War that role would change. In July 1936 Joaquín Peinado was instructed to purge the office by Enrique Ramos, the minister of finance, who considered it to be "a nest of Fascists."[82] Peinado, a prominent member of the Paris School of Spanish painters, had settled in the city in November 1923, rubbing shoulders there with such expatriate *señoritos* as Buñuel, Vicens, José María Ucelay, and Francisco García Lorca. (His presence can be glimpsed in both *Un chien andalou* and *L'Âge d'or.*) With Josep Lluis Sert and the Ultraísta poet and literary critic Guillermo de la Torre, Peinado sought, and got, Araquistáin's assistance in converting the Spanish Tourist Office into the headquarters of the Delegation of Propaganda. On 2 April 1937 Carlos Esplá, minister of propaganda between November

1936 and the following May, wrote from Valencia to Araquistáin, proposing Adolfo Salazar, composer, music critic, and cofounder of the Alliance of Anti-Fascist Intellectuals for the Defense of Culture, as director of the Propaganda Office "organized in Paris by Ilya Eheremburg [*sic*]."[83] Given the imminent exit from power of the two politicians, this appointment came to nothing. The reference to the Soviet writer and journalist, however, is curious and begs the question: is the same institution involved?

The overarching objective of the office was to influence public opinion by endorsing the Comintern/PCF campaign, waged in the pages of *L'Humanité*, *Regards*, *Commune*, and elsewhere, against the "Hitlerization" of Spain and for the maintenance of trade between the latter and France. Keeping the border between the two countries open was a priority in order for the Soviet, European, and American arms that were secretly crossing the Hexagon to reach Spain. While the Léon Blum–led Front Populaire was in power, from June 1936 to April 1938, this occurred. However, in June 1938 the recently elected Daladier government, bending to British pressure, closed the border. The Delegation of Propaganda had forty-five feet of window space at its disposal along the Boulevard de la Madelaine. Displayed there were blowups of the photos of Capa or Chim—a resource for Buñuel and Dreyfus in *Espagne 1936*, remember—plus posters, publications from the front, and bulletins like those of Agence Espagne. An eyewitness, Guillermina Medrano, Republican Youth representative in the Youth Anti-Fascist Alliance, whose head office was in the same building, would state that "in the big display windows that gave onto the boulevard there was, when I arrived, a big photo of Pasionaria and other photos of the generals and heroes in our war. Almost all the propaganda, I quickly ascertained, showed celebrities who were members of the Communist Party or sympathizers with its slogans."[84]

In his late-1960s interview with Aub, Peinado highlighted the collaboration of Aragon, Tzara, and César Vallejo in the activities of the Spanish Tourist Office. Tzara had broken with the Surrealists in 1935 over the issue of Stalinism, an event signaled by his debut in July in number 23 of *Commune*; in number 42 (February 1937) he would contribute a poem called "Espagne 1936." In January 1937 he had taken over from Aragon as secretary of the Committee for the Defense of Spanish Culture, founded by the author of *Les Beaux Quartiers* in September 1936 under the umbrella of the Comintern's International Association of Writers for the Defense of Culture (AIEDC), itself a mutation of an old acquaintance, the UIER. Liaising with Aub, Bergamín, and Larrea, the committee "organized artistic events to draw attention to Spanish culture, the Paris tour of a popular Catalan orchestra, the Cobla de Barcelona, in September 1936, it supported the performing of Cervantes' *Numancia* at the Théâtre Antoine; it sent material aid to servicemen and writers, in the form of newspapers, books and magazines."[85] The Paris-based Peruvian poet, journalist, and translator César Vallejo had, in the space of a single year (1931), converted to the PCE and published an enthusiastic account of his guided tour of the USSR—*Rusia en 1931 (reflexiones al pie del Kremlin)*—as well as a "proletarian" novel, *El tungsteno*. He was to remain a fervent opponent of Surrealism until his early death in 1938.

Shortly after the accession of the Negrín government on 17 May 1937, Sánchez Arcas, the undersecretary of propaganda, asked party comrade Juan Vicens to direct the office (Vicens had already been earmarked for a post in Agence Espagne). As a library inspector—a profession he'd entered after giving up the Librairie Espagnole and returning to Spain—he'd been active in the mass acculturation programs instaured by the Pedagogical Missions (1931–36), programs that went into overdrive with the arrival of the Frente Popular. Buñuel would later claim, exaggeratedly perhaps, that it was he who engineered Vicens's move to Paris, along with that of Eduardo Ugarte and Luis Lacasa: "What were they doing in Spain? Scared stiff, they were. In Paris they performed a brilliant role."[86] Vicens and Ugarte did in fact arrive at the Spanish Embassy at the same time, March 1937, the former as a propaganda delegate and the latter as an attaché.[87] Lacasa was the least likely to have profited from Buñuel's string pulling, however, since Renau had named him in an official capacity for the forthcoming International Exhibition as early as December 1936.

By the beginning of August 1937 Vicens had the diverse elements of his propaganda operation in place: press, publications, radio, general propaganda, and cinema.[88] The press campaign would be mounted in collaboration with Agence Espagne and Agence Fabra. The publications program included two (unnamed) books, one in French, the other in English, about intervention and international politics. The Republican-friendly stations of Radio Paris and Radio Colonial were to be kept informed by Agence Espagne and the Press Office at the Spanish Embassy. General propaganda would be aimed, in France and other countries, at well-disposed committees, organizations, and embassies and would also take on board the travel arrangements of delegations to Spain. As for cinema, Vicens made a thought-provoking allusion to Buñuel, "who joins the general organization under the control of this delegation."[89] An ever-present theme in Vicens's correspondence at this time is the difficulty he has in getting his hands on campaign funding from central government. For example, the sum agreed with Valencia for the initial month of August was 500,000 FF—out of which Agence Espagne was to receive 255,270 FF—but suffering from cash-flow problems, the propaganda delegate had already been obliged to put several projects on hold.

Juan Vicens and his wife, María Luisa González (aka "Comrade Justine"), with their sons Juan and Manuel in Becedas, Ávila, 1932. (Archivo de la Residencia de Estudiantes, Madrid)

Vicens's activities were long the object of surveillance by the French authorities, as a report sent by the director general of the Sûreté Nationale to the prefect of police on 29 December 1938 makes clear:

> A reliable source reveals that the distribution of propaganda funding from the government in Barcelona is effected by M. Juan Vicens, director of the Spanish Tourist Office, Boulevard de la Madeleine.
>
> It is he who remits to the World Committee Against War and Fascism, to the groups Paix et Liberté, Paix et Democratie, etc., the sums intended to pay for the booklets published in favor of Republican Spain; he also hands over gratuities to journalists who defend the cause of the Spanish Republicans.
>
> He has dealt with M. Joseph Kessel for the newspaper report the latter undertook recently in Republican Spain on behalf of *Paris-Soir.*
>
> M. Vicens, a former teacher, is an influential member of the Spanish Communist Party.[90]

The Buñuelophile will have remarked the name of the author of *Belle de jour* (1928). Effectively, in October 1938 Kessel—novelist, scriptwriter (of two recent Anatole Litvak melodramas), and journalist—had been dispatched with photographer Jean Moral to do a reportage on the last, traumatic days of Republican Spain, a reportage duly published (albeit in censored form) in the daily *Paris-Soir* and the magazine *Match.*

Of the other Spanish Tourist Office personnel, our knowledge is sketchy. Although Peinado, Sert, and Guillermo de la Torre had been instrumental in setting it up, their involvement is difficult to quantify and was certainly short-lived. We know that under Vicens's command Loulou Viñes was put in charge of distributing the printed material generated by the propaganda operation. The spokesman on religious matters was José Manuel Gallegos Rocafull, former canon lector of Córdoba Cathedral and friend of prominent French Catholics Jacques Maritain and François Mauriac (whom the Communists were courting in their general campaign to win over the faithful to their cause). From Paris, Gallegos would attempt to mediate between the Republican government and the Catholic Church. He was also writing a book about religion in the rebel zone for the Spanish Tourist Office. In 1939, accused of being a "Red" for having worked "in favor and in defense of the Marxist Red revolution condemned by the Pope and the Spanish episcopacy," he would have to emigrate to Mexico.[91] It appears that Pedro Elviro "Pitouto" was employed as a concierge.[92] Since the advent of sound, this comedy actor from Valencia had worked in the French film industry for the likes of Autant-Lara, Clair, Epstein, Gréville, Robert Siodmak, and Jacques Tourneur (plus a dozen or so less illustrious directors); in 1952

Buñuel would give him a bit part in *Subida al cielo*. Another helper was the young Surrealist painter José Luis González Bernal, who had lived in Paris since 1932, working there as a proofreader on *Minotaure*. In the early days of the *contienda* he'd been in Madrid, helping to organize the intelligence-gathering service of the University Students Federation (FUE), before being sent back to Paris to aid the propaganda effort.

The demise of Vicens's operation was no less forlorn than the illustrated articles Kessel and Moral sent back from Madrid and Barcelona. As early as June 1938 Pascua had begun complaining to Negrín about the unfittedness for effective propaganda work of Vicens. On 12 January 1939 he was officially replaced by Ugarte, who picked up the baton until 28 February, the day on which Franco was recognized by France and Great Britain as head of state.[93] Following that, the Boulevard de la Madeleine premises were sequestered at the demand of the Francoist Committee for Recovering Spanish Property in France. By then Vicens had gone into hiding. On 18 May 1940, with the Wehrmacht already in Paris, he boarded a ship in Saint-Nazaire, destination New York and eventually Mexico. In August 1942 a note emanating from the Paris Customs Board notified the Prefecture of Police that some thirty boxes and packets of propaganda material sent from Barcelona in January 1939 to the Spanish Tourist Office, but never collected, were about to be pulped. Although the contents amounted to 1,170 copies, just three titles were involved. Inexplicably, given the date of dispatch, one of these was meant to have been distributed at the International Exhibition eighteen months before.[94]

The detailed history remains to be written of Paris as the hub of the Comintern-led mobilization of anti-Fascism in Western Europe between the accession of Hitler and the German–Soviet Non-Aggression Pact of August 1939. In our all too schematic account of how the propaganda arm of the Spanish Embassy liaised with different front organizations, Buñuel's name has cropped up several times. As so often with him, a "Harry Lime" or "Scarlet Pimpernel" quality accretes to his presence/absence in affairs that are, if not epoch making, of utmost importance. This is by way of returning to the 464,000 FF he received between October 1936 and May 1937 from, in the last analysis, Araquistáin. This was money for which Buñuel did not need to account; in short, it was money to be used for undercover work.[95]

"Backward" Spain was not a participant in the generalized efflorescence of European espionage following the post–World War I redrawing of the continental map and the mutation of Russia into the USSR. This state of affairs did not change during the Second Republic: the embassy in Paris, for instance, remained the very image of disorganization when it came to security and information gathering. Staffed largely by monarchists who would side with Franco, it remained chaotic until its restructuring under Araquistáin in September 1936. One of the new ambassador's innovations, in line with the State Department—that is, Álvarez del Vayo—was the setting up of an intelligence service, which was seen as an essential adjunct to any performative propaganda operation. As head of the new spy ring, Araquistain installed mural painter Luis Quintanilla, an intimate friend and political co-religionist who'd been civilian head of the Cuartel de la Montaña in Madrid after 19 July and an organizer of the siege of the Alcázar in Toledo in September, before briefly taking up arms in the defense of the capital. The muralist proved to be an able administrator, for the so-called Quintanilla network was up and running by mid-October, as the triple appearance of his name on the embassy's secret balance sheet demonstrates: like Buñuel's, his first entry, dated 3 October, is annotated "intelligence service." Although the Paris-centered network had outposts in Toulouse, Nice, Pau, Perpignan, and Marseille, its frontline was in Biarritz, the French Basque resort being, along with nearby Bayonne, Saint-Jean-de-Luz, and Hendaye, a crucial interface of covert activity, Republican and Francoist. Protected by Right-wing French aristocrats and financed by Francesc Cambó of the Lliga Catalana and millionaire businessman Juan March, Franco's agents had inherited earlier military surveillance systems and were somewhat better organized than the Republicans; in addition they had the backup of the Germans—the Gestapo—and the Italian Organization for the Vigilance and Repression of Antifascism (OVRA).

In the absence of trained personnel, the Spanish Embassy's information-gathering service had an informal, improvisational quality, although one neither more nor less amateur than the other novice networks of entities like the Generalitat de Catalunya, the Basque Nationalist Party, or the CNT. Things were to change with the ascendancy after spring 1937 of the Soviet secret police, the NKVD, under Aleksandr Orlov, which would train the first professional Republican agents, civilian as well as military, to eliminate their enemies both outside and inside the Loyalist camp. Quintanilla's recruitment was paradigmatic: "Araquistáin called me as a result of some things Hemingway said about how it wasn't right to risk the life of artists [in street fighting]. . . . I arrived in Paris. There was nothing. Organize it as best you can, he told me."[96] Yet things were not as rickety as all that, for as a cover for his espionage activities in the Basque border country the ambassador provided Quintanilla with the documentation of a Spanish Consulate inspector. To help the artist in his mission, Araquistáin's wife, Gertrudis (Trudi), put him touch with a Biarritz importer of Spanish vegetables, Saturnino Lasa, a recent convert to Communism who would function as his secretary from a fake business address in the town. Lasa knew the police commissioner in Bayonne, a Socialist who was only too ready to collaborate with the group. In order to further the bilateral exchange of information about the insurgents, who had recently taken Irún and sealed off the border, Commissioner Sangla in turn set up a meeting between Quintanilla and one Gascon, an agent of the French secret service, the Deuxième Bureau. With the same end in view, contact was also made with a British intelligence officer in Hossegor who went by the name of François Perraud. This, then, was the nucleus of the thinly manned Quintanilla network, which remained operative until at least June 1937, when, with Araquistáin out of office, the artist resigned and devoted the next five months to making 140 eyewitness drawings of the disasters of war. An internal embassy report, written by an anonymous diplomat and dated 12 June, reveals how fragile things were after the departure of the Socialist diplomat: "[The intelligence service] was reduced to Sr. Buñuel in Paris with an office [in the Rue de la Pépinière], Sr. Quintanilla touring the border area and ports, and another man in Marseille [the consul, Plácido Álvarez-Buylla]. I know nothing of the efficiency of this setup, but can guarantee that it can't have been up to much because all their collaborators were known to the enemy more than to the friends, and that they were reduced to seeking the collaboration of the French Communist and Socialist organizations."[97]

Buñuel was Quintanilla's liaison with Araquistáin. In Paris, they would also work together on at least one occasion as the armed bodyguards of Juan Negrín when he was still minister of finance.[98] Given their political differences, their relationship was not of the chummiest. The American artist and socialite Ione Robinson has recounted a violent encounter between the two men. The entry for 20 July 1938 in her autobiography reads:

> Mr. Quintanilla arrived in Paris on his way back to Barcelona. He came out for the weekend with Buñuel. It was so rainy and cold; the house [in Samoreau, near Fontainebleau] seemed buried under the tall trees surrounding it. At dinner the two Spaniards had a heated discussion about the war. Mr. Quintanilla, who is a socialist, accused the Communists (especially the French) of squandering the money belonging to the Republican government which was sent to Paris to publish the newspaper, *Ce Soir*. Mr. Buñuel, who is sympathetic to the Communists, argued against this until Ocky [Baroness Ocky van Boetzaler] and I had to leave the table. She sat at the piano playing Bach, trying to drown out the profanity of the Spaniards. She told me no "monarchist" would ever speak in such a manner! Finally the two came into the drawing room, and Mr. Quintanilla settled down to sketch Ocky at the piano. I was glad when both Spaniards left for Paris the next morning![99]

Conceived by PCF general secretary Thorez as a direct competitor to the much-vilified *Paris-Soir*, the first issue of *Ce Soir*, which was announced as the "great independent fact-finding daily," appeared on 1 March 1937. With Louis Aragon and Jean-Richard Bloch as its editors, the paper, heavily subsidized by the Republican government, would become famous for its coverage of the Civil War by such names as Paul Nizan, Édith Thomas, Andrée Viollis, and Georges Soria among the writers and Capa, Gerda Taro, and Chim among the photographers. Not long after its launch, *Ce Soir* had printed the interview with Buñuel, syndicated, so to speak, from the Münzenberg paper, *Pariser Tageszeitung*.[100] Moreover, the paper would set up the first of its three movie theaters, the Ce Soir-Italiens, at 2, Rue des Italiens in the second arrondissement, which opened on 9 April with a week-long double bill of *Espagne 1936*, "the film you have to see, a document in the service of peace," and Jacques de Baroncelli's seafaring drama *Nitchevo*, starring Harry Baur, Marcelle Chantal, and a Franco-Argentinean actor who will reappear in this narrative: Georges Rigaud.[101]

Ione Robinson had met Buñuel ten days before that Samoreau soirée while visiting the Spanish Embassy in Paris. Sent there by Quintanilla, whom she'd encountered (and seduced) in New York in May—he had a show of his Civil War drawings at the MoMA from 15 March to 18 April 1938—Robinson was seeking a visa to visit Barcelona, where, accompanied by the muralist from Santander, she too would produce a portfolio of Social-Realist pictures.

Years later, Quintanilla's sarcasm about Buñuel would be unsparing. He described arriving at the embassy in October 1936 in the company of Sancho, his ex-policeman driver:

> Joining us from time to time was the Surrealist filmmaker who would act as my liaison agent. He'd lived in the city [Paris] for some time, and, as is only natural, he asked us for details about what was happening in Spain, showing a preference, perhaps Surrealist, for the persecution and the killings. Sancho and I observed that, although being of an ultra-Left persuasion, the filmmaker was influenced by all the ferocious Fascist propaganda about the "terrible crimes of the Reds," and Sancho, with great seriousness, outstripped his macabre imagination. Among lots of other things, he explained to him the origin of my clothing. In Madrid, when I knew I was to go to France, I went along to my tailor, who made a present to me, since he didn't want to charge for them, of two magnificent English suits, of perfect fit and sporty appearance, which were much praised by the filmmaker. Sancho changed their provenance, telling the filmmaker that as I only had battledress, he looked for an aristocrat of my build, shot him twice and took the suits, but the aristocrat's shoes weren't my size, so he killed three more until he found the shoes to fit me. The important thing about all this

> extraordinary fantasy was that, having read and heard things of the kind put out by the Fascists, the filmmaker first of all believed it, only reacting later when he got our joke, and if this happened to him, who is not an ingenuous person, it's easy to imagine how history-making legends are created.[102]

In a late-1960s interview with Max Aub for the latter's *Buñuel: Novela* project, an interview not included in the project's final form, *Conversaciones con Buñuel,* Quintanilla provided more detail on their day-to-day dealings: "Buñuel's usefulness, with regard to my thing, and with espionage, was limited to him getting the money together that I asked for from Biarritz and sending it to me. And from time to time for a code service we had, to pass on important direct news."[103] The service involved the communicating of secret ciphers to be used in the encoding and decoding of messages. When it came to communicating with Buñuel by letter, Quintanilla addressed himself to a "Monsieur Dubois," c/o the Librairie Espagnole, owned by Georgette Rucar. Obsessed with digging ever deeper, Aub was not convinced that, as the cineaste himself claimed, he had done little to help the espionage effort. Quintanilla, on the other hand, was of the same opinion as Buñuel, and even went so far as to accuse him of the sin of omission, in that he had stood by while Francoist agents emanating from Colonel José Ungría Jiménez's Military Police Intelligence Service, whose specialty was sabotaging or capturing Loyalist ships and aircraft on French territory, had done just that with a number of planes. "My message was, this is happening," Quintinilla said, "and as such communications go, keep an eye on this or that, and I spoke to him [i.e., Buñuel] to that effect, that he was the one who had to receive my news. They didn't do anything and the planes went missing. . . . We lost some, and the others went to Franco's lot."[104]

After Araquistáin's resignation, which marked the end of the more amateurish, "romantic" phase of the Republican espionage operation, Buñuel and his team continued working under first the febrile Ángel Ossorio y Gallardo and later the more cogent and combative Marcelino Pascua, much of whose diplomatic activity had to do with keeping the Franco-Spanish border open for the passage of armaments. Once the border was closed, Pascua would get the agreement of the French to permit the transit of matériel by sea from Marseille to the eastern coast of Spain.[105] With Quintanilla out of the picture, Buñuel liaised, albeit less so, with his successor in southwest France, Anastasio Blanco Elola, Socialist chancellor of the Spanish Consulate in Hendaye. Blanco was also the local head of the Diplomatic and Special Intelligence Service (SIDE), formed in April 1937 by the industrial engineer Anselmo Carretero, also a Socialist, to centralize the different covert operations in the name of the State

Department in Valencia, and later Barcelona. Blanco's expertise would refine and reinvigorate Republican espionage activity in the region, thus undermining the central status of both Paris and the embassy, which, reduced to a "paymaster" role, went into a decline. Given the exit, following the second change of government in April 1938, of Indalecio Prieto, defense minister and the protector of both Carretero and Blanco, the latter's star faded, however; in October 1938 he was dismissed and his network dismantled. By then Buñuel was in America.

15

Final Flight to the United States

With Negrín's assumption of the presidency in May 1937, Buñuel's team would be extended to include his old friend Rafael Sánchez Ventura, assistant director on *Terre sans pain*, who arrived as a cultural attaché and secretary at the embassy in June. Since the beginning of the Civil War, Sánchez Ventura, a fellow traveler, had served on a committee to safeguard the Prado's art treasures, before being appointed head of the European Section at the State Department in January 1937. In Paris, his duties were to include liaising, in the short term, with José Gaos on the Spanish Pavilion and also serving as Buñuel's aide in his activities to do with information gathering, propaganda, and protocol. Sánchez Ventura would remain in harness after Buñuel's flight to the United States in September 1938—indeed he would lend the cineaste money to pay for his transatlantic crossing. Ione Robinson has left us a moving portrait of Rafael and Maruja Sánchez Ventura at the very end of the Civil War. On 26 March 1939 Robinson was with the couple in Paris: "This evening, when we had just finished dinner, the radio announced the surrender of Madrid. Sánchez Ventura and his wife sat motionless—their grief was the kind of grief that is beyond all sorrow. They didn't even wait to hear the end of the broadcast. I followed them out into the hall of the elevator, and after I had pushed the button, they left me standing by the shaft, and walked down the stairs. I knew there was nothing I could say."[1]

In the interview literature, Buñuel was circumspect about naming his Paris staff, but he did offer clues: in *Mon dernier soupir*, for instance, he spoke of his "secretary, Rue de la Pépinière, [who] was the daughter of the treasurer of the French Communist Party."[2] Mounette Dutilleul was her name, and she was an

Back row from left: Rafael Sánchez Ventura, Conchita Monrás, and Ramón Acín on Torredembarra Beach, Catalonia, 1933. (Courtesy Fundación Ramón y Katia Acín, Zaragoza / Photo: Museo de Huesca)

agent of the Comintern.[3] Born in 1910, at age nineteen she had married the German Communist Aloys Bayer, and the couple spent six months in Moscow in 1930–31, he as an SOI representative, she as a translator and shorthand typist at Comintern headquarters. On her return to Paris in 1931, Mounette joined the PCF. In 1932 she acted as a messenger between Münzenberg (still in Berlin) and the party apparatus in the French capital. Due to the secret nature of her liaison activities with foreign militants, she was instructed to keep a low profile. In 1937 she served on the PCF's cadre commission as an assistant to its head, Maurice Tréand; the commission controlled the recruitment, promotion, and purging of key members.[4] Mounette Dutilleul is said to have told her boss that if the Central Committee had misgivings about her marriage to a German—in 1937 Bayer was in Spain, disseminating Communist propaganda in the Francoist zone—she and her husband were willing to terminate it in order for her to wholeheartedly serve the party. This they did. Mounette began working for Buñuel on 15 October 1936, that is, when he moved into his new office in the eighth arrondissement. Her in-house autobiography for the Comintern, submitted on 15 December 1937, reads: "On 15 October, placed on the recommendation of Mareck, with the consent of the PCF, in Bunuel's office (Propagande par le Film, an antifascist information service concerning Spain). (Salary: 1,500, 1,700 then 2,000 francs a month)."[5] This is the last employment she gives in this document, which would suggest that fourteen months later she was still working with Buñuel. Mareck (or Marek) was the pseudonym of Polish Communist Michel Feintuch, known in France as Jean Jérôme. Jérôme was a Comintern operative responsible for the supplying of weapons and provisions to the Republicans, as well as for the setting up of arms factories in Spain and the equipping of the International Brigades.[6] This is not the first time we've come across La Propagande par le Film: it was this PCF front organization that helped pay for the sonorization of *Las Hurdes*. Here, though, it is linked more closely to Buñuel's name.

Émile Dutilleul was Mounette's father.[7] A typographer by profession, the young Émile had frequented the anarchist milieus of Paris between 1905 and 1911, breaking with it at the time of the founding of the Bonnot Gang. After World War I he turned to Communism. By 1924 he was general secretary of the French section of SOI and a member of the administrative council of both *L'Humanité* and the Banque Ouvrière et Paysanne, which controlled the PCF's finances between 1925 and 1930. In 1932 Émile Dutilleul was appointed national treasurer and played an important part in the direction of the party long before his incorporation as a Central Committee member in December 1937. Two months after the outbreak of the Civil War, Thorez would entrust him with organizing financial aid to Republican Spain.

At a meeting in late September 1936 attended by Thorez, Émile Dutilleul, Tréand, Giulio Ceretti (an Italian Comintern agent who served on the PCF Central Committee under the name of Pierre Allard), and Eugen Fried (the covert power behind the Thorez throne during the 1930s, a high-ranking Slovak Cominternian known as "the mirror," so faithfully did he reflect the general line laid down by Stalin), it was decided to organize a transport network to supply arms to the Loyalists. On 15 April 1937 the shipping company France-Navigation was set up for that purpose, its director being Ceretti ("Monsieur Pierre"), aided by Tréand and Georges Gosnat, a twenty-two-year-old navy officer and cadre who had met Thorez and Fried at age fourteen when, obliged to go underground, the two Communists had been sheltered by his father.[8] With Marek/Jérôme taking care of the financial side of the operation, during the first three years of its existence France-Navigation's capital increased fifty-fold, enabling it to become the country's fourth-ranking shipping company.[9] Once a week Fried and Ceretti would go to the Soviet Embassy in Paris to liaise with representatives of the Spanish Embassy and with Gaston Cusin, who, using the cover of a series of spurious government posts, was the delegate charged by every French administration between Blum and Daladier with helping clandestine aid get to the Republic. It is estimated that this high-ranking customs official and CGT (General Confederation of Labor) syndicalist facilitated the arrival in Spain of some four hundred boats loaded with Soviet military equipment.[10]

We still lack the information to quantify Buñuel's role in facilitating the supply of weapons to the Republic and can only put forward the hypothesis that given his contacts—the Dutilleuls being a prime example—he must have been involved in one way or another. Arms dealing is by definition a hypersecret activity. We have little to go on, then, and what we do have in the interview literature often smacks of the story repeated so many times by this gifted raconteur (often over an aperitif or three) as to be at odds with real events. For instance, there is the tale of Dalí introducing Buñuel to Edward James, who proposed exchanging a bomber, which the English millionaire and eccentric had waiting "on a Czech airfield," for the loan of "a few masterpieces" from the Prado, to be exhibited as a pro-Republican propaganda exercise in Paris and elsewhere.[11] That is Buñuel's version. More plausibly, Ian Gibson tells us that it was the loan of some El Grecos from the same museum that were to be exhibited at the Royal Academy in London in order to raise money for the Republic to purchase bomber planes (Álvarez del Vayo turned the offer down).[12] At times even the fresh information we do possess has a phantasmal quality to it. Witness this note, penned by Aub during, or after, an interview with Wenceslao Roces circa 1970 and never used in *Conversaciones con Buñuel*: "In the 40s of Georges V, opposite, they sent him [Roces] to see what could be done to buy arms. Then to Georges V with the Frente Popular delegation, with Dolores [Ibárruri]. Much interest in Buñuel going. Buñuel: I can't. I'm in the French party. What's more, they've sent me here on a major secret mission." "Georges V" is the Avenue George V, number 13 being the address of the Chancery of the Spanish Embassy, number 15 the ambassador's residence, and number 55 the embassy proper. The date cannot be long after Buñuel's arrival at the latter. What he says and how he says it is not new to us, although here he says it in the presence of a member of the PCE politburo, and the ambiguity exists as to whether the delegation is asking him to go and buy arms, or simply to turn up for the meeting. But what *is* curious is that this note, communicated to us by the Tenerifean historian Fernando Gabriel Martín, who copied it on a visit to the Fundación Max Aub in Segorbe years ago, has since gone astray and cannot be referenced as a bona fide piece of evidence.

As to other evidence, we have discovered that the cineaste was acquainted with Georges Gosnat of France-Navigation; the testimony is Santiago Carrillo's: "I get the impression Buñuel always had a very fluid relationship with the PCF. Not only was he very friendly with Aragon, he was also very friendly with the leaders of the PCF, like Georges Gosnat, who was the person who did all the PCF's business deals."[13] By his own account, Buñuel, that "agent of the Valencia government," as the Sûreté Nationale defined him in their counterespionage fiche dating from 6 October 1937, made trips on behalf of said government to London, Antwerp, and Stockholm, all of them ports.[14] Given what we have said of maritime weapons shipments, the suggestion is that he might have played some part in it.

The idea that the cineaste would travel all the way to Stockholm just to recruit, on the say-so of Trudi Araquistáin, "an extremely beautiful Swedish woman, Kareen, a member of the Swedish Communist Party," so that she might spy for the Quintanilla network seems more than a little flimsy.[15] On the other hand, Buñuel would surely have had diplomatic business—if only as a messenger or bagman—with the ambassadress in the Spanish Legation there. Isabel de Palencia, former Republican representative on the Administration Council of the League of Nations in Geneva (where she worked with Álvarez del Vayo) and member of the World Committee of Women Against War and Fascism, a Münzenberg front, was active in the signing of commercial contracts with neutral Sweden. Were these contracts for the shipping of arms? We do not know, but Palencia was certainly in the intelligence network mounted from Paris by Araquistáin.[16] Another important figure in Communist culture was also to be found in Stockholm: Olaf Aschberg, the "Bolshevik banker" who financed various anti-Fascist fronts in France, as well as such Münzenberg ventures as Éditions du Carrefour and *Pariser Tageszeitung*. Aschberg, who spent six months in Sweden, six in France, was an intimate friend of the del Vayos and the Araquistáins.[17]

The plasticity of some of Buñuel's anecdotes is remarkable. Take the story of the Papal encyclical *Rerum novarum*. In one telling, with the complicity of the PCF, which, in an attempt to win over Catholic voters, would give extended coverage to the persecution of the church in Hitler's Germany, Buñuel delivers five thousand examples of this mildly anti-Nazi tract to a pro-Republican German captain in Antwerp, who is to ship it to the Francoist zone.[18] Published on 14 March 1937, Pius XI's pastoral letter was, in fact, *Mit brennender Sorge* (With Burning Concern), about the situation of the Catholic Church in the Third Reich. *Rerum novarum* dates from May 1891, in fact, and was issued by the first pope ever to be filmed, Leo XIII, who subsequently blessed W. K. Dickson's camera. Since the signing in 1933 of the *Reichskonkordat* between Germany and the Vatican, the National-Socialist state had propagated an aggressive neopaganism, much to the consternation of the Vicar of Christ: "None but superficial minds could stumble into concepts of a national God, of a national religion; or attempt to lock within the frontiers of a single people, within the narrow limits of a single race, God, the Creator of the universe, King and Legislator of all nations before whose immensity they are 'as a drop of a bucket' (*Isaiah* 40, 15)."[19] Aside from a single reply to this embarrassing critique in the official Nazi organ, *Völkischer Beobachter*, Goebbels ordered the German media to keep silent about it. This is why, in a propaganda exercise that is pure Münzenberg, copies of it were dispatched to the compulsorily Catholic and Apostolic part of Spain. Was Mounette Dutilleul's husband Aloys Bayer involved in disseminating the nine-thousand-word pamphlet, one wonders.

Elsewhere, Buñuel is sending copies of the same document by another means: "The last thing I did was the balloons with the encyclicals, which was an idea of Fisher's, an Austrian."[20] This final act of political commitment is dated to just before Buñuel's flight to the United States in September 1938. In another version, he is in Bayonne in 1939, where his role "consisted in taking care of the launching of little hot-air balloons laden with tracts over the Pyrenees. A number of Communist friends, who were to be shot some time later by the Nazis, took care of launching the balloons. . . . This activity seemed completely ridiculous to me. . . . The inventor of this system [was] an American journalist, a friend of Spain's."[21] The dates are all wrong: *Mit brennender Sorge* is from March 1937; the Bayonne espionage operation was in decline by April 1938; by 1939 Buñuel was an ocean away. "Fisher" is Louis Fischer, the American fellow-traveling journalist who resided in Moscow between 1923 and 1936, where he worked as a correspondent for *The Nation* and wrote five pro-Soviet studies. In 1936 he journeyed to Spain to report on the Civil War; there he served as an officer in the International Brigades. In 1949 he would be one of the contributors to *The God That Failed*, an autobiographical collection of essays written by ex-Communists and disillusioned fellow-travelers (the others were Gide, Koestler, Ignazio Silone, Stephen Spender, and Richard Wright). When Fischer broke with the Stalinoid *Nation* in June 1945, his post went to the exiled Álvarez del Vayo. Stephen Koch has categorized Fischer as an out-and-out "Münzenberg man."[22] But did Buñuel really embark on such a "ridiculous" (and convoluted) propaganda exercise? Or did he co-opt a story he'd heard about and simply slot himself into it? In *The Invisible Writing*, Koestler describes the dynamic style of "ideas man" Münzenberg in Paris. Charismatic Willi instructs his secretary Hans Schultz to "buy a book on meteorology, find out about highs and lows and so on, find out how the wind blows over the Rhine, how many quarto handbills you can hang on a toy balloon, in which area of Germany balloons released on the French side are likely to come down, and so on. Then, Hans, you contact a few wholesale manufacturers of toy balloons, tell them it's for export to Venezuela, ask them for estimates for ten thousand balloons. Next, Hans . . ."[23]

There is another unlikely, and equally protean, story of Buñuel's Pyrenean exploits: namely that in the winter of 1936–37 he was one of a group of people who personally directed mule trains from the French side of the mid-Pyrenees to take supplies to a division of Loyalist soldiers cut off in the snow-covered peaks of the Valle de Arán. This is the tale Buñuel told Francisco Aranda, who communicated it to Manuel Rotellar.[24] In another version, recounted to Jean-Claude Carrière, it's a Republican brigade, not a division, that is under attack from Nationalist army units, and it is French sympathizers who supply them from Gavarnie, a ski resort on the other side of the border. Buñuel claims to have gone there with Ugarte, where their car was involved in a collision, leaving them stranded for three days.[25] The Forty-Third Division of the Popular Army, along with several thousand refugees in its care, did spend over a couple of months under heavy siege in their mountain fastness, as reported in *L'Humanité* on various occasions during May and June 1938.[26] Indeed, something of a cult to Lieutenant-Colonel Ángel Beltrán, a former smuggler and, since the outbreak of the Civil War, Republican commissar of the International Station of Canfranc in the Pyrenees, and his nine thousand men was orchestrated by the PCF, which mobilized its followers to fund the sending of tons of food and clothing to the Forty-Third. In mid-June the Spanish Embassy in Paris requested the Central Sanitaire Internationale, which was liaising on the production of *Victoire de la vie* at the time, to send two ambulances to the border to help evacuate the wounded. On 18 June *L'Humanité* published an interview with Ángel Beltrán about the division's tactical retreat into France.

The plot, however, thickens, for it has been claimed that the saga of the stoical soldiery formed the basis of a docudrama, *La división perdida*, directed and photographed by José María Beltrán, who'd shot all four Filmófono productions for Buñuel and Urgoiti, as well as filming the Velo and Mantilla titles that were screened in the Spanish Pavilion during the 1937 International Exhibition. However, as Santiago de Pablo has recently argued, *La división perdida* never existed: it is a myth.[27] And the source of this myth? Aranda, abetted by two of his interlocutors, Fernández Cuenca and Rotellar—although it has to be said that Buñuel's "nephew" was, doubtless in all good faith, trying to square the circle from the scraps of information supplied by his "uncle" and by Beltrán himself. As Roger Caillois would write, "The archaeology of memory is just as inventive as memory itself, and equally as anxious about continuity."[28] In Fernández Cuenca's rerun, *La división perdida* was "a French feature-length production, which reconstituted, with improvised actors and the odd professional of little renown a deed occurring during the previous winter in the Spanish Pyrenees area, when an avalanche of snow cut off a unit of the Republican army, which had to undergo a veritable odyssey in order to get its bearings and recover its former positions; the sudden change is concentrated and combines intimist elements to do with soldiers in an extreme situation with a few bellicose skirmishes."[29] One cannot help thinking that certain elements of the legend originate in an imaginary reworking of John Ford's *The Lost Patrol* (1934), or rather of Mikhail Romm's Socialist-Realist remake, *The Thirteen* (1937). The latter was first shown in Paris, where Beltrán was based at the time, in October 1937 in the Soviet Pavilion at the International Exhibition. In Rotellar's retread, *La división perdida* was made as the events themselves unfolded: "According to Beltrán, some footage was shot directly where the besieged were, but most of the filming was done on the other side of the border, in France, a few miles away from the besieged, with the information and news that arrived from there. . . . The documentary had a storyline, and after various adventures the division finds its 'liaison' and manages to slip past the encirclement and get away."[30] Although it involved his ex-cinematographer—and, as legend has it, Nemesio M. Sobrevila, the scriptwriter of *La hija de Juan Simón*, who was collaborating with Beltrán on propaganda work for the autonomous Basque government—and was, on the face of it, a likely project for Buñuel to be involved in, he purportedly knew nothing of this specular venture. (Quite so, since it never existed!) That said, in June 1938 Beltrán (no relation to Ángel Beltrán) did in fact film the Forty-Third

Division in the Aragonese part of the Pyrenees, more particularly the visit to it by Manuel Irujo, head of the Basque Nationalist Party and minister of justice in the Republican government, and the ascent to the snowbound peaks of a long mule train bringing provisions for the besieged soldiers and civilians. Did Buñuel see a lavender copy of this in Paris and once again "insert" himself into it as a muleteer? Beltrán's footage would ultimately be ceded by the Basque government to Laya Films, seventy-five seconds of it finding its way into an *Espanya al dia* newsreel.[31]

It is not our intention to go on trawling through the accounts Buñuel gave of his Civil War activities and to gauge their truthfulness. Instead, we refer to one or two events to which we can add something by way of information. Thus far, we have spoken of his interventions as a cineaste, as an intelligence agent, and as a facilitator of matériel. Here, we address some of his political activities.

First, the episode of "the three bombs," as it is known in *Mon dernier soupir*. In what follows, we combine this version with the one given by Aub.[32] During Araquistáin's mandate, Buñuel is visited at the embassy by a debonair Colombian claiming to be the member of an action group from Burgos involved in recent bomb outrages on the Republican consulate in Toulouse and Perpignan and on the Bordeaux–Marseille train. As proof, he shows Buñuel several small but powerful bombs he has in a suitcase. Consumed by an intense hatred for the leader of his terrorist cell, the Colombian wishes to betray the latter to the Republicans: if Buñuel will come to La Coupole the next day all will be revealed. Buñuel informs Araquistáin, who in turn informs the French authorities: the bombs are examined and are indeed incredibly powerful. Accompanied by Finki Araquistáin, the ambassador's son, and actress Germaine Montero, our man goes to the rendezvous, where the informer fingers his boss: a Latin American screen actor known to both Buñuel and Montero. Buñuel gives the information to the local prefect of police, a Socialist: the whole group is detained, but released shortly afterward. Sometime later, Buñuel and Sánchez Ventura spot the actor supping in Le Sélect. Under the blind eye of the police, the cell continues to function, blowing up a trade union headquarters near the Place de l'Étoile. The holder of a diplomatic passport from his country, which permits him to travel to Madrid where he continues with his misdeeds, the actor is decorated by Franco at the end of the Civil War.

Jorge Rigaud was that actor.[33] Born Pedro Jorge Rigato Delissetche in Buenos Aires in 1905, but resident in Paris from an early age, Jorge (Georges) Rigaud's first screen appearance was as the journalist Fandor in Paul Fejos's version of *Fantômas*, produced in 1932 by Pierre Braunberger. This is the film put on hold at the beginning of 1932 due to money problems, the same problems that

Franco-Argentinean film star Georges Rigaud as taxi driver Jean in René Clair's *Quatorze Juillet* (1932). (Hulton Archive / Getty Images)

postponed Buñuel's then-current plan to direct *Wuthering Heights* for Braunberger. Between 1932 and 1938 Rigaud made a name for himself as a dashing beau in over twenty-five films by René Clair and Maurice L'Herbier, Robert Siodmak and Max Ophüls, as well as lesser lights like Victor Tourjansky, Jacques de Baroncelli, and Henri Fescourt. In 1933 he appeared in a Ufa-Alliance Cinématographique Européenne co-production entitled *Saison in Kairo*, the French version of which, *Idylle au Caire*, was directed by Claude Heymann (the assistant on *L'Âge d'or*), while a year later he had a role alongside Modot in a medium-length movie directed by former Surrealist Albert Valentin, *Taxi de minuit*, a title written, moreover, by Jacques Prévert. In March 1938 the magazine *Cinématographie Française* announced that "French actor Georges Rigaud, who has been in Hollywood for several months under contract to Paramount, is to begin his first American role in *Café Society*. Frances Dee, Ray Milland and Shirley Ross will be his co-stars."[34]

It is tempting to think that Rigaud's sojourn in California, which logically dates to the end of 1937, was due to a need to quit France after Buñuel's whistleblowing. Rigaud would not appear in the romantic comedy directed by Edward H. Griffith in 1939, nor would Milland and Dee. In one filmography he is credited with appearances in two other Paramount pictures, released in July and August

1938: *Tropic Holiday*, a musical by Theodore Reed, and *Spawn of the North*, an action movie by Henry Hathaway.[35] By early September he was back in Europe, where he played the lead in a Franco-Swiss co-production called *Accord final*, released on 30 December 1938 in Switzerland and 17 February 1939 in France. Directed by I. R. Bay, this lightweight love story with a "conservatoire" setting—the kind of melomaniac kitsch to which Dalí was partial—was supervised, uncredited, by Detlef Sierck (the future Douglas Sirk). A year later the actor turned up in Italy as Giorgio Rigato in *Abbandono* (Mario Mattoli, 1940). In 1941 he landed in Argentina, this time as Jorge Rigaud. In 1957 he'd settle definitively in Spain, where he would prove popular as Saint Valentine in *El día de los enamorados* (Fernando Palacios, 1959) and its sequel, *Vuelve San Valentín* (Fernando Palacios, 1962). The identification of the terrorist leader as Georges Rigaud, communicated to us by the late Emilio Sanz de Soto, an infallible source, is, it has to be said, difficult to square with Buñuel's assertion that the actor "had worked in the cinema with us in Madrid."[36] Filmófono appears out of the question, and the possibility of Rigaud doing dubbing work for Warner Bros. seems unlikely, but he may have worked in Joinville.

We can identify the bomb outrages cited by Buñuel. On 8 March 1937 *L'Humanité* reported an incident in which a device was tossed into the garden of the Spanish Consulate in Perpignan but failed to go off.[37] Two months later, on 5 May, the Bordeaux-Marseille express was brought to a halt in the village of Saint-Martin-de-Crau, just south of Arles, by an explosion that gutted one carriage, killing a passenger and injuring twenty more.[38] In late June a series of exposés by Lucien Sampaix, the PCF paper's general secretary, ascribed these and other attacks to the "Légion Noire," an arm of the German secret service. The bombings, he claimed, were masterminded by Karl Grandt, one of Nazism's main propagandists in Argentina and Paraguay, while the actual devices were prepared in Salamanca by a chemist called Bauer, who'd been smuggled into Spain aboard a German submarine. According to the journalist—one of whose sources may have been Buñuel—the attacks were planned in Biarritz by Count Julián Troncoso y Sagrado, Fascist military governor of Irún and head of border control, and implemented in the Hexagon by a band of terrorists.[39] Due to the slowness of the French authorities in tracking down the terrorists, a slowness that Buñuel read as being politically motivated, the provocations were to continue (and here we can only admire his excellent memory), for on 13 September the news broke of a couple of almost simultaneous explosions that had taken place near the Place de l'Étoile on 11 September in the headquarters of two trade unions. In one, the attack on the Confédération Générale du Patronat Français in Rue de Presbourg, two policemen were killed by falling masonry.[40] A week later the arrests were made of a dozen members of La Cagoule, an ultra-violent organization modeled on the Falange and considered so extreme as to be disavowed by even the French far-Right.[41] In a further article, Sampaix referred to a "mysterious Mexican" known as José Noguera (real name, Luis Salazar), "agent of a foreign power," who'd handed over a number of Bauer's bombs to the police. Was Noguera-Salazar in fact the "Colombian" who'd called on Buñuel?[42]

A similarly murky episode in this dirty war centers on the figure of Agapito García Atadell, the notorious *chekista*. Again, we combine two renderings: Buñuel's in *Mon dernier soupir* and Ricardo Muñoz Suay's in Aub's *Conversaciones*.[43] During the first few months of the Civil War, García Atadell, a militant Socialist, and his "dawn brigade" mount a terror campaign against their class enemies in Madrid. However, under the cover of revolutionary justice, the vigilante and his *sbirri* are purloining the belongings of their aristocratic and clerical victims for themselves. It is estimated that some eight hundred people were murdered and expropriated by the forty-eight members of García Atadell's Popular Investigation Militia. Buñuel, outraged by this vendetta, hears from a French syndicalist that the assassin is heading for South America with the spoils. Our man informs Araquistáin, who informs a neutral embassy, which informs the Francoist authorities in Santa Cruz de Tenerife that García Atadell's ship is due to call there. The perfidious Republican is arrested and, much to the satisfaction of both the Fascists and the Communists, is tried and hanged.

Of late, another account of these events permits us to redefine the outline presented by Buñuel.[44] On 24 November 1936 the French liner *Mexique*, proceeding from Saint-Nazaire and La Coruña en route for Havana, arrived at the port of Santa Cruz de La Palma; among the 213 passengers on board were García Atadell and his henchman, Pedro Penabad. A month earlier, threatened by Communists and anarcho-syndicalists alike for his excesses and fearful of the imminent arrival of the Franco forces, García Atadell had fled from Madrid to Alicante along with three underlings, Penabad, Luis Ortuño, and Ángel Pedrero. There the Cuban vice-consul was inveigled to supply the team with false papers, permitting them to leave on an Argentinean boat bound for Marseille. From Marseille García Atadell and Penabad traveled to Saint-Nazaire, where on 19 November they boarded the *Mexique*. During the crossing of the Bay of Biscay García Atadell fell in with a passenger called Ernesto Ricord, whom he convinced to go ashore at La Coruña and, under the pretense of being a Falangist, to seek information from the local head of the Falange, who told him he suspected that "Spanish Reds" were on board the steamer. Ricord was asked to keep an eye on the passengers. When the *Mexique* reached Santa

Cruz de la Palma, where the authorities had been forewarned by the La Coruña police, Ricord accused two innocent passengers—Gustavo Zaldivea, a Bilbao solicitor, and Rafart, a journalist from Madrid—of being the guilty parties, and they were arrested. In the face of Rafart's protests, however, the real identities of the two fugitive *brigadistas* were eventually discovered, and they were arrested in turn, along with Ricord. Moved first to Santa Cruz de Tenerife and afterward to the Central Prison in Sevilla—where, by a quirk of fate, they rubbed shoulders for a time with Arthur Koestler, who'd been detained by the Fascists after the fall of Málaga in February 1937—García Atadell and Penabad were condemned to death and garroted on 15 July 1937. Just what part Buñuel played in these events, given the detail we now have about them, is that much more difficult to assess. What comes over in this case—as in that of Georges Rigaud—is his "expanded" sense of moral rectitude.

The high spot of Buñuel's visibility as the Spanish Embassy's head of protocol—an unofficial designation, according to him—came about with the mounting of the Second International Congress of Writers for the Defense of Culture in Spain in July 1937, another in the list of committed cultural conventions stage-managed by the Comintern that commenced with the Second International Conference of Proletarian and Revolutionary Writers in Kharkov in 1930 and took in the International Congress of Writers for the Defense of Culture in Paris in 1935. On 30 June Buñuel was present, along with other embassy staff such as Aub and Xammar, at a tea party of honor presided over by Ambassador Ángel Ossorio that marked the official opening ceremony of a congress that would bring together delegates from twenty-two countries. Among those who attended were the French members of the international bureau of the AIEDC: Aragon, Julien Benda, Chamson, Luc Durtain, and Malraux. These, and several other invitees—Martin Andersen Nexö, Lion Feuchtwanger, Alexei Tolstoy—were veterans of the Paris congress in 1935 (Fadaev went back to Kharkov, even). Americans Malcolm Cowley and Langston Hughes were AIEDC activists. Other writers of the same persuasion had recently militated in Spain: Ludwig Renn, Kurt Stern, and Louis Fischer, for instance. Contemporary reports in the Republican press assert that the reception took place "in an atmosphere of enthusiasm, cordiality and adherence to the cause of Spanish democracy," with those present manifesting "absolute faith in the triumph of the soldiers of freedom and in the moral importance this has for the Congress intellectuals."[45]

The project to organize the Second International Congress of Writers for the Defense of Culture had been confirmed in the Spanish capital on 4 October 1936 at an AIEDC meeting attended by Alberti, Aragon, Bergamín, Ehrenburg,

Fischer, Koltsov, Antonio Machado, Malraux, Regler, Renn, Soria, Stern, and Viollis. Planned for May 1937, the itinerant congress proper, like the Spanish Pavilion, the propaganda event that complements it, would open late. Finally getting under way in Valencia on 4 July, it was to continue in Madrid between 5 and 8 July, go back to Valencia on 10 July, move to Barcelona on 11 July, and finally return to Paris on 16 and 17 July. By then the pavilion was into its first week of receiving visitors. The ministers present at the inaugural session of the congress included Juan Negrín, Jesús Hernández, José Giral, and Julián Zugazagoitia. Aside from the writers mentioned above, those who took the floor in Spain included Álvarez del Vayo, Aveline, Nicolas Guillén, Anna Seghers, Tzara, and Vallejo. Many of them were captured by the Eyemo of Roman Karmen, prior to his departure from Spain, and would appear that same July in cinemas across the Soviet Union in the newsreel *Events in Spain no. 20 (I)*.[46] When the road show wound up again in Paris, Bertolt Brecht, Heinrich Mann, Sender, Bloch, and Vaillant-Couturier were among the speakers. An urgent item on the agenda was the condemnation, which fell to congress president Bergamín, of André Gide, that high-profile fellow-traveler at the 1935 Paris congress who had since become a pariah on account of his *Retour de l'U.R.S.S.* (November 1936) and *Retouches à mon Retour de l'U.R.S.S.* (June 1937), essays that have an honorable place among prescient early critiques of Stalinist totalitarianism by André Breton, Ante Ciliga, Panaït Istrati, George Orwell, Victor Serge, and Boris Souvarine.

If, as Buñuel boasted to Aub, he was called upon to ensure that Gide and Aragon did not sit together at an embassy do, this must have been before the Second Congress, at which Gide was emphatically persona non grata.[47] Indeed, in his 16 July declaration to the assembled fideists in Paris, Aragon called Gide nothing less than a "traitor to the people." In her notebooks, Maria van Rysselberghe reveals that on 28 January 1937 Gide lunched with Aragon and Elsa Triolet at the Spanish Embassy. Although this encounter took place a few weeks after the publication of Gide's book on the Soviet Union, it was not uncordial.[48] However, the gap between the two writers would grow relentlessly between January and the July congress, so much so that were they ever to have been in the same room, the intercession of a third party to keep them apart would have been unnecessary. What's more, the fact that Buñuel told Aub that he was present in Madrid in July while Malraux tried to convince Gide to change the final page of a book that had already been published suggests this whole account be taken with a grain of salt.

Not being a scrivener, Buñuel's signature is logically absent from any anti-Fascist tract published by the writing fraternity alone, but it does appear on a couple of wartime declarations on the part of Spanish intellectuals. The first is dated Valencia, 6 June 1937, and is a manifesto protesting recent attacks by German and Italian submarines against Spanish shipping, as well as the shelling of Almería by the battleship *Deutschland.* Signed by Buñuel, along with Alberti, Jacinto Benavente, Bergamín, Ventura Gassol, Miró, Picasso, Sert, and a number of university rectors, the manifesto read: "The signatories of this document . . . address themselves to the men and women of all countries, not in order to launch a useless protest, but to appeal to that universal conscience which cannot remain indifferent towards such events, as the undersigned would not be towards similar events that might occur tomorrow in some other place."[49] The second was published in the Barcelona newspaper *La Vanguardia* on 1 March 1938, shortly after the retaking of Teruel by the Francoists and as the first Negrín government lurched toward a rift between the Communists and Socialists at its core. In this manifesto signed by seventy-five academics, fifty writers, a dozen members of the liberal professions, and thirty artists, including Buñuel, "The intellectuals of Spain for the total victory of the people, March 1938" emphasized the fidelity of the signatories to the Negrín administration and to the Republic per se: "The war has hardened us and made our patriotic feeling even more intense. Today, more than ever, we feel part of our people. And we know that there is no sacrifice capable of holding back the Spanish people in its unyielding resolve to win the war by serving as a basis, a sustenance and a help to the glorious Popular Army."[50] Among the artists, Buñuel rubbed shoulders with Manuel Ángeles Ortiz, Carlos Arniches (the architect), Ángel Ferrán, Halffter, Lacasa, Renau, Alberto Sánchez, and Sánchez Arcas. In the ranks of the writers were Alberti, Álvarez del Vayo, Aub, Bergamín, Pedro Garfias, León, Antonio Machado, Margarita Nelken, Emilio Prados, Sender, and María Zambrano.

The signatures appended to a communication at once triumphalist and vapid would, in the unlikely event that one were still needed, have provided the Francoists with a convenient roll call for future reprisals. In Buñuel's case, only eight weeks were to pass before, on the advice of the chief of police in La Coruña, an order of pursuit and capture was issued against him by the civil governor of the province. Describing him as a "morphine addict and alcoholic," the document specifies that Buñuel "who during recent times has been in Paris at the service of Red propaganda, appears to be trying to enter our territory."[51] Buñuel's espionage activities were doubtless long known to the enemy, although his criminalization (not to say, demonization) would not end there, for on 27 November 1937 the Falangist Ángel Baselga, promoter of a new National Cinema Section of the Fifth Army Corps, an initiative to fill the vacuum in propaganda filmmaking by the rebels, condemned Buñuel to a kind of blacklist as a professional, "unfitted today due to being at the service of the Surrealist-Judeo-Soviet group in Paris, where with Dalí and a few others, he did his artistic training."[52]

In our attempt to describe the polyvalence of Buñuel's activities between September 1936 and 1938, we have rather lost sight of his strictly cinematic endeavors, endeavors that overlapped with the media war effort per se. In general terms, a tailing off is discernible of the exhibition (and therefore production) of pro-Republican film propaganda some twelve months after the Civil War had begun. If, using the daily entertainment column of *L'Humanité* as a yardstick, we focus on the cinemas of Paris, we find that the commercial screening of documentaries during 1937 is restricted to the following: *Espagne 1936* (release date: 9 April 1937); *Attentat contre Madrid* (Arnold (?), 3 May); *Aragon travaille et combat* (Félix Marquet, 7 May); *The Defense of Madrid* (Ivor Montagu, 8 May); *Le Bombardement de Valence* (untraced, 5 June); *Événements d'Espagne* (untraced, 12 June); *Actualités d'Espagne* (untraced, 2 July); *Guernika* (*Au secours des enfants d'Euzkadi*, Nemesio M. Sobrevila, 8 December). Interestingly, all but the latter and *Le Bombardement de Valence* played with a Soviet movie, although *Espagne 1936*, which was the film that enjoyed greatest exposure, supported a variety of features, Hollywood, French, and Russian. Being French in origin, *Attentat contre Madrid* and *Aragon travaille et combat* may well have been compiled from footage that had been vetted by Buñuel; so might *The Defense of Madrid*, as we've already suggested. Missing from this list are the newsreels issued by the seven companies operating at the time in France—*Éclair Journal*, *Gaumont Actualités*, *Pathé Journal*, *Actualities Paramount*, *Fox Movietone*, *Metrotone News*, and *Paris Actualités*—which formed part of many a cinema program but never appeared in newspaper listings. These were homegrown newsreels, but the same stricture holds true for a Spanish "import": Film Popular's monthly *Nouvelles d'Espagne*, the French version of *España al día* (perhaps the three untraced titles cited above belong to this series). Absent, too, are Civil War documentaries that were screened in a politicized, semiprivate context, like *À l'aide du peuple basque* (Jean-Paul Dreyfus, 16 September), part of the PCF's 1937 electoral package that could be rented from Films Populaires by party members; the other films in it, all from that year, were *Le Temps des cerises* (Jean-Paul Dreyfus), *14 juillet 1789–14 juillet 1937* (Ciné-Liberté collective), and *Hommage à la Commune* (Ciné-Liberté collective). Nor are the three films that played in the Spanish Pavilion on the list. What is remarkable, for reasons at which we can only guess, is the concentration of releases in the middle of the year, especially in May; but then May 1937 was a highly charged month, politically speaking. What does come across is the relative paucity and patchiness of the propaganda campaign. As if ideological battle fatigue had quickly begun to take its toll.

In the preceding paragraph we have concentrated on 1937 alone: this is because at the end of that year Buñuel was once again involved in the production of an in-house documentary. The ground for this compilation film, *Espagne 1937*, was prepared by Juan Vicens. Recall that the latter had stated on 5 August that Buñuel had joined the ranks of the Delegation of Propaganda. Part of Vicens's game plan was the relaunching of the cinema campaign, communicated to Ambassador Ossorio in a letter: "As Buñuel so rightly says, the service for distributing films was something that was rather neglected and lacks the means to be developed. All the same, films are an element of propaganda of the first order. On the other hand, the films that were arriving here were few and rarely of good quality; and then again, the service that existed here didn't usually have the means to print copies or to sonorize films or to edit them with dialogues or explanations in French."[53] Buñuel's Rue de la Pépinière operation had been undermined by insufficient funding then. Henceforth, the distribution of film material would be handled by the Boulevard de la Madeleine office, with Buñuel inducted onto the team.

The earliest documentary reference we have found to *Espagne 1937* appears in an 18 November 1937 letter from Vicens to Ossorio. "They've just finished the French and English versions of the film *Espagne 1937*, but in order to exploit it it's necessary to print copies that cost money," money that Vicens knew from bitter experience would take forever to arrive. "The film I was speaking about before is finished," he continued. "The cinema section people request me to ask you if you would like to see it. If so, I'd be grateful if you'd give me a date and a time, because we have to book a private viewing theater. Right now, we've received an acceptance of sale for England; we'll be paid 10,000 francs cash down; with that we'll be able to make three copies and to start distributing it."[54] Just what these French and English versions actually were is a moot point, especially since the English version has proved to be untraceable (but see below). Were they master copies with a soundtrack? Or mute masters with a commentary written but not yet recorded? Were they derivatives of an original Spanish version? Or did the latter not yet exist?

On 3 December the ambassador wrote from Paris to Secretary of State José Giral in Barcelona: "I have the honor to send you, attached, a project for a propaganda film, *España 37*, the author of which is Don Juan Vicens, propaganda delegate in Paris. Indicated in the same are the means necessary to obtain the negative of another film, *Atentado contra Madrid*, and to distribute said film. Likewise, the norms are described for the general propaganda of films useful to our cause."[55] It would seem that Ossorio was acting upon the contents of Vicens's 18 November letter, namely to facilitate funding from central government to pay for prints of the finished movie. The way he tells it, however, suggests that the latter, which he calls *España 37*, rather than *Espagne 1937*, was yet to be begun, thus contradicting Vicens. As things stood, the diplomat was not completely au fait with the dossier he was sending, for he had to ask Juan Guixé, first secretary at the embassy, for verification of who had sent him the project: Buñuel, was it? "Buñuel tells me that it is, in effect, his," was Guixé's reply. Ossorio would pen a further memo to him: "Send it with a dispatch to the Undersecretariat of Propaganda so that they can study and resolve it. Say it's from Buñuel."[56]

The Undersecretariat of Propaganda was, of course, a department of the State Department—the current undersecretary was the geographer L. Martín Echeverría—but the final recipient of this communication must have been the head of the department's Film Service, Manuel Villegas López. This media critic and *cineclubista* was on the point of completing his first documentary, *Madrid*, and had recently helped program the screenings in the Spanish pavilion. Under his guidance the Undersecretariat would produce twenty or so documentaries, of which Villegas López put his name to two titles: *Madrid* and *Blanco* (1938). He would also direct five of the twelve "trailers" released by the Film Service.

On 21 December the ministry acknowledged receipt of the *España 37* proposal. Ossorio instructed Guixé to communicate this to the proposer of the project, Vicens; the secretary did so on 31 December. On 10 January 1938 the ambassador received a letter from Étiennette Bénichou, a relative, perhaps, of Paul Bénichou, the anti-Fascist activist, translator of Ramón J. Sender, and future literary historian. With others, she was mounting a pro-Republican "Centre Cervantes des Amis de l'Espagne," which was to open to the public in early February. The program planned for the new center—not to be confused with the Instituto Cervantes, which dates from 1991—included a conference, convoked by Miró, to be delivered by the "great painters of Paris who are friends of Spain," at which Picasso, André Lhote, Fernand Léger, and Miró himself would appear, plus another conference on the theme of "the Catholics and Spain," with speakers Bergamín, Gallegos Rocafull, Louis Martin-Chauffier, and Mauriac. A further manifestation of the new society, as Guixé explained to Ossorio, who couldn't read Mme Bénichou's French, "will be cinematic. On that score, they only need a technician to commentate on the film *Espagne 37*, which Buñuel has placed at their disposition" (that of the Centre Cervantes).[57] The need for a live commentary would imply that at this point the new movie still lacked a soundtrack.

Albeit corroborated by the documents cited above, the addition of this title to the Buñuel filmography may disconcert some readers. In a sense, however, *Espagne 1937* has always been present in his filmography—present, but occluded, because of its conflation with *Espagne 1936*, two films that, moreover, have no credits. It is worth looking at the historiography, some of it illuminating, some of it confusing, that has allowed us to begin disentangling these two propaganda compilations.

In 1994 the editor of the French magazine *Jeune cinéma*, Lucien Logette, published a transcript of the commentary of *Espagne 1937*, attributing it to Luis Buñuel and Pierre Unik.[58] This document was preceded by a short introduction in which Logette states: "Even if the copy we've been able to consult . . . includes no name in the credits, *Espagne 1937* is without mystery today."[59] If only things were that simple! For although the commentary is indeed that of *Espagne 1937*, all the background information Logette provides relates to *Espagne 1936* and is elaborated from Aranda's biography. The most important consequence of this is that there is no reason whatsoever to accept the attribution of the *Espagne 1937* commentary to both Buñuel and Unik, the supposed writers of *Espagne 1936*, a supposition upon which doubt has already been cast.[60]

It was German historian Wolf Martin Hamdorf who really began to unravel the mystery in his 1995 essay "'Espagne 1936' y 'Espagne 1937': Propaganda para la República (Luis Buñuel y la Guerra Civil Española)." Hamdorf evokes Jay Leyda's discovery in 1966 in the Staatliches Filmarchiv in East Berlin of the complete French and Spanish versions of a Civil War documentary that Leyda subsequently misconstrued as being the Buñuel/Dreyfus opus, based on information provided by the director. Not yet knowing of the existence of *two* documentaries, the American scholar cited the title appearing on the French print, *Espagne 1937*, thus turning Buñuel/Dreyfus into the authors of the wrong film. We know that Leyda wasn't speaking of *Espagne 1936*, however, because he alluded to the soundtrack music of Beethoven, music that indeed accompanies the images of *Espagne 1937*. Once he'd communicated his partly garbled discovery to Aranda in 1967, the latter would quote it in his biography, thus unwittingly repeating an error of attribution that still dogs Buñuel scholarship. Having viewed both films in 1989, Hamdorf made a formal comparison between them, coming to the conclusion that "While *Espagne 1936* has a more intellectual editing style, utilizing not only images by Roman Karmen but also bits of fiction film and bits of direct sound, the editing style of *España 1937* is simpler and visibly involves a film whose original version is in Spanish. . . . Very probably the two emerged from the studio Luis Buñuel was to mount in the Spanish Embassy in Paris."[61]

Pace Leyda, the Spanish version of *Espagne 1937* was incomplete, Hamdorf found—only the second of four reels had survived. He subsequently provided a transcript of the voice-over of this surviving reel, which, when compared to the corresponding section of the French commentary, as supplied by Logette, is highly revealing of the very different ideological tone of the two versions.

Although Natalia Nussinova's "*España-36* ¿Es una producción de Luis Buñuel?" was published in the West in 1996, her essay had originally appeared in Russian seven years before, which in chronological terms makes it the first to propose that *Espagne 1936* and *Espagne 1937* are two separate films, customarily taken to be one. Moscow's Gosfilmfond had prints of both, doubtless as Soviet war booty from Berlin in 1945, where they'd arrived as Nazi war booty from Paris. In a footnote, Nussinova suggested that "it is very possible that the film [*Espagne 1937*] was shot by followers of Buñuel anxious to resume his labors [on *Espagne 1936*]."[62] She was right, if one takes the verb *to shoot* to mean *to compile.*

Published in 1996, the *Catálogo general del cine de la Guerra Civil* lists *España 1937* but is most sparing in its attribution: "1937 Spain / Original language: Spanish / Length of French v[ersion]: 34 minutes (including 2′ 55″ of ambient sound and opening title text)."[63] The synopsis given by Alfonso del Amo and María Luisa Ibáñez, both of the Preservation and Restoration Department of Filmoteca Española, shows that they are indeed speaking of *Espagne 1937*. Like Hamdorf they claim that the original version of the film was in Spanish, yet without presenting any hard evidence for this.

La Guerra Civil Española y el cine francés (2005), by Inmaculada Sánchez Alarcón, professor of documentary and news cinema at Málaga University, represented an important advance in that the author offered new documentary evidence to substantiate her claim that *Espagne 1937* was attributable "without discussion to members of the office operated by Luis Buñuel in Paris."[64] The documents suggest that Juan Vicens was the writer of at least the Spanish commentary, although nothing can be deduced from them as to whether he might have written the French one, too.

The most recent addition to this micro-historiography is "Sobre los documentales de guerra de Buñuel: Aclaraciones y nuevas aportaciones," a lecture from 2006 by Javier Herrera Navarro, keeper of the Buñuel Bequest at Filmoteca Española in Madrid. Herrera accepts Logette's unproven attribution of the *Espagne 1937* voice-over commentary to Unik and Buñuel and is emphatic about the latter's imprint being visible in this film and in *Espagne 1936* "as regards the planning, ordering and editing of material within the model of reportage that he inaugurates with *Las Hurdes–Tierra sin pan.*"[65]

Espagne 1937 is a companion piece to *Espagne 1936*; their titles underline this (just as their similarity has fomented decades of confusion). That the Republicans might have wanted to emulate the success of *Espagne 1936* by making a "sequel" to it is understandable. Of the seven documentaries on the Civil War that were screened commercially in Paris between April and July 1937, *Espagne 1936* was the first and by far the most visible: it played for a total of five weeks at five different cinemas. We might describe it as the flagship of the Republican film propaganda campaign up to that time. Moreover, the hiatus in the cinematic war effort in France between July and December 1937 would have made the reinvigoration of the campaign dependent upon jogging people's memories of an earlier propaganda success, *Espagne 1936*. Hence *Espagne 1937*. As it was, coverage of the Spanish Civil War had been progressively shrinking on the front pages of that fiercely pro-Republican organ, *L'Humanité*. Several factors contributed to this: the military successes of the Axis insurgents; the indefatigable immovability of the Non-Intervention Committee in London, which proved less and less newsworthy; and the outbreak of the Sino-Japanese War on 7 July, with which the Spanish conflict had to share double billing, as it were. Not only would the conflict in China summon Ivens, Karmen, and Capa, but it would also divert Soviet aid from Spain to Asia. Meanwhile, that other ideological window, the International Exhibition, had closed on 25 November; thirty million tickets to it had been sold. By the time of Ossorio's 3 December letter to Giral, resuscitating the film propaganda program had become a priority.

This is the context of the ambassador's allusion to the document he is sending to the secretary of state containing "norms . . . for the general propaganda of films useful to our cause"—guidelines that, in relation to cinema, Buñuel must have played a part in formulating—and to the obtaining of the negative of a French compilation, *Attentat contre Madrid*, doubtless to revamp the voice-over in Spanish and to distribute it in the Republican zone (the Generalitat de Catalunya would eventually take care of this). *Attentat contre Madrid* had been shown in Paris between 3 and 13 May 1937 at the Ce Soir-Italiens and the Ce Soir-Pigalle, with *Vous n'avez rien à déclarer?* (Léo Joannon, 1937) at the former and *Cabin in the Cotton* (Michael Curtiz, 1933) at the latter. Ramón Sala Noguer identifies the eleven-minute *Attentat contre Madrid*, which used some Karmen footage, as a Films Liberté production, with a commentary by Henri Jeanson, who was not only a leading light in Ciné-Liberté, being coeditor of the organization's monthly magazine, but also the screenwriter of *Pépé le Moko* and *Un carnet de bal* (both Julien Duvivier, 1937).[66]

Vicens would divulge that Ilya Ehrenburg had been the hidden hand behind the *Attentat contre Madrid* project in his report for the government in Valencia, a report that has, fortunately, come down to us.[67] Albeit undated, it appears to be written just before or after the end of the International Exhibition, for it hints that the latter has a certain actuality. Although a variety of media are addressed in this document, the section to do with cinema is our focus. Using the first person plural—a "we" that must be taken to include Buñuel—the report sums up a year of activity in Paris. In the main, that activity has been hamstrung by the lack of foreign versions of the copious material originated in Spain: "of the five 'official' films we've managed to bring, only one was explained in French and English." All from 1937, the five titles, which omitted the movies brought solely for the programming of the pavilion, were *Defensa del campo* (Alliance of Anti-Fascist Intellectuals for the Defense of Culture, 1937), *Los Yunteros* (Ministry of Agriculture), *España por Europa* (General Commisariat of War), *Nuestros prisioneros* (General Commisariat of War)—all of these in Spanish only—plus *18 de julio* (Alliance of Anti-Fascist Intellectuals for the Defense of Culture), in French and English.[68] This lack of usable material—or excess of unusable material—had been compensated for by twelve films received from Film Popular in Barcelona, nine of them newsreels (to wit, episodes of *Nouvelles d'Espagne*). The three others were *Guerra en el campo*, *El Tribunal de las Aguas*, and *Galicia Saudade*: Spanish Pavilion material. Vicens drew attention to the fact that a further two titles, having been finalized in France, were not included in the list of propaganda: *Tierra sin pan* and *Espagne 1936*. Supplementing all these films were a number of Cifesa productions that had been screened in the pavilion in French versions, but that could not be shown commercially due to rights problems with the parent company, whose owner had set up in business in the Francoist zone. These Cifesa titles presumably included the prewar documentaries of Velo and Mantilla.

Vicens went on to list the priorities of the film propaganda department during the four months following its reorganization in early August:

1. To bring together as many films as were capable of serving their ends or of being screened in the Spanish Pavilion, ordering them from Spain, censoring and adapting them to the necessities imposed by the French censors.
2. The ongoing programming of the Spanish Pavilion, from 2 August until today's date, presenting seven different programs.
3. The distribution of films, with the charging of rental fees, to charitable entities, film companies and political groups. No special consideration is shown when it comes to charging, due to the need to send unexposed film to Spain along with other raw materials with which they may carry on with production, since it is this that forms the basis of all our potential activity.
4. The continual plea made to Spain for new films and our request to official bodies for them to support our demands and organize production so that the supply of film prints is constant and that they come ready prepared in French or English.
5. Dealings with the business concerns of France and other countries in order to organize the commercial distribution and sale of our films.[69]

If certain remedies were not adopted, Vicens warned, this entire strategy would suffer from the same shortfall in viable material as during the first year's activity between September 1936 and August 1937, that is, although he doesn't name him, when Buñuel was in charge. For a good Marxist-Leninist like Vicens, the long-term solution lay in complete state control within Republican Spain itself. (In a sense, his proposals were a rerun of the history of Soviet centralization, from the mixed economy of the NEP [New Economic Policy] to the full-fledged state capitalism of Stalin.) During a first phase, a specially appointed individual was to buy or rent films worthy of foreign exposure from commercial or political entities in Spain. Once in Paris, these films were to be adapted to suit the strictures of local censorship and then subtitled. Payment to the producers would be made, not in cash, but in virgin negative or positive film stock, which was impossible to find in Spain and could not easily be bought on the international market due to a lack of foreign currency. In a second phase, a state-created delegation would centralize film production still further, obliging producers who received government funding to make films compatible with Frente Popular ideology. This delegation would control each film's budget as well as its content, censoring this if necessary, and oblige the producer to hand over a silent lavender negative so that export prints could be struck. It would also prepare the French- and English-language adaptation for recording in situ and send a copy of this to friendly propaganda agencies abroad.

December 1937 is the moment in which the Republican propaganda campaign gets its second wind in Paris, due in part to the activism of Vicens. On 8 December, Sobrevila's *Guernika* (*Au secours des enfants d'Euzkadi*) opened for a week's run at the Ce Soir-Italiens, with Max Ophüls's *Yoshiwara* (1937). On 10 December, Louis Chéronnet, *L'Humanité*'s film critic and a Ciné-Liberté stalwart, signed a glowing review of Joris Ivens's *Terre d'Espagne* (the French version of *The Spanish Earth*), which he'd seen at a private screening: "This is THE documentary we were waiting for on the war in Spain."[70] On 17 December, the exhibition *L'Espagne vous parle*, which used photographs, artwork, and artifacts to describe the country's history between the fall of the monarchy and the uprising of the generals, opened on the Boulevard Bonne-Nouvelle. Sponsored by the International Committee for Aid to the Spanish People—whose president was Francis Jourdain, and whose honorary board included Bloch, Cachin, Langevin, and Malraux—the show was much panegyrized by Paul Bénichou in *L'Humanité*. On 21 December, the Civil War returned to the front pages of that newspaper in the wave of euphoria elicited by the taking of Teruel from the Fascists. Teruel in the hands of the Franco forces also featured in the last chapter of *L'Espoir*, Malraux's epic novel in praise of the Loyalist cause, which appeared to great acclaim at the end of December. On 28 December *Terre d'Espagne* was screened before the party faithful at the suburban Cinéma Familia, to an introduction by Moussinac. Only on 2 April 1938 would it be commercially released—with the contentious voice-over by the doyen of Ciné-Liberté, Jean Renoir—at the Studio de l'Étoile in the seventeenth arrondissement, with a musical comedy, *Hitting a New High* (Raoul Walsh, 1937). Before moving on to a couple of other cinemas, *Terre d'Espagne* would play there until 10 May, making it the longest running of all the Civil War documentaries, with *Espagne 1936* coming in a close second.

On 11 January 1938 Ossorio paid a visit to the *L'Espagne vous parle* exhibition, which was shortly due to close. (In fact it would give way to another show, *L'Espagne se défend*, about the Popular Army, which ran until late March.) As *L'Humanité* reported, "The Ambassador stopped for a long time in front of each of the paintings and objects. . . . On seeing the moving film that was unfolding before his eyes, a film which evokes the entire history of the Republic of his country, the Ambassador thanked the organizers for managing to convey the Spanish tragedy through this exhibition."[71] Given this description, it is legitimate to ask if this movie was not *Espagne 1937*, a version of which was ready by then: the 11 January date tallies with Étiennette Bénichou's letter of 10 January to Ossorio, announcing that Buñuel had offered her the film for the embryonic Centre Cervantes. Were this to be so, it would mean that the International Committee for Aid to the Spanish People, a classic Communist front organization, was first (and last?) host to the film.

The period between early November 1937 and early February 1938 forms the time frame for the creation of *Espagne 1937*, for in the second week of February the film was presented to the French Board of Film Censors. In a 9 February *L'Humanité* review of two other titles—*Les Bâtisseurs* and *Cœur d'Espagne*—Chéronnet divulged: "The French censors have refused their visa to a documentary film called *Espagne 1937*, a follow-up to *Espagne 1936*, put together from bits of newsreel footage. We have seen this film, which retraces, with objectivity, a decisive year in the development of the Spanish Republic. . . . Such a refusal is beyond our understanding. This movie simply records events. It could even be said to err, in our opinion, on account of a lack of care in its presentation. It aims at no effect. Its editing lacks emphasis. Because the problem the tragic situation of Spain poses goes beyond simple newsreel, it attains a sense of the human in all that is most immense, most profound, most moving."[72]

Hitherto free of centralized censorship, newsreels and documentaries employing *actualité* footage had become subject to state control with the passing of the Sarrault Decree on 7 May 1936. After that date, any producer of such films had to present a detailed list of the material to be projected to the French minister of the interior and the Prefecture of Police. In practice, there was a weekly screening of forthcoming newsreels and documentaries before the authorities, with cuts and outright bans ever in the offing. One French scholar gives a list of repressed subject matter, 1936–39: the activities of La Cagoule; the destruction by fire of the *Lafayette*, the liner on which Buñuel returned from New York in March 1931; the duel between playwrights Henri Bernstein and Édouard Bourdet; the signing of the Anti-Comintern Pact between Germany, Italy, and Japan.[73] The relative dearth of commercial screenings of Civil War documentaries in France suggests a falling foul of the censors. This is confirmed by a remark made at the beginning of 1938 by Sobrevila that "of the films that have been presented as propaganda by the Spanish Republic to the French censors, *Guernika* [by Sobrevila himself] is the only one that's been accepted for showing in public."[74]

A couple of days after the *L'Humanité* revelation of 9 February, the trade magazine *La Cinématographie Française* carried the following item: "*Espagne 1937*. Documentary. Origin: Spanish. Edited by the Spanish Delegation of Propaganda. This documentary relates the main events of the Spanish revolution, as the representatives of Republican Spain see them. It begins with an exposé of the different political and electoral developments that preceded the civil war. It shows, apart from the war, the efforts made by the government forces to do with education and improving the living conditions of the people. A propaganda film, the goal of which is to show, in the most favorable light, the action and influence of the Republican government."[75]

The "follow-up" to *Espagne 1936* opens with a rolling title, which reads:

> *Espagne 1937* / A documentary on the events in Spain during the first year of civil war / The origin of the events that are to unfold before the eyes of the public, goes back to the military defeat Spain experienced in Morocco in 1921. In order to try and allay the discontent that this rout had stirred up in the country at the time, the monarchy had recourse to the dictatorship of Primo de Rivera. But, combated by all, including those who had supported it, this dictatorship could not last. Royalty was abolished. The Republic succeeded it. After two years of a Republic, the popular vote went to the government of Right-wing parties that wanted to back-pedal and return to the retrograde politics that had been those of the decadent monarchy. A revolt breaks out: these were the terrible October Days of 1934. The governments that came after those October Days attempted to direct the course of events, but without being able to avoid new legislative elections that, this time, ensured an overwhelming majority for

> the Frente Popular / "Espagne 37"—a compilation of veracious documents, often filmed at the risk of the life of the cameramen—relates the events that have taken place since then.

These events are organized in a smooth metonymic sequencing that often relies on the banner headlines of liberal, Socialist, and Communist newspapers to convey historical detail. And never with a French translation, thus suggesting that the original version was in Spanish, as Hamdorf argued in his day. After describing the February 1936 election that established the Frente Popular, thus ending a baleful two-year period—the *bienio negro*—remembered for its repression of the October 1934 revolution, we glimpse the comeback of such castigated politicians as the Catalan president Lluís Companys, as well as the arrival of new or reelected deputies like Ibárruri, Prieto, and Negrin, but also the parliamentary opposition of Gil Robles and the Count de Romanones. The much-applauded proclamation of Azaña as president does not, however, stay the hand of the Right: agents provocateurs are at work in those factories that remain open; a reactionary army is on the march. Announced by an intertitle—"18 de julio"—the military uprising is met by fierce worker resistance in the cities; in the countryside armed peasants get on with the harvest. In Madrid the popular militias receive basic training from the Fifth Regiment—its Communist loyalties go unstated—and march off to fight in Somosierra and Toledo. The aerial bombing of the capital's civilian population by the Fascists begins. By now the Fifth Regiment has welded the militias into the Popular Army. A further intertitle, "6 de noviembre," announces the arrival of the Franco forces at the gates of Madrid; for a whole year the populace is to keep this enemy at bay. At this point *Espagne 1937* shifts ground: we observe the literacy (and political indoctrination) campaign aimed at the new Republican frontline infantryman. In the rear we see women doing war work in the factories, and we witness the care and attention lavished on wounded soldiers and refugee children alike. Such disasters of war are linked, via images of Italian arms captured at the battle of Guadalajara to the reality of foreign intervention. The film ends with a last parade of the by now perfectly trained Popular Army, units of which are addressed by General Miaja and Jesús Hernández. Such land forces are supplemented by those of air and sea. The final shot is of a five-pointed star that has not been identified as pertaining to any given Republican entity, but that is a symbol commonly associated with Communist imagery.

Formally, *Espagne 1937* is much less heterogeneous than its predecessor and even gives the impression that its footage (which emanates from many different sources) has been carefully graded at the printing stage to appear more uniform.

It even looks more "modern": a series of decorative wipes are a departure from the customary devices of the genre. Voice-over aside, the soundtrack consists of incessant Beethoven, which is not only overlaid at times with ambient noise but also with other music. In that respect, the soundtrack is less effective than in *Espagne 1936*, for it dispenses with silence. If Buñuel was the supervisor of that very different soundtrack, then it appears unlikely that he watched over the soundtrack of its successor. However, we ought to bear in mind the sustained use of Brahms in *Terre sans pain*. Discretion would suggest that we attribute an inspirational role to Buñuel here, nothing more.

Unlike *Espagne 1936*, of whose voice-over we have only the French version, in the case of *Espagne 1937* both the French and at least part of the Spanish commentary exist. In keeping with Vicens's guidelines of November 1937, we would opt for the primacy of a Spanish version, a silent copy of which was dispatched to Paris for the elaboration of French and English "editions." Upon comparing that single Spanish and French reel at the same point in the voice-over, not only do we find that the former is much wordier than the latter, but also that a very different discourse emerges: the discourse of, on the one hand, class-conscious stridency in *España 1937* and of terse populism in *Espagne 1937*. A couple of examples: "The barbarous powers, caught up in feudalism, begin a war of extermination; they call it the 'renovation' of Spain" (Spanish) versus "The rebels wage a war of extermination" (French). "But the peasants, stooping over Mother Earth, hear the whine of the cannon in the distance. As it is for the proletariat of the cities, the war is a threat to them as well. They are prepared; with weapons and ploughs they alternate between war and peace" (Spanish) versus "The peasant hears the distant noise of cannon. For him too the military uprising is a threat. He also carries his rifle while he drives the plough" (French).[76] Such changes of register may be ascribed to the differing strategies of the PCF and the PCE vis-à-vis their respective Popular Fronts, and to the need, or otherwise, to negotiate the forces of censorship: to tone down the message or to intensify it.

The documents cited earlier in this chapter suggest that Vicens was the author of the *España 1937* commentary. Its rhetoric would certainly square with his militancy in the PCE. Furthermore, he was a bona fide writer: *L'Espagne vivante: Le peuple à la conquête de la culture*, his account of recent mass literacy campaigns in Spain, appeared in February 1938 under the Éditions Sociales Internationales imprint.[77] Léon Moussinac directed this PCF publishing house. He and Vicens had first made contact in May 1936, probably through Sadoul, apropos of the mounting of a counterinformation campaign. The less intrusive, less histrionic commentary of *Espagne 1937* could easily have been written by the same hand as *Espagne 1936*: the sentences in both have the same cadence, weight, didacticism. Witness: "The Frente Popular government is formed and begins to apply the Popular Front program: agrarian reform for our peasants, equivalent to the reforms granted in the revolution of 1789 to the French peasantry" (*Espagne 1936*) versus "The next day, the victory of the Frente Popular results in the formation of a new government. The Republic resumes its forward march" (*Espagne 1937*). "Equipped with war material that is not entirely Spanish, the [Francoist] troops leave for the front" (*Espagne 1936*) versus "After preparing sizeable arms depots, the military rises up against the lawful power" (*Espagne 1937*). If this were so, then in keeping with our reasoning vis-à-vis *Espagne 1936*, the commentary of *Espagne 1937* could also be attributed to Pierre Unik.

We have found no evidence that once *Espagne 1937* was refused a certificate it was ever shown in the kind of politicized semiprivate settings in which films deemed unsuitable for popular consumption by the French censors might still be projected. Did Chéronnet's negative review help bury the movie in such circles? The same holds true for *España 1937* in the rapidly shrinking areas of the peninsula that remained viable as a venue. The historian who has most deeply researched the Republican press during the Civil War, José Cabeza San Deogracias, has confirmed that no Madrid newspaper records a screening of *España 1937*.[78] With regard to the English-language version of the film, however, we have come across a curious allusion to the showing in Australia of a film called *New Spain*, "directed by Luis Buñuel," according to a reference in number 4 of the *Spanish Relief Committee News Bulletin*, published in January 1939.[79] Could this be the "edition" Vicens referred to in his 18 November 1937 missive to Ambassador Ossorio?

As we did with *Espagne 1936*, we will chance our arm and propose a new fiche for its "sequel." It will be immediately obvious that there are many gaps therein, gaps we can only hope other historians might one day fill in. Moreover, some attributions are tentative and thus open to revision:

Espagne 1937
Title of the Spanish version: *España 1937*
Title of the English version: [unknown]
1938 France
35 mm, b & w
Refused a visa by the French Board of Film Censors in the first week of February 1938
Release date of the Spanish version: unknown; ditto, the English version
Producer in Barcelona: Film Service of the Undersecretariat of Propaganda of the State Department

Producer in Paris: Delegation of Spanish Propaganda (i.e., the Spanish Tourist Office) / International Committee for Aid to the Spanish People
Executive producer in Barcelona: Manuel Villegas López
Executive producer in Paris: Luis Buñuel
Original idea: Juan Vicens
Commentary of the Spanish version: Juan Vicens
Commentary of the French version: Pierre Unik
Voice-over of the French version: Gaston Modot (?)
Music: Beethoven's Seventh and Eighth Symphonies
Length: 34 minutes (including 90 seconds of music and singing over black leader, prior to title credit and rolling title)

In order to tie up some of the loose ends as to Buñuel's film-related activities, we must mention, in keeping with the logistic aid he gave to Ivens and Ferno on *The Spanish Earth* in January 1937, the official help he gave to the *Return to Life* and *Heart of Spain* projects. As Sánchez Alarcón tells us, "The Spanish Embassy in Paris [took] charge, for example, of facilitating the trip to Spain of its prime mover, the American filmmaker Herbert Kline, as well as of the transfer by diplomatic bag and the customs arrangements to get the five reels of the copy of *Return to Life* edited in Spain into France."[80]

Further evidence of the reactivation of the Paris propaganda operation at the end of 1937 comes in the form of a letter Ambassador Ossorio wrote to Secretary of State José Giral on 3 January 1938, telling him that he (Ossorio) had received a visit from Charles Desage, director general of the Agence d'Informations et Actualités Cinématographiques in Paris, a visit at which Buñuel must have been present. Desage had just returned from Barcelona, where he'd spoken with defense minister Prieto and undersecretary of war Antonio Fernández Bolaños about a project to, as the ambassador put it, "reveal, through film, on the one hand: 1) the perfect organization of the Republican Army; 2) the importance and activity of our war industries; and 3) the quality of our aviation."[81] To do this, Desage proposed to return to Spain with a film unit consisting of three cameramen, one of whom was Robert Petiot, who was already in the Catalan capital filming for the American newsreel outfit Metrotone News, dependent on press baron William Randolph Hearst and on MGM, for which Desage had also worked; between May and June 1937 Petiot had been in the Basque Country, where he'd shot material for Sobrevila's *Guernika* and for Dreyfus's *À l'aide du peuple basque*.[82] The other technicians were Gaston Chelle (another Metrotone cameraman), Misive (who'd worked at Paramount-Joinville), and sound engineer André Caillat. The last three were in Paris and were ready to leave for Spain immediately, providing the proper funding for the project could be found. It was about this that Ossorio was writing to the minister. Such seed money was not forthcoming, apparently, for Petiot, the most experienced member of the team, returned definitively to France in January.[83] The lack of political will on the part of the Republican government to provide the funding for foreign film propaganda—explainable in part by the scarcity of foreign currency—is manifest here. Although Film Popular would continue to produce the monthly newsreel *Nouvelles d'Espagne*—the French version of *España al día*—until January 1939, the only commercially promoted title we have come across in the listings in *L'Humanité*—prior to Buñuel's departure for the United States—is *Le Bombardement de Barcelona par les avions fascistes* (untraced), which played for a week in March 1938 at all three Ce Soir cinemas in Paris. Apart from this, only *Victoire de la vie* and *Cœur d'Espagne* were shown in 1938—not to the general public, though, but in semi-private screenings, and rare ones at that.

The year 1937 is often given in the literature as the year in which Buñuel composed his film treatment of *The Duchess of Alba and Goya*.[84] This attribution is extremely flimsy, because it indicates he wrote the treatment in Paris in perfect English at the height of the Spanish Civil War. In his old age Braunberger even evoked Buñuel writing the script of *Le Moine*—based on M. G. Lewis's Gothic novel—during the same period. Lodged in the Department of Film at the MoMA, the English-language original of *The Duchess of Alba and Goya* bears no date. Neither is there any record of when the manuscript was deposited in the archive there.[85] Our belief is that it ought to be dated to between September 1939 and June 1943. That is, between the invitation made to Buñuel by Iris Barry, curator of the MoMA Film Library, that he move from Los Angeles to New York, where she helped him survive until he found work at the museum in January 1941 on the "Good Neighbor" Latin American film project sponsored by the U.S. Office of Inter-American Affairs (OIAA), and his politically motivated departure from said museum. Moreover, the flawless English of the film treatment bespeaks the intervention of a sophisticated native speaker. With one likely candidate, Barry herself, Buñuel, whose English was wanting, could always communicate in their common language, French—in 1938 she'd published her translation of Bardèche and Brasillach's *Histoire du cinéma* as *The History of Motion Pictures*.[86] Another possibility is that the provider of linguistic assistance was Jay Leyda, a former editor at Frontier Films during 1937–38 and a Film Library employee, until forced to resign in mid-1940 for being a "Red"—a fate that was to befall Buñuel three years later. Although the future author of *Kino* had left the MoMA before the Spaniard was taken on there, the two men were to see much of each other. Moreover, Leyda had an intimate knowledge of the treatment, since he was able to inform Aranda of imagery that had been edited out of the version we know.[87] Of *The Duchess of Alba and Goya*, with its obvious echoes of the 1926 script the would-be director had submitted for the centenary of the painter's death, Buñuel himself said: "Wretched, it seems to me. I did it to see if I could sell it to Paramount."[88] In his "Auto-Biography," or curriculum vitae, compiled in July 1939, Buñuel did mention his work as a writer of Spanish adaptations for Paramount-Joinville in 1932; that is, the studio was present in his mind as one with which he had a track record good enough to exploit in the United States.[89] Unfortunately, the cineaste gave no indication of the date of the treatment to Aranda, who contradicts himself by ascribing it to 1938 in his filmography, but introducing it in the main text of his biography at the point where Buñuel has left New York and returned to Hollywood for two years, thus implicitly dating it to 1944–46, a hypothesis with which another historian, Nigel Glendinning, concurs. Whatever the truth of the matter, 1937 is too early a date for the writing of this irremediably conventional costume picture in keeping with the commercial criteria of the Hollywood majors of the time.

Opening on 19 December 1936, the twelve-week run of *Terre sans pain* had restored Buñuel's name to a prominence of sorts among the cinephile public of Paris. There were lacunae in his trajectory, however; the director himself made sure of that. Nothing was known of his production work on the four Filmófono pictures, although *La hija de Juan Simón* had been shown in the Spanish Pavilion. And while word had leaked out of his involvement with *Espagne 1936*, his activities as a movie propagandist at the embassy were kept under wraps. For the average movie buff Buñuel remained the notorious Surrealist experimenter of 1929–30, and given the repression of *L'Âge d'or*, his first film tended to function as a synecdoche for his œuvre to date.

On 12 October 1937 Buñuel personally introduced a program in his honor at Henri Langlois and Georges Franju's Cercle du Cinéma, a forerunner of the Cinémathèque Française, a program that opened with *Un chien andalou*. Also on the heterodox bill were *La Route de Don Quichotte* (*La ruta de Don Quijote*, Ramón Biadiu, 1934) and *Les Rois d'Espagne* (*El Escorial de Felipe II*, Carlos Velo and Fernando G. Mantilla, 1935)—these last "borrowed" from the Spanish Pavilion—along with a Belgian Surrealist short, *Mr. Fantômas* (Ernst Moerman, 1937).[90] The members of this Champs Élysées cine sanctum included Yves Allégret, Duvivier, Georges Lacombe, Sadoul, and Paolo Emilio Sales Gomes, Vigo's future biographer. Among the habitués were Becker, Gide, Malraux, Jean Painlevé, and Renoir.[91] On 16 February 1938, in its tenth anniversary year, Studio 28 programmed *Un chien andalou* with Cocteau's *Le Sang d'un poète* for a month's run.

In March the organizers of the Venice Film Festival expressed an interest in showing Buñuel and Dalí's first opus. In July the Paris-based company Intercontinental Film wrote to Buñuel, c/o the Spanish Tourist Office, to confirm that Langlois, who was organizing a retrospective of recent French cinema for Venice, wanted to include the short. Was Buñuel prepared to let it be shown?[92] We haven't been able to ascertain whether he allowed it to appear alongside recent classics by Carné, Clair, Duvivier, and Renoir. To begin with, the Venice Film Festival was a brazen move by Italian Fascism to seek international ideological legitimacy through a spurious appeal to pluralism—the very first director's prize was awarded, in 1932, to Nikolai Ekk for *Road to Life*—but between 1937 and 1942 the régime showed its true colors, with the Mussolini Cup for best foreign film going on four occasions to Nazi filmmakers Veit Harlan, Leni Riefenstahl, Hans Steinhoff, and Gustav Ucicky. Buñuel and Langlois were firm friends by this time: before departing for the States the Spaniard would donate documentary film material on the Spanish Civil War to the fledgling Cinémathèque.[93]

As discussed in an earlier chapter, *Un chien andalou* also entered the 1938 plans of André Breton. On 17 May he presented the movie to an audience in Mexico City during the trip on which he and Trotsky coauthored their famous manifesto, the founding text of the short-lived International Federation of Independent Revolutionary Art (FIARI), created to combat the Stalinist AEAR, although at the behest of Aragon, Tzara, and others, the Mexican branch of the latter did its utmost to sabotage Breton's mission. In that presentation the Surrealist leader criticized Buñuel's "submission to the orders of a party, a submission that has deprived us, unfortunately in my opinion, of a fresh opportunity to appreciate the very rare gifts we knew he had."[94] (In passing, Breton stoked the fires of myth by claiming that the only extant copy of *L'Âge d'or*, the one he'd taken to Santa Cruz de Tenerife in May 1935, had been destroyed by the Francoists.) A few months before this public disqualification, however, Buñuel merited his own entry in the *Dictionnaire abrégé du surréalisme*, compiled by Breton and Éluard and published in January 1938 as the catalog of the International Surrealist Exhibition at the Galerie des Beaux-Arts, a show remembered for its street of erotic mannequins and for Duchamp's twelve hundred hanging coal sacks. Unlike "practicing" Surrealists, who were defined in lavish terms—for instance, "DALI, Salvador, born in 1904. 'Prince of the Catalan intelligentsia, colossally rich.' Painter, poet and Surrealist theorist since 1929"—Buñuel's entry was perfunctory in the extreme: "Filmmaker. His Surrealist activity takes place from 1928 to 1932."[95] Note that, by implication, the date of *Un chien andalou* is given as 1928, an error one still sees repeated in the

Buñuel literature.[96] The criticism Breton would level at him in Mexico City is already latent in the very brevity of this entry. And part of that disapproving vision bore upon Buñuel's actuation during the Spanish Civil War, namely, as a cog in the Stalinist propaganda machine.

On 15 October 1936 Benjamin Péret, in Spain since early August as a militant of the Fourth International's International Workers Party (POI), with a mission to liaise with the POUM, wrote from Barcelona to Breton: "It may be that I return soon to Madrid. Can you tell me if Buñuel will be there and what his address is?"[97] Péret's query indicates that Buñuel and the Surrealists were still on speaking terms, although given the chaotic state of communications, the future author of *Le Déshonneur des poètes* was not to know that the Spaniard had skipped the country a month previously. (In *Mon dernier soupir* Buñuel turns the anecdote around: it is Breton who asks *him* for news of Péret, seemingly under threat of execution at the hands of the POUM.)[98] Two years later, on 11 November 1938, Breton delivered a speech to the POI about his visit to Trotsky, a speech that provides a convenient summary of the Surrealist stance on the Civil War in Spain. Ever since the attempted military coup, Breton argued, the Surrealists have condemned the regressive forces that were behind it and have placed their hopes in the insurgent working class and its revolutionary activity—particularly the anti-religious form of this—as expressed through the FAI, CNT, POUM, and PSUC, assuming that these anarchist and Marxist organizations could fight alongside, and not against, each other. The Surrealists have consistently objected to the non-intervention policy of the Western democracies. What has gained them the greatest ostracism, however, is their contention that the USSR is one of the chief obstacles to the victory of the Spanish proletariat: "For Stalin it is a question of preventing at all costs a new revolutionary wave from spreading across the world."[99] The October 1938 trial by the Negrín government of the POUM leaders for the May Events of the year before is tantamount to a Spanish version of the Moscow Trials. Accordingly, Breton claimed: "Working-class Spain, revolutionary Spain, *the reality of which we refuse to replace with the concept of Republican Spain*, remains on its feet. It is to it, and to it alone, that our ardent fraternity goes: despite all the corrupt attempts, neither Stalin nor Franco is yet its master."[100]

Any reader who has gotten this far will know that this was not a view that Buñuel shared, whence the "disgrace" he would endure in the eyes of Breton until the release of *Los olvidados* in 1951 and the director's subsequent lionization by the young Surrealists of *L'Âge du cinéma* and *Positif* (specifically Ado Kyrou and Robert Benayoun). Buñuel was no one-off aberration, mind you. Of the Surrealists who in 1930–31 had signed tracts like "Seconde prière d'insérer du

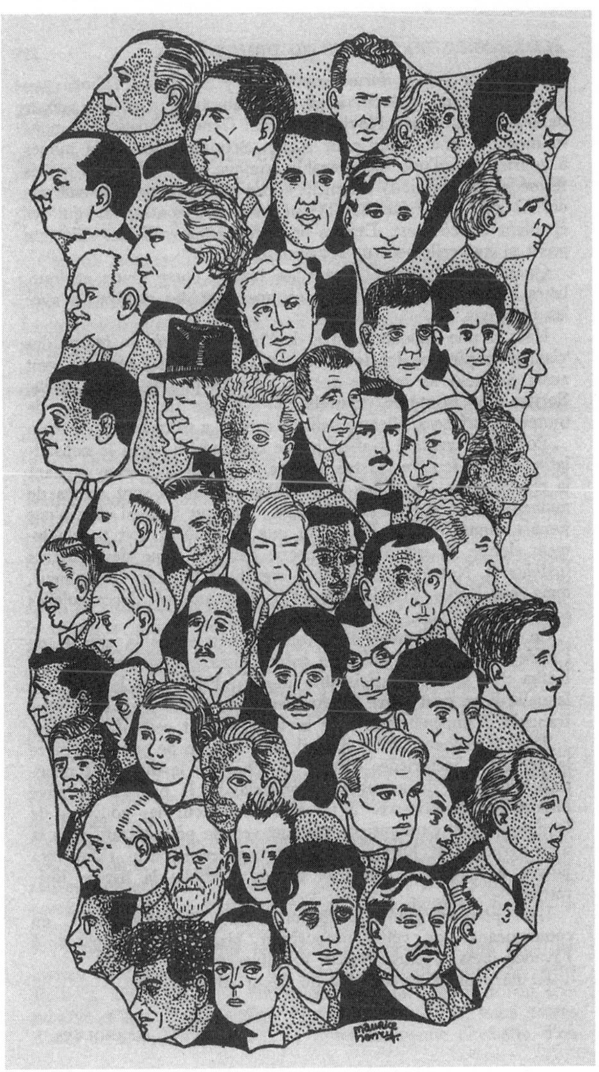

In the eyes of André Breton, Buñuel remained in disgrace until 1951, the year *Los olvidados* was released in France. This disqualification is graphically shown by Maurice Henry in a drawing published in the *Almanach surréaliste du demi-siècle*, a special number of the Paris magazine *La Nef*, 63–64, March 1950, page 22. In this amalgam of precursors and members of the Surrealist Group, the dots on their faces denote the degree of disgrace or dissidence into which the subject has sunk, often for having adhered to Stalinism. Buñuel is the fourth face descending by the left, beneath Trotsky and beside film comedian W. C. Fields, whose immaculate features contrast with the cineaste's "contamination." In the center is a highly contaminated Dalí and at the right, Louis Aragon, the spottiest of all. (© Maurice Henry, VEGAP, Barcelona, 2010)

'Second Manifeste du Surréalism"' and "L'Affaire de 'L'Âge d'or,'" only Péret and Tanguy remained at Breton's side by the end of 1938. Aragon, Buñuel, Crevel, Sadoul, Tzara, and Unik had all thrown in their lot with the Stalinists. Éluard was in the process of doing so. Ernst would quit in sympathy with him. Dalí, too, was poised to exit the group: by February 1939 his racist opinions, not to mention the monotony of his recent pictorial output, were deemed sufficient to eject him.

By the time Breton communicated his sanguine perception of events in Spain to the Trotskyist POI, the more pessimistic, and panicky, Buñuel had put three thousand miles between himself and the Old World. "With the Munich Pact," wrote Max Aub, "this prophet (aided somewhat by the opinions of his better-informed friends) will willingly go to North America, fleeing the future conflagration."[101] Aub's chronology is a little awry, since Buñuel left Paris a couple of weeks before the mendacious non-aggression agreement, formulated to resolve the "Czech crisis," was signed on 30 September between the appeasers, Chamberlain and Daladier, and the appeased, Hitler and Mussolini, but his general point is well made. Things looked exceedingly grim in Europe, while in Spain the war had but months to run, having reached a critical stage with the long, drawn-out Battle of the Ebro, which began on 24 July and would end on 16 November with the retreat of the Popular Army. Six weeks after that the Francoists marched into Barcelona.

Forty-odd years later, the old master scriptwriter spun something of a yarn about his flight. Unable to reconcile himself to the absurdity of ballooning tracts over the Pyrenees Buñuel goes to see Ambassador Pascua and expresses his doubts to the ambassador: isn't there some better way to serve the propaganda effort? "At that time films were being made in the United States that showed the war in Spain. Henry Fonda acted in one of these. In Hollywood they were preparing *Cargo of Innocents*, about the evacuation of Bilbao. These films were often marked by glaring errors whenever it was a matter of local color. As a result Pascua proposed I return to Hollywood and get taken on as a technical or historical adviser."[102] This is the account given in *Mon dernier soupir*; elsewhere, it is the cineaste who suggests to Pascua that he undertake the trip, paying for it himself.[103] Before looking at some of the contemporary documents about this episode, it is worth remarking that aside from the alarming political situation, an important motive for beating a retreat was that Buñuel's two-year diplomatic passport was due to expire on 22 December 1938; to justify its usage, and the privileges that went with this, an official mission (however contrived) made sense.

There was another urgent reason for organizing such a mission, as Buñuel hinted in an 11 August 1938 letter to Ricardo Urgoiti, now exiled in Buenos

Aires, where he'd set up Filmófono Argentina: "From my personal point of view, things are going badly and it's possible they'll call up my *quinta* [draft year] soon."[104] That is, the threat was hanging over him that before long he might be wielding a rifle in Cherta, Gandesa, or Villalba de los Arcos: the Ebro front line. It was time to talk business: he wanted to formalize the monies still due to him—or to his family, were he to die in combat—for his prewar work on their four Filmófono pictures and for their exploitation in Argentina since Urgoiti's arrival there in July 1937.

On 9 September 1938 Buñuel addressed his first missive in five years to Charles de Noailles, informing him that he was to leave for several months for Hollywood "on a so-called 'official' mission."[105] Although he had money enough for his own passage and living expenses, could the Viscount lend him $425 to cover the cost of the Atlantic crossing for his wife and son? Noailles complied with his habitual cordiality. At this point the exact nature of Buñuel's assignment remained as enigmatic as the government mission about which he'd spoken to Alberti in August 1936, when the need arose to flee terror-stricken Madrid; or the mission he'd evoked in Paris to Roces and Ibárruri. To the money the Viscount was prepared to lend were added the sums Buñuel had managed to borrow from Sánchez Ventura and Ione Robinson.

On 11 September Buñuel had his first opportunity to view the one incisive film made in Hollywood about the war in Spain, *Blockade* (William Dieterle, 1938), which opened that day at the Caméo on the Boulevard des Italiens. (He may already have seen James Hogan's *The Last Train from Madrid*, released in France on 25 August 1937, a trivial adventure-cum-love story that had as much to do with the Spanish conflict as its model, Josef von Sternberg's *Shanghai Express* [1932], did with the Chinese Revolution of 1925–27.) Perhaps "incisive" is a misnomer when it comes to *Blockade*: based on a screenplay by CPUSA member John Howard Lawson, from the first this timidly pro-Republican Walter Wanger production, starring Henry Fonda and Madeleine Carroll, is vitiated by a convoluted artificialness attributable to the dead hand of censorship.[106] As Frank S. Nugent noted in a lucid contemporary review, the movie "has a curious unreality considering the grim reality behind it. *Blockade* is a story of Spain: we are reminded of it now and again; but more often it is a story of Zenda or Ruritania or any place where a young patriot falls in love with a beautiful spy." Nugent, the future scriptwriter of John Ford's *Fort Apache*, *The Quiet Man*, and *The Searchers*, continued: "Since no one expects Hollywood to take sides, Walter Wanger's *Blockade*, which is the first fiction film to deal at all seriously with the Spanish civil war, is not to be damned for its failure to mention Loyalist and Rebel, Franco or Mussolini. If it expresses an honest hatred of war, if it deplores

In *Blockade* (William Dieterle, 1938) Henry Fonda wore a military cap with a star that was decidedly *not* the five-pointed kind identifiable as both Republican and Communist. (United Artists / Archive Photos / Getty Images)

the bombing of civilian populations and if it closes with an appeal to the 'conscience of the world,' it is doing the most we can expect an American picture to do."[107] Quite. However, what must also have grabbed the attention of any viewer familiar with Spain were the picture's monumental errors of setting and its confused geographical situations. Was it now that Buñuel glimpsed a less vague job opportunity opening up for him in California on the handful of movies Hollywood was preparing on a civil war few believed had more than a few months to run?

The viewing of *Blockade* took place five days (or fewer) before the Buñuel family left for Le Havre and the ship that would take them to the United States. Much too late, then, for the historical-adviser scheme to have been the *original* reason for the trip. On the point of quitting Paris on 16 September, a grateful evacuee asked Noailles to send the $425 c/o the Spanish Consulate in New York, before expressing his delight at the idea that "I return anew to cinema and this time for quite a while if my luck holds."[108] Four days later, outward-bound on the Cunard White Star Line's *Britannic*—in whose passenger list he appears as a "diplomat"—Buñuel wrote to Urgoiti: "Here I am bound for America, accompanied by my distinguished wife and lovely child. I'm going officially, albeit in an honorary capacity since I'm covering the costs of the trip myself, that is, a number of friends I've asked money from are covering them. I'm going to Hollywood with the aim of finding work, *if possible*, on the films they're making about Spain. I have enough to live well on for four months."[109] Things were far from being cut and dried.

In New York the Buñuels were met by Augusto Centeno, cofounder of the Order of Toledo, Luis's roommate in the Residencia, and now professor of classics at Princeton University, who drove them the fifty miles to his house, where they rested for a week. After an eleven-day crossing of the continent in Buñuel's newly purchased V8 Ford, the family set up house at 8802 Ashcroft Avenue, Los Angeles. Brandishing the talismanic "hasta la vista" letter written on 27 February 1931 by producer Frank Davis, Buñuel turned up at the MGM studios. There, Davis, a CPUSA member by this time, following an "initiatory trip to Russia" in 1935, was preparing the pro-Republican *Cargo of Innocence* project, based on a treatment by Salka Viertel and James Hilton.[110] The story involved the Royal Navy's evacuation across the Bay of Biscay of children from the loyalist zone—a shipboard narrative that would have little need of any insider Spanish expertise. The fact that the treatment was okayed by the censors of the Breen Office on 14 September—two days before Buñuel left Le Havre—did not mean that the project would reach safe haven. In fact, by the time our man got to LA in mid-October, *Cargo of Innocence* was dead in the water. Given the storms that had greeted the release on 3 June of *Blockade*, and the ingrained resistance of censors and producers alike to projects dealing with the *contienda*, the order had finally come through from the Motion Picture Producers and Distributors Association of America (MPPDAA) to cancel all projects about the Spanish Civil War.[111] Buñuel's notion of working as a historical adviser for MGM had never been feasible: "I'm still *idle* here," he would announce to Urgoiti a couple of months later. "I've lots of prospects of work but the hard thing is getting started, although I trust, first, in my lucky star, and second, when I've already got work, in my own powers."[112]

At this point the issue of Buñuel's conscription arose again: "I learned of the call-up of my annual contingent, my *quinta*. I had to go to the front. I wrote to our ambassador in Washington to place myself at his disposal, asking him to repatriate me along with my wife."[113] Surely not! Would the Republican régime, on the point of total collapse, bother about locating one more infantryman and shipping him (and his spouse) across the Atlantic? Why would an individual given to running from physical danger suddenly head straight toward it? Unless, of course, this was a crazy scheme by an impoverished, disorientated pessimist to *get back to* Europe. Be that as it may, on 19 January 1939 the ambassador, Fernando de los Ríos, wrote to Buñuel telling him to sit tight and wait for orders, orders that never came.[114]

The next letter to Noailles sheds more light on Buñuel's parlous situation: "As I told you before my departure, I have come here on an official, albeit honorary, mission, with the intention of collaborating on films whose subject has to do with Spain or with its current struggle. Events force me to enlarge upon my original idea and now I'm trying to direct or at least collaborate on any film whatsoever."[115] The events alluded to must be the recent MPPDAA embargo and the Republican mass retreat from Barcelona to the French frontier. A day later, on 30 January 1939, Buñuel informed Urgoiti: "Hereabouts, all is still promises and bluff. . . . I've been 'on the point of' getting into MGM as a technical adviser, but haven't got past that point."[116] Moreover, the ever-imminent Hollywood project to make Spanish-language fiction films, which might have solved his employment problems, had been reduced to a single title: a Twentieth Century-Fox period melodrama set in Madrid called *Los hijos mandan*, with a Mexican director, Gabriel Soria, and a Mexican cast including Fernando Soler and Arturo de Córdova, two actors Buñuel would call upon years later as the leading players in *La hija del engaño* and *Él*, respectively.[117] On top of that, a scheme to sell gags to Chaplin had failed dismally. "The main aim of this letter," he revealed to Urgoiti, "is to tell you . . . that I'm prepared to leave here as soon as my money runs out—I calculate I have enough for one more month—and that if there's a chance you're going to do something I'd like to be a Filmófonist again, but as a director this time, or whatever. Buñuel is dead. . . . Now, without my artistic prejudices, I think I can be more useful than before."[118] This document is not only revealing of Buñuel's isolation—his *desolation*—but it also displays his willingness to put his politico-aesthetic priorities behind him, to forgo his identity as a highly visible *cinéaste maudit* or, alternatively, as an invisible wirepuller, and to append his name as a director or producer to the kind of lightweight popular movies typical of the Filmófono operation of 1935–36. In that sense, this change of heart already announces Buñuel's Mexican "comeback" in 1947 with *Gran Casino*.

The 30 January letter bore a postscript: "I'm not saying anything about something important I'm pursuing here and that'll give us money to produce in Argentina. I'll only let you in on it if it comes off." Four days later Buñuel wrote again to tell Urgoiti that he was hoping to set up a company in Los Angeles with Tom Kilpatrick, his old interpreter at MGM, with a view to co-producing movies with Filmófono Argentina.[119] The project depended upon Kilpatrick, the moneyman, clinching a contract with Paramount. In the meantime could Urgoiti send detailed information about the movie business in Buenos Aires? The new company would include Buñuel, Kilpatrick, Ugarte (who was still at the embassy in Paris), and the prolific Chilean filmmaker Carlos F. Borcosque, who'd been involved in three Frank Davis Spanish-language productions in 1930–31 as a writer and dialogue director. Borcosque was already in Argentina, surveying the lie of the land. In 1939 he'd script and direct the macho-sounding *Alas de mi patria* and *Y mañana serán hombres* there. As things panned out, the project foundered, in part due to Urgoiti's silence. With an eye to returning to Francoist Spain, he was anxious to have an unblemished biographical record and thus paid heed to a missive that came a week or so after Buñuel's own from a relative, Bartolomé Moreno, who warned him that further contact with the cineaste could only compromise him more in the eyes of the régime.[120]

By now Buñuel was desperate enough to turn to a perennial object of love and hate: Dalí. Kicked out of Surrealism by Breton in February 1939, the artist-showman was in New York a month later, grabbing the headlines with his trashing of Bonwit Teller's store window and his kitsch-erotic *Dream of Venus* pavilion for the World's Fair. And he was rolling in money. Although the letters Buñuel addressed to him have disappeared, Dalí's two replies, the second of which contained a refusal to lend him a red cent, have survived. It is to the first of these, probably written in early April, shortly after Franco's declaration of the end of the Civil War, that we wish to draw attention, on two counts. First, because in it the new convert to Falangist ideology belittles his Republican friend's difficulties in making headway in Hollywood by arguing, in typically megalomaniac fashion, that being so wealthy, he (Dalí) didn't need to seek work there, and that "the cleverest thing for me to do is wait and to refuse any proposition until the moment (which will *inevitably* arrive, with the gathering speed of my *fame and popularity*) they get me to go as a DICTATOR—*as many dollars* to make my film with as I *fucking fancy*, and as much time—this is the only basis for a contract that *I'll agree to*, and this would be impossible were I to accept anything *provisionally*—Do you get my drift?"[121] And second, because from Dalí's crowing reply we can deduce the contents of Buñuel's original letter, in which he must have announced a change of political heart: "Your new position seems much more realistic to me than those Marxist idealisms. Here's the

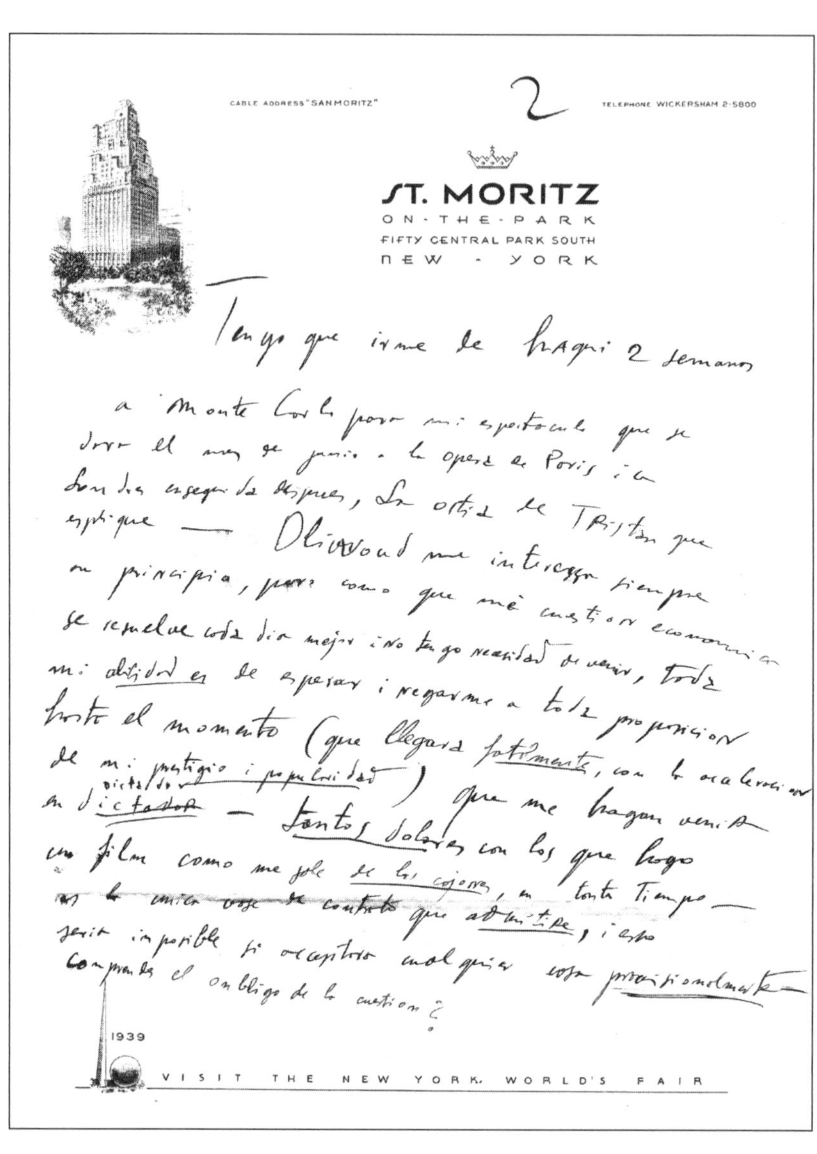

CABLE ADDRESS "SANMORITZ" TELEPHONE WICKERSHAM 2-5800

ST. MORITZ
ON-THE-PARK
FIFTY CENTRAL PARK SOUTH
NEW - YORK

Tengo que irme de haqui 2 semanas a Monte Carlo para mi espectaculo que se dara el mes de junio a la opera de Paris i a Londres enseguida despues, la obra de Tristan que expliqué — Oliwood me interesa siempre en principio, pero como que mi cuestion economica se resuelve cada dia mejor i no tengo necesidad de venir, toda mi actitud es de esperar i negarme a toda proposicion hasta el momento (que llegara fatalmente, con la acceleracion de mi prestigio i popularidad) en dictador — que me hagan venir tantos dolares con los que hago un film como me sale de los cojones, en tanto tiempo — que admitire, seria imposible si acceptara cualquier cosa provisionalmente — i esto comprendes el ombligo de la cuestion?

1939 VISIT THE NEW YORK WORLD'S FAIR

Page 2 of the scathing four-page letter Dalí sent from New York at the beginning of April 1939 to Buñuel in Los Angeles. (Archivo Buñuel, Filmoteca Española, Madrid) advice of a friend, of the Dalí of Toledo: disinfect yourself of all Marxist points of view, since philosophically and from every angle Marxism is our civilization's daftest theory. Everything's false, and Marx is probably the height of abstraction and stupidity—it'd be terrible if you were to quit political Marxism and to go on thinking as a Marxist as to the rest, since Marxism lets us see nothing of the phenomena of our era."[122]

Treading water among the flotsam of his American shipwreck, Buñuel's Red years were seemingly behind him. Overt Red years, that is. Or "overt" Red years, for, as we've seen time and again in this book, taking an unambiguous stand was hardly a penchant of his.

Buñuel's playing down of his CP past is understandable, so as to avoid problems as a resident and employee in the United States. Despite this, he experienced some problems. His troubles began in 1942: in May of that year the FBI began their surveillance of him as a known Communist.[123] Meanwhile, the Republican Right embarked on a campaign against the OIAA/MoMA propaganda film program on which Buñuel was working. In concert, the pro-Catholic *Motion Picture Herald* and the National League of Decency targeted him as a Red and as an atheist, charges not helped by the publication of Dalí's *Secret Life*. In June 1943 Buñuel resigned from the MoMA.[124]

Once he'd quit the States for good—he left Los Angeles in October 1946 to direct *Gran Casino* in Mexico City, where he would reside for the rest of his life—Buñuel's Cold War years would be dotted with collaborations with exiled Communists. He penned scripts with old comrades such as Charles Goldblatt (on *La Fièvre monte à El Pao*, 1959), with blacklisted writers such as Jean and Hugo Butler (on *Robinson Crusoe*, 1952, and *The Young One*, 1960, both of which were produced by the blacklisted George Pepper) or Dalton Trumbo (on Trumbo's *Johnny Got His Gun*, 1971). He would also liaise with PCE production company UNINCI on *Viridiana* (1960), use Communist film stars like Gérard Philipe and Simone Signoret, and direct a handful of films that are, to say the least, informed by a Communist vision: *Cela s'appelle l'aurore* (1955), *La Mort en ce jardin* (1956), and *La Fièvre monte à El Pao*.

According to Max Aub, Buñuel dated his deception with the Soviet system to April 1971 and his reading of *Cancer Ward* (1967), Aleksandr Solzhenitsyn's novel about the *gulag*. On hearing the director say, "We didn't know a thing," Aub scoffed: "Pretending to be surprised at this point! He knew perfectly well what to expect, but he was in agreement with the Stalinist way of organizing the world as long, that is, as it didn't have to do with him."[125] By the time Buñuel came to narrate his life, starting with Aub's post–May 1968 project to use him as a synecdoche for a generation of Leftist Spanish intellectuals and culminating in Jean-Claude Carrière's filial ghosted memoirs in 1982, to have been a Stalinist had no kudos—having been a Surrealist did. And thus far it is as cinema's most unswerving Surrealist that Luis Buñuel has gone down in history.

Notes

Chapter 1. The Militant Surrealist

1. Ian Gibson, *The Shameful Life of Salvador Dalí* (London: Faber and Faber, 1997), 210.

2. Agustín Sánchez Vidal, *El mundo de Luis Buñuel* (Zaragoza: Caja de Ahorros de la Inmaculada de Aragón, 1993), 68–69.

3. Paul Éluard, *Lettres à Gala 1924–1948* (1984; repr., Paris: Gallimard, 1996), 79, letter from the first half of July 1929 from Paul Éluard in Paris to Gala Éluard in Switzerland.

4. See Víctor Fernández Puertas, "Sobre una amistat: Dalí i Buñuel," *Revista de Catalunya*, no. 112 (November 1996): 85–112.

5. Although we use the abbreviations of parties, associations, etc., in their original language, we cite such names in English only. The reader can find the original formulation in the list of abbreviations at the front of the book.

6. Carole Reynaud Paligot, *Parcours politique des surréalistes 1919–1969* (Paris: CNRS Éditions, 2001), 69–104.

7. Georges Sadoul, *Rencontres 1: Chroniques et entretiens* (Paris: Denoël, 1984), 138. The original text, "Mon ami Buñuel, d'*Un chien andalou* à *Los olvidados*," was published in *L'Écran Français*, no. 335 (12–18 December 1951): 12.

8. Elsa Triolet in Sadoul, *Rencontres 1*, 46. The original text, "Souvenirs d'un témoin," was published in *Études cinématographiques*, no. 38–39 (Spring 1965): 9–28. Louis Aragon, *Je n'ai jamais appris à écrire ou* Les incipit (1969; repr., Paris: Flammarion, 1981), 62.

9. André Breton, "Desesperada y apasionada," in *¿Buñuel! La mirada del siglo*, edited by Yasha David (Madrid: MNCARS, 1996; Mexico City: Museo del Palacio de Bellas Artes, 1997), 35. The original, previously unpublished text from 1951, "Sur *Los olvidados*," appears in André Breton, *Œuvres Complètes III*, edited by Marguerite Bonnet, published, for this volume, under the direction of Étienne-Alain Hubert, with the collaboration of Philippe Bernier, Marie-Claire Dumas, and José Pierre (Paris: Gallimard/Bibliothèque de la Pléiade, 1999), 1124–30.

10. Luis Buñuel, *Mon dernier soupir* (Paris: Éditions Robert Laffont, 1982), 128. Because the text of the English version of this book—*My Last Sigh*—is (unbeknownst to the reader) sometimes cut or rearranged, we have preferred to translate from the definitive French edition.

11. Max Aub, *Conversaciones con Buñuel: Seguidas de 45 entrevistas con familiares, amigos y colaboradores del cineasta aragonés* (Madrid: Aguilar, 1985), 361.

12. *Variétés*, for instance, was never slated to publish the scenario, although it did publish some stills from the film in its July 1929 number.

13. Buñuel, *Mon dernier soupir*, 131–32. There is a copy of this letter in the Archives Moussinac of the Bibliothèque Nationale de France, Département des Arts du Spectacle, Paris, 4°-COL-10/013 (027).

14. [The Surrealist Group], *Variétés: Le Surréalisme en 1929*, special number (June 1929): 62–63.

15. In the meantime much of their work was self-published under the "Éditions Surréalistes" imprint.

16. Georges Bataille, "Œil," *Documents*, no. 4 (September 1929): 216. The page with the reproduction of Dalí's painting is unnumbered. On that occasion it was entitled *Blood Is Sweeter Than Honey*.

17. Jean-Michel Bouhours and Nathalie Schoeller, eds., *L'Âge d'or: Correspondance Luis Buñuel–Charles de Noailles; Lettres et documents (1929–1976)* (Paris: Les Cahiers du Musée National d'Art Moderne, Hors série/Archives, 1993), 39, letter of 10 December 1929 from Charles de Noailles in Hyères to Luis Buñuel in Zaragoza.

18. Georges Bataille, "Le 'Jeu lugubre,'" *Documents*, no. 7 (December 1929): 369–72.

19. Bouhours and Schoeller, *L'Âge d'or: Correspondance*, 40, letter of 14 December 1929 from Luis Buñuel in Zaragoza to Charles de Noailles in Hyères.

20. Luis Buñuel and Salvador Dalí, "Un chien andalou," *LRS*, no. 12 (15 December 1929): 34–37.

21. André Breton, *Œuvres Complètes I*, edited by Marguerite Bonnet, with the collaboration of Philippe Bernier, Étienne-Alain Hubert, and José Pierre (Paris: Gallimard/Bibliothèque de la Pléiade, 1988), 783. The enlarged *Second Manifeste du surréalisme* was published in book form by Simon Kra, Paris, 1930.

22. J. Bernard Brunius, "Un chien andalou: Film par Louis Buñuel," *Cahiers d'Art*, no. 5 (July 1929): 230–31.

23. Georges Sebbag, *André Breton: L'Amour-folie* (Paris: Éditions Jean-Michel Place, 2004), 92.

24. Ian Walker argues that it was Magritte who had the Surrealists pose with their eyes closed. See Ian Walker, *City Gorged with Dreams: Surrealism and Documentary Photography in Interwar Paris* (Manchester: Manchester University Press, 2002), 17.

25. See Jean-Michel Goutier, ed., *André Breton: 42, rue Fontaine* (Paris: Calmels Cohen, 2003). This is a catalogue in eight volumes of the auction at Drouot-Richelieu of the contents of Breton's studio. Cited here is the volume "Photographies," 59 and 142 for Buñuel, as well as 234–37 and 325–27 for the other Surrealists.

26. [The Surrealist Group et al.], "Enquête," *LRS*, no. 12 (15 December 1929): 73.

27. See Penelope Rosemont, ed., *Women Surrealists: An International Anthology* (London: Athlone Press, 1998), 16–17.

28. [The Surrealist Group et al.], "Enquête," 65. The compiler was Breton. For Buñuel's replies, see 71.

29. [The Surrealist Group], "Recherches sur la sexualité," *LRS*, no. 11 (15 March 1928): 32–40.

30. [The Surrealist Group], "Hands Off Love," *LRS*, no. 9–10 (1 October 1927): 1–6.

31. Louis Aragon, *L'Œuvre Poétique*, vol. 2, *1927–1935*, edited by Jean Ristat, 2nd ed. (Paris: Livre Club Diderot-Messidor, 1989), 29.

Chapter 2. The Production of *L'Âge d'or*

1. Bouhours and Schoeller, *L'Âge d'or: Correspondance*, 33, letter of 7 July 1929 from Charles de Noailles to Luis Buñuel, both in Paris.

2. Ibid., 35, letter of 19 November 1929 from Charles de Noailles to Luis Buñuel, both in Paris.

3. Ibid., 35.

4. Ibid., 37, letter of 29 November 1929 from Luis Buñuel in Cadaqués to Charles de Noailles in Paris.

5. Luis Buñuel, "'Découpage' o segmentación cinegráfica," *La Gaceta Literaria*, no. 43 (1 October 1928): 1.

6. Studio 28 revue-programme (Paris, 1930): 1. A partial facsimile of this booklet is inserted in Bouhours and Schoeller, *L'Âge d'or: Correspondance*.

7. Salvador Dalí, *The Secret Life of Salvador Dali*, first British edition (London: Vision Press, 1948), 429. All other citations are to the 1942 edition. It is only in recent years that Dalí's name has been spelled with an accent in Anglo-American and French culture.

8. Bouhours and Schoeller, *L'Âge d'or: Correspondance*, 51, letter written between 10 January and 8 March 1930 by Salvador Dalí in Carry-le-Rouet to Luis Buñuel in Paris.

9. Ibid., 47, letter of 8 February 1930 from Luis Buñuel in Paris to Charles de Noailles in Hyères.

10. Claude Heymann, "Sur le tournage de *L'Âge d'or*," *Jeune Cinéma*, no. 134 (April–May 1981): 6.

11. Bouhours and Schoeller, *L'Âge d'or: Correspondance*, 37, letter of 29 November 1929 from Luis Buñuel in Cadaqués to Charles de Noailles in Paris.

12. Ibid., 58, letter of 26 February 1930 from Luis Buñuel in Paris to Charles de Noailles in Hyères.

13. Heymann, "Sur le tournage," 7.

14. Bouhours and Schoeller, *L'Âge d'or: Correspondance*, 47, letter of 8 February 1930 from Luis Buñuel in Paris to Charles de Noailles in Hyères.

15. *LSASDLR*, no. 1 (July 1930): in a signature of photos between 16 and 17.

16. Heymann, "Sur le tournage," 9.

17. Bouhours and Schoeller, *L'Âge d'or: Correspondance*, 63, letter of 15 March 1930 from Luis Buñuel in Paris to Charles de Noailles in Hyères.

18. Francesc Miralles, *Llorens Artigas: Catálogo de obra* (Barcelona: Fundación Llorens Artigas/Polígrafa, 1992), 34. Probably apocryphal.

19. This and other details, which rectify the credits in Paul Hammond, *L'Âge d'or* (London: British Film Institute, 1997), 72–73, are taken from program notes prepared for the New London Film Society by Jacques Brunius for a screening of the film in London on 24 April 1949.

20. Buñuel, *Mon dernier soupir*, 142.

21. Heymann, "Sur le tournage," 6.

Chapter 3. A Fecund Scandal

1. Bouhours and Schoeller, *L'Âge d'or: Correspondance*, 73, note of 30 June 1930 from Luis Buñuel to Charles de Noailles, both in Paris.

2. Aub, *Conversaciones*, 65.

3. Éluard, *Lettres à Gala*, 114, letter of 5 June 1930 from Paul Éluard in Cernay-la-Ville (Seine-et-Oise) to Gala Éluard in Port Lligat.

4. Bouhours and Schoeller, *L'Âge d'or: Correspondance*, 45, letter of 24 January 1930 from Luis Buñuel in Paris to Charles de Noailles in Hyères.

5. André Thirion, *Révolutionnaires sans Révolution* (Paris: Robert Laffont, 1972), 244–45. For another account of the same events, see Georges Hugnet, *Pleins et déliés: Témoignages et souvenirs, 1926–1972* (Paris: Guy Authier, 1972), 396–98.

6. Bouhours and Schoeller, *L'Âge d'or: Correspondance*, 64, letter of 23 March 1930 from Luis Buñuel in Paris to Charles de Noailles in Hyères.

7. See "Second Prière d'insérer du 'Second Manifeste du surréalisme,'" in *Tracts surréalistes et déclarations collectives (1922/1969)*, edited by José Pierre (Paris: Éric Losfeld, 1980), 1:151–52; here 151.

8. [The Surrealist Group], "Déclaration," *LSASDLR*, no. 1 (July 1930): 41. The signatories are Alexandre, Aragon, Joë Bousquet, Buñuel, Char, Crevel, Dalí, Éluard, Ernst, Fourrier, Goemans, Malkine, Paul Nougé, Péret, Francis Ponge, Marco Ristich, Sadoul, Tanguy, Thirion, Tzara, and Albert Valentin.

9. [The Surrealist Group], "Question et réponse," *LSASDLR*, no. 1 (July 1930): 1.

10. Bouhours and Schoeller, *L'Âge d'or: Correspondance*, 74–75, letter of 10 July 1930 from Charles de Noailles in Paris to Luis Buñuel in Zaragoza.

11. Ibid., 76, letter of 16 July 1930 from Luis Buñuel in Zaragoza to Charles de Noailles in Paris.

12. See Manuel Pérez Lizano, *Focos del surrealismo español: Artistas aragoneses, 1929–1991* (Zaragoza: Mira Editores, 1992), 30–33.

13. Andrés Ruiz Castillo, "Luis Buñuel, 'Un chien andalou' y el superrealismo," *El Heraldo de Aragón* (26 July 1930): 1–2. A few extracts from this interview were published in "Planos de Madrid," *Popular Film*, no. 209 (31 July 1930): n.p. Spanish fan magazines of the 1930s such as *Popular Film* and *Cinegramas* were erratic in their pagination, sometimes with page numbers, but more generally without.

14. Bouhours and Schoeller, *L'Âge d'or: Correspondance*, 78, letter of 15 August 1930 from Luis Buñuel in San Sebastián to Charles de Noailles in Paris (?). See ibid., 76–77, for the letter of 14 August 1930 from Charles de Noailles in Paris to Luis Buñuel in San Sebastián.

15. François Buot, *René Crevel: Biographie* (Paris: Bernard Grasset, 1991), 276.

16. Bouhours and Schoeller, *L'Âge d'or: Correspondance*, 80–81, letter of 29 September 1930 from Luis Buñuel to Charles de Noailles, both in Paris.

17. Robert Kiefé, "Pour une réforme de la Censure," *La Revue du cinéma*, no. 21 (1 April 1931): 22.

18. Buñuel, *Mon dernier soupir*, 155; Tomás Pérez Turrent and José de la Colina, *Buñuel por Buñuel* (Madrid: Plot, 1993), 33.

19. Thirion, *Révolutionnaires*, 283–84.

20. Bouhours and Schoeller, *L'Âge d'or: Correspondance*, 84n1.

21. Letter of 22 October 1930 from Pierre Drieu la Rochelle to the Noailles, and letter of 23 October 1930 from Gaston Bergery to the Noailles, Archivo Luis Buñuel, Filmoteca Española, Madrid.

22. Bouhours and Schoeller, *L'Âge d'or: Correspondance*, 89, letter of 29 November 1930 from Salvador Dalí to Charles de Noailles, both in Paris.

23. Jean-Paul Dreyfus, "*L'Âge d'or*, par Louis Buñuel, scénario de Louis Buñuel et Salvador Dalí," *La Revue du cinéma*, no. 17 (1 December 1930): 55–56.

24. Ruiz Castillo, "Luis Buñuel," 2.

25. There is a facsimile of "L'Affaire de 'L'Âge d'or'" in Bouhours and Schoeller, *L'Âge d'or: Correspondance*, 111–16. For Mauclaire's declaration to the police, see ibid., 101–3.

26. The telegram is reproduced in David, *¿Buñuel!*, 255.

27. Bouhours and Schoeller, *L'Âge d'or: Correspondance*, 104, telegram of 13 December 1930 from Charles de Noailles in Hyères to Luis Buñuel in Hollywood.

28. Ibid., 105, letter of 14 December 1930 from Charles de Noailles in Hyères to Luis Buñuel in Hollywood.

29. Marie Seton, *Eisenstein: A Biography* (London: Bodley Head, 1952), 167–86.

30. Bouhours and Schoeller, *L'Âge d'or: Correspondance*, 106, letter of 16 December 1930 from Juan Vicens to Charles de Noailles, both in Paris.

31. Ibid., 108, letter of 26 December 1930 from Luis Buñuel in Hollywood to Charles de Noailles in Hyères.

32. Jean Cocteau, *Opium: Journal d'une désintoxication* (Paris: Librairie Stock, Delamain & Boutelleau, 1930), 203–4.

33. See Bouhours and Schoeller, *L'Âge d'or: Correspondance*, 111–16. The Surrealist signatories are Alexandre, Aragon, Breton, Char, Crevel, Dalí, Éluard, Malkine, Péret, Man Ray, Sadoul, Tanguy, Thirion, Tzara, Unik, and Valentin.

34. The letters in question are reproduced in Emmanuelle Toulet, ed., *Le Cinéma au rendez-vous des arts: France, années 20 et 30* (Paris: Bibliothèque nationale de France, 1995), 24–25.

35. Arthur Koestler, *The Invisible Writing* (London: Collins, 1954), 271.

36. See the letters sent by these three to Breton in the first week of January 1933 and included in Bouhours and Schoeller, *L'Âge d'or: Correspondance*, 117–19.

37. Buot, *René Crevel*, 408.

38. To get the measure of said scholarship, we encourage the reader to refer to the copious notes in Bouhours and Schoeller, *L'Âge d'or: Correspondance.*

Chapter 4. A Brief Stay in Hollywood

1. Salvador Dalí, "Documental-Paris-1929 [VI]," *La Publicitat* (26 June 1929): 1.

2. Aub, *Conversaciones*, 75.

3. Augusto Martínez Torres, "José López Rubio: Un memorión nostálgico," *El País Semanal* (30 November 1986): 29.

4. Aub, *Conversaciones*, 75.

5. [Luis Buñuel], "Buñuel y el surrealismo," *ABC* (25 February 1931): 14.

6. Florentino Hernández Girbal [as Joaquín Zaldívar], "Los que pasaron por Hollywood," interview with Tono, *Cinegramas*, no. 94 (28 June 1936): n.p.

7. Buñuel, *Mon dernier soupir*, 157.

8. Martínez Torres, "José López Rubio," 30.

9. Don Q., "Hollywood," *Cine Mundial* (June 1931): 456.

10. Bouhours and Schoeller, *L'Âge d'or: Correspondance*, 90–91.

11. Buñuel, *Mon dernier soupir*, 160–61.

12. Manuel del Arco, "Mano a mano con Benito Perojo," *La Vanguardia Española* (30 September 1959): 20.

13. "Altavoz de Hollywood," *Popular Film*, no. 257 (16 July 1931): n.p.; Jesús García de Dueñas, *¡Nos vamos a Hollywood!* (Madrid: Nickel Odeon, 1993), 282.

14. Claude Autant-Lara, *Hollywood Cake-Walk (1930–1932)* (Paris: Henri Veyrier, 1985), 133.

15. Luis Gómez Mesa, "La generación del cine y los deportes," interview with Luis Buñuel, *Popular Film*, no. 128 (10 January 1929): 4.

16. Salvador Dalí, "Luis Buñuel (entrevista)," *L'Amic de les Arts*, no. 31 (31 March 1929): 16.

17. Buñuel, *Mon dernier soupir*, 164.

18. Ernesto Giménez Caballero, "Noticiemos sobre cinema," *La Gaceta Literaria*, no. 112 (15 August 1931): 9.

19. Aub, unpublished ms., ref. ARA c. 17/5, document 39-508, Archivo de la Fundación Max Aub, Segorbe.

20. Jacques Feyder, *Le Cinéma notre métier* (Vésenaz-Près-Genève: Pierre Cailleur Éditeur, 1946).

21. Dominique Lebrun, *Paris-Hollywood: Les Français dans le cinéma américain* (Poitiers: Hazan, 1987), 105; Juan B. Heinink and Robert G. Dickson, *Cita en Hollywood* (Bilbao: Ediciones Mensajero, 1990).

22. Robert Florey, *Hollywood d'hier et d'aujourd'hui* (Paris: Prisma, 1948), 86.

23. Ivor Montagu, *With Eisenstein in Hollywood* (Berlin: Seven Seas Books, 1968), 88–89.

24. Florentino Hernández Girbal [as Joaquín Zaldívar], "Los que pasaron por Hollywood," interview with Roberto Rey, *Cinegramas*, no. 37 (26 March 1935): n.p.

25. Martín Abizanda, "López Rubio cuenta sus aventuras," *Cámara*, no. 27 (December 1943): n.p.

26. Buñuel, *Mon dernier soupir*, 164.

27. Interview by the authors with Emilio Sanz de Soto in his house in Madrid, 11 June 2006.

28. Hernández Girbal, "Los que pasaron por Hollywood," interview with Tono.

29. "Chismes y cuentos," *Cinelandia* 5, no. 2 (February 1931): 75.

30. Luis Buñuel, "Variaciones sobre el bigote de Menjou," *La Gaceta Literaria*, no. 35 (1 June 1928): 4.

31. Don Q., "Hollywood," 454–56.

32. Ginette Vicendeau, "Les films en versiones multiples: Un échec édifiant," in *Le Passage du muet au parlant*, edited by Christian Belaygue (Toulouse: Cinémathèque de Toulouse/Éditions Milan, 1988), 34.

33. "Echos," *Ciné-Journal*, no. 1145 (7 August 1931): 3.

34. Bouhours and Schoeller, *L'Âge d'or: Correspondance*, 133.

35. "U.S. Sends 125 Films South in 2 Years," *Motion Picture Herald* (22 May 1943): 36.

Chapter 5. The Coming of the Spanish Second Republic

1. Aub, *Conversaciones*, 71. While for the most part accurate in terms of dates, it is untrue that the jubilant music that announced the proclamation of the Second Republic awakened him on the Tuesday or Wednesday after Good Friday, since this event took place on 14 April, eleven days later.

2. María Teresa León, *Memoria de la melancolía* (1970; repr., Madrid: Castalia, 1998), 201.

3. Gabriel Jackson, *La República española y la Guerra Civil* (Mexico City: Grijalbo, 1967), 35.

4. Stanley G. Payne, *La primera democracia española: La Segunda República, 1931–1936* (Barcelona: Paidós, 1995), 56; Antonio Elorza and Marta Bizcarrondo, *Queridos camaradas: La Internacional comunista y España* (Barcelona: Planeta, 1999), 143; Joan Estruch, *Historia oculta del PCE* (Madrid: Temas de Hoy, 2000), 75.

5. José Bullejos, *La Comintern en España: Recuerdos de mi vida* (Mexico City: Impresiones Modernas S.A., 1972), 122.

6. Jackson, *La República española*, 113.

7. Pérez Turrent and de la Colina, *Buñuel por Buñuel*, 18.

8. Aub, *Conversaciones*, 68, 106.

9. Ibid., 47–48, 95. Liberal Party politician Canalejas was elected prime minister of Spain in 1910. Conservative politician Dato served three times as prime minister, in 1913–15, 1917, and 1920–21; Buñuel, *Mon dernier soupir*, 66.

10. Buñuel, *Mon dernier soupir*, 167.

11. Salvador Dalí, *The Secret Life of Salvador Dali* (New York: Dial Press, 1942), 323.

12. Ibid., 320–22; Gibson, *Shameful Life*, 287–89.

13. Payne, *La primera democracia española*, 62, 71.

14. Namely, Alexandre, Aragon, Breton, Char, Crevel, Éluard, Malkine, Péret, Sadoul, Tanguy, Thirion, and Unik.

15. [The Surrealist Group], "Au feu!," May 1931, in Pierre, *Tracts surréalistes*, 196.

16. Bouhours and Schoeller, *L'Âge d'or: Correspondance*, 92–93.

17. Dalí, *Secret Life*, 308.

18. Bouhours and Schoeller, *L'Âge d'or: Correspondance*, 148.

19. Jeanne Rucar de Buñuel, *Memorias de una mujer sin piano* (Madrid: Alianza Editorial, 1990), 58.

20. Aub, *Conversaciones*, 69.

21. Bouhours and Schoeller, *L'Âge d'or: Correspondance*, 149, letter of 5 December 1931 from Luis Buñuel in Zaragoza to Charles de Noailles in Paris. *L'Âge d'or* would be shown again in the same cinema on 29 October 1933, along with *Un chien andalou.*

22. Ernesto Giménez Caballero, "Las tripas del silencio español," *La Gaceta Literaria*, no. 119 (1 December 1931): 9–10.

23. Bouhours and Schoeller, *L'Âge d'or: Correspondance*, 149, letter of 5 December 1931 from Luis Buñuel in Zaragoza to Charles de Noailles in Paris.

24. Ibid., 149, letter of 27 January 1932 from Luis Buñuel to Charles de Noailles, both in Paris.

25. Jackson, *La república española*, 101.

26. Julio Caro Baroja, *Los Baroja (Memorias familiares)* (Madrid: Editorial Caro Raggio, 1997), 233, 245–46.

27. Bullejos, *La Comintern en España*, 156.

28. Federico García Lorca, "Alocución al pueblo de Fuente Vaqueros," in *Obras Completas III*, edited by Miguel García Posada (Barcelona: Galaxia Gutenberg, 1996), 205.

29. Federico García Lorca, "Charlando con García Lorca," in García Posada, *Obras Completas III*, 447.

30. Bullejos, *La Comintern en España*, 157.

31. Stanley G. Payne, *Unión Soviética, comunismo y revolución en España (1931–1939)* (Barcelona: Plaza y Janés, 2003), 48–49.

32. Bullejos, *La Comintern en España*, 165–66.

33. Elorza and Bizcarrondo, *Queridos camaradas*, 208.

34. Ibid., 93; Payne, *Unión Soviética*, 47.

35. Estruch, *Historia oculta del PCE*, 90–91.

36. Manuel Tuñón de Lara, "La Segunda República," in *La crisis del Estado: Dictadura, república, guerra (1923–1939)*, edited by Manuel Tuñón de Lara (Barcelona, Labor, 1981), 178.

Chapter 6. A Stormy Year

1. Jean-Pierre Morel, *Le Roman insupportable: L'Internationale littéraire et la France (1920–1932)* (Paris: Gallimard, 1985), 364.

2. Stephen Koch, *Double Lives: Stalin, Willi Münzenberg and the Seduction of the Intellectuals* (1994; repr., London: Harper Collins, 1996), 231.

3. Morel, *Le Roman insupportable*, 382.

4. Ibid., 384. The neologism *chekaization* alludes to the Cheka, the Bolshevik state security organization (1917–22), and connotes the secret policing of Communist and fellow-traveling intellectual life.

5. See Pierre, *Tracts surréalistes*, 186–88.

6. Bouhours and Schoeller, *L'Âge d'or: Correspondance*, 145, letter of 30 April 1931 from Luis Buñuel in Paris to Charles de Noailles in Hyères.

7. See Román Gubern, "La traumática transición del cine español del mudo al sonoro," in *El paso del mudo al sonoro en el cine español: Actas del IV Congreso de la AEHC [Asociación Española de Historiadores del Cine]*, edited by Joan M. Minguet Batllori and Julio Pérez Perucha (Madrid: Editorial Complutense, 1993), 17–19.

8. See Paul Rivet et al., "Mission Dakar-Djibouti 1931–1933," *Minotaure*, no. 2 (1 June 1933): 3–88; and Jean Jamin, "Présentation de l'Afrique Fantôme," in Michel Leiris, *Miroir de l'Afrique*, edited by Jean Jamin (Paris: Gallimard, 1995), 65–85.

9. Buñuel, *Mon dernier soupir*, 167–68.

10. This tract is published in Pierre, *Tracts surréalistes*, 196–97; here 197.

11. Report of 12 May 1931, four-page typed manuscript, ref. 551, Fonds Georges Sadoul, Cinémathèque Française, Paris.

12. For this document, see *Europe: Revue mensuelle*, no. 475–76 (November–December 1968): after 32.

13. Robert Stuart Short, "The Political History of the Surrealist Movement in France, 1918–1940" (PhD diss., University of Sussex, 1965), 332.

14. Purnal, the hitherto unrecorded member of the group, was probably the Sacher Purnal who contributed to the Belgian proto-Surrealist magazine *Variétés* in 1929.

15. Bouhours and Schoeller, *L'Âge d'or: Correspondance*, 145, letter of 29 June 1931 from Luis Buñuel to Charles de Noailles, both in Paris.

16. For both tracts, see Pierre, *Tracts surréalistes*, 194–95 and 198–200, respectively.

17. Bouhours and Schoeller, *L'Âge d'or: Correspondance*, 148, letter of 17 September 1931 from Luis Buñuel to Charles de Noailles, both in Paris.

18. Thirion, *Révolutionnaires*, 313–14.

19. Ibid., 323–24.

20. Bouhours and Schoeller, *L'Âge d'or: Correspondance*, 148, letter of 19 October 1931 from Luis Buñuel in Paris to Charles de Noailles in Hyères (?).

21. According to the architect and La Barraca actor Arturo Sáenz de la Calzada, in Aub, *Conversaciones*, 279.

22. Bouhours and Schoeller, *L'Âge d'or: Correspondance*, 149, letter of 5 December 1931 from Luis Buñuel in Zaragoza to Charles de Noailles in Hyères (?). *L'Âge d'or* would be shown again in the same cinema on 29 October 1933, together with *Un chien andalou*.

23. Tota Cuevas, so generous in her emotional and financial support of the fragile Crevel until his suicide in 1935, would have a somewhat asymmetrical affair with Buñuel in the mid-1930s. Cf. Javier Herrera Navarro, "A la sombra de Buñuel: Tota Cuevas de Vera—condesa, surrealista y comunista—a través de un epistolario inédito (1934–1936)," *El Maquinista de la Generación*, no. 17 (2009): 32–55.

24. Bouhours and Schoeller, *L'Âge d'or: Correspondance*, 149.

25. Maurice Heine, "Lettre ouverte à Luis Buñuel," *LSASDLR*, no. 3 (December 1931): 12–13; here 13.

26. Buñuel, *Mon dernier soupir*, 270.

27. See Pierre, *Tracts surréalistes*, 204–5, 456–58. The signatories are Alexandre, Breton, Char, Crevel, Éluard, Malkine, Pierre de Massot, Péret, Sadoul, Tanguy, Thirion, and Unik.

28. Aub, *Conversaciones*, 72.

29. Letter of 30 January 1932 from Pierre Utik to Maurice Thorez, Nouv. Acq. fr. 25094, folios 33, 34, and 35, Département des Manuscrits occidentaux, Bibliothèque nationale de France, Paris. We thank Julie Jones for advising us of the existence of this letter.

30. José Gotovich et al., *Komintern: L'Histoire et les hommes; Dictionnaire biographique de l'Internationale Communiste* (Paris: Éditions de l'Atelier, 2001), 510–11.

31. See Maxime Alexandre, *Mémoires d'un surréaliste* (Paris: La Jeune Parque, 1968), 209–11. Alexandre doesn't mention Buñuel in the group harangued by the PCF in January 1932.

32. According to a statement made by Santiago Carrillo, ex-general secretary of the PCE, to Román Gubern (29 September 2005), prior to the Liberation in 1944, when the PCE was organized in France, and at a time in which one could be a member without a party card, the Communist Party being an international party, a Communist Spanish citizen who resided in France would militate in the PCF. Thus, when the Third Congress of the PCE was held in Paris in August 1929, Joaquín Maurín, a comrade who'd lived in France since his release from prison in 1927, was rejected, not only because his political views were thought to be heterodox but also with the argument that he lived in Paris and was a member of the PCF alone.

33. Bouhours and Schoeller, *L'Âge d'or: Correspondance*, 149, letter of 27 January 1932 from Luis Buñuel in Paris to Charles de Noailles in Hyères.

34. Éluard, *Lettres à Gala*, 154, letter of 30 January 1932 from Paul Éluard in Paris to Gala Éluard in Port Lligat.

35. Bouhours and Schoeller, *L'Âge d'or: Correspondance*, 150, letter of 27 January 1932 from Luis Buñuel in Paris to Charles de Noailles in Hyères.

36. Buñuel, *Mon dernier soupir*, 169; Paul Vaillant-Couturier, *Les Bâtisseurs de la vie nouvelle*, 3 vols. (Paris: Bureau d'Éditions, 1932). The first volume is called *Terre du pain, champs de blé et champs de pétrole*. We would draw attention to the proximity of *Terre du pain* to the title of Buñuel's third film.

37. See Valérie Posener, "Les scénaristes," in Aïcha Kherroubi et al., *Le Studio Mejrabpom ou l'aventure du cinéma privé au pays des bolsheviks*, Les Dossiers du Musée d'Orsay 59 (Paris: La Documentation Française, 1996), 80.

38. *L'Humanité*, no. 12140 (10 March 1932): 2.

39. Éluard, *Lettres à Gala*, 163, letter of 14 March 1932 (dating by the authors) from Paul Éluard in Grimaud (Var) to Gala Éluard in Port Lligat.

40. [AEAR], "Le Manifeste de l'Association des Écrivains et Artistes Révolutionnaires," *L'Humanité*, no. 12152 (22 March 1932): 4.

41. Bouhours and Schoeller, *L'Âge d'or: Correspondance*, 150–51, letter of 17 March 1932 from Luis Buñuel in Paris to Charles de Noailles in Hyères.

42. See Pierre, *Tracts surréalistes*, 223–28, 470–74.

43. Buñuel, *Mon dernier soupir*, 135. Over the years Aragon's threat to kill himself was repeated whenever he had a difference of opinion with the PCF politburo; see Dominique Desanti, *Les Staliniens: Une expérience politique, 1944–1956* (1975; repr., Verviers: Marabout, 1985), 167–68, 376.

44. Éluard, *Lettres à Gala*, 167, letter of 22 March 1932 (dating by the authors) from Paul Éluard in Grimaud (Var) to Salvador Dalí in Port Lligat.

45. Letter of 10–16 March 1932 (dating by the authors) from Salvador Dalí to Luis Buñuel, ref. ARA c. 23-19, Archivo de la Fundación Max Aub, Segorbe.

46. *Films Selectos*, no. 71 (20 February 1932): 21.

47. Éluard, *Lettres à Gala*, 173, letter of 23 March 1932 (dating by the authors) from Paul Éluard in Grimaud (Var) to Gala Éluard in Port Lligat.

48. Bouhours and Schoeller, *L'Âge d'or: Correspondance*, 153, letter of 23 March 1932 from Luis Buñuel in Paris to Charles de Noailles in Hyères.

49. Ibid., 154, letter of 25 March 1932 from Charles de Noailles in Hyères to Luis Buñuel in Paris.

50. Luis Buñuel, "Une girafe," *LSASDLR*, no. 6 (15 May 1933): 34–36. Translated by Garrett White as "A Giraffe," in Luis Buñuel, *An Unspeakable Betrayal: Selected Writings of Luis Buñuel* (Berkeley: University of California Press, 2000), 44–48, here 44. Translation slightly altered.

51. Buñuel, *Mon dernier soupir*, 143.

52. Ibid., 143–44.

53. See Pierre, *Tracts surréalistes*, 230–34, 475.

54. Bouhours and Schoeller, *L'Âge d'or: Correspondance*, 155, letter of 10 May 1932 from Luis Buñuel to Charles de Noailles, both in Paris.

55. Pierre Lherminier, *Jean Vigo* (Paris: Éditions Seghers, 1967), 130. Storck includes Joris Ivens in those April 1932 meetings. However, the latter's biographer dates those

same encounters to summer 1933: see Hans Schoots, *Living Dangerously: A Biography of Joris Ivens* (Amsterdam: Amsterdam University Press, 2000), 85.

56. Only with the restoration and cataloguing of the PCF's film collection, now in the Archives Français du Film, will we know more about the AEAR's early production.

57. Buñuel, *Mon dernier soupir*, 134.

58. Letter of 6 May 1932 from Luis Buñuel to André Breton, both in Paris, ref. Nouv. Acq. fr. 25094, folios f. 102 and 103, Département des Manuscrits occidentaux, Bibliothèque nationale de France, Paris. First published in French in Paul Louis Thirard, "Colloque à Pordenone," *Positif*, no. 471 (May 2000): 64–65. Javier Herrera Navarro published the first translation in Spanish in the *El Cultural* supplement to *El Mundo* (13 February 2000): 6–7. In France Buñuel was accustomed to signing his name without the "ñ."

59. Buñuel, *Mon dernier soupir*, 168–69.

60. Dossier "Communistes Espagnols, mars 1922–1947," correspondence of 23 April 1932, ref. 100-900-K, Préfecture de Police, Paris.

61. Buñuel, *Mon dernier soupir*, 136.

62. Aragon, *L'Œuvre Poétique*, 2:473, 497.

63. Bouhours and Schoeller, *L'Âge d'or: Correspondance*, 156, letter of 6 June 1932 from Luis Buñuel to Charles de Noailles, both in Paris.

64. Ernesto Giménez Caballero, *Retratos españoles (bastante parecidos)* (Barcelona: Planeta, 1985), 165.

65. Carlos Fernández Cuenca, *La guerra de España y el cine* (Madrid: Editora Nacional, 1972), 147–48.

66. Marisol Carnicero and Daniel Sánchez Salas, eds., *En torno a Buñuel*, Cuadernos de la Academia 7–8 (Madrid: Academia de las Artes y las Ciencias Cinematográficas de España, 2000), 259.

67. Santiago Carrillo interviewed by Román Gubern, 29 September 2005.

68. Letter from Rafael Alberti to Max Aub, n.d., ref. c. 17/5, document 1085, Archivo de la Fundación Max Aub, Segorbe.

69. Bouhours and Schoeller, *L'Âge d'or: Correspondance*, 153, letter of 23 March 1932 from Luis Buñuel in Paris to Charles de Noailles in Hyères.

70. Salvador Dalí, *Babaouo, scénario inédit: Précedé d'un Abrégé d'une histoire critique du cinéma et suivi de Guillaume Tell, ballet portugais* (Paris: Éditions des Cahiers Libres, 1932).

Chapter 7. Time-Serving at Paramount-Joinville

1. Luis Buñuel, "Auto-Biography," 28 July 1939, Museum of Modern Art Film Study Center, New York, 12. In this thirty-two-page typescript the exiled cineaste offered his services to MoMA or the American Film Center in Los Angeles.

2. Bouhours and Schoeller, *L'Âge d'or: Correspondance*, 145, letter of 30 April 1931 from Luis Buñuel in Paris to Charles de Noailles in Hyères.

3. *Cinémagazine*, no. 51 (20 December 1929): 472.

4. *La Cinématographie Française*, no. 610 (21 July 1930): 11.

5. Roger Icart, *La Révolution du parlant vue par la presse française* (Perpignan: Institut Jean Vigo, 1988), 56.

6. Donald Crafton, *The Talkies: American Cinema's Transition to Sound, 1926–1931* (Berkeley: University of California Press, 1999), 431.

7. Luis Buñuel, "Una noche en el Studio des Ursulines," *La Gaceta Literaria*, no. 2 (15 January 1927): 6.

8. Juan Piqueras, "Visitas de cinema: Alberto Cavalcanti nos concreta," *La Gaceta Literaria*, no. 99 (15 February 1931): 8.

9. Georges Sadoul, *Dictionnaire des cinéastes* (Paris: Seuil, 1965), 129.

10. Ricardo Baroja, *Gente del 98: Arte, cine y ametralladora* (Madrid: Cátedra, 1989), 291, 310, 311.

11. Paul Éluard and René Crevel, "Un film commercial," *LSASDLR*, no. 4 (December 1931): 29.

12. Geoffrey Donaldson, "Adelqui Millar, fascino latino," *Immagine: Note di Storia del Cinema*, new series, no. 16 (1991): 19–29.

13. Juan Piqueras, "Afirmación del cine europeo y desvalorización del yanqui," *El Sol* (22 February 1931), repr. in *Juan Piqueras: El "Delluc" español*, edited by Manuel Llopis, vol. 1 (Valencia: Filmoteca de la Generalitat Valenciana, 1988), 251.

14. "Claudio de la Torre ingresa en los estudios de Joinville," *Popular Film*, no. 253 (18 June 1931): n.p.

15. Claudio de la Torre, "El tranvía al ralenti (Caminos para Luis Buñuel)," *La Gaceta Literaria*, no. 34 (15 May 1928): 5.

16. Harry Waldman, *Paramount in Paris: 300 Films Produced at the Joinville Studios, 1930–1933* (Lanham, Md.: Scarecrow Press, 1988), 31.

17. Llopis, *Juan Piqueras*, 1:82.

18. *La Semana Gráfica*, no. 258 (20 June 1931), repr. in Llopis, *Juan Piqueras*, 1:81.

19. Luis Vicens, "Coup d'œil sur le marché de langue espagnole: Faut-il faire des versions espagnoles?" *La Cinématographie Française*, no. 686 (26 December 1931); "L'Amortissement des versions espagnoles: Une enquête américaine," *La Cinématographie Française*, no. 689 (16 January 1932), unpaginated press cuttings in the Bibliothèque du film, Paris.

20. "Ecos de París," *Popular Film*, no. 289 (25 February 1932): 14.

21. "Se producirán 16 películas en español," *Cinelandia* 5, no. 12 (December 1932): 9.

22. Ilya Ehrenburg, *Fábrica de sueños* (Madrid: Editorial Cenit, 1932).

23. Aub, *Conversaciones*, 92; Buñuel, *Mon dernier soupir*, 174.

24. Pérez Turrent and de la Colina, *Buñuel por Buñuel*, 39.

25. Bouhours and Schoeller, *L'Âge d'or: Correspondance*, 160.

26. Antonina Rodrigo, *Memoria de Granada: Manuel Ángeles Ortiz y Federico García Lorca* (Granada: Diputación Provincial de Granada, 1993), 222–23.

27. Florentino Hernández Girbal [as Joaquín Zaldívar], "Los que pasaron por Hollywood," interview with José Nieto, *Cinegramas*, no. 47 (4 August 1935): n.p.

28. Christopher Brien, Laurent Ikor, and J. Michel Vignier, *Joinville le Cinéma: Le Temps des Studios* (Paris: Ramsay, 1985), 6.

Chapter 8. The Mutations of *L'Âge d'or* and Other Projects

1. Bouhours and Schoeller, *L'Âge d'or: Correspondance*, 80, letter of 22 September 1930 from Charles de Noailles in Paris to Salvador Dalí in Port Lligat.

2. Gibson, *Shameful Life*, 243.

3. Janine Bouissounouse, *La Nuit d'Autun: Le Temps des illusions* (Paris: Calmann-Lévy, 1977), 46.

4. See Dawn Ades, "Unpublished Film Scenario by Salvador Dalí," *Studio International* 195, no. 993–94 (1982): 62–77; here 70.

5. Dawn Ades, "*Contre la famille*," in *Dalí & Film*, edited by Matthew Gale (London: Tate, 2007), 116.

6. Agustín Sánchez Vidal, "Introducción," in Salvador Dalí, *Obra Completa III: Poesía, prosa, teatro y cine* (Barcelona: Ediciones Destino/Fundación Gala-Salvador Dalí/Sociedad Estatal de Conmemoraciones Culturales, 2004), 117.

7. Dalí, *Obra Completa III*, 1082.

8. Ades, "*Contre la famille*," 116.

9. Salvador Dalí, "La cabra sanitaria," in *Obra Completa III*, 1083–98; Sánchez Vidal, "Introducción," in ibid., 119–22; Agustín Sánchez Vidal, "*La Chèvre sanitaire*," in Gale, *Dalí & Film*, 104–9.

10. Joan M. Minguet Batllori, *Salvador Dalí, cine y surrealismo(s)* (Barcelona: Parsifal Ediciones, 2003), 202.

11. Mark Polizzotti, *Revolution of the Mind: The Life of André Breton* (London: Bloomsbury, 1995), 356.

12. Dalí, "La cabra sanitaria," 1087.

13. See Vicent Santamaría de Mingo, "Dalí i el tango: Entre Paris i Barcelona," *L'Avenç*, no. 332 (February 2008): 42–46.

14. Dalí, *Secret Life*, 318.

15. See, for example, Román Gubern, *Proyector de luna: La generación del 27 y el cine* (Barcelona: Anagrama, 1999), 61; Salvador Dalí, *La Vie secrète de Salvador Dalí: Suis-je un génie?*, edited by Frédérique Joseph-Lowery (Lausanne: L'Âge d'Homme, 2007), 600n39.

16. Letter of 16 August 1932 from Luis Buñuel in San Sebastián to Pierre Unik in Paris (?), ref. ARA c. 23-19, Archivo de la Fundación Max Aub, Segorbe. Pierre Braunberger had a holiday home in Saint-Jean-de-Luz. Man Ray was there filming *corridas* for the producer, a recent convert to bullfighting.

17. Signed copy of *Babaouo*, ref. AB-419, Archivo Luis Buñuel, Filmoteca Española, Madrid.

18. Sánchez Vidal, "Introducción," in Dalí, *Obra Completa III*, 126.

19. Bouhours and Schoeller, *L'Âge d'or: Correspondance*, 158, letter of 18 August 1932 from Luis Buñuel in San Sebastián to Charles de Noailles in Hyères (?).

20. Salvador Dalí, *Abrégé d'une histoire critique du cinéma*, in *Babaouo*, 13–14. English translation in Paul Hammond, ed., *The Shadow and Its Shadow: Surrealist Writings on the Cinema* (San Francisco: City Lights Books, 2000), 63–67; here 64.

21. Juan Gabriel Tharrats, *Los 500 films de Segundo de Chomón* (Zaragoza: Universidad de Zaragoza, 1988), 217.

22. See, for example, Georgina Torello, "Con el demonio en el cuerpo: La mujer en el cine mudo italiano (1913–1920)," *Secuencias: Revista de Historia del Cine*, no. 23 (January–June 2006): 7–19.

23. Dalí, *Abrégé*, in *Babaouo*, 19.

24. Bouhours and Schoeller, *L'Âge d'or: Correspondance*, 148, letter of 19 October 1931 from Luis Buñuel in Paris to Charles de Noailles in Hyères (?).

25. Dalí, *Abrégé*, in *Babaouo*, 20; Hammond, *Shadow*, 67.

26. Salvador Dalí, "Derniers modes d'excitation intellectuelle pour l'été 1934," *Documents 34: Intervention surréaliste* (June 1934): 35.

27. Salvador Dalí, *Abrégé*, in *Babaouo*, 20–21; Hammond, *Shadow*, 67.

28. Pierre Unik, *Le Héros du vide: Roman inachevé* (Paris: Les Éditeurs Français Réunis, 1972). The most complete account of Unik's life and work appears in Emmanuel Hutin, *Pierre Unik 1909/1945* (Paris: Librairie-Galerie Emmanuel Hutin, 2009).

29. Buñuel, *Mon dernier soupir*, 134.

30. Bouhours and Schoeller, *L'Âge d'or: Correspondance*, 149, letter of 5 December 1931 from Luis Buñuel in Zaragoza to Charles de Noailles in Hyères (?).

31. Aub, *Conversaciones*, 319.

32. *Pneumatique* of 19 June 1932 from Luis Buñuel to Pierre Unik, both in Paris, ref. ARA c. 23-19, Archivo de la Fundación Max Aub, Segorbe.

33. Santiago Ontañón and José María Moreiro, *Unos pocos amigos verdaderos* (Madrid: Fundación Banco Exterior, 1988), 73.

34. Letter of 21 July 1932 from Luis Buñuel in Sallent de Gallego (Huesca) to Pierre Unik in Paris, ref. ARA c. 23-19, Archivo de la Fundación Max Aub, Segorbe.

35. Letter of 11 August 1932 from Pierre Unik in Isle-Adam (Seine-et-Oise) to Georges Sadoul in Hamburg (?), Inventaire/annexe 2, lettre 313, Fonds Georges Sadoul, Cinémathèque Française, Paris.

36. Letter of 21 July 1932 from Luis Buñuel in San Sebastián to Pierre Unik in Paris (?), ref. ARA c. 23-19, Archivo de la Fundación Max Aub, Segorbe.

37. Bouhours and Schoeller, *L'Âge d'or: Correspondance*, 158, letter of 18 August 1932 from Luis Buñuel in San Sebastián to Charles de Noailles in Hyères (?).

38. Ibid., 159, letter of 24 September 1932 from Luis Buñuel in Paris to Charles de Noailles in Hyères (?).

39. Pierre Braunberger, *Pierre Braunberger producteur: Cinémamémoire*, edited by Jacques Berger (Paris: Centre Georges Pompidou/Centre Nationale de la Cinématographie, 1987), 201, 203.

40. Bouhours and Schoeller, *L'Âge d'or: Correspondance*, 159, letter of 24 September 1932 from Luis Buñuel in Paris to Charles de Noailles in Hyères (?).

41. Letter of 6 May 1932 from Luis Buñuel to André Breton, quoted in full in chapter 6.

42. André Breton, "Le Château étoilé," *Minotaure*, no. 8 (1936): 29, repr. in André Breton, *L'Amour fou* (Paris: Gallimard, 1937).

43. André Breton, "Présentation d'*Un chien andalou*," in *Œuvres Complètes II*, edited by Marguerite Bonnet et al. (Paris: Gallimard/Bibliothèque de La Pléiade, 1992), 1266.

44. Dalí, *Secret Life*, 284n1.

45. Dalí, *La Vie secrète*, 556.

46. Edmond T. Gréville, *Trente-cinq ans dans la jungle du cinéma* (Arles: Institut Lumière/Actes Sud, 1995), 116–17. The text dates from ca. 1965.

47. Bouhours and Schoeller, *L'Âge d'or: Correspondance*, 159, letter of 24 September 1932 from Luis Buñuel in Paris to Charles de Noailles in Hyères (?).

48. Breton, "Le Château étoilé."

49. Georges Bataille, *L'Apprenti Sorcier: Du Cercle Communiste Démocratique à Acéphale* (Paris: Éditions de la Différence, 1999), 166.

50. Letter of 27 December 1934 from André Breton in Paris to Luis Buñuel in Madrid, ref. R. 355, Archivo Luis Buñuel, Filmoteca Española, Madrid.

51. Fernando Gabriel Martín, "El cine y la izquierda en Tenerife durante la República: Progresía, producción y cultura," in *Internacional constructivista frente a internacional surrealista*, edited by María Isabel Navarro Segura (Tenerife: Cabildo Insular de Tenerife, 1999), 77–79.

52. Domingo Pérez Minik, *Facción española surrealista de Tenerife* (Barcelona: Tusquets, 1975), 98–99.

53. See the statement by André Thirion in Pierre, *Tracts surréalistes*, 472.

54. André Breton, *Entretiens (1913–1952) avec André Parinaud* (Paris: Gallimard, 1952), 169.

55. "Protestez!," March 1933, is reprinted in Pierre, *Tracts surréalistes*, 238–40. The other tracts, not signed by Buñuel, are "L'AEAR s'incline devant les victimes et fait appel aux Correspondants Ouvriers," of February 1933, in ibid., 238; and "Contre le fascisme mais aussi contre l'impérialisme français," of May 1933, in Claude Cahun, *Écrits* (Paris: Jean-Michel Place, 2002), 547.

56. Letter of 11 March 1933 from André Breton to Paul Éluard, cited in Breton, *Œuvres Complètes II*, xxxviii.

57. Letter of 23 February 1933 from Luis Buñuel to Pierre Unik, both in Paris, ref. ARA c. 23-19, Archivo de la Fundación Max Aub, Segorbe.

58. Paul Nizan, *Articles littéraires et politiques*, vol. 1, *1923–1935* (Paris: Joseph K., 2005), 147.

59. Jean-Paul Sartre, *Écrits de jeunesse* (Paris: Gallimard, 1990), 27, cited in Nizan, *Articles littéraires*, 147n9.

60. Paul Vaillant-Couturier et al., *Ceux qui ont choisi: Contre le fascisme en Allemagne; Contre l'impérialisme français* (Paris: AEAR, 1933).

61. Léon Moussinac, "État du cinéma international" (1933), in *L'Âge ingrat du cinéma* (Paris: Éditions du Sagittaire, 1946), 160–73.

62. Ibid., 167–68.

63. Maria Van Rysselberghe, *Les Cahiers de la Petite Dame: Notes pour l'histoire authentique d'André Gide*, vol. 2, *1929–1937*, Cahiers André Gide 5 (Paris: Gallimard, 1975), 241.

64. Ibid., 305.

65. Buñuel, *Mon dernier soupir*, 169–70.

66. Van Rysselberghe, *Les Cahiers de la Petite Dame*, 2:310.

67. Another attempt at filming *Les Caves du Vatican* would be made in 1949, with Yves Allégret as director. Based on a script by Allégret, Jacques Prévert, and Gide, the project was dropped after a month's work because the producer feared a backlash from the Vatican.

68. Letter of 10 January 1934 from Luis Buñuel in Madrid to Pierre Unik in Paris (?), ref. ARA c. 23-19, Archivo de la Fundación Max Aub, Segorbe.

69. Aragon, *L'Œuvre Poétique*, 2:997.

70. Marcel Martin, "Lods (Jean)," in *Larousse Dictionnaire du cinéma*, edited by Jean-Loup Passek (Paris: Larousse, 1995), 2:1340.

71. Letter of 20 December 1934 from Louis Aragon in Odessa to Luis Buñuel in Madrid, ref. R. 000, Archivo Luis Buñuel, Filmoteca Española, Madrid. The attribution by Paul Hammond of a date of 20 December 1932 is incorrect in *Tierra sin pan: Luis Buñuel y los nuevos caminos de las vanguardias*, edited by Mercè Ibarz (Valencia: IVAM, Centre Julio González, 1999), 93, 93n14, 215, 217n13.

72. Aragon, *L'Œuvre Poétique*, 2:996.

73. Letter of 10 February 1935 from Pierre Unik in Paris to Luis Buñuel in Madrid, ref. R. 389, Archivo Luis Buñuel, Filmoteca Española, Madrid.

74. See Toulet, *Le Cinéma au rendez-vous des arts*, 24.

75. Artur London, *The Confession* (New York: Ballantine Books, 1970), 252.

76. See François de la Breteque, "La première de *L'Âge d'or* à Toulouse et à Montpellier," *Les Cahiers de la Cinémathèque*, no. 30–31 (Summer–Autumn 1980): 179–82.

77. Ferdinand Alquié, "Correspondance II: À André Breton," *LSASDLR*, no. 5 (15 May 1933): 43.

78. Salvador Dalí, *Diary of a Genius* (London: Hutchinson, 1966), 76, originally published as *Journal d'un génie* (Paris: Éditions de la Table Ronde, 1964).

79. Benjamín Péret, "La Conversion de Gide," *LSASDLR*, no. 5 (15 May 1933): 29.

80. Buñuel, *Mon dernier soupir*, 169.

Chapter 9. From *Las Hurdes* to *Terre sans pain*

1. Jordana Mendelson, *Documenting Spain: Artists, Exhibition Culture, and the Modern Nation, 1929–1939* (University Park: Pennsylvania State University Press, 2005), 69.

2. Maurice Legendre, *Las Jurdes: Étude de géographie humaine* (Bordeaux: Feret & Fils, 1927), 1. The book was still in print seventy-five years later. Subsequent page citations are listed in the text.

3. Robert Desnos, *Le Soir* (19 May 1927), repr. in Robert Desnos, *Cinéma* (Paris: Gallimard, 1966), 178.

4. Colette, *Colette au cinéma* (Paris: Flammarion, Paris, 1975), 31.

5. Joris Ivens, *The Camera and I* (New York: International, 1969), 55.

6. Jay Leyda, *Kino: A History of the Russian and Soviet Film* (London: George Allen & Unwin, 1960), 293.

7. Harry Alan Potamkin, "Light and Shade in the Soviet Cinema," *Theatre Guild Magazine* (July 1930), repr. in *The Compound Cinema*, edited by Lewis Jacobs (New York: Teachers College Press, 1977), 317.

8. Pierre Billard, *L'Âge classique du cinéma français: Du cinéma parlant à la nouvelle vague* (Paris: Flammarion, 1995), 52–53.

9. Bernard Chardère, *Le Cinéma de Jacques Prévert* (Bordeaux: Le Castor Astral, 2001), 47.

10. Ibid., 53.

11. Bouhours and Schoeller, *L'Âge d'or: Correspondance*, 153.

12. Mercè Ibarz, *Buñuel documental*: Tierra sin pan *y su tiempo* (Zaragoza: Prensas Universitarias de Zaragoza, 1999), 108, 50–51.

13. Pierre Kast, "À la recherche de Luis Bunuel avec Jean Grémillon, Jean Castanier, Eli Lotar, L. Viñes et Pierre Prévert," *Cahiers du cinéma*, no. 7 (December 1951): 20.

14. Buñuel, *Mon dernier soupir*, 170–71; Pérez Turrent and de la Colina, *Buñuel por Buñuel*, 34; Aub, *Conversaciones*, 76.

15. Aranda, *Luis Buñuel: Biografía crítica*, 2nd ed. (Barcelona: Lumen, 1975), 136n1; Aub, *Conversaciones*, 235.

16. Aub, *Conversaciones*, 289, 307; Rafael Alberti, *La arboleda perdida II* (Barcelona: Seix y Barral, 1987), 262.

17. León, *Memoria de la melancolía*, 232.

18. Buñuel, *Mon dernier soupir*, 173; Pérez Turrent and de la Colina, *Buñuel por Buñuel*, 35; Aub, *Conversaciones*, 78.

19. Pérez Turrent and de la Colina, *Buñuel por Buñuel*, 36.

20. Luis Buñuel, "Land without Bread," nine-page manuscript in English of the introductory talk given by Buñuel to students of Columbia University in the MacMillan Academic Theater, New York, on 18 March 1940 , ref. 1485, Archivo Luis Buñuel, Filmoteca Española, Madrid. The same archive also contains the Spanish original, which runs to ten pages with variations and additions. The quote comes from the latter, 10.

21. Pérez Turrent and de la Colina, *Buñuel por Buñuel*, 35.

22. Carlos Rebolledo, *Luis Bunuel* (Paris: Éditions Universitaires, 1964), 43.

23. Buñuel, "Land without Bread," English version, 5.

24. Agustín Sánchez Vidal, "De Las Hurdes a *Tierra sin pan*," in *Las Hurdes: Un documental de Luis Buñuel*, edited by Javier Herrera Navarro (Cáceres: Museo Extremeño e Iberoamericano de Arte Contemporáneo, 1999), 40.

25. Payne, *La primera democracia española*, 111.

26. Georges Sadoul, "Las Hurdes," *Regards*, no. 146 (29 October 1936): 19.

27. Kast, "À la recherche de Luis Bunuel," 21.

28. Letter of 16 April 1933 from Rafael Sánchez Ventura in Las Batuecas to Eli Lotar and Pierre Unik in Paris, ref. c. 23-19, Archivo de la Fundación Max Aub, Segorbe.

29. Braunberger, *Pierre Braunberger producteur*, 118.

30. Aranda, *Luis Buñuel: Biografía crítica*, 139.

31. Braunberger, *Pierre Braunberger producteur*, 118.

32. Sadoul, "Mon ami Buñuel," 12.

33. Fonds Georges Sadoul, Cinémathèque Française, Paris, ref. 310.

34. *Pneumatique* dated 22 July 1933, ref. c. 23-19, Archivo de la Fundación Max Aub, Segorbe.

35. Buñuel, *Mon dernier soupir*, 171; Aub, *Conversaciones*, 76; Pérez Turrent and de la Colina, *Buñuel por Buñuel*, 36.

36. Buñuel, "Land without Bread," Spanish version, 10.

37. Ibarz, *Buñuel documental*, 113.

38. Kast, "À la recherche de Luis Bunuel," 22.

39. André Bazin, "Los Olvidados," *Esprit* 10, no. 186 (January 1952), repr. in André Bazin, *El cine de la crueldad* (Bilbao: Mensajero, 1977), 73.

40. Javier Herrera Navarro, "Pretexto, contexto e hipertexto en *Las Hurdes/Tierra sin pan* de Buñuel," in Herrera Navarro, *Las Hurdes: Un documental de Luis Buñuel*, 26.

41. Aub, *Conversaciones*, 41, 44.

42. Sánchez Vidal, "De Las Hurdes a *Tierra sin pan*," 68.

43. Alberto Farassino, *Tutto il cinema di Luis Buñuel* (Milan: Baldini & Castoldi, 2000), 136.

44. Pérez Turrent and de la Colina, *Buñuel por Buñuel*, 15; Buñuel, *Mon dernier soupir*, 17; Aub, *Conversaciones*, 41.

45. Ado Kyrou, *Le Surréalisme au cinéma* (Paris: Éditions Arcanes, 1953), 230; Ado Kyrou, *Luis Bunuel* (Paris: Seghers, 1962), 38.

46. Kyrou, *Luis Bunuel*, 36.

47. Freddy Buache, *Luis Buñuel* (Lausanne: La Cité, 1970), 33.

48. Patrick Bureau, "Un poème de l'horreur: *Terre sans pain*," *Études cinématographiques*, no. 22–23 (January–March 1963): 165.

49. Giménez Caballero, *Retratos españoles*, 165.

50. Aub, *Conversaciones*, 77.

51. Buñuel, "Una noche en el Studio des Ursulines," 6.

52. Pérez Turrent and de la Colina, *Buñuel por Buñuel*, 37.

53. Bullejos, *La Comintern en España*, 206–8; Elorza and Bizcarrondo, *Queridos camaradas*, 169–70; Estruch, *Historia oculta del PCE*, 79–81; Payne, *Unión Soviética*, 50–51.

54. Hutin, *Pierre Unik*, 43.

55. *Nueva Cultura*, no. 6 (August–September 1935): 13.

56. Alberti, *La arboleda perdida II*, 19.

57. Pierre Robin, "Cinéma," *Commune*, no. 42 (February 1937): 762–63.

58. Laura Vicchi, *Henri Storck: De l'avant-garde au documentaire social* (Crisnée: Yellow Now Éditions, 2002), 43, 188n35; Schoots, *Living Dangerously*, 90.

59. Buñuel, *Mon dernier soupir*, 171–72.

60. Aranda, *Luis Buñuel: Biografía crítica*, 142.

61. Carlos Serrano de Osma, "El documental en el recuerdo," in *El cine de las organizaciones populares republicanas entre 1936 y 1939*, vol. 2, *Las organizaciones marxistas*, edited by Rosa Álvarez, Julio Pérez Perucha, and Ramón Sala (Bilbao: Certamen de Cine Documental, 1981), 48.

62. Carnicero and Sánchez Salas, *En torno a Buñuel*, 261.

63. Kast, "À la recherche de Luis Bunuel," 18.

64. César M. Arconada, "Luis Buñuel y *Las Hurdes*: El film," *Nuestro Cinema*, 2nd ser., no. 2 (15) (February 1935): 8–9.

65. Pérez Turrent and de la Colina, *Buñuel por Buñuel*, 35.

66. Letter of 10 January 1934 from Luis Buñuel in Madrid to Pierre Unik in Paris (?), ref. c. 23-19, Archivo de la Fundación Max Aub, Segorbe.

67. Javier Herrera Navarro, *Estudios sobre* Las Hurdes *de Buñuel: Evidencia fílmica, estética y recepción* (Sevilla: Renacimiento, 2006), 54–63.

68. Buñuel, *Mon dernier soupir*, 173; Pérez Turrent and de la Colina, *Buñuel por Buñuel*, 36.

69. Edward Mortimer, *The Rise of the French Communist Party, 1920–1947* (London: Faber and Faber, 1984), 214.

70. Ibarz, *Buñuel documental*, 136.

71. Letter of 26 May 1937 from Eloy Sota (?), public order delegate in La Coruña, to the chief commissioner of investigation and surveillance of the same city, legajo 2121, Expediente 55, H13179, Archivo Histórico Nacional, Madrid.

72. Antonio del Amo, "Galería de nuevos realizadores: Nacimiento del cinema hispano," *Cinegramas*, no. 89 (24 May 1936): n.p.

73. Letter of 15 April 1936 from Pedro Garrigós to minister of state education Marcelino Domingo, ref. 384/187, Archivo General de la Guerra Civil Española, Salamanca, Político Social, Madrid.

74. Aub, *Conversaciones*, 73, 80, 93.

75. Ibarz, *Buñuel documental*, 145.

76. Victor Fuentes, *Los mundos de Buñuel* (Madrid: Akal, 2000), 51; Victor Fuentes, *La mirada de Buñuel: Cine, literatura y vida* (Madrid: Tabla Rasa, 2005), 61.

77. Sánchez Vidal, "De Las Hurdes a *Tierra sin pan*," 47.

78. Pérez Turrent and de la Colina, *Buñuel por Buñuel*, 36.

79. Javier Herrera Navarro, "Recepción crítica de *Las Hurdes* de Buñuel en Europa durante la Guerra Civil Española," *Secuencias: Revista de Historia del Cine*, 2nd ser., no. 11 (January–March 2000): 72–87.

80. Sadoul, "Las Hurdes," 19.

81. Inmaculada Sánchez Alarcón, *La Guerra Civil Española y el cine francés* (Sant Cugat del Vallès: Los Libros de la Frontera, 2005), 203–4.

82. Basil Wright, "*Land without Bread* and *Spanish Earth*," *World Film News* (December 1937), in *The Documentary Tradition: From Nanook to Woodstock*, edited by Lewis Jacobs (New York: Hopkinson & Blake, 1971), 146.

83. Elsa Triolet, *Dix jours en Espagne* (Paris: Société des Amis de Louis Aragon et Elsa Triolet, 2005), 51. Although written in 1937, this work was first published in 2005.

84. Haidee Wasson, *Museum Movies: The Museum of Modern Art and the Birth of Art Cinema* (Berkeley: University of California Press, 2005), 163.

85. Mary Iea Bandy, *Circulating Film Library Catalog* (New York: Museum of Modern Art, 1984), 116.

86. Emeterio Díez Puertas, *El montaje del franquismo: La política cinematográfica de las fuerzas sublevadas* (Barcelona: Laertes, 2002), 172–73, 200.

87. Braunberger, *Pierre Braunberger producteur*, 118.

88. Ibid., 202.

Chapter 10. Dubbing at Warner Bros.

1. "Controversia literario-cinematográfica," *La Vanguardia* (7 January 1933): 13; "'L'Âge d'or' de Dalí i Buñuel" and "Carnet cinematogràfic," *La Publicitat* (11 January 1933): 8.

2. Rafael Santos Torroella, ed., *Salvador Dalí corresponsal de J. V. Foix 1932–1936* (Barcelona: Editorial Mediterránea, 1986), 129.

3. "El correu d'avui," *La Publicitat* (7 June 1934): 2.

4. Pérez Turrent and de la Colina, *Buñuel por Buñuel*, 34.

5. Buñuel, "Auto-Biography," 12.

6. The remaining titles were *Los que danzan* (1930), a version of *Those Who Dance* (William Beaudine, 1930); *La llama sagrada* (1931), a version of *The Sacred Flame* (Archie Mayo, 1929); *La dama atrevida* (1931), a version of *The Lady Who Dared* (William Beaudine, 1931); and *La buenaventura* (1934).

7. Advertisement for *I Am a Fugitive from a Chain Gang* announcing its first screening at the Cineclub Mirador, *Films Selectos*, no. 127 (18 March 1933): 10.

8. José Castellón Díaz, "Luis Buñuel y *Las Hurdes*: El realizador," *Nuestro Cinema*, 2nd ser., no. 2 (15) (February 1935), repr. in *Del cinema como arma de clase: Antología de* Nuestro Cinema *1932–1935*, edited by Carlos Pérez Merinero and David Pérez Merinero (Valencia: Fernando Torres Editor, 1975), 142.

9. Juan Piqueras, "Nuevos films en París," *Nuestro Cinema*, no. 10 (March 1933): 136–37.

10. Aub, *Conversaciones*, 77.

11. Augusto M. Torres, "El culto al hermano," interview with Jerónimo Mihura, *Archivos de la Filmoteca*, no. 9 (Spring–Summer 1991): 47–48.

12. Eduardo García Maroto, *Aventuras y desventuras del cine español* (Barcelona: Plaza y Janés, 1988), 84.

13. Letter of 16 August 1934 from Luis Buñuel in Madrid to Georges Sadoul in Barcelona (?), ref. GS-C 064, Fonds Georges Sadoul, Cinémathèque Française, Paris.

14. Georges Sadoul, "Bunuel, Viridiana et quelques autres," in *Viridiana* (Paris: InterSpectacles, 1962), 18.

15. Payne, *Unión Soviética*, 75.

16. Letter of 10 January 1934 from Luis Buñuel in Madrid to Pierre Unik in Paris (?), ref. c. 23-19, Archivo de la Fundación Max Aub, Segorbe.

17. Aub, *Conversaciones*, 125. Buñuel and Durán would coincide again during World War II at the MoMA in New York.

18. "Nuevo gerente de la agencia Warner Bros. en Madrid," *Popular Film*, no. 440 (24 January 1935): n.p.

19. Rucar de Buñuel, *Memorias*, 52–53.

20. Buñuel, *Mon dernier soupir*, 193.

21. Ibid., 123.

22. Luis M. Serrano, "Pintura y cinema: Picasso y Buñuel," *Popular Film*, no. 435 (20 December 1934): n.p.

23. These films included *Fashions of 1934* (William Dieterle, 1934); *Ever in My Heart* (Archie Mayo, 1933); *Lady Killer* (Roy Del Ruth, 1933); *Massacre* (Alan Crosland, 1934); *Mandalay* (Michael Curtiz, 1934); *Midnight Alibi* (Alan Crosland, 1934); *A Midsummer Night's Dream* (Max Reinhardt and William Dieterle, 1935); *Bordertown* (Archie Mayo, 1935); *In Caliente* (Busby Berkeley and Lloyd Bacon, 1935); *G-Men* (William Keighley, 1935); *The Circus Clown* (Ray Enright, 1934); *The St. Louis Kid* (Ray Enright, 1934); *Here Comes the Navy* (Lloyd Bacon, 1934); *Living on Velvet* (Frank Borzage, 1935); *Sweet Adeline* (Mervyn Le Roy, 1934); *Wonder Bar* (Busby Berkeley and Lloyd Bacon, 1934); *Female* (Michael Curtiz, 1933); *Flirtation Walk* (Frank Borzage, 1934); and *Heroes for Sale* (William Wellman, 1933).

24. Díez Puertas, *El montaje del franquismo*, 204.

Chapter 11. Commerce, Art, and Politics

1. Ricardo Urgoiti, inscription on 1934–35 *Anuario Rotario*, ref. S.E. Rotarios 13/21, Archivo General de la Guerra Civil Española, Salamanca.

2. Ernesto Giménez Caballero published a colorful anonymous portrait of this character in "Visitas de cinema: Los empresarios: Armenta (Madrid)," *La Gaceta Literaria*, no. 51 (1 February 1929): 6.

3. "Desde Madrid," *Arte y Cinematografía*, no. 334 (February 1929): n.p.

4. "De nuestros corresponsales: Madrid," *Arte y Cinematografía*, no. 383–90 (March–October 1933): n.p.

5. J. Francisco Aranda, "La etapa española 1932–37," in *Luis Buñuel*, edited by Edoardo Bruno (Venice: XLI Mostra Internazionale del Cinema, 1984), 48.

6. "Noticias," *Arte y Cinematografía*, no. 403 (June 1935): n.p.

7. The standard work on Urgoiti is Luis Fernández Colorado and Josetxo Cerdán, *Ricardo Urgoiti: Los trabajos y los días* (Madrid: Filmoteca Española, 2007).

8. Ernesto Giménez Caballero, "Historia del Cineclub Español," *La Gaceta Literaria*, no. 105 (1 May 1931): 3.

9. "Primera producción española completamente hablada y sincronizada," *Arte y Cinematografía*, no. 345 (January 1930): n.p.

10. Manuel Rotellar, *Cine español de la República* (San Sebastián: XXV Festival Internacional de Cine de San Sebastián, 1977), 64; "Hablando con Rosario Pi," *Films Selectos*, no. 112 (3 December 1932): 5.

11. M. A., "María Fernanda Ladrón de Guevara en el cinema hispano," *Popular Film*, no. 294 (31 March 1932): 10. García Sanchiz's trip to Hollywood and the monologues that followed on this subject are documented in "Itinerarios: García Sanchiz a Hollywood," *La Gaceta Literaria*, no. 94 (15 November 1930): 13; "Centelleos," *Popular Film*, no. 244 (16 April 1931): n.p.; "Planos de Madrid," *Popular Film*, no. 248 (14 May 1931): n.p.; "Cine Urquinaona: Tres charlas de Federico García Sanchiz," *Popular Film*, no. 250 (28 May 1931): n.p.; and "García Sanchiz concede una charla para 'Films Selectos,'" *Films Selectos*, no. 34 (6 June 1931): 6–7, 22.

12. Douglas Gomery, *The Hollywood Studio System* (New York: St. Martin's Press, 1986), 104.

13. Garth Jowett, *Film: The Democratic Art* (Boston: Little, Brown, 1976), 196.

14. Llopis, *Juan Piqueras*, 1:77.

15. Ibid., 104.

16. "Selecciones Filmófono ante la nueva temporada cinematográfica," *Arte y Cinematografía*, no. 365 (September 1931): n.p.

17. Ernesto Giménez Caballero, "Nuestros cinempresarios: Ricardo Urgoiti," *La Gaceta Literaria*, no. 112 (15 August 1931): 10.

18. Llopis, *Juan Piqueras*, 1:104.

19. Ibid., 144n39.

20. Ernesto Giménez Caballero, "Muerte y resurrección del Cineclub," *La Gaceta Literaria*, no. 121 (15 January 1932): 11–12.

21. Antonio Guzmán Merino, "Planos de Madrid," *Popular Film*, no. 282 (7 January 1932): n.p.

22. Juan Piqueras, "La Atlántida: Film Franco-Alemán de G. W. Pabst," *Nuestro Cinema*, no. 2 (July 1932): 53.

23. The twelve films were *The Ghost That Will Not Return* (Abram Room, 1929); *The Yellow Ticket* (Fyodor Otsep, 1928); *Cain and Artem* (Pavel Petrov-Bytov, 1929); *Blue Express* (Ilya Trauberg, 1929); *Fragment of an Empire* (Friedrich Ermler, 1929); *The Man from the Restaurant* (Yakov Protazanov, 1927); *Ranks and People* (Yakov Protazanov, 1929); *Mother*

(V. I. Pudovkin, 1926); *The End of St. Petersburg* (V. I. Pudovkin, 1927); and *October* (1927), *Old and New* (1929), and *Romance sentimentale* (1930), all three by Eisenstein, the final one being filmed in Paris with the collaboration of Grigori Alexandrov.

24. François Albera, "La réception du cinéma soviétique en France, dans les années 1920–1930," in *Le Studio Mejrabpom ou l'aventure du cinéma privé au pays des bolsheviks*, edited by Aïcha Kherroubi et al., Les Dossiers du Musée d'Orsay 59 (Paris: La Documentation Française, 1996), 126.

25. Antonio Guzmán Merino, "Planos de Madrid," *Popular Film*, no. 291 (19 March 1932): n.p.

26. Juan Piqueras, "*Kuhle Wampe* y el cine proletario," *Octubre*, no. 1 (June–July 1933): 20–21.

27. Juan Medina, "Revisión de cineclubs," *Popular Film*, no. 362 (20 July 1933): n.p.; Luis M. Serrano, "'El mar de los cuervos' y 'Morgenrot,'" *Popular Film*, no. 378 (9 November 1933): n.p.; Antonio del Amo, "Temporada 1933–34: Revisión de cineclubs," *Popular Film*, no. 413 (12 July 1934): n.p.

28. Antonio del Amo, "Los cineclubs y el cinema," *Popular Film*, no. 383 (14 December 1933): n.p.

29. Juan Piqueras, "Hacia una Federación Española de Cineclubs Proletarios," *Nuestro Cinema*, no. 13 (October 1933): 214–16.

30. Juan Piqueras, "Segunda encuesta: Convocatoria y cuestionario," *Nuestro Cinema*, 2nd ser., no. 4 (August 1935): 66.

31. Juan Piqueras, "Films soviéticos: 'Los tártaros,'" *Popular Film*, no. 214 (4 September 1930): 8.

32. Juan Piqueras, "Cuatro notas de cinema soviético," *La Gaceta Literaria*, no. 87 (1 August 1930): 5.

33. Juan Piqueras, "Colofón a la primera encuesta de *Nuestro Cinema*," *Nuestro Cinema*, no. 7 (October 1932): 203.

34. César M. Arconada, "Hacia un cinema proletario," *Nuestro Cinema*, no. 8–9 (January–February 1933): 92–94.

35. Koch, *Double Lives*, 27–28.

36. Peter B. Schumann, "Le cinéma prolétarien allemand," *Écran 73*, no. 20 (December 1973): 38.

37. Buñuel, *Mon dernier soupir*, 106.

38. Jorge Luis Borges, "Films," *Sur*, no. 3 (Winter 1931), cited in Edgardo Cozarinsky, *Borges en/y/sobre el cine* (Madrid: Editorial Fundamentos, 1981), 30.

39. "Noticiario Films Selectos," *Films Selectos*, no. 153 (16 September 1933): 23.

40. Roger Mortimer, "Buñuel, Sáenz de Heredia and Filmófono," *Sight and Sound*, no. 44 (Summer 1975): 180.

41. Ibid.

42. "Las actividades de 'Selecciones Filmófono,'" *Popular Film*, no. 356 (8 June 1933): n.p.

43. "Hablando con don Ricardo Urgoiti," *Popular Film*, no. 372 (28 September 1933): 5.

44. Piqueras, "Nuevos films en París," 168–69.

45. *Anuario Cinematográfico Español* (Madrid: Unión Poligráfica S.A., 1935), 13–14.

Chapter 12. Filmófono

1. Buñuel, "Auto-Biography," 12–13.

2. Luis Buñuel, debate with students of Columbia University, New York, 10 April 1940, sixteen-page manuscript, Museum of Modern Art Film Study Center, New York, p. 14.

3. Aub, *Conversaciones*, 204.

4. Fernández Colorado and Cerdán, *Ricardo Urgoiti*, 202.

5. Castellón Díaz, "Luis Buñuel y 'Las Hurdes,'" 143.

6. Léon Moussinac, "Muerte de la vanguardia," *Nuestro Cinema*, no. 7 (December 1932): 204–5.

7. Buñuel, *Mon dernier soupir*, 175.

8. Fernández Colorado and Cerdán, *Ricardo Urgoiti*, 99.

9. Gómez Mesa, "La generación del cine," 4.

10. Salvador Dalí, "Luis Buñuel (entrevista)," *L'Amic de les Arts*, no. 31 (31 March 1929): 16.

11. Aranda, "La etapa española 1932–37," 48.

12. Manuel Rotellar, "Luis Buñuel en Filmófono," *Cinema 2002*, no. 37 (March 1978): 39.

13. Buñuel, *Mon dernier soupir*, 175.

14. Antonio de Jaén, "¡Directores a examen! Luis Marquina," *Cinegramas*, no. 88 (17 May 1936): n.p.

15. Pérez Turrent and de la Colina, *Buñuel por Buñuel*, 40.

16. Aub, *Conversaciones*, 77.

17. José Luis Sáenz de Heredia, "Cómo y por qué fui director cinematográfico," *Radiocinema*, no. 122 (1 April 1946): n.p.; Antonio Castro, *El cine español en el banquillo* (Valencia: Fernando Torres, 1974), 368–69; R. Mortimer, "Buñuel, Sáenz de Heredia and Filmófono," 181.

18. Florentino Hernández Girbal, "De fuera vendrán," *Cinema Sparta* (28 December 1935), cited in Fernández Colorado and Cerdán, *Ricardo Urgoiti*, 105–7.

19. Carnicero and Sánchez Salas, *En torno a Buñuel*, 263.

20. Ibid., 101.

21. Aub, *Conversaciones*, 82.

22. Aranda, *Luis Buñuel: Biografía crítica*, 155–56.

23. Carnicero and Sánchez Salas, *En torno a Buñuel*, 102.

24. Fernández Colorado and Cerdán, *Ricardo Urgoiti*, 217.

25. Juan Piqueras, "Prolongación de la falsa españolada," *Siluetas*, no. 5 (1 February 1930), repr. in Llopis, *Juan Piqueras*, 2:18.

26. Jo Labanyi, "Buñuel's Cinematic Collaboration with Sáenz de Heredia, 1935–36," in *Buñuel, siglo XXI*, edited by Isabela Santaololla et al. (Zaragoza: Prensas Universitarias de Zaragoza, 2004), 298.

27. Pérez Merinero and Pérez Merinero, "Introducción," in *Del cinema como arma de clase*, 12.

28. Aub, *Conversaciones*, 77, 91.

29. Gonzalo Torrente Ballester, *Panorama de la literatura española contemporánea* (Madrid: Guadarrama, 1965), 176.

30. Edgar Neville, "Defensa del sainete," *Primer Plano*, no. 216 (3 December 1944): n.p.

31. Julio Romano, "El público de los sainetes madrileños se ha pasado al cine," *Cinegramas*, no. 90 (31 May 1936): n.p.

32. "*Don Quintín el amargao* va a ser llevado a la pantalla," *Popular Film*, no. 454 (2 May 1935): n.p.

33. "Benito Perojo hace un buen contrato con Cifesa," *Popular Film*, no. 442 (7 February 1935): n.p.

34. "Noticias y comentarios en montaje," *Nuestro Cinema*, 2nd ser., no. 2 (15) (February 1935): 16.

35. José Cabeza San Deogracias, *El descanso del guerrero: El cine en Madrid durante la Guerra Civil Española (1936–1939)* (Madrid: Rialp, 2005), 77.

36. Fernández Colorado and Cerdán, *Ricardo Urgoiti*, 101.

37. "Ha terminado el rodaje de *Don Quintín, el amargao*," *El Sol* (21 July 1935): 2.

38. García Maroto, *Aventuras y desventuras del cine español*, 87.

39. "La prensa madrileña en los estudios CEA durante el rodaje de *Don Quintín, el amargao*," *Popular Film*, no. 466 (25 July 1935): n.p.

40. Santiago Aguilar, who was present during the first day's shooting of *Don Quintín, el amargao*, noted the similarity between its urban setting and the world of René Clair in "Cómo se filma una producción nacional: El primer día de rodaje de *Don Quintín, el amargao*," *Cinegramas*, no. 38 (2 June 1935): n.p.

41. Jean-André Fieschi, "L'Ange et la bête (croquis méxicains de Luis Buñuel)," *Cahiers du cinéma*, no. 176 (March 1966): 39.

42. Pérez Turrent and de la Colina, *Buñuel por Buñuel*, 61.

43. *El Sol* (4 October 1935): 2.

44. José Moreno Villa, "Don Quintín y el mundo," *El Sol* (18 October 1935): 1. The "two-tone little flag" is the Monarchist (and later Francoist and "democratic") red and yellow one; the Second Republic's banner was tricolor: red, yellow, and indigo.

45. "Ziff," "Don Quintín el amargao (Don Quintin, the Bitter)," *Variety* (30 October 1935), repr. in *Variety Film Reviews: 1934–1937*, vol. 5 of *Variety Film Reviews: 1907–1980* (New York: Garland, 1983), n.p.

46. "Informaciones: Filmófono adquiere los derechos de adaptación de *La Papirusa*," *Popular Film*, no. 467 (1 August 1935): n.p.

47. "Informaciones: 'La hija de Juan Simón,'" *Popular Film*, no. 468 (8 August 1935): n.p.

48. Payne, *La primera democracia española*, 232.

49. On the interesting and eccentric personality of Sobrevila, see Gubern, *Proyector de luna*, 175–95.

50. R. Mortimer, "Buñuel, Sáenz de Heredia and Filmófono," 181.

51. Sáenz de Heredia, "Cómo y por qué fui director cinematográfico," n.p.

52. Castro, *El cine español en el banquillo*, 368–69.

53. R. Mortimer, "Buñuel, Sáenz de Heredia and Filmófono," 181.

54. Ibid., 182.

55. Aranda, *Luis Buñuel: Biografía crítica*, 163.

56. Rotellar, "Luis Buñuel en Filmófono," 39–40.

57. Aranda, *Luis Buñuel: Biografía crítica*, 164.

58. *La Voz* (17 December 1935), unpaginated press cutting in the Hemeroteca Municipal, Madrid.

59. *Cine Español*, no. 22 (December 1935), unpaginated press cutting in the Hemeroteca Municipal, Madrid.

60. *Arte y Cinematografía*, no. 408 (January 1936): n.p.

61. Lope F. Martínez de Ribera,"Pantallas de Barcelona," *Popular Film*, no. 488 (26 December 1935): n.p.

62. "Federico García Lorca parla per als obrers catalans," *L'Hora* (27 September 1935), repr. in García Lorca, *Obras Completas III*, 597–98.

63. García Lorca, *Obras Completas III*, 607–8, 6 October 1935.

64. Ibid., 604, 4 October 1935.

65. "El Sábado de Gloria en el Palacio de la Música, presenta Filmófono su producción nacional '¿Quién me quiere a mí?,'" *El Sol* (5 April 1936): 9.

66. Juan Julio de Abajo de Pablo, *Mis charlas con José Luis Sáenz de Heredia* (Valladolid: Quirón, 1996), 24; R. Mortimer, "Buñuel, Sáenz de Heredia and Filmófono," 182; Agustín Sánchez Vidal, *Luis Buñuel: Obra cinematográfica* (Madrid: Ediciones JC, 1984), 99–100.

67. *Films Selectos*, no. 276 (1 February 1936): 8.

68. Sáenz de Heredia, "Cómo y por qué fui director cinematográfico," n.p.

69. Santiago Aguilar, "Interviú del momento: La estrella mayor y la estrella menor; Lina Yegros y Mari-Tere," *Cinegramas*, no. 78 (8 March 1936): n.p.

70. "Informaciones: Actividad en los estudios madrileños," *Popular Film*, no. 481 (7 November 1935): n.p.

71. Aranda, *Luis Buñuel: Biografía crítica*, 169.

72. "En Madrid ha comenzado el rodaje de la tercera producción nacional de Filmófono," *Arte y Cinematografía*, no. 408 (January 1936): n.p.

73. De Abajo de Pablo, *Mis charlas con José Luis Sáenz de Heredia*, 24.

74. Emilio García Fernández, "¿Quién me quiere a mí?," *Secuencias: Revista de Historia del Cine*, no. 7 (October 1997): 25.

75. Announcement in *Cinegramas*, no. 12 (2 December 1934): n.p.

76. "También nuestras artistas se divorcian," *Cinegramas*, no. 12 (2 December 1934): n.p.; "Un año de divorcios," *Cinegramas*, no. 23 (17 February 1935): n.p.

77. García Fernández, "¿Quién me quiere a mí?," 25.

78. *El Sol* (5 April 1936): 9.

79. Labanyi, "Buñuel's Cinematic Collaboration with Sáenz de Heredia," 296.

80. Unsigned review in *El Sol* (12 April 1936): 4.

81. Antonio Guzmán Merino, "¿Quién me quiere a mí?," *Cinegramas*, no. 84 (19 April 1936): n.p.

82. Lope F. Martínez de Ribera, "¿Quién me quiere a mí?," *Popular Film*, no. 504 (16 April 1936): n.p.

83. Aranda, "La etapa española," 51.

84. Interview by the authors with Emilio Sanz de Soto in his house in Madrid, 11 June 2006.

85. "Informaciones," *Popular Film*, no. 508 (14 May 1936): n.p.

86. Juan Antonio Ríos Carratalá, *A la sombra de Lorca y Buñuel: Eduardo Ugarte* (Alicante: Universidad de Alicante, 1995), 76.

87. Santiago Aguilar, "Nueve horas en la vida de Angelillo," *Cinegramas*, no. 72 (26 January 1936): n.p.; "Angelillo ha firmado en exclusiva de sus films con la editora Filmófono," *Cine Español*, no. 23 (January 1936): n.p.; *Arte y Cinematografía*, no. 410–11 (March–April 1936): n.p.; advertisement for *¡Centinela alerta!*, *Popular Film*, no. 505 (23 April 1936): n.p.

88. Kast, "À la recherche de Luis Buñuel," 18.

89. Buñuel, *Mon dernier soupir*, 177.

90. Pèrez Turrent and de la Colina, *Buñuel por Buñuel*, 40.

91. Aranda, *Luis Buñuel: Biografía crítica*, 170; Carlos Fernández Cuenca, *Imágenes de Jean Grémillon* (San Sebastián: VIII Festival Internacional de Cine de San Sebastián, 1960), 21; Fernández Cuenca, *La Guerra de España y el cine*, 65; Manuel Rotellar, "Un gran iluminador: José María Beltrán," *Aragoneses en el cine 3* (Zaragoza: Ayuntamiento de Zaragoza, 1972), 15.

92. Aranda, *Luis Buñuel: Biografía crítica*, 172.

93. Pierre Kast, *Jean Grémillon*, Premier plan 5 (Lyon: SERDOC, 1960), 8–9.

94. Fernández Colorado and Cerdán, *Ricardo Urgoiti*, 131.

95. Rafael Abella, *La vida cotidiana durante la Guerra Civil: La España republicana* (Barcelona: Planeta, 1975), 352.

96. Ramón Sala Noguer, *El cine en la España republicana durante la Guerra Civil* (Bilbao: Mensajero, 1993), 27.

97. Review in *El Sol* (1 September 1937): 3.

98. Cabeza San Deogracias, *El descanso del guerrero*, 45.

99. Fernández Cuenca, *Imágenes de Jean Grémillon*, 21.

100. Fiche dated 14 February 1939, caja 36/03145, legajo 212, Archivo de la Administración General del Estado, Alcalá de Henares. This and other information about the censorship records of *¡Centinela, alerta!* has been supplied to us by Christian Franco Torre, an expert on the work of Edgar Neville.

101. Letter of 5 February 1940 from the secretary of the Technical Secretary's Office of Press and Propaganda to His Excellency the Head of State, (03) 049 21/1366, Archivo de la Administración General del Estado, Alcalá de Henares.

102. José Rubia Barcia, *Con Luis Buñuel en Hollywood y después* (La Coruña: Edició Do Castro, 1992), 40.

103. Aranda, "La etapa española," 48.

104. Pérez Turrent and de la Colina, *Buñuel por Buñuel*, 19; David, *¿Buñuel!*, 312; Arantxa Aguirre Carballeira, *Buñuel, lector de Galdós* (Las Palmas de Gran Canaria: Cabildo de Gran Canaria, 2006), 33.

105. Díez Puertas, *El montaje del franquismo*, 197.

Chapter 13. The Outbreak of the Spanish Civil War

1. Julián Zugazagoitia, *Guerra y vicisitudes de los españoles* (1940; repr., Barcelona: Tusquets, 2001), 76.

2. Santiago Carrillo, *Memorias*, rev. ed. (Barcelona: Planeta, 2006), 182.

3. José Moreno Villa, "La Orden de Toledo," *El Nacional* (12 October 1947), unpaginated press cutting in Buñuel's private scrapbook, Archivo Luis Buñuel, Filmoteca Española, Madrid.

4. Aranda, *Luis Buñuel: Biografía crítica*, 179.

5. Buñuel, *Mon dernier soupir*, 187–88.

6. Santiago Carrillo interviewed by Román Gubern, 29 September 2005.

7. Carrillo, *Memorias*, 183.

8. Aub, *Conversaciones*, 92; Buñuel, *Mon dernier soupir*, 192.

9. Carnicero and Sánchez Salas, *En torno a Buñuel*, 103.

10. Ibid.; Aub, *Conversaciones*, 238.

11. Jesús Vived Mairal, *Ramón J. Sender: Biografía* (Madrid: Páginas de Espuma, 2002), 326–27.

12. Zugazagoitia, *Guerra y vicisitudes*, 137.

13. Ontañón and Moreiro, *Unos pocos amigos verdaderos*, 196.

14. Jackson, *La República española*, 243.

15. Buñuel, *Mon dernier soupir*, 185.

16. Aub, *Conversaciones*, 149.

17. Buñuel, *Mon dernier soupir*, 190.

18. Ibid., 190–91.

19. Félix Fanès, ed., *Dalí, Arquitectura* (Barcelona: Fundació Caixa de Catalunya/Fundació Gala-Salvador Dalí, 1996), 2–3.

20. Dalí, *Secret Life*, 360.

21. Obituaries of Leo Fleischman were published in the *Daily Worker* on 19 October and in *Mundo Obrero* and *El Sol* on 21 October 1936. See Arthur Landis, *The Abraham Lincoln Brigade* (New York: Citadel Press, 1967), 14.

22. Castro, *El cine español en el banquillo*, 43.

23. Mario León, "La cinematografía en el frente," *Popular Film*, no. 525 (17 September 1936): n.p.

24. Juan Julio de Abajo de Pablo, *Mis charlas con Antonio del Amo* (Valladolid: Fancy, 1998), 18.

25. Antonio del Amo, "Mi experiencia personal," in *El cine de las organizaciones populares republicanas entre 1936 y 1939*, vol. 2, *Las organizaciones marxistas*, edited by Rosa Álvarez, Julio Pérez Perucha, and Ramón Sala (Bilbao: Certamen de Cine Documental, 1981), 41–42; Sala Noguer, *El cine en la España republicana*, 134.

26. Dossier, Político Social Bilbao 30, Archivo General de la Guerra Civil Española, Salamanca.

27. Llopis, *Juan Piqueras*, 1:134.

28. Ibid., 120.

29. Ibid., 130.

30. Georges Sadoul, "L'assassinat de Juan Piqueras par les rebelles espagnols," *Commune*, no. 43 (March 1937): 840–44; Georges Sadoul, "La Mort de Juan Piqueras: Le 'Delluc español' fusillé par les rebelles," *L'Humanité*, no. 13964 (11 March 1937): 8.

31. Leocadio Mejías, "La novela de un director," interview with José Luis Sáenz de Heredia, *Radiocinema*, no. 107 (30 December 1944): n.p.

32. Ontañón and Moreiro, *Unos pocos amigos verdaderos*, 196–97.

33. Buñuel, *Mon dernier soupir*, 187.

34. Castro, *El cine español en el banquillo*, 369.

35. Carnicero and Sánchez Salas, *En torno a Buñuel*, 417.

36. María Zambrano, "La Alianza de Intelectuales Antifascistas," in *Los intelectuales en el drama de España y escritos de la Guerra Civil* (Madrid: Trotta, 1998), 148.

37. The signatories were Adolphe Acker, Breton, Claude Cahun, Éluard, Arthur Harfaux, Maurice Henry, Georges Hugnet, Marcel Jean, Dora Maar, Léo Malet, Georges Mouton, Henri Pastoureau, Péret, Guy Rosey, Tanguy, "and a certain number of foreign comrades."

38. Miguel A. Gamonal Torres, *Arte y política en la Guerra Civil Española: El caso republicano* (Granada: Diputación Provincial de Granada, 1987), 23.

39. [Association Internationale des Écrivains], *Conférence extraordinaire tenue à Paris le 25 juillet 1938* (Paris: Denoël, 1938), 78.

40. Alberti, *La arboleda perdida II*, 98.

41. Fernández Colorado and Cerdán, *Ricardo Urgoiti*, 138.

42. Alberti, *La arboleda perdida II*, 307; Llopis, *Juan Piqueras*, 1:134.

43. Buñuel, *Mon dernier soupir*, 74, 118; Aub, *Conversaciones*, 93; Pérez Turrent and de la Colina, *Buñuel por Buñuel*, 40.

44. Cabeza San Deogracias, *El descanso del guerrero*, 15.

45. [Association Internationale des Écrivains], *Conférence extraordinaire tenue à Paris*, 91.

46. Estruch, *Historia oculta del PCE*, 137.

47. Jackson, *La República española*, 220. The most detailed description of Soviet military aid to the Republic is found in Yuri Rybalkin, *Stalin y España* (Madrid: Marcial Pons Historia, 2007).

48. Ernesto Giménez Caballero, "Eisenstein gira un film y cuenta su vida," *El Sol* (6 October 1929), unpaginated press cutting in the Hemeroteca Municipal, Madrid.

49. Aurelio de los Reyes, *El nacimiento de "¡Que viva México!"* (Mexico City: Universidad Nacional Autónoma de México-Instituto de Investigaciones Estéticas, 2006), 211.

50. Julio Álvarez del Vayo, "Diez minutos de cine ruso," *La Gaceta Literaria*, no. 75 (1 February 1930): 7.

51. Payne, *La primera democracia española*, 375.

52. Carrillo, *Memorias*, 148.

53. Manuel Azaña, *Diarios completes: Monarquía, República, Guerra Civil* (Barcelona: Crítica, 2004), 970.

54. Eugeni Xammar, *Seixanta anys d'anar pel món* (Barcelona: Editorial Pòrtic, 1974), 405–6.

55. "Notas políticas," *La Vanguardia* (25 September 1936): 1.

56. Buñuel, *Mon dernier soupir*, 72; Aub, *Conversaciones*, 107–8.

57. Juan Francisco Fuentes, "La arboleda encontrada: *¿Qué es España?* Un documental atribuido a Luis Araquistáin," in *El laboratorio de España: La Junta para Ampliación de Estudios e Investigaciones Científicas 1907–1939* (Madrid: Sociedad Estatal de Conmemoraciones Culturales/Residencia de Estudiantes, 2007), 251–61.

58. Aub, *Conversaciones*, 289.

59. Buñuel, *Mon dernier soupir*, 194.

60. Aub, *Conversaciones*, 80.

61. Ibid., 82.

62. Ibid., 93.

63. Ramón Salas Larrázabal, *Historia del Ejército Popular de la República* (1973; repr., Madrid: La Esfera de los libros, 2006), 1:602, 659.

64. Aub, *Conversaciones*, 419–21; Esteve Riambau, *Ricardo Muñoz Suay: Una vida en sombras* (Barcelona: Tusquets, 2007), 326.

65. Buñuel, *Mon dernier soupir*, 194–95; Aub, *Conversaciones*, 84–85.

66. Buñuel, *Mon dernier soupir*, 196.

67. José Andrés Rojo, *Vicente Rojo* (Barcelona: Tusquets, 2006), 96; Jorge M. Reverte, *La batalla de Madrid* (Barcelona: Crítica, 2004), 503.

68. Buñuel, *Mon dernier soupir*, 196.

69. Luis Gómez Mesa, "Situación actual del cine español," *Blanco y Negro* (1 April 1938): 33.

70. Francisco Ayala, *Recuerdos y olvidos* (Madrid: Alianza, 1988), 246–47.

Chapter 14. A Two-Year Mission in Paris

1. Karl Obermann, "Der neue Spanische Film: Ein Interview mit L. Buñuel, dem Regisseur von 'Erde ohne Brot,'" *Pariser Tageszeitung* (22 February 1937), translated into French and published as "À propos d'*Espagne 36*: Le nouveau film espagnol," *Ce Soir* (10 April 1937), unpaginated press cuttings in Buñuel's private scrapbook, Archivo Luis Buñuel, Filmoteca Española, Madrid.

2. Aub, *Conversaciones*, 78.

3. Fernando G. Mantilla, "Los cameraman en el frente," *Nuevo Cinema Revista Cinematográfica*, no. 1 (October 1937): 9, cited in Cabeza San Deogracias, *El descanso del guerrero*, 93.

4. Aub, *Conversaciones*, 361.

5. Rucar de Buñuel, *Memorias*, 64. The address comes from an official form asking for a resident's card, dated 28 October 1936, dossier Luis Buñuel 921-241, Archives of the Préfecture de Police, Paris.

6. Jeanne Rucar, cited in Aub, *Conversaciones*, 326–27.

7. Official form asking for a resident's card, 28 October 1936, dossier Luis Buñuel 921-241, Archives of the Préfecture de Police, Paris.

8. Sala Noguer, *El cine en la España republicana*, 153–54.

9. Aub, *Conversaciones*, 79.

10. Xammar, *Seixanta anys*, 406, 408.

11. Buñuel, *Mon dernier soupir*, 192.

12. Xammar, *Seixanta anys*, 445.

13. Pérez Turrent and de la Colina, *Buñuel por Buñuel*, 35; Aub, *Conversaciones*, 81.

14. Román Gubern, *1936–1939: La guerra de España en la pantalla; De la propaganda a la historia* (Madrid: Filmoteca Española, 1986), 21, 24. See also the respective entries in Juan Manuel Bonet, *Diccionario de las vanguardias en España, 1907–1936* (Madrid: Alianza Editorial, 1995).

15. Obermann, "À propos d'*Espagne 36*." Louis Aragon and Jean-Richard Bloch were coeditors of *Ce Soir*, in which this article appeared. In calling the interviewee "Brunel," the translator of this *Ce Soir* article made an amusing lapsus, confusing Buñuel's name with that of a character in Aragon's *Les Cloches de Bâle* (1934), the first French Socialist-Realist novel.

16. Lucien Logette, "Jacques-Bernard Brunius (1906–1967), ou du violon d'Ingres considéré comme un des beaux arts" (PhD diss., Université de la Sorbonne Nouvelle–Paris III, 1981), 79.

17. Jonathan Buchsbaum, *Cinéma Engagé: Film in the Popular Front* (Urbana: University of Illinois Press, 1988), 86. *La Vie est à nous* would not be commercially exhibited until 1969.

18. Unik was to die in 1945, after escaping from a German prison camp in Silesia.

19. See Oksana Boulgakova, "Les rapports avec l'Allemagne," in *Le Studio Mejrabpom ou l'aventure du cinéma privé au pays des bolsheviks*, edited by Aïcha Kherroubi et al., Les Dossiers du Musée d'Orsay 59 (Paris: La Documentation Française, 1996), 105–15.

20. For a detailed study of this series—called *K Sobitiyam v Ispanii* in Russian—see Alfonso del Amo García and María Luisa Ibáñez Ferradas, eds., *Catálogo general del cine de la Guerra Civil* (Madrid: Cátedra/Filmoteca Española, 1996), 570–82. On Karmen and Makaseev's Spanish campaign, see Sala Noguer, *El cine en la España republicana*, 367–76; and Daniel Kowalsky, "The Soviet Cinematic Offensive in the Spanish Civil War," *Film History* 19 (2007): 7–19, especially 10–13.

21. A lavender copy is an internegative or second negative arrived at by first striking an interpositive print from the precious original negative; the internegative from which all prints are henceforth to be made is then struck from this interpositive.

22. Wolf Martin Hamdorf, *Zwischen ¡No pasarán! und ¡Arriba España! Film und Propaganda im Spanischen Bürgerkrieg* (Münster: MAkS, 1991), 106.

23. Buñuel, *Mon dernier soupir*, 196.

24. Natalia Nussinova, "*España-36* ¿Es una producción de Luis Buñuel?" *Archivos de la Filmoteca*, no. 22 (February 1996): 84.

25. Schoots, *Living Dangerously*, 118.

26. Contract of 14 January 1937 between Luis Buñuel and Joris Ivens, European Foundation Joris Ivens, Nijmegen. We thank Sonia García López for providing us with a copy of this document.

27. Schoots, *Living Dangerously*, 120; Abraham Segal, "Entretien avec Joris Ivens," *L'Avant-Scène du cinéma*, no. 259–60 (1–15 January 1981): 6. See also the paper by Esteve Riambau, "*Tierra(s) de España*: Nueve versiones del film de Joris Ivens," presented at the international congress "La Guerra Civil Española 1936–1939," Madrid, 27–29 November 2006, http://www.secc.es/media/docs/20_1_Esteve_Riambau.pdf.

28. Pérez Turrent and de la Colina, *Buñuel por Buñuel*, 41.

29. Gubern, *1936–1939: La guerra de España en la pantalla*, 44.

30. Schoots, *Living Dangerously*, 133.

31. Sala Noguer, *El cine en la España republicana*, 320. In all probability Buñuel and Montagu collaborated closely during this period. In fact, Buñuel related that in one of his many trips to London during the Civil War he was invited by two people, an unnamed Labour Party MP and Ivor Montagu, president of the Film Society, to give a short propaganda speech in English before twenty Republican sympathizers, including Roland Penrose (who'd appeared in *L'Âge d'or*) and Conrad Veidt. See Buñuel, *Mon dernier soupir*, 196–97.

32. Aub, *Conversaciones*, 86–87.

33. Del Amo García and Ibáñez Ferradas, *Catálogo general del cine de la Guerra Civil*, 425.

34. Aranda, *Luis Buñuel: Biografía crítica*, 455.

35. David, *¿Buñuel!*, 349.

36. Fernández Cuenca, *La guerra de España y el cine*, 151.

37. Magí Crusells, "Cinema as Political Propaganda during the Spanish Civil War: *España 1936*," *Ebre 38: Revista Internacional de la Guerra Civil 1936–1939*, no. 2 (2004): 162.

38. According to an anonymous review in *El Sol* (6 June 1937): 3. We owe the information about *España 1936*'s one-week run to José Cabeza San Deogracias. For *¡Centinela alerta!*, see Cabeza San Deogracias, *El descanso del guerrero*, 44.

39. See Wolf Martin Hamdorf, "'Espagne 1936' y 'Espagne 1937': Propaganda para la República (Luis Buñuel y la Guerra Civil Española)," *Secuencias: Revista de Historia del Cine*, no. 3 (October 1995): 86–94; and Sánchez Alarcón, *La Guerra Civil Española y el cine francés*.

40. Aranda, *Luis Buñuel: Biografía crítica*, 179.

41. Aub, *Conversaciones*, 93.

42. Pérez Turrent and de la Colina, *Buñuel por Buñuel*, 41.

43. Aranda, "La etapa española," 51.

44. Jean-Paul Le Chanois, *Le Temps des cérises: Entretiens avec Philippe Esnault* (Arles: Institut Lumière/Actes Sud, 1996), 96–97.

45. Sánchez Alarcón, *La Guerra Civil Española y el cine francés*, 328–29.

46. We cite this text from *Catalogue 71*, Summer 2006, of the Avignon bookshop L'Ami-Voyage, where it is indexed as "Claude Aveline-Présentation de 'Espagne 1936.'" The document in question is a rough draft of the article published in *Soutes*, no. 8 (July 1937). We thank Dominique Rabourdin for this information.

47. We take this quotation from Javier Herrera Navarro, "Sobre los documentales de guerra de Buñuel: Aclaraciones y nuevas aportaciones" (paper presented at the international congress "La Guerra Civil Española 1936–1939" organized by the Sociedad Estatal de Conmemoraciones Culturales, Madrid, November 2006). Herrera's information proceeds from the filmmaker's personal scrapbooks in the Archivo Buñuel of the Filmoteca Española in Madrid.

48. Álvaro Custodio, "Pequeña historia de un surrealista," *La Semana Cinematográfica* (29 January 1949): 12.

49. Telegram of 20 February 1937 from Luis Buñuel in Paris to Francisco García Lorca in Brussels, cote 19940435, art. 16, dossier no. 1487, under the name of Luis Buñuel, Centre des Archives Contemporaines, Fontainebleau.

50. Report on Buñel prepared for the French minister of the interior, cote 19940435, art. 16, dossier no. 1487, Centre des Archives Contemporaines, Fontainebleau.

51. Aranda, *Luis Buñuel: Biografía crítica*, 182.

52. Carlos Clarens, *Crime Movies: An Illustrated History* (New York: W.W. Norton, 1980), 59.

53. Much of the information on this subject comes from the following sources: Fernando Martín Martín, *El Pabellon Español en la Exposición Universal de París en 1937* (Sevilla: Servicio de Publicaciones de la Universidad de Sevilla, 1983), 28–54, 215–16; Mendelson, *Documenting Spain*, particularly chapter 5, "Josep Renau and the 1937 Spanish Pavilion in Paris," 125–83, 230–40; Miguel Cabañas Bravo, *Josep Renau, arte y propaganda en guerra* (Madrid: Ministerio de Cultura, 2007), 167–215, 258–66.

54. Mariano Rawicz, *Confesionario de papel* (Valencia and Granada: IVAM/Editorial Comares, 1997), 200.

55. The Breton quote is from "Visite à Léon Trotsky: Discours prononcé au meeting anniversaire de la Révolution d'Octobre, tenu par le P.O.I. à Paris, le 11 novembre 1938," a speech delivered on 11 November 1938 and included in Breton, *Œuvres Complètes III*, 692–704, here 695. On Georges Soria, see José Gotovitch et al., *Komintern: L'Histoire et les hommes*, 513–14. In Spain it has been rumored that Rieger was Wenceslao Roces.

56. See Gabrielle Morelli, ed., *Ilegible, hijo de flauta: Argumento cinematográfico original de Juan Larrea y Luis Buñuel, basado en un libro perdido de Juan Larrea* (Sevilla: Editorial Renacimiento, 2007), 146–51.

57. "La participation de l'Espagne républicaine à l'Exposition," *L'Humanité*, no. 14059 (15 June 1937): 7.

58. Cabañas Bravo, *Josep Renau*, 264n317.

59. Crusells, "Cinema as Political Propaganda," 165.

60. See Román Gubern, "Exhibiciones cinematográficas en el pabellón español," in *El pabellón español en la Exposición Internacional de París*, edited by Josefina Alix Trueba (Madrid: MNCARS/Ministerio de Cultura, Dirección General de Bellas Artes y Cultura, 1987), 174–80.

61. Martín Martín, *El Pabellon Español*, 201. The International Exhibition had its own "Pavilion of Cinema," where documentaries were screened.

62. Manuel Aznar Soler, "Los años de la Segunda República (1931–1939)," in *Max Aub en el laberinto del siglo XX*, edited by Juan María Calles (Valencia: Biblioteca Valenciana/ Generalitat Valenciana, 2003), 79–84.

63. Fernández Colorado and Cerdán, *Ricardo Urgoiti*, 137.

64. See the relevant advertising in *L'Humanité*, no. 13993 (9 April 1937): 7; no. 14000 (16 April 1937): 7; no. 14007 (23 April 1937): 7; no. 14034 (21 May 1937): 7.

65. See *L'Humanité*, no. 14083 (9 July 1937): 7.

66. Mendelson, *Documenting Spain*, 163.

67. Juan Larrea, *Guernica: Pablo Picasso* (New York: Curt Valentin, 1947), 72, cited in Gertje R. Utley, *Picasso: The Communist Years* (New Haven, Conn.: Yale University Press, 2000), 24.

68. Aub, *Conversaciones*, 552. Dalí's testimony dates from August 1969.

69. Cabañas Bravo, *Josep Renau*, 170. The source is an unpublished manuscript finished by Renau in 1981, entitled "Albures y cuitas con el 'Guernica' y su madre." On this, see Cabañas Bravo, *Josep Renau*, 239n1.

70. The document is reproduced in Calles, *Max Aub en el laberinto del siglo XX*, 102.

71. Buñuel, *Mon dernier soupir*, 205.

72. Félix Luengo Teixidor, *Espías en la embajada: Los servicios de información secreta republicanos en Francia durante la Guerra Civil* (Bilbao, Servicio Editorial, Universidad del País Vasco/EHU, 1996), 102–3, 122.

73. Aub, *Conversaciones*, 82. Arthur Koestler described his three trips to Francoist Spain in *The Invisible Writing*, 314–64.

74. Luengo Teixidor, *Espías en la embajada*, 55.

75. Letter of 30 October 1936 from Willi Münzenberg to Luis Araquistáin, legajo 34/M448, Archivo Araquistáin, Archivo Histórico Nacional, Madrid. We owe the translation from German of this letter to Dietmar Obermüller.

76. Parts of the text of *L'Espagne ensanglantée* found their way into Koestler's *Spanish Testament* (London: Victor Gollancz/Left Book Club, 1937). The Left Book Club (May 1936–October 1948) was initially a Münzenberg operation.

77. [Otto Katz], *The Nazi Conspiracy in Spain*, by the Editor of *The Brown Book of the Hitler Terror* (London: Victor Gollancz/Left Book Club, 1937). The German edition, *Spione und Verschwörer in Spanien*, was published by Éditions de Carrefour, Paris, 1936, under the pseudonym "Franz Spielhagen."

78. Koestler, *Invisible Writing*, 328.

79. Thierry Wolton, *Le Grand Recrutement* (Paris: Éditions Grasset, 1993), 195.

80. Three copies of the bulletin are preserved: cote F714741, dossier "Agences de presse," Centre historique des Archives nationales, Paris.

81. Sala Noguer, *El cine en la España republicana*, 332–39.

82. The account that follows is based on the interview with Peinado in Aub, *Conversaciones*, 345–60.

83. Letter of 2 April 1937 from Carlos Esplá in Valencia to Luis Araquistáin in Paris, legajo 28/E, no. 35-37, Archivo Araquistáin, Archivo Histórico Nacional, Madrid. For information about Adolfo Salazar, see Bonet, *Diccionario de las vanguardias*, 549–50.

84. Ramón Salaberría, "Vicens y Mantecón, el siglo XX de dos bibliotecarios republicanos," *Trébede: Mensual aragonés de análisis, opinión y cultura*, no. 43 (October 2000), available at http://www.redaragon.com/trebede/oct2000/articulo2.asp.

85. Nicole Racine, "Aragon, militant du mouvement communiste international (1930–1939)," in *Les Engagements d'Aragon*, edited by Jacques Girault and Bernard Lecherbonnier (Paris: L'Harmattan, 1998), 82.

86. Aub, *Conversaciones*, 86.

87. Ugarte's biographer is of the opinion that it was his brother-in-law, José Bergamín, who got him his post in Paris. See Ríos Carratalá, *A la sombra de Lorca y Buñuel*, 92.

88. The information on this propaganda exercise comes from a letter of 5 August 1937 from Juan Vicens to Ángel Ossorio, both in Paris, caja 54/11065, paquete 49, carpeta 6324, Archivo General de la Administración del Estado, Alcalá de Henares.

89. Ibid.

90. Report dated 23 December 1938 from the director general of the Sûreté Nationale to the prefect of police, dossier Juan Vicens, cote 19940482, art. 120, dossier no. 11874, Centre des Archives Contemporaines, Archives de la Sûreté Générale, Fontainebleau.

91. Jean Meyer, "Con la Iglesia hemos topado, Sancho," *Istor: Revista de la historia internacional*, no. 25 (Summer 2006): 114, available at http://www.istor.cide.edu/archivos/num_25/coincidencias.pdf.

92. Information communicated by Ricardo Muñoz Suay to Román Gubern.

93. Hugo García, "La Delegación de propaganda de la República en París, 1936–1939," in *Ayeres en discusión: Temas clave de Historia Contemporánea hoy; IX Congreso de la Asociación de Historia Contemporánea*, edited by María Encarna Nicolás Marín and Carmen González Martínez (Murcia: Universidad de Murcia, 2008), available at http://www.ahistcon.org/docs/murcia/contenido/pdf/15/hugo_garcia_fernandez_taller15.pdf.

94. Note dated August 1942 from the Paris Customs Board to the Prefecture of Police, dossier "Communistes espagnols mars 1922–1947," cote BA 2157, Archives de la Préfecture de Police, Paris.

95. The account that follows draws on Luengo Teixidor, *Espías en la embajada*, 44–60. Although generally well documented, when the author speaks of Buñuel he bases

himself on the version given by the filmmaker, adding little to what we already know. Also of interest here is Pedro Barruso Barés, "El servicio secreto republicano en el sudoeste de Francia (1936–1939)," available at http://www.ciere.org/CUADERNOS/Art%2049/servicio.htm.

96. Luis Quintanilla, interview with Max Aub in Paris, ca. 1969, manuscript, ref. ADVC 18-30, Quintanilla, 1, Archivo de la Fundación Max Aub, Segorbe.

97. Cited in Luengo Teixidor, *Espías en la embajada*, 56.

98. Buñuel, *Mon dernier soupir*, 192.

99. Ione Robinson, *A Wall to Paint On* (New York: E. P. Dutton, 1946), 308–9. We thank Fernando Gabriel Martín for alerting us to the existence of this book.

100. See note 1 in this chapter.

101. See *L'Humanité*, no. 13994 (19 March 1937): 6.

102. Luis Quintanilla, *"Pasatiempo": La vida de un pintor (Memorias)* (La Coruña: Edicios do Castro, 2004), 403.

103. Quintanilla, interview with Aub, Quintanilla, 3.

104. Ibid., 5.

105. On Marcelino Pascua, see Ricardo Miralles, "La embajada de Marcelino Pascua en París durante la Guerra Civil Española (21 de abril de 1938–28 de febrero de 1939)," *Bulletin d'histoire contemporaine de l'Espagne*, no. 28–29 (1999): 135–58.

Chapter 15. Final Flight to the United States

1. Robinson, *A Wall to Paint On*, 392.

2. Buñuel, *Mon dernier soupir*, 203.

3. On Mounette Dutilleul, see Gotovitch et al., *Komintern: L'Histoire et les hommes*, 275–77. The text is an abbreviated version of the entry by the same author, Claude Pennetier, in *Dictionnaire biographique du mouvement ouvrier français*, edited by Jean Maitron (Paris: Éditions de l'Atelier, 1997), available at http://trcamps.free.fr/Mounette%20Maitron.html.

4. On Maurice Tréand, see Gotovitch et al., *Komintern: L'Histoire et les hommes*, 547–49.

5. Mounette Dutilleul, "Auto-biographie," Paris, 15 December 1937, in the collection of RGASPI (the Russian State Archive of Social and Political History), Moscow, kindly communicated to us by Claude Pennetier and Macha Tournié of the Centre d'Histoire Sociale du XXe Siècle, Université de Paris I-CNRS.

6. On Jean Jérôme, see Gotovitch et al., *Komintern: L'Histoire et les hommes*, 357–60.

7. On Émile Dutilleul, see ibid., 274–75.

8. On Giulio Ceretti and Georges Gosnat, see ibid., 206–7 and 312–13, respectively.

9. On France-Navigation, see Pierre Broué, *Staline et la Révolution: Le Cas espagnol* (Paris: Fayard, 1993), 125–29.

10. Claude Pennetier, "Gaston Cusin," in Maitron, *Dictionnaire biographique du mouvement ouvrier français*; résumé available at http://edechambost.ifrance.com/Cusin.htm.

11. Buñuel, *Mon dernier soupir*, 203.

12. Gibson, *Shameful Life of Salvador Dalí*, 361–62.

13. Santiago Carrillo interview with Román Gubern, 29 September 2005.

14. Fiche, cote 19940508, art. 8, under the name of Luis Buñuel, Centre des Archives Contemporaines, Fontainebleau.

15. Buñuel, *Mon dernier soupir*, 197.

16. On Isabel de Palencia, see Antonina Rodrigo, "Isabel Oyarzábal de Palencia, primera embajadora de la República," in *El exilio literario español de 1939: Actas del primer Congreso Internacional (Bellaterra, 27 de noviembre–1 de diciembre de 1995)*, edited by Manuel Aznar Soler, vol. 1 (Alicante: Biblioteca Virtual Miguel de Cervantes, Alicante), available at http://www.cervantesvirtual.com/servlet/SirveObras/08140621955770639732268/p0000011.htm.

17. A report of an interview with the Swedish banker by André Baillet, dated 18 September 1939, in relation to incriminating documents to do with Münzenberg and his wife, Babette Gross, found in Aschberg's Paris apartment, dossier Olaf Aschberg, A3, Archives de la Préfecture de Police, Paris.

18. Aub, *Conversaciones*, 85.

19. The full text of *Mit brennender Sorge* is available at http://www.vatican.va/holy_father/pius_xi/encyclicals/documents/hf_p-xi_enc_14031937_mit-brennender-sorge_en.html.

20. Aub, *Conversaciones*, 93.

21. Buñuel, *Mon dernier soupir*, 218.

22. Koch, *Double Lives*, 384n73.

23. Koestler, *Invisible Writing*, 205–6.

24. Rotellar, "Un gran iluminador: José María Beltrán," 16.

25. Buñel, *Mon dernier soupir*, 206.

26. See, for example, "L'héroïque résistance de la 43e division dans les Pyrenées, à l'arrière des rebelles," *L'Humanité*, no. 14390 (14 May 1938): 4; "43e division: Division de héros! Encerclés dans les montagnes, quelques milliers d'hommes, accrochés aux rochers, se battent farouchement et mettent les rebelles en échec," *L'Humanité*, no. 14399 (23 May 1938): 1; "Franco s'acharne sur la 43e Division: Venons en aide aux combattants républicains et à la population civile qu'ils protègent," *L'Humanité*, no. 14419 (12 June 1938): 3.

27. Santiago de Pablo, *Tierra sin paz: Guerra Civil, cine y propaganda en el País Vasco* (Madrid: Editorial Biblioteca Nueva, 2006), 316–20.

28. Roger Caillois, *Le Fleuve Alphée* (Paris: Gallimard, 1992), 63.

29. Fernández Cuenca, *La Guerra de España y el cine*, 123.

30. Rotellar, "Un gran iluminador: José María Beltrán," 16–17.

31. Del Amo García and Ibáñez Ferradas, *Catálogo general del cine de la Guerra Civil*, 409–10. Entry (289) 37/31 (427), 410, is accompanied by a frame still with Irujo and, one supposes, Lieutenant-Colonel Ángel Beltrán. There are more frame stills of the visit in ibid., entry 847 D9, 876.

32. Buñuel, *Mon dernier soupir*, 200–202; Aub, *Conversaciones*, 79.

33. This information comes from an interview by the authors with Emilio Sanz de Soto in his house in Madrid, 11 June 2006.

34. "Georges Rigaud va commencer son premier film américain," *La Cinématographie Française*, no. 1009 (4 March 1938): 14.

35. Carlos Aguilar and Jaume Genover, *Las estrellas de nuestro cine* (Madrid: Alianza Editorial, 1996), 536. The Internet Movie Database does not include Rigaud in the cast list of these films.

36. Aub, *Conversaciones*, 79.

37. "Deux attentats signés Franco," *L'Humanité*, no. 13961 (8 March 1937): 3.

38. "Criminal attentat dans l'express Bordeaux-Marseille," *L'Humanité*, no. 14019 (6 May 1937): 2.

39. Lucien Sampaix, "Les bombes de la Légion Noire," *L'Humanité*, no. 14071 (27 June 1937): 1, 4; no. 14072 (28 June 1937): 1–2; no. 14073 (29 June 1937): 1–2; no. 14075 (1 July 1937): 1–2. Between 25 April and 3 May 1937 the journalist had published a series of articles in *L'Humanité* under the heading of "Les agents de Franco à Paris." According to his version, the Fascist band included two relatives of the founder of Falange Española, Josefa and Isidro Sáenz de Heredia. In Francoist Spain, the latter would mount the production company Chapalo Films with director José Luis Sáenz de Heredia.

40. "La sanglante provocation de l'Étoile," *L'Humanité*, no. 14148 (13 September 1937): 2. The article included a photo of a defused Bauer bomb.

41. See Ariane Chebel d'Appollonia, *L'Extrême-Droite en France: De Maurras à Le Pen* (Paris: Éditions Complexe, 1996), 205–7.

42. Lucien Sampaix, "La 'Grande Frégate' est fermée," *L'Humanité*, no. 14158 (23 September 1937): 2.

43. Buñuel, *Mon dernier soupir*, 206–7; Aub, *Conversaciones*, 422.

44. José María Zavala, *Los gángsters de la Guerra Civil* (Barcelona: Plaza y Janés, 2006). See the chapter entitled "Atadell, el asesino enmascarado," 143–90. Although novelized, Zavala's account is based on contemporary documents.

45. See Luis Mario Schneider, *II Congreso Internacional de Escritores Antifascistas (1937)*, vol. 1, *Inteligencia y guerra civil en España* (Barcelona: Editorial Laia, 1978), 46–47.

46. Del Amo García and Ibáñez Ferradas, *Catálogo general del cine de la Guerra Civil*, 581–82. The entry for *K Sobitiyam v Ispanii n° 20 (I)* is accompanied by six frame stills.

47. Aub, *Conversaciones*, 74.

48. Van Rysselberghe, *Les Cahiers de la Petite Dame*, 633.

49. "Les intellectuels espagnols dénoncent les agressions allemandes et italiennes," *Ce Soir* (7 June 1937), cited from press cuttings in Buñuel's private scrapbook, Archivo Luis Buñuel, Filmoteca Española, Madrid.

50. The manifesto is reproduced in Manuel Aznar Soler, *II Congreso Internacional de Escritores Antifascistas (1937)*, vol. 2, *Pensamiento literario y compromiso antifascista de la inteligencia española republicana* (Barcelona: Editorial Laia, 1978), 194–97.

51. Official letter of 26 May 1937 from Eloy Sota (?), public order delegate in La Coruña to the chief commissioner of investigation and surveillance of the same city, legajo 2121, expediente 55, H13179, Archivo Histórico Nacional, Madrid.

52. Ángel Baselga, "Memoria sobre el establecimiento de una Sección Nacional de Cinematografía, 25 noviembre 1937 / II Año Triunfal," cultura 21/0001, sobre 58, Archivo General de la Administración, Alcalá de Henares.

53. Letter of 2 October 1937 from Juan Vicens to Ángel Ossorio, both in Paris, caja 54/11065, paquete 49, carpeta 6324, Archivo General de la Administración, Alcalá de Henares.

54. Letter of 18 November 1937 from Juan Vicens to Ángel Ossorio, both in Paris, caja 54/11065, paquete 49, carpeta 6324, Archivo General de la Administración, Alcalá de Henares.

55. Letter of 3 December from the ambassador in Paris to secretary of state José Giral in Barcelona, expediente 6.606, caja 11.1103, sección AAEE, Archivo General de la Administración, Alcalá de Henares. This document was first published in Sánchez Alarcón, *La Guerra Civil Española y el cine francés*, 329. We thank the author for supplying us with a copy.

56. Ibid. Guixé was the author of *Le Vrai Visage de la République espagnole* (Paris: Imprimerie Coopérative Étoile, 1938), among other political works.

57. Ibid. The "Cercle Cervantes," as it would be known, held its constituent session on 28 March 1938, according to the information that Juan Larrea, secretary of the Delegate Committee for the Expansion of Culture Abroad, gave to Ossorio in a letter of 29 March, expediente 6.598, caja 11.1103, sección AAEE, Archivo General de la Administración, Alcalá de Henares.

58. Lucien Logette, "Espagne 37: Documentaire sur les événements d'Espagne au cours de la première année de la guerre civile," *Jeune Cinéma*, no. 225 (January 1994): 11–17.

59. Ibid., 11. The copy Logette saw had been restored by the Archives Françaises du Film in 1993, from negative materials in its possession and from a duplicate from the BundesArchiv in Berlin. Its only identification was a card with the title of the film, without further data.

60. In fact, no documentary proof exists to prove that Buñuel and Unik wrote the commentary.

61. Hamdorf, "'Espagne 1936' y 'Espagne 1937,'" 90–91.

62. Nussinova, "*España-36* ¿Es una producción de Luis Buñuel?," 81n6.

63. Del Amo García and Ibáñez Ferradas, *Catálogo general del cine de la Guerra Civil*, 427.

64. Sánchez Alarcón, *La Guerra Civil Española y el cine francés*, 329.

65. Herrera Navarro, "Sobre los documentales de guerra de Buñuel," n.p.

66. Sala Noguer, *El cine en la España republicana*, 362, 432.

67. Juan Vicens, "Resumen de la memoria acerca de las actividades del departamento de propaganda (cine)," caja 5/11065, paquete 49, carpeta 6324, Archivo General de la Administración, Alcalá de Henares.

68. The producers of these films are cited in Vicens's report. Three of the five titles do not appear in del Amo García and Ibáñez Ferradas, *Catálogo general del cine de la Guerra Civil.*

69. Vicens, "Resumen de la memoria acerca de las actividades del departamento de propaganda (cine)."

70. Louis Chéronnet, "Cinéma, *Terre d'Espagne*," *L'Humanité*, no. 14236 (10 December 1937): 4.

71. "L'Ambassadeur d'Espagne à Paris a visité l'exposition 'l'Espagne vous parle,'" *L'Humanité*, no. 14269 (12 January 1938): 8.

72. Louis Chéronnet, "Cinéma: *Les Bâtisseurs* et *Cœur d'Espagne*," *L'Humanité*, no. 14297 (9 February 1938): 4.

73. See Marcel Huret, *Ciné actualités: Histoire de la presse filmée 1895–1980* (Paris: Henri Veyrier, 1984), 93.

74. Cited (without a date) in de Pablo, *Tierra sin paz*, 127.

75. *La Cinématographie Française*, no. 1006 (11 February 1938): 29.

76. See Hamdorf, "'Espagne 1936' y 'Espagne 1937,'" 92–93; Logette, "Espagne 37," 14–15.

77. Juan Vicens, *L'Espagne vivante: Le peuple à la conquête de la culture* (Paris: Éditions Sociales Internationales, 1938). The Spanish translation, *España viva: El pueblo a la conquista de la cultura* (Madrid: Asociación Educación y Bibliotecas / Ediciones VOSA, 2002), has an informative introduction by Ramón Salaberría, "La larga marcha de Juan Vicens."

78. Email of 16 June 2008 from José Cabeza San Deogracias to Román Gubern.

79. See Agnes Hodgson, *A una milla de Huesca: Diario de una enfermera australiana en la Guerra Civil Española* (Zaragoza: Prensas Universitarias de Zaragoza, 2006), 116n139. Another possibility is that the film was *Espagne 1936*.

80. Sánchez Alarcón, *La Guerra Civil Española y el cine francés*, 330–31.

81. Letter of 3 January 1938 from Ángel Ossorio in Paris to José Giral in Barcelona, (10) 96-54/11209, carpeta 7364, Archivo General de la Administración, Alcalá de Henares.

82. It has recently been claimed that *Guernika* and *À l'aide du peuple basque* are the same film, since Dreyfus was recruited by Sobrevila. See De Pablo, *Tierra sin paz*, 313.

83. On the figure of Robert Petiot, see ibid., 87–89.

84. For example, see Luis Buñuel, *Goya* (Teruel: Instituto de Estudios Turolenses, 1992).

85. Our investigation into *The Duchess of Alba and Goya* owes much to a stimulating correspondence with Ron Magliozzi, assistant curator, Research and Collections of the Department of Film at MoMA. Buñuel's treatment runs to twenty-three typed pages.

86. Buñuel and Barry did in fact correspond in French. See Fernando Gabriel Martín, *El ermitaño errante: Buñuel en Estados Unidos* (Murcia: Tres Fronteras Ediciones / Filmoteca Regional Francisco Rabal, 2010), 216, 247.

87. Aranda, *Luis Buñuel: Biografía crítica*, 196.

88. Ibid., 195. Leyda thought the synopsis was "magnificent" (ibid., 196), an affirmation that was eliminated from the English edition of the book in 1975.

89. Luis Buñuel, "Auto-Biography." Contains "Auto-Biography of Luis Buñuel / My Present Plans / Land without Bread (press cuttings in French) / L'Âge d'or (cuttings in English) / Un chien andalou (cuttings in English) / Bibliography."

90. "Les projets du 'Cercle du Cinéma,'" *L'Indépendance Belge* (17 September 1937), unpaginated cutting in Buñuel's private scrapbook, Archivo Luis Buñuel, Filmoteca Española, Madrid.

91. See Laurent Mannoni, *Histoire de la Cinémathèque Française* (Paris: Gallimard, 2006), 36–37.

92. Letter of 11 July 1938 from an executive at Intercontinental Film to Luis Buñuel, both in Paris, included in Buñuel's private scrapbook, Archivo Luis Buñuel, Filmoteca Española, Madrid.

93. Mannoni, *Histoire de la Cinémathèque Française*, 60.

94. André Breton, "Présentation d' 'Un chien andalou,'" *Œuvres Complètes II*, 1266.

95. André Breton and Paul Éluard, eds., *Dictionnaire abrégé du surréalisme* (Paris: Galerie des Beaux-Arts, 1938), repr. in Breton, *Œuvres Complètes II*, 803, 796.

96. This error extends to the customary attribution of *Las Hurdes* to 1932, which appears to legitimate the inclusion of the film in a Surrealist triad.

97. Letter of 15 October 1936 from Benjamin Péret in Barcelona to André Breton in Paris, cited in Claude Courtot, *Introduction à la lecture de Benjamin Péret* (Paris: Le Terrain Vague, 1965), 33.

98. Buñuel, *Mon dernier soupir*, 192.

99. Breton, "Visite à Léon Trotsky," 695.

100. Ibid, 695–96, our emphasis.

101. Max Aub, "Buñuel," undated manuscript [ca. 1970?], ref. ARA c. 17-5/1 369, Archivo de la Fundación Max Aub, Segorbe.

102. Buñuel, *Mon dernier soupir*, 218–19.

103. Aub, *Conversaciones*, 93.

104. Fernández Colorado and Cerdán, *Ricardo Urgoiti*, 192, letter of 11 August 1938 from Luis Buñuel in Paris to Ricardo Urgoiti in Buenos Aires.

105. Bouhours and Schoeller, *L'Âge d'or: Correspondance*, 164, letter of 9 September 1938 from Luis Buñuel in Paris to Charles de Noailles in Hyères.

106. For a detailed analysis of *Blockade*, see Sonia García López, "Spain Is Us: La Guerra Civil Española en el cine del 'Popular Front': 1936–1939" (PhD diss., Universitat de València, 2008), 191–236.

107. Frank S. Nugent, "Blockade," *New York Times* (17 June 1938): 25.

108. Bouhours and Schoeller, *L'Âge d'or: Correspondance*, 166, letter of 9 September 1938 from Luis Buñuel in Paris to Charles de Noailles in Hyères.

109. Fernández Colorado and Cerdán, *Ricardo Urgoiti*, 193, letter of 20 September 1938 from Buñuel on board the *Britannic* to Ricardo Urgoiti in Buenos Aires.

110. The most exhaustive account of this episode appears in Martín, *El ermitaño errante*, 174–95; see also Salka Viertel, *Los extranjeros de Mabery Road* (Madrid: Ediciones El Imán, 1995), 330–31, 334.

111. See Fernando Gabriel Martín, "El artista aislado: Buñuel en/y Estados Unidos," *Turia*, no. 50 (October 1999): 168.

112. Fernández Colorado and Cerdán, *Ricardo Urgoiti*, 197, letter of 2 January 1939 from Luis Buñuel in Los Angeles to Ricardo Urgoiti in Buenos Aires.

113. Buñuel, *Mon dernier soupir*, 220.

114. Agustín Sánchez Vidal dates this letter to 19 January 1939 in his *Buñuel, Lorca, Dalí: El enigma sin fin* (Barcelona: Planeta, 1988), 284.

115. Bouhours and Schoeller, *L'Âge d'or: Correspondance*, 167, letter of 29 January 1939 from Luis Buñuel in Los Angeles to Charles de Noailles in Hyères.

116. Fernández Colorado and Cerdán, *Ricardo Urgoiti*, 198, letter of 30 January 1939 from Luis Buñuel in Los Angeles to Ricardo Urgoiti in Buenos Aires.

117. We owe this identification to Javier Herrera. See Javier Herrera Navarro, "The Decisive Moments of Buñuel's Time in the United States: 1938–40; An Analysis of Previously Unpublished Letters," in *Luis Buñuel: New Readings*, edited by Peter William Evans and Isabel Santaolalla (London: British Film Institute, 2004), 59n11.

118. Fernández Colorado and Cerdán, *Ricardo Urgoiti*, 198, letter of 30 January 1939 from Luis Buñuel in Los Angeles to Ricardo Urgoiti in Buenos Aires.

119. Ibid., p. 199, letter of 3 February 1939 from Luis Buñuel in Los Angeles to Ricardo Urgoiti in Buenos Aires.

120. Ibid., p. 140, letter of 8 February 1939 from Bartolomé Moreno to Ricardo Urgoiti in Buenos Aires.

121. Letter of early April 1939 from Salvador Dalí in New York to Luis Buñuel in Los Angeles, ref. 572.49 a 44330, Archivo Luis Buñuel, Filmoteca Española, Madrid. We have modified the lax grammar of the original.

122. Ibid.

123. This surveillance intensified between July 1945 and February 1947, when Buñuel was deemed not to be a subversive. Until 1970 he would still be watched whenever he entered the country, however.

124. For an exhaustive account of these machinations, see Martín, *El ermitaño errante*, 423–98.

125. Aub, *Conversaciones*, 142.

Bibliography

Archives

Alcalá de Henares: Archivo General de la Administración del Estado.
Figueres: Archivo de la Fundació Gala-Salvador Dalí.
Fontainebleau: Centre des Archives Contemporaines.
Madrid: Archivo de la Residencia de Estudiantes.
Madrid: Archivo Histórico Nacional.
Madrid: Archivo Juan Vicens, Residencia de Estudiantes.
Madrid: Archivo Luis Buñuel, Filmoteca Española.
Madrid: Hemeroteca Municipal.
New York: Film Study Center, Department of Film, Museum of Modern Art.
Paris: Bibliothèque du film.
Paris: Bibliothèque nationale de France.
Paris: Centre Historique des Archives Nationales.
Paris: Cinémathèque Française.
Paris: Préfecture de Police.
Salamanca: Archivo General de la Guerra Civil Española.
Segorbe: Archivo de la Fundación Max Aub.

Printed Sources

Abella, Rafael. *La vida cotidiana durante la Guerra Civil: La España republicana.* Barcelona: Planeta, 1975.

Abizanda, Martín. "López Rubio cuenta sus aventuras." *Cámara*, no. 27 (December 1943): n.p.

Ades, Dawn. "*Contre la famille.*" In *Dalí & Film*, edited by Matthew Gale, 116–21. London: Tate, 2007.

———. "Unpublished Film Scenario by Salvador Dalí." *Studio International* 195, no. 993–94 (1982): 62–77.

[AEAR]. "Le Manifeste de l'Association des Écrivains et Artistes Révolutionnaires." *L'Humanité*, no. 12152 (22 March 1932): 4.

Aguilar, Carlos, and Jaume Genover. *Las estrellas de nuestro cine.* Madrid: Alianza Editorial, 1996.

Aguilar, Santiago. "Cómo se filma una producción nacional: El primer día de rodaje de *Don Quintín, el amargao.*" *Cinegramas,* no. 38 (2 June 1935): n.p.

———. "Interviú del momento: La estrella mayor y la estrella menor; Lina Yegros y Mari-Tere." *Cinegramas,* no. 78 (8 March 1936): n.p.

———. "Nueve horas en la vida de Angelillo." *Cinegramas,* no. 72 (26 January 1936): n.p.

Aguirre Carballeira, Arantxa. *Buñuel, lector de Galdós.* Las Palmas de Gran Canaria: Cabildo de Gran Canaria, 2006.

Albera, François. "La reception du cinema soviétique en France, dans les années 1920–1930." In *Le Studio Mejrabpom ou l'aventure du cinéma privé au pays des bolsheviks,* edited by Aïcha Kherroubi et al., 117–26. Les Dossiers du Musée d'Orsay 59. Paris: La Documentation Française, 1996.

Alberti, Rafael. *La arboleda perdida II.* Barcelona: Seix y Barral, 1987.

Alexandre, Maxime. *Mémoires d'un surréaliste.* Paris: La Jeune Parque, 1968.

Alix Trueba, Josefina, ed. *El pabellón español en la Exposición Internacional de París.* Madrid: MNCARS/Ministerio de Cultura, 1987.

Alquié, Ferdinand. "Correspondance II: À André Breton." *LSASDLR,* no. 5 (15 May 1933): 43.

Álvarez del Vayo, Julio. "Diez minutos de cine ruso." *La Gaceta Literaria,* no. 75 (1 February 1930): 7.

Anuario Cinematográfico Español. Madrid: Unión Poligráfica S.A., 1935.

Aragon, Louis. "Front rouge." *Littérature de la Révolution Mondiale* (July 1931).

———. *Je n'ai jamais appris à écrire ou* Les incipit. 1969. Reprint, Paris: Flammarion, 1981.

———. *L'Œuvre Poétique.* Vol. 2, *1927–1935.* Edited by Jean Ristat. 2nd ed. Paris: Livre Club Diderot-Messidor, 1989–90.

Aragon, Louis, and Georges Sadoul. "Aux Intellectuels révolutionnaires." December 1930. Tract.

Aranda, J. Francisco. "La etapa española 1932–37." In *Luis Buñuel,* edited by Edoardo Bruno, 46–53. Venice: XLI Mostra Internazionale del Cinema, 1984.

———. *Luis Buñuel: Biografía crítica.* 2nd ed. Barcelona: Lumen, 1975.

———. *Luis Buñuel: A Critical Biography.* London: Secker and Warburg, 1975.

Arconada, César M. "Hacia un cinema proletario." *Nuestro Cinema,* no. 8–9 (January–February 1933): 92–94.

———. "Luis Buñuel y *Las Hurdes*: El film." *Nuestro Cinema,* 2nd ser., no. 2 (February 1935): 8–9.

[Association Internationale des Écrivains]. *Conférence extraordinaire tenue à Paris le 25 juillet 1938.* Paris: Denoël, 1938.

Aub, Max. *Conversaciones con Buñuel: Seguidas de 45 entrevistas con familiares, amigos y colaboradores del cineasta aragonés.* Madrid: Aguilar, 1985.

Autant-Lara, Claude. *Hollywood Cake-Walk (1930–1932).* Paris: Henri Veyrier, 1985.

Aveline, Claude. "Présentation de 'Espagne 1936.'" *Soutes: Revue de Culture Révolutionnaire Internationale*, no. 8 (July 1937).

Ayala, Francisco. *Recuerdos y olvidos*. Madrid: Alianza Editorial, 1988.

Azaña, Manuel. *Diarios completos: Monarquía, República, Guerra Civil*. Barcelona: Crítica, 2004.

Aznar Soler, Manuel, ed. "Los años de la Segunda República (1931–1939)." In *Max Aub en el laberinto del siglo XX*, edited by Juan Manuel Calles, 62–93. Valencia: Biblioteca Valenciana/Generalitat Valenciana, 2003.

———. *II Congreso Internacional de Escritores Antifascistas (1937)*. Vol. 2, *Pensamiento literario y compromiso antifascista de la inteligencia española republicana*. Barcelona: Editorial Laia, 1978.

Bandy, Mary Iea. *Circulating Film Library Catalog*. New York: Museum of Modern Art, 1984.

Baroja, Ricardo. *Gente del 98: Arte, cine y ametralladora*. Madrid: Cátedra, 1989.

Barruso Barés, Pedro. "El servicio secreto republicano en el sudoeste de Francia (1936–1939)." http://www.ciere.org/CUADERNOS/Art%2049/servicio.htm.

Bataille, Georges. *L'Apprenti sorcier: Du Cercle Communiste Démocratique à Acéphale*. Paris: Éditions de la Différence, 1999.

———. "Le Jeu lugubre." *Documents*, no. 7 (December 1929): 369–72.

———. "Œil." *Documents*, no. 4 (September 1929): 216.

Bazin, André. "Los Olvidados." *Esprit* 10, no. 186 (January 1952): 85–89. Reprinted in André Bazin, *El cine de la crueldad* (Bilbao: Mensajero, 1977), 67–74.

Bazin, André, and Jacques Doniol Valcroze. "Entretien avec Luis Buñuel." *Cahiers du cinéma*, no. 36 (June 1954): 2–14.

Billard, Pierre. *L'Âge classique du cinéma français: Du cinéma parlant à la nouvelle vague*. Paris: Flammarion, 1995.

Bonet, Juan Manuel. *Diccionario de las vanguardias en España, 1907–1936*. Madrid: Alianza Editorial, 1995.

Borges, Jorge Luis. "Films." *Sur*, no. 3 (Winter 1931). Reprinted in Edgardo Cozarinsky, *Borges en/y/sobre el cine* (Madrid: Editorial Fundamentos, 1981), 30.

Bouhours, Jean-Michel, and Nathalie Schoeller, eds. *L'Âge d'or: Correspondance Luis Buñuel—Charles de Noailles; Lettres et documents (1929–1976)*. Paris: Les Cahiers du Musée National d'Art Moderne, Hors série/Archives, 1993.

Bouissounouse, Janine. *La Nuit d'Autun: Le Temps des illusions*. Paris: Calman-Lévy, 1977.

Boulgakova, Oksana. "Les rapports avec l'Allemagne." In *Le Studio Mejrabpom ou l'aventure du cinéma privé au pays des bolsheviks*, edited by Aïcha Kherroubi et al., 105–15. Les Dossiers du Musée d'Orsay 59. Paris: La Documentation Française, 1996.

Braunberger, Pierre. *Pierre Braunberger producteur: Cinémamémoire*. Edited by Jacques Berger. Paris: Centre Georges Pompidou/Centre Nationale de la Cinématographie, 1987.

Breton, André. "À propos du concours de littérature prolétarienne organisé par 'l'Humanité.'" *LSASDLR*, no. 5 (15 May 1933): 16–18.

———. *L'Art magique*. Paris: Amis du Club Français du Livre, 1957.

———. "Le Château étoilé." *Minotaure*, no. 8 (15 June 1936): 25–39. Reprinted in André Breton, *L'Amour fou* (Paris: Gallimard, 1937).

———. *Entretiens (1913–1952) avec André Parinaud*. Paris: Gallimard, 1952.

———. *Misère de la poésie: 'L'Affaire Aragon' devant l'opinion publique.* Paris: Éditions Surréalistes, 1932.

———. *Œuvres Complètes I.* Edited by Marguerite Bonnet, with the collaboration of Philippe Bernier, Étienne-Alain Hubert, and José Pierre. Paris: Gallimard/Bibliothèque de la Pléiade, 1988.

———. *Œuvres Complètes II.* Edited by Marguerite Bonnet, with the collaboration of Philippe Bernier, Étienne-Alain Hubert, and José Pierre. Paris: Gallimard/Bibliothèque de la Pléiade, 1992.

———. *Œuvres Complètes III.* Edited by Marguerite Bonnet, published, for this volume, under the direction of Étienne-Alain Hubert, with the collaboration of Philippe Bernier, Marie-Claire Dumas, and José Pierre. Paris: Gallimard/Bibliothèque de la Pléiade, 1999.

———. "Présentation d' 'Un Chien andalou.'" In *Œuvres Complètes II,* edited by Marguerite Bonnet et al., 1263–67. Paris: Gallimard/Bibliothèque de la Pléiade, 1992.

———. "Second Manifeste du surréalisme." *LRS,* no. 12 (15 December 1929): 1–17.

———. *Second Manifeste du surréalisme.* Paris: Simon Kra, 1930. Enlarged book version.

———. "Visite à Léon Trotsky: Discours prononcé au meeting anniversaire de la Révolution d'Octobre, tenu par le P.O.I. à Paris, le 11 novembre 1938." In *Œuvres Complètes III,* edited by Marguerite Bonnet et al., 692–704. Paris: Gallimard/Bibliothèque de la Pléiade, 1999.

Breton, André, and Paul Éluard. *Dictionnaire abrégé du surréalisme.* Paris: Galerie des Beaux-Arts, 1938. Reprinted in *Œuvres Complètes II,* edited by Marguerite Bonnet et al., 787–862 (Paris: Gallimard/Bibliothèque de la Pléiade, 1992).

Brien, Christopher, Laurent Ikor, and J. Michel Vignier. *Joinville le cinéma: Le Temps des studios.* Paris: Ramsay, 1985.

Brunius, J. Bernard. "Un chien andalou: Film par Louis Buñuel." *Cahiers d'Art,* no. 5 (July 1929): 230–31.

Broué, Pierre. *Staline et la Révolution: Le Cas espagnol.* Paris: Fayard, 1993.

Buache, Freddy. *Luis Buñuel.* Lausanne: La Cité, 1970.

Buchsbaum, Jonathan. *Cinéma Engagé: Film in the Popular Front.* Urbana: University of Illinois Press, 1988.

Bullejos, José. *La Comintern en España: Recuerdos de mi vida.* Mexico City: Impresiones Modernas, 1972.

Buñuel, Luis. "Auto-Biography." Thirty-two-page manuscript dated 28 July 1939. Museum of Modern Art Film Study Center, New York.

———. Debate with students of Columbia University, New York, 10 April 1940. New York: Museum of Modern Art Film Study Center, New York. Sixteen-page typescript.

———. "'Découpage' o segmentación cinegráfica." *La Gaceta Literaria,* no. 43 (1 October 1928): 1.

———. *The Duchess of Alba and Goya.* New York: Museum of Modern Art Film Study Center. Twenty-three-page manuscript, undated (1939–1943?).

———. "Une girafe." *LSASDLR,* no. 6 (15 May 1933): 34–36.

———. *Goya.* Teruel: Instituto de Estudios Turolenses, 1992.

———. "Land without Bread." Madrid: Buñuel Archive, Filmoteca Española, ref. 1485. Nine-page manuscript of an introductory talk given by the author in English to students of Columbia University in the MacMillan Academic Theater, New York, on 18 March 1940. The same archive also contains the Spanish original, which runs to ten pages, with variants and additions.

———. *Mon dernier soupir.* Paris: Éditions Robert Laffont, 1982.

———. *My Last Sigh: The Autobiography of Luis Buñuel.* New York: Alfred A. Knopf, 1983.

———. "Una noche en el Studio des Ursulines." *La Gaceta Literaria*, no. 2 (15 January 1927): 6.

———. *An Unspeakable Betrayal: Selected Writings of Luis Buñuel.* Berkeley: University of California Press, 2000.

———. "Variaciones sobre el bigote de Menjou." *La Gaceta Literaria*, no. 35 (1 June 1928): 4.

[Buñuel, Luis]. "Buñuel y el surrealismo." *ABC* (25 February 1931): 14.

Buñuel, Luis, and Salvador Dalí. "Un chien andalou." *LRS*, no. 12 (15 December 1929): 34–37.

Buot, François. *René Crevel: Biographie.* Paris: Bernard Grasset, 1991.

Bureau, Patrick. "Un poème de l'horreur: *Terre sans pain.*" *Études cinématographiques*, no. 22–23 (January–March 1963): 163–68.

Cabañas Bravo, Miguel. *Josep Renau, arte y propaganda en guerra.* Madrid: Ministerio de Cultura, 2007.

Cabeza San Deogracias, José. *El descanso del guerrero: El cine en Madrid durante la Guerra Civil Española (1936–1939).* Madrid: Rialp, 2005.

Cahun, Claude. *Écrits.* Paris: Jean-Michel Place, 2002.

Caillois, Roger. *Le Fleuve Alphée.* 1978. Reprint, Paris: Gallimard, 1992.

Calles, José María, ed. *Max Aub en el laberinto del siglo XX.* Valencia: Biblioteca Valenciana/Generalitat Valenciana, 2003.

Carnicero, Marisol, and Daniel Sánchez Salas, eds. *En torno a Buñuel.* Cuadernos de la Academia 7–8. Madrid: Academia de las Artes y las Ciencias Cinematográficas de España, 2000.

Caro Baroja, Julio. *Los Baroja (Memorias familiares).* Madrid: Editorial Caro Raggio, 1997.

Carrillo, Santiago. *Memorias.* Rev. ed. Barcelona: Planeta, 2006.

Casellón Díaz, José. "Luis Buñuel y *Las Hurdes*: El realizador." *Nuestro Cinema*, 2nd ser., no. 2 (February 1935). Reprinted in *Del cinema como arma de clase: Antología de* Nuestro Cinema *1932–1935*, edited by Carlos Pérez Merinero and David Pérez Merinero (Valencia: Fernando Torres Editor, 1975), 142.

Castro, Antonio. *El cine español en el banquillo.* Valencia: Fernando Torres Editor, 1974.

Chardère, Bernard. *Le Cinéma de Jacques Prévert.* Bordeaux: Le Castor Astral, 2001.

Chebel d'Appollonia, Ariane. *L'Extrême-Droite en France: De Maurras à Le Pen.* Paris: Éditions Complexe, 1996.

Chéronnet, Louis. "Cinéma: *Les Bâtisseurs* et *Cœur d'Espagne.*" *L'Humanité*, no. 14297 (9 February 1938): 4.

———. "Cinéma. *Terre d'Espagne*." *L'Humanité*, no. 14236 (10 December 1937): 4.

Clarens, Carlos. *Crime Movies: An Illustrated History*. New York: W.W. Norton, 1980.

Cocteau, Jean. *Opium: Journal d'une désintoxication*. Paris: Librairie Stock, Delamain et Boutelleau, 1930.

Colette. *Colette au cinema*. Paris: Flammarion, 1975.

Courtot, Claude. *Introduction à la lecture de Benjamin Péret*. Paris: Le Terrain Vague, 1965.

Crafton, Donald. *The Talkies: American Cinema's Transition to Sound, 1926–1931*. Berkeley: University of California Press, 1999.

Crevel, René. *Les Sœurs Brontë, filles du vent*. Paris: Éditions des Quatre-Chemins, 1930.

Crussels, Magí. "Cinema as Political Propaganda during the Spanish Civil War: *España 1936*." *Ebre 38: Revista Internacional de la Guerra Civil 1936–1939*, no. 2 (2004): 157–68.

Custodio, Álvaro. "Pequeña historia de un surrealista." *La Semana Cinematográfica* (29 January 1949): 12–13, 34.

Dalí, Salvador. *Babaouo, scénario inédit: Précedé d'un Abrégé d'une histoire critique du cinéma et suivi de Guillaume Tell, ballet portugais*. Paris: Éditions des Cahiers Libres, 1932.

———. "Derniers modes d'excitation intellectuelle pour l'été 1934." *Documents 34: Intervention surréaliste* (June 1934): 33–35.

———. *Diary of a Genius*. London: Hutchinson, 1966. Originally published as *Journal d'un génie* (Paris: Éditions de la Table Ronde, 1964).

———. "Documental-París 1929 [VI]." *La Publicitat* (26 June 1929): 1.

———. "Luis Buñuel (entrevista)." *L'Amic de les Arts*, no. 31 (31 March 1929): 16.

———. *Obra Completa III: Poesía, prosa, teatro y cine*. Introduction and notes by Agustín Sánchez Vidal. Barcelona: Ediciones Destino/Fundación Gala-Salvador Dalí/Sociedad Estatal de Conmemoraciones Culturales, 2004.

———. "Rêverie." *LSASDLR*, no. 4 (December 1931): 31–36.

———. *The Secret Life of Salvador Dali*. New York: Dial Press, 1942.

———. *The Secret Life of Salvador Dali*. London: Vision Press, 1948. First British edition with 3 new appendices.

———. *La Vie secrète de Salvador Dalí: Suis-je un génie?* Edited by Frédérique Joseph-Lowery. Lausanne: L'Âge d'Homme, 2006.

David, Yasha, ed. *¿Buñuel! La mirada del siglo*. Madrid: MNCARS, 1996; Mexico City: Museo del Palacio de Bellas Artes, 1997.

de Abajo de Pablo, Juan Julio. *Mis charlas con Antonio del Amo*. Valladolid: Fancy, 1998.

———. *Mis charlas con José Luis Sáenz de Heredia*. Valladolid: Quirón, 1996.

de Jaén, Antonio. "¡Directores a examen! Luis Marquina." *Cinegramas*, no. 88 (17 May 1936): n.p.

de la Breteque, François. "La première de *L'Âge d'or* à Toulouse et à Montpellier." *Les Cahiers de la Cinémathèque*, no. 30–31 (Summer–Autumn 1980): 179–82.

del Amo, Antonio. "Los cineclubs y el cinema." *Popular Film*, no. 383 (14 December 1933): n.p.

———. "Galería de nuevos realizadores: Nacimiento del cinema hispano." *Cinegramas*, no. 89 (24 May 1936): n.p.

———. "Mi experiencia personal." In *El cine de las organizaciones populares republicanas entre 1936 y 1939*, vol. 2, *Las organizaciones marxistas*, edited by Rosa Álvarez, Julio Pérez Perucha, and Ramón Sala, 41–43. Bilbao: Certamen de Cine Documental, 1981.

———. "Temporada 1933–34: Revisión de cineclubs." *Popular Film*, no. 413 (12 July 1934): n.p.

del Amo García, Alfonso, and María Luisa Ibáñez Ferradas, eds. *Catálogo general del cine de la Guerra Civil*. Madrid: Cátedra/Filmoteca Española, 1996.

del Arco, Manuel. "Mano a mano con Benito Perojo." *La Vanguardia Española* (30 September 1959): 20.

de la Torre, Claudio. "El tranvía al ralentí (Caminos para Luis Buñuel)." *La Gaceta Literaria*, no. 34 (15 May 1928): 5.

de los Reyes, Aurelio. *El nacimiento de "¡Qué viva México!"* Mexico City: Universidad Nacional Autónoma de México-Instituto de Investigaciones Estéticas, 2006.

de Pablo, Santiago. *Tierra sin paz: Guerra Civil, cine y propaganda en el País Vasco*. Madrid: Editorial Biblioteca Nueva, 2006.

Desanti, Dominique. *Les Staliniens: Une expérience politique; 1944–1956*. 1975. Reprint, Verviers: Marabout, 1985.

Desnos, Robert. *Cinéma*. Paris: Gallimard, 1966.

Díez Puertas, Emeterio: *El montaje del franquismo: La política cinematográfica de las fuerzas sublevadas*. Barcelona: Laertes, 2002.

Donaldson, Geoffrey. "Adelqui Millar, fascino latino." *Immagine: Note di Storia del Cinema*, new series, no. 16 (1991): 19–29.

Don Q. "Hollywood." *Cine Mundial* (June 1931): 454–56.

Dreyfus, Jean-Paul. "*L'Âge d'or*, par Louis Buñuel, scénario de Louis Buñuel et Salvador Dalí." *La Revue du cinéma*, no. 17 (1 December 1930): 55–56.

Ehrenburg, Ilya. *Fábrica de sueños*. Madrid: Editorial Cenit, 1932.

Elorza, Antonio, and Marta Bizcarrondo. *Queridos camaradas: La Internacional Comunista y España*. Barcelona: Planeta, 1999.

Éluard, Paul. "Certificat." 23 March 1932. Tract. In *Tracts surréalistes et déclarations collectives (1922/1969)*, edited by José Pierre, 1:229–30. Paris: Eric Losfeld, 1980.

———. *Lettres à Gala 1924–1948*. 1984. Reprint, Paris: Gallimard, 1996.

Éluard, Paul, and René Crevel. "Un film commercial." *LSASDLR*, no. 4 (14 December 1931): 29.

Estruch, Joan. *Historia oculta del PCE*. Madrid: Temas de Hoy, 2000.

Fanès, Félix, ed. *Dalí, Arquitectura*. Barcelona: Fundació Caixa de Catalunya/Fundació Gala-Salvador Dalí, 1996.

Farassino, Alberto. *Tutto il cinema di Luis Buñuel*. Milan: Baldini & Castoldi, 2000.

Fernández Colorado, Luis, and Josetxo Cerdán. *Ricardo Urgoiti: Los trabajos y los días*. Madrid: Filmoteca Española, 2007.

Fernández Cuenca, Carlos. *La guerra de España y el cine*. Madrid: Editora Nacional, 1972.

———. *Imágenes de Jean Grémillon*. San Sebastián: VIII Festival Internacional de Cine de San Sebastián, 1960.

Fernández Puertas, Víctor. "Sobre una amistat: Dalí i Buñuel." *Revista de Catalunya*, no. 112 (November 1996): 85–112.

Feyder, Jacques. *Le Cinéma notre métier*. Vésenaz-Près-Genève: Pierre Cailleur Éditeur, 1946.

Fieschi, Jean-André. "L'Ange et la bête (croquis méxicain de Luis Buñuel)." *Cahiers du Cinema*, no. 176 (March 1966): 32–40.

Florey, Robert. *Hollywood d'hier et d'aujourd'hui*. Paris: Prisma, 1948.

Fuentes, Juan Francisco. "La arboleda encontrada: *¿Qué es España?* Un documental atribuido a Luis Araquistáin." In *El laboratorio de España: La Junta para Ampliación de Estudios e Investigaciones Científicas 1907–1939*, 251–61. Madrid: Sociedad Estatal de Conmemoraciones Culturales/Residencia de Estudiantes, 2007.

Fuentes, Víctor. *La mirada de Buñuel: Cine, literatura y vida*. Madrid: Tabla Rasa, 2005.

———. *Los mundos de Buñuel*. Madrid: Akal, 2000.

Gale, Matthew, ed. *Dalí & Film*. London: Tate, 2007.

Gamonal Torres, Miguel A. *Arte y política en la Guerra Civil Española: El caso republicano*. Granada: Diputación Provincial de Granada, 1987.

García, Hugo. "La Delegación de propaganda de la República en París, 1936–1939." In *Ayeres en discusión: Temas clave de Historia Contemporánea hoy; IX Congreso de la Asociación de Historia Contemporánea*, edited by María Encarna Nicolás Marín and Carmen González Martínez. Murcia: Universidad de Murcia, 2008. http://www.ahistcon.org/docs/murcia/contenido/pdf/15/hugo_garcia_fernandez_taller15.pdf.

García de Dueñas, Jesús. *¡Nos vamos a Hollywood!* Madrid: Nickel Odeon, 1993.

García Fernández, Emilio. "¿Quién me quiere a mí?" *Secuencias: Revista de Historia del Cine*, no. 7 (October 1997): 24–25.

García López, Sonia. "Spain Is Us: La Guerra Civil Española en el cine del 'Popular Front': 1936–1939." PhD diss., Universitat de València, 2008.

García Lorca, Federico. "Federico García Lorca parla per als obrers catalans." *L'Hora* (27 September 1935). Reprinted in *Obras Completas III*, edited by Miguel García Posada (Barcelona: Galaxia Gutenberg, 1997), 597–98.

———. *Obras Completas III*. Edited by Miguel García Posada. Barcelona: Galaxia Gutenberg, 1997.

García Maroto, Eduardo. *Aventuras y desventuras del cine español*. Barcelona: Plaza y Janés, 1988.

Gibson, Ian. *The Shameful Life of Salvador Dalí*. London: Faber and Faber, 1997.

Giménez Caballero, Ernesto. "Eisenstein gira un film y cuenta su vida." *El Sol*, 6 October 1929. Unpaginated press cutting in the Hemeroteca Municipal, Madrid.

———. "Historia del Cineclub Español." *La Gaceta Literaria*, no. 105 (1 May 1931): 3.

———. "Muerte y resurrección del Cineclub." *La Gaceta Literaria*, no. 121 (15 January 1932): 11–12.

———. "Noticiemos sobre cinema." *La Gaceta Literaria*, no. 112 (15 August 1931): 9.

———. "Nuestros cinempresarios: Ricardo Urgoiti." *La Gaceta Literaria*, no. 112 (15 August 1931): 10.

———. *Retratos españoles (bastante parecidos)*. Barcelona: Planeta, 1985.

———. "Las tripas del silencio español." *La Gaceta Literaria*, no. 119 (1 December 1931): 9–10.

———. "Visitas de cinema: Los empresarios; Armenta (Madrid)." *La Gaceta Literaria*, no. 51 (1 February 1929): 6.

Gomery, Douglas. *The Hollywood Studio System*. New York: St. Martin's Press, 1986.

Gómez Mesa, Luis. "La generación del cine y los deportes." *Popular Film*, no. 128 (10 January 1929): 4. Interview with Luis Buñuel.

———. "Situación actual del cine español." *Blanco y Negro* (1 April 1938). Cited in José Cabeza San Deogracias, *El descanso del guerrero: El cine en Madrid durante la Guerra Civil Española (1936–1939)* (Madrid: Rialp, 2005), 90.

Gotovich, José, et al. *Komintern: L'Histoire et les hommes; Dictionnaire biographique de l'Internationale Communiste*. Paris: Éditions de l'Atelier, 2001.

Goutier, Jean-Michel, ed. *André Breton: 42, rue Fontaine*. Paris: Calmels Cohen, 2003.

Gréville, Edmond T. *Trente-cinq ans dans la jungle du cinema*. Arles: Institut Lumière/Actes Sud, 1995.

Gubern, Román. *1936–1939: La guerra de España en la pantalla; De la propaganda a la historia*. Madrid: Filmoteca Española, 1986.

———. "Exhibiciones cinematográficas en el pabellón español." In *El pabellón español en la Exposición Internacional de París*, edited by Josefina Alix Trueba, 174–80. Madrid: MNCARS/Ministerio de Cultura, 1987.

———. *Proyector de luna: La Generación del 27 y el cine*. Barcelona: Anagrama, 1999.

———. "La traumática transición del cine español del mudo al sonoro." In *El paso del mudo al sonoro en el cine español: Actas del IV Congreso de la AEHC [Asociación Española de Historiadores del Cine]*, edited by Joan M. Minguet Batllori and Julio Pérez Perucha, 3–24. Madrid: Editorial Complutense, 1993.

Guzmán Merino, Antonio. "Don Quintín el amargao." *Cinegramas*, no. 57 (13 October 1935): n.p.

———. "La hija de Juan Simón." *Cinegramas*, no. 67 (22 December 1935): n.p.

———. "Planos de Madrid." *Popular Film*, no. 282 (7 January 1932): n.p.

———. "Planos de Madrid." *Popular Film*, no. 291 (10 March 1932): n.p.

———. "¿Quién me quiere a mí?" *Cinegramas*, no. 84 (19 April 1936): n.p.

Hamdorf, Wolf Martin. "'Espagne 1936' y 'Espagne 1937': Propaganda para la República (Luis Buñuel y la Guerra Civil Española)." *Secuencias: Revista de Historia del Cine*, no. 3 (October 1995): 86–94.

———. *Zwischen ¡No pasarán! und ¡Arriba España! Film und Propaganda im Spanischen Bürgerkrieg*. Münster: MAkS, 1991.

Hammond, Paul. *L'Âge d'or*. London: British Film Institute, 1997.

———, ed., *The Shadow and Its Shadow: Surrealist Writings on the Cinema*. 3rd ed. San Francisco: City Lights Books, 2000.

Heine, Maurice. "Lettre ouverte à Luis Buñuel." *LSASDLR*, no. 3 (December 1931): 12–13.

Heinink, Juan B., and Robert G. Dickson. *Cita en Hollywood*. Bilbao: Ediciones Mensajero, 1990.

Hernández Girbal, Florentino. "De fuera vendrán." *Cinema Sparta* (28 December 1935). Cited in Luis Fernández Colorado and Josetxo Cerdán, *Ricardo Urgoiti: Los trabajos y los días* (Madrid: Filmoteca Española, 2007), 105–7.

——— [as Joaquín Zaldívar]. "Los que pasaron por Hollywood." *Cinegramas*, no. 37 (26 March 1935): n.p. Interview with Roberto Rey.

——— [as Joaquín Zaldívar]. "Los que pasaron por Hollywood." *Cinegramas*, no. 47 (4 August 1935): n.p. Interview with José Nieto.

——— [as Joaquín Zaldívar]. "Los que pasaron por Hollywood." *Cinegramas*, no. 94 (28 June 1936): n.p. Interview with Tono.

Herrera Navarro, Javier. "A la sombra de Buñuel: Tota Cuevas de Vera—condesa, surrealista y comunista—a través de un epistolario inédito (1934–1936)." *El Maquinista de la Generación*, no. 17 (2009): 32–55.

———. "The Decisive Moments of Buñuel's Time in the United States: 1938–40; An Analysis of Previously Unpublished Letters." In *Luis Buñuel: New Readings*, edited by Peter William Evans and Isabel Santaolalla, 43–61. London: British Film Institute, 2004.

———. *Estudios sobre* Las Hurdes *de Buñuel: Evidencia fílmica, estética y recepción*. Sevilla: Renacimiento, 2006.

———. "Pretexto, contexto e hipertexto en *Las Hurdes/Tierra sin pan* de Buñuel." In *Las Hurdes: Un documental de Luis Buñuel*, edited by Javier Herrera Navarro, 10–35. Cáceres: Museo Extremeño e Iberoamericano de Arte Contemporáneo, 1999.

———. "Recepción crítica de *Las Hurdes* de Buñuel en Europa durante la Guerra Civil Española." *Secuencias: Revista de Historia del Cine*, 2nd ser., no. 11 (January–March 2000): 72–87.

———. "Sobre los documentales de guerra de Buñuel: Aclaraciones y nuevas aportaciones." Paper presented at the international congress "La Guerra Civil Española 1936–1939" organized by the Sociedad Estatal de Conmemoraciones Culturales, Madrid, November 2006.

Heymann, Claude. "Sur le tournage de *L'Âge d'or*." *Jeune Cinéma*, no. 134 (April–May 1981): 6–11.

Hodgson, Agnes. *A una milla de Huesca: Diario de una enfermera australiana en la Guerra Civil Española*. Zaragoza: Prensas Universitarias de Zaragoza, 2006.

Hugnet, Georges. *Pleins et déliés: Témoignages et souvenirs 1926–1972*. Paris: Guy Authier, 1972.

Huret, Marcel. *Ciné actualités: Histoire de la presse filmée 1895–1980*. Paris: Henri Veyrier, 1984.

Hutin, Emmanuel. *Pierre Unik 1909/1945*. Paris: Librairie-Galerie Emmanuel Hutin, 2009.

Ibarz, Mercè. *Buñuel documental*: Tierra sin pan *y su tiempo*. Zaragoza: Prensas Universitarias de Zaragoza, 1999.

———, ed. *Tierra sin pan: Luis Buñuel y los nuevos caminos de las vanguardias*. Valencia: IVAM/Centre Julio González, 1999.

Icart, Roger. *La Révolution du parlant vue par la presse française*. Perpignan: Institut Jean Vigo, 1988.

Ivens, Joris. *The Camera and I*. New York: International, 1969.

Jackson, Gabriel. *La República española y la Guerra Civil*. Mexico City: Grijalbo, 1967.

Jacobs, Lewis, ed. *The Documentary Tradition: From Nanook to Woodstock*. New York: Hopkinson and Blake, 1971.

Jamin, Jean. "Présentation de L'Afrique Fantôme." In Michel Leiris, *Miroir de l'Afrique*, edited by Jean Jamin, 65–85. Paris: Gallimard, 1995.

Jowett, Garth. *Film: The Democratic Art*. Boston: Little, Brown, 1976.

Kast, Pierre. "À la recherché de Luis Bunuel avec Jean Grémillon, Jean Castanier, Eli Lotar, L. Viñes et Pierre Prévert." *Cahiers du cinéma*, no. 7 (December 1951): 17–23.

———. *Jean Grémillon*. Premier plan 5. Lyon: SERDOC, 1960.

[Katz, Otto]. *The Nazi Conspiracy in Spain*. By the editor of *The Brown Book of the Hitler Terror*. London: Victor Gollancz/Left Book Club, 1937.

Kiefé, Robert. "Pour une réforme de la Censure." *La Revue du cinéma*, no. 21 (1 April 1931): 21–36.

Koch, Stephen. *Double Lives: Stalin, Willi Münzenberg and the Seduction of the Intellectuals*. 1994. Reprint, London: Harper Collins, 1996.

Koestler, Arthur. *The Invisible Writing*. London: Collins/Hamish Hamilton, 1954.

———. *Spanish Testament*. London: Victor Gollancz/Left Book Club, 1937.

Kowalsky, Daniel. "The Soviet Cinematic Offensive in the Spanish Civil War." *Film History* 19, no. 1 (2000): 7–19.

Kyrou, Ado. *Luis Bunuel*. Paris: Seghers, 1962.

———. *Le Surréalisme au cinema*. Paris: Éditions Arcanes, 1953.

Labanyi, Jo. "Buñuel's Cinematic Collaboration with Sáenz de Heredia, 1935–36." In *Buñuel, siglo XXI*, edited by Isabel Santaolalla et al., 293–301. Zaragoza: Prensas Universitarias de Zaragoza, 2004.

Landis, Arthur. *The Abraham Lincoln Brigade*. New York: Citadel Press, 1967.

Larrea, Juan. *Guernica: Pablo Picasso*. New York: Curt Valentin, 1947.

Lebrun, Dominique. *Paris-Hollywood: Les Français dans le cinéma américain*. Poitiers: Hazan, 1987.

Le Chanois, Jean-Paul. *Le Temps des cérises: Entretiens avec Philippe Esnault*. Arles: Institut Lumière/Actes Sud, 1996.

Legendre, Maurice. *Las Jurdes: Étude de géographie humaine*. Bordeaux: Feret & Fils, Éditeurs, 1927.

Leiris, Michel. *Miroir de l'Afrique*. Paris: Gallimard, 1995.

León, María Teresa. *Memoria de la melancolía*. 1970. Reprint, Madrid: Castalia, 1998.

León, Mario. "La cinematografía en el frente." *Popular Film*, no. 525 (17 September 1936): n.p.

Leyda, Jay. *Kino: A History of the Russian and Soviet Film*. London: George Allen & Unwin, 1960.

Lherminier, Pierre. *Jean Vigo*. Paris: Seghers, 1967.

Llopis, Juan Manuel, ed. *Juan Piqueras: El "Delluc" español.* 2 vols. Valencia: Filmoteca de la Generalitat Valenciana, 1988.

Logette, Lucien. "Espagne 37: Documentaire sur les événements d'Espagne au cours de la première année de la guerre civile." *Jeune Cinéma*, no. 225 (January 1994): 11–17.

———. "Jacques-Bernard Brunius (1906–1967), ou du violon d'Ingres considéré comme une des beaux arts." PhD diss., Université de la Sorbonne Nouvelle–Paris III, 1981.

London, Artur. *The Confession.* New York: Ballantine Books, 1970.

Luengo Teixidor, Félix. *Espías en la embajada: Los servicios de información secreta republicanos en Francia durante la Guerra Civil.* Bilbao: Servicio Editorial, Universidad del País Vasco/EHU, 1996.

M. A. "María Fernanda Ladrón de Guevara en el cinema hispano." *Popular Film*, no. 294 (31 March 1932): 10.

Maitron, Jean, ed. *Dictionnaire biographique du mouvement ouvrier français.* Paris: Éditions de l'Atelier, 1997.

Mannoni, Laurent. *Histoire de la Cinémathèque Française.* Paris: Gallimard, 2006.

Martín, Fernando Gabriel. "El artista aislado: Buñuel en/y Estados Unidos." *Turia*, no. 50 (October 1999): 164–75.

———. "El cine y la izquierda en Tenerife durante la República: Progresía, producción y cultura." In *Internacional constructivista frente a internacional surrealista*, edited by María Isabel Navarro Segura, 69–92. Tenerife: Cabildo Insular de Tenerife, 1999.

———. *El ermitaño errante: Buñuel en Estados Unidos.* Murcia: Tres Fronteras Ediciones/Filmoteca Regional Francisco Rabal, 2010.

Martín, Fernando Martín. *El Pabellón Español en la Exposición Universal de París en 1937.* Sevilla: Servicio de Publicaciones de la Universidad de Sevilla, 1983.

Martínez de Ribera, Lope F. "Pantallas de Barcelona." *Popular Film*, no. 488 (26 December 1935): n.p.

———. "¿Quién me quiere a mí?" *Popular Film*, no. 504 (16 April 1936): n.p.

Martínez Torres, Augusto. "El culto al hermano." *Archivos de la Filmoteca*, no. 9 (Spring–Summer 1991): 47–48. Interview with Jerónimo Mihura.

———. "José López Rubio: Un memorión nostálgico." *El País Semanal* (30 November 1986): 29.

Medina, Juan. "Revisión de cineclubs." *Popular Film*, no. 362 (20 July 1933): n.p.

Mejías, Leocadio. "La novela de un director." *Radiocinema*, no. 107 (30 December 1944): n.p. Interview with José Luis Sáenz de Heredia.

Mendelson, Jordana. *Documenting Spain: Artists, Exhibition Culture, and the Modern Nation, 1929–1939.* University Park: Pennsylvania State University Press, 2005.

Meyer, Jean. "Con la Iglesia hemos topado, Sancho." *Istor: Revista de la historia internacional*, no. 25 (Summer 2006): 99–121. http://www.istor.cide.edu/archivos/num_25/coincidencias.pdf.

Minguet Batllori, Joan M. *Salvador Dalí, cine y surrealismo(s).* Barcelona: Parsifal Ediciones, 2003.

Minguet Batllori, Joan M., and Julio Pérez Perucha, eds. *El paso del mudo al sonoro en el cine español: Actas del IV Congreso de la AEHC [Asociación Española de Historiadores del Cine].* Madrid: Editorial Complutense, 1993.

Miralles, Francesc. *Llorens Artigas: Catálogo de obra.* Barcelona: Fundación Llorens Artigas/Polígrafa, 1992.

Miralles, Ricardo. "La embajada de Marcelino Pascua en París durante la Guerra Civil Española (21 abril 1938–28 febrero 1939)." *Bulletin d'histoire contemporaine de l'Espagne,* no. 28–29 (1999): 135–58.

Montagu, Ivor. *With Eisenstein in Hollywood.* Berlin: Seven Seas Books, 1968.

Morel, Jean-Pierre. *Le Roman insupportable: L'Internationale littéraire et la France (1920–1932).* Paris: Gallimard, 1985.

Morelli, Gabrielle. *Ilegible, hijo de flauta: Argumento cinematográfico original de Juan Larrea y de Luis Buñuel, basado en un libro perdido de Juan Larrea.* Sevilla: Renacimiento, 2007.

Moreno Villa, José. "Don Quintín y el mundo." *El Sol,* 18 October 1935, 1.

———. "La Orden de Toledo." *El Nacional,* 12 October 1947. Unpaginated press cutting in Buñuel's private scrapbook, Archivo Luis Buñuel, Filmoteca Española, Madrid.

Mortimer, Edward. *The Rise of the French Communist Party, 1920–1947.* London: Faber and Faber, 1984.

Mortimer, Roger. "Buñuel, Sáenz de Heredia and Filmófono." *Sight and Sound,* no. 44 (Summer 1975): 180–82.

Moussinac, Léon. *L'Âge ingrat du cinéma.* Paris: Éditions du Sagittaire, 1946.

———. "Muerte de la vanguardia." *Nuestro Cinema,* no. 7 (December 1932): 204–5.

Neville, Edgar. "Defensa del sainete." *Primer Plano,* no. 216 (3 December 1944): n.p.

Nizan, Paul. *Articles littéraires et politiques.* Vol. 1, *1923–1935.* Paris: Joseph K., 2005.

Nugent, Frank S. "Blockade." *New York Times,* 17 June 1938, 25.

Nussinova, Natalia. "*España-36* ¿Es una producción de Luis Buñuel?" *Archivos de la Filmoteca,* no. 22 (February 1996): 79–95.

Obermann, Karl. "Der neue Spanische Film: Ein Interview mit L. Buñuel, dem Regisseur von 'Erde ohne Brot.'" *Pariser Tageszeitung* (22 February 1937). Translated into French and published as "À propos d'*Espagne 36*: Le nouveau film espagnol." *Ce Soir* (10 April 1937). Unpaginated press cuttings in Buñuel's private scrapbook, Archivo Luis Buñuel, Filmoteca Española, Madrid.

Ontañón, Santiago, and José María Moreiro. *Unos pocos amigos verdaderos.* Madrid: Fundación Banco Exterior, 1988.

Passek, Jean-Loup, ed. *Larousse Dictionnaire du cinéma.* Paris: Larousse, 1995.

Payne, Stanley G. *La primera democracia española: La Segunda República, 1931–1936.* Barcelona: Paidós, 1995.

———. *Unión Soviética, comunismo y revolución en España (1931–1939).* Barcelona: Plaza y Janés, 2003.

Péret, Benjamin. "La Conversion de Gide." *LSASDLR,* no. 5 (15 May 1933): 29.

Pérez Lizano, Manuel. *Focos del surrealismo español: Artistas aragoneses, 1929–1991.* Zaragoza: Mira Editores, 1992.

Pérez Merinero, Carlos, and David Pérez Merinero, eds. *Del cinema como arma de clase: Antología de* Nuestro Cinema *1932–1935*. Valencia: Fernando Torres Editor, 1975.

Pérez Minik, Domingo. *Facción surrealista de Tenerife*. Barcelona: Tusquets, 1975.

Pérez Turrent, Tomás, and José de la Colina. *Buñuel por Buñuel*. Madrid: Plot, 1993.

Pierre, José, ed. *Tracts surréalistes et déclarations collectives (1922/1969)*. Vol. 1. Paris: Eric Losfeld, 1980.

Piqueras, Juan. "Afirmación del cine europeo y desvalorización del yanqui." *El Sol*, 22 February 1931. Reprinted in *Juan Piqueras: El "Delluc" español*, edited by Juan Manuel Llopis (Valencia: Filmoteca de la Generalitat Valenciana, 1988), 1:250–51.

———. "La Atlántida: Film Franco-Alemán de G. W. Pabst." *Nuestro Cinema*, no. 2 (July 1932): 52–54.

———. "Colofón a la primera encuesta de *Nuestro Cinema*." *Nuestro Cinema*, no. 7 (October 1932): 203.

———. "Cuatro notas de cinema soviético." *La Gaceta Literaria*, no. 87 (1 August 1930): 5.

———. "Films soviéticos: 'Los tártaros.'" *Popular Film*, no. 214 (4 September 1930): 8.

———. "Hacia una Federación Española de Cineclubs Proletarios." *Nuestro Cinema*, no. 13 (October 1933): 214–16.

———. "*Kuhle Wampe* y el cine proletario." *Octubre*, no. 1 (June–July 1933): 20–21.

———. "Nuevos films en París." *Nuestro Cinema*, no. 10 (March 1933): 136–37.

———. "Nuevos films en París." *Nuestro Cinema*, no. 11 (April–May 1933): 167–69.

———. "Paris-Cinema: La traducción de los films yanquis es un peligro para el cine europeo." *El Sol*, 29 June 1930. Reprinted in *Juan Piqueras: El "Delluc" español*, edited by Juan Manuel Llopis (Valencia: Filmoteca de la Generalitat Valenciana, 1988), 1: 234–35.

———. "Posición actual del cinema francés." *Nuestro Cinema*, no. 8–9 (January–February 1933): 50–52.

———. "Prolongación de la falsa españolada." *Siluetas*, no. 5 (1 February 1930). Reprinted in *Juan Piqueras: El "Delluc" español*, edited by Juan Manuel Llopis (Valencia: Filmoteca de la Generalitat Valenciana, 1988), 2:18.

———. "Segunda encuesta: Convocatoria y cuestionario." *Nuestro Cinema*, 2nd ser., no. 4 (August 1935): 66.

———. "Visitas de cinema: Alberto Cavalcanti nos concreta." *La Gaceta Literaria*, no. 99 (15 February 1931): 8.

Polizzotti, Mark. *Revolution of the Mind: The Life of André Breton*. London: Bloomsbury, 1995.

Posener, Valérie. "Les scénaristes." In Aïcha Kherroubi et al., *Le Studio Mejrabpom ou l'aventure du cinéma privé au pays des bolsheviks*, 75–83. Les Dossiers du Musée d'Orsay 59. Paris: La Documentation Française, 1996.

Potamkin, Harry Alan. "Light and Shade in the Soviet Cinema." *Theatre Guild Magazine*, July 1930. Reprinted in *The Compound Cinema: The Film Writings of Harry Alan Potamkin*, edited by Lewis Jacobs (New York: Teachers College Press, 1977), 316–17.

Quintanilla, Luis. *"Pasatiempo": La vida de un pintor (Memorias)*. La Coruña: Ediciós do Castro, 2004.

Racine, Nicole. "Aragon, militant du movement communiste international (1930–1939)." In *Les Engagements d'Aragon*, edited by Jacques Girault and Bernard Lecherbonnier, 77–85. Paris: L'Harmattan, 1998.

Rawicz, Mariano. *Confesionario de papel.* Valencia and Granada: IVAM/Editorial Comares, 1997.

Rebolledo, Carlos. *Luis Bunuel.* Paris: Éditions Universitaires, 1964.

Renard, Philippe. *Un cinéaste des années 50: Jean-Paul Le Chanois* Paris: Dreamland Éditeur, 2000.

Reverte, Jorge M. *La batalla de Madrid.* Barcelona: Crítica, 2004.

Reynaud Paligot, Carole. *Parcours politique des surréalistes 1919–1969.* Paris: CNRS Éditions, 2001.

Riambau, Esteve. *Ricardo Muñoz Suay: Una vida en sombras.* Barcelona: Tusquets, 2007.

———. "*Tierra(s) de España*: Nueve versiones del film de Joris Ivens." Paper presented at the international congress "La Guerra Civil Española 1936–1939" organized by the Sociedad Estatal de Conmemoraciones Culturales, Madrid, 27–29 November 2006. http://www.secc.es/media/docs/20_1_Esteve_Riambau.pdf.

Ríos Carratalá, Juan Antonio. *A la sombra de Lorca y Buñuel: Eduardo Ugarte.* Alicante: Universidad de Alicante, 1995.

Rivet, Paul, et al. "Mission Dakar-Djibouti 1931–1933." *Minotaure*, no. 2 (1 June 1933): 3–88.

Robin, Pierre. "Cinéma." *Commune*, no. 42 (February 1937): 762–63.

Robinson, Ione. *A Wall to Paint On.* New York: E. P. Dutton, 1946.

Rodrigo, Antonina. "Isabel Oyarzábal de Palencia, primera embajadora de la República." In *El exilio literario español de 1939: Actas del primer Congreso Internacional (Bellaterra, 27 de noviembre–1 de diciembre de 1995)*, edited by Manuel Aznar Soler, 1:341–48. Alicante: Biblioteca Virtual Miguel de Cervantes, 1995. http://www.cervantesvirtual.com/servlet/SirveObras/08140621955770639732268/p0000011.htm#I_57.

———. *Memoria de Granada: Manuel Ángeles Ortiz y Federico García Lorca.* Granada: Diputación Provincial de Granada, 1993.

Rojo, José Andrés. *Vicente Rojo.* Barcelona: Tusquets, 2006.

Romano, Julio. "El público de los sainetes madrileños se ha pasado al cine." *Cinegramas*, no. 90 (31 May 1936): n.p.

Rosemont, Penelope, ed. *Women Surrealists: An International Anthology.* London: Athlone Press, 1998.

Rotellar, Manuel. *Cine español de la República.* San Sebastián: XXV Festival Internacional de Cine de San Sebastián, 1977.

———. "Un gran iluminador: José María Beltrán." In Manuel Rotellar, *Aragoneses en el cine 3*, 15–17. Zaragoza: Ayuntamiento de Zaragoza, 1972.

———. "Luis Buñuel en Filmófono." *Cinema 2002*, no. 37 (March 1978): 37–40.

Rubia Barcia, José. *Con Luis Buñuel en Hollywood y después.* La Coruña: Ediciós Do Castro, 1992.

Rucar de Buñuel, Jeanne. *Memorias de una mujer sin piano.* Madrid: Alianza Editorial, 1991.

Ruiz Castillo, Andrés. "Luis Buñuel, 'Un Chien andalou' y el superrealismo." *El Heraldo de Aragón*, 26 July 1930, 1–2. Interview with Luis Buñuel.

Rybalkin, Yuri. *Stalin y España*. Madrid: Marcial Pons Historia, 2007.

Sadoul, Georges. "L'assassinat de Juan Piqueras par les rebelles espagnols." *Commune*, no. 43 (March 1937): 840–44.

———. "Bunuel, Viridiana et quelques autres." Preface to *Viridiana* by Luis Buñuel. Paris: InterSpectacles, 1962.

———. *Dictionnaire des cinéastes*. Paris: Seuil, 1965.

———. "Las Hurdes." *Regards*, no. 146 (29 October 1936): 19.

———. "La Mort de Juan Piqueras: Le 'Delluc espagnol' fusillé par les rebelles." *L'Humanité*, no. 13964 (11 March 1937): 8.

———. "Mon ami Buñuel, d'*Un chien andalou* à *Los olvidados*." *L'Écran Français*, no. 335 (12–18 December 1951): 12.

———. *Rencontres I: Chroniques et entretiens*. Paris: Denoël, 1984.

———. "Souvenirs d'un témoin." *Études Cinématographiques*, no. 38–39 (Spring 1965): 9–28.

Sáenz de Heredia, José Luis. "Cómo y por qué fui director cinematográfico." *Radiocinema*, no. 122 (1 April 1946): n.p.

Salaberría, Ramón. "Vicens y Mantecón, el siglo XX de dos bibliotecarios republicanos." *Trébede: Mensual aragonés de análisis, opinión y cultura*, no. 43 (October 2000). http://www.redaragon.com/trebede/oct2000/articulo2.asp.

Sala Noguer, Ramón. *El cine en la España republicana durante la Guerra Civil*. Bilbao: Mensajero, 1993.

Salas Larrazábal, Ramón. *Historia del Ejército Popular de la República*. 1973. Reprint, Madrid: La Esfera de los Libros, 2006.

Sampaix, Lucien. "La 'Grande Frégate' est fermée." *L'Humanité*, no. 14158 (23 September 1937): 2.

———. "Les bombes de la Légion Noire." *L'Humanité*, no. 14071 (27 June 1937): 1, 4; no. 14072 (28 June 1937): 1–2; no. 14073 (29 June 1937): 1–2; no. 14075 (1 July 1937): 1–2.

Sánchez Alarcón, Inmaculada. *La Guerra Civil Española y el cine francés*. Sant Cugat del Vallès: Los Libros de la Frontera, 2005.

Sánchez Vidal, Agustín. *Buñuel, Lorca, Dalí: El enigma sin fin*. Barcelona: Planeta, 1988.

———. "*La Chèvre sanitaire*." In *Dalí & Film*, edited by Matthew Gale, 104–9. London: Tate, 2007.

———. "De Las Hurdes a *Tierra sin pan*." In *Las Hurdes: Un documental de Luis Buñuel*, edited by Javier Herrera Navarro, 37–75. Cáceres: Museo Extremeño e Iberoamericano de Arte Contemporáneo, 1999.

———. *Luis Buñuel: Obra cinematográfica*. Madrid: Ediciones JC, 1984.

———. *El mundo de Luis Buñuel*. Zaragoza: Caja de Ahorros de la Inmaculada de Aragón, 1993.

Santamaría de Mingo, Vicent. "Dalí i el tango: Entre Paris i Barcelona." *L'Avenç*, no. 332 (February 2008): 42–46.

Santos Torroella, Rafael, ed. *Salvador Dalí corresponsal de J. V. Foix 1932–1936*. Barcelona: Editorial Mediterránea, 1986.

Sartre, Jean-Paul. *Écrits de jeunesse*. Paris: Gallimard, 1990.

Schneider, Luis Mario. *II Congreso Internacional de Escritores Antifascistas (1937)*. Vol. 1, *Inteligencia y guerra civil en España*. Barcelona: Editorial Laia, 1978.

Schoots, Hans. *Living Dangerously: A Biography of Joris Ivens*. Amsterdam: Amsterdam University Press, 2000.

Schumann, Peter B. "Le cinéma prolétarien allemand." *Écran 73*, no. 20 (December 1973): 37–43.

Sebbag, Georges. *André Breton: L'Amour-folie*. Paris: Éditions Jean-Michel Place, 2004.

Segal, Abraham. "Entretien avec Joris Ivens." *L'Avant-Scène du cinéma*, no. 259–60 (1–15 January 1981): 4–8.

Serrano, Luis M. "'El mar de los cuervos' y 'Morgenrot.'" *Popular Film*, no. 378 (9 November 1933): n.p.

———. "Pintura y cinema: Picasso y Buñuel." *Popular Film*, no. 435 (20 December 1934): n.p.

Serrano de Osma, Carlos. "El documental en el recuerdo." In *El cine de las organizaciones populares republicanas entre 1936 y 1939*, vol. 2, *Las organizaciones marxistas*, edited by Rosa Álvarez, Julio Pérez Perucha, and Ramón Sala, 47–50. Bilbao: Certamen de Cine Documental, 1981.

Seton, Marie. *Eisenstein: A Biography*. London: Bodley Head, 1952.

Short, Robert Stuart. "The Political History of the Surrealist Movement in France, 1918–1940." PhD diss., University of Sussex, 1965.

[The Surrealist Group]. "L'Affaire Aragon." January 1932. Tract.

———. "L'Affaire de 'L'Âge d'or.'" January 1931. Tract.

———. *L'Âge d'or*. November 1930. Revue-programme published by Studio 28.

———. "Arrêtez Gil Robles." 20 July 1936. Tract.

———. "Au feu!" May 1931. Tract.

———. "Déclaration." *LSASDLR*, no. 1 (July 1930): 41.

———. "Du temps que les surréalistes avaient raison." August 1935. Tract.

———. "Hands Off Love." *LRS*, no. 9–10 (1 October 1927): 1–6.

———. "Paillasse! (Fin de l'Affaire Aragon)." March 1932. Tract.

———. "Question et réponse." *LSASDLR*, no 1 (July 1930): 1.

———. "Recherches sur la sexualité." *LRS*, no. 11 (15 March 1928): 32–40.

———. *Variétés: Le Surréalisme en 1929*. Special number, June 1929.

[The Surrealist Group et al.] "Enquête." *LRS*, no. 12 (15 December 1929): 65–76.

Tharrats, Juan Gabriel. *Los 500 films de Segundo de Chomón*. Zaragoza: Universidad de Zaragoza, 1988.

Thirard, Paul Louis. "Colloque à Pordenone." *Positif*, no. 471 (May 2000): 64–65.

Thirion, André. *Révolutionnaires sans Révolution*. Paris: Robert Laffont, 1972.

Torello, Georgina. "Con el demonio en el cuerpo: La mujer en el cine mudo italiano (1913–1920)." *Secuencias: Revista de Historia del Cine*, no. 23 (2006): 6–19.

Torrente Ballaster, Gonzalo. *Panorama de la literatura española contemporánea*. Madrid: Guadarrama, 1965.

Toulet, Emmanuelle, ed. *Le Cinéma au rendez-vous des arts: France, années 20 et 30*. Paris: Bibliothèque nationale de France, 1995.

Triolet, Elsa. *Dix jours en Espagne*. Paris: Société des Amis de Louis Aragon et Elsa Triolet, 2005.

Tuñon de Lara, Manuel, ed. *La crisis del Estado: Dictadura, república, guerra (1923–1939)*. Historia de España 9. Barcelona: Labor, 1981.

Unik, Pierre. *Le Héros du vide: Roman inachevé*. Paris: Les Éditeurs Français Réunis, 1972.

Utley, Gertje R. *Picasso: The Communist Years*. New Haven, Conn.: Yale University Press, 2000.

Vaillant-Couturier, Paul. *Les Bâtisseurs de la vie nouvelle: Neuf mois de voyage dans l'URSS du plan quinquénal*. Vol. 1, *Terres du pain, champs de blé et champs de pétrole*; vol. 2, *Au pays de Tamerlan*; vol. 3: *Les Géants industriels*. Paris: Bureau d'Éditions, 1932.

Vaillant-Couturier, Paul, et al. *Ceux qui ont choisi: Contre le fascisme en Allemagne; Contre l'impérialisme français*. Paris: AEAR, 1933.

Van Rysselberghe, Maria. *Les Cahiers de la Petite Dame: Notes pour l'histoire authentique d'André Gide*. Vol. 2, *1929–1937*. Cahiers André Gide 5. Paris, Gallimard, 1975.

[Various authors]. "A favor de nuestros camaradas: Protestemos contra la barbarie fascista que encarcela a los escritores alemanes." Supplement to *Octubre*, 1 May 1933.

[Various authors]. "Manifiesto fundacional de la Alianza de Intelectuales Antifascistas para la Defensa de la Cultura." July 1936.

Vicchi, Laura. *Henri Storck: De l'avant-garde au documentaire social*. Crisnée: Yellow Now Éditions, 2002.

Vicendeau, Ginette. "Les films en versions multiples: Un échec édifiant." In *Le Passage du muet au parlant*, edited by Christian Belaygue, 29–35. Toulouse: Cinémathèque de Toulouse/Éditions Milan, 1988.

Vicens, Juan. *L'Espagne vivante: Le peuple à la conquête de la culture*. Paris: Éditions Sociales Internationales, 1938. Translated into Spanish as *España viva: El pueblo a la conquista de la cultura* (Madrid: Asociación Educación y Bibliotecas/Ediciones VOSA, 2002).

Viertel, Salka. *Los extranjeros de Mabery Road*. Madrid: Ediciones El Imán, 1995.

Vived Mairal, Jesús. *Ramón J. Sender: Biografía*. Madrid: Páginas de Espuma, 2002.

Waldman, Harry. *Paramount in Paris: 300 Films Produced at the Joinville Studios: 1930–1933*. Lanham, Md.: Scarecrow Press, 1988.

Walker, Ian. *City Gorged with Dreams: Surrealism and Documentary Photography in Interwar Paris*. Manchester: Manchester University Press, 2002.

Wasson, Haidee. *Museum Movies: The Museum of Modern Art and the Birth of Art Cinema*. Berkeley: University of California Press, 2005.

Wolton, Thierry. *Le Grand Recrutement*. Paris: Éditions Grasset, 1993.

Wright, Basil. "*Land without Bread* and *Spanish Earth*." *World Film News* (December 1937). Reprinted in *The Documentary Tradition: From Nanook to Woodstock*, edited by Lewis Jacobs (New York: Hopkinson & Blake, 1971), 146.

Xammar, Eugeni. *Seixanta anys d'anar pel món*. Barcelona: Editorial Pórtic, 1974.
Zambrano, María. *Los intelectuales en el drama de España y escritos de la Guerra Civil*. Madrid: Editorial Trotta, 1998.
Zavala, José María. *Los gángsters de la Guerra Civil*. Barcelona: Plaza y Janés, 2006.
"Ziff." "Don Quintín el amargao (Don Quintin, the Bitter)." *Variety*, 30 October 1935. Reprinted in *Variety Film Reviews: 1934–1937*, vol. 5 of *Variety Film Reviews: 1907–1980* (New York: Garland, 1983), n.p.
Zugazagoitia, Julián. *Guerra y vicisitudes de los españoles*. 1940. Reprint, Barcelona: Tusquets, 2001.

Index

WISCONSIN FILM STUDIES

The Foreign Film Renaissance on American Screens, 1946–1973
Tino Balio

Marked Women: Prostitutes and Prostitution in the Cinema
Russell Campbell

Depth of Field: Stanley Kubrick, Film, and the Uses of History
Edited by Geoffrey Cocks, James Diedrick, and Glenn Perusek

Tough as Nails: The Life and Films of Richard Brooks
Douglass K. Daniel

Luis Buñuel: The Red Years, 1929–1939
Román Gubern and Paul Hammond

Glenn Ford: A Life
Peter Ford

Escape Artist: The Life and Films of John Sturges
Glenn Lovell

I Thought We Were Making Movies, Not History
Walter Mirisch

Giant: George Stevens, a Life on Film
Marilyn Ann Moss